THE CRICKETERS'
WHO'S WHO
1989

THE
CRICKETERS'
WHO'S WHO
1989

**compiled and edited by
IAIN SPROAT**

WILLOW BOOKS
Collins
8 Grafton Street, London W1
1989

Willow Books
William Collins Sons & Co. Ltd
London · Glasgow · Sydney · Auckland
Toronto · Johannesburg

First published in Great Britain in 1989 by
William Collins Sons & Co. Ltd, 8 Grafton Street,
London W1X 3LA in association with The
Cricketers' Who's Who Limited
© Iain Sproat 1989

British Library Cataloguing in Publication Data
The Cricketers' who's who – 10th ed.
1. Cricket players – Biography
I. Sproat, Iain
796.35'8'0922   GV915.A1
ISBN 0-00-218288-2 hardback
ISBN 0-00-218287-4 paperback

Cover photographs of
Robin Smith and Jonathan Agnew
by Adrian Murrell/Allsport

Portraits by Bill Smith

Typeset by Rowland Phototypesetting Ltd
Bury St Edmunds, Suffolk
Printed and bound in Great Britain by
Butler and Tanner Ltd, Frome, Somerset

PREFACE

THE CRICKETERS listed in this volume include those who played for their county at least once last season, either in the County Championship, Refuge Assurance League, Benson & Hedges or NatWest matches. The statistics are accurate up to the end of the last English season – with one exception: it has proved impossible to guarantee the accuracy of the statistics of certain matches, classified as first-class, in India and Pakistan. However, Test match figures in those countries have been included. Figures about 1000 runs in a season refer to matches in England only. First-class figures do not include figures for Test matches which are listed separately. One-day 50s and 100s are for English domestic competitions plus all Internationals, home and abroad. The RAL figures do not include the Refuge Assurance Cup knock-out games.

The following abbreviations apply: * means not out; RAL means Refuge Assurance League; and B & H means Benson & Hedges. The figures for batting and bowling averages refer to the full first-class English list (including the year's visiting tourists and University players) for 1988, followed in brackets by the 1987 figures. Inclusion in the batting averages depends on a minimum of eight innings, and an average of at least 10 runs; a bowler has had to have taken at least 10 wickets in at least 10 innings. The same qualification has been used for compiling the bowlers' strike rate.

Readers will notice certain occasional differences in the way the same kind of information is presented. This is because I have usually tried to follow the way in which the cricketers themselves have provided the relevant information.

A book of this complexity and detail has to be prepared several months in advance of the cricket season, and occasionally there are recent changes in a player's circumstances which cannot be included in time. Many examples of facts and statistics which can quickly become outdated in the period between the actual compilation of the book and its publication, months later, will spring to the reader's mind, and I ask him or her to make the necessary commonsense allowance and adjustments.

I am indebted to Mr Les Hatton for his splendidly professional work in the collection of statistics, and to Mr Bill Smith, FRPS, who personally took most of the photographs. I should also like to thank Mr James Vyvyan and Mr Charles Shaw for their help in the production of this book; and Mr Oliver Pawle and Mr Peter Brooke for contributing some baffling questions. Above all I am grateful to the cricketers themselves without whose support this book could not have been compiled.

Finally, to celebrate the 10th anniversary of *The Cricketers' Who's Who* annual, there is a special competition linked to the 200 quiz questions which appear throughout the book. The entry form appears on page 525. Good luck and enjoy your cricket!

Iain Sproat
January 1989

FOREWORD

V. G. RAMSDEN
Chairman, Refuge Assurance p.l.c.

As MAJOR SPONSORS of cricket in Britain, Refuge Assurance is delighted once again to be supporting *The Cricketers' Who's Who*, a feast of fascinating facts for all lovers of this great game.

This is the third season of the Refuge Assurance League, and we are sure it will provide some classic cricketing entertainment during 1989 as the counties seek to topple Worcestershire from the top-of-the-table place they have held for the past two years.

It is also the second season of the Refuge Assurance Cup, our end-of-season knockout contest for the top four League teams. The success of this new event was assured when some 17,000 enthusiasts packed into Edgbaston last September for a debut final that gave Lancashire a thrilling victory over Worcestershire.

Now we can all enjoy the excitement of the 1989 cricketing season, made doubly pleasurable by the mass of essential information that this book presents.

ABRAHAMS, J.   Lancashire

Full Name: John Abrahams
Role: Left-hand bat, off-break
bowler
Born: 21 July 1952, Cape Town,
South Africa
Height: 5′ 7″ **Weight:** 10st 8lbs
Nickname: Abey
County debut: 1973
County cap: 1982
Benefit: 1988
1000 runs in a season: 4
1st-Class 50s scored: 53
1st-Class 100s scored: 13
1st-Class 200s scored: 1
One-Day 50s: 17
One-Day 100s: 1
Place in batting averages: —
(1987 54th av. 37.50)
1st-Class catches 1988: 2
(career 162)
Parents: Cecil John and Cynthia Jean
Wife and date of marriage: Debbie, 5 April 1986
Family links with cricket: Father was professional with Milnrow and Radcliffe
in Central Lancashire League. Brothers Basil and Peter have both pro'd in the
Leagues for Uppermill CC and Heyside CC
Education: Moorhouse County Primary School; Heywood Grammar School
(later became Heywood Senior High School)
Qualifications: 9 O-levels, 1 A-level, Senior Coaching Certificate
Jobs outside cricket: Shop manager and representative, Beaverwise Plant
Hire, Oldham; coaching community groups through GMYA
Overseas teams played for: Player-coach for Mowbray CC, Tasmania
1980–81; Western Creek CC, Canberra 1983–84, 1984–85
Cricketers particularly learnt from: David Lloyd, Clive Lloyd
Cricketers particularly admired: Clive Lloyd, Mike Brearley
Other sports played: Badminton, golf
Other sports followed: Watching rugby union on TV. Almost all sports
Relaxations: Music and reading
Extras: Has lived in UK since 1962. Substitute for England in place of Brian
Rose in Fifth Test against West Indies at Headingley in August 1980. 'Would
very much like to be a physiotherapist when I retire.' Gold award winner in
1984 B & H final. Captain 1984 and 1985
Opinions on cricket: 'The game's getting harder!'
Best batting performance: 201* Lancashire v Warwickshire, Nuneaton 1984

Best bowling performance: 3-27 Lancashire v Worcestershire, Old Trafford 1981

LAST SEASON: BATTING

	I.	N.O.	R.	H.S.	AV.
TEST					
1ST-CLASS	4	0	58	39	14.50
INT					
RAL					
NAT.W.					
B & H	1	0	7	7	7.00

LAST SEASON: BOWLING

	O.	M.	R.	W.	AV.
TEST					
1ST-CLASS					
INT					
RAL					
NAT.W.					
B & H					

CAREER: BATTING

	I.	N.O.	R.	H.S.	AV.
TEST					
1ST-CLASS	390	52	10059	201*	29.76
INT					
RAL	122	23	2442	103*	24.66
NAT.W.	24	3	491	67*	23.38
B & H	32	6	634	66*	24.38

CAREER: BOWLING

	O.	M.	R.	W.	AV.
TEST					
1ST-CLASS	948.1	201	2811	56	50.19
INT					
RAL	86.2	6	439	13	33.76
NAT.W.	44	6	176	5	35.20
B & H	39	4	166	4	41.50

AFFORD, J. A.   Nottinghamshire

Full Name: John Andrew Afford
Role: Right-hand bat, slow left-arm bowler and 'far-flung fielder!'
Born: 12 May 1964, Crowland, Nr. Peterborough
Height: 6' 2½" **Weight:** 13st
Nickname: Aff
County debut: 1984
1st-Class 5 w. in innings: 4
1st-Class 10 w. in match: 1
Place in bowling averages: — (1987 52nd av. 28.03)
1st-Class catches 1988: 2 (career 10)
Parents: Jill
Wife and date of marriage: Lynn, 1 October 1988
Family links with cricket: 'Uncle played for school 2nd XI!'
Education: Spalding Grammar School; Stamford College for Further Education
Qualifications: 5 O-levels, NCA Coaching Certificate
Off-season 1988–89: Playing and coaching at Taita CC in New Zealand
Cricketing superstitions or habits: 'Always like to have a confident LBW shout against me in the first two balls!'

Overseas teams played for: Upper Hutt CC, New Zealand 1985–87
Cricketers particularly learnt from: 'David Johnson at Bourne CC and everyone at Nottinghamshire, especially Eddie Hemmings. In last couple of seasons Bruce French has been a strong influence.'
Cricketers particularly admired: Richard Hadlee, Bishan Bedi, Derek Underwood
Other sports followed: 'Will give anything a whirl, but nothing too serious. Able to watch most things – just can't fathom out people's fascination for horse racing. Follow Peterborough United FC through thick and thin – mainly thin!'
Injuries 1988: 'Stress fracture of spine caused me to miss most of the season.'
Relaxations: 'Hanging about at home!'
Opinions on cricket: 'I know this is a terrible cliche, but the double standards and rule bending concerning trade with, and sport with, South Africa really galls me!'
Best batting performance: 16 Nottinghamshire v Surrey, Trent Bridge 1987
Best bowling performance: 6-81 Nottinghamshire v Kent, Trent Bridge 1986

LAST SEASON: BATTING

	I.	N.O.	R.	H.S.	AV.
TEST					
1ST-CLASS	8	3	4	3	0.80
INT					
RAL					
NAT.W.					
B & H					

CAREER: BATTING

	I.	N.O.	R.	H.S.	AV.
TEST					
1ST-CLASS	31	16	48	16	3.20
INT					
RAL	–	–	–	–	–
NAT.W.					
B & H	–	–	–	–	–

LAST SEASON: BOWLING

	O.	M.	R.	W.	AV.
TEST					
1ST-CLASS	83	19	270	9	30.00
INT					
RAL					
NAT.W.					
B & H					

CAREER: BOWLING

	O.	M.	R.	W.	AV.
TEST					
1ST-CLASS	965.6	275	2787	89	31.31
INT					
RAL	8	1	27	1	27.00
NAT.W.					
B & H	8	0	55	0	–

1. How tall is Curtley Ambrose?
2. Who is taller: Curtley Ambrose or Joel Garner?
3. What have the following players in common: Tavaré, Lamb, Gatting, Cowley and Marks?

AGNEW, J. P. — Leicestershire

Full Name: Jonathan Philip Agnew
Role: Right-hand bat, right-arm fast bowler, outfielder
Born: 4 April 1960, Macclesfield, Cheshire
Height: 6' 4" **Weight:** 12st 6lbs
Nickname: Spiro (after former US Vice-President Spiro Agnew), Rambo
County debut: 1978
County cap: 1984
Test debut: 1984
No. of Tests: 3
No. of One-Day Internationals: 3
50 wickets in a season: 5
1st-Class 50s scored: 2
1st-Class 5 w. in innings: 29
1st-Class 10 w. in match: 5
Place in batting averages: 242nd av. 12.90 (1987 201st av. 16.82)
Place in bowling averages: 50th av. 25.45 (1987 25th av. 24.26)
Strike rate 1988: 50.56 (career 51.20)
1st-Class catches 1988: 2 (career 31)
Parents: Philip and Margaret
Wife and date of marriage: Beverley, 8 October 1983
Children: Jennifer, 31 October 1985; Rebecca, 18 September 1988
Family links with cricket: First cousin, Mary Duggan, Captain of England's Women's XI in 1960s. Father very keen cricketer
Education: Taverham Hall Prep School; Uppingham School
Qualifications: 9 O-levels, 2 A-levels in German and English
Jobs outside cricket: Cricket Coach. Spent 1981–82 off-season coaching at Sindia High School, Zimbabwe. Production control at T. L. Bennett's Windows Ltd. Sports producer at BBC Radio Leicester
Off-season 1988–89: Leicestershire's Cricket Development Officer, selling cricket to children and particularly teachers. Doing a weekly evening programme on BBC Radio Leicester
Cricketing superstitions or habits: 'I never use a bowling marker so am never popular with groundsmen! Don't whiten boots.'
Overseas tours: Young England to Australia, 1978–79; Leicestershire CCC to Zimbabwe, 1981; England to India and Australia, 1984–85; England B to Sri Lanka, 1986
Overseas teams played for: Whitbread scholarship, playing for Essendon CC,

Melbourne, 1978, 1980; Alexandra CC, Harare, Zimbabwe, 1981–82; Central Cumberland District Cricket Club, Sydney, 1982–83

Cricketers particularly learnt from: Ken Higgs, Frank Tyson, Peter Willey, Ken Shuttleworth

Cricketers particularly admired: Imran Khan, Wayne Larkins

Other sports played: Hockey, golf

Relaxations: Music (all kinds). Playing piano and tuba. Coaching cricket. 'I became very interested in game viewing in Zimbabwe. I spent days driving around to study and photograph – particularly elephants. Watching "Only Fools and Horses", "Minder", and "Blackadder".'

Extras: Played for Surrey 2nd XI 1976–77. Leicestershire CCC Player of the Year 1987. One of *Wisden*'s Five Cricketers of the Year 1987. Writes weekly column in *Today*. Author of *Eight Days a Week* published in 1988

Opinions on cricket: 'Now we have had a taster, let's have a 16 four-day match championship.'

Best batting performance: 90 Leicestershire v Yorkshire, Scarborough 1987

Best bowling performance: 9-70 Leicestershire v Kent, Leicester 1985

LAST SEASON: BATTING

	I.	N.O.	R.	H.S.	AV.
TEST					
1ST-CLASS	29	8	271	38	12.90
INT					
RAL	9	4	87	19*	–
NAT.W.	1	0	1	1	1.00
B & H	2	1	8	5*	8.00

CAREER: BATTING

	I.	N.O.	R.	H.S.	AV.
TEST	4	3	10	5	10.00
1ST-CLASS	171	33	1572	90	11.39
INT	1	1	2	2*	–
RAL	24	13	145	23*	13.18
NAT.W.	6	4	28	8*	14.00
B & H	12	3	64	23*	7.11

LAST SEASON: BOWLING

	O.	M.	R.	W.	AV.
TEST					
1ST-CLASS	783.5	166	2367	93	25.45
INT					
RAL	80.1	6	303	14	21.64
NAT.W.	19	3	62	1	62.00
B & H	25	2	113	1	113.00

CAREER: BOWLING

	O.	M.	R.	W.	AV.
TEST	92	22	373	4	93.25
1ST-CLASS	4456.3	868	14594	533	27.38
INT	21	0	120	3	40.00
RAL	371.3	17	1731	57	30.36
NAT.W.	132	21	481	15	32.06
B & H	231.2	34	885	34	26.02

4. Which county had the most people on its playing staff in 1988, and how many?

5. Which county had the least people on its playing staff in 1988, and how many?

ALDERMAN, T. M.   Gloucestershire

Full Name: Terence Michael Alderman
Role: Right-hand bat, right arm fast-medium bowler
Born: 12 June 1956, Perth, Western Australia
Height: 6′ 3″ **Weight:** 13st 7lbs
Nickname: Clem
County debut: 1984 (Kent), 1988 (Gloucestershire)
County cap: 1984 (Kent)
Test debut: 1981
No. of Tests: 22
No. of One-Day Internationals: 23
50 wickets in a season: 2
1st-Class 50s scored: 1
1st-Class 5 w. in innings: 39
1st-Class 10 w. in match: 7
Place in batting averages: 247th av. 12.27
Place in bowling averages: 33rd av. 22.81
Strike rate 1988: 48.00
1st-Class catches 1988: 12 (career 148)
Parents: William and Joan
Wife and date of marriage: Jane Elizabeth, 1977
Family links with cricket: Grandfather umpire; father W.A. colts team; sister Australian ladies
Education: Aquinas College, Perth; Churchlands College of Advanced Education
Qualifications: Teacher's Certificate

LAST SEASON: BATTING

	I.	N.O.	R.	H.S.	AV.
TEST					
1ST-CLASS	22	11	135	43*	12.27
INT					
RAL					
NAT.W.	1	0	0	0	0.00
B & H	1	0	8	8	8.00

LAST SEASON: BOWLING

	O.	M.	R.	W.	AV.
TEST					
1ST-CLASS	601	135	1711	75	22.81
INT					
RAL					
NAT.W.	34.1	6	127	9	14.11
B & H	40	7	133	7	19.00

CAREER: BATTING

	I.	N.O.	R.	H.S.	AV.
TEST	33	15	113	23	6.27
1ST-CLASS	168	73	897	52*	9.44
INT	9	3	27	9*	4.50
RAL	5	4	21	11	21.00
NAT.W.	1	0	0	0	0.00
B & H	3	1	12	8	6.00

CAREER: BOWLING

	O.	M.	R.	W.	AV.
TEST	895.3	202	2597	79	32.87
1ST-CLASS	4779.5	1112	14271	632	22.58
INT	215	31	803	29	27.69
RAL	105	9	477	21	22.71
NAT.W.	91.1	16	349	19	18.36
B & H	80	14	246	14	17.57

Jobs outside cricket: Corporate officer for Town and County W.A. Building Society (Perth)
Off-season 1988–89: Playing for W.A. and Australia
Overseas teams played for: Watsonians (Scotland) 1980 and Western Australia
Cricketers particularly learnt from: Dennis Lillee
Other sports played: Golf, Aussie rules football, squash
Other sports followed: All sports
Injuries 1988: Hamstring injury
Relaxations: Antique hunting, old cars, golf, wine
Extras: Played one season for Kent while Eldine Baptiste was on West Indies tour of England. Would have played for Worcestershire in 1983 if had not been injured. One of *Wisden*'s Five Cricketers of the Year, 1981. Was banned from playing for Australia for three years for going on rebel tour to South Africa
Best batting performance: 52* Sussex v Kent, Hastings, 1984
Best bowling performance: 8-46 Kent v Derbyshire, Derby 1986

ALIKHAN, R. K. Sussex

Full Name: Rehan Kebal Alikhan
Role: Right-hand bat
Born: 28 December 1962, London
Height: 6′ 1½″ **Weight:** 13st
Nickname: Prince, Oily, Pretty Polly, Munch
County debut: 1986
1st-Class 50s scored: 15
One-Day 50s: 2
Place in batting averages: 161st av. 22.57 (1987 162nd av. 21.48)
1st-Class catches 1988: 8 (career 34)
Parents: Akbar and Farida
Marital status: Single
Education: King's College School, Wimbledon
Qualifications: 2 A-levels, 8 O-levels
Jobs outside cricket: Insurance Broker

Cricketing superstitions or habits: 'I never bat with a cap on.'
Overseas tours: King's College School, Wimbledon to Holland 1978 and 1980; Surrey Schools U-19 to Australia 1979–80; Club Cricket Conference to Kenya 1985

Overseas teams played for: Mosman Middle Harbour District CC 1982–83 and 1983–84
Cricketers particularly learnt from: Imran Khan, Paul Parker, Monty Lynch
Cricketers particularly admired: Zaheer Abbas, Imran Khan, Viv Richards, Greg Chappell
Other sports played: Squash, soccer, rugby
Other sports followed: American football, Aussie rules, hockey, golf, tennis
Relaxations: Reading, music, theatre, watching sport
Extras: Released by Sussex at end of 1988 season
Best batting performance: 98 Sussex v Somerset, Bath 1988
Best bowling performance: 2-19 Sussex v West Indies, Hove 1988

LAST SEASON: BATTING

	I.	N.O.	R.	H.S.	AV.
TEST					
1ST-CLASS	19	0	429	98	22.57
INT					
RAL	1	1	0	0*	–
NAT.W.	1	0	9	9	9.00
B & H					

LAST SEASON: BOWLING

	O.	M.	R.	W.	AV.
TEST					
1ST-CLASS	7.3	0	26	2	13.00
INT					
RAL	8	0	42	0	–
NAT.W.					
B & H					

CAREER: BATTING

	I.	N.O.	R.	H.S.	AV.
TEST					
1ST-CLASS	103	8	2350	98	24.73
INT					
RAL	8	2	72	23	12.00
NAT.W.	8	1	125	41	17.85
B & H					

CAREER: BOWLING

	O.	M.	R.	W.	AV.
TEST					
1ST-CLASS	27.4	1	124	3	41.33
INT					
RAL	9	0	47	0	–
NAT.W.					
B & H					

6. What was Graeme Pollock's Test batting average: 60.97, 50.97 or 40.97?
7. In how many Tests did W. G. Grace play: 22, 52, 82?

ALLEYNE, H. L.   Kent

Full Name: Hartley Leroy Alleyne
Role: Right-hand bat; right-arm
fast bowler
Born: 28 February 1957, Barbados
Height: 6′ **Weight:** 12st 3lbs
County debut: 1980 (Worcestershire),
1988 (Kent)
County cap: 1981 (Worcestershire)
1st-Class 50s scored: 1
1st-Class 5 w. in innings: 9
1st-Class 10 w. in match: 2
1st-Class catches 1988: 0
(career 16)
Parents: Ruth and Norman
Marital status: Single
Family links with cricket: Brother
played club cricket in Barbados
Off-season 1988–89: 'On the
beach watching the sun set.'
Cricketing superstitions or habits: 'Joking with spectators.'
Overseas tours: West Indies to Zimbabwe 1981
Overseas teams played for: Club cricket in Victoria for St Kilda 1981–82,
1982–83; Natal
Cricketers particularly learnt from: Joel Garner, Norman Gifford
Cricketers particularly admired: Vivian Richards, Malcolm Marshall,
Graham Gooch 'and lots more'
Other sports played: Golf
Other sports followed: Football, tennis and Ben Johnson v Carl Lewis

LAST SEASON: BATTING

	I.	N.O.	R.	H.S.	AV.
TEST					
1ST-CLASS	7	1	24	9	4.00
INT					
RAL	1	0	25	25	25.00
NAT.W.					
B & H	1	1	8	8*	–

CAREER: BATTING

	I.	N.O.	R.	H.S.	AV.
TEST					
1ST-CLASS	84	19	648	72	9.96
INT					
RAL	17	3	177	32	12.64
NAT.W.	4	1	27	19	9.00
B & H	7	2	30	10	6.00

LAST SEASON: BOWLING

	O.	M.	R.	W.	AV.
TEST					
1ST-CLASS	94.3	17	322	12	26.83
INT					
RAL	22.2	0	95	7	13.57
NAT.W.					
B & H	36	2	184	2	92.00

CAREER: BOWLING

	O.	M.	R.	W.	AV.
TEST					
1ST-CLASS	2014	375	6330	238	26.59
INT					
RAL	210.2	12	831	38	21.86
NAT.W.	42	7	134	7	19.14
B & H	142.1	22	519	13	39.92

Injuries 1988: Heel trouble
Relaxations: Music, swimming and beach cricket
Extras: Banned from playing for West Indies because of playing in South Africa. Recommended to Kent by Mike Procter
Best batting performance: 72 Worcestershire v Lancashire, Stourport-on-Severn, 1980
Best bowling performance: 8-43 Worcestershire v Middlesex, Lords 1981

ALLEYNE, M. W. Gloucestershire

Full Name: Mark Wayne Alleyne
Role: Right-hand bat, medium pace bowler, cover fielder, occasional wicket-keeper
Born: 23 May 1968, Tottenham
Height: 5′ 10½″ **Weight:** 12st 10lbs
Nickname: Boo-Boo
County debut: 1986
1st-Class 50s scored: 7
1st-Class 100s scored: 1
Place in batting averages: 229th av. 15.00 (1987 128th av. 27.30)
Place in bowling averages: —
(1987 141st av. 64.45)
1st-Class catches 1988: 15
(career 27 + 1 stumping)
Parents: Euclid Clevis and Hyacinth Cordeilla
Marital status: Single
Family links with cricket: Brother played for Gloucestershire 2nd XI and Middlesex YCs. Father played club cricket in Barbados and England
Education: Harrison College, Barbados and Cardinal Pole School, E London
Qualifications: 6 O-levels, NCA senior coaching award, and volleyball coaching certificate
Jobs outside cricket: Accounts clerk, office junior with ANZ Bank
Off-season 1988–89: In Barbados and London with Deluxe Coachlines
Overseas tours: South of England YC to Bermuda; England YC to Sri Lanka 1987; Gloucestershire CC to Sri Lanka 1987; England YC to World Cup, Australia, 1988
Overseas teams played for: Preston CC, Melbourne, 1987–88
Cricketers particularly learnt from: Seymour Nurse (former coach)
Cricketers particularly admired: Gordon Greenidge, Viv Richards
Other sports played: Basketball

Other sports followed: Football, volleyball, athletics
Relaxations: Watching films and sport; listening to music
Extras: Youngest player to score a century for Gloucestershire. Kept wicket for the first time in first-class game v Hampshire
Best batting performance: 116* Gloucestershire v Sussex, Bristol 1986
Best bowling performance: 4-48 Gloucestershire v Glamorgan, Bristol 1988

LAST SEASON: BATTING

	I.	N.O.	R.	H.S.	AV.
TEST					
1ST-CLASS	21	1	300	56	15.00
INT					
RAL	11	6	256	49*	51.20
NAT.W.	2	1	2	2*	2.00
B & H	2	0	11	9	5.50

LAST SEASON: BOWLING

	O.	M.	R.	W.	AV.
TEST					
1ST-CLASS	68	13	227	6	37.83
INT					
RAL	62	2	298	13	22.92
NAT.W.	6	1	37	0	–
B & H	28.1	3	94	6	15.66

CAREER: BATTING

	I.	N.O.	R.	H.S.	AV.
TEST					
1ST-CLASS	69	13	1321	116*	23.58
INT					
RAL	25	12	408	49*	31.38
NAT.W.	6	3	11	9	3.66
B & H	6	0	64	36	10.66

CAREER: BOWLING

	O.	M.	R.	W.	AV.
TEST					
1ST-CLASS	243.4	48	951	17	55.94
INT					
RAL	142	4	694	29	23.93
NAT.W.	20	2	85	1	85.00
B & H	45.1	3	169	10	16.90

ALLOTT, P. J. W.   Lancashire

Full Name: Paul John Walter Allott
Role: Right-hand bat, right-arm fast-medium bowler
Born: 14 September 1956, Altrincham, Cheshire
Height: 6′ 4″ **Weight:** 14st
Nickname: Walt
County debut: 1978
County cap: 1981
Test debut: 1981
No. of Tests: 13
No. of One-Day Internationals: 13
50 wickets in a season: 4
1st-Class 50s scored: 9
1st-Class 5 w. in innings: 29
Place in batting averages: 244th av. 12.83 (1987 122nd av. 27.86)
Place in bowling averages: 15th av. 20.56 (1987 9th av. 20.71)
Strike rate 1988: 52.86 (career 57.67)
1st-Class catches 1988: 13 (career 93)

Parents: John Norman and Lillian Patricia
Wife and date of marriage: Helen, 27 October 1979
Family links with cricket: Father was dedicated club cricketer for 20 years with Ashley CC and is now active with Bowdon CC (Cheshire County League) as a selector, administrator and junior organiser
Education: Altrincham Grammar School; Bede College, Durham
Qualifications: Qualified teacher; cricket coach
Jobs outside cricket: Teacher; cricket coach for Manchester Education Committee; coach in Tasmania for Tasmanian Cricket Association
Off-season 1988–89: Working as director of Blackspur Advertising and Marketing Ltd
Overseas tours: With England to India 1981–82; India and Australia 1984–85; International XI to Jamaica 1982–83
Cricketers particularly learnt from: Dennis Lillee, Steve Murrills
Other sports played: Golf, football, squash, rugby, tennis
Relaxations: Playing golf, watching all sports, listening to music, eating out, photography
Extras: Played as goalkeeper for Cheshire schoolboys. Took part in 10th wicket record partnership for England with Bob Willis, 70 v India, at Lord's, June 1982. Wears contact lenses. Forced by injury to return early from Indian tour in 1984–85
Best batting performance: 88 Lancashire v Hampshire, Southampton 1987
Best bowling performance: 8-48 Lancashire v Northamptonshire, Northampton 1981

LAST SEASON: BATTING

	I.	N.O.	R.	H.S.	AV.
TEST					
1ST-CLASS	28	4	308	29*	12.83
INT					
RAL	9	1	118	43	14.75
NAT.W.	2	0	14	14	7.00
B & H	4	2	20	14*	10.00

LAST SEASON: BOWLING

	O.	M.	R.	W.	AV.
TEST					
1ST-CLASS	590.2	162	1378	67	20.56
INT					
RAL	103.1	5	374	7	53.42
NAT.W.	18	3	45	2	22.50
B & H	41	10	133	8	16.62

CAREER: BATTING

	I.	N.O.	R.	H.S.	AV.
TEST	18	3	213	52*	14.20
1ST-CLASS	205	51	2750	88	17.85
INT	6	1	15	8	3.00
RAL	52	23	465	43	16.03
NAT.W.	10	3	54	19*	7.71
B & H	20	7	130	23*	10.00

CAREER: BOWLING

	O.	M.	R.	W.	AV.
TEST	370.5	75	1084	26	41.69
1ST-CLASS	5185.1	1438	13226	552	23.96
INT	136.3	19	552	15	36.80
RAL	756	65	3006	111	27.08
NAT.W.	196.4	39	580	36	16.11
B & H	358.1	63	1145	51	22.45

8. Who played more Tests, Harold Larwood or Douglas Jardine, and how many each?

ANDERSON, P. N.   Yorkshire

Full Name: Paul Napier Anderson
Role: Right-hand bat, right-arm
seam bowler
Born: 28 April 1966, Driffield,
East Yorkshire
Height: 6′ ½″ **Weight:** 12st 12lbs
Nickname: Rash
County debut: 1988
Parents: Charles Stanley and Dorothy
Marital status: Single
Family links with cricket: Father
was a useful league player
Education: Driffield School;
Humberside College of Higher
Education
Qualifications: 3 A-levels,
9 O-levels; Accountancy foundation
course
Jobs outside cricket: Accountancy
clerk, building labourer, barman at Scarborough Cricket Club
Off-season 1988–89: 'I am going to play cricket in New Zealand for the winter.
The club is based in Napier.'
Cricketing superstitions or habits: 'Favourite shirt. I can't find anything which
makes any difference to my performance – tried everything.'
Cricketers particularly learnt from: 'Have been encouraged and advised by
Steve Oldham – also helped by, and learnt from, Simon Dennis.'
Cricketers particularly admired: Dennis Lillee, Geoff Boycott
Other sports played: Golf, hockey and fitness training
Other sports followed: Golf, football, snooker

LAST SEASON: BATTING

	I.	N.O.	R.	H.S.	AV.
TEST					
1ST-CLASS	1	0	0	0	0.00
INT					
RAL					
NAT.W.					
B & H					

CAREER: BATTING

	I.	N.O.	R.	H.S.	AV.
TEST					
1ST-CLASS	1	0	0	0	0.00
INT					
RAL					
NAT.W.					
B & H					

LAST SEASON: BOWLING

	O.	M.	R.	W.	AV.
TEST					
1ST-CLASS	17.3	4	47	1	47.00
INT					
RAL					
NAT.W.					
B & H					

CAREER: BOWLING

	O.	M.	R.	W.	AV.
TEST					
1ST-CLASS	17.3	4	47	1	47.00
INT					
RAL					
NAT.W.					
B & H					

Injuries 1988: Sprained ankle for a couple of weeks
Relaxations: Eating out, watching television
Extras: Once took nine wickets for one run at school. Never represented Yorkshire at any junior levels
Opinions on cricket: 'I don't think there should be so many overseas players playing in English cricket. Also don't want to see cricket going the way of football in terms of crowd violence and its transfer system of players.'
Best bowling performance: 1-47 Yorkshire v Sri Lankans, Leeds 1988

ANDREW, S. J. W. Hampshire

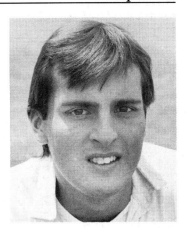

Full Name: Stephen Jon Walter Andrew
Role: Right-hand bat, right-arm medium bowler
Born: 27 January 1966, London
Height: 6′ 3″ **Weight:** 13st
Nickname: Rip
County debut: 1984
1st-Class 5 w. in innings: 4
Place in batting averages: 187th av. 20.50
Place in bowling averages: 47th av. 24.67 (1987 14th av. 21.29)
Strike rate 1988: 52.03 (career 39.52)
1st-Class catches 1988: 1 (career 11)
Parents: Jon Trevor and Victoria Julia Maud
Marital status: Single
Education: Hordle House Prep. School; Milton Abbey Public School
Qualifications: 3 O-levels
Overseas teams played for: Pirates CC, Durban, South Africa, 1983–84; South African Police CC, 1984
Overseas tours: Young England to West Indies 1985
Cricketers particularly learnt from: Peter Sainsbury, Malcolm Marshall
Cricketers particularly admired: Dennis Lillee, Malcolm Marshall
Other sports played: Squash, golf
Other sports followed: Interested in most sports
Injuries 1988: Stress fracture of the spine caused him to miss the last part of the season
Relaxations: Listening to music
Extras: Youngest bowler to have opened bowling for Hampshire

Best batting performance: 12* Hampshire v Middlesex, Basingstoke 1988
Best bowling performance: 7-92 Hampshire v Gloucestershire, Southampton 1987

LAST SEASON: BATTING

	I.	N.O.	R.	H.S.	AV.
TEST					
1ST-CLASS	9	7	41	12*	20.50
INT					
RAL	1	1	1	1*	–
NAT.W.	–	–	–	–	–
B & H	1	1	4	4*	–

CAREER: BATTING

	I.	N.O.	R.	H.S.	AV.
TEST					
1ST-CLASS	27	18	84	12*	9.33
INT					
RAL	1	1	1	1*	–
NAT.W.	1	1	0	0*	–
B & H	2	2	5	4*	–

LAST SEASON: BOWLING

	O.	M.	R.	W.	AV.
TEST					
1ST-CLASS	268.5	68	765	31	24.67
INT					
RAL	46	0	228	5	45.60
NAT.W.	24	3	69	2	34.50
B & H	75	7	245	9	27.22

CAREER: BOWLING

	O.	M.	R.	W.	AV.
TEST					
1ST-CLASS	1172.4	257	3728	134	27.82
INT					
RAL	121.3	1	600	12	50.00
NAT.W.	50	5	185	5	37.00
B & H	109	11	363	20	18.15

ASIF DIN, M.   Warwickshire

Full Name: Mohamed Asif Din
Role: Right-hand bat, leg-break bowler
Born: 21 September 1960, Kampala, Uganda
Height: 5′ 10″ **Weight:** 10st
Nickname: Gunga 'and many others'
County debut: 1981
County cap: 1987
1000 runs in a season: 2
1st-Class 50s scored: 28
1st-Class 100s scored: 5
1st-Class 5 w. in innings: 1
One-Day 50s: 9
One-Day 100s: 2
Place in batting averages: 42nd av. 38.51 (1987 89th av. 33.00)
1st-Class catches 1988: 18 (career 80)
Parents: Jamiz and Mumtaz
Marital status: Married
Family links with cricket: Brothers Khalid and Abid play in Birmingham League
Education: Ladywood Comprehensive School, Birmingham

Qualifications: CSEs and O-levels
Jobs outside cricket: Argos Distributors Limited
Cricketing superstitions: 'Mixing my batting gloves around every time.'
Overseas tours: MCC to East Africa 1981; MCC to Bangladesh 1980–81; Dennis Amiss XI to Barbados 1985
Overseas teams played for: Rugby Union CC, Bathurst, New South Wales, 1984–85; Blayney CC, Blayney, New South Wales, 1985–86
Cricketers particularly admired: Zaheer Abbas, Majid Khan
Other sports played: Squash, badminton, golf, snooker
Other sports followed: American football, basketball
Relaxations: Staying in
Opinions on cricket: 'Too much cricket. Would like to see 16 four-day matches.'
Best batting performance: 158* Warwickshire v Cambridge University, Cambridge 1988
Best bowling performance: 5-100 Warwickshire v Glamorgan, Edgbaston 1982

LAST SEASON: BATTING

	I.	N.O.	R.	H.S.	AV.
TEST					
1ST-CLASS	41	4	1425	158*	38.51
INT					
RAL	14	2	310	93*	25.83
NAT.W.	2	0	53	28	26.50
B & H	5	1	246	107	61.50

CAREER: BATTING

	I.	N.O.	R.	H.S.	AV.
TEST					
1ST-CLASS	227	35	5837	158*	30.40
INT					
RAL	89	15	1881	108*	25.41
NAT.W.	15	4	274	45	24.90
B & H	23	4	598	107	31.47

LAST SEASON: BOWLING

	O.	M.	R.	W.	AV.
TEST					
1ST-CLASS	101	17	387	6	64.50
INT					
RAL					
NAT.W.	8	1	19	1	19.00
B & H	9	0	42	1	42.00

CAREER: BOWLING

	O.	M.	R.	W.	AV.
TEST					
1ST-CLASS	718.5	125	2899	50	57.98
INT					
RAL	15.3	1	90	3	30.00
NAT.W.	9.1	1	24	2	12.00
B & H	11	0	62	1	62.00

9. Who was chosen as captain and vice-captain of the cancelled England tour to India, in 1988–89?

10. Which West Indian Test cricketer was released by Northamptonshire at the end of the 1988 season?

ATHERTON, M. A.   Lancashire

Full Name: Michael Andrew Atherton
Role: Right-hand bat, leg-break bowler
Born: 23 March 1968, Manchester
Height: 6′ **Weight:** 12st
Nickname: Athers
County debut: 1987
1000 runs in a season: 2
1st-Class 50s scored: 7
1st-Class 100s scored: 6
One-Day 50s: 1
Place in batting averages: 14th av. 48.73 (1987 50th av. 38.48)
Place in bowling averages: 135th av. 75.18
Strike rate 1988: 146.81 (career 129.60)
1st-Class catches 1988: 15 (career 22)
Parents: Alan and Wendy
Marital status: Single
Family links with cricket: Father plays club cricket with Widhowes CC in Lancashire and Cheshire League
Education: The Manchester Grammar School; Downing College, Cambridge
Qualifications: 10 O-levels, 3 A-levels; 2:1 in Part 1 History BA Degree
Off-season 1988–89: Studying at Cambridge University
Cricketing superstitions or habits: Always put left pad on first; won't eat curry before a match

LAST SEASON: BATTING

	I.	N.O.	R.	H.S.	AV.
TEST					
1ST-CLASS	27	4	1121	152*	48.73
INT					
RAL					
NAT.W.					
B & H	4	0	84	38	21.00

CAREER: BATTING

	I.	N.O.	R.	H.S.	AV.
TEST					
1ST-CLASS	62	8	2314	152*	42.85
INT					
RAL	3	0	25	22	8.33
NAT.W.					
B & H	7	0	171	57	24.42

LAST SEASON: BOWLING

	O.	M.	R.	W.	AV.
TEST					
1ST-CLASS	269.1	42	827	11	75.18
INT					
RAL					
NAT.W.					
B & H	1	0	8	0	–

CAREER: BOWLING

	O.	M.	R.	W.	AV.
TEST					
1ST-CLASS	432	58	1371	20	68.55
INT					
RAL					
NAT.W.					
B & H	3	0	30	0	–

Overseas tours: NCA to Bermuda 1985; Young England to Sri Lanka 1986; Young England to Australia 1987
Cricketers particularly learnt from: Father, Graham Saville (Cambridge coach), Gehan Mendis
Cricketers particularly admired: Gehan Mendis, David Gower
Other sports played: Football, golf, squash
Other sports followed: Most sports except horse racing, wrestling and boxing
Opinions on cricket: 'Over-rate fines should be abolished. Four-day cricket is extremely boring. County cricket too often takes the brunt for failures in the Test arena (e.g. the substitute rule in 1988).'
Best batting performance: 152* Lancashire v Sussex, Hove 1988
Best bowling performance: 3-32 Lancashire v Middlesex, Old Trafford 1988

ATHEY, C. W. J.   Gloucestershire

Full Name: Charles William Jeffrey Athey
Role: Right-hand bat, right-arm medium bowler
Born: 27 September 1957, Middlesbrough
Height: 5′ 10″ **Weight:** 12st 3lbs
Nickname: Bumper, Wingnut, Ath
County debut: 1976 (Yorkshire), 1984 (Gloucestershire)
County cap: 1980 (Yorkshire), 1985 (Gloucestershire)
Test debut: 1980
No. of Tests: 23
No. of One-Day Internationals: 31
1000 runs in a season: 7
1st-Class 50s scored: 70
1st-Class 100s scored: 31
One-Day 50s: 55
One-Day 100s: 6
Place in batting averages: 4th av. 66.50 (1987 22nd av. 44.65)
1st-Class catches 1987: 18 (career 281 + 2 stumpings)
Parents: Peter and Maree
Wife and date of marriage: Janet Linda, 9 October 1982
Family links with cricket: 'Father played league cricket in North Yorkshire and South Durham League for 29 years, 25 of them with Middlesbrough. President of Middlesbrough CC since 1975. Brother-in-law Colin Cook played for Middlesex, other brother-in-law (Martin) plays in Thames Valley League. Father-in-law deeply involved in Middlesex Youth cricket.'

Education: Linthorpe Junior School; Stainsby Secondary School; Acklam Hall High School

Qualifications: 4 O-levels, some CSEs, National Cricket Association Coaching Certificate

Jobs outside cricket: Barman, building labourer, sports shop assistant

Overseas tours: D. H. Robins' XI to Canada 1976; South America 1979; Australasia 1980; England U-19 to West Indies 1976; England to West Indies 1981; Barbican XI to Gulf States 1983; England B to Sri Lanka 1985–86; England to Australia 1986–87; World Cup, Pakistan, Australia and New Zealand 1987–88

Overseas teams played for: Manly Warringah, Sydney, Australia, 1977–78, 1978–79, 1979–80; Balmain, Sydney, 1980–81; Schoeman Park, Bloemfontein, South Africa, 1981–82; Papatoetoe, Auckland, New Zealand, 1983–84

Cricketers particularly learnt from: Doug Padgett

Cricketers particularly admired: Gordon Greenidge, Malcolm Marshall, Chris Smith

Off-season 1988–89: Working for ADG Group (financial services company) in Bristol

Other sports played: Squash, tennis, soccer

Other sports followed: Most sports

Injuries 1988: Double break in knuckle joint on right hand. Out for last weeks of season

Relaxations: Music, good films, good food

Extras: Played for Teeside County Schools U-16s at age 12. Made debut in 1972 North Yorkshire and South Durham League. Played for Yorkshire Colts 1974. Played for North of England Young Cricketers XI v West Indies Young Cricketers at Old Trafford in 1974. Played football for Middlesbrough Schools U-16 XI 1972–74. Played for Middlesbrough Juniors 1974–75. Offered but declined apprenticeship terms with Middlesbrough FC. Captained North Riding U-19 XI 1975–76. Has Union Jack tattoo on left shoulder

Opinions on cricket: 'Tighten up on "qualifying for England" rules; too many overseas players. Must play on better wickets. Impressed by four-day experi-

LAST SEASON: BATTING

	I.	N.O.	R.	H.S.	AV.
TEST	2	0	27	16	13.50
1ST-CLASS	20	6	1037	168*	74.07
INT					
RAL	10	1	411	67	45.66
NAT.W.	2	0	73	62	36.50
B & H	4	1	177	82	59.00

CAREER: BATTING

	I.	N.O.	R.	H.S.	AV.
TEST	41	1	919	123	22.97
1ST-CLASS	449	46	14059	184	34.88
INT	30	3	848	142*	31.40
RAL	148	13	4786	121*	35.45
NAT.W.	28	4	899	115	37.45
B & H	47	7	1395	95	34.87

LAST SEASON: BOWLING

	O.	M.	R.	W.	AV.
TEST					
1ST-CLASS	5	0	20	0	—
INT					
RAL					
NAT.W.					
B & H					

CAREER: BOWLING

	O.	M.	R.	W.	AV.
TEST					
1ST-CLASS	503	88	1706	37	46.10
INT	1	0	10	0	—
RAL	95.4	1	545	21	25.95
NAT.W.	19.1	1	106	1	106.00
B & H	56.4	4	242	12	20.16

ment. Continually disappointed with press attacks on all and sundry in cricket.'

Best batting performance: 184 England B v Sri Lanka XI, Galle 1985–86
Best bowling performance: 3-3 Gloucestershire v Hampshire, Bristol 1985

ATKINS, P. D. Surrey

Full Name: Paul David Atkins
Role: Right-hand bat, right-arm bowler
Born: 11 June 1966, Aylesbury
Height: 6′ 1″ **Weight:** 13st 7lbs
Nickname: Ripper
County debut: 1988
1st-Class 50s scored: 1
1st-Class 100s scored: 1
One-Day 50s scored: 1
Place in batting averages: 55th av. 35.70
Parents: Brian Alan Arthur and Thelma
Marital status: Single
Family links with cricket: Father plays club cricket for Dinton CC
Education: Aylesbury Grammar School
Qualifications: 7 O-levels, 3 A-levels
Off-season 1988–89: Playing for Perth CC, Western Australia
Cricketing superstitions or habits: Always bats with cap or helmet
Overseas tours: NAYC U-19 to Bermuda 1985; Surrey CCC to United Arab Emirates 1988
Overseas teams played for: Pietermaritzburg University 1985–86; Alexandrians 1986–88, South Africa
Circketers particularly learnt from: Roy Wills, Chris Waller
Cricketers particularly admired: Gordon Greenidge
Other sports played: Golf, football
Other sports followed: Follows Portsmouth FC
Injuries 1988: Hernia operation. Missed last 6 weeks of season
Relaxations: Listening to music. Member of OTT Club with G. E. Brown and J. D. Robinson
Extras: Won Gold Award on Nat West debut. Seventh Surrey player to score hundred on debut. Scored 99 on County Championship debut.

Opinions on cricket: 'Avoid politics and play cricket with all races and anywhere in the world.'
Best batting performance: 114* Surrey v Cambridge University, Cambridge 1988

LAST SEASON: BATTING

	I.	N.O.	R.	H.S.	AV.
TEST					
1ST-CLASS	11	1	357	114*	35.70
INT					
RAL	1	0	2	2	2.00
NAT.W.	2	0	82	82	41.00
B & H					

CAREER: BATTING

	I.	N.O.	R.	H.S.	AV.
TEST					
1ST-CLASS	11	1	357	114*	35.70
INT					
RAL	1	0	2	2	2.00
NAT.W.	2	0	82	82	41.00
B & H					

ATKINSON, J. C. M.   Somerset

Full Name: Jonathan Colin Mark Atkinson
Role: Right-hand bat, right-arm medium bowler
Born: 10 July 1968, Butleigh
Height: 6′ 4″ **Weight:** 14st 7lbs
Nickname: Ako, Atki
County debut: 1985
1st-Class 50s scored: 2
Place in batting averages: 177th av. 21.41
Parents: Colin (C. R. M.) and Shirley
Marital status: Single
Family links with cricket: Father captain of Somerset CCC 1965–67. On TCCB
Education: Millfield School; Cambridge University
Qualifications: 11 O-levels, 3 A-levels
Off-season 1988–89: At Cambridge University
Overseas tours: Millfield School to Barbados 1986
Cricketers particularly learnt from: Father, Gerry Wilson (Millfield pro.), Martin Crowe, Peter Robinson (Somerset CC coach)
Cricketers particularly admired: 'Vivian Richards and Ian Botham for their competitive natures, Imran Khan, Dennis Lillee, Richard Hadlee and Paul Veness.'
Other sports played: Rugby, hockey, basketball, golf
Relaxations: 'Socialising and vodka.'
Injuries 1988: Twisted knee

Extras: Hit highest score of 79 v Northamptonshire on his first-class debut 1985

Opinions on cricket: 'I think it's upsetting that politics should interfere with cricket re South Africa with so much talent in that country. I found the politics of a cricket dressing-room sometimes volatile and juvenile, but most of all interesting. Things are finally going right at Somerset CCC.'

Best batting performance: 79 Somerset v Northamptonshire, Weston 1985

Best bowling performance: 2-80 Somerset v India, Taunton 1986

LAST SEASON: BATTING

	I.	N.O.	R.	H.S.	AV.
TEST					
1ST-CLASS	12	0	257	73	21.41
INT					
RAL	1	0	2	2	2.00
NAT.W.					
B & H	3	0	35	24	11.66

LAST SEASON: BOWLING

	O.	M.	R.	W.	AV.
TEST					
1ST-CLASS	17	1	86	1	86.00
INT					
RAL					
NAT.W.					
B & H					

CAREER: BATTING

	I.	N.O.	R.	H.S.	AV.
TEST					
1ST-CLASS	23	3	495	79	24.75
INT					
RAL	2	0	2	2	1.00
NAT.W.	–	–	–	–	–
B & H	3	0	35	24	11.66

CAREER: BOWLING

	O.	M.	R.	W.	AV.
TEST					
1ST-CLASS	116	17	468	5	93.60
INT					
RAL					
NAT.W.	6	2	16	1	16.00
B & H					

AUSTIN, I. D.   Lancashire

Full Name: Ian David Austin

Role: Left-hand bat, right-arm medium bowler

Born: 30 May 1966, Haslingden, Lancashire

Height: 5′ 10″ **Weight:** 14st 7lbs

Nickname: Oscar, Bully

County debut: 1986

One-Day 50s: 2

1st-Class 5 w. in innings: 2

One-Day 50s: 1

Place in batting averages: 84th av. 30.85

Place in bowling averages: 35th av. 23.13

Strike rate 1988: 54.86 (career 57.00)

Parents: Jack and Ursula

Marital status: Single

Family links with cricket: Father opened batting for Haslingden CC
Education: Haslingden High School
Qualifications: NCA coach
Jobs outside cricket: Carpet fitter and cabinet maker
Overseas tours: NCA North U-19 to Bermuda 1985; Lancashire CCC to Jamaica 1987
Overseas teams played for: Morochydore, Queensland 1987
Cricketers particularly learnt from: Hartley Alleyne, Robby Bentley
Cricketers particularly admired: Ian Botham, Collis King, Mudassar Nazar
Other sports played: Football, snooker, golf
Relaxations: Listening to music, playing snooker, reading
Extras: Holds amateur Lancashire League record for highest individual score for amateur since limited overs (149*)
Opinions on cricket: 'I think the game would benefit from playing four-day county games. It would cut down the number of games played and save the clubs money in the long run, making results more possible and therefore more enjoyable to watch.'
Best batting performance: 64 Lancashire v Derbyshire, Old Trafford 1988
Best bowling performance: 5-79 Lancashire v Surrey, The Oval 1988

LAST SEASON: BATTING

	I.	N.O.	R.	H.S.	AV.
TEST					
1ST-CLASS	9	2	216	64	30.85
INT					
RAL	8	4	102	41	25.50
NAT.W.					
B & H	2	0	29	20	14.50

CAREER: BATTING

	I.	N.O.	R.	H.S.	AV.
TEST					
1ST-CLASS	10	2	253	64	31.62
INT					
RAL	14	5	136	41	15.11
NAT.W.	1	0	10	10	10.00
B & H	4	0	111	80	27.75

LAST SEASON: BOWLING

	O.	M.	R.	W.	AV.
TEST					
1ST-CLASS	137.1	43	347	15	23.13
INT					
RAL	74	3	330	13	25.38
NAT.W.					
B & H	28	3	112	2	56.00

CAREER: BOWLING

	O.	M.	R.	W.	AV.
TEST					
1ST-CLASS	171	50	411	18	22.83
INT					
RAL	126	4	612	16	38.25
NAT.W.	12	1	50	0	–
B & H	50	6	197	3	65.66

11. Who resigned as Somerset captain in 1988 and who succeeded him?
12. How many players appeared for England v West Indies in 1988?
13. Which former England captain is chairman of Glamorgan?

AYLING, J. R.　　　　Hampshire

Full Name: Jonathan Richard Ayling
Role: Right-hand bat, right-arm
medium bowler
Born: 13 June 1967, Portsmouth
Height: 6′ 4½″ **Weight:** 13st 7lbs
Nickname: Victor
County debut: 1987 (RA Sunday
League)
1st-Class 50s scored: 4
Place in batting averages: 143rd
av. 24.51
Place in bowling averages: 38th
av. 23.36
Strike rate 1988: 55.17 (career 55.17)
1st-Class catches 1988: 5 (career 5)
Parents: Christopher Jeremy and
Mary
Marital status: Single
Education: Portsmouth Grammar
School, Hampshire
Qualifications: 8 O-levels, 1 A-level
Jobs outside cricket: Cricket coach
Off-season 1988–89: Improving fitness for new season
Overseas teams played for: Pinelands CC, Cape Town 1986–87, 1987–88
Cricketers particularly learnt from: John Rice, Robin and Chris Smith,
Jimmy Gray, Peter Sainsbury, Mark Nicholas
Cricketers particularly admired: Barry Richards, Gordon Greenidge, Malcolm Marshall, Paul Terry
Other sports played: Snooker, squash, tennis

LAST SEASON: BATTING

	I.	N.O.	R.	H.S.	AV.
TEST					
1ST-CLASS	33	4	711	88*	24.51
INT					
RAL	9	1	153	41*	19.12
NAT.W.	3	2	33	25	33.00
B & H	1	0	1	1	1.00

CAREER: BATTING

	I.	N.O.	R.	H.S.	AV.
TEST					
1ST-CLASS	33	4	711	88*	24.51
INT					
RAL	10	1	168	41*	18.66
NAT.W.	3	2	33	25	33.00
B & H	1	0	1	1	1.00

LAST SEASON: BOWLING

	O.	M.	R.	W.	AV.
TEST					
1ST-CLASS	432.1	97	1098	47	23.36
INT					
RAL	81	2	362	12	30.16
NAT.W.	47	9	154	5	30.80
B & H	31	7	99	3	33.00

CAREER: BOWLING

	O.	M.	R.	W.	AV.
TEST					
1ST-CLASS	432.1	97	1098	47	23.36
INT					
RAL	97	2	429	15	28.60
NAT.W.	47	9	154	5	30.80
B & H	31	7	99	3	33.00

Other sports followed: Soccer, rugby, golf, tennis, athletics
Relaxations: Fell walking in Lake District, reading, listening to music, evenings out with friends
Opinions on cricket: 'The four-day experiment has proved a success. Players should be able to play or coach world-wide without interference from politicians.'
Best batting performance: 88* Hampshire v Lancashire, Liverpool 1988
Best bowling performance: 4-57 Hampshire v Gloucestershire, Gloucester 1988
4-57 Hampshire v Sussex, Eastbourne 1988

AYMES, A. N. Hampshire

Full Name: Adrian Nigel Aymes
Role: Right-hand bat, wicket-keeper
Born: 4 June 1964, Southampton
Height: 6′ **Weight:** 13st 4lbs
Nickname: Ady
County debut: 1987
1st-Class 50s scored: 1
Parents: Michael and Barbara
Marital status: Single
Education: Shirley Middle; Bellemoor Secondary; Hill College
Qualifications: 3 O-levels, 1 A-level
Jobs outside cricket: Sports shop salesman, labourer
Off-season 1988–89: Playing football and relaxing

LAST SEASON: BATTING

	I.	N.O.	R.	H.S.	AV.
TEST					
1ST-CLASS	–	–	–	–	–
INT					
RAL	–	–	–	–	–
NAT.W.					
B & H					

CAREER: BATTING

	I.	N.O.	R.	H.S.	AV.
TEST					
1ST-CLASS	1	0	58	58	58.00
INT					
RAL					
NAT.W.					
B & H					

LAST SEASON: WICKET KEEPING

	C.	ST.			
TEST					
1ST-CLASS	3	–			
INT					
RAL	–	–			
NAT.W.					
B & H					

CAREER: WICKET KEEPING

	C.	ST.			
TEST					
1ST-CLASS	4	–			
INT					
RAL	2	1			
NAT.W.					
B & H					

Cricketing superstitions or habits: Tap four corners of the batting crease
Cricketer particularly learnt from: Andy Brassington
Cricketers particularly admired: Bob Taylor
Other sports played: Football, tennis
Other sports followed: American football, Australian rules football, golf
Injuries 1988: Dislocated finger and knee injury
Relaxations: 'Watching video films; keeping fit; working on my car; taking my girl-friend's dog for a walk.'
Extras: Half century on debut v Surrey
Best batting performance: 58 Hampshire v Surrey, Southampton 1987

BABINGTON, A. M. Sussex

Full Name: Andrew Mark Babington
Role: Left-hand bat, right-arm fast-medium bowler
Born: 22 July 1963, London
Height: 6′ 2″ **Weight:** 13st
Nickname: Hagar, Vinny Jones
County debut: 1986
Place in bowling averages: 102nd av. 33.22 (1987 125th av. 42.76)
Strike rate 1988: 67.93 (career 65.00)
1st-Class catches 1988: 8 (career 15)
Parents: Roy and Maureen
Family links with cricket: 'Father played good club cricket. Mother used to wash my whites.'
Education: Reigate Grammar School; Borough Road PE College
Qualifications: 5 O-levels, 2 A-levels; Member of Institute of Legal Executives
Jobs outside cricket: Work for father's and other firms of solicitors as legal executive. Worked on building sites. Associate with Abbey Life Assurance Company
Off-season 1988–89: Working as Sales Associate with Abbey Life, Crawley branch
Cricketing superstitions or habits: 'Always put my kit on in the same order.'
Overseas tours: Surrey Schools Cricket Association to Australia 1980
Cricketers particularly learnt from: Bob Cottam, Kevin Gibbs, John Snow, John Goodey and staff at Sussex CCC

Cricketers particularly admired: Dennis Lillee, John Snow, Andy Roberts, Michael Holding
Other sports played: Football, squash, golf, snooker, shooting
Other sports followed: All motor sports
Injuries 1988: Damaged finger
Relaxations: Eating out, social drinking with friends, playing golf, reading, listening to music, driving. Helping Kevin Gibbs run his business
Opinions on cricket: 'Cricketers should be free to play anywhere in the world without political repercussions. After all Indian and Pakistani players play in one game alongside South Africans and their governments do not complain then. Overseas players should be limited to one per county, that is, one registered and only one eligible.'
Best batting performance: 16 Sussex v Middlesex, Lord's 1987
Best bowling performance: 4-18 Sussex v Gloucestershire, Bristol 1986

LAST SEASON: BATTING

	I.	N.O.	R.	H.S.	AV.
TEST					
1ST-CLASS	26	8	87	12	4.83
INT					
RAL	–	–	–	–	–
NAT.W.	1	1	0	0*	–
B & H	1	1	4	4*	–

LAST SEASON: BOWLING

	O.	M.	R.	W.	AV.
TEST					
1ST-CLASS	554.5	111	1628	49	33.22
INT					
RAL	78	3	353	7	50.42
NAT.W.	6	0	32	1	32.00
B & H	37	0	155	6	25.83

CAREER: BATTING

	I.	N.O.	R.	H.S.	AV.
TEST					
1ST-CLASS	44	17	146	16	5.40
INT					
RAL	4	1	1	1	0.33
NAT.W.	2	2	4	4*	–
B & H	2	1	5	4*	5.00

CAREER: BOWLING

	O.	M.	R.	W.	AV.
TEST					
1ST-CLASS	920.5	171	2874	85	33.81
INT					
RAL	160	7	779	16	48.68
NAT.W.	41	0	195	7	27.85
B & H	62	3	273	13	21.00

14. Which former captain of an English county played for Scotland in 1988?

15. Which England Test player called his house 'Dunbolin', when he retired?

16. Who played more Tests, Greg or Ian Chappell, and how many?

BAILEY, R. J. — Northamptonshire

Full Name: Robert John Bailey
Role: Right-hand bat, off-break bowler
Born: 28 October 1963, Biddulph, Stoke-on-Trent
Height: 6′ 3″ **Weight:** 14st
Nickname: Bailers, Nose Bag ('I eat a lot!')
County debut: 1982
County cap: 1985
Test debut: 1988
No. of Tests: 1
No. of One-Day Internationals: 2
1000 runs in a season: 5
1st-Class 50s scored: 37
1st-Class 100s scored: 13
1st-Class 200s scored: 2
One-Day 50s: 20
One-Day 100s: 4
Place in batting averages: 48th av. 36.20 (1987 56th av. 37.47)
1st-Class catches 1988: 23 (career 90)
Parents: John and Marie
Wife and date of marriage: Rachel, 11 April 1987
Family links with cricket: Father played in North Staffordshire League for 30 years for Knypersley and Minor Counties cricket for Staffordshire as wicket-keeper. Second cousin to Phil Bainbridge of Gloucestershire
Education: Biddulph High School
Qualifications: 6 CSEs, 1 O-level
Jobs outside cricket: Worked for three winters in electrical trade

LAST SEASON: BATTING

	I.	N.O.	R.	H.S.	AV.
TEST	2	0	46	43	23.00
1ST-CLASS	40	2	1402	127*	36.89
INT					
RAL	12	0	291	78	24.25
NAT.W.	1	0	7	7	7.00
B & H	3	0	168	89	56.00

LAST SEASON: BOWLING

	O.	M.	R.	W.	AV.
TEST					
1ST-CLASS	76.1	10	278	7	39.71
INT					
RAL					
NAT.W.					
B & H	3	0	7	0	—

CAREER: BATTING

	I.	N.O.	R.	H.S.	AV.
TEST	2	0	46	43	23.00
1ST-CLASS	216	35	7300	224*	40.33
INT	2	1	52	41*	52.00
RAL	70	9	2119	125*	34.73
NAT.W.	14	4	314	56*	31.40
B & H	22	1	933	134	44.42

CAREER: BOWLING

	O.	M.	R.	W.	AV.
TEST					
1ST-CLASS	149	35	462	14	33.00
INT	6	0	25	0	—
RAL	10	0	82	3	27.33
NAT.W.	2	0	16	1	16.00
B & H	10	3	29	1	29.00

Off-season 1988–89: Was picked for cancelled England tour to India
Overseas tours: England to Sharjah 1985 and 1987 for Rothmans One-Day International tournament
Overseas teams played for: Rhodes University, Grahamstown, 1982–83; Witenhage CC, South Africa, 1983–84, 1984–85; Fitzroy CC, Melbourne 1985–86; Gosnells CC, Perth 1987–88
Cricketers particularly learnt from: My father, Stan Crump, Dennis Lillee (since his arrival at Northampton)
Other sports played: Badminton, football, golf
Other sports followed: 'Like to see Port Vale and Stoke City doing well.'
Relaxations: Listening to music
Extras: Played for Young England v Young Australia, 1983. Scored two hundreds in match v Middlesex 2nd XI 1984. The only Northants batsman to score 1000 championships runs in 1988
Best batting performance: 224* Northamptonshire v Glamorgan, Swansea 1986
Best bowling performance: 3-27 Northamptonshire v Glamorgan, Wellingborough 1988

BAINBRIDGE, P.   Gloucestershire

Full Name: Philip Bainbridge
Role: Right-hand bat, right-arm medium bowler
Born: 16 April 1958, Stoke-on-Trent
Height: 5′ 9½″ **Weight:** 12st 7lbs
Nickname: Bains, Robbo
County debut: 1977
County cap: 1981
Benefit: 1989
1000 runs in a season: 7
1st-Class 50s scored: 59
1st-Class 100s scored: 18
1st-Class 5 w. in innings: 7
One-Day 50s: 16
One-Day 100s: 1
Place in batting averages: 51st av. 36.05 (1987 69th av. 35.15)
Place in bowling averages: 133rd av. 62.00 (1987 105th av. 37.26)
Strike rate 1988: 114.35 (career 72.75)
1st-Class catches 1988: 9 (career 102)
Parents: Leonard George and Lilian Rose

Wife and date of marriage: Barbara, 22 September 1979
Children: Neil, 11 January 1984; Laura, 15 January 1985
Family links with cricket: Cousin, Stephen Wilkinson, played for Somerset 1969–72. Second cousin to Rob Bailey of Northants
Education: Hanley High School; Stoke-on-Trent Sixth Form College; Borough Road College of Education
Qualifications: 9 O-levels, 2 A-levels, BEd, MCC Coaching Certificate
Jobs outside cricket: PE Lecturer, Marketing Executive with Gloucs CCC until 1988, sales representative
Off-season 1988–89: Working on Benefit year
Overseas tours: Holland with NCA North of England Youth team 1976; Barbados, Trinidad and Tobago with British Colleges 1978; Barbados with Gloucestershire CCC 1980; Pakistan for two Zaheer Abbas benefit matches 1983; Zimbabwe with English Counties XI 1985; Barbados with David Graveney Benefit Tour 1986; Sri Lanka with Gloucestershire 1987; Zimbabwe with Gloucestershire CCC 1988; Sri Lanka with Gloucestershire 1989
Cricketers particularly learnt from: All senior players at Gloucestershire – and county coach
Cricketers particularly admired: Mike Procter
Other sports played: Football, rugby, squash, golf
Other sports followed: All sports
Injuries 1988: Recurrent knee injury resulting in operation in October 1988
Relaxations: Photography, wine-making, beer-making, listening to music. 'Walking in the country with my Golden Retriever dog and my wife, entertaining my children.'
Extras: Played for four 2nd XIs in 1976 – Gloucestershire, Derbyshire, Northamptonshire and Warwickshire. Played for Young England v Australia 1977. Won Commercial Union U-23 Batsman of the Year 1981. Scored first century for Stoke-on-Trent aged 14. One of *Wisden*'s Five Cricketers of the Year, 1985. Stood down from vice captaincy of the county to concentrate on Benefit in 1989
Opinions on cricket: 'The four-day cricket experiment went extremely well in 1988 and I think the authorities should consider 16 four-day games in future.

LAST SEASON: BATTING

	I.	N.O.	R.	H.S.	AV.
TEST					
1ST-CLASS	38	1	1334	169	36.05
INT					
RAL	13	2	378	81	34.36
NAT.W.	2	0	101	89	50.50
B & H	4	0	160	96	40.00

CAREER: BATTING

	I.	N.O.	R.	H.S.	AV.
TEST					
1ST-CLASS	363	54	10291	169	33.30
INT					
RAL	118	23	1991	106*	20.95
NAT.W.	18	2	528	89	33.00
B & H	34	8	757	96	29.11

LAST SEASON: BOWLING

	O.	M.	R.	W.	AV.
TEST					
1ST-CLASS	324	62	1054	17	62.00
INT					
RAL	87.4	4	429	16	26.18
NAT.W.	35	7	85	3	28.33
B & H	35	5	113	3	37.66

CAREER: BOWLING

	O.	M.	R.	W.	AV.
TEST					
1ST-CLASS	2873.4	653	8708	237	36.74
INT					
RAL	777.2	25	3915	135	29.00
NAT.W.	204	26	690	24	28.75
B & H	292.3	31	1062	32	33.18

Refuge knock-out worked well, but colour clothes as well as ball should be introduced to increase interest.'
Best batting performance: 169 Gloucestershire v Yorkshire, Cheltenham 1988
Best bowling performance: 8-53 Gloucestershire v Somerset, Bristol 1986

BAIRSTOW, D. L. Yorkshire

Full Name: David Leslie Bairstow
Role: Right-hand bat, wicket-keeper, occasional medium pacer
Born: 1 September 1951, Bradford
Height: 5′ 10″ **Weight:** 14st 7lbs
Nickname: Bluey
County debut: 1970
County cap: 1973
Benefit: 1982 (£56,913)
Test debut: 1979
No. of Tests: 4
No. of One-Day Internationals: 21
1000 runs in a season: 3
1st-Class 50s scored: 71
1st-Class 100s scored: 9
One-Day 50s: 16
One-Day 100s: 1
Place in batting averages: 182nd
av. 20.80 (1987 82nd av. 33.45)
Wife and date of marriage: Janet, 14 October 1988
Children: Andrew David
Family links with cricket: Father, Lesley, played cricket for Laisterdyke
Education: Hanson Grammar School, Bradford
Qualifications: O and A-levels
Jobs outside cricket: Runs his own office automation company
Off-season 1988–89: Working for his own company
Cricketing superstitions or habits: 'I will pat the ground three times or fiddle with my gloves three times. It is ridiculous but I do not want to stop it. I was in a pub a couple of days before the Leeds Test, and a lad I had never seen before gave me a medallion, and told me to keep it in my pocket for luck. Many people would have forgotten completely, but that medallion went into the pocket of my flannels, and stayed there for the whole match.'
Overseas tours: Australia 1978–79 and 1979–80; West Indies 1981
Overseas teams played for: Griqualand West 1966–67 and 1977–78
Cricketers particularly learnt from: Laurie Bennett (maths and sports master at school), Mike Fearnley

Relaxations: Gardening
Other sports played: Golf
Extras: Turned down an offer to play for Bradford City FC. Played for MCC Schools at Lord's in 1970. First Yorkshire wicket-keeper to get 1000 runs in a season (1982) since Arthur Wood in 1935. Set Yorkshire record of seven catches v Derbyshire at Scarborough, 1982. 133 consecutive John Player League matches. His 145 for Yorkshire v Middlesex is the highest score by a Yorkshire wicket-keeper. Allowed to take an A-level at 6 am at school in order to make Yorkshire debut. Published *A Yorkshire Diary – a year of crisis* 1984. Captain 1984–86. Completed his 1000 dismissals for Yorkshire in last match of 1988 season
Best batting performance: 145 Yorkshire v Middlesex, Scarborough 1980
Best bowling performance: 3-25 Yorkshire v MCC, Scarborough 1987

LAST SEASON: BATTING

	I.	N.O.	R.	H.S.	AV.
TEST					
1ST-CLASS	23	3	416	94*	20.80
INT					
RAL	9	1	47	22*	5.87
NAT.W.	1	0	36	36	36.00
B & H	2	1	21	13	21.00

CAREER: BATTING

	I.	N.O.	R.	H.S.	AV.
TEST	7	1	125	59	20.83
1ST-CLASS	617	115	13330	145	26.55
INT	20	6	206	23*	14.71
RAL	213	47	3416	83*	20.57
NAT.W.	27	5	492	92	22.36
B & H	53	10	803	103*	18.67

LAST SEASON: BOWLING

	O.	M.	R.	W.	AV.
TEST					
1ST-CLASS					
INT					
RAL					
NAT.W.					
B & H					

CAREER: BOWLING

	O.	M.	R.	W.	AV.
TEST					
1ST-CLASS	97	19	308	9	34.22
INT					
RAL					
NAT.W.					
B & H	3	0	17	0	–

LAST SEASON: WICKET KEEPING

	C.	ST.
TEST		
1ST-CLASS	38	1
INT		
RAL	10	1
NAT.W.	5	–
B & H	4	–

CAREER: WICKET KEEPING

	C.	ST.
TEST	12	1
1ST-CLASS	914	136
INT	17	4
RAL	222	21
NAT.W.	38	3
B & H	113	5

17. Which current Australian Test cricketer was awarded the MBE in 1988?

18. Which current New Zealand Test cricketer was awarded the MBE in 1988?

19. Who is captain of Oxford this season?

BAKKER, P.-J.　　　Hampshire

Full Name: Paul-Jan Bakker
Role: Right-hand bat, right-arm medium pace bowler
Born: 19 August 1957, Vlaardingen, Holland
Height: 6' 1" **Weight:** 14st
Nickname: Nip, Grandad, Peech, Dutchie
County debut: 1986
No. of One-Day Internationals: 17 for Holland
1st-Class 5 w. in innings: 2
Place in batting averages: 213th av. 16.66
Place in bowling averages: 29th av. 22.33
Strike rate 1988: 38.73 (career 56.67)
Parents: Hubertus Antonius Bakker and Wilhelmina Hendrika Bakker-Goos
Marital status: Single
Family links with cricket: Father is the scorer for the first team of my club in The Hague, and has been scorer of Hague CC for 15 years
Education: I^e VCL and Hugo de Groot College, The Hague, Holland
Qualifications: 'We have a different school system but finished my HAVO schooling.' Ski-instructor
Jobs outside cricket: Ski-instructor, public relations officer
Off-season 1988–89: Holiday; skiing in Switzerland, then to Cape Town to prepare for 1989 season
Cricketing superstitions or habits: 'I need coffee before a game and cigarettes at tea when my side is fielding. I always wear a T-shirt and short-sleeved sweater.'
Overseas tours: South Africa 1978 with Klaas Vervelde XI; several tours to England with Dutch clubs
Overseas teams played for: Green Point CC, Cape Town 1981–86; Flamingo Touring Club, Kent and Essex 1983; Holland, Gloucester, Essex and MCC 1984 and ICC trophy 1986
Cricketers particularly learnt from: Laddy Outschoorn, Hylton Ackerman
Cricketers particularly admired: Malcolm Marshall
Other sports played: 'I ski, play a bit of golf and like to drive fast.'
Other sports followed: Formula One motor racing, tennis, football, golf and most other sports
Injuries 1988: Shoulder; groin strains; ligaments in both ankles

Relaxations: Social visits to pubs, bars and restaurants; films and newspapers
Extras: First ever Dutch player to play professional cricket
Opinions on cricket: 'I think this South African issue has been blown out of all proportion. It must be my right as a professional cricketer, living in a "free" world to travel when and where I want to, and to make a living out of cricket as I please.'
Best batting performance: 16 Hampshire v Kent, Bournemouth 1988
Best bowling performance: 7-31 Hampshire v Kent, Bournemouth 1987

LAST SEASON: BATTING

	I.	N.O.	R.	H.S.	AV.
TEST					
1ST-CLASS	11	8	50	16	16.66
INT					
RAL	1	1	6	6*	–
NAT.W.	1	0	2	2	2.00
B & H					

LAST SEASON: BOWLING

	O.	M.	R.	W.	AV.
TEST					
1ST-CLASS	293.4	86	670	30	22.33
INT					
RAL	35.3	2	144	12	12.00
NAT.W.	23.4	3	70	5	14.00
B & H					

CAREER: BATTING

	I.	N.O.	R.	H.S.	AV.
TEST					
1ST-CLASS	14	9	56	16	11.20
INT					
RAL	1	1	6	6*	–
NAT.W.	1	0	2	2	2.00
B & H					

CAREER: BOWLING

	O.	M.	R.	W.	AV.
TEST					
1ST-CLASS	453.2	129	1139	48	23.72
INT					
RAL	70.1	2	311	19	16.36
NAT.W.	23.4	3	70	5	14.00
B & H	11	5	19	2	9.50

BALL, M. C. J.　　Gloucestershire

Full Name: Martyn Charles John Ball
Role: Right-hand bat, off-break bowler
Born: 26 April 1970, Bristol
Height: 5' 8" **Weight:** 11st 4lbs
Nickname: Baton, Bouncy, Medicine (anything to do with ball, e.g. 'cricket' ball)
County debut: 1988
Parents: Kenneth Charles and Pamela Wendy
Marital status: Single
Education: King Edmund Secondary School, Yate; Bath College of Further Education
Qualifications: 7 O-levels, 2 A-levels (Mathematics and Computer Science)

Jobs outside cricket: Full-time student up until June 1988
Off-season 1987–1988: In Melbourne, Australia, playing for Brunswick CC in the Sub-District Cricket League
Cricketing superstitions or habits: When bowling in long sleeve shirt always have right cuff undone
Overseas teams played for: Brunswick CC winter 1988–89 in Melbourne
Cricketers particularly learnt from: Graham Wiltshire, John Shepherd, Simon Packer (school PE Teacher who played for Young England and Gloucestershire)
Cricketers particularly admired: Ian Botham, John Emburey, Vic Marks
Other sports played: Football, rugby, most other sports
Other sports followed: All sport, especially football
Relaxations: Following Manchester City FC and listening to music, especially Sade and The Smiths
Extras: Represented County at rugby and football.
Opinions on cricket: 'Haven't got enough experience for valid opinions.'
Best batting performance: 2 Gloucestershire v Hampshire, Southampton 1988
Best bowling performance: 1-2 Gloucestershire v Hampshire, Southampton 1988

LAST SEASON: BATTING

	I.	N.O.	R.	H.S.	AV.
TEST					
1ST-CLASS	1	0	2	2	2.00
INT					
RAL					
NAT.W.					
B & H					

LAST SEASON: BOWLING

	O.	M.	R.	W.	AV.
TEST					
1ST-CLASS	34	8	90	2	45.00
INT					
RAL					
NAT.W.					
B & H					

CAREER: BATTING

	I.	N.O.	R.	H.S.	AV.
TEST					
1ST-CLASS	1	0	2	2	2.00
INT					
RAL					
NAT.W.					
B & H					

CAREER: BOWLING

	O.	M.	R.	W.	AV.
TEST					
1ST-CLASS	34	8	90	2	45.00
INT					
RAL					
NAT.W.					
B & H					

20. Who is captain of Cambridge this season?
21. What was special about Jack Simmons bowling Glamorgan's John Derrick at Swansea last season?
22. Whose nickname is Legger?

BANKS, D. A.   Warwickshire

Full Name: David Andrew Banks
Role: Right-hand bat, occasional seamer 'but trying to develop "offies"'
Born: 11 January 1961, Pensnett
Height: 6' 3" **Weight:** 15st
Nickname: Banksy, Old Dog
County debut: 1983 (Worcestershire), 1988 (Warwickshire)
1st-Class 50s scored: 3
1st-Class 100s scored: 1
One-Day 50s: 1
Place in batting averages: 145th av. 24.37
Parents: William and Betty
Marital status: Single
Family links with cricket: Father and brother both played for same club – Brierley Hill Athletic Club
Education: Biros Meadow Infants (Pensnett); St Marks Primary (Pensnett); The Pensnett School and Dudley Technical College
Qualifications: 4 O-levels, 4 CSEs (City and Guilds Fabrication, Mechanical and Electrical Engineering); NCA Coaching Certificate
Jobs outside cricket: Engineering apprenticeship (4 years) with Gibbons Bros; Groundsman (2 years) with Stourbridge Cricket Club
Off-season 1988–89: Playing/coaching in Western Australia
Cricketing superstitions or habits: Left pad on first
Overseas tours: Tour to Barbados 1981
Overseas teams played for: North Perth CC (Western Australia) 1982–83; Melville CC (Western Australia) 1983–84 and 1984–85; Collingwood Park CC (Albany, Western Australia) 1986–88
Cricketers particularly learnt from: Gordon Smith (Stourbridge CC), 'the best bowler outside first class cricket and still playing at 52.'
Cricketers particularly admired: Graeme Hick, Gordon Greenidge (consistency on all wickets at the highest level), Dennis Lillee, Michael Holding
Other sports played: Soccer, golf, tennis
Other sports followed: Aussie rules
Injuries 1988: Shin soreness, broken thumb
Relaxations: 'Music (mainly soul). Read the occasional book.'
Extras: Left Worcestershire to join Warwickshire in 1988
Opinions on cricket: 'A cricketer should be allowed to earn his living anywhere (without complications) as in other professions. The game is bigger than any person/s.'

Best batting performance: 100 Worcestershire v Oxford University, Oxford 1983 (on debut)

LAST SEASON: BATTING

	I.	N.O.	R.	H.S.	AV.
TEST					
1ST-CLASS	9	1	195	61	24.37
INT					
RAL	5	1	128	51*	32.00
NAT.W.					
B & H					

CAREER: BATTING

	I.	N.O.	R.	H.S.	AV.
TEST					
1ST-CLASS	38	4	896	100	26.05
INT					
RAL	16	2	219	51*	15.64
NAT.W.	3	1	66	37	33.00
B & H					

BARNETT, K. J. Derbyshire

Full Name: Kim John Barnett
Role: Right-hand bat, leg-break or seam bowler, cover fielder
Born: 17 July 1960, Stoke-on-Trent
Height: 6′ 1″ **Weight:** 13st 7lbs
Nickname: Wristy
County debut: 1979
County cap: 1982
Test debut: 1988
No. of Tests: 1
No of One-Day Internationals: 1
1000 runs in a season: 6
1st-Class 50s scored: 67
1st-Class 100s scored: 24
1st-Class 200s scored: 1
1st-Class 5 w. in innings: 1
One-Day 50s: 29
One-Day 100s: 4
Place in batting averages: 9th
av. 57.96 (1987 63rd av. 36.64)
Place in bowling averages: 79th av. 29.57 (1987 3rd av. 17.30)
Strike rate 1988: 69.07 (career 83.30)
1st-Class catches 1988: 16 (career 152)
Parents: Derek and Doreen
Wife and date of marriage: Nancy, 30 September 1984
Children: Rebecca, 13 September 1986
Education: Leek High School, Staffs
Qualifications: 7 O-levels
Jobs outside cricket: Bank clerk, National Westminster Bank 1978
Overseas tours: With England Schools to India 1977; Young England to

Australia 1978–79; Derrick Robins XI to New Zealand and Australia 1979–80; England B to Sri Lanka 1986 (vice-captain)

Overseas teams played for: Boland, South Africa, 1982–83, 1984–85, 1987–88

Cricketers particularly learnt from: Eddie Barlow

Off-season 1988–89: Picked for England team for the cancelled tour to India

Other sports played: Football (has played soccer semi-professionally for Cheshire League side, Leek Town FC), tennis, squash

Other sports followed: Horse racing

Injuries 1988: Broken nose, torn thumb ligament. Had to step down from Fourth Test v West Indies which would have been his Test debut. But his hand recovered for him to make his debut in the Fifth Test

Relaxations: Watching racing on TV, reading, eating

Extras: Played for Northants 2nd XI when aged 15. Played one Minor County match for Staffordshire; also for Warwickshire 2nd XI. Became youngest captain of a first-class county when appointed in 1983. Chris Cowdrey of Kent and England was best man at his wedding

Opinions on cricket: 'I would like to see a more general acceptance of wickets which have a fair balance between bat and ball, and produce results. Wickets should not be "up and down" in bounce, but neither should they be so fast that batsmen completely dominate the game resulting in boredom for spectators.'

Best batting performance: 239* Derbyshire v Leicestershire, Leicester 1988

Best bowling performance: 6-115 Derbyshire v Yorkshire, Bradford 1985

LAST SEASON: BATTING

	I.	N.O.	R.	H.S.	AV.
TEST	2	0	66	66	33.00
1ST-CLASS	28	2	1557	239*	59.88
INT	1	0	84	84	84.00
RAL	13	2	501	90*	45.54
NAT.W.	3	0	82	49	27.33
B & H	6	1	347	85	69.40

LAST SEASON: BOWLING

	O.	M.	R.	W.	AV.
TEST					
1ST-CLASS	161.1	37	414	14	29.57
INT					
RAL	4	0	22	0	—
NAT.W.					
B & H					

CAREER: BATTING

	I.	N.O.	R.	H.S.	AV.
TEST	2	0	66	66	33.00
1ST-CLASS	382	33	12784	239*	36.63
INT	1	0	84	84	84.00
RAL	134	22	3787	131*	33.81
NAT.W.	21	2	667	88	35.10
B & H	38	2	1068	115	29.66

CAREER: BOWLING

	O.	M.	R.	W.	AV.
TEST					
1ST-CLASS	1041.2	217	3367	75	44.89
INT					
RAL	46.3	2	300	7	42.85
NAT.W.	29.4	5	107	11	9.72
B & H	9	2	33	2	16.50

23. Whose nickname is Teflon?

24. Whose nickname is Ned?

BARTLETT, R. J. Somerset

Full Name: Richard James
Bartlett
Role: Right-hand bat
Born: 8 October 1966, Ash
Priors, Somerset
Height: 5′ 9″ **Weight:** 12st
Nickname: Pumpy
County debut: 1986
1st-Class 50s scored: 2
1st-Class 100s scored: 2
One-day 50s: 5
Place in batting averages: 133rd
av. 25.25
1st-Class catches 1988: 12 (career 16)
Parents: Richard and Barbara
Family links with cricket: Father
plays for local club side. Both
parents are members of Somerset CCC
Education: Taunton School
Jobs outside cricket: Worked for British Van Heusen and British Gas as an
office clerk. Worked at Bingo Club for five months. Indoor cricket umpire,
coach, and bar worker in Australia
Off-season 1988–89: Was going to go to university, but decided against it.
Working in Taunton
Overseas tours: Taunton School Under-15s to Sri Lanka 1982; England South
to Bermuda 1985
Overseas teams played for: Manly CC, Sydney, 1986–87, 1987–88
Cricketers particularly learnt from: Andrew Kennedy, Martin Crowe, Steve
Waugh

LAST SEASON: BATTING

	I.	N.O.	R.	H.S.	AV.
TEST					
1ST-CLASS	31	3	707	102*	25.25
INT					
RAL	12	1	319	55	29.00
NAT.W.	2	1	91	85	91.00
B & H					

CAREER: BATTING

	I.	N.O.	R.	H.S.	AV.
TEST					
1ST-CLASS	41	5	1014	117*	28.16
INT					
RAL	13	1	342	55	28.50
NAT.W.	3	1	147	85	73.50
B & H	2	0	4	4	2.00

LAST SEASON: BOWLING

	O.	M.	R.	W.	AV.
TEST					
1ST-CLASS	30	4	145	4	36.25
INT					
RAL					
NAT.W.					
B & H					

CAREER: BOWLING

	O.	M.	R.	W.	AV.
TEST					
1ST-CLASS	30	4	145	4	36.25
INT					
RAL					
NAT.W.					
B & H					

Cricketers particularly admired: Dennis Breakwell, Trevor Gard, Colin Dredge, Steve Waugh

Other sports played: Represented Somerset at U-21 hockey. Golf

Injuries 1988: Injured back falling on advertising board. Also left fore-arm

Relaxations: Watching TV, music, socialising

Extras: First Somerset player to score a century on first-class debut since Harold Gimblett. Won Gray-Nicholls Trophy 1985 as most improved schools cricketer. Represented England Schools and England Young Cricketers

Opinions on cricket: 'The county cricketer should have a larger say in the running of the game, i.e. the Players Association should be a bigger voice in cricket. Sides should only have *one* registered overseas player attached to the club. All committee members should get to know the names of *all* the players on their staff.'

Best batting performance: 117* Somerset v Oxford University, Oxford 1986

Best bowling performance: 1-9 Somerset v Glamorgan, Taunton 1988

BARWICK, S. R.   Glamorgan

Full Name: Stephen Royston Barwick

Role: Right-hand bat, right-arm medium bowler

Born: 6 September 1960, Neath

Height: 6′ 2″ **Weight:** 13st 2lbs

Nickname: Baz

County debut: 1981

County cap: 1987

50 wickets in a season: 1

1st-Class 5 w. in innings: 6

Place in bowling averages: 104th av. 33.25 (1987 108th av. 38.27)

Strike rate 1988: 76.65 (career 69.22)

1st-Class catches 1988: 2 (career 24)

Parents: Margaret and Roy

Wife and date of marriage: Margaret, 12 December 1987

Family links with cricket: 'My Uncle David played for Glamorgan 2nd XI.'

Education: Cwrt Sart Comprehensive School; Dwr-y-Felin Comprehensive School

Qualifications: 'Commerce, human biology, mathematics, English.'

Jobs outside cricket: Ex-steel worker

Other sports played: Badminton, squash, table tennis, football

Other sports followed: Watching Swansea City FC
Injuries 1988: Car accident
Extras: Made debut on 25 April 1981 v Oxford University, and took 4 wickets in 1st innings
Opinions on cricket: 'I think there should be more four-day cricket played.'
Best batting performance: 30 Glamorgan v Hampshire, Bournemouth 1988
Best bowling performance: 8-42 Glamorgan v Worcestershire, Worcester 1983

LAST SEASON: BATTING

	I.	N.O.	R.	H.S.	AV.
TEST					
1ST-CLASS	7	2	40	30	8.00
INT					
RAL	2	2	7	4*	–
NAT.W.	1	1	0	0*	–
B & H	2	2	3	3*	–

CAREER: BATTING

	I.	N.O.	R.	H.S.	AV.
TEST					
1ST-CLASS	108	42	562	30	8.51
INT					
RAL	22	14	86	29*	10.75
NAT.W.	6	3	18	6	6.00
B & H	14	9	52	18	10.40

LAST SEASON: BOWLING

	O.	M.	R.	W.	AV.
TEST					
1ST-CLASS	408.5	112	1064	32	33.25
INT					
RAL	87	5	358	17	21.05
NAT.W.	33.2	9	85	4	21.25
B & H	60	13	197	6	32.83

CAREER: BOWLING

	O.	M.	R.	W.	AV.
TEST					
1ST-CLASS	2780.3	646	8148	241	33.80
INT					
RAL	462.1	29	2065	67	30.82
NAT.W.	96.4	25	251	17	14.76
B & H	207.1	34	734	29	25.31

BASE, S. J.   Derbyshire

Full Name: Simon John Base
Role: Right-hand bat, right-arm medium bowler
Born: 2 January 1960, Maidstone
Height: 6′ 3″ **Weight:** 13st 9lbs
Nickname: Basey, Herman
County debut: 1986 (Glamorgan), 1988 (Derbyshire)
1st-Class 5 w. in innings: 4
Place in batting averages: —
(1987 236th av. 12.70)
Place in bowling averages: 105th av. 33.40 (1987 19th av. 23.57)
Strike rate 1988: 53.18 (career 48.00)
1st-Class catches 1988: 3 (career 9)
Parents: Christine and Peter
Family links with cricket: Grandfather used to play

Education: Fish Hoek Primary School, Fish Hoek High School, Cape Town, South Africa

Qualifications: High School, School Certificate Matriculation. Refrigeration and air conditioning technician

Jobs outside cricket: Hall-Thermotank in South Africa as a technician and S.A. Sea Products. G.S.P.K. Electronics in North Yorkshire, England

Off-season 1988–89: Playing for Boland, Cape Town

Overseas teams played for: Western Province B 1982–83; Boland 1986–87

Cricketers particularly learnt from: Stuart Leary, Graham Gooch, Kevin Lyons, Alan Jones, James Crawford-Porter

Cricketers particularly admired: Eddie Barlow, Graham Gooch, Graeme Pollock

Other sports played: Football, golf, windsurfing

Other sports followed: Golf, tennis, snooker, all sports

Relaxations: Windsurfing and golf. Reading science fiction, watching films and music

Extras: Suspended from first-class cricket for ten weeks during 1988 season for a supposed breach of contract, joining Derbyshire when he was still said to be contracted to Glamorgan. The TCCB fined Derbyshire £2000

Cricketing opinions: 'I feel that politics should not interfere with international sport at any level.'

Best batting performance: 38 Glamorgan v Gloucestershire, Swansea 1987

Best bowling performance: 6-28 Boland v Border, Stellenbosch 1987–88

LAST SEASON: BATTING

	I.	N.O.	R.	H.S.	AV.
TEST					
1ST-CLASS	10	3	59	15	8.42
INT					
RAL	4	1	4	3	1.33
NAT.W.					
B & H					

LAST SEASON: BOWLING

	O.	M.	R.	W.	AV.
TEST					
1ST-CLASS	195	20	735	22	33.40
INT					
RAL	47	3	166	8	20.75
NAT.W.					
B & H					

CAREER: BATTING

	I.	N.O.	R.	H.S.	AV.
TEST					
1ST-CLASS	46	14	292	38	9.12
INT					
RAL	9	1	41	19	5.12
NAT.W.	2	0	6	4	3.00
B & H	3	1	20	12	10.00

CAREER: BOWLING

	O.	M.	R.	W.	AV.
TEST					
1ST-CLASS	888	174	2771	111	24.96
INT					
RAL	96	3	437	15	29.13
NAT.W.	15	0	61	2	30.50
B & H	28	1	147	3	49.00

25. Whose nickname is Fergie?

26. Whose nickname is Kudu?

27. Who won the 1988 Benson & Hedges Cup?

BASTIEN, S.   Glamorgan

Full name: Steven Bastien
Role: Right-hand bat, right-arm
fast-medium bowler, 'outstanding'
fielder
Born: 13 March 1963, Stepney
Height: 6' 1" **Weight:** 12st
Nickname: Bassie
County debut: 1988
1st-Class 5w in innings: 1
1st-Class catches 1988: 1 (career 1)
Parents: Francesca and Anthony
Marital status: Single
Education: St Mary's Academy
School, Dominica, West Indies;
St Bonaventure School, London E7
Qualifications: 3 CSEs;
NCA Coaching Course; Carpentry;
CCPR Course

Jobs outside cricket: Salesman,
labourer, carpenter
Off-season 1988–89: 'I intend to spend the close season with Haringey Cricket
College, working on approaching closer to stumps and bowling at a target.'
Cricketing superstitions or habits: 'I don't believe in any luck.'
Overseas tours: Haringey Cricket College to Barbados, Trinidad and Tobago
1986–87 and Jamaica 1988
Cricketers particularly learnt from: 'My cousin G. Thomas.'
Cricketers particularly admired: Viv Richards, David Gower, Ian Botham,
Michael Holding, Joel Garner, Clive Lloyd
Other sports played: Table tennis, volleyball, basketball

LAST SEASON: BATTING

	I.	N.O.	R.	H.S.	AV.
TEST					
1ST-CLASS	6	2	57	36*	14.25
INT					
RAL					
NAT.W.					
B & H					

LAST SEASON: BOWLING

	O.	M.	R.	W.	AV.
TEST					
1ST-CLASS	119.1	35	289	8	36.12
INT					
RAL					
NAT.W.					
B & H					

CAREER: BATTING

	I.	N.O.	R.	H.S.	AV.
TEST					
1ST-CLASS	6	2	57	36*	14.25
INT					
RAL					
NAT.W.					
B & H					

CAREER: BOWLING

	O.	M.	R.	W.	AV.
TEST					
1ST-CLASS	119.1	35	289	8	36.12
INT					
RAL					
NAT.W.					
B & H					

Other sports followed: Football, boxing, wrestling
Injuries 1988: Muscle strain in chest
Relaxations: Watching movies, listening to reggae, soul and calypso music
Opinions on cricket: 'There is too much three-day cricket. I think we should have more four-day games instead, because there is a better chance of getting a result.'
Best batting performance: 36 Glamorgan v Warwickshire, Edgbaston 1988
Best bowling performance: 5-90 Glamorgan v Leicester, Neath 1988

BENJAMIN, W. K. M. Leicestershire

Full name: Winston Keithroy Matthew Benjamin
Role: Right-hand bat, right-arm fast bowler
Born: 31 December 1964, All Saints, Antigua
County debut: 1986
Test debut: 1987–88
No. of Tests: 7
No. of One-Day Internationals: 30
1st-Class 50s scored: 3
1st-Class 10 w. in match: 1
1st-Class 5 w. in innings: 8
Place in batting averages: 209th av. 17.00
Place in bowling averages: 3rd av. 14.15 (1987 96th av. 35.00)
Strike rate 1988: 33.30 (career 50.08)

LAST SEASON: BATTING

	I.	N.O.	R.	H.S.	AV.
TEST	2	0	9	9	4.50
1ST-CLASS	8	4	93	21*	23.25
INT	–	–	–	–	–
RAL					
NAT.W.					
B & H					

CAREER: BATTING

	I.	N.O.	R.	H.S.	AV.
TEST	9	1	118	41*	14.75
1ST-CLASS	62	21	943	95*	23.00
INT	16	3	79	31	6.07
RAL	15	4	125	19*	11.36
NAT.W.	2	1	7	5	7.00
B & H	6	2	60	21	15.00

LAST SEASON: BOWLING

	O.	M.	R.	W.	AV.
TEST	67	17	151	12	12.58
1ST-CLASS	116.1	27	316	21	15.04
INT	9	0	38	0	–
RAL					
NAT.W.					
B & H					

CAREER: BOWLING

	O.	M.	R.	W.	AV.
TEST	197	36	537	26	20.65
1ST-CLASS	1288.5	285	3841	152	25.26
INT	259.1	20	1056	30	35.20
RAL	122.1	5	537	19	28.26
NAT.W.	45	6	131	7	18.71
B & H	78.4	11	271	19	14.26

1st-Class catches 1988: 6 (career 26)
Education: All Saints School, Antigua
Overseas teams played for: Leeward Islands since 1985
Extras: Played Minor Counties cricket for Cheshire since 1985. Appeared for Rest of the World XI v D. B. Close's XI at Scarborough 1985
Best batting performance: 95* Leicestershire v India, Leicester 1986
Best bowling performance: 6-33 Leicestershire v Nottinghamshire, Leicester 1986

BENSON, J. D. R.   Leicestershire

Full name: Justin David Ramsay Benson
Role: Right-hand bat, wicket-keeper
Born: 1 March 1967, Dublin
Height: 6′ 3″ **Weight:** 13st
Nickname: Rambo, Larger Monster, Beast
County debut: 1988
Parents: Malcolm and Elizabeth
Marital status: Single
Family links with cricket: Father is a qualified first-class umpire
Education: St Faith, The Leys, Cambridge
Qualifications: 10 O-levels; draughtsman, salesman
Jobs outside cricket: Coach and social organiser

LAST SEASON: BATTING

	I.	N.O.	R.	H.S.	AV.
TEST					
1ST-CLASS	1	0	3	3	3.00
INT					
RAL	5	1	119	42*	29.75
NAT.W.					
B & H	1	1	37	37*	–

CAREER: BATTING

	I.	N.O.	R.	H.S.	AV.
TEST					
1ST-CLASS	1	0	3	3	3.00
INT					
RAL	5	1	119	42*	29.75
NAT.W.					
B & H	1	1	37	37*	–

LAST SEASON: WICKET KEEPING

	C.	ST.		
TEST				
1ST-CLASS				
INT				
RAL	1	–		
NAT.W.				
B & H				

CAREER: WICKET KEEPING

	C.	ST.		
TEST				
1ST-CLASS				
INT				
RAL	1	–		
NAT.W.				
B & H				

Off-season 1988–89: Coaching
Overseas teams played for: Durbanville, Cape Town, South Africa 1988–89; Cottonground, Nevis, West Indies 1987–88
Cricketers particularly learnt from: Derek Parry, Terry Hale, Ken Higgs and the lads at Leicester
Cricketers particularly admired: Derek Parry, Derek Randall, Gary Sobers
Other sports played: Rugby, hockey
Other sports followed: Athletics, golf, any sport on TV
Relaxations: Reggae music, drinking, socialising
Opinions on cricket: 'Youngsters should be given a chance to prove themselves at first-class level. Too much "old school tie" still involved in cricket. Overseas players should be restricted to one or none per county and a player should be able to play anywhere in the world he so chooses!'
Best batting performance: 3 Leicestershire v Northamptonshire, Leicester 1988

BENSON, M. R.   Kent

Full Name: Mark Richard Benson
Role: Left-hand bat, off-break bowler
Born: 6 July 1958, Shoreham, Sussex
Height: 5′ 9½″ **Weight:** 12st 7lbs
Nickname: Benny
County debut: 1980
County cap: 1981
Test debut: 1986
No. of Tests: 1
No. of One-Day Internationals: 1
1000 runs in a season: 7
1st-Class 50s scored: 67
1st-Class 100s scored: 24
One-Day 50s: 27
One-Day 100s: 3
Place in batting averages: 64th
av. 34.08 (1987 24th av. 44.23)
1st-Class catches 1988: 13 (career 90)
Parents: Frank and Judy
Wife and date of marriage: Sarah, 20 September 1986
Children: Laurence Mark Edward, 16 October 1987
Family links with cricket: Father played for Ghana
Education: Sutton Valence School
Qualifications: O- and A-levels and 1 S-level. Qualified tennis coach

Jobs outside cricket: Marketing assistant with Shell UK Oil; Financial adviser
Cricketing superstitions or habits: Left pad on first
Overseas teams played for: Balfour Guild CC, 1979–80; Johannesburg Municipals, 1980–81; Port Adelaide CC, 1981–82
Cricketers particularly learnt from: Derek Aslett, Bob Woolmer, Brian Luckhurst
Cricketers particularly admired: Malcolm Marshall, Neal Radford, Ian Botham, Alan Knott, Graham Clinton, Imran Khan
Off-season 1988–89: Working for Stanford Benson & Co.
Other sports played: Golf, table tennis, windsurfing
Other sports followed: Rugby, horse racing
Injuries 1988: Back-spasm for most of season
Relaxations: Windsurfing
Extras: Scored 1000 runs in first full season. Record for most runs in career and season at Sutton Valence School
Opinions on cricket: 'We play too much cricket, thus breeding mediocrity. Four-day cricket is a must.'
Best batting performance: 162 Kent v Hampshire, Southampton 1985
Best bowling performance: 2-55 Kent v Surrey, Dartford 1986

LAST SEASON: BATTING

	I.	N.O.	R.	H.S.	AV.
TEST					
1ST-CLASS	37	1	1227	110	34.08
INT					
RAL	8	0	145	66	18.12
NAT.W.	3	0	46	38	15.33
B & H	4	0	194	113	48.50

LAST SEASON: BOWLING

	O.	M.	R.	W.	AV.
TEST					
1ST-CLASS	3.3	0	39	0	–
INT					
RAL					
NAT.W.					
B & H					

CAREER: BATTING

	I.	N.O.	R.	H.S.	AV.
TEST	2	0	51	30	25.50
1ST-CLASS	298	21	10703	162	38.63
INT	1	0	24	24	24.00
RAL	90	1	2525	97	28.37
NAT.W.	22	1	768	113*	36.57
B & H	36	6	1067	113	35.56

CAREER: BOWLING

	O.	M.	R.	W.	AV.
TEST					
1ST-CLASS	45.5	1	312	3	104.00
INT					
RAL					
NAT.W.					
B & H					

28. Which is the only county to have won the Benson & Hedges Cup two years running?

29. Which first-class umpire stands on one leg if the score is 111?

30. Which first-class umpire played for Kent and Leicestershire?

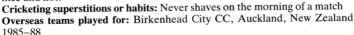

Full Name: Paul Bent
Role: Right-hand bat, off-break bowler
Born: 1 May 1965, Worcester
Height: 6′ 1″ **Weight:** 12st 5lbs
Nickname: Benty, Bodell
County debut: 1985
1st-Class 50s scored: 1
Parents: Emily and Roy
Family links with cricket: Brother plays local club cricket
Education: Worcester Royal Grammar School
Qualifications: 7 O-levels, 2 A-levels; Senior award coach
Jobs outside cricket: Coaching abroad
Off-season 1988–89: 'Hopefully coaching, preferably somewhere nice and hot.'
Cricketing superstitions or habits: Never shaves on the morning of a match
Overseas teams played for: Birkenhead City CC, Auckland, New Zealand 1985–88
Cricketers particularly learnt from: County team mates, particularly Mark Scott
Cricketers particularly admired: Geoff Boycott, Ian Botham, Richard Stemp
Other sports played: Soccer
Other sports followed: Supports West Bromwich Albion
Relaxations: Sleeping-in, dining out, listening to music
Extras: Hat-trick v Leicestershire 2nd XI (1988 season). Fielded as 12th man for England v India, Lord's Test while still on Lord's ground staff
Opinions on cricket: 'The standard of 2nd XI cricket would greatly improve if the wickets played on came up to somewhere near first-class standard.'
Best batting performance: 50 Worcestershire v Yorkshire, Worcester 1988

LAST SEASON: BATTING

	I.	N.O.	R.	H.S.	AV.
TEST					
1ST-CLASS	6	1	111	50	22.20
INT					
RAL	2	0	49	36	24.50
NAT.W.					
B & H					

CAREER: BATTING

	I.	N.O.	R.	H.S.	AV.
TEST					
1ST-CLASS	7	1	125	50	20.83
INT					
RAL	2	0	49	36	24.50
NAT.W.					
B & H					

BERRY, P. J.   Yorkshire

Full Name: Philip John Berry
Role: Right-hand bat, off-break bowler
Born: 28 December 1966, Saltburn, Cleveland
Height: 6′ **Weight:** 11st 7lbs
Nickname: 'Chuck, Goose, Bill, Charlie Chin and anymore they can think of.'
County debut: 1986
1st-Class catches 1988: 1 (career 5)
Parents: John and Beryl
Family links with cricket: Brother Stephen played for Saltburn in North Yorkshire and South Durham Cricket League
Education: Saltscar Comprehensive; Longlands College of Further Education

Qualifications: 1 O-level, City and Guilds passes in Recreational and Leisure Services
Jobs outside cricket: Worked for Redcar Racecourse as a groundsman
Cricketing superstitions or habits: Put left pad on first. Try to change in same place in a changing room if I have done well from that place before. Wear same kit as day before if successful
Overseas tours: NCA North U-19 to Bermuda in July 1985 for the International Youth Tournament
Cricketers particularly learnt from: 'Steve Oldham, Doug Padgett and Brian

LAST SEASON: BATTING

	I.	N.O.	R.	H.S.	AV.
TEST					
1ST-CLASS	2	1	27	23*	27.00
INT					
RAL					
NAT.W.					
B & H					

CAREER: BATTING

	I.	N.O.	R.	H.S.	AV.
TEST					
1ST-CLASS	3	2	31	23*	31.00
INT					
RAL					
NAT.W.					
B & H					

LAST SEASON: BOWLING

	O.	M.	R.	W.	AV.
TEST					
1ST-CLASS	38.2	13	91	3	30.33
INT					
RAL					
NAT.W.					
B & H					

CAREER: BOWLING

	O.	M.	R.	W.	AV.
TEST					
1ST-CLASS	91.2	29	229	5	45.80
INT					
RAL					
NAT.W.					
B & H					

Bainbridge, who taught me everything about the game, when I joined Middlesbrough.'

Cricketers particularly admired: Brian Bainbridge for showing keeness at 56 years old, turning out for Middlesbrough 1st Team every week

Off-season 1988–89: Keeping fit

Other sports played: Snooker, football, badminton

Other sports followed: Rugby union, Middlesbrough FC, American football

Relaxations: Reading, snooker, rugby, listening to music, passing racing tips to the other lads (but they always tend to lose)

Extras: Played for young Young England in the Final Test against Sri Lanka at Trent Bridge which England won by 6 wkts to win series 1–0

Best batting performance: 23* Yorkshire v Cambridge University, Cambridge 1988

Best bowling performance: 2-35 Yorkshire v Cambridge University, Cambridge 1988

BICKNELL, D. J. Surrey

Full Name: Darren John Bicknell

Role: Opening bat, short-leg fielder

Born: 24 June 1967, Guildford

Height: 6' 4½" **Weight:** 13½st

Nickname: Denzil, Razor

County debut: 1987

1st-Class 50s scored: 6

1st-Class 100s scored: 1

Place in batting averages: 199th av. 19.05 (1987 68th av. 35.29)

1st-Class catches 1988: 2 (career 7)

Parents: Vic and Valerie

Marital status: Single

Family links with cricket: Brother plays for Surrey, father is a qualified umpire; little brother Stuart plays for Guildford CC

Education: Robert Haining County Secondary, Mychett, Hampshire

Qualifications: 2 O-levels, 5 CSEs, City and Guilds qualification in Recreation Administration and Sports Studies

Jobs outside cricket: Sports centre lifeguard and sales rep for Notts. Sport

Off-season 1988–89: Playing football

Cricketing superstitions or habits: 'If I score runs in a particular shirt, pair of trousers or pair of boots, I try to bat in the same gear next time.'

Overseas teams played for: Cobury CC, Melbourne 1987–88
Cricketers particularly learnt from: David Smith, Geoff Arnold, Graham Clinton
Cricketers particularly admired: Graham Gooch, Graham Clinton
Other sports played: Football, golf, snooker
Other sports followed: Aldershot FC
Relaxations: Listening to music, playing golf, eating out
Extras: Supporters Young Player of the Year 1987. 'Paul Atkins and myself were both out for 99, LBW on the same day, Paul at Southport on his first-class debut, and I at Chelmsford in a 2nd XI game.'
Opinions on cricket: 'Four-day cricket should be a matter of course. Second Eleven cricket should be played on more first-class grounds.'
Best batting performance: 105 Surrey v Hampshire, The Oval 1987

LAST SEASON: BATTING

	I.	N.O.	R.	H.S.	AV.
TEST					
1ST-CLASS	19	1	343	62	19.05
INT					
RAL	1	0	31	31	31.00
NAT.W.					
B & H					

CAREER: BATTING

	I.	N.O.	R.	H.S.	AV.
TEST					
1ST-CLASS	39	4	943	105	26.94
INT					
RAL	1	0	31	31	31.00
NAT.W.					
B & H	1	0	17	17	17.00

BICKNELL, M. P. Surrey

Full Name: Martin Paul Bicknell
Role: Right-hand bat, right-arm fast medium bowler
Born: 14 January 1969, Guildford
Height: 6′ 3½″ **Weight:** 13½st
Nickname: Bickers, Spandau
County debut: 1986
1st-Class 5 w. in innings: 3
Place in batting averages: —
(1987 117th av. 15.42)
Place in bowling averages: 84th
av. 30.22 (1987 21st av. 23.73)
Strike rate 1988: 61.96 (career 54.23)
1st-Class catches 1988: 4 (career 13)
Parents: Vic and Valerie
Marital status: Single
Family links with cricket: Brother Darren plays for Surrey. Father is
qualified umpire. Younger brother Stuart plays for Guildford Colts

Education: Robert Haining County Secondary, Mychett, Hampshire
Qualifications: 2 O-levels, 5 CSEs
Cricketing superstitions or habits: 'Left pad on first, not that it helps!'
Overseas tours: Surrey Young Cricketers to Australia 1985–86; Young England to Sri Lanka 1987
Overseas teams played for: Suburbs, New Zealand 1987–88
Cricketers particularly learnt from: Geoff Arnold, Mickey Stewart, Graham Saville, Tim Lamb, Bob Cottam
Cricketers particularly admired: Richard Hadlee, Dennis Lillee, Sylvester Clarke
Off-season 1988–89: Keeping fit and playing football
Other sports played: Football, golf
Other sports followed: Anything except horse racing
Injuries 1987: Bruised heel for two weeks, back strain for one week
Relaxations: Watching greyhound racing, music
Extras: Youngest player to play for Surrey since David Smith. On County debut first two overs were maidens. Scored four successive ducks in June. Played in successful series win for Young England against Sri Lanka. Finished 11th in National Bowling Averages. 1986 won Supporters Young Player of the Year, also George Brittain Young Player of the Year. Best bowling figures for Surrey for 30 years, 9 for 45
Opinions on cricket: 'Championship should be 16 four-day games. Too many boring captains; there is nothing to lose by going for a result. The better team will always come out on top.'
Best batting performance: 33 Surrey v Sri Lanka, The Oval 1988
Best bowling performance: 9-45 Surrey v Cambridge University, Cambridge 1988

LAST SEASON: BATTING

	I.	N.O.	R.	H.S.	AV.
TEST					
1ST-CLASS	13	3	93	33	9.30
INT					
RAL	4	1	13	9*	4.33
NAT.W.	2	1	2	1*	2.00
B & H	1	0	0	0	0.00

CAREER: BATTING

	I.	N.O.	R.	H.S.	AV.
TEST					
1ST-CLASS	37	12	222	33	8.88
INT					
RAL	9	5	41	13	10.25
NAT.W.	6	3	7	2*	2.33
B & H	2	1	1	1*	1.00

LAST SEASON: BOWLING

	O.	M.	R.	W.	AV.
TEST					
1ST-CLASS	516.2	136	1511	50	30.22
INT					
RAL	92	4	325	11	29.54
NAT.W.	31	2	124	2	62.00
B & H	11	1	46	2	23.00

CAREER: BOWLING

	O.	M.	R.	W.	AV.
TEST					
1ST-CLASS	1075.4	273	3108	119	26.11
INT					
RAL	206	8	802	21	38.19
NAT.W.	92	12	300	7	42.85
B & H	36	5	118	9	13.11

BIRCH, J. D. Nottinghamshire

Full Name: John Dennis Birch
Role: Right-hand bat, right-arm
medium bowler, gully fielder
Born: 18 June 1955, Nottingham
Height: 6′ 1″ **Weight:** 13st
Nickname: Bonk, Denzil
County debut: 1973
County cap: 1981
1000 runs in a season: 2
1st-Class 50s scored: 51
1st-Class 100s scored: 6
1st-Class 5 w. in innings: 1
One-Day 50s: 17
Place in batting averages: 167th
av. 22.17 (1987 98th av. 31.51)
1st-Class catches 1988: 14
(career 182)
Parents: Bill and Mavis
Wife and date of marriage: Linda,
15 May 1980
Children: Nathalie and Daniel (twins), 31 January 1981
Family links with cricket: Father was a local cricketer
Education: William Crane School
Qualifications: O-levels and CSEs
Jobs outside cricket: Runs a small building firm with a friend and brothers;
player-manager, Arnold Town FC; coaching director at Nottingham Cricket
Centre
Off-season 1988–89: Organising benefit year in 1989
Cricketing superstitions or habits: Right pad on first

LAST SEASON: BATTING

	I.	N.O.	R.	H.S.	AV.
TEST					
1ST-CLASS	39	4	776	114*	22.17
INT					
RAL	13	5	306	65*	38.25
NAT.W.	2	2	56	55*	–
B & H	3	0	33	15	11.00

CAREER: BATTING

	I.	N.O.	R.	H.S.	AV.
TEST					
1ST-CLASS	374	59	8673	125	27.53
INT					
RAL	139	35	2765	92	26.58
NAT.W.	19	4	273	55*	18.20
B & H	41	8	698	85	21.15

LAST SEASON: BOWLING

	O.	M.	R.	W.	AV.
TEST					
1ST-CLASS	123.2	35	379	7	54.14
INT					
RAL	9	0	77	5	15.40
NAT.W.					
B & H	2	1	8	1	8.00

CAREER: BOWLING

	O.	M.	R.	W.	AV.
TEST					
1ST-CLASS	667.3	115	2446	50	48.92
INT					
RAL	161	12	796	25	31.84
NAT.W.	14	1	73	1	73.00
B & H	61	8	245	9	27.22

Cricketers particularly learnt from: Clive Rice, Richard Hadlee
Cricketers particularly admired: Clive Rice, Richard Hadlee, Geoffrey Boycott
Other sports played: Soccer, golf, snooker, all sports
Other sports followed: Watching any other sports
Relaxations: 'Gardening, fishing and the odd pint of good beer.'
Extras: 'Would like to thank Frank Woodhead for giving me the chance to play for Notts and all who have helped me at the club.' Captained Nottinghamshire in 1988 when Tim Robinson was off injured
Opinions on cricket: 'We need someone to sort out the problems of Test cricket, arising from South Africa.'
Best batting performance: 125 Nottinghamshire v Leicestershire, Trent Bridge 1982
Best bowling performance: 6-64 Nottinghamshire v Hampshire, Bournemouth 1975

BLAKEY, R. J. — Yorkshire

Full Name: Richard John Blakey
Role: Right-hand bat, occasional wicket-keeper, right-arm medium bowler
Born: 15 January 1967, Huddersfield
Height: 5' 9" **Weight:** 11st 6lbs
Nickname: Dick, Mutley, Warren
County debut: 1985
County cap: 1987
1st-Class 50s scored: 11
1st-Class 100s scored: 3
1st-Class 200s scored: 1
One-Day 50s: 2
Place in batting averages: 164th av. 22.30 (1987 33rd av. 41.30)
1st-Class catches 1988: 7 (career 36)
Parents: Brian and Pauline
Marital status: Single
Family links with cricket: Father played league cricket
Education: Woodhouse Primary; Rastrick Grammar School
Qualifications: 4 O-levels, NCA Coaching Certificate
Overseas tours: Young England to West Indies 1985; Yorkshire CCC to Saint Lucia 1987
Overseas teams played for: Waverley CC, Melbourne 1985–86, 1986–87

Cricketers particularly learnt from: My father Brian, Doug Padgett, Steve Oldham, Martyn Moxon and all Yorkshire's capped players
Cricketers particularly admired: Ian Botham, Martyn Moxon
Off-season 1988–89: Keeping as fit as possible
Other sports played: Golf, squash, snooker
Other sports followed: 'Football, most other sports but not ice skating.'
Relaxations: Music and watching Leeds United FC. Rabbit keeping
Extras: Made record 2nd XI score – 273* v Northamptonshire 1986
Opinions on cricket: 'In our climate I would like to see 16 four-day matches. With three-day fixtures you seem to spend the first 2½ days jockeying for position, using declaration bowlers, forfeits etc, in order to try to manufacture a result.'
Best batting performance: 204* Yorkshire v Gloucestershire, Leeds 1987
Best bowling performance: 1-68 Yorkshire v Nottinghamshire, Sheffield 1986

LAST SEASON: BATTING

	I.	N.O.	R.	H.S.	AV.
TEST					
1ST-CLASS	24	4	446	85*	22.30
INT					
RAL	5	3	92	40*	46.00
NAT.W.					
B & H	1	0	9	9	9.00

CAREER: BATTING

	I.	N.O.	R.	H.S.	AV.
TEST					
1ST-CLASS	93	11	2563	204*	31.25
INT					
RAL	6	3	95	40*	31.66
NAT.W.	3	1	18	14	9.00
B & H	7	2	164	58	32.80

LAST SEASON: WICKET KEEPING

	C.	ST.
TEST		
1ST-CLASS	20	2
INT		
RAL	4	–
NAT.W.		
B & H		

CAREER: WICKET KEEPING

	C.	ST.
TEST		
1ST-CLASS	32	2
INT		
RAL	4	–
NAT.W.		
B & H		

31. What is the badge of Kent CCC?

32. Who wrote these famous lines on that legendary, early cricketer, Alfred Mynn: 'Proudly, sadly, will we name him – to forget him were a sin. Lightly lie the turf on thee, kind and manly Alfred Mynn'?

Full Name: James Boiling
Role: Right-hand bat, off-break bowler
Born: 8 April 1968, New Delhi, India
Height: 6′ 4″ **Weight:** 12st 12lbs
Nickname: Boilers, Viv, Hamish
County debut: 1988
Parents: Graham and Geraldine
Marital status: Single
Family links with cricket: 'Both grandfathers played club cricket. Mother played rounders!'
Education: Rutlish School, Merton; Durham University
Qualifications: 10 O-levels, 3 A-Levels; studying for a BA Hons Degree in History
Jobs outside cricket: Stacking shelves in Sainsbury's, clerical assistant in passport office
Off-season 1988–89: At university
Cricketing superstitions or habits: Haddock for breakfast on match days; left shoe on first
Overseas tours: Surrey Schools U-19 to Australia 1985–86; Young England to Australia, Youth World Cup 1988
Cricketers particularly learnt from: Jim Laker, Michael Edwards, Mickey Stewart, Bob Cottam
Cricketers particularly admired: Jim Laker, Nasser Hussain, Sylvester Clarke, Keith Medlycott

LAST SEASON: BATTING

	I.	N.O.	R.	H.S.	AV.
TEST					
1ST-CLASS	2	1	9	8*	9.00
INT					
RAL					
NAT.W.					
B & H	4	3	16	9*	16.00

CAREER: BATTING

	I.	N.O.	R.	H.S.	AV.
TEST					
1ST-CLASS	2	1	9	8*	9.00
INT					
RAL					
NAT.W.					
B & H	4	3	16	9*	16.00

LAST SEASON: BOWLING

	O.	M.	R.	W.	AV.
TEST					
1ST-CLASS	15	3	40	0	—
INT					
RAL					
NAT.W.					
B & H	39.1	0	170	5	34.00

CAREER: BOWLING

	O.	M.	R.	W.	AV.
TEST					
1ST-CLASS	15	3	40	0	—
INT					
RAL					
NAT.W.					
B & H	39.1	0	170	5	34.00

Other sports played: Rowing, swimming
Other sports followed: Soccer
Injuries 1988: Dislocated finger, Achilles tendon strain
Relaxations: 'Playing and watching most sports; enjoying my girlfriend's company; signing autographs; listening to good music; dancing to good music; discussing life with Graham Thorpe.'
Extras: Surrey Young Cricketer of the Year 1985 and 1987. *Daily Telegraph* Bowler of Year (U-19) 1986
Opinions on cricket: 'There should be 16 four-day matches. Young players should be more disciplined, and have more respect for senior players and umpires. First-class status of Oxford and Cambridge Universities should be abolished, and there should be a national Combined Universities side. England "B" or Under 25 should tour each winter to give promising youngsters a chance to get the feel of international cricket. Heavy bats should be banned to give spinners more of a chance!'
Best batting performance: 8* Surrey v Glamorgan, Swansea 1988

BOON, T. J.   Leicestershire

Full Name: Timothy James Boon
Role: Right-hand bat,
right-arm medium bowler
Born: 1 November 1961,
Doncaster, South Yorkshire
Height: 5' 11½" **Weight:** 12st 3lbs
Nickname: Ted Moon, Cod
County debut: 1980
County cap: 1986
1000 runs in a season: 3
1st-Class 50s scored: 25
1st-Class 100s scored: 6
One-Day 50s: 3
Place in batting averages: 158th
av. 22.95 (1987 30th av. 42.04)
1st-Class catches 1988: 8 (career 54)
Parents: Jeffrey and Elizabeth
Marital status: Single
Family links with cricket: Father
played club cricket

Education: Mill Lane Primary; Edlington Comprehensive. Three months at Doncaster Art School
Qualifications: 1 A-level, 6 O-levels. Coaching qualifications
Jobs outside cricket: Worked with Leicester Dyers, 1986–1987

Cricketing superstitions or habits: 'Constantly changing.'

Overseas tours: Toured the Caribbean with England Young Cricketers 1980, as captain; Leicestershire CCC to Zimbabwe 1981

Overseas teams played for: Old Hararians, Zimbabwe, 1980–81; Ceylon CC, Colombo, 1981–82; Pirates CC, Durban, 1982–83, 1984–85

Cricketers particularly learnt from: The late Mike Fearnley, Ken Higgs, Chris Balderstone, Peter Willey

Cricketers particularly admired: 'Those who make the most of their ability.'

Other sports played: 'Enjoy playing and watching all sports.'

Injuries 1988: Arm broken in May by a delivery from Devon Malcolm

Relaxations: Sleeping, barbecue in garden, dining out

Extras: Captain England Young Cricketers Tour West Indies 1980; Captain England Young Cricketers v Indian Young Cricketers 1981; Most Promising Schoolboy Cricketer 1979. Missed 1985 season due to broken leg sustained in a car crash in South Africa the previous winter. Had sixteen inch nail removed in October 1986

Best batting performance: 144 Leicestershire v Gloucestershire, Leicester 1984

Best bowling performance: 3-40 Leicestershire v Yorkshire, Leicester 1986

LAST SEASON: BATTING

	I.	N.O.	R.	H.S.	AV.
TEST					
1ST-CLASS	23	1	505	131	22.95
INT					
RAL	3	0	44	22	14.66
NAT.W.					
B & H	3	1	96	53	48.00

LAST SEASON: BOWLING

	O.	M.	R.	W.	AV.
TEST					
1ST-CLASS	–	–	–	–	–
INT					
RAL	–	–	–	–	–
NAT.W.	–	–	–	–	–
B & H					

CAREER: BATTING

	I.	N.O.	R.	H.S.	AV.
TEST					
1ST-CLASS	185	25	4900	144	30.62
INT					
RAL	53	9	856	61	19.45
NAT.W.	6	3	72	22*	24.00
B & H	11	4	251	58*	35.85

CAREER: BOWLING

	O.	M.	R.	W.	AV.
TEST					
1ST-CLASS	49.3	7	249	5	49.80
INT					
RAL	2	0	14	0	–
NAT.W.	1	0	2	0	–
B & H					

33. Who was acting captain of England when Graham Gooch dislocated his finger in the Fifth Test v West Indies in 1988?

34. Who opened the batting with Desmond Haynes in both innings for the West Indies in the Fourth Test v England in 1988?

BOOTH, P. A. Yorkshire

Full Name: Paul Antony Booth
Role: Left-hand bat,
left-arm spin bowler
Born: 5 September 1965, Huddersfield
Height: 6′ 0″ **Weight:** 11st 12lbs
Nickname: Boot, Spike
County debut: 1982
1st-Class 5 w. in innings: 1
Place in batting averages: 220th
av. 16.00
Place in bowling averages: 99th
av. 32.81
Strike rate 1988: 74.00
(career 110.62)
1st-Class catches 1988: 1 (career 5)
Parents: Colin and Margaret
Marital status: Single
Family links with cricket: Father
played local cricket for
over 30 years

Education: Honley High School
Qualifications: Mathematics, Woodwork
Jobs outside cricket: Joiner, postman
Off-season 1988–89: Training and getting fit for the new season
Overseas tours: Young England to the West Indies 1985
Cricketers particularly learnt from: Doug Padgett, Phil Carrick
Cricketers particularly admired: Derek Underwood
Other sports played: Football, golf
Other sports followed: Football – Leeds United

LAST SEASON: BATTING

	I.	N.O.	R.	H.S.	AV.
TEST					
1ST-CLASS	8	2	96	33*	16.00
INT					
RAL					
NAT.W.					
B & H					

CAREER: BATTING

	I.	N.O.	R.	H.S.	AV.
TEST					
1ST-CLASS	26	6	178	33*	8.90
INT					
RAL					
NAT.W.	1	1	6	6*	–
B & H	1	0	1	1	1.00

LAST SEASON: BOWLING

	O.	M.	R.	W.	AV.
TEST					
1ST-CLASS	135.4	35	361	11	32.81
INT					
RAL					
NAT.W.					
B & H					

CAREER: BOWLING

	O.	M.	R.	W.	AV.
TEST					
1ST-CLASS	626.5	205	1470	34	43.23
INT					
RAL	8	0	57	1	57.00
NAT.W.	11	2	33	0	–
B & H	8	0	28	2	14.00

Relaxations: Listening to tapes and records; round of golf
Extras: Made debut when 17 years 3 days. First wicket was A. Lamb
Opinions on cricket: 'Sport should be left out of politics.'
Best batting performance: 33* Yorkshire v Lancashire, Old Trafford 1988
Best bowling performance: 5-98 Yorkshire v Lancashire, Old Trafford 1988

BORDER, A. R. Essex

Full Name: Allan Robert Border
Role: Left-hand bat, slow
left-arm bowler
Born: 27 July 1955, Cremorne,
Sydney
Height: 5′ 9″
Nickname: AB, Herby
(from Herbaceous)
County debut: 1977 (Gloucestershire),
1986 (Essex)
County cap: 1986 (Essex)
Test debut: 1978–79
No. of Tests: 94
No. of One-Day Internationals: 170
1000 runs in a season: 3
1st-Class 50s scored: 89
1st-Class 100s scored: 56
1st-Class 200s scored: 2
One-Day 50s: 33
One-Day 100s: 3
Place in batting averages: 8th av. 58.04
1st-Class catches 1988: 27 (career 240)
Wife and date of marriage: Jane, 12 April 1980
Children: Dene and Nicole
Family links with cricket: Father-in-law, president of Mosman CC
Education: Mosman Primary; North Sydney Technical School; North Sydney
Boys High
Jobs outside cricket: 'Clerk; working in motor-trade, mainly of a promotional
nature, for Ron McConnell (who brought me to Queensland).'
Off-season 1988–89: Playing for Queensland and Australia
Overseas tours: With Australia to England for World Cup, 1979, and for tour
in 1980, 1981, 1985; West Indies 1983–84; New Zealand 1981–82, 1986; India
1979–80, 1986, Pakistan 1979–80, 1982–83; Sri Lanka 1982–83; to India and
Pakistan for World Cup 1987
Overseas teams played for: New South Wales 1976–80; Queensland 1980–86

Cricketers admired: Gary Sobers, Barry Knight, Mark Williamson (elder half-brother)

Other sports played: Baseball (when younger), golf

Injuries 1988: Hospitalised after being hit on the head by Warwickshire's Tony Merrick

Extras: Played for Gloucestershire 2nd XI in 1977 and one match for Gloucestershire 1st XI that year. Captained North Sydney High. Made A-grade debut for Mosman at 16. One of *Wisden*'s Five Cricketers of the Year, 1981. Captained Australia World Cup-winning side 1987. Has appeared in more one-day internationals than any other player in the world. Captain of Queensland since 1983–84; captain of Australia since 1985. Played for East Lancashire in Lancashire League 1978, scoring 1100 odd runs, a club record. Also took about 50 wickets with medium-pace slingers, as opposed to the normal slow left-arm. Joined Essex on 2-year contract in 1986. Published autobiography in 1986

Opinions on cricket: 'I have always regarded Headingley as a sub-standard Test wicket. The unpredictable nature of it makes team selection and captaincy a bit of a nightmare. Overseas tours have been too long. I'd strongly favour reducing future tours to three months. I also advocate less cricket and oppose players' wives coming on tour.'

Best batting performance: 205 Australia v New Zealand, Adelaide 1987–88

Best bowling performance: 4-61 Queensland v New South Wales, Sydney 1980–81

LAST SEASON: BATTING

	I.	N.O.	R.	H.S.	AV.
TEST					
1ST-CLASS	32	8	1393	169*	58.04
INT					
RAL	11	3	344	77	43.00
NAT.W.	2	0	36	35	18.00
B & H	5	2	173	75*	57.66

LAST SEASON: BOWLING

	O.	M.	R.	W.	AV.
TEST					
1ST-CLASS	36	9	113	1	113.00
INT					
RAL	11.4	1	39	1	39.00
NAT.W.					
B & H	11	0	70	0	—

CAREER: BATTING

	I.	N.O.	R.	H.S.	AV.
TEST	164	27	7343	205	53.59
1ST-CLASS	245	35	11467	200	54.60
INT	160	22	4316	127*	31.27
RAL	24	4	674	77	33.70
NAT.W.	5	1	111	46*	27.75
B & H	10	2	254	75*	31.75

CAREER: BOWLING

	O.	M.	R.	W.	AV.
TEST	49 / 231.3	18 / 64	699	16	43.68
1ST-CLASS	243.6 / 328.1	35 / 73	1633	45	36.28
INT	203	5	980	29	33.79
RAL	16.4	1	65	4	16.25
NAT.W.	2.4	0	12	1	12.00
B & H	11	0	70	0	—

BORE, M. K.   Nottinghamshire

Full Name: Michael Kenneth Bore
Born: 2 June 1947, Hull
Height: 5′ 10″ **Weight:** 14st
Nickname: Nod
County debut: 1969 (Yorkshire), 1979 (Nottinghamshire)
County cap: 1980 (Nottinghamshire)
1st-Class 5 w. in innings: 9
1st-Class catches 1988: 0 (career 51)
Parents: Kenneth and Cicely
Wife and date of marriage: Ann, 30 September 1972
Children: Christopher Mark, 17 July 1977; Suzanne, 23 July 1979
Family links with cricket: Father played a good level of local amateur league cricket
Education: Maybury High School
Qualifications: NCA Advanced Coach
Jobs outside cricket: Full-time coach with Nottinghamshire CC
Off-season 1988–89: Coaching children and club players, running courses and seminars at college and university level
Cricketing superstitions or habits: Always put right pad on first. When not captain, prefer to follow wicket-keeper on to field
Overseas tours: Gibraltar with Yorkshire CCC, 1976–77
Cricketers particularly learnt from: 'Most I've played with and against.'
Cricketers particularly admired: Richard Hadlee, Jimmy Binks
Other sports played: Badminton, squash, snooker, golf (badly)
Other sports followed: Football, Rugby League

LAST SEASON: BATTING

	I.	N.O.	R.	H.S.	AV.
TEST					
1ST-CLASS	2	0	5	5	2.50
INT					
RAL	–	–	–	–	–
NAT.W.					
B & H					

LAST SEASON: BOWLING

	O.	M.	R.	W.	AV.
TEST					
1ST-CLASS	9	2	41	0	–
INT					
RAL	8	0	30	1	30.00
NAT.W.					
B & H					

CAREER: BATTING

	I.	N.O.	R.	H.S.	AV.
TEST					
1ST-CLASS	158	52	874	37*	8.24
INT					
RAL	32	14	129	28*	7.16
NAT.W.	7	4	9	4*	3.00
B & H	10	7	27	7*	9.00

CAREER: BOWLING

	O.	M.	R.	W.	AV.
TEST					
1ST-CLASS	4609.1	1561	11243	372	30.22
INT					
RAL	776	81	3082	97	31.77
NAT.W.	109.2	19	327	11	29.72
B & H	259.4	59	736	29	25.38

Relaxations: Family, gardening, driving, watching out for younger cricketers at Sunday matches

Extras: Having just retired from first-class cricket was reinstated for 1987 and 1988

Opinions on cricket: 'Reservations on four-day cricket. More time should be spent by the TCCB into looking into better quality pitches and facilities for 2nd XI cricket, and to help the counties with more funding, especially covering the cost of first-class umpires standing in 2nd XI games.'

Best batting performance: 37* Yorkshire v Nottinghamshire, Bradford 1973

Best bowling performance: 8-89 Nottinghamshire v Kent, Folkestone 1979

BOTHAM, I. T. Worcestershire

Full Name: Ian Terrence Botham
Role: Right-hand bat, right-arm fast-medium bowler, slip fielder
Born: 24 November 1955, Heswall, Cheshire
Height: 6′ 2″ **Weight:** 15st 5lbs
Nickname: Guy, Both, Beefy
County debut: 1974 (Somerset), 1987 (Worcestershire)
County cap: 1976 (Somerset), 1987 (Worcestershire)
Benefit: 1984 (£90,822)
Test debut: 1977
No. of Tests: 94
No. of One-Day Internationals: 95
1000 runs in a season: 4
50 wickets in a season: 7
1st-Class 50s scored: 81
1st-Class 100s scored: 31
1st-Class 200s scored: 2
1st-Class 5 w. in innings: 53
1st-Class 10 w. in match: 7
One-Day 50s: 54
One-Day 100s: 7
Place in batting averages: — (1987 108th av. 29.90)
Place in bowling averages: — (1987 121st av. 42.04)
1st-Class catches 1988: 4 (career 303)
Parents: Les and Marie
Wife and date of marriage: Kathryn, 31 January 1976
Children: Liam James, 26 August 1977; Sarah Lianne, 3 February 1979; Rebecca Kate, 13 November 1985

Family links with cricket: Father played for Navy and Fleet Air Arm; mother played for VAD nursing staff
Education: Millford Junior School; Buckler's Mead Secondary School, Yeovil
Overseas tours: Pakistan and New Zealand 1977–78; Australia 1978–79; Australia and India, 1979–80; West Indies 1981 as captain; India 1981–82; Australia and New Zealand 1982–83; West Indies 1986
Cricketers particularly learnt from: Brian Close
Cricketers particularly admired: Viv Richards, David Gower, Allan Border
Off-season 1988–89: Getting fit
Other sports played: Captained school soccer team, and has played for Scunthorpe United, making debut as striker v Bournemouth in March 1980. Offered terms by Crystal Palace. Now plays for Yeovil Town. U-16 Somerset champion, badminton doubles
Injuries 1988: Missed nearly whole season because of back operation
Relaxations: Golf, shooting, fishing (salmon and trout). Has learned to fly
Extras: Captain of England 1980–81. Took five Australian wickets in his first day of Test Match cricket aged 21. Played for County 2nd XI 1971. On MCC staff 1972–73. One of *Wisden*'s Five Cricketers of the Year, 1977. Subject of 'This is Your Life' television programme in November 1981. Was Best Man at Viv Richards' wedding in March 1981 in Antigua. Voted BBC TV Sportsview Sporting Personality of 1981. Having a go at baseball in Los Angeles in September 1981 easily exceeded the striking rate of established American baseball stars: he complained that Americans could not pitch the ball fast enough. Scored fastest 100 of 1982 and 1985 seasons. Scored 200 in 272 minutes for England v India at The Oval, 9 July 1982, third fastest Test double century by an Englishman, after Walter Hammond (240 mins v New Zealand in 1932) and Denis Compton (245 mins v Pakistan in 1954). Crashed two £12,000 sports cars at 100 mph in same afternoon in May 1982. Among the books he chose to take to a desert island was Jack Fingleton's book on the great Australian cricketer *The Immortal Victor Trumper*. Published books

LAST SEASON: BATTING

	I.	N.O.	R.	H.S.	AV.
TEST					
1ST-CLASS	4	0	18	7	4.50
INT					
RAL	4	0	80	39	20.00
NAT.W.					
B & H	3	0	54	43	18.00

LAST SEASON: BOWLING

	O.	M.	R.	W.	AV.
TEST					
1ST-CLASS	43	11	125	1	125.00
INT					
RAL	28.4	2	157	5	31.40
NAT.W.					
B & H	28	4	100	8	12.50

CAREER: BATTING

	I.	N.O.	R.	H.S.	AV.
TEST	150	5	5057	208	34.87
1ST-CLASS	359	32	11365	228	34.75
INT	86	11	1693	72	22.57
RAL	139	22	3843	175*	32.84
NAT.W.	30	6	926	101	38.58
B & H	55	7	1121	126*	23.35

CAREER: BOWLING

	O.	M.	R.	W.	AV.
TEST	259.4 / 3120.5	42 / 705	10392	373	27.86
1ST-CLASS	190.3 / 7725	43 / 1782	16588	632	26.24
INT	38.7 / 794.4	2 / 93	3398	116	29.29
RAL	997.2	61	4416	195	22.64
NAT.W.	353.3	56	1191	42	28.35
B & H	630.4	120	2138	103	20.75

include *High, Wide and Handsome*, an account of his record-breaking 1985 season and *It Sort of Clicks*, in collaboration with his former Somerset colleague Peter Roebuck. First cricketer since W. G. Grace to have painting commissioned by National Portrait Gallery. Captain of Somerset 1984–85. Holds record for having scored 1000 runs and taken 100 wickets in fewest Test matches. First player to score a century and take 8 wickets in an innings in a Test Match, v Pakistan at Lord's in 1978. Most sixes in a first-class season 1985. Left Somerset at the beginning of 1987 to join Worcestershire after Somerset had decided not to renew the contracts of Richards and Garner

Opinions on cricket: 'Too many people live in the past.'

Best batting performance: 228 Somerset v Gloucestershire, Taunton 1980

Best bowling performance: 8-34 England v Pakistan, Lord's 1978

BOWLER, P. D. Derbyshire

Full Name: Peter Duncan Bowler
Role: Right-hand opening bat, off-spinner
Born: 30 July 1963, Plymouth, Australia
Height: 6′ 2″ **Weight:** 13st
Nickname: Skippy
County debut: 1986 (Leicestershire), 1988 (Derbyshire)
1000 runs in a season: 1
1st-Class 50s scored: 10
1st-Class 100s scored: 5
One-Day 50s: 3
Place in batting averages: 21st av. 46.62
1st-Class catches 1988: 13 (career 15)
Parents: Peter and Etta
Marital status: Single
Education: Daramalan College, Canberra, Australia
Qualifications: Australian Yr 12 Certificate
Overseas teams played for: Manly CC 1982; Westbury CC 1983–87
Cricketers particularly learnt from: Rob Jeffery, Bill Carracher, Gus Valence
Cricketers particularly admired: Greg Chappell, Richard Hadlee, Dennis Lillee
Other sports played: Rugby union
Relaxations: Music, reading, newspapers. Playing sports other than cricket. Relaxing with family

Extras: First Leicestershire player to score a first-class hundred on debut (100 not out v Hampshire 1986). Moved to Derbyshire at end of 1987 season and then scored a century for Derbyshire on his debut for them v Cambridge University
Best batting performance: 159* Derbyshire v Essex, Chesterfield 1988
Best bowling performance: 2-63 Derbyshire v Worcestershire, Derby 1988

LAST SEASON: BATTING

	I.	N.O.	R.	H.S.	AV.
TEST					
1ST-CLASS	42	5	1725	159*	46.62
INT					
RAL	14	0	292	44	20.85
NAT.W.	3	0	65	46	21.66
B & H	6	0	191	64	31.83

CAREER: BATTING

	I.	N.O.	R.	H.S.	AV.
TEST					
1ST-CLASS	56	6	1989	159*	39.78
INT					
RAL	25	1	463	55	19.29
NAT.W.	3	0	65	46	21.66
B & H	6	0	191	64	31.83

LAST SEASON: BOWLING

	O.	M.	R.	W.	AV.
TEST					
1ST-CLASS	169.5	28	577	7	82.42
INT					
RAL	32	1	185	4	46.25
NAT.W.	3	0	14	0	–
B & H	41	7	125	4	31.25

CAREER: BOWLING

	O.	M.	R.	W.	AV.
TEST					
1ST-CLASS	195.3	38	634	7	90.57
INT					
RAL	32	1	185	4	46.25
NAT.W.	3	0	14	0	–
B & H	41	7	125	4	31.25

BRASSINGTON, A. J.   Gloucestershire

Full Name: Andrew James Brassington
Role: Right-hand bat, wicket-keeper
Born: 9 August 1954, Bagnall, Stoke-on-Trent
Height: 6′ 0″ **Weight:** 11st 9lbs
Nickname: Imma
County debut: 1974
County cap: 1978
Benefit: 1988
Parents: Joan Ursula and John Reginald
Wife and date of marriage: Rosalyn, 26 February 1977
Children: Emma Louisa
Education: Endon Secondary Modern
Qualifications: 6 CSEs
Jobs outside cricket: Salesman and promotional work

Overseas tours: To Malawi with Gloucestershire 1978
Cricketers particularly learnt from: Bob Taylor
Cricketers particularly admired: Alan Knott, Bob Taylor, Greg Chappell, Rod Marsh, Viv Richards, Mike Procter
Other sports played: Football (goalkeeper)
Relaxations: Watching TV, playing Scrabble and music
Extras: Retired at end of 1988 season to become Gloucestershire's full-time marketing manager
Best batting performance: 35 Gloucestershire v Sussex, Hastings 1982

LAST SEASON: BATTING

	I.	N.O.	R.	H.S.	AV.
TEST					
1ST-CLASS	1	0	1	1	1.00
INT					
RAL					
NAT.W.					
B & H	—	—	—	—	—

LAST SEASON: WICKET KEEPING

	C.	ST.		
TEST				
1ST-CLASS	1	1		
INT				
RAL				
NAT.W.				
B & H	1	—		

CAREER: BATTING

	I.	N.O.	R.	H.S.	AV.
TEST					
1ST-CLASS	156	46	882	35	8.01
INT					
RAL	21	12	93	14*	10.33
NAT.W.	2	1	0	20	20.00
B & H	7	2	21	9*	4.20

CAREER: WICKET KEEPING

	C.	ST.		
TEST				
1ST-CLASS	216	49		
INT				
RAL	33	9		
NAT.W.	3	—		
B & H	9	2		

BRIERS, N. E. Leicestershire

Full Name: Nigel Edwin Briers
Role: Right-hand bat, right-arm medium bowler, cover fielder
Born: 15 January 1955, Leicester
Height: 6′ 0″ **Weight:** 12st 5lbs
Nickname: Kudu
County debut: 1971 (aged 16 yrs 104 days)
County cap: 1981
1000 runs in a season: 5
1st-Class 50s scored: 51
1st-Class 100s scored: 13
1st-Class 200s scored: 1
One-Day 50s: 29
One-Day 100s: 3
Place in batting averages: 63rd av. 34.23 (1987 21st av. 44.89)
1st-Class catches 1988: 14 (career 100)

Parents: Leonard Arthur Roger and Eveline
Wife and date of marriage: Suzanne Mary Tudor, 3 September 1977
Children: Michael Edward Tudor, 25 March 1983; Andrew James Tudor, 30 June 1986
Family links with cricket: Father was captain and wicket-keeper of Narborough and Littlethorpe Cricket Club, first division of Leicestershire League, for 15 years. Mother was scorer for team. Father was Captain of South Leicestershire Representative XI and played for the Royal Marines in the same team as Trevor Bailey. Cousin, Norman Briers, played for Leicestershire once in 1967
Education: Lutterworth Grammar School; Borough Road College
Qualifications: Qualified teacher (Certificate of Education), BEd Hons, MCC Advanced Coach
Jobs outside cricket: Lecturer in Physical Education at Leicester Polytechnic
Off-season 1988–89: Teaching PE and history at Ludgrove School
Overseas tours: Derrick Robins' XI to South America, 1979; MCC to Far East, 1981; Leicestershire CCC to Zimbabwe, 1981
Cricketers particularly learnt from: 'My father, Maurice Hallam, Jack Birkenshaw, Ray Illingworth.'
Extras: Captained Leicestershire in David Gower's absence in 1988
Best batting performance: 201* Leicestershire v Warwickshire, Edgbaston 1983
Best bowling performance: 4-29 Leicestershire v Derbyshire, Leicester 1985

LAST SEASON: BATTING

	I.	N.O.	R.	H.S.	AV.
TEST					
1ST-CLASS	41	2	1335	125*	34.23
INT					
RAL	14	2	373	37	9.25
NAT.W.	2	0	58	42	29.00
B & H	3	0	50	44	16.66

LAST SEASON: BOWLING

	O.	M.	R.	W.	AV.
TEST					
1ST-CLASS					
INT					
RAL					
NAT.W.					
B & H					

CAREER: BATTING

	I.	N.O.	R.	H.S.	AV.
TEST					
1ST-CLASS	374	37	10063	201*	29.86
INT					
RAL	136	21	3972	119*	34.53
NAT.W.	23	2	410	59	19.52
B & H	32	2	486	71*	16.20

CAREER: BOWLING

	O.	M.	R.	W.	AV.
TEST					
1ST-CLASS	338.5	70	988	32	30.87
INT					
RAL	80.2	5	384	10	38.40
NAT.W.	14	0	75	6	12.50
B & H	55	3	266	3	88.66

35. What is unusual about Derek Pringle's boots?

36. Graham Gooch has taken over 200 first-class wickets. True or false?

37. Who has taken more first-class wickets, Graham Gooch or Viv Richards?

BROAD, B. C.   Nottinghamshire

Full Name: Brian Christopher Broad
Role: Left-hand bat, right-arm medium bowler
Born: 29 September 1957, Bristol
Height: 6′ 4″ **Weight:** 14st 7lbs
Nickname: Walter, Broadie, Whoda (by Mike Gatting, as in 'Whoda thought of you')
County debut: 1979 (Gloucestershire), 1984 (Nottinghamshire)
County cap: 1981 (Gloucestershire), 1984 (Nottinghamshire)
Test debut: 1984
No. of Tests: 23
No. of One-Day Internationals: 34
1000 runs in a season: 6
1st-Class 50s scored: 74
1st-Class 100s scored: 25
One-Day 50s: 41
One-Day 100s: 3
Place in batting averages: 132nd av. 25.64 (1987 92nd av. 32.18)
1st-Class catches 1988: 13 (career 125)
Parents: Nancy and Kenneth
Wife and date of marriage: Carole Ann, 14 July 1979
Children: Gemma Joanne, 14 January 1984; Stuart Christopher John, 24 June 1986
Education: Colston's School, Bristol; St Paul's College, Cheltenham
Qualifications: 5 O-levels, NCA advanced coach
Family links with cricket: Father and grandfather both played local cricket. Father member of Gloucestershire Committee until retired
Cricketing superstitions or habits: Puts left pad on first
Overseas tours: Gloucestershire CCC to Malawi 1978 and Barbados 1980; British Colleges to Trinidad and Barbados 1979; English Counties to Zimbabwe, 1985; International XI to Jamaica, 1985; England to West Indies 1986; World Cup, Pakistan, New Zealand and Australia 1987–88
Overseas teams played for: Somerville CC, Melbourne, 1979–80, Takapuna CC, Auckland 1982–83, 1983–84, Orange Free State 1985–86 (Captain)
Cricketers particularly learnt from: Reg Sinfield, Sadiq Mohammed, John Sullivan
Cricketers particularly admired: Graham Gooch, Richard Hadlee, Clive Rice

Other sports played: Played Rugby for English Colleges, Bristol United, St Paul's College, and Clifton

Relaxations: 'Playing any sport, spending time with my family.'

Extras: Struck down by osteomyelitis at age 15. First played adult cricket for Downend CC, where W. G. Grace learnt to play; then Long Ashton CC; Gloucestershire U-19s; Gloucestershire Young Cricketers'; NAYC v MCC Schools. Played with Allan Border in Gloucestershire 2nd XI. Played with Tim Robinson in 1977 for NAYC v Young Australians. Published autobiography *Home Thoughts from Abroad* in 1987. Hit three centuries in a row in Test series v Australia, 1986–87. Uses a bat weighing 3lbs

Opinions on cricket: 'I would have loved playing as an amateur. I am an unashamed traditionalist.'

Best batting performance: 171 Nottinghamshire v Derbyshire, Derby 1985

Best bowling performance: 2-14 Gloucestershire v West Indies, Bristol 1980

LAST SEASON: BATTING

	I.	N.O.	R.	H.S.	AV.
TEST	4	0	71	54	17.75
1ST-CLASS	30	0	801	73	26.70
INT	3	0	82	35	27.33
RAL	9	1	304	96*	38.00
NAT.W.	2	0	29	27	14.50
B & H	4	0	146	52	36.50

LAST SEASON: BOWLING

	O.	M.	R.	W.	AV.
TEST					
1ST-CLASS	4	0	30	0	–
INT					
RAL					
NAT.W.					
B & H					

CAREER: BATTING

	I.	N.O.	R.	H.S.	AV.
TEST	40	2	1579	162	41.55
1ST-CLASS	360	26	11765	171	35.22
INT	34	0	1154	106	33.94
RAL	109	6	3363	104*	32.65
NAT.W.	23	0	820	98	35.65
B & H	39	2	1035	122	27.97

CAREER: BOWLING

	O.	M.	R.	W.	AV.
TEST	1	0	4	0	–
1ST-CLASS	269.5	60	1032	16	64.50
INT	1	0	6	0	–
RAL	111.3	4	602	19	31.68
NAT.W.					
B & H	50.4	2	282	5	56.40

38. How many Tests had England gone without a win before they beat Sri Lanka in August 1988?

39. Who captained Sri Lanka v England in August 1988 at Lord's?

40. How many captains did England have v West Indies in 1988, and who were they, in correct order?

BROWN, A. D. Essex

Full Name: Adrian Desmond Brown
Role: Right-hand bat,
wicket-keeper
Born: 18 May 1962, Clacton-on-Sea
Height: 5′ 11″ **Weight:** 12st
Nickname: Doey, Hovis, Smurf,
Brownie
County debut: 1988
Parents: Desmond and Kathleen
Marital status: Single
Family links with cricket: Father
played for local club side,
Clacton
Education: Clacton County High
School; Magdalene College,
Cambridge
Qualifications: 8 O-levels –
all 'A' grade; 3 A-Levels
(French 'A', German 'A',
Latin 'A'); II. I in Modern Languages and MA; Post Graduate Certificate of
Education; Senior Coaching Award NCA

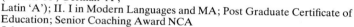

Jobs outside cricket: Teaching: King's College Taunton 1986–87; Colbayno
High School 1987–88
Cricketing superstitions or habits: Keeping wicket in a cap. Wearing long
sleeved shirt to keep wicket
Cricketers particularly learnt from: David East, Bob Richards, Ray East,
John Childs
Cricketers particularly admired: Jack Russell, Bob Taylor, Alan Knott
Other sports played: Football, tennis

LAST SEASON: BATTING

	I.	N.O.	R.	H.S.	AV.
TEST					
1ST-CLASS	5	3	13	6*	6.50
INT					
RAL	1	1	1	1*	–
NAT.W.	–	–	–	–	–
B & H					

LAST SEASON: WICKET KEEPING

	C.	ST.
TEST		
1ST-CLASS	9	2
INT		
RAL	1	–
NAT.W.	1	–
B & H		

CAREER: BATTING

	I.	N.O.	R.	H.S.	AV.
TEST					
1ST-CLASS	16	4	99	30	8.25
INT					
RAL	1	1	1	1*	–
NAT.W.	2	0	10	9	5.00
B & H	4	2	24	10*	12.00

CAREER: WICKET KEEPING

	C.	ST.
TEST		
1ST-CLASS	24	4
INT		
RAL	1	–
NAT.W.	4	2
B & H	1	1

Other sports followed: Rugby
Relaxations: Cinema, theatre, holding intellectual conversations with Don Topley, keeping chickens
Extras: Cambridge Blue. Played against touring Indians and New Zealanders for Combined Universities plus B & H 1986. Released by Essex at end of 1988
Opinions on cricket: 'Cricket will benefit from more four-day cricket providing the pitches are up to standard. Counties should do more for their players in the close season – particularly if they stay in England: employers are not very interested in six month employees.'
Best batting performance: 30 Cambridge University v Surrey, Cambridge 1986

BROWN, G. E. Surrey

Full Name: Graham Elliott Brown
Role: Right-hand bat, wicket-keeper
Born: 11 October 1966, Balham
Height: 5' 7" **Weight:** 11st
Nickname: Browny, Stumper, Pipsqueak, Reggie Perrin, Reg
County debut: 1986
Parents: Alan and Dorothy
Wife and date of marriage: Pamela, January 1987
Family links with cricket: 'Father and uncles avid watchers. Father an avid moaner on my performance!'
Education: Spencer Park School, Wandsworth; South London College, West Norwood

Qualifications: 6 CSEs, 3 O-levels
Jobs outside cricket: Postman, sports coach, insurance broker, painter and decorator
Cricketing superstitions or habits: Left keeping pad on first; left inner glove on first; being first out onto the middle to get new ball off umpire
Overseas tours: London Schools U-16s to Jamaica 1983; Surrey to La Manga 1986 and Dubai 1988
Cricketers particularly learnt from: Jack Richards, Ray Jackson, Ron Brown, Ray East
Cricketers particularly admired: Jack Richards, Alan Knott
Off-season 1988–89: Working for Video Arts
Other sports played: Football, baseball

Injuries 1988: Broken finger in right hand; out for three weeks
Relaxations: Reading, travelling, sleeping
Best batting performance: 13* Surrey v Pakistanis, The Oval 1987

LAST SEASON: BATTING

	I.	N.O.	R.	H.S.	AV.
TEST					
1ST-CLASS	2	0	10	10	5.00
INT					
RAL					
NAT.W.					
B & H					

LAST SEASON: WICKET KEEPING

	C.	ST.		
TEST				
1ST-CLASS	6	1		
INT				
RAL				
NAT.W.				
B & H				

CAREER: BATTING

	I.	N.O.	R.	H.S.	AV.
TEST					
1ST-CLASS	11	8	59	13*	19.66
INT					
RAL					
NAT.W.					
B & H					

CAREER: WICKET KEEPING

	C.	ST.		
TEST				
1ST-CLASS	19	2		
INT				
RAL				
NAT.W.				
B & H				

BROWN, K. R. Middlesex

Full Name: Keith Robert Brown
Role: Right-hand bat, wicket-keeper
Born: 18 March 1963, Edmonton
Height: 5′ 11″ **Weight:** 13st 7lbs
Nickname: Browny, Gloves, Scarface, Pigsy
County debut: 1984
1st-Class 50s scored: 10
1st-Class 100s scored: 3
One-Day 50s: 1
One-Day 100s: 1
Place in batting averages: 110th av. 28.34 (1987 126th av. 27.57)
1st-Class catches 1988: 32 (career 64)
Parents: Kenneth William and Margaret Sonia
Wife and date of marriage: Marie, 3 November 1984

Children: Zachary, 24 February 1987
Family links with cricket: Brother Gary was on Middlesex staff for 3 years. Father is qualified umpire and played club cricket
Education: Chance Boys' School, Enfield

Qualifications: French O-level; Junior and Senior Cricket Coach
Jobs outside cricket: Plasterer, light engineering, painter, decorator
Cricketing superstitions or habits: Nelson 111. Wear same gear if successful
Overseas tours: NCA to Denmark 1981. Pre-season trips with Middlesex to La Manga 1985 and 86
Cricketers particularly learnt from: Father and Don Bennett, Clive Radley
Cricketers particularly admired: Clive Radley
Off-season 1988–89: In Sydney, Australia
Other sports played: Rugby, tennis, snooker
Other sports followed: All of them, especially boxing and football
Relaxations: Exercising Golden Retriever Wesley, looking after baby Zachary – not relaxing but enjoyable
Extras: Had promising boxing career but gave it up in order to concentrate on cricket. Picked to play rugby for Essex
Opinions on cricket: 'Four-day cricket may benefit county players with a view to representing their country. Over rate fines should be abolished. New law about bringing protective equipment onto the field should be scrapped.'
Best batting performance: 131* Middlesex v Nottinghamshire, Lord's 1988
Best bowling performance: 2-7 Middlesex v Gloucestershire, Bristol 1987

LAST SEASON: BATTING

	I.	N.O.	R.	H.S.	AV.
TEST					
1ST-CLASS	34	5	822	131*	28.34
INT					
RAL	11	1	213	102	21.30
NAT.W.	3	1	68	37*	34.00
B & H	4	1	73	32*	24.33

CAREER: BATTING

	I.	N.O.	R.	H.S.	AV.
TEST					
1ST-CLASS	86	12	2072	131*	28.00
INT					
RAL	24	5	491	102	22.35
NAT.W.	4	1	92	37*	30.66
B & H	4	1	73	32*	24.33

LAST SEASON: BOWLING

	O.	M.	R.	W.	AV.
TEST					
1ST-CLASS	2	2	0	0	–
INT					
RAL					
NAT.W.					
B & H	1	1	0	0	–

CAREER: BOWLING

	O.	M.	R.	W.	AV.
TEST					
1ST-CLASS	16.4	4	64	3	21.33
INT					
RAL	1	0	1	0	–
NAT.W.					
B & H	1	1	0	0	–

41. Who headed the England batting averages v Sri Lanka, and what was his average?

42. True or false: Trevor Bailey of Essex and England once bowled an orange instead of a cricket ball at Len Hutton of Yorkshire and England?

BROWN, S. J.   Northamptonshire

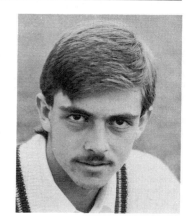

Full Name: Simon John Brown
Role: Right-hand bat, left-arm medium pace bowler
Born: 29 June 1969, Cleadon Village, Sunderland
Height: 6′ 3″ **Weight:** 12st
Nickname: Chubby, Biffo
County debut: 1987
1st-Class catches 1988: 2 (career 3)
Parents: Ernie and Doreen
Marital status: Single
Education: Boldon Comprehensive, Tyne & Wear
Qualifications: 5 O-levels, 5 CSEs
Jobs outside cricket: Sales assistant, part-time groundsman, furniture van driver
Off-season 1988–89: Taxi driving, playing basketball
Cricketing superstitions or habits: Always to be last onto the field
Cricketers particularly learnt from: Alec Coxon, Dennis Lillee, Bob Carter
Cricketers particularly admired: John Lever, Dennis Lillee, Richard Hadlee
Other sports played: Basketball, football, tennis, golf, snooker, squash
Other sports followed: Basketball, snooker
Relaxations: Fishing, cycling, playing snooker, restoring old cars
Extras: Offered basketball scholarship in America. Also professional terms with Sunderland FC. Took wicket with first ball in Sunday League
Opinions on cricket: 'Too many three-day games depend entirely on the last day, and the first two days are pointless.'

LAST SEASON: BATTING

	I.	N.O.	R.	H.S.	AV.
TEST					
1ST-CLASS	6	1	34	25*	6.80
INT					
RAL	1	0	1	1	1.00
NAT.W.					
B & H	–	–	–	–	–

CAREER: BATTING

	I.	N.O.	R.	H.S.	AV.
TEST					
1ST-CLASS	11	4	59	25*	8.42
INT					
RAL	1	0	1	1	1.00
NAT.W.					
B & H	–	–	–	–	–

LAST SEASON: BOWLING

	O.	M.	R.	W.	AV.
TEST					
1ST-CLASS	102	34	221	9	24.55
INT					
RAL	33.3	0	177	6	29.50
NAT.W.					
B & H	7	0	33	0	–

CAREER: BOWLING

	O.	M.	R.	W.	AV.
TEST					
1ST-CLASS	184	57	437	18	24.27
INT					
RAL	44.3	1	241	8	30.12
NAT.W.					
B & H	7	0	33	0	–

Best batting performance: 25* Northamptonshire v Gloucestershire, Northampton 1988
Best bowling performance: 3-20 Northamptonshire v Oxford University, Oxford 1988

BULLEN, C. K. Surrey

Full Name: Christopher Keith Bullen
Role: Right-hand bat, off-break bowler, slip fielder
Born: 5 November 1962, Clapham
Height: 6' 5" **Weight:** 14st 7lbs
Nickname: CB, Jasper, Bullo, Roadrunner, Steeley
County debut: 1985
1st-Class 50s scored: 4
1st-Class 5 w. in innings: 1
Place in batting averages: 171st av. 21.75 (1987 138th av. 25.90)
Place in bowling averages: 70th av. 28.72 (1987 48th av. 26.85)
Strike rate 1988: 58.45 (career 65.26)
1st-Class catches 1988: 8 (career 24)
Parents: Keith Thomas and Joan
Marital status: Single
Family links with cricket: 'Parents are enthusiastic cricket watchers. Father claims he played cricket at a high standard, but there's no evidence! Cousin David is an up-an-coming Under 12 with Cornwall Schools.'
Education: Glenbrook Primary; Chaucer Middle; Rutlish School
Qualifications: 6 O-levels
Jobs outside cricket: Labourer, car washer, packer
Off-season 1988–89: Working for Notts Sport selling artificial cricket pitches; playing rugby and football
Cricketing superstitions or habits: Always put left things on first, i.e. socks, shoes, batting gloves. Always brush hair before going out to field
Overseas tours: Surrey Schools U-19 to Australia 1980–81
Overseas teams played for: Claremont Cottesloe, Perth, 1984–85, 1985–86
Cricketers particularly learnt from: Mickey Stewart, Geoff Arnold, Chris Waller
Cricketers particularly admired: Jim Laker, Chris Brown
Other sports played: Golf, rugby

Other sports followed: Soccer, American football, Aussie rules
Injuries 1988: Badly swollen ankle – suspected broken
Relaxations: Listening to music, leisurely walk after a golf ball
Extras: Spends free time playing club cricket for Wimbledon and Old Rutlishians. Captain of Surrey U-25 side which won Warwick Trophy in 1986. Once a night-watchman in B & H semi-final. Member of Surrey 2nd XI which won 2nd XI Championship in 1988
Opinions on cricket: 'Four-day county games should be played on good wickets. English registration is given too freely. 2nd XI matches should be played under same conditions as first-class games. More should be done by clubs to look after their players during the winter, especially those staying in this country.'
Best batting performance: 65 Surrey v Pakistanis, The Oval 1987
Best bowling performance: 6-119 Surrey v Middlesex, Lord's, 1987

LAST SEASON: BATTING

	I.	N.O.	R.	H.S.	AV.
TEST					
1ST-CLASS	14	2	261	59*	21.75
INT					
RAL	8	2	83	23	13.83
NAT.W.	4	1	32	22	10.66
B & H	2	1	25	21	25.00

CAREER: BATTING

	I.	N.O.	R.	H.S.	AV.
TEST					
1ST-CLASS	31	5	573	65	22.03
INT					
RAL	20	7	176	25	13.53
NAT.W.	5	2	33	22	11.00
B & H	3	1	58	33	29.00

LAST SEASON: BOWLING

	O.	M.	R.	W.	AV.
TEST					
1ST-CLASS	107.1	25	316	11	28.72
INT					
RAL	96	2	503	19	26.47
NAT.W.	44	3	144	5	28.80
B & H	34.5	1	182	2	91.00

CAREER: BOWLING

	O.	M.	R.	W.	AV.
TEST					
1ST-CLASS	369.5	107	984	34	28.94
INT					
RAL	215.3	11	1023	37	27.64
NAT.W.	68	8	218	6	36.33
B & H	89.5	6	362	7	51.71

43. What unique feat did Graham Gooch perform on 30 August 1988?

44. Which two West Indian fast bowlers playing first-class cricket in 1988 have exactly the same initials?

BUNTING, R. A.

Sussex

Full Name: Rodney Alan Bunting
Role: Right-hand bat, right-arm
fast-medium bowler
Born: 25 April 1965, King's Lynn
Height: 6′ 5″ **Weight:** 13st 9lbs
Nickname: Herman, Tiddler
County debut: 1988
1st-Class 5 w. in innings: 3
Place in bowling averages: 96th
av. 32.19
Strike rate 1988: 58.54
(career 58.54)
1st-Class catches 1988: 2 (career 2)
Parents: Geoffrey Thomas and
Frances
Wife and date of marriage:
Christine Antoinette, 7 March 1986
Children: Jonathan Charles,
16 September 1986
Family links with cricket: Two elder brothers played county schools cricket.
Parents very interested in cricket
Education: King Edward VII Grammar School
Qualifications: 6 O-levels
Jobs outside cricket: Farm work
Off-season 1988–89: Coaching and playing in South Africa
Cricketing superstitions or habits: Tapping bat twice on the floor before going
out to bat
Overseas teams played for: Uitenhage, South Africa 1983–84; Humansdorp,
South Africa 1984–85, 1985–86

LAST SEASON: BATTING

	I.	N.O.	R.	H.S.	AV.
TEST					
1ST-CLASS	21	5	96	17*	6.00
INT					
RAL	1	1	5	5*	–
NAT.W.					
B & H	1	0	0	0	0.00

LAST SEASON: BOWLING

	O.	M.	R.	W.	AV.
TEST					
1ST-CLASS	400	69	1320	41	32.19
INT					
RAL	8	0	49	2	24.50
NAT.W.					
B & H	22	0	88	3	29.33

CAREER: BATTING

	I.	N.O.	R.	H.S.	AV.
TEST					
1ST-CLASS	21	5	96	17*	6.00
INT					
RAL	1	1	5	5*	–
NAT.W.					
B & H	1	0	0	0	0.00

CAREER: BOWLING

	O.	M.	R.	W.	AV.
TEST					
1ST-CLASS	400	69	1320	41	32.19
INT					
RAL	8	0	49	2	24.50
NAT.W.					
B & H	22	0	88	3	29.33

Cricketers particularly learnt from: 'All of the players at Sussex during the last season. Dennis Lillee during Northants game.'
Cricketers particularly admired: Bob Willis, Mike Hendrick
Other sports played: Occasional golf, soccer
Other sports followed: Soccer, American football
Relaxations: Easy crosswords, playing with young son, drinking when allowed
Opinions on cricket: 'Disagree with politics interfering with sport.'
Best batting performance: 17* Sussex v Hampshire, Southampton 1988
Best bowling performance: 5-44 Sussex v Warwickshire, Hove 1988

BURNS, N. D. Somerset

Full Name: Neil David Burns
Role: Left-hand bat, wicket-keeper
Born: 19 September 1965, Chelmsford
Height: 5' 10" **Weight:** 11½st
Nickname: Burnsie, Ernie
County debut: 1986 (Essex), 1987 (Somerset)
County cap: 1987 (Somerset)
1st-Class 50s scored: 6
1st-Class 100s scored: 2
One-Day 50s: 1
Place in batting averages: 127th av. 26.22 (1987 136th av. 26.03)
Parents: Roy and Marie
Wife and date of marriage: Anne, 26 September 1987
Family links with cricket: Father Roy played club cricket for Finchley CC; brother Ian captained Essex U-19 and plays for Chelmsford CC and Stock Exchange CC
Education: Mildmay Junior and Moulsham High School
Qualifications: 5 O-levels, Advanced Cricket Coach
Jobs outside cricket: Worked in a sports shop one winter
Cricketing superstitions or habits: Must go through a particular warm-up and practice before every day's play. Always keep wicket in a cap
Overseas tours: Young England to West Indies 1985
Overseas teams played for: Northerns-Goonwood CC (Cape Town) 1984–85, 1985–86; Western Province B in Sach Castle Bowl 1985–86

Cricketers particularly learnt from: Ray East, Graham Saville, Alan Knott, Robin Jackman, Martin Crowe

Cricketers particularly admired: Alan Knott, Bob Taylor, Rod Marsh, Graham Gooch, Martin Crowe, John Lever

Other sports followed: Most sports particularly soccer and West Ham United FC

Relaxations: Relaxing at home, music, theatre, watching and playing sport, TV, sleeping

Extras: Former schoolboy footballer with Spurs and Orient FC. Joined Somerset in 1987 on two-year contract to further career after spending four years at Essex. Once took 8 stumpings in match v Kent 2nd XI at Dartford 1984. Essex Young Player of Year 1984. Trained with West Ham United FC. Joined Somerset in 1987. Scored maiden 1st-class century against old county at Chelmsford

Opinions on cricket: 'Should be a regular overseas tour in the winter of an England U-25 or B team to bridge gap between young England and the full side. More should be done by clubs to encourage players to work for the club in winter months in some promotional capacity. Bowlers run-ups should be uncovered, if pitches are. 16 four-day matches for 1st-class games. 2nd XI competition to be 16 three-day games playing each county once with venues switching alternate seasons. Better quality pitches at 2nd XI level and one 1st-class umpire to stand to raise umpiring level. All grounds should have top quality grass practice pitches available.'

Best batting performance: 133* Somerset v Sussex, Hove 1988

LAST SEASON: BATTING

	I.	N.O.	R.	H.S.	AV.
TEST					
1ST-CLASS	34	7	708	133*	26.22
INT					
RAL	12	2	148	34	14.80
NAT.W.	2	1	19	18	19.00
B & H	2	0	7	5	3.50

CAREER: BATTING

	I.	N.O.	R.	H.S.	AV.
TEST					
1ST-CLASS	67	14	1521	100*	28.69
INT					
RAL	23	4	223	34	11.73
NAT.W.	3	1	36	18	18.00
B & H	6	3	152	51	50.66

LAST SEASON: WICKET KEEPING

	C.	ST.			
TEST					
1ST-CLASS	57	2			
INT					
RAL	16	2			
NAT.W.	1	1			
B & H	4	–			

CAREER: WICKET KEEPING

	C.	ST.			
TEST					
1ST-CLASS	111	10			
INT					
RAL	29	5			
NAT.W.	2	2			
B & H	10	1			

BUTCHER, A. R.   Glamorgan

Full Name: Alan Raymond Butcher
Role: Left-hand bat, slow left-arm
or medium pace bowler
Born: 7 January 1954, Croydon
Height: 5' 8" **Weight:** 11st 7lbs
Nickname: Butch, Budgie
County debut: 1972 (Surrey),
1987 (Glamorgan)
County cap: 1975 (Surrey),
1987 (Glamorgan)
Benefit: 1985 (Surrey)
Test debut: 1979
No. of Tests: 1
No. of One-Day Internationals: 1
1000 runs in a season: 9
1st-Class 50s scored: 82
1st-Class 100s scored: 33
1st-Class 200s scored: 1
1st-Class 5 w. in innings: 1
One-Day 50s: 43
One-Day 100s: 4
Place in batting averages: 68th av. 33.73 (1987 41st av. 40.36)
1st-Class catches 1988: 13 (career 151)
Parents: Raymond and Jackie
Wife and date of marriage: Elaine, 27 September 1972
Children: Mark, Gary, Lisa
Family links with cricket: Brother, Martin, played for MCC Young Professionals. Brother, Ian, plays for Gloucestershire CC
Education: Heath Clark Grammar School

LAST SEASON: BATTING

	I.	N.O.	R.	H.S.	AV.
TEST					
1ST-CLASS	40	2	1282	166	33.73
INT					
RAL	10	4	122	34*	20.33
NAT.W.	3	0	153	80	51.00
B & H	6	0	115	57	19.16

CAREER: BATTING

	I.	N.O.	R.	H.S.	AV.
TEST	2	0	34	20	17.00
1ST-CLASS	555	47	16991	216*	33.44
INT	1	0	14	14	14.00
RAL	182	22	4469	113*	27.93
NAT.W.	28	3	768	86*	30.72
B & H	61	4	1426	80	25.01

LAST SEASON: BOWLING

	O.	M.	R.	W.	AV.
TEST					
1ST-CLASS	54	10	198	5	39.60
INT					
RAL	5	0	25	0	—
NAT.W.					
B & H	7	2	19	0	—

CAREER: BOWLING

	O.	M.	R.	W.	AV.
TEST	2	0	9	0	—
1ST-CLASS	1590.2	327	5049	134	37.67
INT					
RAL	328.2	22	1445	36	40.13
NAT.W.	67.2	10	249	5	49.80
B & H	175.3	32	526	24	21.91

Qualifications: 5 O-levels, 1 A-level
Jobs outside cricket: Football coach, PE master
Other sports played: Football
Relaxations: Most sport, rock music, reading
Extras: Scored a century before lunch v Glamorgan at The Oval, 1980. Released by county at end of 1986 season. Joined Glamorgan in 1987
Best batting performance: 216* Surrey v Cambridge University, Cambridge 1980
Best bowling performance: 6-48 Surrey v Hampshire, Guildford 1972

BUTCHER, I. P. Gloucestershire

Full Name: Ian Paul Butcher
Role: Right-hand bat, slip fielder
Born: 1 July 1962, Farnborough, Kent
Height: 6' 0" **Weight:** 14st
Nickname: Butch, Dog
County debut: 1980 (Leicestershire), 1988 (Gloucestershire)
County cap: 1984 (Leicestershire)
1000 runs in a season: 2
1st-Class 50s scored: 21
1st-Class 100s scored: 9
One-Day 50s: 7
One-Day 100s: 2
Place in batting averages: —
(1987 78th av. 33.91)
1st-Class catches 1988: 2 (career 79)
Parents: Raymond and Jackie
Wife and date of marriage: Marie, 12 March 1983
Children: Marie
Family links with cricket: Brother, Alan, Glamorgan CCC and England. Brother, Martin, MCC ground-staff and captains club side
Education: John Ruskin High School
Qualifications: Preliminary Coaching Certificate
Jobs outside cricket: Football coach, Cumnor House School, South Croydon. Asst Sports Director, Leicester University
Off-season 1988–89: Working at Leicester University as assistant director of sport and recovering from football injury
Cricketing superstitions or habits: 'I have many . . . If I score runs I like to do

everything (if possible) the same, the following day. I always wear a sweat-band on left wrist while batting.'

Overseas tours: England Young Cricketers to West Indies 1980
Overseas teams played for: Johannesburg Municipals, 1981–82
Cricketers particularly learnt from: Brian Davison, Graham Gooch, Chris Balderstone, Paddy Clift, David Gower
Other sports played: Football, golf. 'I'll try my hand at anything!'
Injuries 1988: Floating tissue in right knee for whole season
Relaxations: Sleeping, good beer, good food, music, TV
Extras: Made his debut for Leicestershire CCC in the John Player League v Surrey 1979. Scored century on championship debut at Grace Road. Moved to Gloucestershire for 1988, but missed most of season through injury
Opinions on cricket: 'I feel that counties should be limited to one overseas player registered at any one time. It would make counties select their players more wisely, i.e. as regards possible fitness problems having no back-up overseas players and any gambles can be left to home-grown players.'
Best batting performance: 139 Leicestershire v Nottinghamshire, Leicester 1983
Best bowling performance: 1-2 Leicestershire v Essex, Chelmsford 1983

LAST SEASON: BATTING

	I.	N.O.	R.	H.S.	AV.
TEST					
1ST-CLASS	6	0	98	75	16.33
INT					
RAL					
NAT.W.					
B & H					

LAST SEASON: BOWLING

	O.	M.	R.	W.	AV.
TEST					
1ST-CLASS					
INT					
RAL					
NAT.W.					
B & H					

CAREER: BATTING

	I.	N.O.	R.	H.S.	AV.
TEST					
1ST-CLASS	159	9	4530	139	30.20
INT					
RAL	50	3	928	71	19.74
NAT.W.	7	0	172	81	24.57
B & H	18	1	647	103*	38.05

CAREER: BOWLING

	O.	M.	R.	W.	AV.
TEST					
1ST-CLASS	10	2	28	1	28.00
INT					
RAL	1	0	4	0	–
NAT.W.	0.3	0	6	1	6.00
B & H					

45. Which West Indian-born fast bowler called his son Imran?

46. What is Roger Harper's (West Indies and Northants) nickname and why?

47. Which 1988 county cricketer has a middle name of Caleb?

BUTCHER, R. O. Middlesex

Full Name: Roland Orlando Butcher
Role: Right-hand bat, right-arm medium bowler
Born: 14 October 1953, East Point, St Philip, Barbados
Height: 5′ 7″ **Weight:** 12st
Nickname: Butch
County debut: 1974
Benefit: 1989
County cap: 1979
Test debut: 1980–81
No. of Tests: 3
No. of One-Day Internationals: 3
1000 runs in a season: 4
1st-Class 50s scored: 64
1st-Class 100s scored: 16
One-Day 50s: 25
One-Day 100s: 1
Place in batting averages: 88th av. 30.61 (1987 125th av. 67.61)
1st-Class catches 1988: 15 (career 274 + 1 stumping)
Parents: Robert and Doreen
Wife: Cheryl Denise
Children: Paul Nicholas Roland, 2 January 1979; Michelle Denise, 11 November 1982
Family links with cricket: Cousin is Basil Butcher, of Guyana and West Indies
Qualifications: Advanced Cricket Coaching Certificate, Football Association Preliminary Coaching Certificate
Jobs outside cricket: Football coach, insurance salesman

LAST SEASON: BATTING

	I.	N.O.	R.	H.S.	AV.
TEST					
1ST-CLASS	29	3	796	134	30.61
INT					
RAL	12	2	269	77	26.90
NAT.W.	4	1	166	65	55.33
B & H	5	0	165	75	33.00

LAST SEASON: BOWLING

	O.	M.	R.	W.	AV.
TEST					
1ST-CLASS					
INT					
RAL					
NAT.W.					
B & H					

CAREER: BATTING

	I.	N.O.	R.	H.S.	AV.
TEST	5	0	71	32	14.20
1ST-CLASS	399	39	11348	197	31.52
INT	3	0	58	52	19.33
RAL	145	15	2906	100	22.35
NAT.W.	26	5	501	65	23.85
B & H	31	3	697	85	24.89

CAREER: BOWLING

	O.	M.	R.	W.	AV.
TEST					
1ST-CLASS	48.1	10	180	4	45.00
INT					
RAL	1.2	0	5	0	–
NAT.W.	2	0	18	1	18.00
B & H					

Off-season 1988–89: Working on benefit year
Overseas tours: England to West Indies 1981
Overseas teams played for: Barbados in 1974–75 Shell Shield Competition; Tasmania, 1982
Cricketers particularly admired: Sunil Gavaskar, Viv Richards, Ian Chappell, John Inverarity, Colin Bland
Other sports played: Football
Relaxations: Television, horse racing, cinema
Extras: Arrived in England aged 13. Played semi-professional soccer for Biggleswade and Stevenage. Does work for Inter-Action Group in deprived areas of London. A devout member of the Anglican church. Autobiography *Rising to the Challenge* published 1989
Best batting performance: 197 Middlesex v Yorkshire, Lord's 1982
Best bowling performance: 2-37 Middlesex v Gloucestershire, Cheltenham 1986

BYAS, D. Yorkshire

Full Name: David Byas
Role: Left-hand bat, right-arm medium bowler, slip/cover fielder
Born: 26 August 1964, Driffield, East Yorkshire
Height: 6′ 4″ **Weight:** 14st 7lbs
Nickname: Bingo
County debut: 1988
1st-Class 50s scored: 4
1st-Class 100s scored: 1
One-Day 50s: 1
Place in batting averages: 139th av. 24.66
1st-Class catches 1988: 12 (career 13)
Parents: Richard and Anne
Marital status: Single
Family links with cricket: Father played in local league
Education: Scarborough College
Qualifications: 1 O-level (Engineering)

Jobs outside cricket: Working on family farm
Off-season 1988–89: Playing and coaching in Auckland, New Zealand
Cricketing superstitions or habits: Left boot and pad on before right. Always wears same clothing during an innings
Overseas teams played for: Auckland, New Zealand 1988–89

Cricketers particularly learnt from: Doug Padgett
Cricketers particularly admired: David Gower, Viv Richards, Ian Botham
Other sports played: Hockey, squash
Relaxations: Game shooting, rallying, eating out
Best batting performance: 112 Yorkshire v Gloucestershire, Cheltenham 1988

LAST SEASON: BATTING

	I.	N.O.	R.	H.S.	AV.
TEST					
1ST-CLASS	25	1	592	112	24.66
INT					
RAL	10	3	266	69*	38.00
NAT.W.					
B & H					

CAREER: BATTING

	I.	N.O.	R.	H.S.	AV.
TEST					
1ST-CLASS	26	1	592	112	23.68
INT					
RAL	12	3	291	69*	32.33
NAT.W.					
B & H	1	0	2	2	2.00

CAIRNS, C. L. — Nottinghamshire

Full Name: Christopher Lance
Cairns
Role: Right-hand bat, right-arm
fast medium bowler
Born: 13 June 1970, Picton,
New Zealand
Height: 6' 2" **Weight:** 14st
Nickname: Sheep
County debut: 1988
Place in bowling averages: 53rd
av. 25.60
Strike rate 1988: 43.60 (career 43.60)
Parents: Lance and Sue
Marital status: Single
Family links with cricket: Father
played Test cricket, uncle played
first-class cricket in New Zealand
Education: Christchurch Boys'
High School, New Zealand

Qualifications: 5th and 6th form certificates
Jobs outside cricket: Labourer
Off-season 1988–89: Playing in New Zealand
Cricketing superstitions or habits: Putting right pad on first
Overseas tours: New Zealand Youth XI to Australia for Youth World Cup
1988
Cricketers particularly learnt from: Father, Billy Ibadullah, Dennis Lillee,
Bob Carter
Cricketers particularly admired: Mick Newell, Richard Hadlee, Dennis
Lillee

Other sports played: Rugby
Other sports followed: Most sports
Injuries 1988: Sprained ankle
Relaxations: 'Sleeping and ignoring Mick Newell!'
Opinions on cricket: 'Great game.'
Best batting performance: 15 Nottinghamshire v Kent, Dartford 1988
Best bowling performance: 4-70 Nottinghamshire v Kent, Dartford 1988

LAST SEASON: BATTING

	I.	N.O.	R.	H.S.	AV.
TEST					
1ST-CLASS	7	0	78	28	11.14
INT					
RAL					
NAT.W.					
B & H					

LAST SEASON: BOWLING

	O.	M.	R.	W.	AV.
TEST					
1ST-CLASS	14	2	63	4	15.75
INT					
RAL					
NAT.W.					
B & H					

CAREER: BATTING

	I.	N.O.	R.	H.S.	AV.
TEST					
1ST-CLASS	10	3	118	28	16.85
INT					
RAL					
NAT.W.					
B & H	3	1	60	46	30.00

CAREER: BOWLING

	O.	M.	R.	W.	AV.
TEST					
1ST-CLASS	38.5	6	173	5	34.60
INT					
RAL					
NAT.W.					
B & H	27	0	127	2	63.50

CANN, M. J.   Glamorgan

Full Name: Michael James Cann
Role: Left-hand bat, off-break bowler
Born: 4 July 1965, Cardiff
Height: 5' 9" **Weight:** 11½st
Nickname: Tin, Canny, Three Noses
County debut: 1986
1st-Class catches 1988: 5 (career 6)
Parents: Leslie and Catherine
Marital status: Single
Education: St Illtyos College, Cardiff; Swansea University
Qualifications: 10 O-levels, 3 A-levels, Degree in Biochemistry, Senior NCA coach
Cricketers particularly learnt from: Tom Cartwright, Alan Jones, Tony Cordle
Cricketers particularly admired: Barry Lloyd

Cricketing superstitions or habits: 'I don't have any. I don't consider cricket to be a game of luck!'
Other sports played: Squash, cards, snooker
Other sports followed: Football (Cardiff City)
Relaxations: Contract bridge, general socialising, going out for meals, reading cricket books
Extras: Represented Combined Universities in B & H Cup
Opinions on cricket: 'I find it a disgrace that overseas players and foreigners can play county cricket registered as English.'
Best batting performance: 28 Glamorgan v Worcestershire, Worcester 1988
Best bowling performance: 2-20 Glamorgan v Worcestershire, Worcester 1988

LAST SEASON: BATTING

	I.	N.O.	R.	H.S.	AV.
TEST					
1ST-CLASS	5	1	31	15	7.75
INT					
RAL	1	0	4	4	4.00
NAT.W.					
B & H					

CAREER: BATTING

	I.	N.O.	R.	H.S.	AV.
TEST					
1ST-CLASS	5	1	31	15	7.75
INT					
RAL	1	0	4	4	4.00
NAT.W.					
B & H					

LAST SEASON: BOWLING

	O.	M.	R.	W.	AV.
TEST					
1ST-CLASS	109	16	384	15	25.60
INT					
RAL	5	1	30	0	–
NAT.W.					
B & H					

CAREER: BOWLING

	O.	M.	R.	W.	AV.
TEST					
1ST-CLASS	109	16	384	15	25.60
INT					
RAL	5	1	30	0	–
NAT.W.					
B & H					

48. Which Test player believes it is bad luck to wear ironed shirts?

49. Which player in the 1988 Benson & Hedges Cup Final bowled a hat-trick of wides and clean bowled two batsmen in the same over?

CAPEL, D. J.   Northamptonshire

Full Name: David John Capel
Role: Right-hand bat, right-arm fast medium bowler, all-rounder
Born: 6 July 1963, Northampton
Height: 6′ **Weight:** 12st 6lbs
Nickname: Capes
County debut: 1981
County cap: 1986
Test debut: 1987
No. of Tests: 10
No. of One-Day Internationals: 11
1000 runs in a season: 1
1st-Class 50s scored: 31
1st-Class 100s scored: 4
1st-Class 5 w. in innings: 9
One-Day 50s: 9
Place in batting averages: 69th av. 33.54 (1987 153rd av. 23.66)
Place in bowling averages: 112th av. 35.39 (1987 45th av. 26.33)
Strike rate 1988: 63.82 (career 61.43)
1st-Class catches 1988: 4 (career 71)
Parents: John and Angela Janet
Wife and date of marriage: Debbie, 21 September 1985
Children: Jenny, 21 October 1987
Family links with cricket: Father played in local league and brother Andrew in County League
Education: Roade Primary and Roade Comprehensive School
Qualifications: 3 O-levels, 5 CSEs, NCA Coaching Certificate
Jobs outside cricket: Hand-made surgical shoemaker (when 16–17)
Off-season 1988–89: Playing for Scarborough CC in Western Australia
Overseas tours: Dubai with *The Cricketer* XI, 1983; England to Sharjah 1986; England to Pakistan, New Zealand and Australia 1987–88
Overseas teams played for: Latrobe, Tasmania, 1982–83; Westview CC, Port Elizabeth, 1983–84–85; Grey School and Eastern Province, 1985–86
Cricketers particularly learnt from: Brian Reynolds (coach), Wayne Larkins, Peter Willey, Geoff Cook, Kepler Wessels
Cricketers particularly admired: Barry Richards, Richard Hadlee, Ian Botham, Clive Rice, Mike Procter
Cricket superstitions or habits: 'I tend to change in most of the same places in grounds on the circuit.'
Other sports played: Golf, table tennis
Other sports followed: 'I like watching athletics.'

Injuries 1988: Ankle ligaments, knee operation

Relaxations: 'I enjoy good debates on television, but not political ones. Also TV comedy and various types of music, pop, rock and some classical.'

Extras: Played for his village team, Roade, and swam for Northamptonshire, both at age 11. Played for Young England 1982

Opinions on cricket: 'For fast bowlers and all-rounders, there is just a bit too much cricket played at first-class level. More time to train and to build up for games and to wind down would be welcome. I believe that competition would then be even keener, and more of a spectacle to watch. The present fining system on over rates is ridiculous – and if so much money is being collected, where does it go, and who benefits from it? More natural flair should be encouraged in the game, instead of players being restricted to doing a "steady" job. Especially in four-day cricket the wickets should be the best possible: that is, with an even pace and bounce, and quick enough to carry to the keeper. This would give both batsmen and bowlers an equal chance to perform their skills and express their talents. To make the game entertaining to watch, it is then up to the players to use their imagination, to play the game with some endeavour and show some enterprise.'

Best batting performance: 134 Eastern Province v Western Province, Port Elizabeth 1986–87

Best bowling performance: 7-46 Northamptonshire v Yorkshire, Northampton 1987

LAST SEASON: BATTING

	I.	N.O.	R.	H.S.	AV.
TEST	4	0	29	16	7.25
1ST-CLASS	32	5	1011	92	37.44
INT					
RAL	9	1	218	83	27.25
NAT.W.	1	0	4	4	4.00
B & H	3	0	55	25	18.33

CAREER: BATTING

	I.	N.O.	R.	H.S.	AV.
TEST	16	0	272	98	17.00
1ST-CLASS	228	40	5464	134	29.06
INT	11	2	221	50*	24.55
RAL	71	16	1447	83	26.30
NAT.W.	14	6	293	48	36.62
B & H	22	4	420	97	23.33

LAST SEASON: BOWLING

	O.	M.	R.	W.	AV.
TEST	22	2	79	1	79.00
1ST-CLASS	414.1	74	1372	40	34.30
INT					
RAL	58	1	233	3	77.66
NAT.W.	12	3	28	2	14.00
B & H	30	2	107	4	26.75

CAREER: BOWLING

	O.	M.	R.	W.	AV.
TEST	185.2	31	527	10	52.70
1ST-CLASS	2548.2	483	8345	257	32.47
INT	97	6	433	11	39.36
RAL	355.1	13	1642	51	32.19
NAT.W.	89.3	15	309	10	30.90
B & H	195	26	697	29	24.03

CARR, J. D.   Middlesex

Full Name: John Donald Carr
Role: Right-hand bat, off-break
bowler, slip fielder
Born: 15 June 1963, St John's
Wood, London
Height: 6′ **Weight:** 12st
Nickname: Carsy
County debut: 1983
County cap: 1987
1000 runs in a season: 2
1st-Class 50s scored: 23
1st-Class 100s scored: 9
1st-Class 5 w. in innings: 3
One-Day 50s: 6
Place in batting averages: 59th
av 35.05 (1987 32nd av. 41.64)
1st-Class catches 1988: 21 (career 62)
Parents: Donald and Stella
Marital status: Single
Family links with cricket: Father, D. B. Carr, was secretary of TCCB and played for Oxford University, Derbyshire and England, captaining all three at some stage
Education: The Hall School, Repton School and Oxford University (Worcester College)
Qualifications: BA Hons (Philosophy, Politics and Economics)
Jobs outside cricket: Taught one term at St George's School, Windsor. Worked briefly at DHSS in Oxford
Off-season 1988–89: Coaching cricket in Buenos Aires
Overseas tours: Australia with Repton Pilgrims 1982–83; La Manga with Hertfordshire 1983; Australia and Hong Kong with Oxbridge 1985–86; Troubadours tour to Argentina and Brazil 1989
Overseas teams played for: Sydney University, 1986; Western Creek, Canberra, 1986–87
Cricketers particularly learnt from: Eric Marsh, Walter Hadlee, Kevin Hayes, Don Bennett, Donald Carr
Cricketers particularly admired: Viv Richards, Ian Botham, Michael Holding, Graeme Hick, Richard Hadlee, Imran Khan, Malcolm Marshall
Other sports played: Eton fives, golf, squash, soccer
Other sports followed: 'I like watching any sport played well.'
Relaxations: 'Music, films, good food; thinking about what career I want to pursue "next year"; trying to get our bowlers to bowl at me in the nets.'
Extras: Played for Oxford in Varsity Match 1984. Secretary of University in 1984. Came on as substitute fielder for Middlesex in the 1983 Benson and

Hedges Cup Final, holding a vital catch to help his side defeat Essex. Received special clearance to play in the match having previously appeared for Combined Universities in the same competition

Opinions on cricket: 'There should be some small reward for drawing as opposed to losing a Championship game. Perhaps two points. The difference between "win" bonus points and "draw" bonus points would still be great enough to encourage positive and adventurous cricket.'

Best batting performance: 156 Middlesex v Essex, Lord's 1987

Best bowling performance: 6-61 Middlesex v Gloucestershire, Lord's 1985

LAST SEASON: BATTING

	I.	N.O.	R.	H.S.	AV.
TEST					
1ST-CLASS	43	6	1297	144	35.05
INT					
RAL	11	1	192	69	19.20
NAT.W.	5	0	74	42	14.80
B & H	5	0	126	62	25.20

CAREER: BATTING

	I.	N.O.	R.	H.S.	AV.
TEST					
1ST-CLASS	150	18	4629	156	35.06
INT					
RAL	33	5	662	84	23.64
NAT.W.	7	0	101	42	14.42
B & H	15	1	400	67	28.57

LAST SEASON: BOWLING

	O.	M.	R.	W.	AV.
TEST					
1ST-CLASS	84.1	22	196	5	39.20
INT					
RAL	11	0	66	2	33.00
NAT.W.	15	1	48	3	16.00
B & H					

CAREER: BOWLING

	O.	M.	R.	W.	AV.
TEST					
1ST-CLASS	976.4	254	2588	56	46.21
INT					
RAL	34.2	1	179	6	29.83
NAT.W.	15	1	48	3	16.00
B & H	81.2	9	327	7	46.71

CARRICK, P. Yorkshire

Full Name: Phillip Carrick
Role: Right-hand bat, slow left-arm bowler, slip fielder
Born: 16 July 1952, Leeds
Height: 6′ 0″ **Weight:** 14st
Nickname: Fergie
County debut: 1970
County cap: 1976
Benefit: 1985
50 wickets in a season: 8
1st-Class 50s scored: 30
1st-Class 100s scored: 3
1st-Class 5 w. in innings: 38
1st-Class 10 w. in match: 5
One-Day 50s: 2
Place in batting averages: 90th av. 30.18 (1987 197th av. 17.44)

Place in bowling averages: 88th av. 31.02 (1987 40th av. 25.94)
Strike rate 1988: 71.16 (career 71.81)
1st-Class catches 1988: 8 (career 175)
Parents: Arthur (deceased) and Ivy
Wife and date of marriage: Elspeth, 2 April 1977
Children: Emma Elizabeth, 6 May 1980; Philippa Louise, 11 January 1982
Family links with cricket: Father and brother useful league players
Education: Bramley CS, Intake CS, Park Lane College of Further Education
Qualifications: 2 O-levels, 8 CSEs, NCA Coaching Certificate
Jobs outside cricket: Company Director in own promotional business. Cricket coach
Off-season 1988–89: Working in the business
Cricketing superstitions or habits: Left pad on first
Overseas tours: Derrick Robins' XI to South Africa 1975–76; Far East 1977
Overseas teams played for: Eastern Province in 1976–77 Currie Cup Competition; Northern Transvaal 1982–83
Cricketers particularly learnt from: Geoff Boycott, Ray Illingworth, Mike Fearnley
Cricketers particularly admired: Graeme Pollock, Gary Sobers
Other sports played: Golf
Other sports followed: Bradford City FC, rugby league
Relaxation: 'My family.'
Extras: Appointed Yorkshire captain for 1987. Led them to victory in the B & H Cup in first season as captain
Best batting performance: 131* Yorkshire v Northamptonshire 1980
Best bowling performance: 8-33 Yorkshire v Cambridge University, Cambridge 1973

LAST SEASON: BATTING

	I.	N.O.	R.	H.S.	AV.
TEST					
1ST-CLASS	34	7	815	81	30.18
INT					
RAL	10	4	172	41	28.66
NAT.W.	1	0	14	14	14.00
B & H	1	0	15	15	15.00

CAREER: BATTING

	I.	N.O.	R.	H.S.	AV.
TEST					
1ST-CLASS	456	83	8327	131*	21.71
INT					
RAL	108	32	1117	43*	14.69
NAT.W.	18	2	244	68	15.25
B & H	27	4	266	53	11.56

LAST SEASON: BOWLING

	O.	M.	R.	W.	AV.
TEST					
1ST-CLASS	593	175	1551	50	31.02
INT					
RAL	87	2	393	14	28.07
NAT.W.	22	5	69	0	–
B & H	13	0	48	0	–

CAREER: BOWLING

	O.	M.	R.	W.	AV.
TEST					
1ST-CLASS	10293	3293	25705	860	29.88
INT					
RAL	761	31	3455	109	31.69
NAT.W.	192.5	44	513	15	34.20
B & H	354.3	49	1160	31	37.41

CHILDS, J. H. Essex

Full Name: John Henry Childs
Role: Left-hand bat, slow left-arm
orthodox bowler
Born: 15 August 1951, Plymouth
Height: 6′ 0″ **Weight:** 12st 6lbs
Nickname: Charlie
County debut: 1975 (Gloucestershire),
1985 (Essex)
County cap: 1977 (Gloucestershire),
1986 (Essex)
Testimonial: 1985
Test debut: 1988
No. of Tests: 2
50 wickets in a season: 3
1st-Class 5 w. in innings: 30
1st-Class 10 w. in match: 6
Place in batting averages: 261st
av. 10.42 (1987 237th av. 12.55)
Place in bowling averages: 49th
av. 25.12 (1987 88th av. 33.18)
Strike rate 1988: 63.37 (career 67.87)
1st-Class catches 1988: 6 (career 80)
Parents: Sydney and Barbara (both deceased)
Wife and date of marriage: Jane Anne, 11 November 1978
Children: Lee Robert, 28 November 1980; Scott Alexander, 21 August 1984
Education: Audley Park Secondary Modern, Torquay
Qualifications: Advanced Cricket Coach
Jobs outside cricket: Signwriter

LAST SEASON: BATTING

	I.	N.O.	R.	H.S.	AV.
TEST	4	4	2	2*	–
1ST-CLASS	15	8	71	25*	10.14
INT					
RAL	3	2	4	2*	4.00
NAT.W.					
B & H					

CAREER: BATTING

	I.	N.O.	R.	H.S.	AV.
TEST	4	4	2	2*	–
1ST-CLASS	215	101	950	34*	8.33
INT					
RAL	22	12	88	16*	8.80
NAT.W.	4	3	22	14*	22.00
B & H	7	5	25	10	12.50

LAST SEASON: BOWLING

	O.	M.	R.	W.	AV.
TEST	86	29	183	3	61.00
1ST-CLASS	568.5	179	1399	59	23.71
INT					
RAL	22	2	87	4	21.75
NAT.W.					
B & H					

CAREER: BOWLING

	O.	M.	R.	W.	AV.
TEST	86	29	183	3	61.00
1ST-CLASS	6860.1	2034	18072	611	29.57
INT					
RAL	345.1	19	1564	43	36.37
NAT.W.	60	12	180	7	25.71
B & H	156	35	466	14	33.29

Off-season 1988–89: Chosen for cancelled England tour of India. Sales and marketing with Essex CCC
Overseas tours: Zambia, 1977; Barbados, 1983
Cricketers particularly admired: Gary Sobers, Mike Procter
Other sports played: Most ball games
Relaxations: Watching rugby, decorating at home, walking on moors and beaches, enjoying my family
Extras: Played for Devon 1973–74. Released by Gloucestershire at end of 1984 and joined Essex. One of *Wisden*'s Five Cricketers of the Year, 1986
Opinions on cricket: 'Everything I had aimed for in cricket came about in the last three seasons (1986, 1987, 1988) – winning the County Championship, getting an England cap and then being selected for an overseas tour.'
Best batting performance: 34* Gloucestershire v Nottinghamshire, Cheltenham 1982
Best bowling performance: 9-56 Gloucestershire v Somerset, Bristol 1981

CLARKE, A. R.   Sussex

Full Name: Andrew Russell Clarke
Role: Right-hand bat, leg spin bowler
Born: 23 December 1961, Brighton
Height: 5′ 9″ **Weight:** 12st
Nickname: Nobby, Doughnut, Charlie
County debut: 1988
1st-Class 50s: 1
1st-Class 5 w. in innings: 2
Place in batting averages: 235th av. 14.04
Place in bowling averages: 120th av. 37.50
Strike rate 1988: 84.27 (career 84.27)
1st-Class catches 1988: 7 (career 7)
Parents: Ken and Gwen
Wife and date of marriage: Jennifer, 12 September 1987
Family links with cricket: Father played club cricket, as did his two brothers
Education: Longhill High School
Qualifications: 2 O-levels, 7 CSEs; NCA cricket coach
Jobs outside cricket: Insurance clerk for Legal and General
Off-season 1988–89: Working for Legal and General
Cricketers particularly learnt from: Paul Parker, Chris Waller

Cricketers particularly admired: Ian Botham, Mike Gatting, Dennis Lillee, Tony Greig
Other sports played: Football, golf, snooker, squash
Other sports followed: All sports
Injuries 1988: Tendon trouble in right shin
Relaxations: Gambling, reading, watching video films
Extras: 'From the age of 15 to 26 I didn't have any coaching so I had to teach myself.' The only specialist leg spinner playing county cricket in 1988. Played for Preston Nomads in Brighton Club Cricket. Played for South of England Schools. Played four matches for Sussex 2nd XI in 1987. Became Sussex's regular night-watchman in 1988
Opinions on cricket: 'Pitches and run-ups should be uncovered. All championship games should be over four days. There should be a competition comprising of four teams: North, South-East, West, Midlands. They would play against each other in five-day "Test" type matches so selectors could see how potential Test players perform under pressure in five-day games. Batsmen should be given out LBW when not playing a shot when the ball pitches outside the line of leg stump.'
Best batting performance: 68 Sussex v Hampshire, Eastbourne, 1988
Best bowling performance: 5-60 Sussex v Hampshire, Eastbourne, 1988

LAST SEASON: BATTING

	I.	N.O.	R.	H.S.	AV.
TEST					
1ST-CLASS	32	8	337	68	14.04
INT					
RAL	2	0	7	7	3.50
NAT.W.	1	0	24	24	24.00
B & H					

LAST SEASON: BOWLING

	O.	M.	R.	W.	AV.
TEST					
1ST-CLASS	618	157	1650	44	37.50
INT					
RAL	64.4	7	267	17	15.70
NAT.W.					
B & H					

CAREER: BATTING

	I.	N.O.	R.	H.S.	AV.
TEST					
1ST-CLASS	32	8	337	68	14.04
INT					
RAL	2	0	7	7	3.50
NAT.W.	1	0	24	24	24.00
B & H					

CAREER: BOWLING

	O.	M.	R.	W.	AV.
TEST					
1ST-CLASS	618	157	1650	44	37.50
INT					
RAL	64.4	7	267	17	15.70
NAT.W.					
B & H					

50. Who was the Man of the Match in the 1988 Benson & Hedges Cup Final?

Full Name: Sylvester Theophilus Clarke
Role: Right-hand bat, right-arm fast bowler, gully fielder
Born: 11 December 1955, Lead Vale, Christchurch, Barbados
Height: 6′ 2″ **Weight:** 15st
Nickname: Silvers
County debut: 1979
County cap: 1980
Benefit: 1987
Test debut: 1977–78
No. of Tests: 11
No. of One-Day Internationals: 10
50 wickets in a season: 5
1st-Class 50s scored: 5
1st-Class 100s scored: 1
1st-Class 5 w. in innings: 58
1st-Class 10 w. in match: 10
Place in batting averages: 225th av. 15.66
Place in bowling averages: 4th av. 14.49 (1987 4th av. 17.31)
Strike rate 1988: 37.78 (career 45.78)
1st-Class catches 1988: 11 (career 138)
Parents: Marjorie and Ashton
Children: Desiree, 8 December 1974; Dawn, 18 August 1976; Shelly, 2 July 1978
Family links with cricket: Half-brother Damien is professional at Todmorden CC
Education: St Bartholomew Boys' School

LAST SEASON: BATTING

	I.	N.O.	R.	H.S.	AV.
TEST					
1ST-CLASS	10	1	141	28	15.66
INT					
RAL	5	4	24	12*	24.00
NAT.W.	2	0	4	3	2.00
B & H	2	0	36	32	18.00

CAREER: BATTING

	I.	N.O.	R.	H.S.	AV.
TEST	16	5	172	35*	15.63
1ST-CLASS	238	38	2995	100*	14.97
INT	8	2	60	20	10.00
RAL	53	16	479	34*	12.94
NAT.W.	14	4	168	45*	16.80
B & H	26	4	209	39	9.50

LAST SEASON: BOWLING

	O.	M.	R.	W.	AV.
TEST					
1ST-CLASS	396.4	108	913	63	14.49
INT					
RAL	84.4	2	402	13	30.92
NAT.W.	45	2	141	11	12.81
B & H	43	6	120	6	20.00

CAREER: BOWLING

	O.	M.	R.	W.	AV.
TEST	412.5	79	1171	42	27.88
1ST-CLASS	6608	1733	1660	878	18.97
INT	87.2	13	245	13	18.84
RAL	603.1	48	2446	95	25.74
NAT.W.	258.2	56	634	40	15.85
B & H	424.4	89	1182	69	17.13

Jobs outside cricket: Carpenter
Overseas tours: West Indies to India and Sri Lanka, 1978–79. Pakistan 1980–81, Australia 1981, Rebel West Indian XI to South Africa 1982–83 and 1983–84
Overseas teams played for: Local club in Barbados Cricket League; Transvaal; Orange Free State
Cricketers particularly learnt from: Vanburn Holder
Other sports played: Football
Other sports followed: Tennis
Relaxations: 'Music and parties.'
Extras: Made fastest century of the 1981 season in 62 mins v Glamorgan. Took Championship hat-trick in 1980 season v Nottinghamshire
Best batting performance: 100* Surrey v Glamorgan, Swansea 1981
Best bowling performance: 8-62 Surrey v Northamptonshire, The Oval 1987

CLEAL, M. W. Somerset

Full Name: Matthew William Cleal
Role: Right-hand bat, right-arm fast medium bowler
Born: 23 July 1969, Yeovil
Height: 6′ 3″ **Weight:** 13½st
County debut: 1988
Place in bowling averages: 72nd av. 29.10
Strike rate 1988: 50.40 (career 50.40)
1st-Class catches 1988: 2 (career 2)
Parents: Michael Gordon and Diana Alma
Marital status: Single
Family links with cricket: 'None, apart from Dad playing County School cricket.'
Education: Preston Comprehensive, Yeovil

Jobs outside cricket: Apprentice painter and decorator 1985–86
Off-season 1988–89: Playing cricket in New Zealand
Overseas teams played for: Wanganui, New Zealand 1988–89
Cricketers particularly learnt from: Father, Peter Robinson (coach at Somerset), Nigel Felton, Adrian Jones, Neil Mallender
Cricketers particularly admired: Dennis Lillee, Steve Waugh ('very hard, but very fair competitor')

Other sports played: Football, golf, tennis, badminton
Relaxations: Listening to music, playing golf, watching films or video
Extras: Bowler of tournament in 7 Nations International Youth Festival in Ireland 1987. Somerset Young Player of Year 1988. Sponsored by local newspaper
Opinions on cricket: 'Having been a pro for only a year I have not really got any definite opinions on the make up or alterations to the game that would improve it.'
Best batting performance: 19 Somerset v West Indians, Taunton 1988
Best bowling performance: 4-41 Somerset v West Indians, Taunton 1988

LAST SEASON: BATTING

	I.	N.O.	R.	H.S.	AV.
TEST					
1ST-CLASS	12	1	97	19	8.81
INT					
RAL	1	0	1	1	1.00
NAT.W.					
B & H					

CAREER: BATTING

	I.	N.O.	R.	H.S.	AV.
TEST					
1ST-CLASS	12	1	97	19	8.81
INT					
RAL	1	0	1	1	1.00
NAT.W.					
B & H					

LAST SEASON: BOWLING

	O.	M.	R.	W.	AV.
TEST					
1ST-CLASS	168	25	582	20	29.10
INT					
RAL	10	0	66	0	–
NAT.W.					
B & H					

CAREER: BOWLING

	O.	M.	R.	W.	AV.
TEST					
1ST-CLASS	168	25	582	20	29.10
INT					
RAL	10	0	66	0	–
NAT.W.					
B & H					

CLINTON, G. S. Surrey

Full Name: Graham Selvey Clinton
Role: Left-hand bat, right-arm medium bowler
Born: 5 May 1953, Sidcup
Nickname: Clint
County debut: 1974 (Kent), 1979 (Surrey)
County cap: 1980 (Surrey)
Benefit: 1989
1000 runs in a season: 6
1st-Class 50s scored: 60
1st-Class 100s scored: 19
One-Day 50s: 23
One-Day 100s: 4
Place in batting averages: 25th av. 43.91 (1987 106th av. 30.28)
1st-Class catches 1988: 8 (career 83)

Family links with cricket: Younger brothers Neil and Tony regular members of Blackheath CC
Education: Chislehurst and Sidcup Grammar School
Overseas tours: England Young Cricketers to West Indies 1972
Extras: Formerly played for Kent, where he made his debut 1974. Left after 1978 season to join Surrey. Renowned as a dressing-room wit and as being one of the most injury-prone cricketers. At age 11, he played for Kemnal Manor, Kent. Later played club cricket for Sidcup and for Blackheath. Played for London Colts in 1968 with Emburey and Gooch and topped the batting averages
Best batting performance: 192 Surrey v Yorkshire, The Oval 1984
Best bowling performance: 2-8 Kent v Pakistan, Canterbury 1978

LAST SEASON: BATTING

	I.	N.O.	R.	H.S.	AV.
TEST					
1ST-CLASS	29	5	1054	158	43.91
INT					
RAL	3	0	80	47	26.66
NAT.W.	4	0	67	30	16.75
B & H	4	1	153	121*	51.00

LAST SEASON: BOWLING

	O.	M.	R.	W.	AV.
TEST					
1ST-CLASS	0.4	0	16	0	—
INT					
RAL					
NAT.W.					
B & H					

CAREER: BATTING

	I.	N.O.	R.	H.S.	AV.
TEST					
1ST-CLASS	378	46	10956	192	33.00
INT					
RAL	69	9	1958	105*	32.63
NAT.W.	23	1	655	146	29.77
B & H	41	2	1350	121*	34.61

CAREER: BOWLING

	O.	M.	R.	W.	AV.
TEST					
1ST-CLASS	26.4	2	201	4	50.25
INT					
RAL					
NAT.W.	4	2	2	0	—
B & H	1.2	0	10	0	—

COBB, R. A.   Leicestershire

Full Name: Russell Alan Cobb
Role: Right-hand bat, slow left-arm bowler, short-leg fielder
Born: 18 May 1961, Leicester
Height: 5′ 11″ **Weight:** 12st
Nickname: Cobby
County debut: 1980
County cap: 1986
1000 runs in a season: 1
1st-Class 50s scored: 22
One-Day 50s: 1
Place in batting averages: 148th av. 24.00 (1987 116th av. 29.14)
1st-Class catches 1988: 10 (career 65)
Parents: Alan and Betty

Wife and date of marriage: Sharon, 30 March 1985
Family links with cricket: Father a club cricketer. Godfather, Maurice Hallam, former Leicestershire captain
Education: Woodbank School, Leicester, Trent College, Nottingham
Qualifications: 7 O-levels, NCA Advanced Coaching Certificate
Jobs outside cricket: Clerk for British Shoe Corporation, Leicester. Worked on promotion for Leicestershire CCC. Worked for shoe company in Australia
Cricketing superstitions or habits: 'Always put my left pad on first. Must wear some sort of headgear.'
Off-season 1988–89: Playing and coaching abroad
Overseas tours: Young England to Australia 1979; Young England to West Indies 1980; Leicestershire to Zimbabwe 1981; Leicestershire to Holland 1988
Overseas teams played for: Glenelg, Adelaide, South Australia, 1980–81; Teachers Training College, Pretoria, 1983–84, 1984–85
Cricketers particularly learnt from: Jack Birkenshaw, Ken Higgs, Chris Balderstone
Cricketers particularly admired: 'All who have played top class cricket for a number of years.'
Other sports played: Squash, badminton
Other sports followed: Most sports, particularly rugby
Relaxations: 'A little gardening, walking, eating out – good for my back. Flying – I have a private pilot's licence.'
Best batting performance: 91 Leicestershire v Northamptonshire, Leicester 1986

LAST SEASON: BATTING

	I.	N.O.	R.	H.S.	AV.
TEST					
1ST-CLASS	20	2	432	65	24.00
INT					
RAL					
NAT.W.	2	0	42	28	21.00
B & H					

CAREER: BATTING

	I.	N.O.	R.	H.S.	AV.
TEST					
1ST-CLASS	178	15	4072	91	24.98
INT					
RAL	6	4	60	24	30.00
NAT.W.	5	1	125	66*	31.25
B & H	2	0	26	22	13.00

51. Who hit the winning run for Hampshire in the 1988 Benson & Hedges Cup Final?

52. Who were the players dropped from the England Test squad after three disastrous Tests against the West Indies in 1988?

Full Name: Cardigan Adolphus Connor
Role: Right-hand bat, right-arm fast-medium bowler
Born: 24 March 1961, West End, Anguilla
Height: 5′ 10″ **Weight:** 11st 6lbs
Nickname: 'Christy, Cardy and many more.'
County debut: 1984
County cap: 1988
1st-Class 5 w. in innings: 3
Place in bowling averages: 64th av. 27.21 (1987 87th av. 33.15)
Strike rate 1988: 54.05 (career 65.53)
1st-Class catches 1988: 3 (career 29)
Parents: Ethleen Snagg
Marital status: Single
Education: Valley Secondary School, Anguilla; Langley College
Qualifications: Engineer
Jobs outside cricket: Timko Engineering, Slough Trading Estate
Cricketing superstitions or habits: Never change before the end of play
Overseas tours: Hampshire CCC tour of Hong Kong, Singapore, New Zealand and Australia 1983
Overseas teams played for: Merriweather CC, Newcastle, Australia, 1983–84 and 1984–85; West End CC, Anguilla, 1973–76
Cricketers particularly learnt from: Tim Tremlett

LAST SEASON: BATTING

	I.	N.O.	R.	H.S.	AV.
TEST					
1ST-CLASS	22	4	135	24	7.50
INT					
RAL	4	2	16	5*	8.00
NAT.W.	–	–	–	–	–
B & H	1	1	5	5*	–

CAREER: BATTING

	I.	N.O.	R.	H.S.	AV.
TEST					
1ST-CLASS	76	27	337	36	6.87
INT					
RAL	11	9	23	5*	11.50
NAT.W.	2	1	8	5	8.00
B & H	4	3	9	5*	9.00

LAST SEASON: BOWLING

	O.	M.	R.	W.	AV.
TEST					
1ST-CLASS	495.3	92	1497	55	27.21
INT					
RAL	82.2	10	343	11	31.18
NAT.W.	22	4	62	1	62.00
B & H	73.2	13	215	12	17.91

CAREER: BOWLING

	O.	M.	R.	W.	AV.
TEST					
1ST-CLASS	2544.5	548	7590	233	32.57
INT					
RAL	491	30	2151	85	25.30
NAT.W.	93.5	14	293	9	32.55
B & H	183.3	23	663	29	22.86

Cricketers particularly admired: Viv Richards, Andy Roberts, Richard Hadlee
Other sports played: Most other sports
Other sports followed: Football, boxing, tennis
Relaxations: Music, wine bars, meeting people
Extras: Played for Buckinghamshire in Minor Counties before joining Hampshire. First Anguillan-born player to appear in the County Championship
Best batting performance: 36 Hampshire v Northamptonshire, Northampton 1985
Best bowling performance: 7-37 Hampshire v Kent, Bournemouth 1984

COOK, G. Northamptonshire

Full Name: Geoffrey Cook
Role: Right-hand bat, slow left-arm bowler, occasional wicket-keeper
Born: 9 October 1951, Middlesbrough, Yorkshire
Height: 6′ 0″ **Weight:** 12st 10lbs
Nickname: Geoff
County debut: 1971
County cap: 1975
Benefit: 1985
Test debut: 1981–82
No. of Tests: 7
No. of One-Day Internationals: 6
1000 runs in a season: 11
1st-Class 50s scored: 107
1st-Class 100s scored: 32
1st-Class 200s scored: 1
One-Day 50s: 45
One-Day 100s: 4
Place in batting averages: 99th av. 29.31 (1987 105th av. 30.28)
1st-Class catches 1988: 11 (career 410 + 3 stumpings)
Parents: Harry and Helen
Wife and date of marriage: Judith, 22 November 1975
Children: Anna, 21 May 1980
Family links with cricket: Father and brother, David, very keen club cricketers. 'Father was virtually "Mr Cricket" in Middlesbrough cricket in the 1960s being secretary, president and chairman of various leagues at one time or another.'
Education: Middlesbrough High School
Qualifications: 6 O-levels, 1 A-level

Jobs outside cricket: Has taught at Spratton Hall Prep. School
Overseas tours: England to India 1981–82 and Australia 1982–83
Overseas teams played for: Eastern Province, 1978–81
Cricketers particularly learnt from: Wayne Larkins
Cricketers particularly admired: Clive Rice
Other sports played: 'All sports when given opportunity.' Football with Wellingborough in the Southern League
Injuries 1988: Broke his jaw in May
Relaxations: Walking, reading, crosswords
Extras: 'Great believer in organised recreation for young people. Would enjoy time and scope to carry my beliefs through.' Captain from 1981 to 1988. Voluntarily stepped down from captaincy at the end of the 1988 season. Chairman of the Cricketers' Association
Opinions on cricket: Following his departure as captain, Cook said 'It is not only a team that needs motivating. The captain needs a certain amount of motivating as well.'
Best batting performance: 203 Northamptonshire v Yorkshire, Scarborough 1988
Best bowling performance: 3-47 England XI v South Australia, Adelaide 1982–83

LAST SEASON: BATTING

	I.	N.O.	R.	H.S.	AV.
TEST					
1ST-CLASS	30	1	850	203	29.31
INT					
RAL	9	0	163	43	18.11
NAT.W.	1	1	53	53*	–
B & H	2	1	18	18	18.00

CAREER: BATTING

	I.	N.O.	R.	H.S.	AV.
TEST	13	0	203	66	15.61
1ST-CLASS	732	61	21613	203	32.21
INT	6	0	106	32	17.66
RAL	212	19	4518	98	23.40
NAT.W.	39	2	1467	130	39.64
B & H	63	5	1609	108	27.74

LAST SEASON: BOWLING

	O.	M.	R.	W.	AV.
TEST					
1ST-CLASS	5	2	7	0	–
INT					
RAL	1	0	4	0	–
NAT.W.					
B & H					

CAREER: BOWLING

	O.	M.	R.	W.	AV.
TEST	7	3	27	0	–
1ST-CLASS	196.2	40	764	15	50.93
INT					
RAL	2.0	0	10	0	–
NAT.W.					
B & H					

53. Who were the new players in the England Test squad for the Fourth Test v West Indies in 1988?

COOK, N. G. B.   Northamptonshire

Full Name: Nicholas Grant
Billson Cook
Role: Right-hand bat, slow
left-arm bowler, backward
short-leg fielder
Born: 17 June 1956, Leicester
Height: 6′ 0″ **Weight:** 12st 8lbs
Nickname: Beast, Rag'ead
County debut: 1978 (Leicestershire),
1986 (Northamptonshire)
County cap: 1982 (Leicestershire),
1987 (Northamptonshire)
Test debut: 1983
No. of Tests: 12
No. of One-Day Internationals: 2
50 wickets in a season: 5
1st-Class 50s scored: 4
1st-Class 5 w. in innings: 25
1st-Class 10 w. in match: 3

Place in batting averages: — (1987 204th av. 16.61)
Place in bowling averages: 42nd av. 24.04 (1987 62nd av. 29.14)
Strike rate 1988: 67.88 (career 66.59)
1st-Class catches 1987: 14 (career 150)
Parents: Peter and Cynthia
Marital status: Divorced
Family links with cricket: Father played club cricket
Education: Stokes Croft Junior; Lutterworth High; Lutterworth Upper
Qualifications: 7 O-levels, 1 A-level, Advanced Cricket Coach
Jobs outside cricket: Has worked for Leicestershire CCC on promotions, organising lotteries, sponsored walks, general fund-raising projects
Overseas tours: Whitbread Scholarship to Perth, Australia, 1980–81; Far East tour with MCC to Bangkok, Singapore, Hong Kong, 1981; Australia and New Zealand with Derrick Robins XI, 1980; Zimbabwe with Leicestershire CCC, 1981; Dubai with Barbican XI 1982; America with MCC 1982–83; Kuwait with MCC 1983; New Zealand and Pakistan with England 1983–84; Sri Lanka with England B, 1986; Pakistan with England, 1987; MCC to Bermuda, 1987
Overseas teams played for: Claremont-Cottesloe CC, Perth, 1980–81
Cricketers particularly learnt from: Jack Birkenshaw, Roger Tolchard
Other sports followed: Soccer, rugby, horse racing
Injuries 1988: 'Sprained ankle ligaments which forced me out of the Old Trafford Test match. Broken right thumb and split lip against Yorkshire at Scarborough.'

112

Relaxations: Crosswords, watching horse racing and football (especially Leicester City), reading (especially Wilbur Smith), good comedy programmes, good food

Extras: Played for ESCA 1975. Played for Young England v Young West Indies 1975. Played for MCC v Middlesex at start of 1981 season. Played for England B Team v Pakistan, August 1982. Left Leicestershire to join Northamptonshire for 1986 season

Opinions on cricket: 'Overseas players should be limited to one per county team. Loopholes in TCCB rules should be tightened up to prevent overseas players becoming "English". To play for England you should be brought up and educated in England and have at least a father who has been through the same process. The directive from the TCCB that pitches should be cut at one level is wrong. The vast majority of pitches are seamers' paradises. The ends should be shaved but still firm, thus encouraging the spinners, but without making batting a lottery.'

Best batting performance: 75 Leicestershire v Somerset, Taunton 1980

Best bowling performance: 7-63 Leicestershire v Somerset, Taunton 1982

LAST SEASON: BATTING

	I.	N.O.	R.	H.S.	AV.
TEST					
1ST-CLASS	27	2	181	24	7.24
INT					
RAL	6	3	35	13*	11.66
NAT.W.	1	0	9	9	9.00
B & H	2	1	9	8	9.00

CAREER: BATTING

	I.	N.O.	R.	H.S.	AV.
TEST	20	1	134	26	7.05
1ST-CLASS	247	65	2292	75	12.53
INT	–	–	–	–	–
RAL	28	13	143	13*	9.53
NAT.W.	3	0	26	13	8.66
B & H	11	4	106	23	15.14

LAST SEASON: BOWLING

	O.	M.	R.	W.	AV.
TEST					
1ST-CLASS	769.2	264	1635	68	24.04
INT					
RAL	86.3	4	370	9	41.11
NAT.W.	10	1	20	1	20.00
B & H	37	6	103	3	34.33

CAREER: BOWLING

	O.	M.	R.	W.	AV.
TEST	591.5	197	1407	47	29.93
1ST-CLASS	7033.3	2292	18348	640	28.66
INT	14	1	52	3	17.33
RAL	439.5	30	1925	62	31.04
NAT.W.	107	20	351	13	27.00
B & H	223	26	821	15	54.73

54. Who captained the MCC v the Rest of the World in 1987?

55. What great Test player came out of retirement to captain Lancashire against the Rest of the World in August 1987?

COOPER, K. E. — Nottinghamshire

Full Name: Kevin Edwin Cooper
Role: Left-hand bat, right-arm
fast-medium bowler
Born: 27 December 1957,
Sutton-in-Ashfield
Height: 6′ 1″ **Weight:** 12st 4lbs
Nickname: Henry
County debut: 1976
County cap: 1980
50 wickets in a season: 5
1st-Class 5 w. in innings: 20
Place in batting averages: 257th
av. 11.28
Place in bowling averages: 21st
av. 21.57 (1987 37th av. 25.80)
Strike rate 1988: 48.47 (career 58.86)
1st-Class catches 1988: 7 (career 69)
Parents: Gerald Edwin and Margaret
Wife and date of marriage: Linda
Carol, 14 February 1981
Children: Kelly Louise, 8 April 1982; Tara Amy, 22 November 1984
Family links with cricket: Father played local cricket
Jobs outside cricket: Warehouseman and maintenance man, public relations
officer in free trade department of local brewery
Overseas tours: Australasia with Derrick Robins' U-23 XI 1979–80
Cricketers particularly admired: John Snow
Other sports played: Football, golf, shooting
Relaxations: Golf, clay pigeon shooting
Extras: In 1974, playing for Hucknall Ramblers CC, took 10 wickets for 6 runs

LAST SEASON: BATTING

	I.	N.O.	R.	H.S.	AV.
TEST					
1ST-CLASS	34	9	282	39	11.28
INT					
RAL	3	1	4	3*	2.00
NAT.W.	–	–	–	–	–
B & H	3	1	15	9	7.50

CAREER: BATTING

	I.	N.O.	R.	H.S.	AV.
TEST					
1ST-CLASS	226	55	1661	46	9.71
INT					
RAL	39	13	120	31	4.61
NAT.W.	5	1	29	11	7.25
B & H	17	10	81	25*	11.57

LAST SEASON: BOWLING

	O.	M.	R.	W.	AV.
TEST					
1ST-CLASS	816	220	2179	101	21.57
INT					
RAL	79	5	307	13	23.61
NAT.W.	24	3	75	2	37.50
B & H	42	8	139	6	23.16

CAREER: BOWLING

	O.	M.	R.	W.	AV.
TEST					
1ST-CLASS	5798	1599	15459	591	26.15
INT					
RAL	828	56	3664	111	33.00
NAT.W.	217.2	50	598	28	21.35
B & H	443.4	85	1551	51	30.41

in one innings against Sutton College in the Mansfield and District League. First bowler to take 50 first-class wickets in 1988 season
Best batting performance: 46 Nottinghamshire v Middlesex, Trent Bridge 1985
Best bowling performance: 8-44 Nottinghamshire v Middlesex, Lord's 1984

COTTEY, P. A.   Glamorgan

Full Name: Phillip Anthony Cottey
Role: Right-hand opening bat, short leg and cover point fielder
Born: 2 June 1966, Swansea
Height: 5′ 5″ **Weight:** 9st 10lbs
County debut: 1986
Nickname: Colts
1st-Class 50s scored: 5
Place in batting averages: 91st av. 30.15
1st-Class catches 1988: 4 (career 8)
Parents: Bernard John and Ruth
Marital status: Single
Family links with cricket: Father played for Swansea CC
Education: Bishopston Comprehensive School
Qualifications: 9 O-levels

Jobs outside cricket: Played professional soccer for Swansea City until 1985
Off-season 1988–89: Playing and coaching for Benoni in Transvaal, South Africa
Overseas tours: Glamorgan to La Manga 1988
Overseas teams played for: Penrith DCC 1986–87; Benoni 1988–89
Cricketers particularly learnt from: Alan Jones, Tom Cartwright, John Hopkins, A. L. Jones
Cricketers particularly admired: Alan Jones, Ian Botham, Viv Richards, Geoff Boycott
Other sports played: Soccer, golf, squash, weight training
Injuries 1988: 'Nothing too serious.'
Relaxations: Anything revolving around sport. Watching videos, listening to music
Extras: Left school at 16 to play for Swansea City FC for three years as a

professional. Captained Welsh Youth Soccer XI (3 caps). Played in Football League

Opinions on cricket: 'Four-day cricket was a success. I think that 16 four-day games would make for a fairer county championship. Wickets around the country in 1988 were of a generally poor standard. I think there should be an incentive for groundsmen to produce good pitches, i.e. 'Groundsman of the Year', which would be judged by a panel of ex-players, ex-groundsmen and umpires and would involve a worthwhile cash prize.'

Best batting performance: 92 Glamorgan v Cambridge University, Cambridge 1988

LAST SEASON: BATTING

	I.	N.O.	R.	H.S.	AV.
TEST					
1ST-CLASS	23	3	603	92	30.15
INT					
RAL	1	0	4	4	4.00
NAT.W.					
B & H	2	0	29	15	14.50

CAREER: BATTING

	I.	N.O.	R.	H.S.	AV.
TEST					
1ST-CLASS	38	5	788	92	23.87
INT					
RAL	7	0	21	10	3.00
NAT.W.					
B & H	2	0	29	15	14.50

COWANS, N. G. — Middlesex

Full Name: Norman George Cowans
Role: Right-hand bat, right-arm fast bowler
Born: 17 April 1961, Enfield St Mary, Jamaica
Height: 6′ 3″ **Weight:** 14st
Nickname: Flash
County debut: 1980
County cap: 1984
Test debut: 1982–83
No. of Tests: 19
No. of One-Day Internationals: 23
50 wickets in a season: 3
1st-Class 50s scored: 1
1st-Class 5 w. in innings: 21
1st-Class 10 w. in match: 1
Place in bowling averages: 7th av. 18.16 (1987 5th av. 18.78)
Strike rate 1988: 41.56 (career 45.05)
1st-Class catches 1988: 5 (career 50)
Parents: Gloria and Ivan
Marital status: Single

Education: Park High Secondary, Stanmore, Middlesex
Qualifications: Qualified coach
Jobs outside cricket: Squash and real tennis professional. Glassblower with Whitefriars hand-made glass
Overseas tours: Young England to Australia 1979; Middlesex to Zimbabwe 1980; *The Cricketer* to Dubai 1981; England to Australia and New Zealand 1982–83 and New Zealand and Pakistan 1983–84; International tour to Jamaica 1983; India and Australia with England 1984–85; England B to Sri Lanka 1986
Overseas teams played for: Claremont-Cottesloe CC, Perth, Australia
Cricketers particularly learnt from: Dennis Lillee, Wayne Daniel, Michael Holding. 'The aggression of Lillee, the power of Daniel, and the smoothness of Holding.'
Other sports played: Basketball, squash, table tennis, swimming, tennis, real tennis
Other sports followed: Football (Arsenal FC)
Relaxations: Dancing, reading, being with friends, listening to reggae music
Extras: Two Young England Tests, one One-Day Youth International. Has won athletics championships in sprinting and javelin throwing
Best batting performance: 66 Middlesex v Surrey, Lord's 1984
Best bowling performance: 6-31 Middlesex v Leicestershire, Leicester 1985

LAST SEASON: BATTING

	I.	N.O.	R.	H.S.	AV.
TEST					
1ST-CLASS	21	7	119	27*	8.50
INT					
RAL	5	1	13	10	3.25
NAT.W.	–	–	–	–	–
B & H	3	2	5	4*	5.00

CAREER: BATTING

	I.	N.O.	R.	H.S.	AV.
TEST	29	7	175	36	7.96
1ST-CLASS	129	29	916	66	9.16
INT	8	3	13	4*	2.60
RAL	18	7	91	20	8.27
NAT.W.	10	2	33	12*	4.12
B & H	8	4	21	6	5.25

LAST SEASON: BOWLING

	O.	M.	R.	W.	AV.
TEST					
1ST-CLASS	491.5	124	1290	71	18.16
INT					
RAL	90	5	342	11	31.09
NAT.W.	45	9	129	9	14.33
B & H	47.5	5	135	3	45.00

CAREER: BOWLING

	O.	M.	R.	W.	AV.
TEST	575.2	113	2003	51	39.27
1ST-CLASS	2991.2	633	9161	424	21.60
INT	213.4	17	913	23	39.70
RAL	371.2	23	1508	56	26.92
NAT.W.	192	32	626	31	20.19
B & H	197.1	26	616	32	19.25

56. Which current county player scored a century on his first-class debut but had to wait nine seasons before scoring another?

COWDREY, C. S.   Kent

Full Name: Christopher Stuart Cowdrey
Role: Right-hand bat, right-arm medium bowler
Born: 20 October 1957, Farnborough, Kent
Height: 6′ 0″ **Weight:** 14st
Nickname: Cow, Woody
County debut: 1977
County cap: 1979
Test debut: 1984
No. of Tests: 6
No. of One-Day Internationals: 3
1000 runs in a season: 3
1st-Class 50s scored: 46
1st-Class 100s scored: 16
1st-Class 5 w. in innings: 2
One-Day 50s: 34
One-Day 100s: 2
Place in batting averages: 103rd av. 29.06 (1987 102nd av. 30.90)
Place in bowling averages: 75th av. 29.25 (1987 130th av. 45.84)
Strike rate 1988: 60.20 (career 69.40)
1st-Class catches 1988: 33 (career 259)
Parents: Michael Colin and Penelope Susan
Wife and date of marriage: Christel, 1 January 1989
Family links with cricket: Grandfather, Stuart Chiesman, on Kent Committee, 12 years as Chairman. Pavilion on Kent's ground at Canterbury named after him. Father played for Kent and England, brother made Kent debut 1984
Education: Wellesley House, Broadstairs; Tonbridge School
Jobs outside cricket: Director of Ten Tenths Travel. Consultant to Stuart Canvas Products
Overseas tours: Captained Young England to West Indies, 1976; with Derrick Robins XI to Far East, South America and Australasia, 1979–80; India and Australia with England, 1984–85
Overseas teams played for: Avendale CC, Cape Town, 1983–84; Cumberland CC, Sydney, 1978–79 and 1982–83
Cricketers particularly learnt from: Asif Iqbal, Allan Lamb, Clive Radley, John Inverarity
Cricketers particularly admired: David Gower
Other sports played: Golf, tennis, backgammon
Other sports followed: All sports
Injuries 1988: Damaged foot kept him out of Fifth Test v West Indies

Relaxations: Dining at Silks Restaurant with Richard Scott and taking Blaise Craven's money at backgammon

Extras: Played for Kent 2nd XI at age 15. Vice-captain 1984. Captain 1985. Captain of England for one Test v West Indies, 1988. Injury kept him out of next Test; then astonishingly not picked for next Test. Best man at wedding of Kim Barnett of Derbyshire and England. David Gower was his best man. Is credited with the following joke: Scene, Third Test at Calcutta, 1984 v India. Gower, England's captain is discussing field placing, and in particular Gatting at first slip, with the bowler, Cowdrey. Gower: 'Do you want Gatt a foot wider?' Cowdrey: 'No, he would burst.' Published autobiography, *Good Enough?*, 1986

Opinions on cricket: 'None that can be quoted!'

Best batting performance: 159 Kent v Surrey, Canterbury 1985

Best bowling performance: 5-46 Kent v Hampshire, Canterbury 1986

LAST SEASON: BATTING

	I.	N.O.	R.	H.S.	AV.
TEST	2	0	5	5	2.50
1ST-CLASS	34	7	838	124*	31.03
INT					
RAL	13	4	305	63*	33.88
NAT.W.	1	0	10	10	10.00
B & H	4	2	71	40*	35.50

CAREER: BATTING

	I.	N.O.	R.	H.S.	AV.
TEST	8	1	101	38	14.42
1ST-CLASS	379	56	10026	159	31.04
INT	3	1	51	46*	25.50
RAL	149	23	3266	95	25.92
NAT.W.	26	5	709	122*	33.76
B & H	48	8	1280	114	32.00

LAST SEASON: BOWLING

	O.	M.	R.	W.	AV.
TEST	5.3	0	21	0	–
1ST-CLASS	385.5	94	1120	39	28.71
INT					
RAL	75.4	3	356	12	29.66
NAT.W.	26	1	74	1	74.00
B & H	41	3	166	5	33.20

CAREER: BOWLING

	O.	M.	R.	W.	AV.
TEST	66.3	2	309	4	77.25
1ST-CLASS	2038.5	405	6581	178	36.97
INT	8.4	0	55	2	27.50
RAL	553.1	8	2622	95	27.60
NAT.W.	164	17	584	22	26.54
B & H	264.4	12	1170	31	37.74

57. Who replaced Ian Botham when injury forced him to withdraw from the MCC side v Rest of the World in the 1987 Bicentenary Test?

COWDREY, G. R.   Kent

Full Name: Graham Robert
Cowdrey
Role: Right-hand bat, right-arm
medium bowler, cover fielder
Born: 27 June 1964,
Farnborough, Kent
Height: 5′ 10″ **Weight:** 13st
Nickname: Van, Cow
County debut: 1984
County cap: 1988
1st-Class 50s scored: 12
1st-Class 100s scored: 1
One-Day 50s: 6
Place in batting averages: 108th
av. 28.62 (1987 100th av. 31.28)
1st-Class catches 1988: 10 (career 30)
Parents: Michael Colin and
Penelope Susan
Marital status: Single
Family links with cricket: Father played for England and Kent. Brother
captain of Kent
Education: Wellesley House, Broadstairs; Tonbridge School; Durham University
Qualifications: 8 O-levels, 3 A-levels, University entrance
Cricketing superstitions or habits: 'Say a prayer at the top of the steps before
batting. Have to run every day.'
Overseas tours: Australia with Tonbridge School in 1980; Christians in Sport
India tour, 1985–86
Overseas teams played for: Avendale CC, Cape Town, 1983–84; Mosman

LAST SEASON: BATTING

	I.	N.O.	R.	H.S.	AV.
TEST					
1ST-CLASS	33	4	830	145	28.62
INT					
RAL	11	3	232	53	29.00
NAT.W.	1	0	25	25	25.00
B & H	1	0	11	11	11.00

CAREER: BATTING

	I.	N.O.	R.	H.S.	AV.
TEST					
1ST-CLASS	77	8	1723	145	24.97
INT					
RAL	35	6	606	53	20.89
NAT.W.	4	1	74	25	24.66
B & H	13	1	412	69	34.33

LAST SEASON: BOWLING

	O.	M.	R.	W.	AV.
TEST					
1ST-CLASS	94	18	365	6	60.83
INT					
RAL	65	2	281	12	23.41
NAT.W.	22	7	49	4	12.25
B & H	6	2	17	1	17.00

CAREER: BOWLING

	O.	M.	R.	W.	AV.
TEST					
1ST-CLASS	119	23	457	8	57.12
INT					
RAL	87	3	394	21	18.76
NAT.W.	38	11	94	5	18.80
B & H	10	2	35	1	35.00

CC, Sydney, 1985–86
Cricketers particularly learnt from: Mark Benson, Chris Tavaré, Bob Woolmer, Roy Pienaar, Father
Cricketers particularly admired: Richard Hadlee, Chris Cowdrey, Richard Ellison
Other sports played: Most sports, particularly golf, rackets, snooker, tennis
Other sports followed: Rugby union
Extras: Played for Young England and Australia. 1000 runs for Kent 2nd XI first season on staff, captain of Kent 2nd XI in 1984. Very interested in psychology of cricket. Broke 2nd XI record with 1300 runs in 26 innings in 1985
Opinions on cricket: 'Too much travel and staying in hotels. Fitness is an increasingly important part of the game.'
Best batting performance: 145 Kent v Essex, Chelmsford 1988
Best bowling performance: 1-5 Kent v Warwickshire, Edgbaston 1988

COWLEY, N. G.   Hampshire

Full Name: Nigel Geoffrey Cowley
Role: Right-hand bat, off-break bowler
Born: 1 March 1953, Shaftesbury, Dorset
Height: 5′ 7″ **Weight:** 12st 5lbs
Nickname: Dougal
County debut: 1974
County cap: 1978
Benefit: 1988
1000 runs in a season: 1
50 wickets in a season: 5
1st-Class 50s scored: 30
1st-Class 100s scored: 2
1st-Class 5 w. in innings: 5
One-Day 50s: 5
Place in batting averages: —
(1987 178th av. 19.70)
Place in bowling averages: 86th av. 30.36 (1987 94th av. 34.45)
Strike rate 1988: 85.72 (career 72.31)
1st-Class catches 1988: 1 (career 96)
Parents: Geoffrey and Betty
Wife: Susan
Children: Mark and Darren

Family links with cricket: Father played good club cricket, two sons play for Hampshire U-13 and U-11 teams
Education: Mere Dutchy Manor, Mere, Wiltshire
Off-season 1988–89: Completing Benefit
Overseas tours: England to Sri Lanka 1977; West Indies 1980
Overseas teams played for: Paarl CC, Cape Town, 1981–83; Amanzimoti, Durban, 1983–85
Cricketers particularly learnt from: Peter Sainsbury
Other sports played: Golf (9 handicap), football
Injuries 1988: Three weeks out with right thumb injury. Three weeks out at end of season with pulled calf-muscle
Extras: In charge of pre-season and match day training
Best batting performance: 109* Hampshire v Somerset, Taunton 1977
Best bowling performance: 6-48 Hampshire v Leicestershire, Southampton 1982

LAST SEASON: BATTING

	I.	N.O.	R.	H.S.	AV.
TEST					
1ST-CLASS	7	3	168	55	42.00
INT					
RAL	8	4	53	19*	13.25
NAT.W.	3	2	3	1*	3.00
B & H	2	1	25	18*	25.00

CAREER: BATTING

	I.	N.O.	R.	H.S.	AV.
TEST					
1ST-CLASS	356	58	6705	109*	22.50
INT					
RAL	138	31	2022	74	18.89
NAT.W.	24	5	334	63*	17.57
B & H	41	4	512	59	13.83

LAST SEASON: BOWLING

	O.	M.	R.	W.	AV.
TEST					
1ST-CLASS	157.1	47	337	11	30.63
INT					
RAL	82	2	423	12	35.25
NAT.W.	48	5	145	2	72.50
B & H	77	15	166	4	41.50

CAREER: BOWLING

	O.	M.	R.	W.	AV.
TEST					
1ST-CLASS	5098.1	1337	13877	423	32.80
INT					
RAL	963.4	49	4634	155	29.89
NAT.W.	272.1	37	805	28	28.75
B & H	418.3	64	1303	30	43.43

58. Who captained the Rest of the World in the MCC bicentenary game?

CROWE, M. D.   Somerset

Full Name: Mark David Crowe
Role: Right-hand bat, slip
fielder
Born: 22 September 1962,
Auckland, New Zealand
Height: 6′ 1½″ **Weight:** 14st
Nickname: Hogan
County debut: 1984
County cap: 1984
Test debut: 1981–82
No. of Tests: 42
No. of One-Day Internationals: 77
1000 runs in a season: 2
1st-Class 50s scored: 54
1st-Class 100s scored: 44
1st-Class 200s scored: 2
1st-Class 5 w. in innings: 4
One-Day 50s: 24
One-Day 100s: 3
Place in batting averages: 7th av. 60.87 (1987 1st av. 67.79)
1st-Class catches 1988: 4 (career 170)
Parents: David William and Audrey Sybil
Marital status: Single
Family links with cricket: Father played 1st-class cricket for Canterbury and
Wellington. Brother Jeff Captain of New Zealand
Education: Auckland Grammar School
Qualifications: School Certificate, Advanced Coaching Certificate
Off-season 1988–89: In New Zealand, recovering from illness
Overseas tours: New Zealand to Australia 1982, 1984, 1985; to England 1983,

LAST SEASON: BATTING

	I.	N.O.	R.	H.S.	AV.
TEST					
1ST-CLASS	9	1	487	136*	60.87
INT					
RAL	1	0	2	2	2.00
NAT.W.					
B & H	1	0	24	24	24.00

LAST SEASON: BOWLING

	O.	M.	R.	W.	AV.
TEST					
1ST-CLASS					
INT					
RAL					
NAT.W.					
B & H					

CAREER: BATTING

	I.	N.O.	R.	H.S.	AV.
TEST	70	6	2774	188	43.34
1ST-CLASS	204	36	10377	242*	61.76
INT	74	6	2192	105*	32.23
RAL	28	1	841	82	31.14
NAT.W.	4	0	143	114	35.75
B & H	11	2	417	155*	46.33

CAREER: BOWLING

	O.	M.	R.	W.	AV.
TEST	206.3	46	607	13	46.69
1ST-CLASS	1026.5	238	3078	103	29.88
INT	183	16	781	25	31.24
RAL	84	3	426	10	42.60
NAT.W.	30	6	75	6	12.50
B & H	89	3	368	15	24.53

1986; to Sri Lanka 1984, 1985, 1987; to Pakistan 1984, 1987; to West Indies 1985

Overseas teams played for: Auckland 1979–83 ; Central Districts 1984–87
Cricketers particularly learnt from: Greg Chappell, Richard Hadlee
Cricketers particularly admired: Greg Chappell, Richard Hadlee
Other sports played: Golf, tennis
Other sports followed: All Blacks, top golf
Injuries 1988: Back strain caused him to miss season after May
Extras: Crowe sadly told Somerset that he would not be able to return to them in 1989 to fulfil his contract. His illness is said to be a toxic allergy arising from salmonella poisoning in 1986. He had been chosen as vice-captain of New Zealand's touring team to India, but had to bow out of the tour. One of *Wisden*'s Cricketers of the Year, 1984
Best batting performance: 242* New Zealanders v South Australia, Adelaide 1985–86
Best bowling performance: 5-18 Central Districts v Auckland, Auckland 1983–84

CURRAN, K. M. Gloucestershire

Full Name: Kevin Malcolm Curran
Role: Right-hand bat, right-arm fast-medium bowler
Born: 7 September 1959, Rusape, Zimbabwe
Height: 6′ 2″ **Weight:** 13st 9lbs
Nickname: KC
County debut: 1985
County cap: 1985
No. of One-Day Internationals: 11
1000 runs in a season: 3
50 wickets in a season: 1
1st-Class 50s scored: 23
1st-Class 100s scored: 9
1st-Class 5 w. in innings: 6
1st-Class 10 w. in match: 3
One-Day 50s: 14
Place in batting averages: 46th av. 37.22 (1987 28th av. 42.29)
Place in bowling averages: 19th av. 21.30
Strike rate 1988: 38.25 (career 44.96)
1st-Class catches 1988: 15 (career 70)
Parents: Kevin Patrick and Sylvia

Marital status: Single
Family links with cricket: Father played for Rhodesia 1949–53
Education: Marandelias High School
Qualifications: 6 O-levels, 2 M-levels
Jobs outside cricket: Tobacco buyer/farmer
Off-season 1988–89: Resting completely from cricket
Overseas tours: Sri Lanka 1982; World Cup 1983 with Zimbabwe; World XI to West Indies, 1985; World Cup 1987
Cricket superstitions or habits: 111, 222, 333 on the scoreboard while batting
Overseas teams played for: Harare SC, Zimbabwe 1981–85
Cricketers particularly learnt from: Brian Davison, Duncan Fletcher, Mike Procter
Cricketers particularly admired: Keith Fletcher, 'for his approach and understanding of the game. Probably one of the best captains around.'
Other sports played: Touch rugby, squash, tennis
Other sports followed: Rugby union, athletics
Injuries 1988: 'There is always something wrong. Our bodies are not machines.'
Relaxations: 'Both deep-sea and fresh-water fishing. Hunting for guinea-fowl, partridge and spring hares. Music, movies and good restaurants with stimulating company. Running and gym.'
Opinions on cricket: 'The introduction of the four-day game has been a success. 16 four-day games would be the answer. The best sides on the circuit would then be in contention to win the championship, and it would not be so much of a lottery. The top sides would have more time to bowl sides out and to build bigger innings.'
Best batting performance: 142 Gloucestershire v Middlesex, Lord's 1988
Best bowling performance: 7-54 Gloucestershire v Leicestershire, Gloucester 1988

LAST SEASON: BATTING

	I.	N.O.	R.	H.S.	AV.
TEST					
1ST-CLASS	34	7	1005	142	37.22
INT					
RAL	13	3	230	41	23.00
NAT.W.	2	1	111	58*	111.00
B & H	4	1	63	32*	21.00

LAST SEASON: BOWLING

	O.	M.	R.	W.	AV.
TEST					
1ST-CLASS	414.2	86	1385	65	21.30
INT					
RAL	88.3	3	405	19	21.31
NAT.W.	29.5	4	114	4	28.50
B & H	39	6	127	6	21.16

CAREER: BATTING

	I.	N.O.	R.	H.S.	AV.
TEST					
1ST-CLASS	175	31	4959	142	34.43
INT	11	0	287	73	26.09
RAL	55	13	1384	71*	32.95
NAT.W.	11	1	275	58*	27.50
B & H	14	4	387	57	38.70

CAREER: BOWLING

	O.	M.	R.	W.	AV.
TEST					
1ST-CLASS	1356.1	282	4396	181	24.28
INT	114.2	3	398	9	44.22
RAL	215.2	11	1011	52	19.44
NAT.W.	84.5	16	260	11	23.63
B & H	130.1	14	498	19	26.21

CURTIS, T. S. Worcestershire

Full Name: Timothy Stephen Curtis
Role: Right-hand bat, leg-break
bowler
Born: 15 January 1960, Chislehurst,
Kent
Height: 5′ 11″ **Weight:** 12st 5lbs
Nickname: TC, Duracell,
Professor
County debut: 1979
County cap: 1984
Test debut: 1988
No. of tests: 2
1000 runs in a season: 5
1st-Class 50s scored: 50
1st-Class 100s: 12
One-Day 50s: 22
One-Day 100s: 1
Place in batting averages: 37th

av. 39.32 (1987 16th av. 47.08)
1st-Class catches 1988: 21 (career 83)
Parents: Bruce and Betty
Wife and date of marriage: Philippa, 21 September 1985
Family links with cricket: Father played good club cricket in Bristol and
Stafford
Education: The Royal Grammar School, Worcester; Durham University;
Cambridge University
Qualifications: 12 O-levels, 4 A-levels, BA (Hons) English, postgraduate
certificate in Education in English and Games
Overseas tours: NCA U-19 tour of Canada 1979

LAST SEASON: BATTING

	I.	N.O.	R.	H.S.	AV.
TEST	4	0	69	30	17.25
1ST-CLASS	34	4	1268	131	42.26
INT					
RAL	12	1	504	97	45.81
NAT.W.	5	0	249	120	49.80
B & H	4	0	60	52	15.00

LAST SEASON: BOWLING

	O.	M.	R.	W.	AV.
TEST					
1ST-CLASS	14.5	1	74	1	74.00
INT					
RAL					
NAT.W.	2	1	6	1	6.00
B & H					

CAREER: BATTING

	I.	N.O.	R.	H.S.	AV.
TEST	4	0	69	30	17.25
1ST-CLASS	263	36	8541	153	37.62
INT					
RAL	73	12	2318	102	38.00
NAT.W.	18	2	811	120	50.68
B & H	23	2	637	78	30.33

CAREER: BOWLING

	O.	M.	R.	W.	AV.
TEST					
1ST-CLASS	89.2	12	362	7	51.71
INT					
RAL					
NAT.W.	4	1	15	2	7.50
B & H	0.2	0	4	0	—

Cricketers particularly learnt from: Glenn Turner
Off-season 1988–89: Teaching
Other sports played: Rugby, tennis, squash, golf
Extras: Captained Durham University to a UAU Championship. Made highly favourable Test debut v West Indies 1988
Opinions on cricket: '16 four-day matches would seem to be the best combination for championship cricket, with one-day competitions taking place at the weekends. This would reduce the amount of cricket played and place a greater emphasis on the quality of the cricket.'
Best batting performance: 153 Worcestershire v Somerset, Worcester 1986
Best bowling performance: 2-58 Cambridge University v Nottinghamshire, Cambridge 1983

DANIEL, W. W.   Middlesex

Full Name: Wayne Wendell Daniel
Role: Right-hand bat, right-arm fast bowler
Born: 16 January 1956, St Philip, Barbados
Nickname: Diamond
County debut: 1977
County cap: 1977
Benefit: 1985
Test debut: 1975–76
No. of Tests: 10
No. of One-Day Internationals: 18
1st-Class 50s scored: 2
1st-Class 5 w. in innings: 31
1st-Class 10 w. in match: 7
Place in bowling averages: —
(1987 114th av. 39.84)
1st-Class catches 1988: 5 (career 63)
Marital status: Single
Injuries 1988: Broke down in Middlesex's second match of the season and missed the rest of the season
Relaxations: Enjoys listening to soul music
Extras: Toured England with West Indies Schoolboys team 1974. Played for Middlesex 2nd XI 1975. Debut for Barbados 1975–76. Toured with West Indies to England 1976. Spent 1979–80 off-season in Barbados playing island cricket. Best bowling record for B & H competition in 1978 with 7 for 12 v Minor Counties East at Ipswich

Best batting performance: 53* Barbados v Jamaica, Bridgetown 1979–80
53* Middlesex v Yorkshire, Lord's 1981
Best bowling performance: 9-61 Middlesex v Glamorgan, Swansea 1982

LAST SEASON: BATTING

	I.	N.O.	R.	H.S.	AV.
TEST					
1ST-CLASS	2	0	0	0	0.00
INT					
RAL					
NAT.W.					
B & H					

LAST SEASON: BOWLING

	O.	M.	R.	W.	AV.
TEST					
1ST-CLASS	16	2	37	2	18.50
INT					
RAL					
NAT.W.					
B & H					

CAREER: BATTING

	I.	N.O.	R.	H.S.	AV.
TEST	11	4	46	11	6.57
1ST-CLASS	230	102	1505	53*	11.75
INT	5	4	49	16*	49.00
RAL	40	16	105	14	4.37
NAT.W.	18	10	42	14	5.25
B & H	18	5	73	20*	5.61

CAREER: BOWLING

	O.	M.	R.	W.	AV.
TEST	292	61	910	36	25.28
1ST-CLASS	6385.2	1233	18580	831	22.35
INT	152	17	595	23	25.87
RAL	831.3	77	3057	163	18.75
NAT.W.	360	62	1033	70	14.75
B & H	434	71	1370	82	16.70

DAVIS, R. P. Kent

Full Name: Richard Peter Davis
Role: Slow left-arm bowler,
gully fielder
Born: 18 March 1966, Westgate
Height: 6′ 4″ **Weight:** 14st 7lbs
Nickname: Dickie, Doughnut
County debut: 1986
1st-Class 5 w. in innings: 1
Place in bowling averages: 118th
av. 37.07 (1987 134th av. 47.30)
Strike rate 1988: 88.26 (career 85.75)
1st-Class catches 1988: 11 (career 17)
Parents: Brian and Silvia
Marital status: Single
Family links with cricket: Father
played league cricket in
Yorkshire and local cricket
in Kent and is an NCA coach
Education: King Ethelberts School,
Birchington; Thanet Technical College, Broadstairs
Qualifications: 8 CSEs
Jobs outside cricket: Carpenter, builder
Overseas tours: Kent Schools CA U-17s Canadian tour 1983
Overseas team played for: Hutt District CC, New Zealand 1986–87, 1987–88

Cricketers particularly learnt from: Derek Underwood, Eldine Baptiste, Colin Page, Jonathan Longley
Cricketers particularly admired: Derek Underwood, Viv Richards, Clive Lloyd
Off-season 1988–89: At home, building and labouring with colleague, David Sabine
Other sports played: Golf, football, badminton and many others
Other sports followed: American football, rugby
Injuries 1988: Badly bruised toe
Relaxations: Reading, sport, TV, a drink down the local
Extras: Played for Kent Schools, 1983; Kent Colts, 1983. Was offered a contract in 1984 by Derbyshire, but preferred to stay in his native county
Opinions on cricket: 'I would like to see the Championship consist of 16 four-day games, but it would only work if the wickets were produced to last four days. The wickets should be hard and brown so that it encourages quick bowling, and on the third and fourth day the spin bowlers would get a chance to bowl long spells on wickets that would probably assist.'
Best batting performance: 23 Kent v Hampshire, Canterbury 1988
Best bowling performance: 5-132 Kent v Essex, Chelmsford 1988

LAST SEASON: BATTING

	I.	N.O.	R.	H.S.	AV.
TEST					
1ST-CLASS	21	8	115	23	8.84
INT					
RAL	2	0	0	0	0.00
NAT.W.	1	0	0	0	0.00
B & H	1	1	0	0*	–

LAST SEASON: BOWLING

	O.	M.	R.	W.	AV.
TEST					
1ST-CLASS	559	177	1409	38	37.07
INT					
RAL	75.2	6	295	14	21.07
NAT.W.	18.3	3	63	4	15.75
B & H	39.1	2	179	2	89.50

CAREER: BATTING

	I.	N.O.	R.	H.S.	AV.
TEST					
1ST-CLASS	31	13	158	23	8.77
INT					
RAL	5	2	14	7*	4.66
NAT.W.	1	0	0	0	0.00
B & H	1	1	0	0*	–

CAREER: BOWLING

	O.	M.	R.	W.	AV.
TEST					
1ST-CLASS	771.5	234	2003	54	37.09
INT					
RAL	134.2	9	592	23	25.73
NAT.W.	18.3	3	63	4	15.75
B & H	39.1	2	179	2	89.50

59. In what novel does the hero take 8 wickets for 0 in his first serious match, 7 for 7 for England against the Australians, and give up a Test place to propose to his future wife?

Full Name: Winston Walter Davis
Role: Right-hand bat, right-arm fast bowler
Born: 18 September 1958, St Vincent, Windward Islands
Height: 6′ 2″ **Weight:** 12st
Nickname: Davo
County debut: 1982 (Glamorgan), 1987 (Northamptonshire)
County cap: 1987 (Northamptonshire)
Test debut: 1982–83
No. of Tests: 15
No. of One-Day Internationals: 35
1st-Class 50s scored: 5
1st-Class 5 w. in innings: 26
1st-Class 10 w. in match: 7
Place in batting averages: 87th av. 20.40 (1987 125th av. 14.30)
Place in bowling averages: 25th av. 22.10 (1987 50th av. 27.22)
Strike rate 1988: 44.25 (career 53.48)
1st-Class catches 1988: 5 (career 54)
Jobs outside cricket: Clerk
Off-season 1988–89: Playing A Grade cricket for Campbelltown DCC in New South Wales
Overseas tours: Young West Indies to Zimbabwe, 1981–82; West Indies to India 1983–84; Australia 1983–84, 1984–85
Overseas teams played for: Windward Islands, Combined Islands, Campbelltown DCC in Australia

LAST SEASON: BATTING

	I.	N.O.	R.	H.S.	AV.
TEST					
1ST-CLASS	18	3	306	43	20.40
INT					
RAL	7	2	79	34	15.80
NAT.W.	1	0	2	2	2.00
B & H	1	0	8	8	8.00

CAREER: BATTING

	I.	N.O.	R.	H.S.	AV.
TEST	17	4	202	77	15.53
1ST-CLASS	164	48	1589	60	13.69
INT	15	3	28	10	2.33
RAL	11	4	89	34	12.71
NAT.W.	6	3	24	14*	8.00
B & H	9	3	64	15*	10.66

LAST SEASON: BOWLING

	O.	M.	R.	W.	AV.
TEST					
1ST-CLASS	538.2	92	1614	73	22.10
INT					
RAL	66	5	305	7	43.57
NAT.W.	12	1	48	1	48.00
B & H	19	1	77	2	38.50

CAREER: BOWLING

	O.	M.	R.	W.	AV.
TEST	462.1	53	1472	45	32.71
1ST-CLASS	4030.5	775	12530	459	27.29
INT	320.3	31	1186	39	30.41
RAL	222.4	19	954	39	24.46
NAT.W.	91.5	13	306	10	30.60
B & H	130.2	13	515	21	24.52

Cricketers particularly learnt from: Andy Roberts, Joel Garner
Cricketers particularly admired: 'I like watching Viv Richards bat and Malcolm Marshall bowl.'
Other sports played: Table tennis
Other sports followed: Soccer, athletics, lawn tennis
Relaxations: 'Reading, watching television, playing with my children.'
Opinions on cricket: 'I should like to see the leg-bye rule changed for all one-day matches. No runs should be allowed for a ball coming off the batsman's pads. Cricket is a game very true to life, and because of that I believe it helps those who play it to understand and to cope with life's ups and downs better.'
Best batting performance: 77 West Indies v England, Old Trafford 1984
Best bowling performance: 7-52 Northamptonshire v Sussex, Northampton 1988

DEFREITAS, P. A. J.   Lancashire

Full Name: Phillip Anthony Jason DeFreitas
Role: Right-hand bat, right-arm fast-medium bowler, cover fielder
Born: 18 February 1966, Dominica
Height: 5′ 11″ **Weight:** 12st 7lbs
Nickname: Daffy
County debut: 1985 (Leicestershire)
County cap: 1986 (Leicestershire)
Test debut: 1986–87
No. of Tests: 12
No. of One-Day Internationals: 38
1st-Class 50s scored: 8
1st-Class 100s scored: 2
1st-Class 5 w. in innings: 17
1st-Class 10 w. in match: 1
One-Day 50s: 2
Place in batting averages: 175th av. 21.54 (1987 179th av. 19.61)
Place in bowling averages: 44th av. 24.29 (1987 39th av. 25.89)
Strike rate 1988: 52.26 (career 52.84)
1st-Class catches 1988: 8 (career 29)
Parents: Sybil and Martin
Marital status: Single
Family links with cricket: Father played in the Windward Islands. All six brothers play

Education: Willesden High School

Qualifications: 2 CSEs

Off-season 1988–89: 'Moving to my new home in Manchester. Playing for Mosman CC in Sydney.'

Overseas tours: Young England to West Indies 1985; England to Australia 1986–87; World Cup, Pakistan, Australia and New Zealand 1987–88

Overseas teams played for: Port Adelaide CC 1985–86

Cricketers particularly learnt from: Ian Botham, Mike Gatting

Cricketers particularly admired: Viv Richards, Malcolm Marshall

Other sports played: Football, golf

Other sports followed: Rugby union – Leicester Tigers

Extras: Left Leicestershire and joined Lancashire at end of 1988 season

Opinions on cricket: 'Fines on over rates to be abolished. 2nd XI wickets ought to be much better.'

Best batting performance: 113 Leicestershire v Nottinghamshire, Worksop 1988

Best bowling performance: 7-44 Leicestershire v Essex, Southend 1986

LAST SEASON: BATTING

	I.	N.O.	R.	H.S.	AV.
TEST	5	0	36	18	7.20
1ST-CLASS	20	1	481	113	25.31
INT	1	1	15	15*	–
RAL	8	0	74	37	9.25
NAT.W.	2	0	18	11	9.00
B & H	3	0	62	57	20.66

LAST SEASON: BOWLING

	O.	M.	R.	W.	AV.
TEST	92	16	253	3	84.33
1ST-CLASS	465.3	111	1302	61	21.34
INT	31	9	94	3	31.33
RAL	56.5	3	233	5	46.60
NAT.W.	20	1	51	1	51.00
B & H	28.4	1	93	7	13.28

CAREER: BATTING

	I.	N.O.	R.	H.S.	AV.
TEST	17	1	182	40	11.37
1ST-CLASS	94	9	1782	113	20.96
INT	26	10	289	33	18.06
RAL	32	5	306	37	11.33
NAT.W.	6	1	141	69	28.20
B & H	9	2	111	57	15.85

CAREER: BOWLING

	O.	M.	R.	W.	AV.
TEST	389.4	87	1080	23	46.95
1ST-CLASS	2076.3	420	6134	257	23.86
INT	356.2	51	1280	47	27.23
RAL	268.2	13	1281	50	25.62
NAT.W.	81.3	15	263	12	21.91
B & H	115.4	14	351	15	23.40

60. Who said 'Pitches are like wives. You can never tell how they will turn out'?

61. Who said: 'I've never met a yorker – only half-volleys and full tosses'?

DENNIS, S. J.   Glamorgan

Full Name: Simon John Dennis
Role: Right-hand bat, left-arm fast-medium bowler
Born: 18 October 1960, Scarborough
Height: 6′ 1″ **Weight:** 13st
Nickname: Donkey
County debut: 1980 (Yorkshire)
County cap: 1983 (Yorkshire)
1st-Class 50s scored: 1
1st-Class 5 w. in innings: 5
1st-Class catches 1988: 1 (career 20)
Parents: Margaret and Geoff
Marital status: Single
Family links with cricket: Father captained Scarborough for many years. Uncle, Frank Dennis, played for Yorkshire 1928–33. Uncle, Sir Leonard Hutton, played for Yorkshire and England
Education: Northstead County Primary School; Scarborough College
Qualifications: 7 O-levels, 1 A-level, City and Guilds Computer Literacy
Jobs outside cricket: Assistant groundsman at Scarborough CC. Furniture salesman. Worked for a Scarborough printing firm. Worked for G. A. Pinder & Sons Ltd in sales department
Cricketing superstitions or habits: 'If I have a good day I try to do everything the same the next day before the game.'
Overseas tours: ESCA to India, 1978–79; Young England to Australia, 1980; MCC to East and Central Africa, 1981; MCC to America, 1982; Sheffield

LAST SEASON: BATTING

	I.	N.O.	R.	H.S.	AV.
TEST					
1ST-CLASS	5	2	50	36*	16.66
INT					
RAL					
NAT.W.					
B & H					

LAST SEASON: BOWLING

	O.	M.	R.	W.	AV.
TEST					
1ST-CLASS	90	19	262	8	32.75
INT					
RAL					
NAT.W.					
B & H					

CAREER: BATTING

	I.	N.O.	R.	H.S.	AV.
TEST					
1ST-CLASS	71	27	456	53*	10.36
INT					
RAL	19	11	87	16*	10.87
NAT.W.	2	0	14	14	7.00
B & H					

CAREER: BOWLING

	O.	M.	R.	W.	AV.
TEST					
1ST-CLASS	1898	376	6061	194	31.24
INT					
RAL	261	14	1188	27	44.00
NAT.W.	52.2	8	202	6	33.66
B & H	87	15	327	7	46.71

Cricket Lovers to Gibraltar, 1983; Yorkshire to Barbados, 1987; Yorkshire to La Manga, 1988
Overseas teams played for: Orange Free State 1982–83; Durban Collegians 1985–86
Cricketers particularly learnt from: Doug Padgett, Don Wilson, Ray Illingworth
Cricketers particularly admired: Dennis Lillee, John Lever
Injuries 1988: Chipped bone in left ankle, stopping ball off own bowling
Relaxations: Car maintenance, wine- and beer-making. Photography and real ale. Home computer, video games. 'Also terrible snooker player.'
Extras: On debut for Yorkshire v Somerset, at Weston 1980, got Gavaskar as his first wicket. Released by Yorkshire at end of 1988 season. Joined Glamorgan for 1989
Best batting performance: 53* Yorkshire v Nottinghamshire, Trent Bridge 1984
Best bowling performance: 5-35 Yorkshire v Somerset, Sheffield 1981

DERRICK, J.   Glamorgan

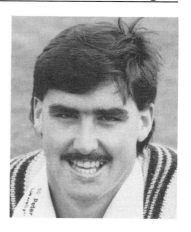

Full Name: John Derrick
Role: Right-hand bat, right-arm medium bowler
Born: 15 January 1963, Aberdare, South Wales
Height: 6' 1" **Weight:** 14st 5lbs
Nickname: JD, Bo
County debut: 1983
County cap: 1988
1st-Class 50s scored: 10
1st-Class 5 w. in innings: 2
Place in batting averages: 260th av. 10.40 (1987 176th av. 19.90)
Place in bowling averages: 95th av. 32.14 (1987 78th av. 31.29)
Strike rate 1988: 68.95 (career 71.76)
1st-Class catches 1988: 10 (career 32)
Parents: John Raymond and Megan Irene
Wife and date of marriage: Anne Irene, 20 April 1985
Children: Liam Kyle, 3 April 1987
Family links with cricket: Father and brother play club cricket for Aberdare
Education: Glynhafod and Blaengwawr Primary Schools; Blaengwawr Comprehensive School

Qualifications: School Certificate
Jobs outside cricket: Coaching cricket
Off-season 1988–89: Playing and coaching with Te Puke CC, New Zealand
Overseas teams played for: Toombul CC, Brisbane, 1982–85; Te Puke CC & Bay of Plenty Red Team New Zealand 1985–86; Northern Districts 1986–87
Cricketers particularly learnt from: Tom Cartwright, Don Wilson, Andy Wagner and senior Glamorgan players, Lance Cairns and Andy Roberts in New Zealand
Cricketers particularly admired: Geoff Boycott, John Snow, Dennis Lillee, Graeme Hick
Other sports played: Soccer, squash, golf – 'give anything a try'
Other sports followed: Rugby, Chelsea FC
Relaxations: 'Days off when I can take my little boy for walks. TV and video.'
Extras: Spent three years on MCC groundstaff 1980–82. Coached at Lord's in winter of 1981. Captained Welsh Schools U-11s on tour to Lancashire and Cheshire. Took 9 for 9 off 9 overs v Lancashire and 6 for 6 off 6 overs v Cheshire
Opinions on cricket: 'Review the points system, i.e. perhaps points for first innings win. Definitely in favour of four-day Championship, but need better wickets.'
Best batting performance: 78* Glamorgan v Derbyshire, Abergavenny 1986
Best bowling performance: 6-54 Glamorgan v Leicestershire, Leicester 1988

LAST SEASON: BATTING

	I.	N.O.	R.	H.S.	AV.
TEST					
1ST-CLASS	28	6	229	50*	10.40
INT					
RAL	6	1	34	15	6.80
NAT.W.	1	0	4	4	4.00
B & H	1	0	4	4	4.00

CAREER: BATTING

	I.	N.O.	R.	H.S.	AV.
TEST					
1ST-CLASS	114	33	1759	78*	21.71
INT					
RAL	40	12	330	26	11.78
NAT.W.	3	1	10	4	5.00
B & H	8	2	87	42	14.50

LAST SEASON: BOWLING

	O.	M.	R.	W.	AV.
TEST					
1ST-CLASS	540.1	138	1511	47	32.14
INT					
RAL	76	3	358	15	23.86
NAT.W.	30	4	116	6	19.33
B & H	55	10	183	13	14.07

CAREER: BOWLING

	O.	M.	R.	W.	AV.
TEST					
1ST-CLASS	1495	326	4650	125	37.20
INT					
RAL	348.3	6	1773	53	33.45
NAT.W.	58.3	10	178	12	14.83
B & H	117	17	414	18	23.00

DILLEY, G. R. Worcestershire

Full Name: Graham Roy Dilley
Role: Left-hand bat, right-arm fast
bowler
Born: 18 May 1959, Dartford
Height: 6′ 4″ **Weight:** 15st
Nickname: Picca
County debut: 1977 (Kent),
1987 (Worcestershire)
County cap: 1980 (Kent),
1987 (Worcestershire)
Test debut: 1979–80
No. of Tests: 39
No. of One-Day Internationals: 36
1st-Class 50s scored: 4
1st-Class 5 w. in innings: 26
1st-Class 10 w. in match: 2
Place in batting averages: 256th

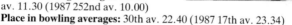

av. 11.30 (1987 252nd av. 10.00)
Place in bowling averages: 30th av. 22.40 (1987 17th av. 23.34)
Strike rate 1988: 47.40 (career 54.02)
1st-Class catches 1988: 2 (career 68)
Parents: Geoff and Jean
Wife and date of marriage: Helen, 6 November 1980
Children: Paul and Christopher
Family links with cricket: Father and grandfather both played local cricket.
Wife is former Kent colleague Graham Johnson's sister
Education: Dartford West Secondary School
Qualifications: 3 O-levels
Jobs outside cricket: Diamond setter. Spent two winters carrying sheets of
plaster-board for uncle's office partitioning company. Doing cricket commentary for Radio Medway
Off-season 1988–89: Picked for England's cancelled tour of India
Overseas tours: With England to Australia 1979–80, West Indies 1981, India
1981–82, New Zealand and Pakistan 1983–84, Australia 1986–87, World
Cup, Pakistan, New Zealand and Australia 1987–88
Cricketers particularly learnt from: Dennis Lillee, John Snow
Other sports played: Golf, squash, badminton
Relaxations: Music
Extras: Got sacked from his first job with a Hatton Garden diamond firm after
taking time off to play for Kent 2nd XI. Suffered from glandular fever at end
of 1980 season, causing him to miss Centenary Test. Voted Young Cricketer
of the Year 1980 by Cricket Writers' Club. Missed 1984 season after suffering

back injury on 1983–84 tour. Joined Worcestershire in 1987. Autobiography *Swings and Roundabouts*, 1988

Opinions on cricket: 'For years counties have held almost a feudal grip on their players. While I accept that some clubs have not been able to pay their players more than the basic minimum agreed by the Professional Cricketers' Association, they have always had a hold over their unhappy employees who have been forced to show a false sense of loyalty with the hope of a lucrative benefit. The system had one merit in that a player around the age of 30 to 35 was given the chance to make enough money in a year to make himself financially secure for life. But it failed to take into account others less fortunate who might have been forced out of the game at a younger age without any lump sum, no formal training in any other profession than cricket, and with little hope for the future.'

Best batting performance: 81 Kent v Northamptonshire, Northampton 1979
Best bowling performance: 7-63 Natal v Transvaal, Johannesburg 1985–86

LAST SEASON: BATTING

	I.	N.O.	R.	H.S.	AV.
TEST	7	1	58	28	9.66
1ST-CLASS	8	1	89	36	12.71
INT	–	–	–	–	–
RAL	–	–	–	–	–
NAT.W.	2	1	3	2*	3.00
B & H	2	0	25	16	12.50

CAREER: BATTING

	I.	N.O.	R.	H.S.	AV.
TEST	55	18	479	56	12.94
1ST-CLASS	157	53	1447	81	13.91
INT	18	8	114	31*	11.40
RAL	27	8	252	33	13.26
NAT.W.	13	4	105	25	11.66
B & H	25	7	154	37*	8.55

LAST SEASON: BOWLING

	O.	M.	R.	W.	AV.
TEST	136.1	26	403	15	26.86
1ST-CLASS	251	44	695	34	20.44
INT	22	0	109	3	36.33
RAL	41	4	162	3	54.00
NAT.W.	46	9	140	11	12.72
B & H	39.3	6	118	6	19.66

CAREER: BOWLING

	O.	M.	R.	W.	AV.
TEST	1280.2	269	3789	133	28.48
1ST-CLASS	3465	730	10440	394	26.49
INT	340.3	33	1291	48	26.89
RAL	465.2	35	1902	74	25.70
NAT.W.	192.4	33	584	34	17.17
B & H	376.2	51	1231	60	20.51

62. What Australian grade cricket club has a name spelled the same way backwards as forwards?

Full Name: Damian Basil D'Oliveira
Role: Right-hand bat, off-break bowler, fields anywhere 'except short leg'
Born: 19 October 1960, Cape Town, South Africa
Height: 5′ 8″ **Weight:** 11st 8lbs
Nickname: Dolly
County debut: 1982
County cap: 1985
1000 runs in a season: 3
1st-Class 50s scored: 25
1st-Class 100s scored: 6
One-Day 50s: 9
One-Day 100s: 1
Place in batting averages: 239th av. 13.20 (1987 81st av. 33.51)
1st-Class catches 1988: 6 (career 99)
Parents: Basil and Naomi
Wife and date of marriage: Tracey, 26 September 1983
Children: Marcus Damian, 27 April 1986; Dominic James, 29 April 1988
Family links with cricket: Father played for Worcestershire and England
Education: St George's RC Primary School; Blessed Edward Oldcorne Secondary School
Qualifications: 3 O-levels, 5 CSEs
Jobs outside cricket: Selling car-phones
Off-season 1988–89: Working for the Carphone Group
Overseas tours: English Counties XI to Zimbabwe 1985

LAST SEASON: BATTING

	I.	N.O.	R.	H.S.	AV.
TEST					
1ST-CLASS	11	1	132	37	13.20
INT					
RAL	9	2	169	54*	24.14
NAT.W.	1	0	0	0	0.00
B & H	3	0	97	35	32.33

LAST SEASON: BOWLING

	O.	M.	R.	W.	AV.
TEST					
1ST-CLASS					
INT					
RAL					
NAT.W.	2	0	12	0	–
B & H					

CAREER: BATTING

	I.	N.O.	R.	H.S.	AV.
TEST					
1ST-CLASS	215	16	5436	146*	27.31
INT					
RAL	80	7	1550	103	21.23
NAT.W.	14	1	326	99	25.07
B & H	24	3	531	66	25.28

CAREER: BOWLING

	O.	M.	R.	W.	AV.
TEST					
1ST-CLASS	257.1	49	923	23	40.13
INT					
RAL	39	2	232	7	33.14
NAT.W.	38	5	134	6	22.33
B & H	38	4	148	5	29.60

Overseas teams played for: West Perth CC, Western Australia, 1979–80; Christchurch Shirley 1982–83 and 1983–84 on a Whitbread scholarship
Cricketers particularly admired: Greg Chappell, Viv Richards, Dennis Lillee, Malcolm Marshall, Richard Hadlee
Other sports played: Football
Other sports followed: 'Most others, but not horse racing.'
Injuries 1988: Pulled hamstring
Relaxations: Watching films, TV and eating out
Best batting performance: 146* Worcestershire v Gloucestershire, Cheltenham 1986
Best bowling performance: 2-17 Worcestershire v Gloucestershire, Cheltenham 1986

DONALD, A. A. Warwickshire

Full Name: Allan Anthony Donald
Role: Right-hand bat, right-arm fast-medium bowler
Born: 20 October 1966, Bloemfontein, South Africa
Height: 6' 3" **Weight:** 13½st
County debut: 1987
1st-Class 5 w. in innings: 7
1st-Class 10 w. in match: 1
Place in batting averages: 259th av. 10.57 (1987 211th av. 15.85)
Place in bowling averages: 14th av. 20.53 (1987 41st av. 25.94)
Strike rate 1988: 41.69 (career 48.58)
1st-Class catches 1988: 4 (career 12)
Parents: Stuart and Francina
Marital status: Single
Education: Grey College High School and Technical High School, Bloemfontein
Qualifications: Matriculation
Off-season 1988–89: Playing cricket in South Africa
Cricketing superstitions or habits: Loves bowling to left-handers
Overseas teams played for: Orange Free State, South Africa
Cricketers particularly learnt from: Chris Broad, Vanburn Holder, Alvin Kallicharran
Cricketers particularly admired: Ian Botham, Imran Khan
Other sports played: Rugby

Other sports followed: Rugby, football
Relaxations: Playing tennis, listening to music
Extras: Played for a South Africa XI v an Australian XI in one 5-day Test and three One-Day Internationals, 1986–87
Opinions on cricket: 'There should not be politics in world sport.'
Best batting performance: 37* Warwickshire v Sussex, Nuneaton 1987
Best bowling performance: 8-37 Orange Free State v Transvaal, Johannesburg 1986–87

LAST SEASON: BATTING

	I.	N.O.	R.	H.S.	AV.
TEST					
1ST-CLASS	10	3	74	29	10.57
INT					
RAL	3	2	25	18*	25.00
NAT.W.					
B & H					

LAST SEASON: BOWLING

	O.	M.	R.	W.	AV.
TEST					
1ST-CLASS	180.4	40	534	26	20.53
INT					
RAL	28	2	133	2	66.50
NAT.W.					
B & H					

CAREER: BATTING

	I.	N.O.	R.	H.S.	AV.
TEST					
1ST-CLASS	55	23	348	37*	10.87
INT					
RAL	7	4	48	18*	16.00
NAT.W.					
B & H	1	0	0	0	0.00

CAREER: BOWLING

	O.	M.	R.	W.	AV.
TEST					
1ST-CLASS	1279.2	219	3921	158	24.81
INT					
RAL	68	7	296	12	24.66
NAT.W.	29.2	4	88	10	8.80
B & H	23.2	3	91	7	13.00

DOWNTON, P. R.   Middlesex

Full Name: Paul Rupert Downton
Role: Right-hand bat, wicket-keeper
Born: 4 April 1957, Farnborough, Kent
Height: 5' 10" **Weight:** 12st 4lbs
Nickname: Nobby
County debut: 1977 (Kent), 1980 (Middlesex)
County cap: 1979 (Kent), 1981 (Middlesex)
Test debut: 1980–81
No. of Tests: 30
No. of One-Day Internationals: 28
1000 runs in a season: 1
1st-Class 50s scored: 36
1st-Class 100s scored: 5
One-Day 50s: 7
Place in batting averages: 77th av. 32.31 (1987 57th av. 37.33)

Parents: George Charles and Jill Elizabeth
Wife and date of marriage: Alison, 19 October 1985
Children: Phoebe Alice, 16 December 1987
Family links with cricket: Father kept wicket for Kent 1948–49
Education: Sevenoaks School; Exeter University
Qualifications: 9 O-levels, 3 A-levels; Law degree (LLB); NCA Coaching Certificate
Jobs outside cricket: Stockbroker
Off-season 1988–89: Working for James Capel (stockbrokers)
Overseas tours: England Young Cricketers to West Indies, 1976; England to Pakistan and New Zealand, 1977; West Indies 1980–81 and 1986; India and Australia 1984–85
Overseas teams played for: Sandgate, Redcliffe 1981–82; Stellenbosch University 1983–84
Cricketers particularly learnt from: Father, Alan Knott, Clive Radley
Cricketers particularly admired: Alan Knott, Rod Marsh
Other sports played: Rugby (played in England U-19 squad 1975 and Exeter University 1st XV), golf, tennis
Other sports followed: American football
Relaxations: Reading
Extras: Made debut for Kent CCC in 1977, gaining cap in 1979. Played for Kent 2nd XI at age 16. Joined Middlesex in 1980
Opinions on cricket: 'We play too much cricket which inevitably leads to a dilution in quality. Each game should be a big game, but the system rarely allows that.'
Best batting performance: 126* Middlesex v Oxford University, Oxford 1986

LAST SEASON: BATTING

	I.	N.O.	R.	H.S.	AV.
TEST	5	1	84	27	21.00
1ST-CLASS	19	4	530	120	35.33
INT	1	0	30	30	30.00
RAL	9	1	178	49	22.25
NAT.W.	4	2	109	43	54.50
B & H		2	51	43	17.00

LAST SEASON: WICKET KEEPING

	C.	ST.		
TEST	9	–		
1ST-CLASS	31	5		
INT	6	–		
RAL	10	1		
NAT.W.	10	1		
B & H	4	1		

CAREER: BATTING

	I.	N.O.	R.	H.S.	AV.
TEST	48	8	785	74	19.62
1ST-CLASS	293	61	6137	126*	26.45
INT	20	5	242	44*	16.13
RAL	89	26	1370	70	21.74
NAT.W.	23	4	409	62	21.52
B & H	32	12	504	80*	25.20

CAREER: WICKET KEEPING

	C.	ST.		
TEST	70	5		
1ST-CLASS	504	74		
INT	26	3		
RAL	113	30		
NAT.W.	42	6		
B & H	38	9		

DREDGE, C. H. Somerset

Full Name: Colin Herbert Dredge
Role: Left-hand bat, right-arm
medium bowler
Born: 4 August 1954, Frome,
Somerset
Height: 6′ 5″ **Weight:** 14st 7lbs
Nickname: Herbie, Bert
County debut: 1976
County cap: 1978
Benefit: 1987 (£59,854)
1st-Class 50s scored: 1
1st-Class 5 w. in innings: 12
1st-Class catches 1988: 1 (85)
Parents: Frederick and Kathleen
Wife and date of marriage: Mandy,
9 December 1978
Children: David, 13 November
1979; Mark, 6 July 1981; Neil,
27 June 1983

Family links with cricket: One of ten children, eight boys and two girls; all the
brothers have played cricket for Frome CC
Education: Wesley Methodist School; Milk Street School; Oakfield School
Qualifications: Qualified toolmaker. Served apprenticeship Rolls Royce Ltd.,
Patchway, Bristol
Jobs outside cricket: Toolmaker
Cricketers particularly learnt from: Peter White, Peter Robinson
Other sports played: Played Western League football for Welton Rovers.
Played for Bristol City Reserves 1974–76 and now for Frome Town AFC
Relaxations: 'Football, watching TV, playing with my children.'

LAST SEASON: BATTING

	I.	N.O.	R.	H.S.	AV.
TEST					
1ST-CLASS	6	0	82	37	13.66
INT				.	
RAL	4	0	20	13	5.00
NAT.W.					
B & H					

LAST SEASON: BOWLING

	O.	M.	R.	W.	AV.
TEST					
1ST-CLASS	68.5	20	225	3	75.00
INT					
RAL	57.4	3	210	6	35.00
NAT.W.					
B & H					

CAREER: BATTING

	I.	N.O.	R.	H.S.	AV.
TEST					
1ST-CLASS	224	68	2182	56*	13.98
INT					
RAL	58	29	337	28*	11.62
NAT.W.	9	4	28	9	5.60
B & H	21	11	99	25	9.90

CAREER: BOWLING

	O.	M.	R.	W.	AV.
TEST					
1ST-CLASS	4735.4	1120	1338	443	30.10
INT					
RAL	946.5	44	4174	154	27.10
NAT.W.	254.3	34	868	39	22.25
B & H	397.4	46	1391	60	23.18

Extras: Released by Somerset at end of 1988 season. Known affectionately as the 'Demon of Frome'
Best batting performance: 56* Somerset v Yorkshire, Harrogate 1977
Best Bowling performance: 6-37 Somerset v Gloucestershire, Bristol 1981

EAST, D. E.   Essex

Full Name: David Edward East
Role: Right-hand bat, wicket-keeper
Born: 27 July 1959, Clapton
Height: 5′ 10″ **Weight:** 12st 10lbs
Nickname: 'Various insults, but Ethel seems popular and Easty.'
County debut: 1981
County cap: 1982
1st-Class 50s scored: 15
1st-Class 100s scored: 4
Place in batting averages: 149th av. 23.89 (1987 215th av. 15.48)
Parents: Edward William and Joan Lillian
Wife and date of marriage: Jeanette Anne, 14 September 1984
Children: Matthew David Leonard, 8 November 1986
Family links with cricket: Father played club cricket for Hadley CC, an Essex touring side
Education: Millfields Primary; Hackney Downs School; University of East Anglia
Qualifications: BSc Hons in Biological Sciences. Advanced Cricket Coach
Jobs outside cricket: Has worked for shipping, insurance and finance brokers, cricket coaching and now cricket administration. Cricket consultant to Pony Sports (UK) Ltd
Off-season 1988–89: With Essex CCC co-ordinating club benefit year and also acting as cricket consultant to Pony Sports (UK) Ltd
Overseas teams played for: Avendale CC, Cape Town, 1984–85
Cricketing superstitions or habits: 'The number 111. When the side are on 111, I join in the usual foot in the air business. Never take wicket-keeping pads off between sessions unless raining hard!'
Cricketers particularly learnt from: 'Keith Fletcher, "the sage of Essex", has always been very helpful.'
Cricketers particularly admired: 'Alan Knott, simply the best as far as I am concerned.'

Injuries 1988: Small fracture in little finger

Other sports played: Hockey, 'poor squash'

Other sports followed: Interested in most but loathes horse and dog racing. 'I have a passing interest in most other sports.'

Relaxations: Playing the piano, listening to various types of music, video, spending time at home; cooking (especially curry and Chinese); home-made wine and beer. 'I went clay pigeon shooting for the first time in 1988 and think I have got the bug for it.'

Extras: Spent 1980 season with Northamptonshire 2nd XI. Played for Essex 2nd XI at 16. Gordon's Gin Wicket-keeper of the Year 1983. World record holder for most catches in an innings in first-class cricket, 8, on his birthday in 1985

Opinions on cricket: 'I believe that the "bad light" law is far too ambiguous and that it is interpreted badly by a great number of umpires, particularly when tail-end batsmen are subjected to fast, often short-pitched, bowling. How about starting the season one month later and finishing in October? The weather is usually pretty good in the autumn and it would stop the need for early games in April, when we all freeze to death. If this is not possible, can we have warmer sweaters, please!'

Best batting performance: 134 Essex v Gloucestershire, Ilford 1988

LAST SEASON: BATTING

	I.	N.O.	R.	H.S.	AV.
TEST					
1ST-CLASS	30	2	669	134	23.89
INT					
RAL	10	3	119	29*	17.00
NAT.W.	1	0	20	20	20.00
B & H		0	17	12	8.50

CAREER: BATTING

	I.	N.O.	R.	H.S.	AV.
TEST					
1ST-CLASS	252	32	4551	134	20.68
INT					
RAL	58	19	508	43	13.02
NAT.W.	16	5	142	28	12.90
B & H	21	4	234	33	13.76

LAST SEASON: WICKET KEEPING

	C.	ST.
TEST		
1ST-CLASS	60	6
INT		
RAL	10	1
NAT.W.	2	–
B & H	7	1

CAREER: WICKET KEEPING

	C.	ST.
TEST		
1ST-CLASS	478	53
INT		
RAL	88	15
NAT.W.	29	3
B & H	49	1

63. Which current Australian Test cricketer has a cricketing twin?

64. What do W. G. Grace's initials stand for?

ELLCOCK, R. M.　　　Worcestershire

Full Name: Ricardo McDonald
Ellcock
Role: Right-hand bat,
right-arm fast bowler
Born: 17 June 1965, Barbados
Height: 5′ 11″ **Weight:** 13st
Nickname: Ricky
County debut: 1982
1st-Class catches 1988: 1 (career 5)
Parents: Everson McDonald
(deceased) and Ione Marian
Marital status: Single
Education: Welches Mixed School,
Combermere, Barbados; Malvern
College, England
Qualifications: 6 O-levels
Overseas tours: Around West
Indies with Barbados
Overseas teams played for:
Combined Schools, Barbados, 1980; Carlton and Barbados
Cricketers particularly learnt from: Malcolm Marshall
Cricketers particularly admired: Alvin Kallicharran, Michael Holding
Other sports played: Table tennis, basketball
Other sports followed: Soccer, motor racing
Relaxations: Movies, music, TV
Best batting performance: 45* Worcestershire v Essex, Worcester 1984
Best bowling performance: 4-34 Worcestershire v Glamorgan, Worcester
1984

LAST SEASON: BATTING

	I.	N.O.	R.	H.S.	AV.
TEST					
1ST-CLASS	4	1	27	13	9.00
INT					
RAL					
NAT.W.					
B & H					

CAREER: BATTING

	I.	N.O.	R.	H.S.	AV.
TEST					
1ST-CLASS	40	11	371	45*	12.79
INT					
RAL	5	2	6	5*	2.00
NAT.W.	1	0	6	6	6.00
B & H	2	1	16	12	16.00

LAST SEASON: BOWLING

	O.	M.	R.	W.	AV.
TEST					
1ST-CLASS	81.1	8	328	7	46.85
INT					
RAL					
NAT.W.					
B & H					

CAREER: BOWLING

	O.	M.	R.	W.	AV.
TEST					
1ST-CLASS	684.5	90	2525	75	33.66
INT					
RAL	61.3	4	235	31	18.07
NAT.W.	10	2	49	3	16.33
B & H	25	4	98	3	32.66

ELLISON, R. M. Kent

Full Name: Richard Mark Ellison
Role: Left-hand bat,
right-arm medium bowler
Born: 21 September 1959,
Ashford, Kent
Height: 6′ 3″ **Weight:** 14st 3lb
Nickname: Elly, Nellie
County debut: 1981
County cap: 1983
Test debut: 1984
No. of Tests: 11
No. of One-Day Internationals: 14
1st-Class 50s: 13
1st-Class 100s: 1
One-Day 50s: 4
Place in batting averages: 215th
av. 16.47
Place in bowling averages: 41st
av. 23.90
Strike rate 1988: 51.01 (career 30.25)
1st-Class catches 1988: 7 (career 52)
Parents: Peter Richard Maxwell (deceased) and Bridget Mary
Wife and date of marriage: Fiona, 28 September 1985
Family links with cricket: Brother Charles Christopher blue at Cambridge University 1981–86. Grandfather played with Grace brothers and was secretary of Derby CCC in about 1915
Education: Friars Preparatory School, Great Chart, Ashford; Tonbridge School; St Lukes College; Exeter University
Qualifications: 8 O-levels, 2 A-levels; Degree B.Ed.; Teacher
Jobs outside cricket: Three months teaching winter 1985. Salesman for Panasonic winter 1987
Off-season 1988–89: Training for 1989 season. Couple of trips abroad
Overseas tours: With England to India and Australia 1984–85; England to Sharjah 1985; England to West Indies 1986
Overseas teams played for: University of Witwatersrand 1982–83, 1983–84; Tasmania 1986–87; Clarence Cricket Club, Hobart 1986–87
Cricketers particularly learnt from: Ray Dovey, Bob Woolmer, John Inverarity, Geoff Arnold
Cricketers particularly admired: Malcolm Marshall, Richard Hadlee, Chris Tavaré
Other sports played: Used to play a lot of hockey; golf, snooker
Other sports followed: Anything but horse racing and greyhounds
Relaxations: Social drinking, good food

Extras: Did not play at all in 1987 due to back injury. One of *Wisden*'s Five Cricketers of the Year, 1985

Opinions on cricket: 'We should not be dictated to in the way in which we select the England teams. Manner in which people qualify for English registration is a joke. One overseas player only. Why should we be prevented going to South Africa? A fair few players, whose governments want players who have been there to be banned, allow their individual Test players to come and play against and with the majority of English pros who have at some stage been to South Africa. If they feel that strongly about it, they could ban their own players from coming over here.'

Best batting performance: 108 Kent v Oxford University, Oxford 1984
Best bowling performance: 7-87 Kent v Northamptonshire, Maidstone, 1985

LAST SEASON: BATTING

	I.	N.O.	R.	H.S.	AV.
TEST					
1ST-CLASS	27	6	346	50*	16.47
INT					
RAL	7	4	157	44	52.33
NAT.W.	1	0	21	21	21.00
B & H	3	1	49	22*	24.50

CAREER: BATTING

	I.	N.O.	R.	H.S.	AV.
TEST	16	1	202	41	13.46
1ST-CLASS	176	44	3228	108	24.45
INT	12	4	86	24	10.75
RAL	53	23	877	84	29.23
NAT.W.	14	6	261	49*	32.62
B & H	19	4	328	72	21.86

LAST SEASON: BOWLING

	O.	M.	R.	W.	AV.
TEST					
1ST-CLASS	603.4	177	1697	71	23.90
INT					
RAL	81.3	6	378	9	42.00
NAT.W.	28.5	4	86	2	43.00
B & H	41.3	4	171	4	42.75

CAREER: BOWLING

	O.	M.	R.	W.	AV.
TEST	377.2	90	1048	35	29.94
1ST-CLASS	1342.2	793	7970	306	26.04
INT	116	9	510	12	42.50
RAL	454.5	26	2035	78	26.08
NAT.W.	174.3	32	542	26	20.84
B & H	239.1	43	786	33	23.81

EMBUREY, J. E. Middlesex

Full Name: John Ernest Emburey
Role: Right-hand bat, off-break bowler, slip or gully fielder
Born: 20 August 1952, Peckham
Height: 6′ 2″ **Weight:** 13st 12lbs
Nickname: Embers, Ernie, Knuckles
County debut: 1973
County cap: 1977
Benefit: 1986
Test debut: 1978
No. of Tests: 57
No. of One-Day Internationals: 55
1st-Class 50s scored: 34
1st-Class 100s scored: 3
1st-Class 5 w. in innings: 52

Place in batting averages: 101st av. 29.26 (1987 91st av. 32.27)
Place in bowling averages: 59th av. 26.60 (1987 106th av. 37.45)
Strike rate 1988: 69.58 (career 63.80)
1st-Class catches 1988: 24 (career 306)
Parents: John and Rose
Wife and date of marriage: Susie, 20 September 1980
Children: Clare, 1 March 1983; Chloe, 31 October 1985
Family links with cricket: Brother, Stephen, represented London Schools Colts in 1977
Education: Peckham Manor Secondary School
Qualifications: O-levels, Advanced Cricket Coaching Certificate
Jobs outside cricket: 'No other jobs. Have been abroad coaching most years.'
Off-season 1988–89: Chosen for England for cancelled tour of India
Overseas tours: With England to Australia 1978–79 and 1979–80 (following injury to Geoff Miller), West Indies 1981 and 1986, India 1981–82; World Cup, Pakistan, Australia and New Zealand 1987–88
Overseas teams played for: St Kilda CC, Melbourne, 1979–80, 1984–85; Prahran, Melbourne, 1977–78; Western Province 1982–83, 1983–84
Cricketers particularly learnt from: 'All.'
Cricketers particularly admired: Ken Barrington
Other sports: Golf, squash
Relaxations: Reading, gardening, going to the theatre
Extras: Played for Surrey Young Cricketers 1969–70. Whitbread scholarship to Australia, 1977–78. P. H. Edmonds of Middlesex and England was the best man at his wedding. Middlesex vice-captain since 1983. One of *Wisden*'s Five Cricketers of the Year, 1983. Banned from Test cricket for three years after playing for England Rebels in South Africa. Hit 6 sixes in 7 balls for Western Province v Eastern Province 1983–84 (52* in 22 balls). Captain of England v West Indies, 1988. Published autobiography *Emburey* in 1988
Opinions on cricket: 'I don't believe that anybody who plays cricket for a living should have his livelihood jeopardised or restricted (by bans on going to

LAST SEASON: BATTING

	I.	N.O.	R.	H.S.	AV.
TEST	6	0	46	30	7.66
1ST-CLASS	21	4	627	102	36.88
INT	1	0	8	8	8.00
RAL	9	1	170	50	21.25
NAT.W.	3	1	61	35	30.50
B & H	4	1	46	18	15.33

LAST SEASON: BOWLING

	O.	M.	R.	W.	AV.
TEST	82	24	266	4	66.50
1ST-CLASS	590.4	192	1277	54	23.64
INT	24.3	2	111	5	22.20
RAL	81	3	354	15	23.60
NAT.W.	58.3	12	179	3	59.66
B & H	46	3	180	6	30.00

CAREER: BATTING

	I.	N.O.	R.	H.S.	AV.
TEST	84	17	1409	75	21.02
1ST-CLASS	351	73	6465	133	23.25
INT	42	10	461	34	14.40
RAL	115	38	1300	50	16.88
NAT.W.	23	7	353	36*	22.06
B & H	37	12	486	50	19.44

CAREER: BOWLING

	O.	M.	R.	W.	AV.
TEST	144.4 2026.3	49 649	4763	130	36.63
1ST-CLASS	155.1 9186.4	39 3047	22788	962	23.68
INT	513.5	38	2087	69	30.24
RAL	1137.5	96	4804	222	21.63
NAT.W.	420.3	76	1118	37	30.21
B & H	457.4	76	1330	45	29.55

South Africa) . . . It can't be right to discriminate against a youngster who is prepared to pay his own fare to coach or play abroad to supplement his income or widen his experience. In fact, it wouldn't be a bad idea if county clubs gave such players a little bit of assistance with their travel costs.'

Best batting performance: 133 Middlesex v Essex, Chelmsford 1983
Best bowling performance: 7-36 Middlesex v Cambridge University, Cambridge 1977

EVANS, K. P.   Nottinghamshire

Full Name: Kevin Paul Evans
Role: Right-hand bat, right-arm medium bowler, slip fielder
Born: 10 September 1963, Calverton, Nottingham
Height: 6′ 1″ **Weight:** 12st 10lbs
Nickname: Ghost
County debut: 1984
1st-Class 50s scored: 1
Place in batting averages: 188th av. 20.30
Place in bowling averages: 121st av. 37.68
Strike-rate 1988: 70.86 (career 81.03)
1st-Class catches 1988: 19 (career 25)
Parents: Eric and Eileen
Marital status: Engaged
Family links with cricket: Brother Russell taken onto Nottinghamshire staff in 1985. Father played local cricket
Education: William Lee Primary; Colonel Frank Seely Comprehensive, Calverton
Qualifications: 9 O-levels, 3 A-levels. Qualified coach
Jobs outside cricket: Bank work
Off-season 1988–89: Coaching and playing in New Zealand
Cricketing superstitions and habits: Left pad on first
Overseas teams played for: Wainuomata, New Zealand, 1986–87
Cricketers particularly learnt from: Bob White, Mike Harris and 'most of the Nottinghamshire staff'
Cricketers particularly admired: Gary Sobers, Clive Rice
Other sports played: Football, tennis
Other sports followed: American football
Relaxations: Listening to music, reading, DIY, gardening

Extras: Together with brother Russell, first brothers to bat together for Nottinghamshire CCC in 1st-class cricket for 50 years

Opinions on cricket: 'Review of the Championship points system. Maybe give points to the team with a first innings lead so that the Championship is not decided totally on declarations and weather. Four-day cricket seems good for the game, but 110 overs per day is too many.'

Best batting performance: 54 Nottinghamshire v Derbyshire, Trent Bridge 1988

Best bowling performance: 3-22 Nottinghamshire v Derbyshire, Trent Bridge 1988

LAST SEASON: BATTING

	I.	N.O.	R.	H.S.	AV.
TEST					
1ST-CLASS	24	4	406	54	20.30
INT					
RAL	9	4	43	11	8.60
NAT.W.	–	–	–	–	–
B & H	3	1	60	31*	30.00

LAST SEASON: BOWLING

	O.	M.	R.	W.	AV.
TEST					
1ST-CLASS	259.5	49	829	22	37.68
INT					
RAL	88.4	2	415	15	27.66
NAT.W.	23	3	90	2	45.00
B & H	31.2	2	138	5	27.60

CAREER: BATTING

	I.	N.O.	R.	H.S.	AV.
TEST					
1ST-CLASS	35	4	514	54	16.58
INT					
RAL	19	7	173	28	14.41
NAT.W.	3	0	19	10	6.33
B & H	5	2	82	31*	27.33

CAREER: BOWLING

	O.	M.	R.	W.	AV.
TEST					
1ST-CLASS	418.4	75	1391	31	44.87
INT					
RAL	177.4	4	953	29	32.86
NAT.W.	59	11	184	8	23.00
B & H	42.2	2	185	6	30.83

EVANS, R. J.   Nottinghamshire

Full Name: Russell John Evans
Role: Right-hand bat, occasional off-spin bowler, gully or slip fielder
Born: 1 October 1965, Calverton, Nottingham
Height: 6′ **Weight:** 11st 11lbs
Nickname: Brains, GC, Rubber-head (by John Birch only)
County debut: 1985
1st-Class 50s scored: 1
1st-Class catches 1988: 2 (career 3)
Parents: Eric and Eileen
Family links with cricket: Brother Kevin on Nottinghamshire staff. Father played local cricket
Education: Colonel Frank Seely Comprehensive, Calverton

Qualifications: 8 O-levels, 3 A-levels
Jobs outside cricket: Driving jobs, warehouse work. Working for Gunn and Moore
Off-season 1988–89: Playing and coaching for Karaka CC and Counties Representative XI in New Zealand
Cricketing superstitions and habits: Left pad on first; if opening, never face first ball
Overseas teams played for: Papakura, New Zealand 1986–87
Cricketers particularly learnt from: Father, Mike Bore, Tim Robinson, Clive Rice, Tony Bunkle, John Laurie, Eddie Hemmings
Cricketers particularly admired: Richard Hadlee, Clive Rice, Graham Gooch, Ian Botham, Geoff Boycott, Derek Randall
Other sports played: Football, tennis, squash, swimming
Other sports followed: Football, golf
Relaxations: Music, crosswords, dining out, social evenings
Injuries 1988: Lacerated shin
Extras: He and Kevin were first brothers to bat together in a first-class match for Nottinghamshire CCC for over 50 years
Opinions on cricket: 'Bonus points should be altered for four-day cricket. There should be no limit of overs to gain bonus points. Playing a limited number of four-day games and the rest three-day games makes it difficult as it depends upon who you play. There will be more chance of a result in four-day cricket so if you get drawn against the weaker counties for the four-day game you can pick up points more easily.'
Best batting performance: 50* Nottinghamshire v Sri Lankans, Trent Bridge 1988
Best bowling performance: 3-40 Nottinghamshire v Oxford University, Oxford 1988

LAST SEASON: BATTING

	I.	N.O.	R.	H.S.	AV.
TEST					
1ST-CLASS	2	1	71	50*	71.00
INT					
RAL	1	0	7	7	7.00
NAT.W.					
B & H					

LAST SEASON: BOWLING

	O.	M.	R.	W.	AV.
TEST					
1ST-CLASS	25	9	63	3	21.00
INT					
RAL					
NAT.W.					
B & H					

CAREER: BATTING

	I.	N.O.	R.	H.S.	AV.
TEST					
1ST-CLASS	4	1	75	50*	25.00
INT					
RAL	5	1	55	20	13.75
NAT.W.					
B & H					

CAREER: BOWLING

	O.	M.	R.	W.	AV.
TEST					
1ST-CLASS	27	9	73	3	24.33
INT					
RAL					
NAT.W.					
B & H					

FAIRBROTHER, N. H.   Lancashire

Full Name: Neil Harvey
Fairbrother
Role: Left-hand bat, left-arm
medium bowler
Born: 9 September 1963,
Warrington, Cheshire
Height: 5' 8" **Weight:** 11st
Nicknames: Harvey, Farnsbarns,
Little Ted
County debut: 1982
County cap: 1985
Test debut: 1987
No. of Tests: 4
No. of One-Day Internationals: 11
1000 runs in a season: 5
1st-Class 50s scored: 43
1st-Class 100s scored: 13
One-Day 50s: 18
One-Day 100s: 3
Place in batting averages: 86th av. 30.64 (1987 29th av. 42.25)
1st-Class catches 1988: 9 (career 83)
Parents: Leslie Robert and Barbara
Wife and date of marriage: Audrey, 23 September 1988
Family links with cricket: Father and two uncles played local league cricket
Education: St Margaret's Church of England School, Oxford; Lymn Grammar School
Qualifications: 5 O-levels
Off-season 1988–89: Playing in Canberra

LAST SEASON: BATTING

	I.	N.O.	R.	H.S.	AV.
TEST					
1ST-CLASS	41	4	1134	111	30.64
INT					
RAL	15	4	422	116*	38.36
NAT.W.	2	1	115	80*	115.00
B & H	3	1	143	116*	71.50

CAREER: BATTING

	I.	N.O.	R.	H.S.	AV.
TEST	4	0	5	3	1.25
1ST-CLASS	216	30	7023	164*	37.75
INT	11	2	232	54	25.77
RAL	69	15	1806	116*	33.44
NAT.W.	12	3	534	93*	59.33
B & H	19	5	531	116*	37.92

LAST SEASON: BOWLING

	O.	M.	R.	W.	AV.
TEST					
1ST-CLASS	10.1	0	59	0	–
INT					
RAL					
NAT.W.					
B & H					

CAREER: BOWLING

	O.	M.	R.	W.	AV.
TEST					
1ST-CLASS	90.2	21	323	4	80.75
INT					
RAL	2	0	15	0	–
NAT.W.	3	0	16	0	–
B & H					

Overseas tours: Denmark 1980 with North of England U-19; England to Sharjah 1987; World Cup, Pakistan, Australia and New Zealand 1987–88
Overseas teams played for: Eastern Suburbs CC, Canberra, Australia 1985–86
Cricketers particularly learnt from: 'All the senior players at Old Trafford have been a great help, particularly Messrs Fowler and Allott.'
Cricketers particularly admired: Clive Lloyd, Allan Border
Other sports played: Rugby, squash
Other sports followed: Football, rugby union, rugby league
Relaxations: Music and playing sport
Extras: 'I was named after the Australian cricketer Neil Harvey, who was my mum's favourite cricketer.' Three Tests and two U-19 one-day internationals v Young Australians 1983. Made full Test debut v Pakistan at Old Trafford 1987
Best batting performance: 164* Lancashire v Hampshire, Liverpool 1985
Best bowling performance: 2-91 Lancashire v Nottinghamshire, Old Trafford 1987

FALKNER, N. J. Sussex

Full Name: Nicholas James Falkner
Role: Right-hand bat, right-arm seamer, cover or mid-wicket fielder
Born: 30 September 1962, Redhill
Height: 5′ 10½″ **Weight:** 12st 3lbs
Nickname: Beefy, Vulture, Falksy
County debut: 1984 (Surrey), 1988 (Sussex)
1st-Class 50s scored: 3
1st-Class 100s scored: 2
One-Day 50s: 3
Place in batting averages: 214th av. 16.57
1st-Class catches 1988: 4 (career 14)
Parents: John and Barbara
Family links with cricket:
Father plays club cricket for Chipstead and Coulsdon

Education: Yardley Court; Reigate Grammar School
Wife and date of marriage: Jacqueline Patricia, 19 March 1988
Qualifications: 5 O-levels

Jobs outside cricket: Assistant buyer for Balfour Beatty Int Construction; worked in insurance company
Cricketing superstitions or habits: Left pad on first. One of the last to leave changing room
Overseas tours: Captained Surrey Schools to Australia 1980–81
Overseas teams played for: Perth Cricket Club 1982–83, 1985–86; University Cricket Club, Perth 1986–87
Cricketers particularly learnt from: Les Smithers, Father ('Always give me sound advice')
Cricketers particularly admired: Ian Botham, John Goddey
Other sports played: Squash, golf, rugby
Other sports followed: All sports
Injuries 1988: Slipped disc in June. Out for one month
Relaxations: Reading, playing chess, sleeping, pottering around in the garden
Extras: Scored a century on first-team debut for Surrey, 101* v Cambridge University. 'I have taken only *one* first-class wicket, namely a Test captain – Imran Khan!' Left Surrey for Sussex during 1988 season
Opinions on cricket: 'When the 110 overs are complete, that should be it for the day, even if all 110 overs are complete by 6.15 pm. Four-day games are a must. Every county would then play each other once only – a much fairer system. Only one overseas player per county staff!'
Best batting performance: 102 Surrey v Middlesex, Lord's 1986
Best bowling performance: 1-3 Surrey v Sussex, Guildford 1986

LAST SEASON: BATTING

	I.	N.O.	R.	H.S.	AV.
TEST					
1ST-CLASS	14	0	232	55	16.57
INT					
RAL	2	0	12	10	6.00
NAT.W.					
B & H	1	0	15	15	15.00

CAREER: BATTING

	I.	N.O.	R.	H.S.	AV.
TEST					
1ST-CLASS	38	3	966	102	27.60
INT					
RAL	6	0	163	52	27.16
NAT.W.	2	0	36	36	18.00
B & H	5	1	76	58	19.00

65. Which Gloucestershire and England cricketer took all ten wickets in an innings v Worcestershire and had it described by which Gloucestershire and England captain as 'not so much good bowling as rank bad batting'?

FARBRACE, P. Kent

Full Name: Paul Farbrace
Role: Right-hand bat,
wicket-keeper
Born: 7 July 1967, Ash, nr
Canterbury
Height: 5′ 10″ **Weight:** 11st 7lbs
Nickname: Farby, Ugly
County debut: 1987
1st-Class 50s scored: 1
Parents: David and Betty
Wife and date of marriage:
Elizabeth Jane, 27 July 1985
Children: Jemma Elizabeth,
30 March 1985; Eleanor Kate,
3 September 1988
Family links with cricket: 'Father
played village cricket, as do my two
brothers – Ian plays in South
Wales and Colin plays for Ash. Dad
and eldest brother both keep wicket.'
Education: Geoffrey Chaucer School, Canterbury
Qualifications: 2 O-levels, 6 CSEs, NCA Cricket Coaching Certificate and
NCA Senior Coaching Award
Jobs outside cricket: Working for HM Customs and Excise
Off-season 1988–89: Coaching at various schools in Kent
Cricketing superstitions or habits: 'Always arrive at ground very early, then
lay all my kit out. Follow captain onto field, then on to collect ball off the
umpire. Fiddle with pads, trousers and then gloves when keeping, in sequence
before every ball. Too many to mention when batting.'
Overseas tours: Kent Schools U-17 XI to Canada 1983
Cricketers particularly learnt from: Alan Knott, Derek Underwood, Bob
Woolmer, Colin Page, Alan Ealham, Steve Marsh
Cricketers particularly admired: Alan Knott, Derek Underwood
Other sports played: Football, golf, rugby, basketball
Other sports followed: All sports except horse racing
Relaxations: 'Reading and spending as much time with my wife and
daughters.'
Extras: Played County Schools football, had England Schools U-18 trial,
attracted attention from Notts County, then had extended trials with
Coventry City when seventeen as a goalkeeper
Opinions on cricket: 'I would like to see wickets uncovered but also leave the
bowlers' run-ups uncovered as well. More spinners would have to be used,
this making the keeper's job a little more interesting. I think that players

155

should not put umpires under too much pressure, forcing them into making bad decisions. In particular, 2nd XI umpires who may not be quite as good as first-class umpires, are put under too much pressure by continual shouting by bowlers and close fielders. We all complain from time to time about decisions that go against us, but I'm sure we could help ourselves by being easier on the umpires. Politicians should be kept out of all sports, especially cricket.'

Best batting performance: 75* Kent v Yorkshire, Canterbury 1987

LAST SEASON: BATTING

	I.	N.O.	R.	H.S.	AV.
TEST					
1ST-CLASS	2	0	15	9	7.50
INT					
RAL					
NAT.W.					
B & H					

CAREER: BATTING

	I.	N.O.	R.	H.S.	AV.
TEST					
1ST-CLASS	9	3	149	75*	24.83
INT					
RAL					
NAT.W.	1	0	4	4	4.00
B & H					

LAST SEASON: WICKET KEEPING

	C.	ST.			
TEST					
1ST-CLASS	2	–			
INT					
RAL					
NAT.W.					
B & H					

CAREER: WICKET KEEPING

	C.	ST.			
TEST					
1ST-CLASS	13	–			
INT					
RAL					
NAT.W.	3	–			
B & H					

FELTHAM, M. A. Surrey

Full Name: Mark Andrew Feltham
Role: Right-hand bat, right-arm fast-medium bowler
Born: 26 June 1963, London
Height: 6' 2" **Weight:** 13st 10bs
Nickname: Felts, Felpsy, Boff or Douglas
County debut: 1983
1st-Class 50s scored: 2
1st-Class 5 w. in innings: 4
Place in batting averages: 160th av. 22.93 (1987 124th av. 14.33)
Place in bowling averages: 82nd av. 29.98 (1987 69th av. 30.05)
Strike rate 1988: 62.53 (career 59.24)
1st-Class catches 1988: 10 (career 22)
Parents: Leonard William and Patricia Louise

Family links with cricket: Mother involved in Ken Barrington Cricket Centre Appeal; brother plays for Surrey Young Cricketers and League cricket
Education: Roehampton Church School; Tiffin Boys' School
Qualifications: 7 O-levels; Advanced Cricket Coach
Jobs outside cricket: Marketing and sales
Off-season 1988–89: Marketing in London and south-east
Cricketing superstitions or habits: 'Left pad on before right. Have favourite trousers, shirt etc, to bat in.'
Overseas tours: Australia, 1980, with Surrey Cricket Association U-19s; Barbados, 1981, with MCC Young Professionals
Overseas teams played for: Glenwood High School Old Boys, Durban, 1984–85
Cricketers particularly learnt from: Sylvester Clarke, Pat Pocock, Mickey Stewart, Geoff Arnold, Trevor Jesty
Cricketers particularly admired: Ian Botham, David Gower, Graham Gooch, Sylvester Clarke, Gordon Greenidge
Other sports played: Football, snooker, golf
Relaxations: Listening to music, crosswords – 'although only in *Sun* and *Star*!'
Extras: Played for England Schools at U-15 and U-19 levels. On the MCC Young Professionals Staff 1981 and 1982
Opinions on cricket: 'With the 1988 first-class programme involving more days cricket, it seems to me that the authorities are trying to get more and more each year from the modern players. Why we couldn't have gone straight to 16 four-day games seems strange to me. Players should be allowed to play and earn a living wherever they wish without being put under pressure by politicians. There is so much hypocrisy on this subject it is disgraceful.'
Best batting performance: 76 Surrey v Gloucestershire, The Oval 1986
Best bowling performance: 5-45 Surrey v Lancashire, The Oval 1988

LAST SEASON: BATTING

	I.	N.O.	R.	H.S.	AV.
TEST					
1ST-CLASS	25	9	367	74	22.93
INT					
RAL	7	2	75	20*	15.00
NAT.W.	3	2	23	16*	23.00
B & H	2	0	3	2	1.50

LAST SEASON: BOWLING

	O.	M.	R.	W.	AV.
TEST					
1ST-CLASS	584	130	1679	56	29.98
INT					
RAL	93.4	1	508	11	46.18
NAT.W.	36	5	160	2	80.00
B & H	41	2	153	6	25.50

CAREER: BATTING

	I.	N.O.	R.	H.S.	AV.
TEST					
1ST-CLASS	68	22	974	76	21.17
INT					
RAL	31	12	254	37	13.36
NAT.W.	7	2	48	16*	9.60
B & H	9	3	75	22*	12.50

CAREER: BOWLING

	O.	M.	R.	W.	AV.
TEST					
1ST-CLASS	1540.5	338	4792	156	30.71
INT					
RAL	324	9	1747	44	39.70
NAT.W.	80	13	324	7	46.28
B & H	153.2	15	614	20	30.70

FELTON, N. A.   Somerset

Full Name: Nigel Alfred Felton
Role: Left-hand bat
Born: 24 October 1960,
Guildford
Height: 5' 7" **Weight:** 10st 7lbs
Nickname: Will, Twiglets
County debut: 1982
1000 runs in a season: 2
1st-Class 50s scored: 28
1st-Class 100s scored: 8
One-Day 50s: 8
Place in batting averages: 106th
av. 28.80 (1987 134th av. 26.68)
1st-Class catches 1988: 7 (career 46)
Parents: Ralph and Enid
Marital status: Single
Family links with cricket:
Father played club cricket
Education: Hawes Down Secondary
School, West Wickham, Kent; Millfield School, Street, Somerset; Loughborough University
Qualifications: 6 O-levels, 2 A-levels, BSc(Hons), Cert of Education PE/Sports Sciences, qualified teacher
Jobs outside cricket: Teaching, digging holes, working with Somerset CCC marketing dept
Cricketing superstitions or habits: Always put right pad on first
Overseas tours: English Schools to India 1976–77; Young England to Australia 1978; Scorpions CC to Sierra Leone 1987
Overseas teams played for: Waneroro CC, Perth, Western Australia 1985–86
Other sports followed: Most ball games
Other sports played: Most winter sports
Relaxations: Music, reading, relaxing at home
Extras: Joined Somerset in July 1981. Played a season for Kent in 1980 after leaving Millfield and before going to Loughborough. Left Kent at pre-season training 1981, due to the size of the staff. Joined Somerset at end of first year at Loughborough. Released by Somerset at end of 1988 season

LAST SEASON: BATTING

	I.	N.O.	R.	H.S.	AV.
TEST					
1ST-CLASS	27	2	720	127	28.80
INT					
RAL	2	0	8	8	4.00
NAT.W.					
B & H	4	0	82	50	20.50

CAREER: BATTING

	I.	N.O.	R.	H.S.	AV.
TEST					
1ST-CLASS	180	7	4987	173*	28.82
INT					
RAL	38	5	773	96	23.42
NAT.W.	8	2	303	87	50.50
B & H	11	0	146	50	13.27

Opinions on cricket: 'In favour of four-day cricket.'
Best batting performance: 173* Somerset v Kent, Taunton 1983

FERRIS, G. J. F. Leicestershire

Full Name: George John Fitzgerald
Ferris
Role: Right-hand bat, right-arm
fast bowler
Born: 18 October 1964, Urlings
Village, Antigua
Height: 6′ 3″ **Weight:** 14st
Nickname: Ferro, Slugo
County debut: 1983
1st-Class 5 w. in innings: 9
1st-Class 10 w. in match: 1
Place in batting averages: 251st
av. 11.58 (1987 248th av. 10.33)
Place in bowling averages: 28th
av. 22.25 (1987 15th av. 21.98)
Strike rate 1988: 43.75 (career 46.74)
1st-Class catches 1988: 1 (career 10)
Children: Imran J., 12 November 1984
Education: Jenning's Secondary
Jobs outside cricket: Physical education teacher
Off-season 1988–89: Coaching and playing in Shell Shield
Overseas tours: With Young West Indies to Zimbabwe 1983
Overseas teams played for: Leeward Islands; Matabeleland
Cricketers particularly learnt from: Andy Roberts (neighbour in Antigua),
Ken Higgs

LAST SEASON: BATTING

	I.	N.O.	R.	H.S.	AV.
TEST					
1ST-CLASS	20	8	139	36*	11.58
INT					
RAL	5	4	21	13*	21.00
NAT.W.	1	1	1	1*	—
B & H	1	1	1	1*	—

CAREER: BATTING

	I.	N.O.	R.	H.S.	AV.
TEST					
1ST-CLASS	82	35	518	36*	11.02
INT					
RAL	9	6	36	13*	12.00
NAT.W.	3	2	3	2*	3.00
B & H	2	2	1	1*	—

LAST SEASON: BOWLING

	O.	M.	R.	W.	AV.
TEST					
1ST-CLASS	452.1	82	1380	62	22.25
INT					
RAL	64.4	4	266	15	17.73
NAT.W.	18	2	90	2	45.00
B & H	21	3	70	6	11.66

CAREER: BOWLING

	O.	M.	R.	W.	AV.
TEST					
1ST-CLASS	1900.5	344	6199	244	25.40
INT					
RAL	156.3	7	678	28	24.21
NAT.W.	52	5	238	5	47.60
B & H	61	6	279	12	23.25

Cricketers particularly admired: Michael Holding, Malcolm Marshall
Other sports played: Soccer, tennis
Other sports followed: Soccer, tennis, American basketball
Relaxations: Listening to music
Extras: Picked out by Viv Richards as one of two future West Indies stars, in 1983. (Richards' other choice was Jeff Dujon)
Best batting performance: 36* Leicestershire v Hampshire, Leicester 1988
Best bowling performance: 7-42 Leicestershire v Glamorgan, Hinckley 1983

FINNEY, R. J. Derbyshire

Full Name: Roger John Finney
Role: Right-hand bat, left-arm slow bowler
Born: 2 August 1960, Darley Dale, Derbyshire
Height: 6' 1" **Weight:** 12st 10lbs
Nickname: Albert
County debut: 1982
County cap: 1985
50 wickets in a season: 2
1st-Class 50s scored: 14
1st-Class 5 w. in innings: 8
One-Day 50s: 1
Place in batting averages: —
(1987 149th av. 24.51)
Place in bowling averages: —
(1987 75th av. 31.07)
1st-Class catches 1988: 2 (career 28)
Parents: Roy and Janet
Wife and date of marriage: Carol, 21 September 1985
Children: Ryan Anthony Edward, 28 April 1987
Family links with cricket: Father played and captained local side for many years
Education: Lady Manners School, Bakewell
Qualifications: O-levels
Jobs outside cricket: Production clerk and sports salesman
Off-season 1988–89: 'Developing my business.'
Cricketing superstitions or habits: Left pad on first
Overseas teams played for: Alexandrians, Pietermaritzburg, South Africa, 1980–82, 1984–85
Cricketers particularly learnt from: Phil Russell (Derbyshire coach), Don Wilson (head coach at Lord's)
Other sports played: Rugby, football, golf

Injuries 1988: Nagging back problem restricted him badly
Relaxations: 'Music, movies, good beer, eating at a good restaurant.'
Extras: Before joining Derbyshire, spent two years with the MCC Young Professionals. Decided to retire at end of 1988 season
Best batting performance: 82 Derbyshire v Gloucestershire, Derby 1985
Best bowling performance: 7-54 Derbyshire v Leicestershire, Leicester 1986

LAST SEASON: BATTING

	I.	N.O.	R.	H.S.	AV.
TEST					
1ST-CLASS	5	2	142	52*	47.33
INT					
RAL	1	0	15	15	15.00
NAT.W.					
B & H	–	–	–	–	–

LAST SEASON: BOWLING

	O.	M.	R.	W.	AV.
TEST					
1ST-CLASS	59	15	168	1	168.00
INT					
RAL	4	0	16	0	–
NAT.W.					
B & H	6	0	23	1	23.00

CAREER: BATTING

	I.	N.O.	R.	H.S.	AV.
TEST					
1ST-CLASS	168	29	2856	82	20.54
INT					
RAL	45	12	538	50*	16.30
NAT.W.	3	1	59	40	29.50
B & H	11	2	160	46	17.77

CAREER: BOWLING

	O.	M.	R.	W.	AV.
TEST					
1ST-CLASS	1982.2	391	6297	202	31.17
INT					
RAL	326.3	18	1605	49	32.75
NAT.W.	40	7	128	4	32.00
B & H	124.5	14	483	16	30.18

FITTON, J. D.　　　　　　　　Lancashire

Full Name: John Dexter Fitton
Role: Left-hand bat, off-break bowler
Born: 24 August 1965, Rochdale
Height: 5′ 10″ **Weight:** 12st
Nickname: Ted, Bert, Lord
County debut: 1987
1st-Class 5 w. in innings: 1
Parents: Derek and Jean
Marital status: Single
Family links with cricket:
Father dedicated cricketer for 20 years with Littleboro in Central Lancashire League and Robinsons in North Manchester League
Education: Redbrook and Auder Hill Upper School
Qualifications: 2 O-levels, Diploma in Business Studies
Jobs outside cricket: Worked for three years as an Export Administrator at a steel springs works

Cricketing superstitions or habits: 'Always clean my teeth prior to the start of a match.'

Cricketers particularly learnt from: Dad, Paul Rocca (Rochdale coach), John Abrahams

Cricketers particularly admired: David Gower, Clive Lloyd, Richard Hadlee, Neil Fairbrother

Other sports played: Football, golf, badminton

Other sports followed: Manchester City FC, greyhound racing at Oldham

Relaxations: Listening to music, watching comedy films and shows

Extras: Youngest player to take 50 wickets and score 500 runs for Rochdale in the Central Lancashire League. Scored 1000 runs a season for three seasons running in the same league

Best batting performance: 36 Lancashire v Yorkshire, Old Trafford 1988

Best bowling performance: 6-59 Lancashire v Yorkshire, Old Trafford 1988

LAST SEASON: BATTING

	I.	N.O.	R.	H.S.	AV.
TEST					
1ST-CLASS	2	1	47	36	47.00
INT					
RAL					
NAT.W.					
B & H					

LAST SEASON: BOWLING

	O.	M.	R.	W.	AV.
TEST					
1ST-CLASS	58	16	120	7	17.14
INT					
RAL					
NAT.W.					
B & H					

CAREER: BATTING

	I.	N.O.	R.	H.S.	AV.
TEST					
1ST-CLASS	3	1	50	36	25.00
INT					
RAL	1	0	0	0	0.00
NAT.W.					
B & H					

CAREER: BOWLING

	O.	M.	R.	W.	AV.
TEST					
1ST-CLASS	65	16	143	8	17.87
INT					
RAL	8	0	25	1	25.00
NAT.W.					
B & H					

66. How many England captains past, present and future represented England v Australia in the Fourth Test at Edgbaston in 1981, and who were they?

67. Who won the 2nd XI Championship in 1988?

FLETCHER, K. W. R.   Essex

Full Name: Keith William Robert Fletcher
Role: Right-hand bat, leg-break bowler
Born: 20 May 1944, Worcester
Height: 5′ 10″ **Weight:** 10st 7lbs
Nickname: Gnome, Fletch
County debut: 1962
County cap: 1963
Benefit: 1973
Testimonial: 1982
Test debut: 1968
No. of Tests: 59
No. of One-Day Internationals: 24
1000 runs in a season: 20
1st-Class 50s scored: 222
1st-Class 100s scored: 61
1st-class 200s scored: 2
1st-Class 5 w. in innings: 1
One-Day 50s: 62
One-Day 100s: 2
Place in batting averages: 115th av. 27.54 (1987 117th av. 28.90)
1st-Class catches 1988: 9 (career 643)
Parents: Joseph and Doris
Wife and date of marriage: Susan Elizabeth, 22 March 1969
Children: Tamara Jane, 2 August 1970; Sara Jane, 19 December 1972
Jobs outside cricket: Has worked as oil representative
Overseas tours: Pakistan 1966–67; Ceylon and Pakistan 1968–69; Australia and New Zealand 1970–71 and 1974–75; India, Sri Lanka and Pakistan 1972–73; West Indies 1973–74; India, Sri Lanka and Australia 1976–77; India and Sri Lanka 1981–82 as captain
Other sports played: Golf, fishing, shooting partridge – 'my second favourite sport after cricket.'
Relaxations: Gardening
Extras: Played for Essex at age of 17. Captained Essex from 1974 and led county to first County Championship in 1979, second in 1983 and third in 1984. Also Benson & Hedges Cup in 1979 and John Player Special League in 1981, 1984 and 1985. Won NatWest Trophy in 1985 to become first captain to win all four domestic competitions. Scored two centuries in a match, 111 and 102* v Nottinghamshire, at Nottingham in 1976. Awarded OBE in 1985 New Year's Honours list. Gave up captaincy at end of 1985 season, but frequently stood in for Graham Gooch to lead Essex in 1986 Championship-winning season. Appointed Essex captain again for 1988. Handed back captaincy to

Graham Gooch and retired from first-class game to take over 2nd XI captaincy for 1989

Opinions on cricket: 'For the first time in my career, I found I wasn't looking forward to batting at the end of last season. With the ball flying off those grassy pitches, I was concerned that one of these days, I wouldn't get my gloves up fast enough to keep the ball out of my face. I still love the game . . . If Essex are in a dire emergency, I may play the odd first-class match.'

Best batting performance: 228* Essex v Sussex, Hastings 1968
Best bowling performance: 5-41 Essex v Middlesex, Colchester 1979

LAST SEASON: BATTING

	I.	N.O.	R.	H.S.	AV.
TEST					
1ST-CLASS	14	3	303	58	27.54
INT					
RAL	10	1	104	24	11.55
NAT.W.	1	0	0	0	0.00
B & H	4	1	88	40*	29.33

CAREER: BATTING

	I.	N.O.	R.	H.S.	AV.
TEST	96	14	3272	216	39.90
1ST-CLASS	1071	156	34393	228*	37.58
INT	22	3	757	131	39.84
RAL	238	39	5726	99*	28.77
NAT.W.	45	4	1036	97	25.26
B & H	78	15	3111	101*	33.50

LAST SEASON: BOWLING

	O.	M.	R.	W.	AV.
TEST					
1ST-CLASS					
INT					
RAL					
NAT.W.					
B & H					

CAREER: BOWLING

	O.	M.	R.	W.	AV.
TEST	20 20.5	1 5	193	2	96.50
1ST-CLASS	64.3 367.3	6 52	2103	49	42.91
INT					
RAL					
NAT.W.	10.3	1	43	2	21.50
B & H	4.4	0	30	1	30.00

FLETCHER, S. D. Yorkshire

Full Name: Stuart David Fletcher
Role: Right-hand bat, right-arm medium bowler
Born: 8 June 1964, Keighley
Height: 5′ 10″ **Weight:** 12st
Nickname: Fletch, Godber, Norman Stanley, Dr Death, Ghostie
County debut: 1983
1st-Class 5 w. in innings: 3
Place in batting averages: —
(1987 249th av. 10.16)
Place in bowling averages: 27th
av. 22.16 (1987 55th av. 28.21)
Strike rate 1988: 41.89 (career 58.82)
1st-Class catches 1988: 8 (career 17)
Parents: Brough and Norma Hilda

Family links with cricket: Father played league cricket
Education: Woodhouse Primary; Reins Wood Scondary
Qualifications: O-level English and Woodwork; City and Guilds in coach-building
Jobs outside cricket: Coachbuilder at Reliance Commercial Vehicles Ltd. Worked at Ben Shaw's Pop Merchants
Overseas tours: Holland 1983 with National Cricket Association U-19s
Cricketers particularly learnt from: Father, Phil Carrick, Steve Oldham
Cricketers particularly admired: Ian Botham, Arnie Sidebottom
Other sports played: Snooker, golf, football
Other sports followed: Watches Leeds United FC
Relaxations: Watching TV, snooker and golf
Extras: Played in the Yorkshire U-19s who were the first Yorkshire side to win the Cambridge and Oxford Festival, 1983
Best batting performance: 28* Yorkshire v Kent, Tunbridge Wells 1984
Best bowling performance: 8-58 Yorkshire v Essex, Sheffield 1988

LAST SEASON: BATTING

	I.	N.O.	R.	H.S.	AV.
TEST					
1ST-CLASS	15	3	81	18	6.75
INT					
RAL	1	1	2	2*	—
NAT.W.	1	0	2	2	2.00
B & H	1	0	1	1	1.00

CAREER: BATTING

	I.	N.O.	R.	H.S.	AV.
TEST					
1ST-CLASS	56	22	294	28*	8.64
INT					
RAL	10	7	23	8	7.66
NAT.W.	4	2	5	2*	2.50
B & H	3	1	2	1	1.00

LAST SEASON: BOWLING

	O.	M.	R.	W.	AV.
TEST					
1ST-CLASS	412	66	1308	59	22.16
INT					
RAL	107.4	3	501	25	20.04
NAT.W.	22.1	2	71	3	23.66
B & H	11	1	55	3	18.33

CAREER: BOWLING

	O.	M.	R.	W.	AV.
TEST					
1ST-CLASS	1666.4	293	5394	170	31.72
INT					
RAL	382.2	12	1957	71	27.56
NAT.W.	102.1	13	336	13	25.84
B & H	142.4	8	604	22	27.45

68. Whose recent cricketing book is called *Fox on the Run*?
69. Who has taken the most Test wickets?

FOLLEY, I. Lancashire

Full Name: Ian Folley
Role: Right-hand bat, slow left-arm bowler, 'night-watchman and Mendo's bag packer'
Born: 9 January 1963
Height: 5' 9½" **Weight:** 11st
Nickname: Thatch, Vicar, Reverend, Foll, Neil
County debut: 1982
County cap: 1987
1st-Class 50s scored: 1
1st-Class 5 w. in innings: 10
1st-Class 10 w. in match: 1
Place in batting averages: 208th av. 17.00 (1987 223rd av. 14.79)
Place in bowling averages: 80th av. 29.84 (1987 31st av. 25.20)
Strike rate 1988: 64.68 (career 67.53)
1st-Class catches 1988: 6 (career 57)
Parents: James and Constance
Wife and date of marriage: Julie, 27 September 1986
Education: Mansfield High School, Nelson; Colne College
Qualifications: 5 O-levels, Business Studies diploma
Jobs outside cricket: 'Too numerous to mention.'
Off-season 1988–89: 'Playing a lot of golf, squash, etc. Generally looking after my fitness – once I get it. Football.'
Cricketing superstitions or habits: 'Pre-match bowling to Mendo. Do it as a pastime.'
Overseas tours: Barbados 1982 with Lancashire; Denmark 1981 with NCA; New York 1985 with Lancashire; Jamaica 1987 and 1988 with Lancashire
Overseas teams played for: Glenorchy, Tasmania, 1985–86; Brighton, Tasmania, 1987–88
Cricketers particularly learnt from: D. Bloodworth
Cricketers particularly admired: Clive Lloyd, Viv Richards, Graeme Hick, Malcolm Marshall
Other sports played: Golf, squash, football
Other sports followed: 'I'm a bad watcher.'
Injuries 1988: Broken finger pre-season in Jamaica; ligament trouble; index-finger of left-hand
Relaxations: Interested in rallying and saloon car racing, listening to music (detests disco music)
Extras: Represented Lancashire Schools U-15s and U-19s as captain. Represented Lancashire Federation 1979–81. Played for England U-19 v India U-19

in three 'Tests' in 1981. Young England v West Indies (three 'Tests') and two One-Day 'Internationals'. Debut for Lancashire v Cambridge University at Fenners. In 1984 changed from left-arm medium pace to slow left-arm bowler
Opinions on cricket: 'Four-day cricket only lasts four days if better pitches are prepared for playing on than were prepared in 1988. Over rate fines should be less severe. The "fixture computer" needs a complete overhaul!'
Best batting performance: 69 Lancashire v Yorkshire, Old Trafford 1985
Best bowling performance: 7-15 Lancashire v Warwickshire, Southport 1987

LAST SEASON: BATTING

	I.	N.O.	R.	H.S.	AV.
TEST					
1ST-CLASS	20	14	102	30	17.00
INT					
RAL					
NAT.W.					
B & H					

LAST SEASON: BOWLING

	O.	M.	R.	W.	AV.
TEST					
1ST-CLASS	614.3	168	1701	57	29.84
INT					
RAL					
NAT.W.					
B & H					

CAREER: BATTING

	I.	N.O.	R.	H.S.	AV.
TEST					
1ST-CLASS	152	48	1353	69	13.00
INT					
RAL	10	6	56	19	14.00
NAT.W.	2	1	4	3*	4.00
B & H	5	5	21	11*	—

CAREER: BOWLING

	O.	M.	R.	W.	AV.
TEST					
1ST-CLASS	3106.4	860	8343	276	30.22
INT					
RAL	144	5	703	14	50.21
NAT.W.	39.3	4	114	7	16.28
B & H	84	17	215	14	15.36

FORDHAM, A.   Northamptonshire

Full Name: Alan Fordham
Role: Right-hand bat, occasional right-arm medium pace bowler
Born: 9 November 1964, Bedford
Height: 6' ½" **Weight:** 13st
Nickname: Forders
County debut: 1986
1st-Class 50s scored: 3
1st-Class 100s scored: 1
Place in batting averages: 114th av. 27.69
1st-Class catches 1988: 13 (career 13)
Parents: Clifford and Ruth
Marital status: Single
Family links with cricket: Brother John played school and college cricket
Education: Bedford Modern School, 1973–83; Durham University, 1984–87

Qualifications: 9 O-levels, 3 A-levels, BSc Honours Degree in Chemistry
Off-season 1988–89: Working in a laboratory. Working and cricketing in Perth, Western Australia
Overseas tours: Barbados, 1983, with Bedford Modern School; Jersey and Guernsey, 1987, with Gentlemen of Leicestershire Cricket Club
Overseas teams played for: Camberwell CC, Melbourne, Australia 1987–88; Curtin University CC, Perth, Australia 1988–89
Cricketers particularly learnt from: Andy Curtis, Brian Reynolds, Bob Carter
Cricketers particularly admired: Allan Lamb, Bob Willis
Other sports played: Squash, used to play table tennis
Other sports followed: Rugby union and most other sports
Relaxations: Rock music, TV
Extras: Also plays for Bedfordshire in Minor Counties Championship where possible
Best batting performance: 125* Northamptonshire v Surrey, The Oval 1988

LAST SEASON: BATTING

	I.	N.O.	R.	H.S.	AV.
TEST					
1ST-CLASS	29	6	637	125*	27.69
INT					
RAL	4	0	67	30	16.75
NAT.W.					
B & H					

CAREER: BATTING

	I.	N.O.	R.	H.S.	AV.
TEST					
1ST-CLASS	32	6	663	125*	25.50
INT					
RAL	4	0	67	30	16.75
NAT.W.					
B & H					

FOSTER, D. J. Somerset

Full Name: Daren Joseph Foster
Role: Right-hand bat, right-arm fast medium bowler
Born: 14 March 1966, London
Height: 5' 9" **Weight:** 9½st
Nickname: DJ
County debut: 1986
Place in batting averages: 119th av. 37.28
Place in bowling averages: —
(1987 107th av. 37.69)
1st-Class catches 1988: 3 (career 3)
Parents: Vivian and Sadie
Children: Marcella and Daren
Education: Somerset School; Southgate Technical College

Qualifications: 2 O-levels, 1 CSE. Pre-vocational Studies pass. Commercial Studies pass and credit
Off-season 1988–89: Playing in Australia
Overseas teams played for: Geelong, Victoria
Cricketers particularly learnt from: Malcolm Marshall, Hallam Moseley
Cricketers particularly admired: Malcolm Marshall, Michael Holding, Gary Sobers, Viv Richards, Ian Botham, Clive Lloyd
Other sports played: Basketball, table tennis
Injuries 1988: Torn ligament in ankle
Other sports followed: American football, athletics
Relaxations: Music
Extras: Appeared for Middlesex and Surrey 2nd XI's in 1985
Best batting performance: 20 Somerset v Hampshire, Southampton 1988
Best bowling performance: 4-46 Somerset v Worcestershire, Worcester 1988

LAST SEASON: BATTING

	I.	N.O.	R.	H.S.	AV.
TEST					
1ST-CLASS	14	9	72	20	14.40
INT					
RAL	2	2	2	2*	–
NAT.W.					
B & H	–	–	–	–	–

CAREER: BATTING

	I.	N.O.	R.	H.S.	AV.
TEST					
1ST-CLASS	18	10	97	20	12.12
INT					
RAL	3	3	5	3*	–
NAT.W.					
B & H	–	–	–	–	–

LAST SEASON: BOWLING

	O.	M.	R.	W.	AV.
TEST					
1ST-CLASS	299.3	46	1044	28	37.28
INT					
RAL	29	1	123	5	24.60
NAT.W.					
B & H	11	0	57	1	57.00

CAREER: BOWLING

	O.	M.	R.	W.	AV.
TEST					
1ST-CLASS	416.2	56	1563	41	38.12
INT					
RAL	49	2	213	5	42.60
NAT.W.					
B & H	11	0	57	1	57.00

70. Which current county player has as one of his relaxations, keeping rabbits?

FOSTER, N. A.   Essex

Full Name: Neil Alan Foster
Role: Right-hand bat, right-arm
fast-medium bowler, outfielder
Born: 6 May 1962, Colchester
Height: 6' 4" **Weight:** 12st 12lbs
Nickname: Fozzy, Stick Insect
County debut: 1980
County cap: 1983
Test debut: 1983
No. of Tests: 25
No. of One-Day Internationals: 45
1st-Class 50s scored: 5
1st-Class 5 w. in innings: 34
1st-Class 10 w. in match: 6
One-Day 50s: 4
Place in batting averages: 262nd
av. 10.05 (1987 175th av. 19.95)
Place in bowling averages: 32nd av. 22.77 (1987 16th av. 22.00)
Strike rate 1988: 44.88 (career 41.59)
1st-Class catches 1988: 8 (career 64)
Parents: Jean and Alan
Wife and date of marriage: Romany, 21 September 1985
Family links with cricket: Father and brother both play local cricket
Education: Broomgrove Infant & Junior Schools; Philip Morant Comprehensive, Colchester
Qualifications: 9 O-levels, 1 A-level, NCA Coaching Award
Jobs outside cricket: Played semi-pro football for some years
Off-season 1988–89: Chosen for cancelled tour of India. 'Decorating the house instead.'
Overseas tours: NCA tour of Canada 1978; Young England XI tour of West Indies 1980; England tour of New Zealand and Pakistan 1983–84, India and Australia 1984–85, West Indies 1986; World Cup, Pakistan, Australia and New Zealand 1987–88
Overseas teams played for: Glenorchy (Tasmania) 1981–82 on Whitbread Scholarship
Cricketers particularly learnt from: All Essex players
Cricketers particularly admired: Dennis Lillee, Richard Hadlee, Imran Khan
Other sports played: Nearly any sport. Has had football trials with Colchester and Ipswich. Golf. 'Nothing horsey.'
Injuries 1988: Knee injury
Relaxations: 'My Boxer dog – Bertie; kennel name: Tropical Burlington Bertie. Playing golf. Avoiding work around the house.'
Extras: Was summoned from school at short notice to play for Essex v Kent at

Ilford to open bowling. First ball went for 4 wides, but he went on to dismiss Woolmer, Tavaré and Ealham for 51 runs in 15 overs. Played for Young England v Young India 1981

Opinions on cricket: 'I'm fed up seeing all the critics always complaining about our performances. This does not just apply to cricket but all our sports with national sides. Those critics build people up to knock them down and I find it incredible that they get paid to do just that. It's about time we gave people a fair chance and showed them some loyalty. Roll-on four-day cricket. As long as the nights are good, it can only be good for the game. Come on, Lord's, stop stalling!'

Best batting performance: 74* England v Queensland, Brisbane 1986–87
Best bowling performance: 8-107 England v Pakistan, Leeds 1987

LAST SEASON: BATTING

	I.	N.O.	R.	H.S.	AV.
TEST	5	2	63	34	21.00
1ST-CLASS	16	2	108	22	7.71
INT	–	–	–	–	–
RAL	4	1	42	40	14.00
NAT.W.	1	0	12	12	12.00
B & H	1	1	9	9*	–

LAST SEASON: BOWLING

	O.	M.	R.	W.	AV.
TEST	127.2	27	399	14	28.50
1ST-CLASS	471.1	95	1423	66	21.56
INT	11	0	47	0	–
RAL	38	2	110	5	22.00
NAT.W.	12	0	51	3	17.00
B & H	22	6	68	2	34.00

CAREER: BATTING

	I.	N.O.	R.	H.S.	AV.
TEST	37	5	342	39	10.68
1ST-CLASS	138	35	2073	74*	20.12
INT	24	11	145	24	11.15
RAL	22	7	243	40	16.20
NAT.W.	8	1	112	26	16.00
B & H	12	6	135	37*	22.50

CAREER: BOWLING

	O.	M.	R.	W.	AV.
TEST	846.3	190	2376	76	31.26
1ST-CLASS	3160.3	725	11564	502	23.03
INT	405.5	23	1706	52	32.80
RAL	294.1	19	1308	56	23.35
NAT.W.	152.2	26	441	28	15.75
B & H	266.3	27	971	48	20.22

FOWLER, G. Lancashire

Full Name: Graeme Fowler
Role: Left-hand opening bat, cover fielder, occasional wicket-keeper
Born: 20 April 1957, Accrington
Height: 5′ 9″ **Weight:** 'Near 11st'
Nickname: Fow, Fox, Foxy
County debut: 1979
County cap: 1981
Test debut: 1982
No. of Tests: 21
No. of One-Day Internationals: 26
1000 runs in a season: 7
1st-Class 50s scored: 67
1st-Class 100s scored: 25
1st-Class 200s scored: 2

One-Day 50s: 27
One-Day 100s: 5
Place in batting averages: 87th av. 30.64 (1987 15th av. 47.36)
1st-Class catches 1988: 19 (career 103 + 5 stumpings)
Education: Accrington Grammar School; Bede College, Durham University
Wife: Stephanie
Jobs outside cricket: Qualified teacher, swimming teacher, Advanced Cricket Coach
Cricketing superstitions or habits: Checks grip before every ball. Likes to chatter away while batting
Overseas tours: England to Australia and New Zealand 1982–83; New Zealand and Pakistan 1983–84; India and Australia 1984–85
Overseas teams played for: Scarborough, Perth, Western Australia; Tasmania, 1981–82
Relaxations: Photography
Extras: At 15 he was the youngest opener in the Lancashire League. Scored two consecutive centuries v Warwickshire in July 1982 with aid of a runner. Never played cricket until he was 12. Played for Accrington and Rawtenstall in Lancashire League. In 1975 and 1976 played for ESCA, NAYC, and MCC Schools and Young England. Published *Fox on the Run*, a cricketing diary from 1984 to 1986, in 1988. First Englishman to score a double century in India
Best batting performance: 226 Lancashire v Kent, Maidstone 1984
Best bowling performance: 2-34 Lancashire v Warwickshire, Old Trafford 1986

LAST SEASON: BATTING

	I.	N.O.	R.	H.S.	AV.
TEST					
1ST-CLASS	38	1	1134	172	30.64
INT					
RAL	13	0	279	70	21.46
NAT.W.	2	0	73	38	36.50
B & H	4	0	126	66	31.50

CAREER: BATTING

	I.	N.O.	R.	H.S.	AV.
TEST	37	0	1307	201	35.32
1ST-CLASS	300	16	10526	226	37.06
INT	26	2	744	81*	31.00
RAL	107	7	2836	112	28.36
NAT.W.	19	0	603	122	31.73
B & H	39	1	937	97	24.65

LAST SEASON: BOWLING

	O.	M.	R.	W.	AV.
TEST					
1ST-CLASS					
INT					
RAL					
NAT.W.					
B & H					

CAREER: BOWLING

	O.	M.	R.	W.	AV.
TEST	3	1	11	0	–
1ST-CLASS	36.5	5	160	7	22.85
INT					
RAL	1	0	1	0	–
NAT.W.					
B & H					

Full Name: Alastair Gregory James Fraser
Role: Right-hand bat, right-arm fast medium bowler
Born: 17 October 1967, Edgware
Height: 6′ 1″ **Weight:** 12st 7lbs
Nickname: Junior
County debut: 1986
Parents: Irene and Don
Marital status: Single
Family links with cricket: Brother Angus on Middlesex staff. Dad played club cricket, Mum keen follower
Education: Gayton High School; John Lyon School, Harrow Weald 6th Form College
Qualifications: 4 O-levels; qualified coach
Jobs outside cricket: Michael Waite's chauffeur
Off-season 1988–89: With Greenpoint CC, Cape Town, South Africa
Overseas tours: England Young Cricketers to Sri Lanka 1987; U-19 NCA to South Bermuda 1985
Overseas teams played for: Plimmerton CC, Wellington, New Zealand 1986–87 and 1987–88
Cricketers particularly learnt from: Don Bennett, Gordon Jenkins
Cricketers particularly admired: Malcolm Marshall, Ian Botham
Other sports played: Football – Southern Amateur League
Other sports followed: Rugby, football

LAST SEASON: BATTING

	I.	N.O.	R.	H.S.	AV.
TEST					
1ST-CLASS	2	1	19	14	19.00
INT					
RAL					
NAT.W.					
B & H					

LAST SEASON: BOWLING

	O.	M.	R.	W.	AV.
TEST					
1ST-CLASS	28	6	82	1	82.00
INT					
RAL					
NAT.W.					
B & H					

CAREER: BATTING

	I.	N.O.	R.	H.S.	AV.
TEST					
1ST-CLASS	5	3	51	19*	25.50
INT					
RAL	1	1	2	2*	–
NAT.W.					
B & H					

CAREER: BOWLING

	O.	M.	R.	W.	AV.
TEST					
1ST-CLASS	84.4	21	247	9	27.44
INT					
RAL	21	0	80	2	40.00
NAT.W.					
B & H					

Injuries 1988: Had glandular fever at the start of the season. Back injury mid-season, missed a month

Relaxations: Watching Liverpool FC when possible, snooker

Opinions on cricket: 'Have realised over the last two years how hard the game is! One overseas player per county staff. 16 four-day games means that the best side generally wins and it's not contrived by declarations meaning silly cricket! England should not be dictated to and told where their players can and cannot play cricket.'

Best batting performance: 19* Middlesex v Warwickshire, Uxbridge 1986

Best bowling performance: 3-46 Middlesex v New Zealaned, Lord's 1986

FRASER, A. R. C.   **Middlesex**

Full Name: Angus Robert Charles Fraser

Role: Right-hand bat, right-arm fast-medium bowler; short-leg and silly-point specialist

Born: 8 August 1965, Billinge, Lancashire

Height: 6' 6" **Weight:** 15st 7lbs

Nickname: Gus, Gnat, Jacques Cousteau ('due to a bad round of golf in La Manga'), Boots, Plod

County debut: 1984

1st-Class 5 w. in innings: 6

1st-Class 10 w. in match: 2

Place in batting averages: 246th av. 12.38 (1987 240th av. 11.88)

Place in bowling averages: 11th av. 19.37 (1987 92nd av. 34.22)

Strike rate 1988: 52.13 (career 54.39)

1st-Class catches 1988: 1 (career 5)

Parents: Don and Irene

Marital status: Single

Family links with cricket: Father played and is now keen follower of cricket; brother Alastair on Middlesex staff. 'Mum is good at cleaning whites!'

Education: Gayton High School, Harrow; Orange High School, Edgware

Qualifications: 7 O-levels, coaching certificate

Jobs outside cricket: Worked at Makro in North Acton 1984–85; labouring for Norwest Holst Construction Ltd 1986–87. Reconciliation officer for National Bank, New Zealand, 1987–88

Off-season 1988–89: Playing for Western Suburbs CC in Sydney

Cricketing superstitions or habits: 'Change in same place at most grounds. Tend to bowl into the wind or up-hill, more often than not.'

Overseas tours: Barbados with Thames Valley Gentlemen 1985; La Manga with Middlesex 1985 and 1986; Lords Taverners to Hong Kong, 1988

Overseas teams played for: Plimmerton CC, Wellington 1985–86, 1987–88; Western Suburbs CC, Sydney 1988–89

Cricketers particularly learnt from: Don Bennett, Don Wilson, Clive Desmond, Norman Jacobs

Cricketers particularly admired: Dennis Lillee, Richard Hadlee, Michael Holding

Other sports played: Rugby, golf, football

Other sports followed: 'Most except horse racing.'

Injuries 1988: Strain in left groin and calf

Relaxations: Playing other sports, watching Liverpool FC, driving, talking cricket

Extras: Took 3 wickets in 4 balls v Glamorgan in 1985. Hat-trick in B & H Cup v Sussex, 1988. Nixdorf Computers Middlesex Player of the Year, 1988. Has size 13 boots specially made!

Opinions on cricket: 'The number of overseas players should be reduced to a maximum of one per county as it is getting ridiculous. If a county has three or four it could use the money to bring on youngsters. Overseas players should have to play a full season, why should they have it easier than our players? England should play who they like, where they like. If other countries don't like it, that's tough. England should not be told what to do by countries who haven't got their own house in order.'

Best batting performance: 41 Middlesex v Sri Lanka, Lord's 1988

Best bowling performance: 6-68 Middlesex v Hampshire, Basingstoke 1988

LAST SEASON: BATTING

	I.	N.O.	R.	H.S.	AV.
TEST					
1ST-CLASS	27	9	223	41	12.38
INT					
RAL	6	4	41	30*	20.50
NAT.W.	–	–	–	–	–
B & H	4	2	27	13*	13.50

LAST SEASON: BOWLING

	O.	M.	R.	W.	AV.
TEST					
1ST-CLASS	695.1	154	1550	80	19.37
INT					
RAL	113	10	383	22	17.40
NAT.W.	58.4	16	144	12	12.00
B & H	54	10	210	6	35.00

CAREER: BATTING

	I.	N.O.	R.	H.S.	AV.
TEST					
1ST-CLASS	57	15	467	41	11.11
INT					
RAL	17	8	81	30*	9.00
NAT.W.	–	–	–	–	–
B & H	7	2	33	13*	6.60

CAREER: BOWLING

	O.	M.	R.	W.	AV.
TEST					
1ST-CLASS	1296.3	349	3669	143	25.65
INT					
RAL	281	20	1114	39	28.56
NAT.W.	70.4	21	168	13	12.92
B & H	114	15	416	9	46.22

FRASER-DARLING, D. Nottinghamshire

Full Name: David Fraser-Darling
Role: Right-hand bat, right-arm fast-medium bowler
Born: 30 September 1963, Sheffield
Height: 6′ 5″ **Weight:** 14st 7lbs
Nickname: Meat, Axe, Lazer, Beefy
County debut: 1984
1st-Class 50s scored: 1
1st-Class 5 w. in innings: 1
1st-Class catches 1988: 2 (career 11)
Parents: Alasdair and Mary
Marital status: Single
Education: Edinburgh University
Qualifications: 7 O-levels, 3 A-levels, Junior Cricket Coach
Jobs outside cricket: Coaching
Cricketing superstitions or habits: Left sock, shoe, pad, etc on first
Overseas teams played for: Upper Hutt CC, Wellington, New Zealand 1987–88
Cricketers particularly learnt from: Mike Hendrick, David Stanley, Tony Dyer and all at Nottinghamshire
Cricketers particularly admired: Mike Hendrick, Richard Hadlee, Geoff Boycott
Other sports played: Football, rugby, golf – 'of a low standard'
Other sports followed: Rugby, horse racing, American football
Relaxations: Eating out in poor restaurants, TV, films
Extras: Played rugby for Scotland U-19 v England, Wales and Ireland 1981. Released at end of 1988 season

LAST SEASON: BATTING

	I.	N.O.	R.	H.S.	AV.
TEST					
1ST-CLASS	1	0	18	18	18.00
INT					
RAL	3	1	29	10*	14.50
NAT.W.					
B & H					

CAREER: BATTING

	I.	N.O.	R.	H.S.	AV.
TEST					
1ST-CLASS	12	2	242	61	24.20
INT					
RAL	9	2	60	11	8.57
NAT.W.					
B & H	–	–	–	–	–

LAST SEASON: BOWLING

	O.	M.	R.	W.	AV.
TEST					
1ST-CLASS	12	4	30	0	–
INT					
RAL	32	0	191	6	31.83
NAT.W.					
B & H					

CAREER: BOWLING

	O.	M.	R.	W.	AV.
TEST					
1ST-CLASS	226	38	876	17	51.52
INT					
RAL	85	4	463	18	25.72
NAT.W.					
B & H	3	0	12	0	–

Best batting performance: 61 Nottinghamshire v Northamptonshire, Northampton 1986
Best bowling performance: 5-84 Nottinghamshire v Northamptonshire, Northampton 1986

FRENCH, B. N.   Nottinghamshire

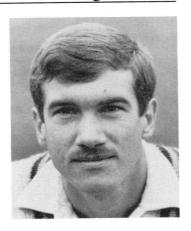

Full Name: Bruce Nicholas French
Role: Right-hand bat, wicket-keeper
Born: 13 August 1959, Warsop, Nottinghamshire
Height: 5′ 8″ **Weight:** 10st
Nickname: Frog
County debut: 1976
County cap: 1980
Test debut: 1986
No. of Tests: 16
No. of One-Day Internationals: 13
1st-Class 50s scored: 18
Place in batting averages: —
(1987 173rd av. 20.27)
Parents: Maurice and Betty
Wife and date of marriage:
Ellen Rose, 9 March 1978
Children: Charles Daniel,
31 August 1978; Catherine Ellen,
28 December 1980
Family links with cricket: Brothers, Neil, David, Charlie, Joe, played for Welbeck CC. Father, Treasurer Welbeck CC. In 1988 Neil played for Lincolnshire.
Education: Meden School, Warsop
Qualifications: O-level and CSE
Jobs outside cricket: Warehouseman, window cleaner, bricklayer's labourer
Overseas tours: England to India and Sri Lanka 1984–85; West Indies 1985–86; Australia 1986–87; World Cup, Pakistan, Australia and New Zealand 1987–88
Cricketing superstitions or habits: Right pad on before left when keeping wicket
Cricketers particularly learnt from: Bob Taylor, Clive Rice
Other sports played: Rock climbing, fell walking and all aspects of mountaineering
Injuries 1988: Missed most of the season following operations in May on index finger of left hand. 'I broke this index finger two years ago and it gave me a lot

of trouble in pre-season work in the nets. The specialist strongly advised immediate surgery to fuse the split bone on the top joint of the finger.'

(French has had a run of extraordinary bad luck with injuries. In 1986 on tour with England in the West Indies he was bitten by a dog whilst jogging. During the Second Test at Lord's in 1986 he had to be carried off the field with a cut head and concussion, after being struck by a short-pitched delivery from Richard Hadlee. In Australia, 1986–87, he was hit in the chest by a ball and later contracted a chest infection. On the 1987–88 winter tour of Pakistan he needed stitches in a cut eye after being hit by a spectator's throw during a practice session. On the way to hospital a car struck his legs and then after treatment he banged his head on a light fitting. In 1988 he missed the Third Test against Pakistan because of chicken pox.)

Relaxations: Reading, pipe smoking and drinking Theakston's Ale

Extras: Youngest player to play for Nottinghamshire, aged 16 years 10 months. Equalled Nottinghamshire record for dismissals in match with 10 (7ct 3st), and dismissals in innings with 6 catches. New Nottinghamshire record for dismissals in a season with 87 (75ct 12st). Wicket-Keeper of the Year 1984

Best batting performance: 98 Nottinghamshire v Lancashire, Trent Bridge 1984

LAST SEASON: BATTING

	I.	N.O.	R.	H.S.	AV.
TEST					
1ST-CLASS	11	1	135	28	13.50
INT					
RAL	3	1	58	23	29.00
NAT.W.					
B & H	–	–	–	–	–

LAST SEASON: WICKET KEEPING

	C.	ST.
TEST		
1ST-CLASS	13	–
INT		
RAL	4	–
NAT.W.		
B & H	4	–

CAREER: BATTING

	I.	N.O.	R.	H.S.	AV.
TEST	21	4	308	59	18.11
1ST-CLASS	313	61	4715	98	18.71
INT	8	3	34	9*	6.80
RAL	67	22	637	37	14.15
NAT.W.	18	5	291	49	22.38
B & H	29	6	219	48*	9.52

CAREER: WICKET KEEPING

	C.	ST.
TEST	38	1
1ST-CLASS	558	60
INT	13	3
RAL	79	12
NAT.W.	28	4
B & H	44	8

71. Which current county cricketer was an undertaker's assistant?

FROST, M. Surrey

Full Name: Mark Frost
Role: Bowler
Born: 21 October 1962, Barking
Height: 6' 2" **Weight:** 14st
Nickname: Harold, Frosty, 'H'
County debut: 1988
1st-Class catches 1988: 1 (career 1)
Parents: George and Joyce
Marital status: Single
Family links with cricket: All
three brothers play
Education: Alexandra High, Tipton;
St Peters, Wolverhampton; University
of Durham
Qualifications: 10 O-levels,
4 A-levels, Hons Degree in Geography
Jobs outside cricket: Senior Buyer,
Lucas Electrical
Off-season 1988–89: Getting my
ankle back in shape and working in sales for SCS, a computer stationery
company
Overseas tours: India 1985, Christians in Sport; Sharjah 1988, Surrey pre-
season tour
Cricketers particularly learnt from: Jack Breakwell, Andy Webster, Mushtaq
Mohammed, Ron Headley, Geoff Arnold
Cricketers particularly admired: Michael Holding, Phil Oliver, Neil Stuart,
Chris Derham, Nick Peters
Other sports played: Football, goalkeeper for Tipton Green Juniors
Other sports followed: Soccer, rugby, tennis, athletics

LAST SEASON: BATTING

	I.	N.O.	R.	H.S.	AV.
TEST					
1ST-CLASS	4	0	11	7	2.75
INT					
RAL					
NAT.W.					
B & H					

CAREER: BATTING

	I.	N.O.	R.	H.S.	AV.
TEST					
1ST-CLASS	4	0	11	7	2.75
INT					
RAL					
NAT.W.					
B & H					

LAST SEASON: BOWLING

	O.	M.	R.	W.	AV.
TEST					
1ST-CLASS	99.5	23	326	10	32.60
INT					
RAL					
NAT.W.					
B & H					

CAREER: BOWLING

	O.	M.	R.	W.	AV.
TEST					
1ST-CLASS	99.5	23	326	10	32.60
INT					
RAL					
NAT.W.					
B & H					

Injuries 1988: Tendon inflammation in ankle – 'never got rid of it!'
Relaxations: Hill walking, climbing, Banks' beer, compact discs
Extras: Member of Christians in Sport. Played for Old Hill CC in Birmingham League 'when we won the National Knockout "Cockspur Cup" in 1987' and for Staffs before joining Surrey. Played for League Cricket Conference against Rest of the World XI 1987
Opinions on cricket: 'Nationally sponsored youth schemes don't solve the problems of the "dreadful" state of cricket in comprehensive schools.'
Best batting performance: 7 Surrey v Sri Lankans, The Oval 1988
Best bowling performance: 4-56 Surrey v Cambridge University, Cambridge 1988

GARNHAM, M. A.   Essex

Full Name: Michael Anthony Garnham
Role: Right-hand bat, wicket-keeper
Born: 20 August 1960, Johannesburg, South Africa
Height: 5' 10" **Weight:** 11st
Nickname: Fred
County debut: 1979 (Gloucestershire), 1980 (Leicestershire)
1st-Class 50s scored: 11
1st-Class 100s scored: 1
One-Day 50s: 2
One-Day 100s: 1
Parents: Pauline Anne and Robert Arthur (divorced)
Wife and date of marriage: Lorraine, 15 September 1984
Family links with cricket: Father was a club cricketer in Essex.
He lost the sight of an eye keeping wicket
Education: Camberwell Grammar, Melbourne, Australia; Scotch College, Perth, Australia; Park School, Barnstaple, North Devon; North Devon College; University of East Anglia (for one year)
Qualifications: 10 O-levels, 2 A-levels
Overseas tours: England Schools tour of India 1977–78; Young England tour of Australia 1979
Overseas teams played for: Melbourne University & North Sydney 1979–80 (as prize for Young Wicketkeeper of the Year award, 1979); Glenelg, South Australia, 1980–81

Cricketers particularly learnt from: Brian Roe (ex-Somerset), Alan Knott, Bob Taylor
Other sports played: Squash
Other sports followed: Athletics
Relaxations: Carpentry, DIY, music, reading
Extras: Moved to England in 1975 after living in Australia for ten years and in South Africa for four years. Played for Devon in 1976 and 1977 (possibly youngest ever) before joining Gloucstershire. Signed for Leicestershire in 1980 and was banned by the registration committee from competitive first-team cricket for a month for breach of registration regulations. Played for Gloucestershire 2nd XI since 1976, making John Player League debut in 1978 v Warwickshire at Birmingham and Championship debut in 1979. Retired at end of 1985. Returned for five one-day games in 1988 following injury to Phil Whitticase. Signed for Essex in 1989
Best batting performance: 100 Leicester v Oxford University, Oxford 1985

LAST SEASON: BATTING

	I.	N.O.	R.	H.S.	AV.
TEST					
1ST-CLASS	–	–	–	–	–
INT					
RAL	1	0	0	0	0.00
NAT.W.	1	0	110	110	110.00
B & H	3	1	24	13*	12.00

CAREER: BATTING

	I.	N.O.	R.	H.S.	AV.
TEST					
1ST-CLASS	104	18	2083	100	24.22
INT					
RAL	64	13	893	79*	17.50
NAT.W.	12	3	278	110	30.88
B & H	24	8	365	55	22.81

LAST SEASON: WICKET KEEPING

	C.	ST.			
TEST					
1ST-CLASS	2	–			
INT					
RAL					
NAT.W.	–	–			
B & H	–	2			

CAREER: WICKET KEEPING

	C.	ST.			
TEST					
1ST-CLASS	162	23			
INT					
RAL	77	10			
NAT.W.	8	1			
B & H	26	3			

72. In what newspaper did the original mention of The Ashes occur, and in what year?

GATTING, M. W.   Middlesex

Full Name: Michael William Gatting
Role: Right-hand bat, right-arm medium bowler, slip fielder
Born: 6 June 1957, Kingsbury, Middlesex
Height: 5′ 10″ **Weight:** 14st
Nickname: Gatt
County debut: 1975
County cap: 1977
Benefit: 1988
Test debut: 1977–78
No. of Tests: 67
No. of One-Day Internationals: 82
1000 runs in a season: 10
1st-Class 50s scored: 109
1st-Class 100s scored: 46
1st-Class 200s scored: 4
1st-Class 5 w. in innings: 2
One-Day 50s: 51
One-Day 100s: 6
Place in batting averages: 19th av. 47.38 (1987 4th av. 60.96)
1st-Class catches 1988: 15 (career 295)
Parents: Bill and Vera
Wife and date of marriage: Elaine, September 1980
Children: Andrew, 21 January 1983; James, 11 July 1986
Family links with cricket: Father used to play club cricket. Brother, Steve, played for Middlesex 2nd XI
Education: Wykeham Primary School; John Kelly Boys' High School
Qualifications: 4 O-levels
Jobs outside cricket: Part-time plumber
Off-season 1988–89: 'Helping to complete my benefit year. Spending time with my wife and two sons.'
Overseas tours: Whitbread scholarship to Australia with Balmain CC. Toured West Indies with England Young Cricketers 1979–80; with England in West Indies 1981 and 1986; India 1981–82; New Zealand and Pakistan 1983–84; World Cup, Pakistan, Australia and New Zealand 1987–88
Overseas teams played for: Club cricket in Sydney, Australia 1979–80
Cricketers particularly learnt from: Ken Barrington, Mike Brearley
Cricketers particularly admired: Sir Gary Sobers, Sir Leonard Hutton
Other sports played: Football, tennis, swimming, golf, squash
Injuries 1988: Broken toe, broken thumb
Relaxations: Reading science fiction thrillers, 'hooked on Tolkien' and a great

fan of 'Dr Who'; music, including Beethoven, Holst, singing Elton John songs – 'the only music I positively dislike is punk rock and heavy metal.'

Extras: Awarded OBE in Queen's Birthday Honours for services to cricket. Played for England Young Cricketers 1974. Young Cricketer of the Year 1981. Captain of Middlesex since 1983. Captain of England from 1986 to 1988, when he was dropped during the Test series v West Indies. Author of *Limited Overs*, *Triumph in Australia* and autobiography *Leading From the Front*, 1988. Won a bronze medal for ballroom dancing at the Neasden Ritz, as did his brother, Steve. Played football for Edgware FC as a teenager. At school was goalkeeper, but also played centre-half for Brent Schools and then Middlesex Schools. Was wicket-keeper at school, though bowled as well. Played cricket for Middlesex U-15s for two seasons. Played for England Schools v Public Schools and hit a century. Gatting was recommended to West Ham in his 5th year at school, but nothing came of it. Had a junior trial for Queen's Park Rangers. By then Steve had played for Arsenal and Southampton. Mike was offered an apprenticeship by Watford FC. One of *Wisden*'s Five Cricketers of the Year, 1983. Led England on victorious tour of Australia, 1986–87, when England won the Ashes, the Perth Challenge Cup and World Series Cup. Led England to victory against West Indies in Texaco One-Day Trophy, 1988. Was relieved of England captaincy after leading them to draw in First Test against West Indies, 1988, being the first time the West Indies had not beaten England in 14 consecutive matches.

Opinions on cricket: 'There seems to be far too much cricket compressed into our domestic season and with all the travelling involved, it leaves most of us rather jaded by the time September comes.'

Best batting performance: 258 Middlesex v Somerset, Bath 1984
Best bowling performance: 5-34 Middlesex v Glamorgan, Swansea 1982

LAST SEASON: BATTING

	I.	N.O.	R.	H.S.	AV.
TEST	4	0	38	29	9.50
1ST-CLASS	29	2	1431	210	53.00
INT	3	2	140	82*	140.00
RAL	11	1	302	105*	30.20
NAT.W.	5	1	196	80*	49.00
B & H	5	1	239	72	59.75

LAST SEASON: BOWLING

	O.	M.	R.	W.	AV.
TEST					
1ST-CLASS	96	22	287	4	71.75
INT					
RAL	10	0	77	1	77.00
NAT.W.	15.5	2	48	1	48.00
B & H	4.3	1	10	0	–

CAREER: BATTING

	I.	N.O.	R.	H.S.	AV.
TEST	115	14	3848	207	38.09
1ST-CLASS	411	62	17212	258	49.31
INT	79	17	1991	115*	32.11
RAL	135	15	3583	109	29.85
NAT.W.	41	10	1324	118*	42.70
B & H	56	16	1935	143*	48.37

CAREER: BOWLING

	O.	M.	R.	W.	AV.
TEST	1 124	0 29	317	4	79.25
1ST-CLASS	19.7 1340.4	3 318	3709	141	26.30
INT	64.2	4	334	10	33.40
RAL	423.5	12	2117	72	29.40
NAT.W.	158.2	23	584	17	34.35
B & H	195.2	16	772	37	20.86

GIFFORD, N. Warwickshire

Full Name: Norman Gifford
Role: Left-hand bat, slow left-arm bowler
Born: 30 March 1940, Ulverston, Cumbria
Height: 5′ 10″ **Weight:** 13st 7lbs
Nickname: Giff
County debut: 1960 (Worcestershire), 1983 (Warwickshire)
County cap: 1961 (Worcestershire), 1983 (Warwickshire)
Benefit: 1974 (£11,047)
Testimonial: 1981
Test debut: 1964
No. of Tests: 15
No. of One-Day Internationals: 2
1st-Class 50s scored: 3
1st-Class 5 w. in innings: 93
1st-Class 10 w. in match: 14
Place in batting averages: — (1987 251st av. 10.07)
Place in bowling averages: 92nd av. 31.48 (1987 77th av. 31.13)
Strike-rate 1988: 82.29 (career 62.08)
1st-Class catches 1988: 3 (career 319)
Family links with cricket: Father played amateur cricket and football, and was also cricket umpire
Qualifications: City & Guilds
Jobs outside cricket: Estimator, industrial decorating
Cricketers particularly learnt from: Charles Hallows (Worcestershire coach)

LAST SEASON: BATTING

	I.	N.O.	R.	H.S.	AV.
TEST					
1ST-CLASS	25	11	104	23*	7.42
INT					
RAL	2	2	2	2*	—
NAT.W.	1	1	3	3*	—
B & H	1	0	0	0	0.00

CAREER: BATTING

	I.	N.O.	R.	H.S.	AV.
TEST	20	9	179	25*	16.27
1ST-CLASS	785	255	6868	89	12.95
INT	1	0	0	0	0.00
RAL	139	62	952	32*	12.36
NAT.W.	34	8	224	38	8.61
B & H	43	14	300	33	10.34

LAST SEASON: BOWLING

	O.	M.	R.	W.	AV.
TEST					
1ST-CLASS	425.1	121	976	31	31.48
INT					
RAL	41	2	184	9	20.44
NAT.W.	12	0	27	1	27.00
B & H	28.5	6	92	6	15.33

CAREER: BOWLING

	O.	M.	R.	W.	AV.
TEST	146.4 514	14 17	1026	33	31.09
1ST-CLASS	20688.3	6968	47705	2035	23.44
INT	20	1	50	4	12.50
RAL	1671.4	98	7541	284	26.55
NAT.W.	491	104	1415	61	23.19
B & H	732.2	108	2465	93	26.50

Overseas tours: Rest of World to Australia 1971–72; India, Pakistan and Sri Lanka 1972–73; Sharjah 1985 as captain
Other sports: Football, golf
Relaxations: Horse racing
Extras: Was awarded MBE in 1979. Played in one match for Rest of World v Australia 1972. Suffers badly from the sun on overseas tours. Took 100 wickets in a season four times. Uncle, Harry Gifford, played rugby union for England. Released by Worcestershire at end of 1982 season. Debut 1960, cap 1961, captain 1971–80. England selector, and assistant manager of England side on tour. Warwickshire captain 1985–87. Retired at the end of 1988
Best batting performance: 89 Worcestershire v Oxford University, Oxford 1963
Best bowling performance: 8-28 Worcestershire v Yorkshire, Sheffield 1968

GOLDSMITH, S. C. Derbyshire

Full Name: Steven Clive Goldsmith
Role: Right-hand bat, right-arm medium or off-break bowler, cover fielder
Born: 19 December 1964, Ashford, Kent
Height: 5′ 10½″ **Weight:** 12st 7lbs
Nickname: Goldy
County debut: 1987 (Kent), 1988 (Derbyshire)
1000 runs in a season: 1
1st-Class 50s scored: 7
One-Day 50s: 1
Place in batting averages: 89th av. 39.60
1st-Class catches 1988: 16 (career 17)
Parents: Tony and Daphne
Marital status: Engaged
Family links with cricket: Father played for Folkestone, captaining them for a few years
Education: Simon Langton Grammar School, Canterbury
Qualifications: 8 O-levels, NCA Coaching Award
Jobs outside cricket: Bar Steward, waiter, undertaker's assistant
Cricketing superstitions or habits: 'I always buckle my pads on the same way and smoke a fair bit as well as biting my nails down to the elbows.'
Overseas tours: ESCA U-19 to Zimbabwe 1982–83; UK Upsetters to Trinidad and Tobago 1985

Overseas teams played for: Essendon, Melbourne 1984
Cricketers particularly learnt from: Colin Page, Chris Tavaré, Simon Hinks
Cricketers particularly admired: Chris Tavaré, David Gower, Eldine Baptiste
Other sports played: Hockey, golf, snooker – 'and anything else where a ball moves'
Other sports followed: All sports
Relaxations: Golf, serious drinking, comedy on TV, Van Morrison's music, Tony Hancock, Richard Pryor
Extras: Spent four years on Kent staff. Only wicket in first-class cricket was David Gower's. Released at end of 1987 season. Joined Derbyshire for 1988
Cricketing opinions: 'With the introduction of uncovered wickets, the bowlers' run-ups should also be uncovered. Four-day cricket would be a good idea but should be confined to say half the matches at the end of the season. All professional cricketers should be made to take an NCA Coaching Award.'
Best batting performance: 89 Derbyshire v Kent, Chesterfield 1988
Best bowling performance: 1-37 Kent v Leicestershire, Canterbury 1987

LAST SEASON: BATTING

	I.	N.O.	R.	H.S.	AV.
TEST					
1ST-CLASS	39	4	1071	89	30.60
INT					
RAL	14	1	299	61	23.00
NAT.W.	3	0	21	10	7.00
B & H	5	1	64	27*	16.00

CAREER: BATTING

	I.	N.O.	R.	H.S.	AV.
TEST					
1ST-CLASS	43	4	1120	89	28.71
INT					
RAL	17	2	348	61	23.20
NAT.W.	3	0	21	10	7.00
B & H	5	1	64	27*	16.00

GOOCH, G. A. Essex

Full Name: Graham Alan Gooch
Role: Right-hand bat, right-arm medium bowler
Born: 23 July 1953, Leytonstone
Height: 6' 0" **Weight:** 13st
Nickname: Zap, Goochie
County debut: 1973
County cap: 1975
Benefit: 1985 (£153,906)
Test debut: 1975
No. of Tests: 68
No. of One-Day Internationals: 67
1000 runs in a season: 12
1st-Class 50s scored: 138
1st-Class 100s scored: 61
1st-Class 200s scored: 5
1st-Class 5 w. in innings: 3

One-Day 50s: 83
One-Day 100s: 23
Place in batting averages: 5th av. 64.55 (1987 48th av. 38.88)
Place in bowling averages: 122nd av. 40.10 (1987 85th av. 32.71)
Strike rate 1988: 91.20 (career 73.31)
1st-Class catches 1988: 27 (career 379)
Parents: Alfred and Rose
Wife and date of marriage: Brenda, 23 October 1976
Children: Hannah, Megan, Sally
Family links with cricket: Father played local cricket for East Ham Corinthians. Second cousin, Graham Saville, played for Essex CCC and is now NCA coach for Eastern England
Education: Norlington Junior High School, Leytonstone
Qualifications: Four-year apprenticeship in toolmaking
Jobs outside cricket: Toolmaker
Off-season 1988–89: Was chosen as captain for cancelled tour of India
Overseas tours: West Indies with England Young Cricketers 1972; England to Australia 1978–79 and 1979–80; West Indies 1981 and 1986; India 1981–82; World Cup, Pakistan and New Zealand 1987–88
Overseas teams played for: Perth CC, Western Australia; Western Province, South Africa
Cricketers particularly admired: Bob Taylor, a model sportsman; Mike Procter for his enthusiasm; Barry Richards for his ability
Other sports played: Squash, soccer, golf. Trains in off-season with West Ham United FC
Injuries 1988: Dislocated finger
Relaxations: 'Relaxing at home.'
Extras: One of *Wisden*'s Five Cricketers of the Year, 1979. Published *Batting* in 1980. Wrote a diary of 1981 cricket year. Autobiography *Out of the Wilderness* published by Collins in 1985. Hit a century before lunch v Leicester, 28 June 1981. Kept wicket for England v India in 2nd innings at

LAST SEASON: BATTING

	I.	N.O.	R.	H.S.	AV.
TEST	12	0	570	146	47.50
1ST-CLASS	25	1	1754	275	73.08
INT	4	0	110	43	27.50
RAL	11	0	301	90	27.36
NAT.W.	2	0	141	71	70.50
B & H	6	2	398	120*	99.50

LAST SEASON: BOWLING

	O.	M.	R.	W.	AV.
TEST					
1ST-CLASS	152	39	401	10	40.10
INT	16	2	50	3	16.66
RAL	76	2	403	9	44.77
NAT.W.	17	3	40	3	13.33
B & H	65	7	249	7	35.57

CAREER: BATTING

	I.	N.O.	R.	H.S.	AV.
TEST	123	4	4541	196	38.15
1ST-CLASS	537	48	22204	275	45.40
INT	66	3	2615	142	41.50
RAL	186	16	5364	176	31.55
NAT.W.	35	1	1479	133	43.50
B & H	75	7	3405	198*	50.07

CAREER: BOWLING

	O.	M.	R.	W.	AV.
TEST	6 230.3	1 67	550	13	42.30
1ST-CLASS	1 2326.1	0 583	6318	197	32.07
INT	205.5	13	966	23	42.00
RAL	746.2	37	3400	118	28.81
NAT.W.	236.1	33	699	24	29.12
B & H	443.5	48	1487	51	29.15

Madras, 1982. Captained English rebel team in South Africa, 1982 and was banned from Test cricket for three years. Hit a hole in one at Tollygunge Golf Club during England's tour in India, 1981–82. Bowled both right and left handed in a Test match (v India at Calcutta, imitating Dilip Doshi). Shared in second wicket record partnership for county, 321 with K. S. McEwan v Northamptonshire, at Ilford in 1978. Holds record (jointly) for Essex for catches in match (6) and innings (5) v Gloucestershire, 1982. Appointed Essex captain 1986. Resigned captaincy at end of 1987 season. Captain of England for last two Tests against West Indies and Sri Lanka in 1988. Picked to captain England on the cancelled tour of India. Reappointed captain of Essex for 1989 following retirement of Keith Fletcher

Best batting performance: 275 Essex v Kent, Chelmsford 1988
Best bowling performance: 7-14 Essex v Worcestershire, Ilford 1982

GOULD, I. J. Sussex

Full Name: Ian James Gould
Role: Left-hand bat, wicket-keeper
Born: 19 August 1957, Taplow, Bucks
Height: 5′ 8″ **Weight:** 11st 12lbs
Nickname: Gunner
County debut: 1975 (Middlesex), 1981 (Sussex)
County cap: 1977 (Middlesex), 1981 (Sussex)
No. of One-Day Internationals: 18
1000 runs in a season: 1
1st-Class 50s scored: 38
1st-Class 100s scored: 3
One-Day 50s: 15
Place in batting averages: 76th av. 32.40 (1987 88th av. 33.00)

Parents: Doreen and George
Wife: Jo
Children: Gemma Louise, 30 June 1984
Family links with cricket: 'Brothers tried!'
Education: Westgate School
Jobs outside cricket: Barman. 'High class dole collector.'
Off-season 1988–89: Coaching in New Zealand
Overseas tours: West Indies with England Young Cricketers 1976; Derrick Robins' XI to Australia, New Zealand and Canada 1978–79; International XI to Pakistan 1980–81; with England in Australia and New Zealand 1982–83

Overseas teams played for: Auckland, 1979–80, 1987–88
Cricketers particularly learnt from: Jamie Hall
Cricketers particularly admired: Richard Hadlee
Other sports played: Amateur footballer for Slough Town FC at full-back; golf, swimming
Other sports followed: American football
Injuries 1988: Back injury; broken thumb
Relaxations: Spending time with the family. Drinking in pubs with the best lager
Extras: Made debut for Middlesex in 1975, gaining cap in 1977. Was offered contract for 1981 by Middlesex but chose to join Sussex. Vice-captain in 1985. Took over captaincy during 1986 and officially appointed for 1987. Resigned captaincy at end of 1987 season
Opinions on cricket: 'Stick to four-day cricket.'
Best batting performance: 128 Middlesex v Worcestershire, Worcester 1978
Best bowling performance: 2-48 Sussex v Hampshire, Eastbourne 1988

LAST SEASON: BATTING

	I.	N.O.	R.	H.S.	AV.
TEST					
1ST-CLASS	31	4	875	82*	32.40
INT					
RAL	12	1	167	59*	15.18
NAT.W.					
B & H	4	0	71	37	17.75

CAREER: BATTING

	I.	N.O.	R.	H.S.	AV.
TEST					
1ST-CLASS	354	57	7651	128	25.76
INT					
RAL	144	23	2241	74	18.52
NAT.W.	21	2	398	88	20.94
B & H	46	7	701	72	17.97

LAST SEASON: WICKET KEEPING

	C.	ST.
TEST		
1ST-CLASS	33	–
INT		
RAL	7	1
NAT.W.		
B & H	4	–

LAST SEASON: BOWLING

	O.	M.	R.	W.	AV.
TEST					
1ST-CLASS	21	2	84	2	42.00
INT					
RAL					
NAT.W.					
B & H					

CAREER: BOWLING

	O.	M.	R.	W.	AV.
TEST					
1ST-CLASS	61	4	305	4	76.25
INT					
RAL					
NAT.W.					
B & H	0.2	0	0	1	0.00

CAREER: WICKET KEEPING

	C.	ST.
TEST		
1ST-CLASS	510	67
INT		
RAL	135	22
NAT.W.	25	7
B & H	52	5

73. Who bowled the most overs in first-class cricket?

74. Who bowled the second most overs in first-class cricket?

GOULDSTONE, M. R. Northamptonshire

Full Name: Mark Roger Gouldstone
Role: Right-hand opening
bat, cover or short-leg
fielder
Born: 3 February 1963, Bishops
Stortford
Height: 6′ **Weight:** 12st
Nickname: Bladder
County debut: 1986
1st-Class 50s scored: 2
Place in batting averages: 172nd
av. 21.72
1st-Class catches 1988: 4 (career 4)
Parents: Roy
Marital status: Single
Family links with cricket: Father
played village cricket
Education: Newport Grammar
School, Essex; Braintree College
of Further Education
Qualifications: 6 O-levels
Off-season 1988–89: Working in England
Cricketing superstitions or habits: Left pad on first
Overseas tours: NCA U-19 tour to Denmark 1981
Overseas teams played for: Penrith CC, Australia 1981–82, 1982–83;
Uitenhage, South Africa 1985–86; Old Grey, South Africa 1987–88
Cricketers particularly learnt from: Duncan Wild
Cricketers particularly admired: Wayne Larkins
Other sports played: Soccer, squash
Other sports followed: Soccer, hockey
Relaxations: Soccer
Extras: Released by Northamptonshire at end of 1988 season
Opinions on cricket: 'Having just been released by Northants, I now appreci-
ate how much it meant to me to have my father show so much faith in me and
give me the confidence to score runs in first-class cricket. Get rid of overseas

LAST SEASON: BATTING

	I.	N.O.	R.	H.S.	AV.
TEST					
1ST-CLASS	12	1	239	71	21.72
INT					
RAL	5	0	34	11	6.80
NAT.W.					
B & H					

CAREER: BATTING

	I.	N.O.	R.	H.S.	AV.
TEST					
1ST-CLASS	13	1	274	71	22.83
INT					
RAL	6	0	38	11	6.33
NAT.W.					
B & H					

players. Too many people in the county game who are inadequate in carrying out their jobs efficiently.'
Best batting performance: 71 Northamptonshire v Essex, Northampton 1988

GOWER, D. I.   Leicestershire

Full Name: David Ivon Gower
Role: Left-hand bat,
off-break bowler
Born: 1 April 1957, Tunbridge
Wells
Height: 5′ 11¾″ **Weight:** 11st 11lbs
Nickname: Lubo, Shaggy
County debut: 1975
County cap: 1977
Benefit: 1987 (£121,546)
Test debut: 1978
No. of Tests: 100
No. of One-Day Internationals: 102
1000 runs in a season: 8
1st-Class 50s scored: 105
1st-Class 100s scored: 38
1st-Class 200s scored: 2
One-Day 50s: 43
One-Day 100s: 17

Place in batting averages: 41st av. 38.76 (1987 23rd av. 44.33)
1st-Class catches 1988: 16 (career 209 + 1 stumping)
Parents: Richard Hallam and Sylvia Mary
Marital status: Single
Family links with cricket: Father was club cricketer
Education: Marlborough House School; King's School, Canterbury; University College, London (did not complete law course)
Qualifications: 8 O-levels, 3 A-levels
Jobs outside cricket: Worked at Bostik Ltd
Off-season 1988–89: 'Waiting for a tour to happen!'
Cricketing superstitions or habits: 'They change every time they go wrong.'
Overseas tours: Toured South Africa with English Schools XI 1974–75 and West Indies with England Young Cricketers 1976; Derrick Robins XI to Canada 1976 and to Far East 1977; with England to Australia 1978–79 and 1979–80, West Indies 1980–1, India 1981–82, Australia and New Zealand 1982–83, New Zealand 1983–84, India and Australia 1984–85, West Indies 1986

Overseas teams played for: Claremont-Cottesloe, Perth, Australia, 1977–78
Cricketers particularly learnt from: 'Ray Illingworth and Jack Birkenshaw, amongst many others whose advice has come my way.'
Cricketers particularly admired: Graeme Pollock and many others
Other sports played: Golf, squash, water and snow skiing. Rode in a British bobsled at Cervinia (Italy) in 1985, diving
Other sports followed: Rugby, bob-sledding
Relaxations: Music, photographs, beaches, vintage port and crosswords
Extras: Played for King's Canterbury 1st XI for three years. One of *Wisden*'s Five Cricketers of the Year, 1978. Has written *Anyone for Cricket* jointly with Bob Taylor about the 1978–79 Australian tour. Also *With Time to Spare*, an autobiography published in 1980, and *Heroes and Contemporaries* (Collins) 1983, *A Right Ambition* (Collins) 1986. Writes regular column for *Wisden Cricket Monthly*. England captain 1984–86; Leicestershire captain 1984–86. Declared himself not available for England tour 1987–88. Reappointed Leicestershire captain for 1988
Best batting performance: 215 England v Australia, Edgbaston 1985
Best bowling performance: 3-47 Leicestershire v Essex, Leicester 1977

LAST SEASON: BATTING

	I.	N.O.	R.	H.S.	AV.
TEST	8	1	211	88*	30.14
1ST-CLASS	30	3	1107	172	41.00
INT					
RAL	11	1	124	50	12.40
NAT.W.	2	0	127	99	63.50
B & H	3	0	82	53	27.33

LAST SEASON: BOWLING

	O.	M.	R.	W.	AV.
TEST					
1ST-CLASS					
INT					
RAL					
NAT.W.	1	0	4	0	—
B & H					

CAREER: BATTING

	I.	N.O.	R.	H.S.	AV.
TEST	172	13	7000	215	44.02
1ST-CLASS	374	37	12890	187	38.24
INT	99	8	2905	158	31.92
RAL	130	20	4024	135*	36.58
NAT.W.	31	4	1392	156	51.55
B & H	48	5	1152	114*	26.79

CAREER: BOWLING

	O.	M.	R.	W.	AV.
TEST	6	1	20	1	20.00
1ST-CLASS	37.1	4	203	3	67.66
INT	0.5	0	14	0	—
RAL					
NAT.W.	2.3	0	16	0	—
B & H					

75. What was John Emburey's first Test Match?

GRAVENEY, D. A.   Gloucestershire

Full Name: David Anthony Graveney
Role: Right-hand bat, slow left-arm bowler
Born: 2 January 1953, Bristol
Height: 6′ 4″ **Weight:** 14st
Nickname: Gravity, Grav
County debut: 1972
County cap: 1976
Benefit: 1986
50 wickets in a season: 4
1st-Class 50s scored: 15
1st-Class 100s scored: 2
1st-Class 5 w. in innings: 31
1st-Class 10 w. in match: 5
One-Day 50s: 1
Place in batting averages: 227th av. 15.40
Place in bowling averages: 51st av. 25.52 (1987 70th av. 30.25)
Strike rate 1988: 69.32 (career 67.41)
1st-Class catches 1988: 6 (career 185)
Parents: Ken and Jeanne (deceased)

Wife and date of marriage: Julie, 23 September 1978
Children: Adam, 13 October 1982
Family links with cricket: Son of J. K. Graveney, captain of Gloucestershire, who took 10 wickets for 66 runs v Derbyshire at Chesterfield in 1949, and nephew of Tom Graveney of Gloucestershire, Worcestershire and England. Brother, John, selected for English Public Schools v English Schools at Lord's
Education: Millfield School, Somerset
Jobs outside cricket: Company director. Accountant
Other sports played: Golf, soccer, squash
Relaxations: 'Playing sport, TV and cinema. Relaxing at a good pub.'
Extras: Treasurer of the County Cricketers' Association. Captain of Gloucestershire, 1981 to 1988. Dropped as captain at end of 1988 season. Third member of the Graveney family to be dismissed by Gloucester CCC – Uncle Tom as captain in 1960 and father Ken as chairman in 1982
Opinions on cricket: 'I must admit I have enjoyed the role of captain, not least the friendships formed with other leaders. Like left-arm spinners, we have our own little "union". Some may think that strange as we spend a fair amount of time trying to do each other out of a job!'
Best batting performance: 119 Gloucestershire v Oxford University, Oxford 1980

Best bowling performance: 8-85 Gloucestershire v Nottinghamshire, Cheltenham 1974

LAST SEASON: BATTING

	I.	N.O.	R.	H.S.	AV.
TEST					
1ST-CLASS	24	9	231	47	15.40
INT					
RAL	2	2	5	4*	–
NAT.W.	1	0	22	22	22.00
B & H	2	2	7	5*	–

CAREER: BATTING

	I.	N.O.	R.	H.S.	AV.
TEST					
1ST-CLASS	451	129	5836	119	18.12
INT					
RAL	129	48	1269	56*	15.66
NAT.W.	25	9	292	44	18.25
B & H	40	13	399	49*	14.77

LAST SEASON: BOWLING

	O.	M.	R.	W.	AV.
TEST					
1ST-CLASS	612.2	179	1353	53	25.52
INT					
RAL	26	2	126	4	31.50
NAT.W.	29	6	92	4	23.00
B & H	30.3	4	105	4	26.25

CAREER: BOWLING

	O.	M.	R.	W.	AV.
TEST					
1ST-CLASS	8416.1	2517	21471	749	28.66
INT					
RAL	923.1	52	4317	128	33.72
NAT.W.	332.5	51	1086	46	23.60
B & H	429.2	41	1545	50	30.90

GRAY, A. H.   Surrey

Full Name: Anthony Hollis Gray
Role: Right-hand bat, right-arm fast bowler
Born: 23 May 1963, Belmont, Port of Spain, Trinidad
Height: 6′ 6″ **Weight:** 15st
Nickname: Big Man
County debut: 1985
County cap: 1985
Test debut: 1986–87
No. of Tests: 5
No. of One-Day Internationals: 21
1st-Class 50s scored: 1
1st-Class 5 w. in innings: 16
1st-Class 10 w. in match: 3
Place in batting averages: —
(1987 232nd av. 13.40)
Place in bowling averages: —
(1987 2nd av. 15.65)
Strike rate 1988: 78.00 (career 59.07)
1st-Class catches 1988: 1 (career 29)
Parents: Anthony and Merle
Education: Marlick Ser. Comprehensive; St Augustine Ser. Comprehensive
Qualifications: 3 O-levels

Cricketing superstitions or habits: Always bats with cap on
Cricketers particularly learnt from: Alf Gover
Cricketers particularly admired: Viv Richards, Mike Holding
Other sports played: Football, basketball, table tennis
Other sports followed: Football
Relaxations: Watching sports, watching movies, music, going to the parks
Extras: The only son in a family of five. Trinidad and Tobago Player of the Year 1985. Surrey CC Supporters' Association Player of the Year 1985. Hat-trick v Yorkshire 1985
Best batting performance: 54* Trinidad v Leeward Islands, Basseterre 1985–86
Best bowling performance: 8-40 Surrey v Yorkshire, Sheffield 1985

LAST SEASON: BATTING

	I.	N.O.	R.	H.S.	AV.
TEST					
1ST-CLASS	–	–	–	–	–
INT					
RAL	–	–	–	–	–
NAT.W.					
B & H					

LAST SEASON: BOWLING

	O.	M.	R.	W.	AV.
TEST					
1ST-CLASS	26	13	38	2	19.00
INT					
RAL	8	0	56	4	14.00
NAT.W.					
B & H					

CAREER: BATTING

	I.	N.O.	R.	H.S.	AV.
TEST	8	2	48	12*	8.00
1ST-CLASS	72	12	734	54*	12.23
INT	8	4	43	10*	10.75
RAL	11	6	115	24*	23.00
NAT.W.	1	0	3	3	3.00
B & H					

CAREER: BOWLING

	O.	M.	R.	W.	AV.
TEST	148	37	377	22	17.13
1ST-CLASS	2815.4	357	6083	279	21.80
INT	174.4	18	635	34	18.67
RAL	173	5	768	39	19.69
NAT.W.	23	3	89	5	17.80
B & H	11	1	33	0	–

76. True or false: Mike Gatting played over 50 innings for England before hitting a century?

Full Name: Allan Michael Green
Role: Right-hand bat, off-break bowler, short-leg fielder
Born: 28 May 1960, Pulborough
Height: 5′ 10″ **Weight:** 11st
Nickname: Gilbert, Greenie, Wedgey
County debut: 1980
County cap: 1985
1000 runs in a season: 3
1st-Class 50s scored: 34
1st-Class 100s scored: 9
1st-Class 5 w. in innings: 1
One-Day 50s: 14
One-Day 100s: 1
Place in batting averages: 150th av. 23.66 (1987 151st av. 24.14)
1st-Class catches 1988: 10 (career 82)
Parents: Sheila Cynthia and Basil Michael
Wife and date of marriage: Kerry Louise, 19 September 1986
Family links with cricket: Father played for Findon CC 'as a fielder'
Education: Knoll School, Hove; Brighton Sixth Form College
Qualifications: 5 O-levels
Jobs outside cricket: Sports shop assistant, labourer
Cricketing superstitions or habits: 'Strap left pad on first and like to bat in same clothes, smell permitting.'
Overseas tours: *The Cricketer* tour to Dubai 1983
Overseas teams played for: Orange Free State, South Africa 1985–87

LAST SEASON: BATTING

	I.	N.O.	R.	H.S.	AV.
TEST					
1ST-CLASS	29	2	639	68	23.66
INT					
RAL	9	2	155	57	22.14
NAT.W.					
B & H	4	0	113	53	28.25

CAREER: BATTING

	I.	N.O.	R.	H.S.	AV.
TEST					
1ST-CLASS	284	17	7734	179	28.96
INT					
RAL	53	5	1314	83	27.37
NAT.W.	12	0	503	102	41.91
B & H	19	0	427	53	22.47

LAST SEASON: BOWLING

	O.	M.	R.	W.	AV.
TEST					
1ST-CLASS	151.5	40	392	10	39.20
INT					
RAL	2.4	1	16	3	5.33
NAT.W.					
B & H					

CAREER: BOWLING

	O.	M.	R.	W.	AV.
TEST					
1ST-CLASS	644.4	119	2081	46	45.23
INT					
RAL	3.4	1	23	3	7.66
NAT.W.	1.3	0	9	0	–
B & H	6	2	26	1	26.00

Cricketers particularly learnt from: Ian Thomson, Chris Waller, Roger Marshall, Tony Buss, Alvin Kallicharran
Other sports played: Golf, snooker, football
Relaxations: 'Sleeping, going to concerts, eating, drinking and watching it rain!'
Opinions on cricket: 'Should play 16 four-day championship matches.'
Best batting performance: 179 Sussex v Glamorgan, Cardiff 1986
Best bowling performance: 6-82 Sussex v Hampshire, Southampton 1988

GREEN, S. J. Warwickshire

Full Name: Simon James Green
Role: Right-hand bat, left-arm bowler
Born: 19 March 1970, Bloxwich, Staffordshire
Height: 6′ 2″ **Weight:** 12st 2lbs
Nickname: Charlie or The Fridge
County debut: 1988
Parents: Albert Ernest and Jennifer
Marital status: Single
Education: West House School (Preparatory), Old Swinford Hospital
Qualifications: 3 O-levels, 5 GSEs; 2 years YTS Scheme Coaching Certificate
Off-season 1988–89: Six months working and playing cricket in Albany, Western Australia
Cricketing superstitions or habits:
'Always wear inners and wear my St Christopher chain.'
Overseas tours: England (South) U-19 XI to Belfast 1987
Cricketers particularly learnt from: Neil Abberley, Steve Rouse, Norman Gifford, Geoff Humpage, David Thomas, Sports Master at Prep School
Cricketers particularly admired: Dennis Lillee, Paul Smith, Joey Benjamin, Simon Myles and the rest of Warwickshire CCC

LAST SEASON: BATTING

	I.	N.O.	R.	H.S.	AV.
TEST					
1ST-CLASS	2	0	28	28	14.00
INT					
RAL	3	1	11	10*	5.50
NAT.W.	1	0	1	1	1.00
B & H					

CAREER: BATTING

	I.	N.O.	R.	H.S.	AV.
TEST					
1ST-CLASS	2	0	28	28	14.00
INT					
RAL	3	1	11	10*	5.50
NAT.W.	1	0	1	1	1.00
B & H					

Other sports played: Football, snooker, hockey, golf
Other sports followed: All sports. Supports Derby County FC
Relaxations: Listening to music
Extras: First 'first-class' innings versus Lancashire was lbw first ball
Opinions on cricket: 'The greatest game known to Mankind and being paid for the privilege of participating.'
Best batting performance: 28 Warwickshire v Lancashire, Nuneaton 1988

GREENE, V. S.   Gloucestershire

Full Name: Victor Sylvester Greene
Role: Right-hand bat, right arm fast-medium bowler
Born: 24 September 1960, Barbados
Nickname: Vibert
County debut: 1987
1st-Class 50s scored: 1
1st-Class 5 w. in innings: 2
Place in batting averages: —
(1987 135th av. 26.57)
Place in bowling averages: —
(1987 56th av. 28.24)
1st-Class catches 1988: 1 (career 10)
Overseas tours: Barbados 1985–86
Best batting performance:
62* Gloucestershire v
Leicestershire, Cheltenham 1987
Best bowling performance: 7-96
Gloucestershire v Nottinghamshire,
Trent Bridge 1987

LAST SEASON: BATTING

	I.	N.O.	R.	H.S.	AV.
TEST					
1ST-CLASS	2	0	2	2	1.00
INT					
RAL	7	6	63	21*	63.00
NAT.W.					
B & H					

CAREER: BATTING

	I.	N.O.	R.	H.S.	AV.
TEST					
1ST-CLASS	27	8	302	62*	15.89
INT					
RAL	7	6	63	21*	63.00
NAT.W.					
B & H					

LAST SEASON: BOWLING

	O.	M.	R.	W.	AV.
TEST					
1ST-CLASS	69	19	180	8	22.50
INT					
RAL	96	4	415	19	21.84
NAT.W.					
B & H					

CAREER: BOWLING

	O.	M.	R.	W.	AV.
TEST					
1ST-CLASS	600	113	1788	76	23.52
INT					
RAL	108	5	462	21	22.00
NAT.W.					
B & H					

GREENIDGE, C. G. — Hampshire

Full Name: Cuthbert Gordon Greenidge
Role: Right-hand bat, right-arm medium bowler
Born: 1 May 1951, St Peter, Barbados
County debut: 1970
County cap: 1972
Benefit: 1983 (£28,648)
Test debut: 1974–75
No. of Tests: 87
No. of One-Day Internationals: 98
1000 runs in a season: 15
1st-Class 50s scored: 172
1st-Class 100s scored: 73
1st-Class 200s scored: 10
1st-Class 5 w. in innings: 1
One-Day 50s: 78
One-Day 100s: 29
Place in batting averages: 12th av. 50.80 (1987 11th av. 49.94)
1st-Class catches 1988: 6 (career 486)
Wife and date of marriage: Anita, September 1977
Children: Carl, 1978
Family links with cricket: Wife is cousin of former West Indian and Leicestershire fast bowler, Andy Roberts
Education: Black Bess School; St Peter's Boys' School; Sutton Secondary School, Reading
Qualifications: Studied accountancy and book-keeping

LAST SEASON: BATTING

	I.	N.O.	R.	H.S.	AV.
TEST	6	0	282	103	47.00
1ST-CLASS	10	1	480	111	53.33
INT	3	0	78	39	26.00
RAL					
NAT.W.					
B & H					

LAST SEASON: BOWLING

	O.	M.	R.	W.	AV.
TEST					
1ST-CLASS					
INT					
RAL					
NAT.W.					
B & H					

CAREER: BATTING

	I.	N.O.	R.	H.S.	AV.
TEST	146	14	6186	223	46.86
1ST-CLASS	616	55	28254	273*	45.86
INT	97	9	4048	115	46.00
RAL	180	12	6348	172	37.78
NAT.W.	33	1	1284	177	40.12
B & H	58	3	2157	173*	39.21

CAREER: BOWLING

	O.	M.	R.	W.	AV.
TEST	4.2	3	4	0	–
1ST-CLASS	155.5	37	468	17	27.53
INT	10	0	45	1	45.00
RAL	18	0	89	1	89.00
NAT.W.	1	0	5	0	–
B & H	12.1	1	57	0	–

Jobs outside cricket: Working for Sutton's Seeds, Reading; Dimplex, Southampton

Off-season 1988–89: Touring with the West Indies in Australia

Overseas tours: Toured with West Indies to India, Sri Lanka and Pakistan 1974–75; Australia 1975–76; England 1976, 1980 and 1984; Australia 1979–80; Pakistan 1980; Australia 1981–82; India 1983; Australia 1984–85; Australia 1988–89

Overseas teams played for: Barbados

Other sports played: Soccer, rugby, golf

Extras: Could have played for either England or West Indies. Persuaded to join Hampshire by John Arlott after playing for Berkshire U-19s. Scored two centuries in one match (134 and 101) for West Indies v England at Manchester 1976, and v Kent at Bournemouth (136 and 120) in 1978. Shared in partnership of 285 for second wicket with D. R. Turner v Minor Counties South at Amersham in 1973, being the record partnership for all one-day competitions. Awarded MBE in 1985. Released by Hampshire at end of 1988 season

Best batting performance: 273* D. H. Robins' XI v Pakistan, Eastbourne 1974

Best bowling performance: 5-49 Hampshire v Surrey, Southampton 1971

GREIG, I. A. Surrey

Full Name: Ian Alexander Greig
Role: Right-hand bat, right-arm medium bowler, slip fielder
Born: 8 December 1955, Queenstown, South Africa
Height: 5′ 11¾″ **Weight:** 12st
Nickname: Washie, Greigy
County debut: 1980 (Sussex), 1987 (Surrey)
County cap: 1981 (Sussex), 1987 (Surrey)
Test debut: 1982
No. of Tests: 2
1st-Class 50s scored: 24
1st-Class 100s scored: 5
1st-Class 5 w. in innings: 10
1st-Class 10 w. in match: 2
One-Day 50s: 3
Place in batting averages: 196th av. 19.59 (1987 103rd av. 30.58)
Place in bowling averages: 37th av. 23.32 (1987 99th av. 35.91)

Strike rate 1988: 49.28 (career 56.33)
1st-Class catches 1988: 17 (career 122)
Parents: Sandy and Joyce
Wife and date of marriage: Cheryl, 8 January 1983
Children: Michelle, 17 December 1984; Andrew, 20 January 1987
Family links with cricket: Brother of Tony, former captain of Sussex and England; brother-in-law Phillip Hodson played for Cambridge University and Yorkshire
Education: Queens College, Queenstown; Downing College, Cambridge
Qualifications: MA Law (Cantab)
Off-season 1988–89: Marketing executive at The Oval
Cricketing superstitions or habits: Left pad on first
Overseas tours: Combined Universities to Australia 1979–80
Overseas teams played for: Border, South Africa 1974–75; Griqualand West, South Africa 1975–76
Cricketers particularly learnt from: Geoff Arnold
Cricketers particularly admired: Garth le Roux, Richard Hadlee
Other sports played: Rugby Union, fishing
Other sports followed: Football
Relaxations: Relaxing with family, barbecues, fly-fishing
Opinions on cricket: 'Get into 16 four-day matches which will surely be a benefit to English cricket fortunes *provided* that the wickets are fully covered.'
Best batting performance: 147* Sussex v Oxford University, Oxford 1983
Best bowling performance: 7-43 Sussex v Cambridge University, Cambridge 1981

LAST SEASON: BATTING

	I.	N.O.	R.	H.S.	AV.
TEST					
1ST-CLASS	28	1	529	67	19.59
INT					
RAL	12	5	258	56*	36.85
NAT.W.	4	1	45	22	15.00
B & H	3	0	8	8	2.66

CAREER: BATTING

	I.	N.O.	R.	H.S.	AV.
TEST	4	0	26	14	6.50
1ST-CLASS	241	30	5393	147*	25.55
INT					
RAL	81	20	1413	56*	23.16
NAT.W.	14	1	242	82	18.61
B & H	40	3	509	51	13.75

LAST SEASON: BOWLING

	O.	M.	R.	W.	AV.
TEST					
1ST-CLASS	402.3	83	1143	49	23.32
INT					
RAL	109.3	3	540	28	19.28
NAT.W.	41	6	147	5	29.40
B & H	39	7	121	6	20.16

CAREER: BOWLING

	O.	M.	R.	W.	AV.
TEST	31.2	6	114	4	28.50
1ST-CLASS	3583.3	747	11029	381	28.94
INT					
RAL	597.4	19	3068	109	28.14
NAT.W.	144.4	17	496	21	23.61
B & H	351	36	1337	50	26.74

GRIFFITH, F. A.   Derbyshire

Full Name: Frank Alexander Griffith
Role: Right-hand bat, right-arm
medium bowler
Born: 15 August 1968, Leyton
Height: 6′ **Weight:** 12st
Nickname: Sir Learie
County debut: 1988
1st-Class catches 1988: 2 (career 2)
Parents: Alex and Daisy
Marital status: Single
Family links with cricket: Charlie
Griffith played Test cricket for
West Indies
Education: William Morris High
School, Walthamstow
Qualifications: Food and
nutrition and art O-levels;
NCA coaching certificate
Jobs outside cricket: Labourer,
salesman
Off-season 1988–89: 'Going back to Haringey Cricket College to work on my game.'
Cricketing superstitions or habits: 'I like to be by myself and think about the game.'
Overseas tours: Haringey Cricket College to Barbados Trinidad and Tobago, 1986–87; Jamaica, 1988
Cricketers particularly learnt from: My brothers Victor and Gline
Cricketers particularly admired: Collis King, Franklyn Stephenson
Other sports played: Table tennis, basketball, football

LAST SEASON: BATTING

	I.	N.O.	R.	H.S.	AV.
TEST					
1ST-CLASS	7	1	105	37	17.50
INT					
RAL	5	1	29	9	7.25
NAT.W.					
B & H					

LAST SEASON: BOWLING

	O.	M.	R.	W.	AV.
TEST					
1ST-CLASS	99.3	20	347	10	34.70
INT					
RAL	28	2	137	3	45.66
NAT.W.					
B & H					

CAREER: BATTING

	I.	N.O.	R.	H.S.	AV.
TEST					
1ST-CLASS	7	1	105	37	17.50
INT					
RAL	5	1	29	9	7.25
NAT.W.					
B & H					

CAREER: BOWLING

	O.	M.	R.	W.	AV.
TEST					
1ST-CLASS	99.3	20	347	10	34.70
INT					
RAL	28	2	137	3	45.66
NAT.W.					
B & H					

Injuries 1988: Pulled hamstring
Relaxations: Listening to music
Opinions on cricket: 'We must play more four-day games and get results, instead of playing three-day games and letting the game end in a draw.'
Best batting performance: 37 Derbyshire v Northamptonshire, Northampton 1988
Best bowling performance: 4-47 Derbyshire v Lancashire, Old Trafford 1988

HARDEN, R. J. Somerset

Full Name: Richard John Harden
Role: Right-hand bat, left-arm medium bowler
Born: 16 August 1965, Bridgwater
Height: 5' 11" **Weight:** 13st 4lbs
Nickname: Rich
County debut: 1985
1000 runs in a season: 1
1st-Class 50s scored: 13
1st-Class 100s scored: 3
One-Day 50s: 5
Place in batting averages: 97th av. 29.50 (1987 154th av. 23.66)
1st-Class catches 1988: 3 (career 37)
Parents: Chris and Ann
Marital status: Single
Family links with cricket: Grandfather played club cricket for Bridgwater
Education: Kings College, Taunton
Qualifications: 8 O-levels, 2 A-levels. Coaching award
Jobs outside cricket: Insurance clerk
Off-season 1987–88: Coaching and playing in New Zealand
Cricketing superstitions or habits: Right pad on first
Overseas teams played for: New Plymouth Old Boys, 1984–85, 1985–86; Central Districts in New Zealand, 1987–88
Cricketers particularly learnt from: Roy Marshall
Cricketers particularly admired: Viv Richards, David Gower, Steve Waugh
Other sports played: Squash, 'struggling golfer'
Injuries 1988: Broke knuckle of right index finger. Out of game for 12 weeks
Relaxations: Listening to music, eating good food, playing snooker or pool, drinking in good wine bars
Opinions on cricket: 'The introduction of four-day cricket is excellent. However, it must be played on decent pitches.'

Best batting performance: 108 Somerset v Sussex, Taunton 1986
Best bowling performance: 2-7 Central Districts v Canterbury, Blenheim 1987–88

LAST SEASON: BATTING

	I.	N.O.	R.	H.S.	AV.
TEST					
1ST-CLASS	11	1	295	78	29.50
INT					
RAL	5	0	109	52	21.80
NAT.W.					
B & H	4	0	69	30	17.25

LAST SEASON: BOWLING

	O.	M.	R.	W.	AV.
TEST					
1ST-CLASS	16	1	61	0	–
INT					
RAL					
NAT.W.					
B & H					

CAREER: BATTING

	I.	N.O.	R.	H.S.	AV.
TEST					
1ST-CLASS	108	15	2731	108	29.36
INT					
RAL	36	6	775	73	25.83
NAT.W.	1	0	17	17	17.00
B & H	13	0	198	35	15.23

CAREER: BOWLING

	O.	M.	R.	W.	AV.
TEST					
1ST-CLASS	115.3	14	434	10	43.40
INT					
RAL	0.1	0	0	0	–
NAT.W.					
B & H					

HARDIE, B. R. Essex

Full Name: Brian Ross Hardie
Role: Right-hand bat, right-arm
medium bowler, bat/pad fielder
Born: 14 January 1950,
Stenhousemuir
Height: 5′ 10″ **Weight:** 12st 7lbs
Nickname: Lager
County debut: 1973
County cap: 1974
Benefit: 1983 (£48,486)
1000 runs in a season: 11
1st-Class 50s scored: 83
1st-Class 100s scored: 23
One-Day 50s: 43
One-Day 100s: 6
Place in batting averages: 168th
av. 22.17 (1987 70th av. 35.12)
1st-Class catches 1988: 9 (career 313)

Parents: James Millar (deceased) and Elspet
Wife and date of marriage: Fiona, 28 October 1977
Family links with cricket: Father and brother, Keith, played for Scotland
Education: Stenhousemuir Primary School; Larbert High School
Qualifications: 7 O-levels, 3 H-levels, NCA Advanced Cricket Coach
Jobs outside cricket: Computer operator, bank clerk, shipping clerk
Off-season 1988–89: Cricket manager in Auckland, New Zealand

Overseas teams played for: Two seasons in New Zealand club cricket 1980–81 and 1981–82
Cricketers particularly learnt from: 'Everyone has something to offer.'
Other sports played: Football, golf
Injuries 1988: Broken arm
Relaxations: Sport
Extras: Played for Stenhousemuir in East of Scotland League. Debut for Scotland 1970. Scored two centuries for Scotland v MCC at Aberdeen in 1971, but not then regarded as first-class match. Man of the Match in 1985 NatWest Final
Best batting performance: 162 Essex v Warwickshire, Edgbaston 1975
162 Essex v Somerset, Southend 1985
Best bowling performance: 2-39 Essex v Glamorgan, Ilford 1979

LAST SEASON: BATTING

	I.	N.O.	R.	H.S.	AV.
TEST					
1ST-CLASS	20	3	377	58	22.17
INT					
RAL	11	1	433	87	43.30
NAT.W.	2	1	88	77	88.00
B & H	6	0	231	53	38.50

CAREER: BATTING

	I.	N.O.	R.	H.S.	AV.
TEST					
1ST-CLASS	564	70	16583	162	33.56
INT					
RAL	190	18	4749	109	27.61
NAT.W.	32	1	1105	110	35.64
B & H	69	15	1687	119*	31.24

LAST SEASON: BOWLING

	O.	M.	R.	W.	AV.
TEST					
1ST-CLASS					
INT					
RAL					
NAT.W.					
B & H					

CAREER: BOWLING

	O.	M.	R.	W.	AV.
TEST					
1ST-CLASS	46	3	238	3	79.33
INT					
RAL	4.5	0	24	1	34.00
NAT.W.	8	1	16	1	16.00
B & H					

77. What was the title of John Emburey's autobiography?

78. Who was the first cricketer to score 30 Test centuries and the first past 10,000 Test runs?

HARDY, J. J. E.   Somerset

Full Name: Jonathan James Ean
Hardy
Role: Left-hand bat
Born: 2 October 1960, Nakuru,
Kenya
Height: 6′ 3″ **Weight:** 13½st
Nickname: JJ
County debut: 1984 (Hampshire),
1986 (Somerset)
County cap: 1987 (Somerset)
1000 runs in a season: 1
1st-Class 50s scored: 30
1st-Class 100s scored: 2
One-Day 50s: 7
One-Day 100s: 1
Place in batting averages: 130th
av. 25.75 (1987 118th av. 28.65)
1st-Class catches 1988: 23 (career 61)
Parents: Ray and Petasue
Wife and date of marriage: Janet,
25 September 1987

Family links with cricket: Father played for Yorkshire Schools; related to
Nottinghamshire Gunn's
Education: Pembroke House, Gilgil, Kenya; Canford School, Dorset
Qualifications: 10 O-levels, 3 A-levels (English, Economics, Geography)
Off-season 1988–89: Captaining Cape Town CC, South African national club
champions. Coaching in Cape Town Schools
Overseas teams played for: Pirates, Durban 1981–85; Paarl CC 1985–86;
Cape Town CC 1987–89
Cricketers particularly admired: Graeme Pollock, Greg Chappell, Malcolm
Marshall
Other sports played: Hockey (captain Dorset U-19), rugby, squash
Relaxations: Photography, walking
Extras: Suffered from bilharzia, a tropical parasitic disease from 1980 to
February 1986. Left Hampshire to join Somerset for 1986 season
Opinions on cricket: 'Would like to see an increasing role in championship

LAST SEASON: BATTING

	I.	N.O.	R.	H.S.	AV.
TEST					
1ST-CLASS	39	3	927	97	25.75
INT					
RAL	12	0	202	45	16.83
NAT.W.	2	0	112	100	56.00
B & H	4	1	172	70*	57.33

CAREER: BATTING

	I.	N.O.	R.	H.S.	AV.
TEST					
1ST-CLASS	162	15	4389	119	29.85
INT					
RAL	46	7	889	94*	22.79
NAT.W.	7	1	190	100	31.66
B & H	14	1	335	70*	25.76

cricket for spinners and No.6 batsmen and a decreased one for contrived finishes and attempts at under-prepared pitches.'
Best batting performance: 119 Somerset v Gloucestershire, Taunton 1987

HARMAN, M. D. Kent

Full Name: Mark David Harman
Role: Right-hand bat, right-arm off-spinner, 1st slip fielder
Born: 30 June 1964, Aylesbury
Height: 5' 11½" **Weight:** 12st 7lbs
Nickname: Harmony, Basil
County debut: 1986 (Somerset), 1988 (Kent)
1st-Class 5 w. in innings: 2
Place in batting averages: 253rd av. 11.42 (1987 213th av. 15.66)
Place in bowling averages: 40th av. 23.72
Strike rate 1988: 64.00 (career 83.30)
1st-Class catches 1988: 8 (career 15)
Parents: Michael and Barbara
Marital status: Single
Family links with cricket: Father played club cricket
Education: Frome College; Loughborough University
Qualifications: 9 O-levels, 3 A-levels, BSc (First-Class Honours) Degree in Financial Management; cricket coaching awards
Jobs outside cricket: Chartered Accountancy
Off-season 1988–89: Playing and coaching in Wellington, New Zealand
Cricketing superstitions or habits: Always put socks on before shoes. Like to do a thorough series of stretching exercises before the day's play. Also brush teeth a lot during a day's play!
Cricketers particularly learnt from: Peter Robinson among many others at Somerset CCC, Roy Pienaar, John Inverarity
Cricketers particularly admired: Vic Marks, Martin Crowe, Steve Waugh, Richard Hadlee, Roger Harper, Chris Tavaré
Other sports played: Soccer, golf, swimming, running
Other sports followed: All sports through TV, media etc
Relaxations: 'Reading, sleeping, walking in the country, listening to music (not all at the same time) and brushing my teeth!'
Extras: 'Nearly run-out from first delivery in first-class cricket! Left Somerset at the end of 1987 season to join Kent to further my career, as first-team

opportunities at Somerset were limited due to presence of Vic Marks in the side.'

Opinions on cricket: 'Four-day cricket appears to have worked – and gradual progressions to 16 four-day games would eventually produce a "fairer" championship. The sides which are the strongest in depth and play the more attacking, inventive cricket will ultimately benefit.'

Best batting performance: 41 Somerset v Kent, Bath 1987
Best bowling performance: 5-55 Kent v Oxford University, Oxford 1988

LAST SEASON: BATTING

	I.	N.O.	R.	H.S.	AV.
TEST					
1ST-CLASS	13	6	80	17*	11.42
INT					
RAL	1	1	8	8*	–
NAT.W.					
B & H					

LAST SEASON: BOWLING

	O.	M.	R.	W.	AV.
TEST					
1ST-CLASS	266.4	86	593	25	23.72
INT					
RAL	6	0	58	2	29.00
NAT.W.					
B & H					

CAREER: BATTING

	I.	N.O.	R.	H.S.	AV.
TEST					
1ST-CLASS	26	10	201	41	12.56
INT					
RAL	2	1	10	8*	10.00
NAT.W.	1	0	0	0	0.00
B & H					

CAREER: BOWLING

	O.	M.	R.	W.	AV.
TEST					
1ST-CLASS	458.1	133	1110	33	33.63
INT					
RAL	14	0	111	2	55.50
NAT.W.	12	1	38	1	38.00
B & H					

HARTLEY, P. J.   *Yorkshire*

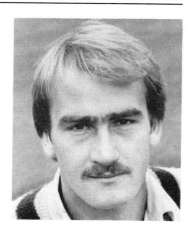

Full Name: Peter John Hartley
Role: Right-hand bat, right-arm fast-medium bowler
Born: 18 April 1960, Keighley
Height: 6′ 0″ **Weight:** 13st 4lbs
Nickname: Daisy, Jack
County debut: 1982 (Warwickshire), 1985 (Yorkshire)
County cap: 1987 (Yorkshire)
1st-Class 50s scored: 4
1st-Class 100s scored: 1
1st-Class 5 w. in innings: 4
Place in batting averages: 71st av. 33.09 (1987 189th av. 18.26)
Place in bowling averages: 116th av. 35.85 (1987 103rd av. 36.72)
Strike rate 1988: 54.26 (career 57.67)
1st-Class catches 1988: 7 (career 24)
Parents: Thomas and Molly

Wife and date of marriage: Sharon, 12 March 1988
Family links with cricket: Father played local league cricket
Education: Greenhead Grammar School; Bradford College
Qualifications: City & Guilds in Textiles
Jobs outside cricket: Textile supervisor
Off-season 1988–89: Playing in South Africa for Orange Free State
Overseas teams played for: Hamilton, Melville, New Zealand, 1983–84; Adelaide CC, 1985–86; Orange Free State, 1988–89
Cricket superstitions or habits: Vortex sighting
Cricketers particularly learnt from: Phil Carrick, Steve Oldham, Mike Page, Doug Padgett
Cricketers particularly admired: Dennis Lillee, Richard Hadlee, Gordon Greenidge
Other sports played: Golf, tennis, football
Other sports followed: Bradford City FC
Injuries 1988: Knee operation. Out for five weeks
Relaxations: Any sport, music, golf, weather forecasts
Best batting performance: 127* Yorkshire v Lancashire, Old Trafford 1988
Best bowling performance: 6-68 Yorkshire v Nottinghamshire, Sheffield 1986

LAST SEASON: BATTING

	I.	N.O.	R.	H.S.	AV.
TEST					
1ST-CLASS	17	6	364	127*	33.09
INT					
RAL	5	2	38	21*	12.66
NAT.W.	1	1	5	5*	–
B & H	1	0	12	12	12.00

LAST SEASON: BOWLING

	O.	M.	R.	W.	AV.
TEST					
1ST-CLASS	307.3	33	1219	34	35.85
INT					
RAL	56	3	288	11	26.18
NAT.W.	12	0	37	2	18.50
B & H	22	3	127	4	31.75

CAREER: BATTING

	I.	N.O.	R.	H.S.	AV.
TEST					
1ST-CLASS	76	21	1354	127*	24.61
INT					
RAL	23	9	148	35	10.57
NAT.W.	4	2	46	23	23.00
B & H	6	3	50	29*	16.66

CAREER: BOWLING

	O.	M.	R.	W.	AV.
TEST					
1ST-CLASS	1499.3	223	5500	156	35.25
INT					
RAL	243.4	7	1177	41	28.70
NAT.W.	59	4	206	14	14.71
B & H	140	12	586	26	22.53

79. Who made a Test double-hundred against New Zealand at the age of 19?

80. Which Australian Test cricketer had a brother who was a successful international golfer?

Full Name: Stuart Neil Hartley
Role: Right-hand bat, right-arm
medium bowler, outfielder
Born: 18 March 1956, Shipley,
West Yorkshire
Height: 5′ 11½″ **Weight:** 13st
Nickname: Tommy
County debut: 1978
County cap: 1981
1st-Class 50s scored: 25
1st-Class 100s scored: 4
One-Day 50s: 13
Place in batting averages: —
(1987 186th av. 18.62)
1st-Class catches 1988: 0 (career 54)
Parents: Marjorie and Horace
Marital status: Divorced
Family links with cricket:
Father played league cricket
Education: Beckfoot Grammar School, Bingley; Cannington High, Perth,
Western Australia
Qualifications: 8 O-levels, 3 A-levels; exam passes in insurance
Jobs outside cricket: Trained insurance underwriter; National Sales Executive for R.B.S. (Financial Services) Ltd
Off-season 1988–89: Working as insurance broker
Overseas tours: Captained North of England NCA team to Holland 1975 and Gibraltar 1981
Overseas teams played for: Orange Free State, 1981–82; Durban Collegians

LAST SEASON: BATTING

	I.	N.O.	R.	H.S.	AV.
TEST					
1ST-CLASS	3	1	60	26*	30.00
INT					
RAL	10	3	207	43*	29.57
NAT.W.	1	0	4	4	4.00
B & H					

CAREER: BATTING

	I.	N.O.	R.	H.S.	AV.
TEST					
1ST-CLASS	215	28	4667	114	24.95
INT					
RAL	113	24	2053	83*	23.06
NAT.W.	11	0	243	69	22.09
B & H	20	5	408	65*	27.20

LAST SEASON: BOWLING

	O.	M.	R.	W.	AV.
TEST					
1ST-CLASS	5	1	25	0	—
INT					
RAL	28	0	133	5	26.60
NAT.W.	2	0	12	0	—
B & H					

CAREER: BOWLING

	O.	M.	R.	W.	AV.
TEST					
1ST-CLASS	597	109	2182	48	45.45
INT					
RAL	254.3	3	1461	45	32.46
NAT.W.	28	2	114	1	114.00
B & H	86	3	336	13	25.84

Cricketers particularly learnt from: Doug Padgett, Mike Fearnley, Yorkshire CCC coaching staff
Cricketers particularly admired: Imran Khan, Clive Rice
Other sports played: Golf, rugby union
Injuries 1988: Broken finger
Extras: 'Started to play cricket in Perth, Western Australia, where I lived for 2½ years, 1967–69. I would like to live in Perth in the future.' Amateur football with Bradford City 1970–75. Rugby Union with Bingley RUFC. Has been acting captain of Yorkshire. Captain of 2nd XI
Best batting performance: 114 Yorkshire v Gloucestershire, Bradford 1982
Best bowling performance: 4-51 Yorkshire v Surrey, The Oval 1985

HAYHURST, A. N. Lancashire

Full Name: Andrew Neil Hayhurst
Role: Right-hand bat, right-arm medium bowler
Born: 23 November 1962, Davyhulme, Manchester
Height: 6' 0" **Weight:** 13st
Nickname: Barney, Ritchie Cunningham
County debut: 1985
1st-Class 50s scored: 2
1st-Class 100s scored: 1
One-Day 50s: 3
Place in batting averages: 153rd av. 23.42
Place in bowling averages: 98th av. 32.52
Strike rate 1988: 64.05 (career 61.16)
1st-Class catches 1988: 2 (career 9)

Parents: William and Margaret
Marital status: Single
Family links with cricket: Father played club cricket
Education: St Mark's Primary School; Worsley Wardley High; Eccles College; Carnegie College, Leeds
Qualifications: 8 O-levels, 3 A-levels, BA(Hons) Human Movement
Jobs outside cricket: Lecturing in winter 1985–86 and 1986–87
Cricketers particularly learnt from: Father and Geoff Ogden (Worsley CC)
Cricketers particularly admired: Geoff Boycott, Ian Botham, Viv Richards
Other sports played: Football, golf – all sports
Relaxations: Watching all sports, good food, good company

Extras: Scored a record 197 runs whilst playing for North of England v South, Southampton 1982. Represented NAYC v MCC 1982. Holds record number of runs for Lancashire Cricket Fed. U-19 (av. 105.00), 1982. Holds record number of runs in Manchester & District Cricket Association League, whilst playing for Worsley CC in 1984: 1193 runs (av. 70.17). Represented Greater Manchester U-19 County at football 1981–82

Opinions on cricket: '2nd XI cricket should be played on better pitches if that cricket is to be a successful grounding for future 1st XI players.'

Best batting performance: 107 Lancashire v Derybshire, Derby 1988

Best bowling performance: 4-27 Lancashire v Middlesex, Old Trafford 1987

LAST SEASON: BATTING

	I.	N.O.	R.	H.S.	AV.
TEST					
1ST-CLASS	23	2	492	107	23.42
INT					
RAL	13	0	411	84	31.61
NAT.W.	2	1	73	38*	73.00
B & H	3	0	15	12	5.00

LAST SEASON: BOWLING

	O.	M.	R.	W.	AV.
TEST					
1ST-CLASS	181.3	41	553	17	32.52
INT					
RAL	84	2	496	10	49.60
NAT.W.	19	3	53	2	26.50
B & H	24	2	100	2	50.00

CAREER: BATTING

	I.	N.O.	R.	H.S.	AV.
TEST					
1ST-CLASS	46	3	892	107	20.74
INT					
RAL	25	4	613	84	29.19
NAT.W.	6	1	148	49	29.60
B & H	4	0	16	12	4.00

CAREER: BOWLING

	O.	M.	R.	W.	AV.
TEST					
1ST-CLASS	438.2	79	1436	43	33.89
INT					
RAL	189.3	7	982	18	54.55
NAT.W.	71.5	6	265	9	29.44
B & H	35	3	150	6	25.00

HEGG, W. K. Lancashire

Full Name: Warren Kevin Hegg
Role: Right-hand bat, wicket-keeper
Born: 23 February 1968, Radcliffe, Lancashire
Height: 5′ 10″ **Weight:** 11st 5lbs
Nickname: Chucky, Chutch
County debut: 1986
1st-Class 50s scored: 1
1st-Class 100s scored: 1
Place in batting averages: 219th av. 16.10 (1987 161st av. 21.87)
Parents: Kevin and Glenda
Marital status: Single
Family links with cricket: Father played in local leagues, as does brother Martin
Education: Unsworth High School; Stand College, Whitefield

Qualifications: 5 O-levels, 7 CSEs; qualified coach
Jobs outside cricket: Groundsman at Old Trafford; worked at warehouse (involved in textiles)
Cricketing superstitions or habits: Left pad on first. Always wears a cap when keeping wicket
Overseas tours: North of England U-19 to Bermuda 1985; England Young Cricketers to Sri Lanka
Cricketers particularly learnt from: Father, Jim Kenyon (old pro), Clive Lloyd
Cricketers particularly admired: Ian Botham, Bob Taylor, Alan Knott
Other sports played: County football, golf, tennis
Other sports followed: Football, golf
Relaxations: Watching TV, sleeping, walking dog, fishing
Extras: First player to make County debut from Lytham CC. Holds Lancashire Schools U-19 record for most dismissals in a match – 6 (previous holder Graeme Fowler). Youngest player to score a 100 for Lancashire for 30 years, 130 v Northants in fourth 1st-class game
Opinions on cricket: 'Over-rate fines should be abolished. Tea sessions should be ten minutes longer.'
Best batting performance: 130 Lancashire v Northamptonshire, Northampton 1987

LAST SEASON: BATTING

	I.	N.O.	R.	H.S.	AV.
TEST					
1ST-CLASS	34	5	467	76	16.10
INT					
RAL	6	3	20	9*	6.66
NAT.W.	2	0	26	20	13.00
B & H	2	0	12	11	6.00

CAREER: BATTING

	I.	N.O.	R.	H.S.	AV.
TEST					
1ST-CLASS	59	9	858	130	17.16
INT					
RAL	9	4	32	9*	6.40
NAT.W.	2	0	26	20	13.00
B & H	2	0	12	11	6.00

LAST SEASON: WICKET KEEPING

	C.	ST.			
TEST					
1ST-CLASS	52	8			
INT					
RAL	13	2			
NAT.W.	1	–			
B & H	7	–			

CAREER: WICKET KEEPING

	C.	ST.			
TEST					
1ST-CLASS	80	22			
INT					
RAL	22	4			
NAT.W.	1	–			
B & H	7	–			

HEMMINGS, E. E. Nottinghamshire

Full Name: Edward Ernest
Hemmings
Role: Right-hand bat, off-break
bowler
Born: 20 February 1949,
Leamington Spa, Warwickshire
Height: 5′ 10″ **Weight:** 13st
Nickname: Eddie
County debut: 1966 (Warwickshire),
1979 (Nottinghamshire)
County cap: 1974 (Warwickshire),
1980 (Nottinghamshire)
Benefit: 1987
Test debut: 1982
No. of Tests: 8
No. of One-Day Internationals: 13
1st-Class 50s scored: 22
1st-Class 100s scored: 1
1st-Class 5 w. in innings: 59
1st-Class 10 w. in match: 14
One-Day 50s: 1
Place in batting averages: 217th av. 16.33 (1987 171st av. 20.47)
Place in bowling averages: 89th av. 31.23 (1987 24th av. 24.07)
Strike rate 1988: 72.69 (career 66.65)
1st-Class catches 1988: 9 (career 178)
Parents: Edward and Dorothy Phyliss
Wife and date of marriage: Christine Mary, 23 October 1971
Children: Thomas Edward, 26 July 1977; James Oliver, 9 September 1979
Family links with cricket: Father and father's father played Minor Counties
and League cricket
Education: Campion School, Leamington Spa
Off-season 1988–89: Chosen for England's cancelled tour of India
Overseas tours: Derrick Robins XI tour to South Africa 1975; International
XI tour to Pakistan 1981; England to Australia and New Zealand 1982–83;
World Cup, Pakistan and New Zealand 1987–88
Cricketers particularly learnt from: John Jameson, Clive Rice
Cricketers particularly admired: Tim Robinson
Other sport played: Golf
Injuries 1988: Tendonitis in groin
Relaxations: 'Watching football at any level – especially junior. Dining out
with my wife. Golf, real ale – and sleeping it off!'
Extras: Debut for Warwickshire 1966, cap 1974. No longer wears glasses,
plays in contact lenses. Started his career as a medium-pacer, and was thought

of as a successor to Tom Cartwright. 'I was even known as "Tommy's Ghost" around Edgbaston.' Suffers from asthma. Took a hat-trick for Warwickshire in 1977 but had to wait four years to receive the inscribed match ball, when he had moved to Nottinghamshire. Hit first century – 127* v Yorkshire at Worksop, July 1982 – after 16 years in first-class game. When playing in a benefit game in Blackpool with Tim Robinson, spotted the potential of Franklyn Stephenson and recommended him to Nottinghamshire as a successor to Richard Hadlee

Best batting performance: 127* Nottinghamshire v Yorkshire, Worksop 1982
Best bowling performance: 10-175 International XI v West Indies XI, Kingston 1982–83

LAST SEASON: BATTING

	I.	N.O.	R.	H.S.	AV.
TEST					
1ST-CLASS	25	10	245	31*	16.33
INT					
RAL	6	4	23	12*	11.50
NAT.W.	–	–	–	–	–
B & H	3	1	26	21*	13.00

LAST SEASON: BOWLING

	O.	M.	R.	W.	AV.
TEST					
1ST-CLASS	508.5	139	1312	42	31.23
INT					
RAL	56	1	261	3	87.00
NAT.W.	24	3	105	2	52.50
B & H	44	5	130	2	65.00

CAREER: BATTING

	I.	N.O.	R.	H.S.	AV.
TEST	12	3	207	95	23.00
1ST-CLASS	525	121	7945	127*	19.66
INT	3	1	8	4*	4.00
RAL	151	45	1428	44*	13.47
NAT.W.	26	9	230	31*	13.52
B & H	42	12	450	61*	15.00

CAREER: BOWLING

	O.	M.	R.	W.	AV.
TEST	388.4	112	876	16	54.75
1ST-CLASS	12754	3623	34006	1185	28.69
INT	119.2	9	538	20	26.90
RAL	1465	96	6796	232	29.29
NAT.W.	401.1	65	1334	39	34.20
B & H	673.4	88	2092	59	35.45

HESELTINE, P. A. W.   Sussex

Full Name: Peter Anthony William Heseltine
Role: Right-hand bat, off-break bowler
Born: 5 April 1965, Barnsley
Height: 5' 10" **Weight:** 10st 10lbs
Nickname: Gonzo, Yorkie, Woodstock, Rigger, Streisand, Manilow
County debut: 1987
Place in batting averages: —
(1987 244th av. 11.46)
Place in bowling averages: —
(1987 131st av. 45.85)
1st-Class catches 1988: 0 (career 3)
Parents: Colin James and Georgina Mae

Marital status: Single
Family links with cricket: Brother Philip gained Oxford Blue 1983
Education: Queen Elizabeth Grammar School, Wakefield; King's College, London
Qualifications: 9 O-levels, 3 A-levels
Jobs outside cricket: Ice-cream man, baker, labourer, quarryman, local government officer
Cricketers particularly learnt from: Steve Oldham, Paul Parker, brother Philip
Cricketers particularly admired: John Emburey, Richard Hadlee, David Gower, Derek Randall
Other sports played: Golf, football
Other sports followed: Barnsley FC when possible and all other sports
Relaxations: Listening to all kinds of music, fly-fishing, watching television
Extras: Released by Sussex at end of 1988 season
Best batting performance: 26 Sussex v Kent, Dartford 1987
Best bowling performance: 3-33 Sussex v Nottinghamshire, Eastbourne 1987

LAST SEASON: BATTING

	I.	N.O.	R.	H.S.	AV.
TEST					
1ST-CLASS	2	0	14	8	7.00
INT					
RAL					
NAT.W.					
B & H					

LAST SEASON: BOWLING

	O.	M.	R.	W.	AV.
TEST					
1ST-CLASS	28	5	106	1	106.00
INT					
RAL					
NAT.W.					
B & H					

CAREER: BATTING

	I.	N.O.	R.	H.S.	AV.
TEST					
1ST-CLASS	20	3	186	26	10.94
INT					
RAL	1	1	6	6*	—
NAT.W.					
B & H					

CAREER: BOWLING

	O.	M.	R.	W.	AV.
TEST					
1ST-CLASS	344.2	81	1069	22	48.59
INT					
RAL	6	0	34	1	34.00
NAT.W.					
B & H	2	0	12	2	6.00

81. Of whom was it said: 'His gift was a capacity to invest cricket and cricketers with heroic stature . . . and he changed the entire shape of writing about the game'?

HICK, G. A. — Worcestershire

Full Name: Graeme Ashley Hick
Role: Right-hand bat, off-break bowler, slip and gully fielder
Born: 23 May 1966, Salisbury, Rhodesia
Height: 6′ 3″ **Weight:** 14½st
Nickname: Hicky, Hickery
County debut: 1984
County cap: 1986
1000 runs in a season: 4
1st-Class 50s scored: 29
1st-Class 100s scored: 29
1st-Class 200s scored: 5
One-Day 50s: 21
One-Day 100s: 6
Place in batting averages: 2nd av. 77.51 (1987 8th av. 52.19)
Place in bowling averages: 85th av. 30.57 (1987 120th av. 41.68)
Strike rate 1988: 58.28 (career 80.95)
1st-Class catches 1988: 28 (career 112)
Parents: John and Eve
Marital status: Single
Family links with cricket: Father connected with cricket administration since 1972 and in 1984 elected to Zimbabwe Cricket Union Board of Control
Education: Banket Primary; Prince Edward Boys' High School, Zimbabwe
Qualifications: 4 O-levels, NCA coaching award
Jobs outside cricket: Zimbabwe Cricket Union coach
Off-season 1988–89: Playing for Northern Districts, New Zealand
Cricketing superstitions or habits: Left pad on first
Overseas tours: Zimbabwe XI 1983 World Cup; Zimbabwe v Sri Lanka in Sri Lanka; Zimbabwe U-23 Triangular Tournament to Zambia; Zimbabwe to UK 1985
Overseas teams played for: Old Harrarians, Zimbabwe, since 1982
Cricketers particularly learnt from: David Houghton, Basil D'Oliveira, Father
Cricketers particularly admired: Duncan Fletcher (Zimbabwe captain) for approach and understanding of the game
Other sports played: Golf, tennis, squash, indoor hockey
Other sports followed: Follows Liverpool FC
Injuries 1988: Chipped knuckle; strained groin
Relaxations: Watching movies, television, listening to music
Extras: Youngest player participating in 1983 Prudential World Cup (aged

17); youngest player to represent Zimbabwe. Scored 1234 runs in 1984 Birmingham League season; scored 964 runs in 1984 2nd XI for Worcestershire; scored 185 in Birmingham League – highest score since the War; scored 11 centuries (including six in a row) in both above competitions. Scored 108* when only 6 years old for school team, Banket Junior. Played hockey for Zimbabwe, on tour in England, Holland and Germany. In 1986, at age 20, he became the youngest player to score 2000 runs in an English season. One of *Wisden*'s Five Cricketers of the Year, 1986. Hit 405* v Somerset, 1988, the highest individual score in England since 1895. Scored 1000 first-class runs by end of May 1988, taking century off West Indies to complete it. Hit record of 410 runs in April, 1988. Has decided to qualify for England

Opinions on cricket: 'The four-day game proved to be a winner. A closer look should be given to the pitches. Surely some of them cannot be good for cricket?'

Best batting performance: 405* Worcestershire v Somerset, Taunton 1988
Best bowling performance: 4-31 Worcestershire v Lancashire, Old Trafford 1987

LAST SEASON: BATTING

	I.	N.O.	R.	H.S.	AV.
TEST					
1ST-CLASS	37	2	2713	405*	77.51
INT					
RAL	14	2	512	111	42.66
NAT.W.	5	0	296	138	59.20
B & H	4	0	87	47	21.75

CAREER: BATTING

	I.	N.O.	R.	H.S.	AV.
TEST					
1ST-CLASS	180	16	9681	405*	59.03
INT					
RAL	54	10	1823	111	41.43
NAT.W.	11	2	560	172*	62.22
B & H	15	3	697	103*	58.08

LAST SEASON: BOWLING

	O.	M.	R.	W.	AV.
TEST					
1ST-CLASS	204	43	642	21	30.57
INT					
RAL	20	0	132	6	22.00
NAT.W.	41.3	3	133	8	16.62
B & H	3	0	8	0	–

CAREER: BOWLING

	O.	M.	R.	W.	AV.
TEST					
1ST-CLASS	931	196	2982	69	43.21
INT					
RAL	113.1	1	602	21	29.66
NAT.W.	51.3	4	158	9	17.55
B & H	23	1	85	3	28.33

82. Who said: 'I tend to believe that cricket is the greatest thing that God ever created on earth'?

Full Name: Simon Graham Hinks
Role: Left-hand bat, bat/pad fielder
Born: 12 October 1960,
Northfleet, Kent
Height: 6′ 2″ **Weight:** 13st 6lbs
Nickname: Hinksy
County debut: 1982
County cap: 1985
1000 runs in a season: 1
1st-Class 50s scored: 19
1st-Class 100s scored: 6
One-Day 50s: 11
Place in batting averages: 98th
av. 29.38 (1987 94th av. 32.00)
1st-Class catches 1988: 12 (career 74)
Parents: Mary and Graham
Marital status: Single
Family links with cricket: Father
captained Gravesend CC and is now chairman. Brother Jonathan plays for
Gravesend (captain) and Kent U-19s
Education: Dover Road Infant and Junior Schools, Northfleet; St George's
C of E School, Gravesend
Qualifications: 5 O-levels, 1 A-level
Jobs outside cricket: Worked for Reed Corrugated Cases for last two years as
a sales representative
Off-season 1988–89: Working for Reed Corrugated Cases
Cricketing superstitions or habits: Puts gear on in set order
Overseas teams played for: Pirates, Johannesburg, 1981–82; University of
Tasmania, 1983–86
Cricketers particularly learnt from: 'Learnt from my father and members of
local club, Gravesend; and past and present members of county.'
Cricketers particularly admired: 'Admire Clive Loyd's style and power and
anyone who has proved themselves over a long period.'
Other sports played: Most ball games
Injuries 1988: 'Mark Benson's back injury and Neil Taylor's finger injury!'
Relaxations: TV, music, papers, books, DIY
Opinions on cricket: 'Young players are still very dependent on going abroad
during the winter months as counties still do very little, if anything, to find
them winter employment. Players, particularly bowlers, therefore do not
have time to recover from injury or rest sufficiently playing overseas, as they
would with the benefit of a winter rest and stable employment. They would
also be able to afford mortgages (at present the wages for six months are so
low they can't afford one) and so feel more secure in the cricketing life, and be

more able to commit themselves to one particular county, rather than going to the highest bidder.'

Best batting performance: 138 Kent v Oxford University, Oxford 1988
Best bowling performance: 1-10 Kent v Oxford Unversity, Oxford 1986

LAST SEASON: BATTING

	I.	N.O.	R.	H.S.	AV.
TEST					
1ST-CLASS	27	1	764	138	29.38
INT					
RAL	13	3	250	55	25.00
NAT.W.	2	2	72	64*	—
B & H	4	1	112	78*	37.33

CAREER: BATTING

	I.	N.O.	R.	H.S.	AV.
TEST					
1ST-CLASS	174	9	4678	138	28.35
INT					
RAL	58	5	1117	99	21.07
NAT.W.	7	2	260	95	52.00
B & H	22	1	599	85	28.52

LAST SEASON: BOWLING

	O.	M.	R.	W.	AV.
TEST					
1ST-CLASS	2	0	28	0	—
INT					
RAL					
NAT.W.					
B & H					

CAREER: BOWLING

	O.	M.	R.	W.	AV.
TEST					
1ST-CLASS	77.4	9	289	4	72.25
INT					
RAL	25	1	139	4	34.75
NAT.W.					
B & H	41	0	198	5	39.60

HOFFMAN, D. S.   Northamptonshire

Full Name: Dean Stuart Hoffman
Role: Right-hand bat, right-arm seam bowler.
Born: 13 January 1966, Birmingham
Height: 6′ 2″ **Weight:** 13st
Nickname: Tootsie, Deano
County debut: 1985 (Warwickshire), 1988 (Northamptonshire)
1st-Class catches 1988: 1 (career 4)
Parents: Ken and Pauline
Marital status: Single
Family links with cricket: Father and brother play for Walmley CC
Education: Moor End Lane School
Qualifications: Cricket coach
Jobs outside cricket: Sales person for Argos
Overseas tours: Young England tour to the West Indies, 1985
Cricketers particularly learnt from: David Brown, Bob Willis
Cricketers particularly admired: Bob Willis, Graham Gooch
Other sports played: Golf, snooker
Other sports followed: Football, tennis
Relaxations: Listening to music, playing golf
Extras: Released by Northamptonshire at end of 1988 season

Best batting performance: 20* Northamptonshire v West Indians, Northampton 1988
Best bowling performance: 4-100 Warwickshire v Nottinghamshire, Nuneaton 1985

LAST SEASON: BATTING

	I.	N.O.	R.	H.S.	AV.
TEST					
1ST-CLASS	1	1	20	20*	–
INT					
RAL					
NAT.W.					
B & H					

LAST SEASON: BOWLING

	O.	M.	R.	W.	AV.
TEST					
1ST-CLASS	32	6	97	2	48.50
INT					
RAL					
NAT.W.					
B & H					

CAREER: BATTING

	I.	N.O.	R.	H.S.	AV.
TEST					
1ST-CLASS	16	5	59	20*	5.36
INT					
RAL	3	2	3	2	3.00
NAT.W.	1	0	3	3	3.00
B & H					

CAREER: BOWLING

	O.	M.	R.	W.	AV.
TEST					
1ST-CLASS	319.1	47	1178	28	42.07
INT					
RAL	57	2	252	5	50.40
NAT.W.	22	1	100	2	50.00
B & H					

HOLDING, M. A.   Derbyshire

Full Name: Michael Anthony Holding
Role: Right-hand bat, right-arm fast bowler
Born: 16 February 1954, Kingston, Jamaica
Nickname: Whispering Death, Mickey
County debut: 1981 (Lancashire), 1983 (Derbyshire)
County cap: 1983 (Derbyshire)
Test debut: 1975–76
No. of Tests: 60
No. of One-Day Internationals: 102
1st-Class 50s scored: 14
1st-Class 5 w. in innings: 38
1st-Class 10 w. in match: 4
One-Day 50s: 7
Place in batting averages: 242nd av. 12.90 (1987 198th av. 17.37)
Place in bowling averages: 110th av. 34.45 (1987 28th av. 24.36)
Strike rate 1988: 69.54 (career 46.41)
1st-Class catches 1988: 7 (career 106)

Off-season 1988–89: 'Doing weight training in Jamaica.'
Overseas tours: With West Indies to Australia 1975–76, 1981–82; to England 1976, 1980, 1984; to India 1983–84; International team to Pakistan 1981–82
Overseas teams played for: Jamaica; Tasmania; Canterbury, New Zealand 1987–88
Extras: One of *Wisden*'s Five Cricketers of the Year, 1976. Played for Lancashire in 1981. Moved to Derbyshire in 1983. Has 'deepest voice in county cricket'. Retired from Test cricket in 1987
Opinions on cricket: 'I am conscious of the fact that I haven't really done very well this season, despite my world-record 8-21 in the NatWest Trophy. I'm particularly disappointed in my form in championship cricket and I don't want to pretend that it has all been down to playing on pitches without real pace or bounce. Derbyshire have been good to me and I am very keen to repay them by going out on a high note next season. It will almost certainly be my last and I'd like to give everybody something to remember me by.'
Best batting performance: 80 Derbyshire v Yorkshire, Chesterfield 1985
Best bowling performance: 8-92 West Indies v England, The Oval 1976

LAST SEASON: BATTING

	I.	N.O.	R.	H.S.	AV.
TEST					
1ST-CLASS	12	2	129	30*	12.90
INT					
RAL	12	0	184	53	15.33
NAT.W.	2	0	1	1	0.50
B & H	4	2	74	35*	37.00

CAREER: BATTING

	I.	N.O.	R.	H.S.	AV.
TEST	76	10	910	73	13.78
1ST-CLASS	187	28	2529	80	15.90
INT	42	11	282	64	9.09
RAL	50	4	691	58	15.02
NAT.W.	8	1	70	27	10.00
B & H	14	4	256	69	25.60

LAST SEASON: BOWLING

	O.	M.	R.	W.	AV.
TEST					
1ST-CLASS	278.1	49	827	24	34.45
INT					
RAL	92.3	5	432	16	27.00
NAT.W.	30.1	8	60	10	6.00
B & H	74.2	11	244	15	16.26

CAREER: BOWLING

	O.	M.	R.	W.	AV.
TEST	140.5 1925.5	15 395	5898	249	23.68
1ST-CLASS	56 3536.5	5 892	11204	491	22.81
INT	912.1	97	3034	142	21.36
RAL	446.5	42	1827	84	21.75
NAT.W.	125.4	26	328	23	14.26
B & H	211.2	32	651	29	22.44

HOLLOWAY, P. C. L. Warwickshire

Full Name: Piran Christopher Laity Holloway
Role: Left-hand bat, wicket-keeper
Born: 1 October 1970, Helston, Cornwall
Height: 5′ 8″ **Weight:** 10st 7lbs
Nickname: Pirras, Oggie, Pil
County debut: 1988
Parents: Chris and Mary
Education: Nansloe CP School, Helston; Taunton School, Somerset
Qualifications: 6 O-levels (English, maths, physics, chemistry, biology, history)
Overseas tours: Millfield School to Barbados 1986
Cricketers particularly learnt from: Father, Bob Cottam, Les Lenham, Andy Kennedy
Cricketers particularly admired: Ian Botham, David Gower, Alan Knott
Other sports played: Rugby, soccer
Other sports followed: Rugby, soccer
Relaxations: Rock music, watching films, keeping fit
Extras: England Schools U-15 – Awarded Jack Hobbs Award by Cricket Society. England Schools U-17 – Wicket-keeping Award. Youngest on staff at Warwickshire 1988. Highest score 151 (Cornwall Schools v Northamptonshire Schools)
Best batting performance: 16 Warwickshire v Glamorgan, Edgbaston 1988

LAST SEASON: BATTING

	I.	N.O.	R.	H.S.	AV.
TEST					
1ST-CLASS	5	0	40	16	8.00
INT					
RAL	2	1	20	13	20.00
NAT.W.					
B & H					

CAREER: BATTING

	I.	N.O.	R.	H.S.	AV.
TEST					
1ST-CLASS	5	0	40	16	8.00
INT					
RAL	2	1	20	13	20.00
NAT.W.					
B & H					

LAST SEASON: WICKET KEEPING

	C.	ST.			
TEST					
1ST-CLASS	8	1			
INT					
RAL	1	–			
NAT.W.					
B & H					

CAREER: WICKET KEEPING

	C.	ST.			
TEST					
1ST-CLASS	8	1			
INT					
RAL	1	–			
NAT.W.					
B & H					

HOLMES, G. C. — Glamorgan

Full Name: Geoffrey Clark Holmes
Role: Right-hand bat, right-arm medium bowler, cover fielder
Born: 16 September 1958, Newcastle-on-Tyne
Height: 5′ 10″ **Weight:** 11st 2lbs
County debut: 1978
County cap: 1985
1000 runs in a season: 3
1st-Class 50s scored: 31
1st-Class 100s scored: 8
1st-Class 5 w. in innings: 2
One-Day 50s: 12
Place in batting averages: 56th av. 35.67 (1987 146th av. 24.91)
Place in bowling averages: 123rd av. 40.45
Strike rate 1988: 66.18 (career 78.12)
1st-Class catches 1988: 6 (career 73)
Parents: George and Rita
Wife: Christine
Children: Victoria
Family links with cricket: Father played in the Northumberland League
Education: West Denton High School
Qualifications: 6 O-levels, 2 A-levels; Advanced Cricket Coach
Jobs outside cricket: Trainee estimator; has worked as milkman
Cricket superstitions or habits: 'When things are going well I try to keep my preparations on the next day as similar as possible.'

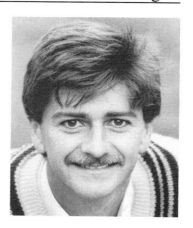

LAST SEASON: BATTING

	I.	N.O.	R.	H.S.	AV.
TEST					
1ST-CLASS	32	4	999	117	35.67
INT					
RAL	12	1	260	47	23.63
NAT.W.	3	0	66	38	22.00
B & H	6	4	157	59*	78.50

CAREER: BATTING

	I.	N.O.	R.	H.S.	AV.
TEST					
1ST-CLASS	281	42	6591	117	27.57
INT					
RAL	94	17	1835	73	23.97
NAT.W.	12	0	229	57	19.08
B & H	23	6	545	70	32.05

LAST SEASON: BOWLING

	O.	M.	R.	W.	AV.
TEST					
1ST-CLASS	121.2	15	445	11	40.45
INT					
RAL	39.3	1	211	8	26.37
NAT.W.	5	0	17	1	17.00
B & H	17	1	68	1	68.00

CAREER: BOWLING

	O.	M.	R.	W.	AV.
TEST					
1ST-CLASS	1041.4	200	3636	80	45.45
INT					
RAL	425.1	13	2245	92	24.40
NAT.W.	78	15	198	10	19.80
B & H	137.2	14	558	22	25.36

Overseas teams played for: Villa CC, Antigua, 1980–81; Bathurst RUCC, New South Wales, 1983–84; Fish Hoek, South Africa, 1984–85
Cricketers particularly learnt from: Javed Miandad
Cricketers admired: Geoff Boycott, John Snow
Other sports played: Soccer, snooker
Relaxations: Reading (especially cricket books), TV, sport, 3-card brag
Extras: Scored a century in each innings v Somerset at Taunton, 1988
Opinions on cricket: 'I think we play too much county cricket and would like to see 16 Championship matches per season with no extra one-day cricket. I would like to see one of the one-day competitions to be played as day–night matches, under floodlights.'
Best batting performance: 117 Glamorgan v Gloucestershire, Bristol 1988
Best bowling performance: 5-38 Glamorgan v Essex, Colchester 1988

HOPKINS, J. A. Glamorgan

Full Name: John Anthony Hopkins
Role: Right-hand bat, occasional wicket-keeper
Born: 16 June 1953, Maesteg
Nickname: Ponty
County debut: 1970
County cap: 1977
Benefit: 1986
1000 runs in a season: 7
1st-Class 50s scored: 64
1st-Class 100s scored: 18
1st-Class 200s scored: 1
One-Day 50s: 33
One-Day 100s: 2
Place in batting averages: 147th av. 24.27 (1987 216th av. 15.15)
1st-Class catches 1988: 9 (career 213 + 1 stumping)

LAST SEASON: BATTING

	I.	N.O.	R.	H.S.	AV.
TEST					
1ST-CLASS	23	1	534	87	24.27
INT					
RAL	14	2	362	60	30.16
NAT.W.	3	0	15	12	5.00
B & H	5	0	179	81	35.80

CAREER: BATTING

	I.	N.O.	R.	H.S.	AV.
TEST					
1ST-CLASS	535	32	13742	230	27.32
INT					
RAL	181	15	3980	130*	23.97
NAT.W.	22	0	409	63	18.89
B & H	49	2	1251	103*	26.61

Family links with cricket: Younger brother of J. D. Hopkins who appeared for Middlesex CCC and formerly on Glamorgan staff
Education: Trinity College of Education, Carmarthen
Qualifications: Trained as a teacher
Jobs outside cricket: Teacher
Extras: Known as fine baritone singer and raconteur in the Glamorgan 'cabaret' act. Retired at end of 1988 season
Best batting performance: 230 Glamorgan v Worcestershire, Worcester 1977

HUGHES, D. P. Lancashire

Full Name: David Paul Hughes
Role: Right-hand bat, slow left-arm bowler
Born: 13 May 1947, Newton-le-Willows
Height: 5′ 11″ **Weight:** 12st
Nickname: Yozzer
County debut: 1967
County cap: 1970
Benefit: 1981
1000 runs in a season: 2
1st-Class 50s scored: 42
1st-Class 100s scored: 8
1st-Class 5 w. in innings: 20
1st-Class 10 w. in match: 2
One-Day 50s: 10
Place in batting averages: 205th av. 17.40 (1987 199th av. 17.34)
1st-Class catches 1988: 25 (career 290)

Parents: Both deceased
Wife and date of marriage: Christine, March 1973
Children: James, July 1975
Family links with cricket: Father, Lloyd, a professional with Bolton League club Walkden, before and after Second World War
Education: Newton-le-Willows Grammar School
Qualifications: NCA Coaching Certificate
Overseas tours: With Derrick Robins XI to South Africa 1972–73; England Counties side to West Indies 1974–75
Overseas teams played for: Tasmania while coaching there in 1975–76 and 1976–77
Cricketers particularly learnt from: 'At the start of my career I spoke to all the leading left-arm spin bowlers in the game for help.'

Relaxations: Golf
Extras: Coached in South Africa 1977–78; coached in Tasmania 1978–79 and 1979–80. Gillette Cup 'specialist'. Hit 24 runs off John Mortimer v Gloucestershire in penultimate over in Gillette semi-final in 1972. Hit 26 runs off last over of innings v Northamptonshire in Gillette Final at Lord's, 1976. Bowled 13 consecutive maiden overs v Gloucestershire at Bristol, 1980. Appointed Lancashire captain 1987. One of *Wisden*'s Five Cricketers of the Year, 1987
Best batting performance: 153 Lancashire v Glamorgan, Old Trafford 1983
Best bowling performance: 7-24 Lancashire v Oxford University, Oxford 1970

LAST SEASON: BATTING

	I.	N.O.	R.	H.S.	AV.
TEST					
1ST-CLASS	34	4	522	62	17.40
INT					
RAL	12	3	111	34	12.33
NAT.W.	2	0	41	23	20.50
B & H	4	0	53	19	13.25

LAST SEASON: BOWLING

	O.	M.	R.	W.	AV.
TEST					
1ST-CLASS					
INT					
RAL					
NAT.W.					
B & H	2	0	8	0	—

CAREER: BATTING

	I.	N.O.	R.	H.S.	AV.
TEST					
1ST-CLASS	535	94	9643	153	21.86
INT					
RAL	203	46	2859	92	18.21
NAT.W.	37	15	801	71	36.40
B & H	54	13	960	52	23.41

CAREER: BOWLING

	O.	M.	R.	W.	AV.
TEST					
1ST-CLASS	23 6748.1	3 2090	18392	614	29.95
INT					
RAL	809.1	62	3568	169	21.11
NAT.W.	300.2	29	1166	44	26.50
B & H	237.2	40	754	29	26.00

HUGHES, S. P.　　　　　　Middlesex

Full Name: Simon Peter Hughes
Role: Right-hand bat, right-arm fast-medium bowler
Born: 20 December 1959, Kingston, Surrey
Height: 5′ 10″ **Weight:** 11st 7lbs
Nickname: Yozzer, Spam, Yule
County debut: 1980
County cap: 1981
1st-Class 50s scored: 1
1st-Class 5 w. in innings: 8
Place in batting averages: 193rd av. 20.06 (1987 227th av. 13.92)
Place in bowling averages: 130th av. 46.59 (1987 117th av. 40.24)
Strike rate 1988: 98.07 (career 57.11)

1st-Class catches 1988: 3 (career 34)
Parents: Peter and Erica
Marital status: Single
Family links with cricket: Father very keen coach and player who owned indoor cricket school. 'Uncle once hit a ball over the school pavilion!'
Education: Latymer Upper School, Hammersmith; Durham University
Qualifications: 10 O-levels, 4 A-levels, BA General Studies
Jobs outside cricket: Writes regular sports column in local weekly paper, and monthly for *The Cricketer*. Also contributes a weekly cricket column to *The Independent*
Off-season 1988–89: Playing for Grafton CC in Auckland, New Zealand
Overseas tours: Personal overseas spell playing in Sri Lanka 1979; Middlesex CCC tour to Zimbabwe winter 1980; with Overseas XI (captained by J. M. Brearley) to Calcutta (v Indian XI) 1980–81; International Ambassadors tour to India 1985; Fred Rumsey Cricket Festival, Barbados, 1987; Bristol University to Sri Lanka, 1987–88
Overseas teams played for: Colts CC, Colombo, Sri Lanka, and Sri Lanka Board President's XI; Northern Transvaal 1982–83; Grosvenor-Fynaland 1983–84; Auckland University 1984–85; Freemantle CC (Perth) 1985–86; Sydney University 1987; Grafton CC (Auckland) 1988–89
Cricketers particularly learnt from: Father, Jack Robertson, Mike Brearley, Mike Selvey, Gubby Allen
Cricketers particularly admired: John Emburey, Clive Radley, Malcolm Marshall, Richard Hadlee
Other sports played: Soccer (for university), tennis, golf
Relaxations: Travelling, slapstick films, jazz and blues piano, eating curry, broadcasting and journalism
Extras: Took 4-82 v Kent on Championship debut, plus played in County Championship and Gillette Cup winning sides (Lord's Final) in 1980 in first season. Selected for England U-25 XI v Sri Lanka (Trent Bridge) July 1981. Awarded cap after only 20 matches. Middlesex/Austin Reed Player of the Year 1986. Won a free holiday as Middlesex leading wicket-taker 1986
Opinions on cricket: 'It is a waste of breath bothering to argue with people's

LAST SEASON: BATTING

	I.	N.O.	R.	H.S.	AV.
TEST					
1ST-CLASS	21	5	321	53	20.06
INT					
RAL	6	5	65	18*	65.00
NAT.W.	3	3	7	4*	—
B & H	3	0	3	2	1.00

CAREER: BATTING

	I.	N.O.	R.	H.S.	AV.
TEST					
1ST-CLASS	142	49	1167	53	12.54
INT					
RAL	27	14	208	22*	16.00
NAT.W.	9	5	20	6	5.00
B & H	10	5	27	8*	5.40

LAST SEASON: BOWLING

	O.	M.	R.	W.	AV.
TEST					
1ST-CLASS	441.2	84	1258	27	46.59
INT					
RAL	107.2	1	590	24	24.58
NAT.W.	41	2	144	7	20.57
B & H	48	5	188	7	26.85

CAREER: BOWLING

	O.	M.	R.	W.	AV.
TEST					
1ST-CLASS	3113	591	9998	327	30.57
INT					
RAL	457.1	9	2252	80	28.15
NAT.W.	169.2	19	630	27	23.33
B & H	127.1	13	494	19	26.00

hypocritical and inaccurate views regarding the South African issue. No one ever seems to change sides in an argument anyway. When a player is on the way up he is not as good as everyone says he is, but on the way down he's not as bad.'

Best batting performance: 53 Middlesex v Cambridge University, Cambridge 1988
Best bowling performance: 7-35 Middlesex v Surrey, The Oval 1986

HUMPAGE, G. W. Warwickshire

Full Name: Geoffrey William Humpage
Role: Right-hand bat, wicket-keeper; can also bowl right-arm medium
Born: 24 April 1954, Birmingham
Height: 5′ 9″ **Weight:** 12st 7lbs
Nickname: Farsley
County debut: 1974
County cap: 1976
Benefit: 1987
No. of One-Day Internationals: 3
1000 runs in a season: 10
1st-Class 50s scored: 87
1st-Class 100s scored: 26
1st-Class 200s scored: 2
One-Day 50s: 33
One-Day 100s: 3
Place in batting averages: 216th av. 16.44 (1987 34th av. 41.18)
Parents: Ernest and Mabel
Wife and date of marriage: Valerie Anne, 14 September 1983 (2nd marriage)
Children: Philip Andrew Guy, 16 November 1977
Education: Golden Hillock Comprehensive School, Birmingham
Jobs outside cricket: Former police cadet, then police constable, Birmingham City Police. Coach, Scarborough CC, Western Australia, 1978–79. Sports executive for Pace Insurance Consultants, Birmingham
Other sports played: Soccer, squash, tennis, swimming, golf, snooker, table tennis
Relaxations: Reading, listening to E.L.O.
Extras: Good impressionist, particularly of Frankie Howerd. Took part in record Warwickshire and English first-class 4th wicket partnership of 470 v Lancashire at Southport, July 1982, with Kallicharran (230*). Humpage made 254* including 13 sixes. Previous 4th wicket record was 448 for Surrey at

The Oval v Yorkshire in 1899, by R. Abel and T. W. Hayward. Joined England Rebels in South Africa in 1982. One of *Wisden*'s Five Cricketers of the Year, 1984

Best batting performance: 254 Warwickshire v Lancashire, Southport 1982
Best bowling performance: 2-13 Warwickshire v Gloucestershire, Edgbaston 1980

LAST SEASON: BATTING

	I.	N.O.	R.	H.S.	AV.
TEST					
1ST-CLASS	26	1	411	80	16.44
INT					
RAL	12	0	327	56	27.25
NAT.W.	2	0	13	11	6.50
B & H	4	0	52	14	13.00

CAREER: BATTING

	I.	N.O.	R.	H.S.	AV.
TEST					
1ST-CLASS	518	65	16429	254	36.26
INT	2	0	11	6	5.50
RAL	171	24	3802	109*	25.86
NAT.W.	31	4	733	77	27.14
B & H	55	7	1309	100*	27.27

LAST SEASON: WICKET KEEPING

	C.	ST.			
TEST					
1ST-CLASS	56	1			
INT					
RAL	9	–			
NAT.W.	2	1			
B & H	6	–			

LAST SEASON: BOWLING

	O.	M.	R.	W.	AV.
TEST					
1ST-CLASS	9	0	38	0	–
INT					
RAL					
NAT.W.					
B & H					

CAREER: BOWLING

	O.	M.	R.	W.	AV.
TEST					
1ST-CLASS	141.1	17	490	10	49.00
INT					
RAL	97.5	2	556	15	37.06
NAT.W.					
B & H	27	2	123	3	41.00

CAREER: WICKET KEEPING

	C.	ST.			
TEST					
1ST-CLASS	600	68			
INT	2	–			
RAL	116	20			
NAT.W.	34	7			
B & H	67	3			

83. Who has scored the most runs for Hampshire?

84. Which famous cricket family were for many years able to assemble their own cricket team?

HUSSAIN, N.   Essex

Full Name: Nasser Hussain
Role: Right-hand bat
Born: 28 March 1968, Madras, India
Height: 6′ 1″
Nickname: Bunny
County debut: 1987
1st-Class 50s scored: 2
1st-Class 100s scored: 1
One-day 50s: 1
1st-Class catches 1988: 5 (career 7)
Parents: Jainad and Shireen
Marital status: Single
Family links with cricket: Father
played for Madras in Ranji
Trophy 1966–67. Uncle played
for Combined Indian Universities.
Brother Amel on Hampshire staff
in 1983 and 1984. Brother Abbas
played for Essex 2nd XI
Education: Forest School; Durham University
Qualifications: 9 O-levels, 3 A-levels; NCA Cricket Coaching Award
Jobs outside cricket: Worked at Morgan Guaranty Bank during holidays
Off-season 1988–89: Studying at Durham University
Overseas tours: Young England to Sri Lanka, 1987; Young England to
Australia for Youth World Cup, 1988
Overseas teams played for: Madras 1986–87
Cricketers particularly learnt from: Father, Ray East, Graham Saville
Cricketers particularly admired: 'They are all in the Essex dressing-room,
plus David Gower.'
Other sports played: Golf, football
Other sports followed: Golf, football, American football
Injuries 1988: Strained wrist, out for two weeks
Relaxations: Music
Extras: Played for England Schools U-15 for two years (one as captain).
Youngest player to play for Essex Schools U-11 at the age of 8 and U-15 at the

LAST SEASON: BATTING

	I.	N.O.	R.	H.S.	AV.
TEST					
1ST-CLASS	13	3	486	165*	48.60
INT					
RAL	6	0	108	38	18.00
NAT.W.					
B & H	4	1	126	76*	42.00

CAREER: BATTING

	I.	N.O.	R.	H.S.	AV.
TEST					
1ST-CLASS	16	3	518	165*	39.84
INT					
RAL	10	1	199	38	22.11
NAT.W.					
B & H	7	2	213	76*	42.60

age of 12. At 15, was considered the best young leg-spin bowler in the country
Best batting performance: 165* Essex v Leicestershire, Chelmsford 1988

HUTCHINSON, I. J. F.   Middlesex

Full Name: Ian James Frederick Hutchinson
Role: Right-hand bat, right-arm medium pace bowler
Born: 31 October 1964, Welshpool
Height: 6′ **Weight:** 13st
County debut: 1987
Nickname: Hutch
Parents: Ann and Michael
Wife and date of marriage: Louise, 19 September 1987
Family links with cricket: Grandfather played for Leicestershire 2nd XI. Father played club cricket
Education: Kingsland Grange Preparatory School; Shrewsbury School
Qualifications: 10 O-levels, 2 A-levels, cricket coach
Jobs outside cricket: Sales consultant with Imperial Trident Life. Coach of Eton fives at eight London public schools
Off-season 1988–89: Working with Imperial Trident Life
Overseas tours: Australia with Bathurst Rugby and Cricket Club, 1984
Cricketers particularly learnt from: Geoff Boycott
Cricketers particularly admired: Geoff Boycott
Other sports played: Eton fives
Other sports followed: 'Any apart from horses!'
Injuries 1988: 'Back injury kept me out of the last two months of the season, but I am fit now.'

LAST SEASON: BATTING

	I.	N.O.	R.	H.S.	AV.
TEST					
1ST-CLASS	4	0	48	25	12.00
INT					
RAL	1	1	22	22*	–
NAT.W.					
B & H					

CAREER: BATTING

	I.	N.O.	R.	H.S.	AV.
TEST					
1ST-CLASS	4	0	48	25	12.00
INT					
RAL	1	1	22	22*	–
NAT.W.					
B & H					

Relaxation: 'At home with Louise. Eating out.'
Extras: Played for Shropshire 1984–85. On MCC groundstaff 1984–86. Was substitute fielder for England v New Zealand at Lord's 1986
Opinions on cricket: 'I think that as I haven't played many 1st team games it is difficult for me to say anything in that respect. I just hope people can still play cricket and enjoy doing so, at every level.'
Best batting performance: 25 Middlesex v Northamptonshire, Luton, 1988

IBADULLA, K. B.   Gloucestershire

Full Name: Kassem Ben Ibadulla
Role: Right-hand bat, off-spin bowler
Born: 13 October 1964, Birmingham
Height: 5′ 6″ **Weight:** 11st 5lbs
Nickname: Kass
County debut: 1987
1st-Class 100s scored: 1
1st-Class 5 w. in innings: 1
Place in batting averages: —
(1987 169th av. 20.57)
1st-Class catches 1988: 1 (career 7)
Parents: Khalid and Gertrude
Marital status: Single
Family links with cricket: Father Khalid 'Billy' Ibadulla played for Warwickshire and Pakistan
Education: Springfield Primary School, Birmingham; St Dunstan's Preparatory School, Catford; Otago Boys High School, New Zealand

LAST SEASON: BATTING

	I.	N.O.	R.	H.S.	AV.
TEST					
1ST-CLASS	7	3	124	77	31.00
INT					
RAL					
NAT.W.					
B & H					

CAREER: BATTING

	I.	N.O.	R.	H.S.	AV.
TEST					
1ST-CLASS	25	6	440	107	23.15
INT					
RAL	1	0	12	12	12.00
NAT.W.					
B & H					

LAST SEASON: BOWLING

	O.	M.	R.	W.	AV.
TEST					
1ST-CLASS	34.2	6	143	3	47.66
INT					
RAL					
NAT.W.					
B & H					

CAREER: BOWLING

	O.	M.	R.	W.	AV.
TEST					
1ST-CLASS	195.4	41	601	16	37.56
INT					
RAL					
NAT.W.					
B & H					

Qualifications: School Certificate and OE New Zealand. Qualified coach
Off-season 1988–89: Playing in New Zealand
Overseas teams played for: Otago, New Zealand 1981
Cricketers particularly learnt from: Father and all at Gloucester
Cricketers particularly admired: Geoff Boycott
Other sports played: Billiards
Injuries 1988: Broken thumb – out for two months
Relaxations: Fishing, sleeping, music
Extras: Scored maiden first class hundred for Otago in New Zealand. Played for Cheshire in 1986
Best batting performance: 107 Otago v Central Districts, New Plymouth 1987–88
Best bowling performance: 5-22 Otago v Canterbury, Invercargill 1982–83

IGGLESDEN, A. P.   Kent

Full Name: Alan Paul Igglesden
Role: Right-hand bat, right-arm fast bowler, outfielder
Born: 8 October 1964, Farnborough, Kent
Height: 6' 6" **Weight:** 14st 8lbs
Nickname: Iggy, Norman
County debut: 1986
1st-Class 5 w. in innings: 8
1st-Class 10 w. in match: 2
Place in bowling averages: 22nd av. 21.75 (1987 43rd av. 25.98)
Strike rate 1988: 38.02 (career 42.74)
1st-Class catches 1988: 1 (career 9)
Parents: Alan Trevor and Gillian Catharine
Marital status: Single
Family links with cricket: Brother Kevin plays for Holmedale in the Kent League
Education: St Mary's Primary School, Westerham; Hosey School, Westerham; Churchill Secondary School, Westerham
Qualifications: 9 CSEs
Jobs outside cricket: 'Since I left school I have had a couple of jobs to fit in with my cricket at Kent.'
Off-season 1988–89: Playing and coaching multi-racial cricket for Avendale in Cape Town

Cricketing superstitions or habits: 'Like to be at the ground early. Try to keep to the same match build-up if things are going well.'
Overseas teams played for: Avendale CC 1985–89
Cricketers particularly learnt from: Terry Alderman, Bob Woolmer, Colin Page, Stuart Leary, Colin Tomlin
Cricketers particularly admired: Terry Alderman, Dennis Lillee, Ian Botham, Imran Khan, Chris Penn
Other sports played: Golf, football, snooker, darts
Other sports followed: Football – 'go to watch Crystal Palace with the lads whenever I can.'
Injuries 1988: Broken thumb – tendons below the right patella
Relaxations: Listening to music (especially The Smiths and Van Morrison), sleeping, watching sport on TV, crosswords
Extras: 'I didn't play any schools representative cricket.'
Best batting performance: 41 Kent v Surrey, Canterbury 1988
Best bowling performance: 6-34 Kent v Surrey, Canterbury 1988

LAST SEASON: BATTING

	I.	N.O.	R.	H.S.	AV.
TEST					
1ST-CLASS	8	2	103	41	17.16
INT					
RAL					
NAT.W.					
B & H					

LAST SEASON: BOWLING

	O.	M.	R.	W.	AV.
TEST					
1ST-CLASS	234.3	47	805	37	21.75
INT					
RAL					
NAT.W.					
B & H					

CAREER: BATTING

	I.	N.O.	R.	H.S.	AV.
TEST					
1ST-CLASS	34	8	263	41	10.11
INT					
RAL	3	1	25	13*	12.50
NAT.W.					
B & H	1	1	5	5*	–

CAREER: BOWLING

	O.	M.	R.	W.	AV.
TEST					
1ST-CLASS	933.2	156	3093	131	23.61
INT					
RAL	53.5	5	217	9	24.11
NAT.W.	19	5	60	4	15.00
B & H	23	2	92	2	46.00

85. Who played first-class cricket and also played soccer for England when they won the 1966 World Cup?

86. How many seasons of first-class cricket did Norman Gifford play for Worcestershire, Warwickshire and England?

ILLINGWORTH, R. K.   Worcestershire

Full Name: Richard Keith Illingworth
Role: Right-hand bat, slow left-arm bowler
Born: 23 August 1963, Bradford
Height: 6′ ½″ **Weight:** 12st 7lbs
Nickname: Lucy, Harry
County debut: 1982
County cap: 1986
1st-Class 50s scored: 4
1st-Class 100s scored: 1
1st-Class 5 w. in innings: 6
1st-Class 10 w. in match: 1
Place in batting averages: 163rd av. 22.44 (1987 5th av. 56.00)
Place in bowling averages: 24th av. 21.96 (1987 122nd av. 42.15)
Strike rate 1988: 61.82 (career 79.92)
1st-Class catches 1988: 18 (career 66)
Parents: Keith and Margaret
Wife and date of marriage: Anne, 20 September 1985
Children: Miles Jonathan, 28 August 1987
Family links with cricket: Father plays Bradford League cricket.
Education: Wrose Brow Middle; Salts Grammar School (same school as the late Jim Laker)
Qualifications: 6 O-levels, senior coaching award holder
Jobs outside cricket: Civil servant
Off-season 1988–89: Playing and coaching cricket overseas
Overseas tours: Denmark Youth Tournament NAYC 1981; Whitbread

LAST SEASON: BATTING

	I.	N.O.	R.	H.S.	AV.
TEST					
1ST-CLASS	22	4	404	60	22.44
INT					
RAL	3	2	0	0	0.00
NAT.W.	2	2	8	6*	—
B & H	1	1	7	7*	—

CAREER: BATTING

	I.	N.O.	R.	H.S.	AV.
TEST					
1ST-CLASS	147	44	2018	120*	19.59
INT					
RAL	35	18	131	21	7.70
NAT.W.	6	2	47	22	11.75
B & H	8	5	59	17*	19.66

LAST SEASON: BOWLING

	O.	M.	R.	W.	AV.
TEST					
1ST-CLASS	597.4	189	1274	58	21.96
INT					
RAL	54.5	1	237	7	33.85
NAT.W.	36	6	96	2	48.00
B & H	6	0	27	0	—

CAREER: BOWLING

	O.	M.	R.	W.	AV.
TEST					
1ST-CLASS	3716.4	1058	9585	279	34.35
INT					
RAL	385	20	1804	80	22.55
NAT.W.	103.1	17	295	9	32.77
B & H	143	18	522	19	27.47

scholarship playing for Colts CC, Brisbane 1982–83; Wisden Cricket XI, Barbados 1983; University of St Heliers, Auckland, New Zealand 1986–87, 1987–88

Cricketers particularly learnt from: Father
Other sports played: Golf, football, snooker
Other sports followed: Football (follows Leeds United and Bradford City)
Relaxations: 'Listening to music. Reading cricket autobiographies. DIY around the house and garden.'
Opinions on cricket: 'Counties should be limited to one overseas player on the staff in any one year. Should be more cricket players in state schools to encourage youngsters.'
Best batting performance: 120* (as nightwatchman) Worcestershire v Warwickshire, Worcester 1987
Best bowling performance: 7-50 Worcestershire v Oxford University, Oxford 1985

ILOTT, M. C. Essex

Full Name: Mark Christopher Ilott
Role: Left-hand bat, left-arm fast bowler
Born: 27 August 1970, Watford
Height: 6' 1" **Weight:** 11st 10lbs
Nickname: Ramble, Muke
County debut: 1988
Parents: John and Glenys
Marital status: Single
Family links with cricket: Father long-time President of Watford Town CC. Brother represents Hertfordshire full team. Grandfather played for Ruislip Manor for many years
Education: Francis Combe School
Qualifications: 6 O-levels
(maths, physics, chemistry, English, technology, computer studies),
2 A/O-levels (maths, general studies),
2 A-levels (physics, chemistry)

Jobs outside cricket: Storeman for R. S. Kennedys, civil and electrical engineers
Off-season 1988–89: Working for the above and getting fit

Cricketers particularly learnt from: John Lever, Ray East, Nick King, Dennis Lillee

Cricketers particularly admired: John Lever, Graham Gooch, Malcolm Marshall, Richard Hadlee

Other sports played: 'None competitively but all for fun!'

Other sports followed: Tennis, football, American football

Injuries 1988: A pull in the lower back towards end of season

Relaxations: Swimming

Opinions on cricket: 'LBW should be given if no shot is played and ball pitches outside leg stump and would have hit the wicket.'

Best batting performance: 6 Essex v Northamptonshire, Northampton 1988

Best bowling performance: 2-23 Essex v Cambridge University, Cambridge 1988

LAST SEASON: BATTING

	I.	N.O.	R.	H.S.	AV.
TEST					
1ST-CLASS	1	0	6	6	6.00
INT					
RAL					
NAT.W.					
B & H					

LAST SEASON: BOWLING

	O.	M.	R.	W.	AV.
TEST					
1ST-CLASS	49	15	111	3	37.00
INT					
RAL					
NAT.W.					
B & H					

CAREER: BATTING

	I.	N.O.	R.	H.S.	AV.
TEST					
1ST-CLASS	1	0	6	6	6.00
INT					
RAL					
NAT.W.					
B & H					

CAREER: BOWLING

	O.	M.	R.	W.	AV.
TEST					
1ST-CLASS	49	15	111	3	37.00
INT					
RAL					
NAT.W.					
B & H					

87. Who scored a century on his debut for one county, and then another century for his new county on his debut for them, the following season?

IMRAN KHAN Sussex

Full Name: Ahmad Khan Niazi Imran
Role: Right-hand bat, right-arm fast bowler
Born: 25 November 1952, Lahore, Pakistan
Height: 6′ 0″ **Weight:** 12st 2lbs
Nickname: Immie
County debut: 1971 (Worcestershire), 1977 (Sussex)
County cap: 1976 (Worcestershire), 1978 (Sussex)
Benefit: 1987
Test debut: 1971
No of Tests: 73
No of One-Day Internationals: 106
1000 runs in a season: 4
1st-Class 50s scored: 85
1st-Class 100s scored: 27
1st-Class 5 w. in innings: 70
1st-Class 10 w. in match: 13
One-Day 50s: 48
One-Day 100s: 4
1st-Class catches 1988: 0 (career 113)
Marital status: Single
Education: Aitchison College; Cathedral School, Lahore; Worcester Royal Grammar School; Keble College, Oxford University
Qualifications: BA Hons in politics and economics
Jobs outside cricket: 'I play cricket all the year round.'
Off-season 1988–89: Captaining Pakistan in Australia
Family links with cricket: Cousin of Pakistan cricketers, Majid Khan and Javed Burki
Overseas tours: Toured with Pakistan to England in 1971, 1974, 1982 and 1983 (World Cup); Australia and West Indies 1976–77; India 1979–80, Australia, 1981–82, 1983–84; Sri Lanka 1985–86; India 1986–87; England 1987; Australia 1988–89
Overseas teams played for: Various Lahore teams
Cricketers particularly learnt from: John Snow, Basil D'Oliviera, Majid Khan
Other sports: Squash, swimming, hockey.
Relaxations: Shooting, listening to music (Western and Eastern)
Extras: Debut for Lahore A 1969–70. Debut for Worcestershire 1971, cap 1976. Left Worcestershire in 1977. Oxford cricket blue 1973–74–75. Captain

in 1974. Scored two centuries in a match, 117* and 106, Oxford University v Nottinghamshire at Oxford in 1974. Had a match double of 111 not out and 13 for 99 v Lancashire at Worcester in 1976. Played World Series Cricket. Has bad scar on left arm resulting from falling off a slide in Lahore, and canot fully extend his arm: 'It affects my batting a bit. My top hand grip is very strange if I don't bat regularly'. Drinks no alcohol. Does not smoke. 'I don't eat pig meat and I wear a verse from the Koran in gold round my neck, which is supposed to protect me. I pray before going to sleep.' Top of Sussex first-class batting and bowling averages in 1982 and 1983. Captain of Pakistan. One of *Wisden*'s Five Cricketers of the Year, 1982

Opinions on cricket: 'I've always treated a game of cricket as something to win and if you can't win, you shouldn't be afraid of losing. Most three-day matches are drawn, and I find it dreary playing in games that are heading nowhere. It is unsuitable for the players, and it is unsuitable for spectators. Young people are watching other sports. I see very few young and enthusiastic people watching three-day matches. Who wants to watch draws? Four-day games are more likely to reach a positive result. It would be necessary to attack. There would be more emphasis on getting batsmen out rather than just containing them. And the crowds would come back.'

Best batting performance: 170 Oxford University v Northamptonshire, Oxford 1974

Best bowling performance: 8-34 Sussex v Middlesex, Lord's 1986

LAST SEASON: BATTING

	I.	N.O.	R.	H.S.	AV.
TEST					
1ST-CLASS	7	1	119	55	19.83
INT					
RAL	10	1	190	50	21.11
NAT.W.	1	0	0	0	0.00
B & H	3	1	104	71	52.00

LAST SEASON: BOWLING

	O.	M.	R.	W.	AV.
TEST					
1ST-CLASS	122.3	27	310	13	23.84
INT					
RAL	72.3	8	285	9	31.66
NAT.W.	10.1	1	49	1	49.00
B & H	27.4	2	112	4	28.00

CAREER: BATTING

	I.	N.O.	R.	H.S.	AV.
TEST	106	18	2860	135*	32.50
1ST-CLASS	445	73	13664	170	36.73
INT	90	24	1898	102*	28.75
RAL	130	18	3410	104*	30.44
NAT.W.	30	6	763	114*	31.79
B & H	47	11	1514	112*	42.05

CAREER: BOWLING

	O.	M.	R.	W.	AV.
TEST	410 2310.3	68 528	7319	334	21.91
1ST-CLASS	1809 6739	87 1728	20125	921	21.85
INT	738.2	74	2788	123	22.66
RAL	948.1	85	3547	175	20.26
NAT.W.	292.4	51	873	39	22.38
B & H	461.1	89	1348	65	20.73

Full Name: Kevan David James
Role: Left-hand bat, left-arm fast-medium bowler, fields 'anywhere but short leg'
Born: 18 March 1961, Lambeth, South London
Height: 6' 0½" **Weight:** 12st 6lbs
Nickname: Jambo, Jaimo
County debut: 1980 (Middlesex), 1985 (Hampshire)
1st-Class 50s scored: 4
1st-Class 100s scored: 3
1st-Class 5 w. in innings: 6
One-Day 50s: 1
Place in batting averages: 220th av. 16.00 (1987 3rd av. 62.00)
Place in bowling averages: 23rd av. 21.80 (1987 113th av. 39.84)
Strike rate 1988: 51.22 (career 60.34)
1st-Class catches 1988: 3 (career 22)
Parents: David and Helen
Wife and date of marriage: Debbie, October 1987
Family links with cricket: Late father played club cricket in North London
Education: Edmonton County High School
Qualifications: 5 O-levels; qualified coach
Overseas tours: Young England tour of Australia, 1978–79; Young England tour of West Indies, 1979–80
Overseas teams played for: Canterbury Province U-23, New Zealand, 1980;

LAST SEASON: BATTING

	I.	N.O.	R.	H.S.	AV.
TEST					
1ST-CLASS	22	2	320	77	16.00
INT					
RAL	9	3	71	24*	11.83
NAT.W.	2	1	16	12	16.00
B & H	2	1	46	25	46.00

CAREER: BATTING

	I.	N.O.	R.	H.S.	AV.
TEST					
1ST-CLASS	84	20	1820	142*	28.43
INT					
RAL	32	13	465	54*	24.47
NAT.W.	5	2	62	19	20.66
B & H	12	1	158	29	14.36

LAST SEASON: BOWLING

	O.	M.	R.	W.	AV.
TEST					
1ST-CLASS	298.5	73	763	35	21.80
INT					
RAL	86.4	3	355	10	35.50
NAT.W.	23	3	82	3	27.33
B & H	43	5	144	5	28.80

CAREER: BOWLING

	O.	M.	R.	W.	AV.
TEST					
1ST-CLASS	1267.2	304	3797	126	30.13
INT					
RAL	391.4	18	1730	46	37.60
NAT.W.	71.4	6	305	10	30.50
B & H	163.5	16	603	19	31.73

Sydenham CC, Christchurch, New Zealand, 1980–81; Wellington, New Zealand, 1982–83, 1984–85; Eden-Roskill, Auckland 1987–88
Cricketers particularly learnt from: Don Bennett (Middlesex coach)
Other sports played: Soccer
Other sports followed: Watches American football, follows Spurs
Relaxations: DIY and making money. Wrote two columns, one in *The Club Cricketer*, the other in a local Southampton paper. 'It would be nice just to have time to relax.'
Extras: Released by Middlesex at end of 1984 season and joined Hampshire
Best batting performance: 142* Hampshire v Nottinghamshire, Bournemouth 1987
Best bowling performance: 6-22 Hampshire v Australia, Southampton 1985

JARVIS, K. B. S.   Gloucestershire

Full Name: Kevin Bertram Sidney Jarvis
Role: Right-hand bat, right-arm fast-medium bowler
Born: 23 April 1953, Dartford, Kent
Height: 6′ 3″ **Weight:** 13st
Nickname: Jarvo, Ferret, KJ
County debut: 1975 (Kent), 1988 (Gloucestershire)
County cap: 1977 (Kent)
Benefit: 1987 (£48,485)
50 wickets in a season: 7
1st-Class 5 w. in innings: 19
1st-Class 10 w. in match: 3
Place in batting averages: —
(1987 245th av. 11.00)
Place in bowling averages: —
(1987 81st av. 31.57)
1st-Class catches 1988: 0 (career 56)
Parents: Herbert John and Margaret Elsie
Wife and date of marriage: Margaret Anne, 16 September 1978
Children: Simon Martin, 16 April 1985; Laura Emily, 6 January 1988
Family links with cricket: Son very keen; father played club cricket; Simon Hinks is a distant relative
Education: Springhead School, Northfleet, Kent; Thames Polytechnic
Qualifications: 6 O-levels, 3 A-levels, NCA coach, ISMA, MAMSA
Jobs outside cricket: Accountancy, insurance, clerical

Off-season 1988–89: 'Looking after juvenile delinquents and underprivileged children!'

Cricketing superstitions or habits: 'I never hook before October and have a habit of not getting any runs.'

Overseas tours: Derrick Robins' XI to Far East 1977; Jamaica 1982

Overseas teams played for: Played and coached for South Melbourne, 1979 and 1981; Tooronga, 1978

Cricketers particularly learnt from: Derek Underwood, Bob Woolmer

Cricketers particularly admired: Richard Hadlee, Dennis Lillee

Other sports played: Squash, badminton, tennis, football, hockey, darts

Other sports followed: 'Watch everything except synchronised swimming.'

Extras: Released by Kent at end of 1987 season. Joined Gloucestershire on a two-year contract in 1988

Opinions on cricket: 'Play more one-day cricket and more exciting three-day cricket. Play on uncovered pitches. I believe four-day cricket will kill the Championship as a spectator sport.'

Best batting performance: 19 Kent v Derbyshire, Maidstone 1984

Best bowling performance: 8-97 Kent v Worcestershire, Worcester 1978

LAST SEASON: BATTING

	I.	N.O.	R.	H.S.	AV.
TEST					
1ST-CLASS	1	1	1	1*	–
INT					
RAL	1	1	1	1*	–
NAT.W.					
B & H					

LAST SEASON: BOWLING

	O.	M.	R.	W.	AV.
TEST					
1ST-CLASS	47	7	165	1	165.00
INT					
RAL	99	7	420	19	22.10
NAT.W.					
B & H					

CAREER: BATTING

	I.	N.O.	R.	H.S.	AV.
TEST					
1ST-CLASS	183	82	337	19	3.33
INT					
RAL	49	30	59	8*	3.10
NAT.W.	11	5	16	5*	2.66
B & H	24	15	16	4*	1.77

CAREER: BOWLING

	O.	M.	R.	W.	AV.
TEST					
1ST-CLASS	5983.2	1309	18928	635	29.80
INT					
RAL	1079.5	88	4526	194	23.32
NAT.W.	236.5	29	874	37	23.62
B & H	532.2	78	1885	86	21.91

88. True or false: Graham Cowdrey, after making his first first-class century for Kent v Essex in April, put his contact lenses in two glasses of water, and room-mate Steven Marsh drank one and swallowed his contact lens?

JARVIS, P. W.   Yorkshire

Full Name: Paul William Jarvis
Role: Right-hand bat, right-arm
fast-medium bowler
Born: 29 June 1965, Redcar,
North Yorkshire
Height: 5′ 11″ **Weight:** 12st 5lbs
Nickname: Jarv, Beaver,
Gnasher
County debut: 1981
County cap: 1986
Test debut: 1987–88
No. of Tests: 4
No. of One-Day Internationals: 5
1st-Class 5 w. in innings: 12
1st-Class 10 w. in match: 2
Place in batting averages: —
(1987 208th av. 16.30)
Place in bowling averages: 6th
av. 17.59 (1987 30th av. 24.58)
Strike rate 1988: 37.83 (career 50.33)
1st-Class catches 1988: 0 (career 30)
Parents: Malcolm and Marjorie
Marital status: Single
Family links with cricket: Father has played league cricket for 30 years with
Marske CC; brother, Andrew, played for English Schools U-15s, and also had
trials for Northamptonshire and Derbyshire
Education: Bydales Comprehensive School, Marske
Qualifications: 4 O-levels
Jobs outside cricket: Trainee groundsman, Marske Cricket Club
Off-season 1988–89: 'Winter at home, training and getting fit for 1989 season.'
Cricketing superstitions: The number 111
Overseas tours: Channel Islands April 1986 and Ireland June 1986 with
Yorkshire; St Lucia and Barbados, 1987, with Yorkshire; with England to
World Cup, Pakistan, Australia and New Zealand 1987–88
Overseas teams played for: Mosman Middle Harbour CC, Sydney, 1984–85;
Avendale CC, Cape Town 1985–86
Cricketers particularly learnt from: Maurice Hill, Phil Carrick, Geoff
Boycott, Albert Padmore
Cricketers particularly admired: Dennis Lillee, Richard Hadlee
Other sports played: Football, running and fitness, golf, squash
Other sports followed: Most sports
Injuries 1988: Lower back strain; had to withdraw from England team for
Third Test in June and did not play again for the rest of the season

Relaxations: Fishing, music, golf
Extras: Youngest player ever to play for Yorkshire 1st XI in John Player League and County Championships (16 years, 2 months, 1 day in John Player League; 16 years, 2 months, 13 days for County Championship). Youngest player to do hat-trick in JPL and Championship. Played for Young England v West Indies 1982 and Australia 1983. Selected for TCCB XI v New Zealand 1986
Opinions on cricket: 'Only people actually born in England should be permitted to play for England. County cricket should be divided into two divisions, 10 in either division. The tables would be chosen on merit and run on a similar basis to the football league, the additional teams would come from either the minor counties, e.g. Northumberland, or counties having two teams in the league. Three-day cricket would be played between the 10 teams in each league – a total of 18 matches as you would play each other home and away. Two top (2nd division) and two bottom (1st division) would be promoted and relegated each season. The B & H Cup and NWT would be run exactly as it is now and the RAL would be played in its divisions – the two winners and runners up in each division (4 teams) would then play off for the overall champions cup – the winners of each division would also win their respective (A division) and (B division) league cups. This system would make the cricket much more interesting for more teams – nearly every team rather than just a few at the end of a season will have something to play for – encouraging better cricket to play and making it more interesting for the spectators to follow. Four-day cricket should be scrapped.'
Best batting performance: 47 Yorkshire v Essex, Chelmsford 1986
Best bowling performance: 7-55 Yorkshire v Surrey, Leeds 1986

LAST SEASON: BATTING

	I.	N.O.	R.	H.S.	AV.
TEST	3	1	42	29*	21.00
1ST-CLASS	9	1	55	13	6.87
INT					
RAL	–	–	–	–	–
NAT.W.	–	–	–	–	–
B & H	–	–	–	–	–

LAST SEASON: BOWLING

	O.	M.	R.	W.	AV.
TEST	57.1	6	217	6	36.16
1ST-CLASS	176.1	46	434	31	14.00
INT					
RAL	24	2	104	5	20.80
NAT.W.	11	2	18	2	9.00
B & H	10	1	43	1	43.00

CAREER: BATTING

	I.	N.O.	R.	H.S.	AV.
TEST	6	2	76	29*	19.00
1ST-CLASS	92	32	847	47	14.11
INT	2	1	5	5*	5.00
RAL	24	12	120	29*	10.00
NAT.W.	4	1	35	16	11.66
B & H	5	1	40	20	10.00

CAREER: BOWLING

	O.	M.	R.	W.	AV.
TEST	155.1	37	418	12	34.83
1ST-CLASS	2218.5	438	7193	271	26.54
INT	47.5	4	187	6	31.16
RAL	375.5	24	1684	81	20.79
NAT.W.	104.5	14	364	15	24.26
B & H	153	26	506	26	19.46

JEAN-JACQUES, M.   Derbyshire

Full Name: Martin Jean-Jacques
Role: Right-hand bat, right-arm
medium pace bowler
Born: 2 July 1960, Dominica
County debut: 1986
1st-Class 50s scored: 1
1st-Class 5 w. in innings: 1
1st-Class 10 w. in match: 1
Place in batting averages: —
(1987 239th av. 12.00)
Place in bowling averages: —
(1987 111th av. 39.55)
1st-Class catches 1988: 2 (career 9)
Extras: Played Minor Counties
cricket for Buckinghamshire since
1983. Formerly played for
Shepherds Bush CC. On debut
for Derbyshire (v Yorkshire)
put on 132 with A. Hill for the
10th wicket – a new Derbyshire record
Best batting performance: 73 Derbyshire v Yorkshire, Sheffield 1986
Best bowling performance: 8-77 Derbyshire v Kent, Derby 1986

LAST SEASON: BATTING

	I.	N.O.	R.	H.S.	AV.
TEST					
1ST-CLASS	4	0	5	5	1.25
INT					
RAL	2	0	20	13	10.00
NAT.W.	–	–	–	–	–
B & H					

CAREER: BATTING

	I.	N.O.	R.	H.S.	AV.
TEST					
1ST-CLASS	36	7	405	73	13.96
INT					
RAL	12	1	69	15	6.27
NAT.W.	5	2	28	16	9.33
B & H	2	1	4	2*	4.00

LAST SEASON: BOWLING

	O.	M.	R.	W.	AV.
TEST					
1ST-CLASS	101.4	16	328	9	36.44
INT					
RAL	22	0	129	1	129.00
NAT.W.	10	0	46	0	–
B & H					

CAREER: BOWLING

	O.	M.	R.	W.	AV.
TEST					
1ST-CLASS	585.4	91	1995	58	34.39
INT					
RAL	130	2	709	20	35.45
NAT.W.	74	7	300	12	25.00
B & H	30	0	164	5	32.80

JEFFRIES, S. T.   Hampshire

Full Name: Stephen Thomas Jefferies
Role: Left-hand bat, left-arm
fast-medium bowler
Born: 8 December 1959, Cape
Town, South Africa
Nickname: Jeffo
County debut: 1982 (Derbyshire),
1983 (Lancashire), 1988 (Hampshire)
1st-Class 50s scored: 14
1st-Class 5 w. in innings: 16
1st-Class 10 w. in match: 3
Place in batting averages: 72nd
av. 33.00
Place in bowling averages: 114th
av. 35.76
Strike rate 1988: 62.67 (career 56.42)
1st-Class catches 1988: 4 (career 43)
Education: Plumstead High School
Jobs outside cricket: Physical

training instructor with South African Navy
Off-season 1988–89: Playing in South Africa for Western Province
Overseas teams played for: Western Province, South Africa
Extras: Professional with Crompton in Central Lancashire League. Played for South African Schools XI in 1978. With Derbyshire in 1982. Left Lancashire staff 1985. Man of the Match B & H Final 1988
Best batting performance: 93 Lancashire v Sussex, Old Trafford 1985
Best bowling performance: 10-59 Western Province v Orange Free State, Cape Town 1987–88

LAST SEASON: BATTING

	I.	N.O.	R.	H.S.	AV.
TEST					
1ST-CLASS	19	5	462	60	33.00
INT					
RAL	10	4	158	39	26.33
NAT.W.	4	0	83	39	20.75
B & H	2	0	8	7	4.00

CAREER: BATTING

	I.	N.O.	R.	H.S.	AV.
TEST					
1ST-CLASS	157	30	3348	93	26.36
INT					
RAL	24	7	496	39	29.17
NAT.W.	6	1	106	39	21.20
B & H	5	0	81	39	16.20

LAST SEASON: BOWLING

	O.	M.	R.	W.	AV.
TEST					
1ST-CLASS	355.1	53	1216	34	35.76
INT					
RAL	70.5	6	277	14	19.78
NAT.W.	48	2	204	8	25.50
B & H	75.2	5	273	18	15.16

CAREER: BOWLING

	O.	M.	R.	W.	AV.
TEST					
1ST-CLASS	3855.5	846	11103	410	27.08
INT					
RAL	194	16	819	32	25.59
NAT.W.	69.5	3	292	11	26.54
B & H	158	22	538	30	17.93

JESTY, T. E. — Lancashire

Full Name: Trevor Edward Jesty
Role: Right-hand bat, right-arm medium bowler
Born: 2 June 1948, Gosport, Hampshire
Height: 5′ 9″ **Weight:** 11st 10lbs
Nickname: Jets
County debut: 1966 (Hampshire), 1985 (Surrey), 1988 (Lancashire)
County cap: 1971 (Hampshire), 1985 (Surrey)
Benefit: 1982
No. of One-Day Internationals: 10
1000 runs in a season: 9
1st-Class 50s scored: 95
1st-Class 100s scored: 32
1st-Class 200s scored: 2
1st-Class 5 w. in innings: 19
One-Day 50s: 42
One-Day 100s: 7
Place in batting averages: 105th av. 28.87 (1987 75th av. 34.64)
Place in bowling averages: — (1987 12th av. 21.20)
1st-Class catches 1988: 0 (career 250 + 1 stumping)
Parents: Aubrey Edward and Sophia
Wife and date of marriage: Jacqueline, 12 September 1970
Children: Graeme Barry, 27 September 1972; Lorna Samantha, 7 November 1976
Family links with cricket: Brother, Aubrey Jesty, wicket-keeper and left-hand bat, could have joined Hampshire staff, but decided to continue with his apprenticeship
Education: Privet County Secondary Modern, Gosport
Jobs outside cricket: Representative for wine company
Overseas teams played for: Border in 1973–74, and Griqualand West in 1974–75 and 1975–76 in the Currie Cup Competition, South Africa
Cricketers particularly learnt from: Barry Richards
Other sports played: Soccer, golf
Relaxations: Watching soccer, gardening
Extras: Took him 10 years to score maiden first-class century. Missed most of 1980 season through injury. Made vice-captain of Hampshire in 1981. Considered to be most unlucky not to be chosen for England tour of Australia 1982–83 after brilliant 1982 season, then was called in as a replacement. One of *Wisden*'s Five Cricketers of the Year, 1982. Left Hampshire at end of 1984 when not appointed captain. Took over captaincy of Surrey in 1985. Replaced

as captain in 1986. Released by Surrey at end of 1987 season. Joined Lancashire 1988

Best batting performance: 248 Hampshire v Cambridge University, Cambridge 1984

Best bowling performance: 7-75 Hampshire v Worcestershire, Southampton 1976

LAST SEASON: BATTING

	I.	N.O.	R.	H.S.	AV.
TEST					
1ST-CLASS	27	3	693	73	28.87
INT					
RAL	12	2	232	41	23.20
NAT.W.	2	0	37	37	18.50
B & H	1	0	57	57	57.00

LAST SEASON: BOWLING

	O.	M.	R.	W.	AV.
TEST					
1ST-CLASS	25	10	56	0	—
INT					
RAL	1	0	5	0	—
NAT.W.	11	1	48	0	—
B & H	11	0	39	5	7.80

CAREER: BATTING

	I.	N.O.	R.	H.S.	AV.
TEST					
1ST-CLASS	714	92	19962	248	24.28
INT	10	4	127	52*	21.17
RAL	250	35	5383	166*	25.03
NAT.W.	33	2	957	118	30.87
B & H	67	10	2073	105	36.36

CAREER: BOWLING

	O.	M.	R.	W.	AV.
TEST					
1ST-CLASS	6125.1	1632	16005	584	27.40
INT	18	0	93	1	93.00
RAL	1297.3	76	6095	248	24.57
NAT.W.	314	52	1038	39	26.61
B & H	514.4	62	1790	74	24.18

JOHNSON, P.   Nottinghamshire

Full Name: Paul Johnson
Role: Right-hand bat, right-arm occasional bowler
Born: 24 April 1965, Newark
Height: 5′ 8″ **Weight:** 11st 7lbs
Nickname: Johno, Dwarf, Gus, Midge
County debut: 1982
County cap: 1986
1000 runs in a season: 3
1st-Class 50s scored: 30
1st-Class 100s scored: 13
One-Day 50s: 9
One-Day 100s: 1
Place in batting averages: 57th av. 35.61 (1987 65th av. 35.91)
1st-Class catches 1988: 12 (career 85 + 1 stumping)
Parents: Donald Edward and Joyce
Wife and date of marriage: Hazel, 17 October 1987
Family links with cricket: Father played local cricket and is a qualified coach
Education: Grove Comprehensive School, Newark

Qualifications: 9 CSEs, senior coaching certificate
Off-season 1988–89: Coaching and playing for Hutt District CC, New Zealand
Cricketing superstitions or habits: Left pad on first
Overseas tours: Keith Pont Benefit tour to Barbados 1987
Overseas teams played for: RAU, Johannesburg, 1985–86; Hutt DCC, New Zealand, 1988–89
Cricketers particularly learnt from: Most of Nottinghamshire staff, Clive Rice
Cricketers particularly admired: Richard Hadlee, Ian Botham, Dennis Lillee, Derek Underwood, Graeme Pollock
Other sports played: Football referee, golf (14 handicap), bowls
Other sports followed: Watches ice-hockey (Nottingham Panthers), football (Forest and County)
Injuries 1988: Missed two Sunday League games with badly bruised shin
Relaxations: 'Sleeping, eating, and company of good friends.'
Extras: Played for English Schools cricket in 1980–81 season. Youngest member ever to join the Nottinghamshire CCC staff. Hit 16 sixes in School County Cup game v Joseph Whittaker, scoring 195*. Played for Young England U-19, 1982 and 1983. Made 235 for Nottinghamshire 2nd XI, July 1982, aged 17. Won man of match award in first NatWest game (101* v Staffordshire); missed 1985 final due to appendicitis
Opinions on cricket: 'Counties should be left to prepare wickets and not have restrictions put upon them, e.g. uncovered pitches, no heavy roller. It seems to be a trial and error exercise at the players' inconvenience, as always! England's cricket media should give more backing to its players. There is enough pressure on players without trash being raked up. This also applies to the coverage on TV with so-called expert views which only seem to belittle today's players which wouldn't have happened in the "experts" day.'
Best batting performance: 140 Nottinghamshire v Hampshire, Basingstoke 1988
Best bowling performance: 1–9 Nottinghamshire v Oxford University, Trent Bridge 1984

LAST SEASON: BATTING

	I.	N.O.	R.	H.S.	AV.
TEST					
1ST-CLASS	42	3	1389	140	35.61
INT					
RAL	11	0	214	82	19.45
NAT.W.	2	0	45	29	22.50
B & H	4	1	98	37	32.66

CAREER: BATTING

	I.	N.O.	R.	H.S.	AV.
TEST					
1ST-CLASS	201	20	6178	140	34.13
INT					
RAL	67	7	1323	90	22.05
NAT.W.	14	2	286	101*	23.83
B & H	18	2	247	49	15.43

LAST SEASON: BOWLING

	O.	M.	R.	W.	AV.
TEST					
1ST-CLASS	2	1	1	0	—
INT					
RAL					
NAT.W.	1	0	11	0	—
B & H					

CAREER: BOWLING

	O.	M.	R.	W.	AV.
TEST					
1ST-CLASS	57	7	353	3	117.66
INT					
RAL					
NAT.W.	2	0	16	0	—
B & H					

JONES, A. N. Somerset

Full Name: Adrian Nicholas Jones
Role: Left-hand bat, right-arm
fast bowler, outfielder
Born: 22 July 1961, Woking
Height: 6′ 2″ **Weight:** 13st 10lbs
Nickname: Quincy, Jonah
County debut: 1981 (Sussex),
1987 (Somerset)
County cap: 1986 (Sussex),
1987 (Somerset)
1st-Class 5 w. in innings: 6
1st-Class 10 w. in match: 1
Place in batting averages: 263rd
av. 10.00
Place in bowling averages: 83rd
av. 30.14 (1987 58th av. 28.57)
1st-Class catches 1988: 8 (career 25)
Parents: William Albert and Emily
Doris
Family links with cricket: Father and brother, Glynne, both fine club
cricketers
Education: Forest Grange Preparatory School; Seaford College
Qualifications: 8 O-levels, 2 A-levels, NCA coaching qualification, consumer
credit licence
Jobs outside cricket: Financial consultant/adviser
Cricketing superstitions or habits: 'Always salute a magpie.'
Overseas teams played for: Old Selbournians and Bohemians, South Africa,
1981–82; Border 1981–82; Red and White CC, Haarlem, Holland, 1980;
Orange Free State, 1986

LAST SEASON: BATTING

	I.	N.O.	R.	H.S.	AV.
TEST					
1ST-CLASS	21	8	130	38	10.00
INT					
RAL	4	3	27	16*	27.00
NAT.W.	–	–	–	–	–
B & H	1	1	1	1*	–

CAREER: BATTING

	I.	N.O.	R.	H.S.	AV.
TEST					
1ST-CLASS	88	36	528	38	10.15
INT					
RAL	13	11	83	17*	41.50
NAT.W.	2	2	4	3*	–
B & H	9	4	42	20	8.40

LAST SEASON: BOWLING

	O.	M.	R.	W.	AV.
TEST					
1ST-CLASS	512	86	1658	55	30.14
INT					
RAL	85	1	508	18	28.22
NAT.W.	16	4	78	0	–
B & H	27	1	107	5	21.40

CAREER: BOWLING

	O.	M.	R.	W.	AV.
TEST					
1ST-CLASS	1869.3	307	6411	213	30.09
INT					
RAL	336.4	15	1657	85	19.49
NAT.W.	68	11	264	9	29.33
B & H	111.4	10	480	24	20.00

Cricketers particularly learnt from: Father, Ian Greig, Geoff Arnold, Imran Khan, Garth le Roux

Cricketers particularly admired: Imran Khan, Geoff Arnold, Richard Hadlee, Garth le Roux, Sylvester Clarke

Other sports played: 'Golf badly; hockey slightly better; rugby like an animal.'

Relaxations: 'UB40, watching Laurel and Hardy films, walking, eating, good wine and port.'

Extras: Played for Young England in 1981. Left Sussex to join Somerset at end of 1986 season

Opinions on cricket: 'There should be an alternative system for the awarding of a benefit than the present haphazard method. Perhaps an endowment scheme taken out when the player is capped.'

Best batting performance: 38 Somerset v Gloucestershire, Bristol 1988

Best bowling performance: 7-30 Somerset v Hampshire, Southampton 1988

KALLICHARRAN, A. I. Warwickshire

Full Name: Alvin Isaac Kallicharran
Role: Left-hand bat, right-arm off-spin bowler
Born: 21 March 1949, Guyana
Height: 5′ 4″
Nickname: Kalli
County debut: 1971
County cap: 1972
Benefit: 1983 (£34,094)
Test debut: 1971–72
No. of Tests: 66
No. of One-Day Internationals: 31
1000 runs in a season: 12
1st-Class 50s scored: 155
1st-Class 100s scored: 78
1st-Class 200s scored: 6
1st-Class 5 w. in innings: 1
One-day 50s: 50
One-day 100s: 11
Place in batting averages: 92nd av. 29.85
1st-Class catches 1988: 4 (career 310)
Marital status: Married
Children: One son, Rohan
Family links with cricket: Brother, Derek Isaac, played for Guyana
Overseas tours: With West Indies to New Zealand 1971; England in 1973 and

1976; India, Sri Lanka and Pakistan, 1974–75; Australia 1975–76 and 1979
–80; India and Sri Lanka, 1978–79 as captain; Pakistan, 1980
Overseas teams played for: Guyana 1966–67 in Shell Shield competition;
Queensland in 1977–78 Sheffield Shield competition; Transvaal and Orange
Free State in South Africa
Extras: Scored 100* and 101 in first two innings in Test matches v New
Zealand in 1971. Signed for World Series Cricket but resigned before playing.
He has made his home in England. With Geoff Humpage took part in record–
for Warwickshire and for all English counties – 4th wicket stand of 470 v
Lancashire at Southport in July 1982. Kallicharran made 230*, Humpage
254*. Previous record was 448 by Abel and Hayward for Surrey v Yorkshire at
The Oval in 1899. Top of Warwickshire batting averages in 1982 and 1983.
Banned from playing in West Indies for going to South Africa. One of
Wisden's Five Cricketers of the Year, 1982
Best batting performance: 243* Warwickshire v Glamorgan, Edgbaston 1983
Best bowling performance: 5-45 Transvaal v Western Province, Cape Town
1982–83

LAST SEASON: BATTING

	I.	N.O.	R.	H.S.	AV.
TEST					
1ST-CLASS	15	1	418	117*	29.85
INT					
RAL	5	1	136	63	34.00
NAT.W.					
B & H	5	1	258	90*	64.50

LAST SEASON: BOWLING

	O.	M.	R.	W.	AV.
TEST					
1ST-CLASS					
INT					
RAL					
NAT.W.					
B & H					

CAREER: BATTING

	I.	N.O.	R.	H.S.	AV.
TEST	109	10	4399	187	44.43
1ST-CLASS	689	73	27420	243*	44.51
INT	28	4	826	78	34.41
RAL	160	18	4340	102*	30.56
NAT.W.	25	2	1169	206	50.82
B & H	56	7	2140	122*	43.67

CAREER: BOWLING

	O.	M.	R.	W.	AV.
TEST	3.1 63.3	1 13	158	4	39.50
1ST-CLASS	1075.3	158	3817	78	48.93
INT	17	3	64	3	21.33
RAL	161.1	5	880	14	62.85
NAT.W.	80.4	9	277	14	19.78
B & H	34	0	153	0	–

89. What did Bill Edrich, Reg Sinfield, Lindsay Hassett and Doug
    Wright have in common?

90. Who was the first Gloucestershire professional to do the double
    in 1934?

KELLEHER, D. J. M.   Kent

Full Name: Daniel John
Michael Kelleher
Role: Right-hand bat, right-arm
medium bowler, outfielder
Born: 5 May 1966, London
Height: 6′ **Weight:** 12st 13lbs
Nickname: Donk, Shots
County debut: 1987
1st-Class 50s scored: 1
1st-Class 5 w. in innings: 2
Place in bowling averages: —
(1987 38th av. 25.82)
1st-Class catches 1988: 2 (career 3)
Parents: John and Joan
Marital status: Single
Family links with cricket: Uncle
played county cricket for Surrey
and Northants. Father played
club cricket

Education: St Mary's Grammar School, Sidcup; Erith College of Technology
Qualifications: O-levels
Jobs outside cricket: Gardener
Cricketing superstitions or habits: Always put gear on in set order
Overseas tours: Kent Schools U-17 to Vancouver and Victoria, Canada, 1984;
UK Upsetters to Trinidad and Tobago, 1986
Overseas teams played for: Doncaster CC Melbourne, 1984–85; Avendale
CC, Cape Town, 1986–87
Cricketers particularly learnt from: My father, Claude Lewis, Alan Spencer,
Colin Page

LAST SEASON: BATTING

	I.	N.O.	R.	H.S.	AV.
TEST					
1ST-CLASS	7	1	150	51	25.00
INT					
RAL					
NAT.W.					
B & H	–	–	–	–	–

CAREER: BATTING

	I.	N.O.	R.	H.S.	AV.
TEST					
1ST-CLASS	19	2	231	51	13.58
INT					
RAL					
NAT.W.	1	1	0	0*	–
B & H	1	1	0	0*	–

LAST SEASON: BOWLING

	O.	M.	R.	W.	AV.
TEST					
1ST-CLASS	94	23	229	9	25.44
INT					
RAL					
NAT.W.					
B & H	11	2	43	1	43.00

CAREER: BOWLING

	O.	M.	R.	W.	AV.
TEST					
1ST-CLASS	395	95	1107	43	25.74
INT					
RAL					
NAT.W.	17.2	2	79	2	39.50
B & H	44	3	156	3	52.00

Cricketers particularly admired: Ian Botham, David Gower, Richard Davis, David Sabine
Other sports played: Golf, skiing
Other sports followed: Rugby, American football, women's tennis
Relaxations: Watching TV, music, watching Richard Davis bat
Extras: Played for Kent Schools from U-11 to U-19. At school played rugby and cricket for Kent
Opinions on cricket: 'Too much cricket played.'
Best batting performance: 51 Kent v West Indians, Canterbury 1988
Best bowling performance: 6-109 Kent v Somerset, Bath 1987

KENDRICK, N. M. Surrey

Full Name: Neil Michael Kendrick
Role: Right-hand bat, left-arm spin bowler
Born: 11 November 1967, Bromley
Height: 6′ **Weight:** 11st 7lbs
Nickname: Kendo, The Rat
County debut: 1988
1st-Class catches 1988: 1 (career 1)
Parents: Michael Hall and Anne Patricia
Marital status: Single
Family links with cricket: Father plays club cricket for Old Wilsonians
Education: Hayes Primary; Wilson's Grammar School
Qualifications: 7 O-levels, 1 A-level
Jobs outside cricket: Stockbroker, hospital porter
Cricketing superstitions or habits: 'Any that I have seem to disappear when I'm doing badly!'
Cricketers particularly learnt from: Alec Stewart, Neil Stewart, Mickey Stewart, Chris Waller, Geoff Arnold, Mike Kendrick
Cricketers particularly admired: Phil Edmonds, Bob 'The Cat' Bevan
Other sports played: Football
Other sports followed: Most ball sports
Relaxations: East Street soulful music
Opinions on cricket: 'The Championship should be 16 four-day games for both 1st and 2nd XI's, played on the best pitches possible. A weight limit should be put on bats so they can't hit me as far!'

Best batting performance: 8* Surrey v Cambridge University, Cambridge 1988
Best bowling performance: 1-92 Surrey v Cambridge University, Cambridge 1988

LAST SEASON: BATTING

	I.	N.O.	R.	H.S.	AV.
TEST					
1ST-CLASS	1	1	8	8*	—
INT					
RAL					
NAT.W.					
B & H					

LAST SEASON: BOWLING

	O.	M.	R.	W.	AV.
TEST					
1ST-CLASS	28.5	7	97	1	97.00
INT					
RAL					
NAT.W.					
B & H					

CAREER: BATTING

	I.	N.O.	R.	H.S.	AV.
TEST					
1ST-CLASS	1	1	8	8*	—
INT					
RAL					
NAT.W.					
B & H					

CAREER: BOWLING

	O.	M.	R.	W.	AV.
TEST					
1ST-CLASS	28.5	7	97	1	97.00
INT					
RAL					
NAT.W.					
B & H					

KIMBER, S. J. S. Sussex

Full Name: Simon Julian Spencer Kimber
Role: Right-hand bat, right-arm fast-medium bowler
Born: 6 October 1963, Ormskirk Lancashire
Height: 6′ 2″ **Weight:** 13st
Nickname: Que, Kipper
County debut: 1985 (Worcestershire), 1987 (Sussex)
1st-Class 50s scored: 1
Place in batting averages: —
(1987 131st av. 26.83)
Place in bowling averages: —
(1987 139th av. 53.25)
1st-Class catches 1988: 2 (career 5)
Parents: Ron and Joan
Marital status: Single

Family links with cricket: Father played good standard of club cricket in England and West Indies (Jamaica) for three years
Education: Thomas More School, South Africa
Qualifications: School matriculation

Jobs outside cricket: Insurance broker
Overseas teams played for: Durban Collegians, South Africa, 1984–85 and 1987–88; Natal B 1986–87
Cricketers particularly learnt from: Father
Cricketers particularly admired: Richard Hadlee, Martin Crowe
Other sports played: Soccer, rugby, tennis, squash, golf
Other sports followed: Soccer, rugby, tennis, athletics
Relaxations: Music, watching sport and films, eating out
Best batting performance: 54 Sussex v Nottinghamshire, Eastbourne 1987
Best bowling performance: 4-76 Natal B v Eastern Province B, Uitenhage 1986–87

LAST SEASON: BATTING

	I.	N.O.	R.	H.S.	AV.
TEST					
1ST-CLASS	7	3	54	32*	13.50
INT					
RAL	7	4	55	15*	18.33
NAT.W.	1	0	0	0	0.00
B & H	3	1	26	15	13.00

LAST SEASON: BOWLING

	O.	M.	R.	W.	AV.
TEST					
1ST-CLASS	83	19	272	7	38.85
INT					
RAL	94.1	2	496	9	55.11
NAT.W.					
B & H	32	4	112	5	22.40

CAREER: BATTING

	I.	N.O.	R.	H.S.	AV.
TEST					
1ST-CLASS	19	7	266	54	22.16
INT					
RAL	9	4	60	15*	12.00
NAT.W.	1	0	0	0	0.00
B & H	3	1	26	15	13.00

CAREER: BOWLING

	O.	M.	R.	W.	AV.
TEST					
1ST-CLASS	334.1	55	1191	31	38.41
INT					
RAL	107.1	2	578	9	64.22
NAT.W.					
B & H	32	4	112	5	22.40

91. What is the subject of Don Mosey's recent book *We Don't Play for Fun*?

92. Which current county and Test cricketer turned down offers to play rugby league and box professionally?

LAMB, A. J. Northamptonshire

Full Name: Allan Joseph Lamb
Role: Right-hand bat, right-arm
medium bowler
Born: 20 June 1954, Langebaanweg,
Cape Province, South Africa
Height: 5′ 8″ **Weight:** 12st 12lbs
Nickname: Lambie, Legger,
Lambo
County debut: 1978
County cap: 1978
Benefit: 1988
Test debut: 1982
No. of Tests: 56
No. of One-Day Internationals: 80
1000 runs in a season: 8
1st-Class 50s scored: 119
1st-Class 100s scored: 54
1st-Class 200s scored: 1
One-Day 50s: 55
One-Day 100s: 12

Place in batting averages: 11th av. 52.86 (1987 90th av. 32.73)
1st-Class catches 1988: 7 (career 245)
Parents: Michael and Joan
Wife and date of marriage: Lindsay St Leger, 8 December 1979
Children: Katie-Ann
Family links with cricket: Father played in the Boland League. Brother
played for Western Province B. Brother-in-law, Tony Bucknall, won 10 caps
for England at rugger
Education: Wynberg Boys' High School; Abbotts College
Qualifications: Matriculation
Jobs outside cricket: Timber representative. Promotions and selling
Off-season 1988–89: Playing in South Africa
Cricketing superstitions or habits: 'Try to use the same batting shirt which I
have scored runs in.'
Overseas tours: With England to Australia and New Zealand 1982–83; New
Zealand and Pakistan 1983–84; India and Australia 1984–85; West Indies
1986; World Cup 1987
Overseas teams played for: Western Province in Currie Cup Competition,
1972–81
Cricketers particularly learnt from: 'Everyone.'
Other sports played: Squash, golf. Rode in a British bobsled at Cervinia
(Italy) in 1985
Other sports followed: Most sports

Relaxations: Shooting, fishing
Extras: Made first-class debut for Western Province in 1972–73 Currie Cup. Applied to be registered as English in 1980 but application deferred. Was top of batting averages 1980. Was primarily a bowler when first played schoolboy cricket in South Africa. One of *Wisden*'s Five Cricketers of the Year, 1980. Missed two years of first-class cricket because of military training. Qualified to play for England 1982. Appointed Northamptonshire captain for 1989
Best batting performance: 294 Orange Free State v Eastern Province, Bloemfontein, 1987–88
Best bowling performance: 1-1 Northamptonshire v Derbyshire, Derby 1978

LAST SEASON: BATTING

	I.	N.O.	R.	H.S.	AV.
TEST	10	2	325	113	40.62
1ST-CLASS	17	3	838	155	59.85
INT	4	1	110	66	36.66
RAL	5	0	215	79	43.00
NAT.W.	1	0	27	27	27.00
B & H	3	0	33	19	11.00

LAST SEASON: BOWLING

	O.	M.	R.	W.	AV.
TEST					
1ST-CLASS	4	0	19	0	–
INT					
RAL					
NAT.W.					
B & H	1	0	11	1	11.00

CAREER: BATTING

	I.	N.O.	R.	H.S.	AV.
TEST	98	9	2969	137*	33.35
1ST-CLASS	450	78	18787	294	50.50
INT	78	14	2724	118	42.56
RAL	115	17	3825	132*	39.03
NAT.W.	28	1	1015	101	37.59
B & H	46	7	1769	126*	45.35

CAREER: BOWLING

	O.	M.	R.	W.	AV.
TEST	4	1	23	1	23.00
1ST-CLASS	39.1	10	141	5	28.20
INT	1	0	3	0	–
RAL					
NAT.W.	1.2	0	12	1	12.00
B & H	1	0	11	1	11.00

LARKINS, W.   Northamptonshire

Full Name: Wayne Larkins
Role: Right-hand bat, right-arm medium bowler
Born: 22 November 1953
Height: 5′ 11″ **Weight:** 12st
Nickname: Ned
County debut: 1972
County cap: 1976
Benefit: 1986
Test debut: 1979–80
No. of Tests: 6
No. of One-Day Internationals: 6
1000 runs in a season: 10
1st-Class 50s scored: 76
1st-Class 100s scored: 40
1st-Class 200s scored: 2
1st-Class 5 w. in innings: 1

One-Day 50s: 43
One-Day 100s: 11
Place in batting averages: 126th av. 26.25 (1987 73rd av. 34.97)
1st-Class catches 1988: 23 (career 201)
Parents: Mavis (father deceased)
Wife and date of marriage: Jane Elaine, 22 March 1975
Children: Philippa Jane, 30 May 1981
Family links with cricket: Father was umpire. Brother, Melvin, played for Bedford Town for many years
Education: Bushmead, Eaton Socon, Huntingdon
Jobs outside cricket: Farming
Overseas tours: England to Australia and India 1979–80
Cricketers particularly learnt from: Mushtaq Mohammad
Other sports played: Golf, football (currently with Buckingham and was on Notts County's books), squash
Relaxations: Gardening
Extras: With Peter Willey, received 2016 pints of beer (seven barrels) from a Northampton brewery as a reward for their efforts in Australia in 1979–80. Hat-trick for Northamptonshire v Combined Universities, Benson & Hedges Cup, 1980. Banned from English Test Cricket for three years for joining rebel tour of South Africa in 1982. Recalled to Test team 1986 but withdrew due to thumb injury. Missed another Test recall in 1987 due to injury sustained whilst playing football
Best batting performance: 252 Northamptonshire v Glamorgan, Cardiff 1983
Best bowling performance: 5-59 Northamptonshire v Worcestershire, Worcester 1984

LAST SEASON: BATTING

	I.	N.O.	R.	H.S.	AV.
TEST					
1ST-CLASS	41	2	1024	134	26.25
INT					
RAL	13	0	289	65	22.23
NAT.W.	1	0	19	19	19.00
B & H	3	0	75	70	25.00

CAREER: BATTING

	I.	N.O.	R.	H.S.	AV.
TEST	11	0	176	34	16.00
1ST-CLASS	596	37	19090	252	34.15
INT	6	0	84	34	14.00
RAL	198	13	5106	172*	27.60
NAT.W.	34	3	1249	121*	40.29
B & H	58	3	1758	132	31.96

LAST SEASON: BOWLING

	O.	M.	R.	W.	AV.
TEST					
1ST-CLASS	35	18	65	3	21.66
INT					
RAL	12	0	51	0	—
NAT.W.					
B & H	7	0	31	0	—

CAREER: BOWLING

	O.	M.	R.	W.	AV.
TEST					
1ST-CLASS	539.1	117	1760	42	41.90
INT	2	0	21	0	—
RAL	321.5	9	1581	54	29.27
NAT.W.	73.5	9	248	4	62.00
B & H	112.3	14	444	16	27.75

LAWRENCE, D. V.   Gloucestershire

Full Name: David Valentine
Lawrence
Role: Right-hand bat, right-arm
fast bowler, slip fielder
Born: 28 January 1964, Gloucester
Height: 6′ 3″ **Weight:** 15st 7lbs
Nickname: Syd, Bruno
County debut: 1981
County cap: 1985
1st-Class 50s scored: 1
1st-Class 5 w. in innings: 14
Place in bowling averages: 65th
av. 27.33 (1987 104th av. 37.10)
Strike rate 1988: 46.23 (career 53.14)
1st-Class catches 1988: 3 (career 26)
Parents: Joseph and Joyce
Education: Linden School, Gloucester
Qualifications: 3 CSEs
Off-season 1988–89: Chosen for England's cancelled tour of India
Overseas tours: England B to Sri Lanka 1986
Overseas teams played for: Scarborough CC, Perth, Western Australia
Cricketers particularly learnt from: Michael Holding, Richard Hadlee,
Dennis Lillee
Cricketers particularly admired: Viv Richards
Other sports played: Rugby football. 'Was offered terms to play professional
rugby league winter 1985–86, but turned them down.'
Relaxations: 'Like listening to jazz, funk and dancing.'
Best batting performance: 65* Gloucestershire v Glamorgan, Swansea 1987
Best bowling performance: 7-47 Gloucestershire v Surrey, Cheltenham, 1988

LAST SEASON: BATTING

	I.	N.O.	R.	H.S.	AV.
TEST	1	0	4	4	4.00
1ST-CLASS	25	3	221	29	10.04
INT					
RAL					
NAT.W.	1	1	2	2*	–
B & H	1	0	6	6	6.00

CAREER: BATTING

	I.	N.O.	R.	H.S.	AV.
TEST	1	0	4	4	4.00
1ST-CLASS	135	26	1036	65*	9.50
INT					
RAL	12	5	79	21*	11.28
NAT.W.	7	3	4	2*	1.00
B & H	8	5	43	22*	14.33

LAST SEASON: BOWLING

	O.	M.	R.	W.	AV.
TEST	36	9	111	3	37.00
1ST-CLASS	611.2	94	2185	81	26.97
INT					
RAL					
NAT.W.	31	4	82	2	41.00
B & H	26	6	75	3	25.00

CAREER: BOWLING

	O.	M.	R.	W.	AV.
TEST	36	9	111	3	37.00
1ST-CLASS	2895.5	419	10896	328	33.21
INT					
RAL	276	2	1484	47	31.57
NAT.W.	149.4	14	621	20	31.05
B & H	170	10	713	25	28.52

LEATHERDALE, D. A. Worcestershire

Full Name: David Anthony
Leatherdale
Role: Right-hand bat, right-arm
medium bowler
Born: 26 November 1967, Bradford
Height: 5′ 10½″ **Weight:** 11st
Nickname: Lugs, Jimmy, Spock
County debut: 1988
One-Day 50s scored: 2
Place in batting averages: 203rd
av. 18.21
1st-Class catches 1988: 3 (career 3)
Parents: Paul Anthony and Rosalyn
Marital status: Single
Family links with cricket: Brother
plays in Bradford League. Brother-
in-law played for Young England in
1979 (toured Canada)

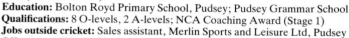

Education: Bolton Royd Primary School, Pudsey; Pudsey Grammar School
Qualifications: 8 O-levels, 2 A-levels; NCA Coaching Award (Stage 1)
Jobs outside cricket: Sales assistant, Merlin Sports and Leisure Ltd, Pudsey
Off-season 1988–89: Playing and coaching overseas
Cricketing superstitions or habits: 'Left pad on first as do 80 per cent of all
cricketers. After taking guard I take a stroll and tap the wicket on a few pitch
marks to settle myself.'
Overseas tours: Barbados 1985 with Bradford Junior League side
Overseas teams played for: Pretoria Police CC, 1987–89
Cricketers particularly learnt from: Mark Scott, George Batty, Peter Kippax
Other sports played: Golf (Yorkshire schools), football, squash
Other sports followed: American football whenever possible
Injuries 1988: Septic arthritis of left knee three weeks before NatWest Final
Relaxations: Listening to music, writing letters
Opinions on cricket: 'A full circuit of 2nd XI cricket as with the 1st XI will only
improve the standards of 2nd-class cricket in England, and make it easier for
2nd XI players to adapt to the move up into 1st-class cricket.'

LAST SEASON: BATTING

	I.	N.O.	R.	H.S.	AV.
TEST					
1ST-CLASS	15	1	255	34*	18.21
INT					
RAL	5	2	128	62*	42.66
NAT.W.	4	1	78	43	26.00
B & H					

CAREER: BATTING

	I.	N.O.	R.	H.S.	AV.
TEST					
1ST-CLASS	15	1	255	34*	18.21
INT					
RAL	5	2	128	62*	42.66
NAT.W.	4	1	78	43	26.00
B & H					

Best batting performance: 34* Worcestershire v Kent, Folkestone 1988
Best bowling performance: 1-17 Worcestershire v Northamptonshire, Worcester 1988

LENHAM, N. J. Sussex

Full Name: Neil John Lenham
Role: Right-hand bat, right-arm medium bowler
Born: 17 December 1965, Worthing
Height: 5′ 11″ **Weight:** 10st 12lbs
Nickname: Archie, Pin
County debut: 1984
1st-Class 50s scored: 3
1st-Class 100s scored: 1
One-Day 50s: 2
Place in batting averages: 144th av. 24.43
1st-Class catches 1988: 7 (career 20)
Parents: Leslie John and Valerie Anne
Marital status: Single
Family links with cricket: Father ex-Sussex county cricketer and now NCA National Coach

Education: Broadwater Manor House Prep School; Brighton College
Qualifications: 5 O-levels, 2 A-levels, Advanced Cricket Coach
Jobs outside cricket: Teacher, grease monkey in a garage
Off-season 1988–89: Playing and coaching at Port Elizabeth CC in South Africa
Cricketing superstitions or habits: Adjusting all equipment to obtain comfort
Overseas tours: 1981 tour to Barbados with Sussex U-16; 1982 tour to Barbados with Sussex Young Cricketers; 1985 England Young Cricketers tour to West Indies (as captain)
Cricketers particularly learnt from: Father, John Spencer
Cricketers particularly admired: Ken McEwan, Barry Richards, Viv Richards
Other sports played: Hockey, squash, golf, snooker
Injuries 1988: Broken finger
Relaxations: Music (Van Morrison and Fleetwood Mac), reading, keeping tropical fish
Extras: Made debut for Young England 1983. Broke record for number of

runs scored in season at a public school in 1984 (1534 av. 80.74). Youngest player to appear for County 2nd XI at 14 years old
Opinions on cricket: 'Over-rate fines should be looked into so they don't end up punishing attacking cricket.'
Best batting performance: 104* Sussex v Pakistanis, Hove 1987
Best bowling performance: 4-88 Sussex v Leicestershire, Leicester 1986

LAST SEASON: BATTING

	I.	N.O.	R.	H.S.	AV.
TEST					
1ST-CLASS	32	2	733	74	24.43
INT					
RAL	7	4	130	39	43.33
NAT.W.					
B & H	4	1	86	55	28.66

CAREER: BATTING

	I.	N.O.	R.	H.S.	AV.
TEST					
1ST-CLASS	83	12	1907	104*	26.85
INT					
RAL	11	7	167	39	41.75
NAT.W.	1	0	6	6	6.00
B & H	9	2	225	82	32.14

LAST SEASON: BOWLING

	O.	M.	R.	W.	AV.
TEST					
1ST-CLASS	28.5	3	101	3	33.66
INT					
RAL	12	0	47	2	23.50
NAT.W.					
B & H	9	0	46	1	46.00

CAREER: BOWLING

	O.	M.	R.	W.	AV.
TEST					
1ST-CLASS	159.5	29	510	12	42.50
INT					
RAL	20	0	87	2	43.50
NAT.W.	9	0	48	1	48.00
B & H	9	0	46	1	46.00

LEVER, J. K.   Essex

Full Name: John Kenneth Lever
Role: Right-hand bat, left-arm fast-medium bowler
Born: 24 February 1949, Stepney
Height: 6' 0" **Weight:** 13st
Nickname: Jake, JK, Stanley
County debut: 1967
County cap: 1970
Benefit: 1980 (£66,250)
Test debut: 1976–77
No. of Tests: 21
No. of One-Day Internationals: 22
50 wickets in a season: 16
1st-Class 50s scored: 3
1st-Class 5 w. in innings: 84
1st-Class 10 w. in match: 12
Place in bowling averages: 84th
av. 30.15 (1987 82nd av. 31.73)
Strike rate 1988: 66.76 (career 52.77)
1st-Class catches 1988: 2 (career 184)
Parents: Ken and Doris

Wife and date of marriage: Chris, 30 July 1983
Children: Jocelyn Jennifer, 9 January 1985; James, 4 March 1988
Education: Highlands Junior; Dane County Secondary School
Qualifications: 3 O-levels, 3 RSAs
Jobs outside cricket: Clerk with Access Social Club; Byron Shipping; Dominion Insurance
Off-season 1988–89: Organising Testimonial Year
Cricketing superstitions or habits: 'Too many to mention.'
Overseas tours: India, Sri Lanka and Australia, 1976–77; Pakistan and New Zealand, 1977–78; Australia, 1978–79 and 1979–80
Cricketers particularly learnt from: 'The Essex team.'
Cricketers particularly admired: Sir Gary Sobers
Other sports played: Football, golf
Injuries 1988: 'Old age!'
Relaxations: Indian food, real ale
Extras: Took 10 wickets on his Test debut in 1976 v India at Delhi. Took 106 wickets at an average of 15.80 in 1978, and 106 wickets at an average of 17.30 in 1979, and 106 wickets at an average of 16.28 in 1983. President of Blythswood CC. Member of Ilford CC since the age of 14. One of *Wisden*'s Five Cricketers of the Year, 1978. Has reputation of 'not breaking down'. On the executive of the Cricketers' Association. Banned from Test Cricket for three years for joining rebel tour of South Africa in 1982. Recalled to England side in 1986 after four-year absence
Opinions on cricket: 'Pitches to be improved if four-day cricket is here to stay.'
Best batting performance: 91 Essex v Glamorgan, Cardiff 1970
Best bowling performance: 8-37 Essex v Gloucestershire, Bristol 1984

LAST SEASON: BATTING

	I.	N.O.	R.	H.S.	AV.
TEST					
1ST-CLASS	13	1	53	20	4.41
INT					
RAL	7	3	12	5*	3.00
NAT.W.	1	1	1	1*	—
B & H	—	—	—	—	—

LAST SEASON: BOWLING

	O.	M.	R.	W.	AV.
TEST					
1ST-CLASS	434	106	1176	39	30.15
INT					
RAL	93.3	3	417	8	52.12
NAT.W.	17	6	32	3	10.66
B & H	62.2	9	222	6	37.00

CAREER: BATTING

	I.	N.O.	R.	H.S.	AV.
TEST	31	5	306	53	11.76
1ST-CLASS	500	187	3316	91	10.59
INT	11	4	56	27*	8.00
RAL	113	68	402	23	8.93
NAT.W.	26	18	94	15*	11.75
B & H	26	18	104	13	13.00

CAREER: BOWLING

	O.	M.	R.	W.	AV.
TEST	166.7 516.2	27 113	1951	73	26.72
1ST-CLASS	210.4 13932.4	3132	39121	1619	24.16
INT	33 148	5 15	713	24	29.70
RAL	1931.1	211	7230	365	19.80
NAT.W.	444.3	105	1177	70	16.81
B & H	852.1	160	2614	143	18.27

LEWIS, C. C.   Leicestershire

Full Name: Christopher Clairmonte Lewis
Role: Right-hand bat, right-arm medium bowler
Born: 14 February 1968, Georgetown, Guyana
Height: 6' 2½" **Weight:** 13st
Nickname: Carl
County debut: 1987
1st-Class 5 w. in innings: 2
1st-Class 10 w. in match: 1
One-Day 50s scored: 1
Place in batting averages: 181st av. 21.05
Place in bowling averages: 71st av. 28.80
Strike rate 1988: 55.95 (career 58.04)
1st-Class catches 1988: 10 (career 11)
Parents: Philip and Patricia
Marital status: Single
Education: Willesden High School
Qualifications: 2 O-levels
Overseas tours: Young England to Australia 1987
Cricketers particularly learned from: Ted Jackson, Paddy Clift
Cricketers particularly admired: Richard Hadlee
Other sports played: Snooker, football
Other sports followed: Snooker, football, darts, American football
Relaxations: Music, sleeping

LAST SEASON: BATTING

	I.	N.O.	R.	H.S.	AV.
TEST					
1ST-CLASS	23	4	400	40	21.05
INT					
RAL	6	2	92	40	23.00
NAT.W.	2	0	63	53	31.50
B & H	3	2	23	13*	23.00

CAREER: BATTING

	I.	N.O.	R.	H.S.	AV.
TEST					
1ST-CLASS	27	4	453	42	19.69
INT					
RAL	10	6	127	40	31.75
NAT.W.	4	0	96	53	24.00
B & H	3	2	23	13*	23.00

LAST SEASON: BOWLING

	O.	M.	R.	W.	AV.
TEST					
1ST-CLASS	391.4	83	1210	42	28.80
INT					
RAL	58.4	1	249	8	31.12
NAT.W.	24	2	86	4	21.50
B & H	28	2	109	4	27.25

CAREER: BOWLING

	O.	M.	R.	W.	AV.
TEST					
1ST-CLASS	454.4	92	1377	47	29.29
INT					
RAL	89.4	2	408	11	37.09
NAT.W.	51	4	189	6	31.50
B & H	28	2	109	4	27.25

266

Best batting performance: 42 Leicestershire v Nottinghamshire, Leicester 1987
Best bowling performance: 6-22 Leicestershire v Oxford University, Oxford 1988

LILLEE, D. K.   Northamptonshire

Full Name: Dennis Keith Lillee
Role: Right-hand bat, right-arm
fast-medium bowler (formerly fast:
'I'm only 70 or 80 per cent of
the bowler I was.')
Born: 18 July, 1949, Subiaco,
Perth, Western Australia
Height: 6' 0" **Weight:** 13st 10lbs
Nickname: Fot
County debut: 1988
Test debut: 1970–71
No. of Tests: 70
No. of One-Day Internationals: 63
1st-Class 50s scored: 2
1st-Class 5w in innings: 50
1st-Class 10w in match: 13
Place in batting averages: 238th
av. 13.33

Place in bowling averages: 117th
av. 37.04
Strike rate 1988: 70.00 (career 50.18)
Wife and date of marriage: Helen, 1969
Children: Adam, Dean
Family links with cricket: Both grandfathers played good club cricket
Education: Belmont Secondary School, Perth
Off-season 1988–89: Playing for Perth CC
Overseas tours: With Australia to England, 1972, 1975, 1980, 1981; to West Indies, 1972–73; to New Zealand 1976–77, 1981–82; to Pakistan, 1979–80; to Sri Lanka, 1982–83; to South Africa, with International XI, 1975–76
Overseas teams played for: Western Australia, Tasmania
Cricketers particularly learnt from: Ray Lindwall
Injuries 1988: Various injuries caused him to miss most of season
Relaxations: Surfing, driving into the country, music
Extras: Taken most Test wickets of any Australian, 355. For a time, held record of most Test wickets ever. Played World Series Cricket for Kerry Packer, 1977–79. In 1981, took Sheffield Shield record of 85 wickets. Taken record 163 wickets in Anglo–Australian Test cricket. Suffers from hay-fever.

Left first-class cricket in 1984, and stayed out for three years. Says he did not even watch cricket. Then in 1987, played for Tasmania, and was offered terms - by Northamptonshire for 1988 season. Hoping to stay on in 1989 as club coach
Best batting performance: 73* Australia v England, Lord's 1975
Best bowling performance: 8-29 Australia v Rest of the World, Melbourne 1971–72

LAST SEASON: BATTING

	I.	N.O.	R.	H.S.	AV.
TEST					
1ST-CLASS	11	2	120	22	13.33
INT					
RAL	1	1	6	6*	–
NAT.W.					
B & H	1	0	7	7	7.00

CAREER: BATTING

	I.	N.O.	R.	H.S.	AV.
TEST	90	24	905	73*	13.71
1ST-CLASS	151	46	1472	54*	14.01
INT	34	8	240	42*	9.23
RAL	1	1	6	6*	–
NAT.W.					
B & H	1	0	7	7	7.00

LAST SEASON: BOWLING

	O.	M.	R.	W.	AV.
TEST					
1ST-CLASS	245	45	778	21	37.04
INT					
RAL	35	2	129	5	25.80
NAT.W.					
B & H	20	2	84	4	21.00

CAREER: BOWLING

	O.	M.	R.	W.	AV.
TEST	732.2 2102.5	105 547	8493	355	23.92
1ST-CLASS	1423.6 2400.2	205 563	12202	527	23.15
INT	8 588.1	1 79	2145	103	20.82
RAL	35	2	129	5	25.80
NAT.W.					
B & H	20	2	84	4	21.00

LILLEY, A. W. Essex

Full Name: Alan William Lilley
Role: Right-hand bat, right-arm medium bowler, cover fielder
Born: 8 May 1959, Ilford, Essex
Height: 6′ 2″ **Weight:** 14st
Nickname: Lil
County debut: 1978
County cap: 1986
1st-Class 50s scored: 22
1st-Class 100s scored: 2
One-Day 50s: 7
One-Day 100s: 2
Place in batting averages: 120th av. 26.76 (1987 99th av. 31.32)
1st-Class catches 1988: 16 (career 56)
Parents: Min and Ron
Wife and date of marriage: Helen, 6 October 1984 (separated)

Family links with cricket: Father played for Osborne CC as a bowler for 18 years
Education: Caterham High School, Ilford
Jobs outside cricket: Shipping broker
Off-season 1987–88: Working in a shipping office
Overseas teams played for: Perth CC, Western Australia, 1979–80
Cricketers particularly learnt from: Stuart Turner, Bill Morris
Other sports played: Most
Injuries 1988: 'None – which is a change!'
Extras: Was on MCC Young Pro staff at Lord's one season after leaving school. Scored century in second innings of debut v Nottinghamshire
Best batting performance: 102 Essex v Middlesex, Chelmsford 1987
Best bowling performance: 3-116 Essex v Glamorgan, Swansea 1985

LAST SEASON: BATTING

	I.	N.O.	R.	H.S.	AV.
TEST					
1ST-CLASS	33	3	803	80*	26.76
INT					
RAL	12	2	217	38*	21.70
NAT.W.	2	0	8	7	4.00
B & H	4	1	68	29	22.66

CAREER: BATTING

	I.	N.O.	R.	H.S.	AV.
TEST					
1ST-CLASS	162	13	3881	102	26.04
INT					
RAL	102	9	1504	60	16.17
NAT.W.	15	2	352	113	27.07
B & H	29	3	537	119	20.65

LAST SEASON: BOWLING

	O.	M.	R.	W.	AV.
TEST					
1ST-CLASS	11	0	119	0	–
INT					
RAL	1	0	3	0	–
NAT.W.					
B & H					

CAREER: BOWLING

	O.	M.	R.	W.	AV.
TEST					
1ST-CLASS	79.3	4	505	7	72.14
INT					
RAL	4.3	0	23	3	7.66
NAT.W.	8	3	33	2	16.50
B & H	1	0	4	1	4.00

93. What do the captain of Dorset and the secretary of Worcestershire have in common?

94. John Childs, making his Test debut at 36, was the oldest England player to do so since whom?

Full Name: Graham David Lloyd
Role: Right-hand bat
Born: 1 July 1969, Accrington
Height: 5′ 9″ **Weight:** 11st 7lbs
Nickname: Bumble
County debut: 1988
1st-Class catches 1988: 1 (career 1)
Parents: David and Susan
Marital status: Single
Family links with cricket: Father
played for Lancashire and England
Education: Hollins County High
School, Accrington
Off-season 1988–89: Playing
cricket in Queensland
Overseas teams played for: Balmain,
Sydney 1986–87, 1987–88
Cricketers particularly learnt from:
Terry Holt (local coach), Dad,
Graeme Fowler
Cricketers particularly admired: Graeme Hick, Allan Lamb, David Makinson
Other sports: Tennis, golf
Other sports followed: All sports
Best batting performance: 22 Lancashire v Derbyshire, Derby 1988

LAST SEASON: BATTING

	I.	N.O.	R.	H.S.	AV.
TEST					
1ST-CLASS	2	0	22	22	11.00
INT					
RAL					
NAT.W.					
B & H					

CAREER: BATTING

	I.	N.O.	R.	H.S.	AV.
TEST					
1ST-CLASS	2	0	22	22	11.00
INT					
RAL					
NAT.W.					
B & H					

95. True or false: in the English summer of 1947, when Denis
Compton scored 18 centuries for Middlesex and England, and a
total of 3816 runs, he also took 73 first-class wickets?

96. Who was top of the 1988 first-class bowling averages for
Derbyshire?

Full Name: Timothy Andrew Lloyd
Role: Left-hand bat, off-break bowler
Born: 5 November 1956, Oswestry
Height: 5′ 10″ **Weight:** 11st 10lbs
Nickname: Teflon
County debut: 1977
County cap: 1980
Test debut: 1984
No. of Tests: 1
No. of One-Day Internationals: 3
1000 runs in a season: 7
1st-Class 50s scored: 65
1st-Class 100s scored: 24
1st-Class 200s scored: 1
One-Day 50s: 42
One-Day 100s: 2
Place in batting averages: 49th
av. 36.20 (1987 73rd av. 34.95)
1st-Class catches 1988: 7 (career 116)
Marital status: Single
Children: Sophie, Georgia
Education: Oswestry Boys' High School; Dorset College of Higher Education
Qualifications: O-levels, A-levels, HND Tourism, NCA Advanced Coach
Jobs outside cricket: Agent for Italian colour printer, book publishing, lorry driver, corporate hospitality
Off-season 1988–89: Working with Elite Promotions
Overseas tours: Derrick Robins' XI to South America 1979; Warwickshire CCC to Zambia 1977; Warwickshire Wanderers to Barbados 1978
Overseas teams played for: Orange Free State, Zingari CC, Waverley CC
Cricketers particularly learnt from: Dennis Amiss
Cricketers particularly admired: Gary Sobers
Other sports: Soccer, golf, tennis, table tennis, squash
Other sports followed: Golf, tennis, horse racing, greyhound racing
Injuries 1988: 'None, miraculously!'
Relaxations: 'Enjoying my home, drinking good wine and beer, eating various cuisines, greyhounds.'
Extras: Scored 202* for Shropshire Schools v Worcestershire. Played for Shropshire and Warwickshire 2nd XI, both in 1975. Appointed captain of Warwickshire for 1988 season
Opinions on cricket: 'Toss should be awarded to visiting captain in Championship cricket in an attempt to prevent home sides preparing pitches geared to their advantage.'

Best batting performance: 208* Warwickshire v Gloucestershire, Edgbaston 1983
Best bowling performance: 3-62 Warwickshire v Surrey, Edgbaston 1985

LAST SEASON: BATTING

	I.	N.O.	R.	H.S.	AV.
TEST					
1ST-CLASS	43	3	1448	160*	36.20
INT					
RAL	14	0	295	66	21.07
NAT.W.	2	0	159	121	79.50
B & H	5	0	248	93	49.60

CAREER: BATTING

	I.	N.O.	R.	H.S.	AV.
TEST	1	1	10	10*	–
1ST-CLASS	410	37	13386	208*	35.88
INT					
RAL	123	12	3263	90	29.39
NAT.W.	23	3	897	121	44.85
B & H	37	3	1153	137*	33.91

LAST SEASON: BOWLING

	O.	M.	R.	W.	AV.
TEST					
1ST-CLASS	31	1	208	2	104.00
INT					
RAL					
NAT.W.					
B & H					

CAREER: BOWLING

	O.	M.	R.	W.	AV.
TEST					
1ST-CLASS	264	42	1189	15	79.26
INT					
RAL	23.1	0	149	1	149.00
NAT.W.	9	1	47	2	23.50
B & H	15	1	76	0	–

LLOYDS, J. W.   Gloucestershire

Full Name: Jeremy William Lloyds
Role: Left-hand bat, off-break bowler, close fielder
Born: 17 November 1954, Penang, Malaya
Height: 5′ 11″ **Weight:** 12st
Nickname: Jo'burg, JJ or Jerry
County debut: 1979 (Somerset), 1985 (Gloucestershire)
County cap: 1982 (Somerset), 1985 (Gloucestershire)
1000 runs in a season: 2
1st-Class 50s scored: 44
1st-Class 100s scored: 10
1st-Class 5 w. in innings: 11
1st-Class 10 w. in match: 1
One-Day 50s: 2
Place in batting averages: 186th av. 20.61 (1987 25th av. 43.32)
Place in bowling averages: 132nd av. 58.23 (1987 118th av. 40.72)
Strike rate 1988: 110.53 (career 67.82)
1st-Class catches 1988: 20 (career 173)
Parents: Edwin William and Grace Cicely
Marital status: Single
Family links with cricket: Father played Blundell's 1st XI 1932–35, selected

for Public Schools Rest v Lord's Schools at Lord's 1935. Played Inter-State cricket in Malaya and Singapore 1950–55. Brother, Christopher Edwin Lloyds, played for Blundell's 1st XI 1964–66 and Somerset 2nd XI in 1966

Education: St Dunstan's Prep School; Blundell's School

Qualifications: 10 O-levels, NCA Advanced Coach

Jobs outside cricket: Lloyds Bank, Taunton, for 1½ years. MCC Young Professionals at Lord's 1975 for 4 years

Off-season 1988–89: Playing cricket in Cape Town for Fishoek CC

Overseas tours: With Somerset to Antigua, 1981; with Gloucestershire to Barbados, 1985; Sri Lanka 1987

Overseas teams played for: St Stithian's Old Boys, Johannesburg, 1978–80; Toombul DCC, Brisbane, 1980–82; North Sydney District 1982–83; Orange Free State 1983–84; Preston (Victoria) 1986

Cricketers particularly learnt from: Don Wilson, Derek Taylor, Brian Davison

Cricketers particularly admired: John Hampshire, Graeme Pollock, Viv Richards, Ian Botham, Derek Underwood, Brian Davison

Other sports played: Golf, swimming, windsurfing

Other sports followed: Motor racing, tennis, American football

Relaxations: Music, cinema, driving, reading

Extras: Scored 132* and 102* for Somerset in same Championship match, June 1982. Took 30 catches in 1982 season for Somerset. Moved to Gloucestershire for 1985 season

Opinions on cricket: 'Coloured clothing worn for all one-day cricket. Covered wickets at all times. If another TV channel wants to cover full Sunday cricket and one-day games, let them. The five over substitute law (which does not affect Test cricket – caused by certain Test countries abusing the rule in one-day cricket in 1987) should be scrapped, for reasons obvious to those who know and play the game!'

Best batting performance: 132* Somerset v Northamptonshire, Northampton 1982

Best bowling performance: 7-88 Somerset v Essex, Chelmsford 1982

LAST SEASON: BATTING

	I.	N.O.	R.	H.S.	AV.
TEST					
1ST-CLASS	24	3	433	102*	20.61
INT					
RAL	6	0	46	18	7.66
NAT.W.					
B & H	4	2	36	20	18.00

CAREER: BATTING

	I.	N.O.	R.	H.S.	AV.
TEST					
1ST-CLASS	300	43	8005	132*	31.14
INT					
RAL	70	11	783	57	13.27
NAT.W.	13	3	181	40	18.10
B & H	19	2	261	51	15.35

LAST SEASON: BOWLING

	O.	M.	R.	W.	AV.
TEST					
1ST-CLASS	239.3	42	757	13	58.23
INT					
RAL					
NAT.W.					
B & H					

CAREER: BOWLING

	O.	M.	R.	W.	AV.
TEST					
1ST-CLASS	2848.3	608	9138	252	36.26
INT					
RAL	92.2	6	461	11	41.90
NAT.W.	38.3	4	120	3	40.00
B & H	29.2	2	97	4	24.25

LORD, G. J. Worcestershire

Full Name: Gordon John Lord
Role: Left-hand bat, slow left-arm
bowler, specialist third-man
Born: 25 April 1961, Birmingham
Height: 5′ 10″ **Weight:** 'Variable
and confidential.'
Nickname: Plum
County debut: 1983 (Warwickshire),
1987 (Worcestershire)
1st-Class 50s scored: 8
1st-Class 100s scored: 2
One-Day 50s: 1
One-Day 100s: 1
Place in batting averages: 112th
av. 27.80 (1987 168th av. 20.76)
1st-Class catches 1988: 4 (career 13)
Parents: Michael David and
Christine Frances
Marital status: Single
Family links with cricket: Uncle Charles Watts played for Leicestershire
Education: Warwick School; Durham University
Qualifications: 7 O-levels, 4 A-levels, BA General Studies, NCA Coaching
Award
Jobs outside cricket: Personnel trainee, Lucas Engineering and Systems;
Assistant Manager, Worcester Country Club
Off-season 1988–89: Working at Worcester Country Club
Overseas tours: England U-19 to Australia 1978–79 and West Indies 1979–80
Cricketers particularly learnt from: Allan Wilkins (school coach), Neal
Abberley (2nd XI coach), Norman Graham (University coach), Peter
Stringer, Tim Curtis, Basil D'Oliveira
Cricketers particularly admired: Dennis Amiss, Graeme Hick
Other sports played: Squash
Other sports followed: Watches rugby, squash, snooker
Injuries 1988: Groin strain and broken finger
Relaxations: All forms of music, particularly church organ music; astronomy,
reading, people, Indian cooking and eating

LAST SEASON: BATTING

	I.	N.O.	R.	H.S.	AV.
TEST					
1ST-CLASS	33	2	862	101	27.80
INT					
RAL					
NAT.W.	1	0	0	0	0.00
B & H	3	0	23	15	7.66

CAREER: BATTING

	I.	N.O.	R.	H.S.	AV.
TEST					
1ST-CLASS	78	6	1723	199	23.93
INT					
RAL	13	1	249	103	20.75
NAT.W.	1	0	0	0	0.00
B & H	4	0	23	15	5.75

Extras: Released by Warwickshire at end of 1986 season. Joined Worcestershire for 1987
Best batting performance: 199 Warwickshire v Yorkshire, Edgbaston 1985

LOVE, J. D.   Yorkshire

Full Name: James Derek Love
Role: Right-hand bat, right-arm medium bowler
Born: 22 April 1955, Leeds
Height: 6′ 2″ **Weight:** 14st
Nickname: Jim
County debut: 1975
County cap: 1980
Benefit: 1989
No. of One-Day Internationals: 3
1000 runs in a season: 2
1st-Class 50s scored: 55
1st-Class 100s scored: 13
One-Day 50s: 17
One-Day 100s: 4
Place in batting averages: 104th
av. 28.88 (1987 123rd av. 27.78)
1st-Class catches 1988: 12 (career 119)
Parents: Derek Oliver and Betty
Wife and date of marriage: Janice Hazel, 28 February 1986
Children: Thomas James, 4 March 1988
Family links with cricket: Father played local cricket; brother Robert plays for Tadcaster CC in Yorkshire League
Education: Brudenell County Secondary, Leeds
Jobs outside cricket: Civil servant for three years until left to become professional cricketer
Overseas teams played for: Whitbread Scholarship to Mosman Middle Harbour and District CC in 1977–78; Scarborough CC, Perth, Western Australia, 1978–79; Mosman Middle Harbour and District CC 1982–83, 1984–85
Cricketers particularly learnt from: Doug Padgett (county coach)
Other sports played: Local football, golf
Other sports followed: Rugby League
Injuries 1988: Right knee ('probably old age')
Relaxations: Shooting
Extras: Man of the Match in Yorkshire's victory in B & H Cup Final 1987. Awarded Benefit 1989

Opinions on cricket: 'I wish employment could be found for more cricketers when the season ends.'
Best batting performance: 170* Yorkshire v Worcestershire, Worcester 1979
Best bowling performance: 2-0 Yorkshire v Windward Islands, Castries 1986–87

LAST SEASON: BATTING

	I.	N.O.	R.	H.S.	AV.
TEST					
1ST-CLASS	28	2	751	93*	28.88
INT					
RAL	9	2	94	43	13.42
NAT.W.	1	0	67	67	67.00
B & H	3	2	66	45*	66.00

CAREER: BATTING

	I.	N.O.	R.	H.S.	AV.
TEST					
1ST-CLASS	376	57	10063	170*	31.54
INT	3	0	61	43	20.33
RAL	136	17	2722	118*	22.87
NAT.W.	17	3	258	67	18.42
B & H	35	12	1069	118*	46.47

LAST SEASON: BOWLING

	O.	M.	R.	W.	AV.
TEST					
1ST-CLASS	2.3	0	11	1	11.00
INT					
RAL	1	0	14	0	–
NAT.W.					
B & H					

CAREER: BOWLING

	O.	M.	R.	W.	AV.
TEST					
1ST-CLASS	231.3	37	815	9	90.55
INT					
RAL	19	1	83	3	27.66
NAT.W.	12	3	39	2	19.50
B & H	1	0	7	0	–

LYNCH, M. A. Surrey

Full Name: Monte Allan Lynch
Role: Right-hand bat, right-arm medium and off-break bowler
Born: 21 May 1958, Georgetown, Guyana
Weight: 12st
Nickname: Mont
County debut: 1977
County cap: 1982
No. of One-Day Internationals: 3
1000 runs in a season: 6
1st-Class 50s scored: 54
1st-Class 100s scored: 28
One-Day 50s: 29
One-Day 100s: 4
Place in batting averages: 35th av. 39.84 (1987 86th av. 33.14)
1st-Class catches 1988: 17 (career 216)
Parents: Lawrence and Doreen Austin
Marital status: Single

Family links with cricket: 'Father and most of family played at some time or another.'
Education: Ryden's School, Walton-on-Thames
Other sports: Football, table tennis
Extras: Hitting 141* for Surrey v Glamorgan at Guildford in August 1982, off 78 balls in 88 minutes, one six hit his captain's, Roger Knight's, car, denting it. Repeated trick in 1983 v Worcestershire in John Player Special League. Joined West Indies Rebels in South Africa 1983–84, although qualified for England. Appeared in all three One-Day Internationals v West Indies 1988
Best batting performance: 152 Surrey v Nottinghamshire, The Oval 1986
Best bowling performance: 3-6 Surrey v Glamorgan, Swansea 1981

LAST SEASON: BATTING

	I.	N.O.	R.	H.S.	AV.
TEST					
1ST-CLASS	29	4	996	103*	39.84
INT	3	0	8	6	2.66
RAL	13	5	427	85*	53.37
NAT.W.	4	0	141	61	35.25
B & H	3	1	132	63*	66.00

CAREER: BATTING

	I.	N.O.	R.	H.S.	AV.
TEST					
1ST-CLASS	385	44	11960	152	35.07
INT	3	0	8	6	2.66
RAL	134	20	3339	136	29.28
NAT.W.	24	4	597	129	29.85
B & H	37	3	975	112*	28.67

LAST SEASON: BOWLING

	O.	M.	R.	W.	AV.
TEST					
1ST-CLASS	29.2	8	88	4	22.00
INT					
RAL	1	0	12	0	–
NAT.W.	7	0	38	0	–
B & H	6	0	42	0	–

CAREER: BOWLING

	O.	M.	R.	W.	AV.
TEST					
1ST-CLASS	294.5	55	1116	24	46.50
INT					
RAL	11.5	0	95	5	19.00
NAT.W.	23	6	80	2	40.00
B & H	6	0	42	0	–

97. Who was top of the 1988 first-class bowling averages for Essex?

98. Who was top of the 1988 first-class bowling averages for Glamorgan?

MACLAURIN, N. R. C.　　　　Middlesex

Full Name: Neil Ralph Charter Maclaurin
Role: Right-hand bat, right-arm medium pace bowler
Born: 22 March 1966, Welwyn Garden City
Height: 5′ 10½″ **Weight:** 11st 5lbs
Nickname: Macca
County debut: 1986
Parents: Ian and Ann
Family links with cricket: Father had a few seasons with Kent CCC
Education: Ardwickbury Preparatory School; Malvern College
Qualifications: 9 O-levels, 2 A-levels
Jobs outside cricket: Retailing, supermarketing
Off-season 1988–89: Working for a corporate entertainment business
Cricketing superstitions or habits: Always puts left pad on first
Overseas tours: School tour to Barbados, 1984
Overseas teams played for: Balmain DCC, Sydney 1985–88
Cricketers particularly learnt from: Clive Radley, Don Bennett, Geoff Boycott
Cricketers particularly admired: Barry and Viv Richards, Alvin Kallicharran
Other sports played: Tennis, soccer, lots of golf
Other sports followed: Soccer, Tottenham Hotspur FC, baseball
Injuries 1988: Ruptured thigh muscle
Relaxations: Golf
Extras: Retired from Middlesex at end of 1988 season
Opinions on cricket: 'No overseas players. Pump more money into youth cricket from money saved. More four-day cricket.'
Best batting performance: 35 Middlesex v Cambridge University, Cambridge 1988

LAST SEASON: BATTING

	I.	N.O.	R.	H.S.	AV.
TEST					
1ST-CLASS	2	0	37	35	18.50
INT					
RAL	1	1	15	15*	–
NAT.W.					
B & H					

CAREER: BATTING

	I.	N.O.	R.	H.S.	AV.
TEST					
1ST-CLASS	2	0	37	35	18.50
INT					
RAL	4	1	20	15*	6.66
NAT.W.					
B & H					

MAHER, B. J. M.   Derbyshire

Full Name: Bernard Joseph Michael Maher
Role: Right-hand bat, wicket-keeper
Born: 11 February 1958, Hillingdon
Height: 5′ 9½″ **Weight:** 11st 7lbs
Nickname: 'Tends to vary but all derogatory!' B.J.
County debut: 1981
County cap: 1987
1st-Class 50s scored: 14
1st-Class 100s scored: 4
One-Day 50s: 2
Place in batting averages: 96th av. 29.51 (1987 164th av. 21.38)
Parents: Francis J. and Mary Ann
Marital status: Single
Family links with cricket: Brother kept wicket for school. Father followed Derbyshire CCC quite closely
Education: St Bernadette's Primary; Abbotsfield Comprehensive; Bishopsmalt Grammar; Loughborough University
Qualifications: 10 O-levels, 3 A-levels, BSc Hons in Economics and Accountancy. NCA Coaching Award. Qualified to professional stage 2 of certified accountancy exams
Jobs outside cricket: Accountant
Off-season 1988–89: Acting as Northland cricket coaching coordinator in New Zealand. Playing in Northland
Overseas tours: With the Middlesex Cricket League touring team to Trinidad and Tobago, 1978; Amsterdam with Loughborough University 1981
Overseas teams played for: Zingari CC, Pietermaritzburg 1982–83, 1983–84; Ellerslie CC, Auckland, New Zealand 1984–85; Kamo CC and Northland, New Zealand 1985–86; Northern Districts B 1986–87
Cricketers particularly learnt from: Bob Taylor, Alan Knott, John Wright
Cricketers particularly admired: Malcolm Marshall, Richard Hadlee, Gordon Greenidge
Other sports played: Badminton
Other sports followed: Athletics, rugby, tennis, boxing
Relaxations: Scuba-diving, fell-walking, coarse- and fly-fishing
Extras: Caught five catches in innings on debut v Gloucestershire. Topped wicket-keepers' dismissals list in 1987 with 76 victims
Opinions on cricket: 'A "transfer system" should operate in cricket allowing both clubs and players to make money. A transfer system would also

indirectly improve youth cricket, because young talent will be sought and coached more effectively, because of the possible earnings potential for county clubs. Television coverage of the Refuge Assurance League is declining in favour of other sports. I believe coloured clothing and floodlights should be used, along with other gimmicks to ensure the public and television coverage on Sundays is maintained. To ensure the best national cricket team is selected a paid national selector should be appointed to watch every county game. A lot has been written and said about ways in which to stop fast bowlers intimidating batsmen by bowling short. Restrictions on the number of short balls per over etc. do not appear to have worked. I believe there should be no restrictions on the bowler, but possibly the answer could be by making the glove no longer part of the bat, i.e. balls which leap at a batsman's throat are often fended away by a player's gloves. By making a player caught off the glove not out it will allow batsmen to defend themselves without fear of getting out.'

Best batting performance: 126 Derbyshire v New Zealand, Derby 1986

Best bowling performance: 2-69 Derbyshire v Glamorgan, Abergavenney 1986

LAST SEASON: BATTING

	I.	N.O.	R.	H.S.	AV.
TEST					
1ST-CLASS	39	6	974	121*	29.51
INT					
RAL	14	5	193	36*	21.44
NAT.W.	3	1	69	44	34.50
B & H	3	0	10	8	3.33

CAREER: BATTING

	I.	N.O.	R.	H.S.	AV.
TEST					
1ST-CLASS	159	29	3061	126	23.54
INT					
RAL	49	9	631	78	15.77
NAT.W.	7	1	82	44	13.66
B & H	9	1	145	50	18.12

LAST SEASON: WICKET KEEPING

	C.	ST.			
TEST					
1ST-CLASS	60	1			
INT					
RAL	13	2			
NAT.W.	5	–			
B & H	9	–			

CAREER: WICKET KEEPING

	C.	ST.			
TEST					
1ST-CLASS	223	12			
INT					
RAL	40	9			
NAT.W.	10	–			
B & H	18	1			

99. Who was top of the 1988 first-class bowling averages for Gloucestershire?

100. Who was top of the 1988 first-class bowling averages for Hampshire?

MAKINSON, D. J. — Lancashire

Full Name: David John Makinson
Role: Right-hand bat, left-arm fast-medium bowler
Born: 12 January 1961, Eccleston, Lancashire
Height: 6′ 4″ **Weight:** 13st
Nickname: Maki
County debut: 1984
1st-Class 50s scored: 1
1st-Class 5 w. in innings: 1
1st-Class catches 1988: 1 (career 10)
Parents: Thomas Andrew and Rhoda
Wife and date of marriage: Susan, 9 April 1983
Education: St Mary's High School; Leyland Motors Technical College; Bolton Institute of Technology
Qualifications: 6 O-levels, ONC in Mechanical Engineering; HNC in Automobile Engineering. Qualified Engineering Technician
Jobs outside cricket: Draughtsman (Leyland Trucks)
Off-season 1988–89: Playing for Maroochydore in Queensland
Overseas tours: New York 1985 with Lancashire
Overseas teams played for: Maroochydore, Queensland, 1984–85
Cricketers particularly learned from: Clive Lloyd, Peter Lever
Cricketers particularly admired: Ian Botham
Other sports played: Football
Other sports followed: Rugby league

LAST SEASON: BATTING

	I.	N.O.	R.	H.S.	AV.
TEST					
1ST-CLASS	–	–	–	–	–
INT					
RAL					
NAT.W.					
B & H					

LAST SEASON: BOWLING

	O.	M.	R.	W.	AV.
TEST					
1ST-CLASS	27	14	50	1	50.00
INT					
RAL					
NAT.W.					
B & H					

CAREER: BATTING

	I.	N.O.	R.	H.S.	AV.
TEST					
1ST-CLASS	39	17	486	58*	22.09
INT					
RAL	14	7	56	13	8.00
NAT.W.	2	1	25	17	25.00
B & H	3	2	5	5	5.00

CAREER: BOWLING

	O.	M.	R.	W.	AV.
TEST					
1ST-CLASS	611.1	164	3097	70	44.24
INT					
RAL	245.1	10	1154	35	32.97
NAT.W.	17	3	86	1	86.00
B & H	53	3	217	8	27.12

Injuries 1988: Missed nearly all season because of back injury. Played only one first-class match
Relaxations: Sunbathing, swimming, eating out
Extras: Writes on cricket for Sunshine Coast newspaper in Queensland. Released by Lancashire at end of 1988 season
Best batting performance: 58* Lancashire v Northamptonshire, Lytham 1985
Best bowling performance: 5-60 Lancashire v Derbyshire, Old Trafford 1985

MALCOLM, D. E. — Derbyshire

Full Name: Devon Eugene Malcolm
Role: Right-hand bat, right-arm fast bowler
Born: 22 February 1963, Kingston, Jamaica
Height: 6′ 3″ **Weight:** 14st 7lbs
Nickname: Dude
County debut: 1984
1st-Class 5 w. in innings: 3
Place in bowling averages: 81st av. 29.92 (1987 95th av. 34.53)
Strike rate 1988: 52.33 (career 52.68)
1st-Class catches 1988: 1 (career 11)
Parents: Albert and Brendalee (deceased)
Marital status: Single
Education: St Elizabeth Technical High School; Richmond College
Qualifications: College certificates, O-levels, coaching certificate

LAST SEASON: BATTING

	I.	N.O.	R.	H.S.	AV.
TEST					
1ST-CLASS	21	5	119	22	7.43
INT					
RAL					
NAT.W.	2	0	0	0	0.00
B & H	2	1	0	0*	0.00

CAREER: BATTING

	I.	N.O.	R.	H.S.	AV.
TEST					
1ST-CLASS	53	14	239	29*	6.12
INT					
RAL	1	0	16	16	16.00
NAT.W.	3	0	1	1	0.33
B & H	2	1	0	0*	0.00

LAST SEASON: BOWLING

	O.	M.	R.	W.	AV.
TEST					
1ST-CLASS	488.1	93	1676	56	29.92
INT					
RAL					
NAT.W.	21	3	72	1	72.00
B & H	47	4	149	8	18.62

CAREER: BOWLING

	O.	M.	R.	W.	AV.
TEST					
1ST-CLASS	1132.5	202	4095	129	31.74
INT					
RAL	16	0	87	3	29.00
NAT.W.	32	3	125	2	62.50
B & H	47	4	149	8	18.62

Jobs outside cricket: Coaching
Overseas teams played for: Ellerslie CC, New Zealand 1985–86
Cricketers particularly admired: Michael Holding, Richard Hadlee
Other sports played: Football
Other sports followed: Football, table tennis
Relaxations: Reggae, funk and soul music
Extras: Wears spectacles when batting
Best batting performance: 29* Derbyshire v Gloucestershire, Gloucester 1986
Best bowling performance: 6-68 Derbyshire v Warwickshire, Derby 1988

MALLENDER, N. A. Somerset

Full Name: Neil Alan Mallender
Role: Right-hand bat, right-arm
fast-medium bowler
Born: 13 August 1961, Kirk
Sandall, Nr Doncaster
Height: 6′ 1″ **Weight:** 13st
Nickname: Ghostie
County debut: 1980
(Northamptonshire), 1987
(Somerset)
County cap: 1984
(Northamptonshire), 1987
(Somerset)
1st-Class 50s scored: 4
1st-Class 5 w. in innings: 11
1st-Class 10 w. in match: 1
Place in batting averages: 248th
av. 12.15 (1987 206th av. 16.37)
Place in bowling averages:
17th av. 20.74 (1987 29th av. 24.54)
Strike rate 1988: 51.98 (career 58.94)
1st-Class catches 1988: 8 (career 77)
Parents: Ron and Jean
Wife and date of marriage: Caroline, 1 October 1983
Family links with cricket: Brother, Graham, used to play good representative
cricket before joining the RAF
Education: Beverley Grammar School, East Yorkshire
Qualifications: 7 O-levels
Cricketing superstitions or habits: Left boot on first
Overseas tours: Young England to West Indies, 1980

Overseas teams played for: Belmont DCC, NSW, 1980–81; Bathurst, NSW, 1982–83; Otago and Kaikorai CC, New Zealand, 1983–87
Cricketers particularly learnt from: Peter Willey, Warren Lees, Martin Crowe
Cricketers particularly admired: Richard Hadlee, Dennis Lillee
Other sports played: Golf
Other sports followed: Rugby league (especially Hull RFC), most sports
Relaxations: Pop/modern music, golf
Extras: Signed a 3-year contract to play for Somerset in 1987. Took hat-trick in first round of 1987 B & H Cup v Combined Universities
Best batting performance: 88 Otago v Central Districts, Oamaru 1984–85
Best bowling performance: 7-27 Otago v Auckland, Auckland 1984–85

LAST SEASON: BATTING

	I.	N.O.	R.	H.S.	AV.
TEST					
1ST-CLASS	20	7	158	44	12.15
INT					
RAL	7	3	46	23*	11.50
NAT.W.	–	–	–	–	–
B & H	2	1	16	16*	16.00

CAREER: BATTING

	I.	N.O.	R.	H.S.	AV.
TEST					
1ST-CLASS	230	75	2174	88	14.02
INT					
RAL	43	22	224	23*	10.66
NAT.W.	9	3	45	11*	7.50
B & H	12	4	40	16*	5.00

LAST SEASON: BOWLING

	O.	M.	R.	W.	AV.
TEST					
1ST-CLASS	433.1	111	1037	50	20.74
INT					
RAL	90.5	6	410	7	24.11
NAT.W.	23	1	76	2	38.00
B & H	37.1	5	101	3	33.66

CAREER: BOWLING

	O.	M.	R.	W.	AV.
TEST					
1ST-CLASS	5030.2	1125	14604	512	28.52
INT					
RAL	696.4	43	3196	126	25.36
NAT.W.	199.4	28	575	30	19.16
B & H	291.3	35	1058	40	26.45

101. How far did Ian Botham walk with his elephants across the Alps, how long did it take, and approximately how much did he raise for leukaemia research?

102. Who was the first Gloucestershire player to score 100 on his Test debut since W. G. Grace?

MARKS, V. J. Somerset

Full Name: Victor James Marks
Role: Right-hand bat, off-break bowler
Born: 25 June 1955, Middle Chinnock, Somerset
Height: 5′ 9″ **Weight:** 11st 8lbs
Nickname: Vic
County debut: 1975
County cap: 1979
Benefit: 1988
Test debut: 1982
No. of Tests: 6
No. of One-Day Internationals: 34
1000 runs in a season: 2
1st-Class 50s scored: 69
1st-Class 100s scored: 5
1st-Class 5 w. in innings: 39
1st-Class 10 w. in match: 5
One-Day 50s: 13
Place in batting averages: 138th av. 24.79 (1987 142nd av. 25.40)
Place in bowling averages: 74th av. 29.13 (1987 73rd av. 30.78)
Strike rate 1988: 68.11 (career 71.64)
1st-Class catches 1988: 8 (career 136)
Parents: Harold and Joan
Wife and date of marriage: Anna, 9 September 1978
Children: Amy, 27 November 1979; Rosie, 8 November 1987
Family links with cricket: 'Father a dangerous village cricketer.'
Education: Blundell's School; Oxford University
Qualifications: MA Classics
Jobs outside cricket: Teaching – but not since March 1981
Overseas tours: Derrick Robins' XI to Canada 1977; England to Australia and New Zealand 1982–83, New Zealand and Pakistan 1983–84, India and Australia 1984–85; Christians in Sport to India 1985
Overseas teams played for: Grade cricket with Bayswater Morley CC in Perth, Western Australia, 1981–82, Western Australia 1986–87
Cricketers particularly learnt from: Tom Cartwright, Arthur Milton
Cricketers particularly admired: Colin Dredge
Other sports played: Squash, golf
Injuries 1988: Had his nose broken in a practice match pre-season
Extras: Half-blue for rugby fives at Oxford University. Debut for Oxford University CC 1975. Blue 1975–76–77–78. Captain 1976–77. Somerset vice-captain 1984. Author of *Somerset County Cricket Scrapbook* (1984), *Marks Out of XI* (1985), *TCCB Guide to Better Cricket* (1987) and *The Ultimate*

One-Day Cricket Match (1988) with Robin Drake. Took over as captain when Peter Roebuck was injured in August 1988. Appointed captain for 1989 season

Opinions on cricket: 'We play too much.'
Best batting performance: 134 Somerset v Worcestershire, Weston-super-Mare 1984
Best bowling performance: 8-17 Somerset v Lancashire, Bath 1985

LAST SEASON: BATTING

	I.	N.O.	R.	H.S.	AV.
TEST					
1ST-CLASS	31	2	719	68	24.79
INT	–	–	–	–	–
RAL	13	4	228	80	25.33
NAT.W.	2	1	66	45*	66.00
B & H	3	0	40	16	13.33

CAREER: BATTING

	I.	N.O.	R.	H.S.	AV.
TEST	10	1	249	83	27.66
1ST-CLASS	458	77	11348	134	29.78
INT	24	3	285	44	13.57
RAL	122	31	2017	80	22.16
NAT.W.	23	7	472	55	29.50
B & H	45	8	968	81*	26.16

LAST SEASON: BOWLING

	O.	M.	R.	W.	AV.
TEST					
1ST-CLASS	862.5	222	2214	76	29.13
INT	11	0	59	0	–
RAL	104	9	420	17	24.70
NAT.W.	24	6	55	1	55.00
B & H	35.5	2	142	1	142.00

CAREER: BOWLING

	O.	M.	R.	W.	AV.
TEST	180.2	54	484	11	44.00
1ST-CLASS	9515.2	2611	25855	801	32.27
INT	306.2	28	1135	44	25.79
RAL	849.4	54	3434	130	26.41
NAT.W.	226.2	41	685	21	32.61
B & H	493.4	82	1525	47	32.44

MARSH, S. A.   Kent

Full Name: Steven Andrew Marsh
Role: Right-hand bat, wicket-keeper
Born: 27 January 1961, Westminster
Height: 5' 11" **Weight:** 12st
County debut: 1982
Nickname: Marshy
1st-Class 50s scored: 9
1st-Class 100s scored: 2
Place in batting averages: 140th
av. 24.58 (1987 185th av. 18.68)
Parents: Melvyn Graham and Valerie Ann
Wife and date of marriage: Julie, 27 September 1986
Family links with cricket: Father played local cricket for Lordswood. Father-in-law, Bob Wilson, played for Kent 1954–66
Education: Walderslade Secondary

School for Boys; Mid-Kent College of Higher and Further Education

Qualifications: 6 O-levels, 2 A-levels, OND in Business Studies
Jobs outside cricket: Office clerk, cricket coach, computer operator
Off-season 1988–89: Working for car sponsor Swale Motor Company
Cricketing superstitions or habits: 'When batting, getting into double figures.'
Overseas tours: Lordswood CC, Kent to Barbados 1979; Fred Rumsey's tour to Barbados 1987, 1988
Overseas teams played for: Avendale CC, South Africa 1985–86
Cricketers particularly learnt from: Alan Igglesden ('I have learnt to keep to leg-side bowling!'), Bob Woolmer
Cricketers particularly admired: Gary Sobers, Alan Knott
Other sports played: Golf, snooker, soccer, horse riding
Relaxations: Horse racing, eating and sleeping
Extras: Once swallowed one of Graham Cowdrey's contact lenses, when Cowdrey left it in a glass of water overnight and Marsh drank the water
Best batting performance: 120 Kent v Essex, Chelmsford 1988

LAST SEASON: BATTING

	I.	N.O.	R.	H.S.	AV.
TEST					
1ST-CLASS	35	6	713	120	24.58
INT					
RAL	7	1	40	9	6.66
NAT.W.	1	1	24	24*	–
B & H	2	0	20	17	10.00

CAREER: BATTING

	I.	N.O.	R.	H.S.	AV.
TEST					
1ST-CLASS	112	22	2161	120	24.01
INT					
RAL	28	7	234	36	11.14
NAT.W.	2	1	25	24*	25.00
B & H	10	2	69	17	8.62

LAST SEASON: WICKET KEEPING

	C.	ST.		
TEST				
1ST-CLASS	56	5		
INT				
RAL	12	5		
NAT.W.	9	1		
B & H	6	1		

CAREER: WICKET KEEPING

	C.	ST.		
TEST				
1ST-CLASS	169	13		
INT				
RAL	46	7		
NAT.W.	11	1		
B & H	22	2		

103. Who said that his bowling was so slow that if he didn't like a ball he'd bowled, he could run after it and fetch it back?

104. Which former England opening bat was the Sussex coach in 1988, and has since joined MCC as assistant secretary?

MARSHALL, M. D.   Hampshire

Full Name: Malcolm Denzil Marshall
Role: Right-hand bat, right-arm fast bowler
Born: 18 April 1958, Barbados
Height: 5′ 10½″ **Weight:** 12st 8lbs
Nickname: Macko
County debut: 1979
County cap: 1981
Benefit: 1987 (£61,006)
Test debut: 1978–79
No. of Tests: 58
No. of One-Day Internationals: 90
50 wickets in a season: 7
1st-Class 50s scored: 34
1st-Class 100s scored: 4
1st-Class 5 w. in innings: 70
1st-Class 10 w. in match: 10
One-Day 50s: 3
Place in batting averages: 78th av. 32.11 (1987 66th av. 35.88)
Place in bowling averages: 1st av. 13.16 (1987 8th av. 19.84)
Strike rate 1988: 33.23 (career 40.82)
1st-Class catches 1988: 3 (career 107)
Parents: Mrs Eleanor Inniss
Children: Shelly, 24 November 1984
Family links with cricket: Cousin Errol Yearwood plays for Texaco in Barbados as a fast bowler
Education: St Giles Boys' School; Parkinson Comprehensive School, Barbados
Qualifications: School passes in Maths and English
Jobs outside cricket: Working for Banks Brewery
Off-season 1988–89: Touring with the West Indies in Australia
Overseas tours: With West Indies to India and Sri Lanka 1978–79; Australia 1979–80, 1981–82, 1984–85; Pakistan 1980–81; India 1983–84; England 1980 and 1984; Zimbabwe 1981; New Zealand 1979–80; England 1988; Australia 1988–89
Overseas teams played for: Barbados (debut 1977–78)
Cricketers particularly learnt from: Wes Hall, Gary Sobers
Other sports played: Tennis, darts, pool, golf
Relaxations: Soul-music, reggae
Extras: Took nine wickets in debut match v Glamorgan in May 1979. Scored his first first-class century (109) in Zimbabwe, October 1981, for the West Indies against Zimbabwe. Most wickets in the Shell Shield Competition (25)

by a Barbadian. Broke record of number of wickets taken in 22-match season (i.e. since 1969) with 133. Published autobiography *Marshall Arts* (1987). Nearly chose to become a wicket-keeper. 'Even now I wish sometimes I was in Jeff Dujon's place behind the stumps.' £61,006 from his benefit was a record for a West Indian in county cricket. One of *Wisden*'s Five Cricketers of the Year, 1982

Opinions on cricket: 'Cricket has been my life since I could stand upright and hold a cricket bat or at least our home-made apology, built from anything that looked like one. I played morning, noon and night every day of my life. Not even school could get in the way of my obsession with the game. There was no question of playing football, or anything else, for very long. It was cricket, cricket and more cricket.'

Best batting performance: 116* Hampshire v Lancashire, Southampton 1982
Best bowling performance: 8-71 Hampshire v Worcestershire, Southampton 1982

LAST SEASON: BATTING

	I.	N.O.	R.	H.S.	AV.
TEST	6	1	135	72	27.00
1ST-CLASS	4	0	154	76	38.50
INT	3	0	48	41	16.00
RAL					
NAT.W.					
B & H					

LAST SEASON: BOWLING

	O.	M.	R.	W.	AV.
TEST	203.1	49	443	35	12.65
1ST-CLASS	42.3	7	110	7	15.71
INT	29	4	82	3	27.33
RAL					
NAT.W.					
B & H					

CAREER: BATTING

	I.	N.O.	R.	H.S.	AV.
TEST	72	7	1278	92	19.66
1ST-CLASS	270	35	5667	116*	24.11
INT	48	15	549	66	16.63
RAL	59	16	742	46	17.25
NAT.W.	13	7	194	51	32.33
B & H	23	1	285	34	12.95

CAREER: BOWLING

	O.	M.	R.	W.	AV.
TEST	2174.3	460	5921	290	20.41
1ST-CLASS	6226.1	1747	15734	920	17.10
INT	797.5	92	2654	115	23.07
RAL	698.4	68	2404	104	23.11
NAT.W.	190.4	36	495	18	27.50
B & H	265.1	51	737	37	19.91

105. True or false: Sussex leg-spinner, Andy Clarke, took a 300 per cent cut in earnings in order to play first-class cricket?

106. How many seasons has Jack Simmons been playing for Lancashire?

MARTINDALE, D. J. R.
Nottinghamshire

Full Name: Duncan John Richardson Martindale
Role: Right-hand bat, cover fielder
Born: 13 December 1963, Harrogate
Height: 5′ 11″ **Weight:** 12st
Nickname: Blowers
County debut: 1985
1st-Class 50s scored: 3
1st-Class 100s scored: 2
Place in batting averages: 192nd av. 20.07 (1987 196th av. 17.45)
1st-Class catches 1988: 3 (career 12)
Parents: Don and Isabel
Marital status: Single
Family links with cricket: Father and grandfather played club cricket in Nottingham; great uncle played for Nottinghamshire 2nd XI

Education: Lymm Grammar School; Trent Polytechnic
Qualifications: 9 O-levels, 2 A-levels, HND Business Studies, NCA Coaching Award
Off-season 1988–89: Playing and working in Australia
Overseas tours: International Ambassadors XI to India, 1985
Overseas teams played for: Prospect and District CC, Adelaide, 1985–86, 1986–87
Cricketers particularly learnt from: 'All professional cricketers'
Cricketers particularly admired: Richard Hadlee, Clive Rice, Vic Marks
Other sports played: All sports, particularly long-distance running, squash and golf
Relaxations: Reading, listening to all types of music, meeting people, good food, travelling
Extras: Scored century (104*) in fifth first-class innings. First one-day match was 1985 NatWest Final. Member of Christians in Sport

LAST SEASON: BATTING

	I.	N.O.	R.	H.S.	AV.
TEST					
1ST-CLASS	14	1	261	52*	20.07
INT					
RAL	1	0	39	39	39.00
NAT.W.					
B & H					

CAREER: BATTING

	I.	N.O.	R.	H.S.	AV.
TEST					
1ST-CLASS	45	6	885	104*	22.69
INT					
RAL	5	0	84	39	16.80
NAT.W.	1	1	20	20*	–
B & H					

Opinions on cricket: 'I believe that cricket has to improve its public appeal. That is, it must generate interest among the "general" public.'
Best batting performance: 104* Nottinghamshire v Lancashire, Old Trafford 1985

MARU, R. J. G. Hampshire

Full Name: Rajesh Jamandass Govind Maru
Role: Right-hand bat, slow left-arm bowler, close fielder
Born: 28 October 1962, Nairobi
Height: 5′ 6″ **Weight:** 10st 7lbs
Nickname: Raj
County debut: 1980 (Middlesex), 1984 (Hampshire)
County cap: 1986 (Hampshire)
50 wickets in a season: 1
1st-Class 50s scored: 2
1st-Class 5 w. in innings: 10
Place in batting averages: 245th av. 12.58
Place in bowling averages: 115th av. 35.84 (1987 60th av. 29.02)
Strike rate 1988: 84.12 (career 67.98)
1st-Class catches 1988: 31 (career 119)
Parents: Jamandass and Prabhavati
Family links with cricket: Brother has played for Middlesex 2nd XI and in Middlesex League
Education: Harrow College
Qualifications: Cricket coach
Jobs outside cricket: Cricket coach
Off-season 1988–89: 'Having a winter off.'
Cricketing superstitions or habits: Nelsons: 111, 222 and 333
Overseas tours: Young England tour of West Indies 1980; NCA tour of Canada; Barbican International XI to Dubai; Middlesex to Zimbabwe 1980–81
Overseas teams played for: Blenheim CC, New Zealand, 1985–86
Cricketers particularly learnt from: Jack Robertson, Derek Underwood, David Graveney, Malcolm Marshall, Peter Sainsbury, Don Bennett, Paul Terry
Cricketers particularly admired: Malcolm Marshall, Mike Gatting, Derek Underwood, Phil Edmonds, Maninder Singh, Gordon Greenidge

Other sports played: Badminton, table tennis, squash, swimming, hockey
Other sports followed: Football, rugby union
Relaxations: Music, reading, TV
Extras: Played for Middlesex 1980–83. Joined Hampshire in 1984
Opinions on cricket: 'If we are going to play four-day cricket, then the wickets have to improve, so that they last the full four days. Practice wickets when you play away from home should be prepared so that you can have decent practice before the game. There should also be wicket inspections more regularly.'
Best batting performance: 74 Hampshire v Gloucestershire, Gloucester 1988
Best bowling performance: 7–79 Hampshire v Middlesex, Bournemouth 1984

LAST SEASON: BATTING

	I.	N.O.	R.	H.S.	AV.
TEST					
1ST-CLASS	29	5	302	74	12.58
INT					
RAL	–	–	–	–	–
NAT.W.					
B & H					

CAREER: BATTING

	I.	N.O.	R.	H.S.	AV.
TEST					
1ST-CLASS	104	30	1130	74	15.27
INT					
RAL	3	3	9	6*	
NAT.W.	–	–	–	–	–
B & H					

LAST SEASON: BOWLING

	O.	M.	R.	W.	AV.
TEST					
1ST-CLASS	701	201	1792	50	35.84
INT					
RAL	8	0	30	3	10.00
NAT.W.					
B & H					

CAREER: BOWLING

	O.	M.	R.	W.	AV.
TEST					
1ST-CLASS	3535	983	9542	312	30.58
INT					
RAL	60	3	288	9	32.00
NAT.W.	2	0	5	2	2.50
B & H					

MATTHEWS, C. D.   Lancashire

Full Name: Christopher Darrell Matthews
Role: Left-hand bat, left-arm fast-medium bowler
Born: 22 September 1962, Cunderin, Perth, Western Australia
Nickname: Chris
County debut: 1988
Test debut: 1986–87
No. of Tests: 2
1st-Class 50s scored: 3
1st-Class 5w in innings: 8
1st-Class catches 1988: 0 (career 10)
Wife: Anne
Jobs outside cricket: Runs own engineering business, Rittco Sales in Perth

Off-season 1988–89: Playing for Western Australia and Australia. Running own engineering business
Overseas teams played for: Mount Lawley, Perth, Western Australia since 1984
Extras: Played in 1988 in Lancashire League. Took 51 Shield wickets in 1987–88 Australian season, at average of 22.29, becoming only the fifth bowler to take 50 wickets in a Sheffield Shield season. Took a wicket with first ball in first RAL match
Best batting performance: 65 Western Australia v Victoria, Perth 1986–87
Best bowling performance: 8-101 Western Australia v Queensland, 1987–88

LAST SEASON: BATTING

	I.	N.O.	R.	H.S.	AV.
TEST					
1ST-CLASS	3	0	38	31	12.66
INT					
RAL	1	1	1	1*	–
NAT.W.					
B & H	1	0	43	43	43.00

CAREER: BATTING

	I.	N.O.	R.	H.S.	AV.
TEST	3	0	21	11	7.00
1ST-CLASS	41	3	777	65	20.44
INT					
RAL	1	1	1	1*	–
NAT.W.					
B & H	1	0	43	43	43.00

LAST SEASON: BOWLING

	O.	M.	R.	W.	AV.
TEST					
1ST-CLASS	77.2	18	225	7	32.14
INT					
RAL	14.1	0	71	3	23.66
NAT.W.					
B & H	5	0	17	0	–

CAREER: BOWLING

	O.	M.	R.	W.	AV.
TEST	70.1	14	233	6	38.83
1ST-CLASS	1290.4	266	3626	149	24.33
INT					
RAL	14.1	0	71	3	23.66
NAT.W.					
B & H	5	0	17	0	–

MAYNARD, M. P.   Glamorgan

Full Name: Matthew Peter Maynard
Role: Right-hand bat, right-arm medium bowler, slip fielder
Born: 21 March 1966, Oldham
Height: 5′ 10½″ **Weight:** 12st 3lbs
Nickname: Walter
County debut: 1985
County cap: 1987
Test debut: 1988
No. of Tests: 1
1000 runs in a season: 3
1st-Class 50s scored: 30
1st-Class 100s scored: 8
One-Day 50s: 7
One-Day 100s: 2
Place in batting averages: 32nd av. 41.25 (1987 38th av. 40.65)

1st-Class catches 1988: 22 (career 66)
Parents: Pat and Ken (deceased)
Wife and date of marriage: Susan, 27 September 1986
Family links with cricket: Father pro'd for Duckinfield. Brother played club cricket. Brother, Charles, started playing again for St Fagans
Education: Ysgol David Hughes, Anglesey
Qualifications: Cricket coach
Jobs outside cricket: Sales rep for Bangor City FC; barman, burger-bar chef, labourer on site
Off-season 1988–89: Playing for Gosnells CC, Perth, Western Australia
Cricketing superstitions or habits: 'Nothing if things are going well. Everything if they aren't!'
Overseas tours: Barbados with North Wales XI, 1982
Overseas teams played for: St Josephs, Whakatane, 1986–87, 1987–88
Cricketers particularly learnt from: Father, Colin Page, Bill Clutterbuck, John Steele and 'everyone at Glamorgan'
Cricketers particularly admired: Richard Hadlee, Ian Botham, Barry Richards
Other sports played: Football, golf, snooker
Other sports followed: Rugby
Injuries 1988: Broken finger
Relaxations: Socialising
Extras: Scored century on debut v Yorkshire at Swansea. Also youngest centurion for Glamorgan. Scored 1000 runs in first full season. Fastest ever 50 for Glamorgan (14 mins) v Yorkshire. Youngest player to be awarded Glamorgan cap. Fastest TV 50 in Refuge Assurance League 1987. Leading 6-hitter in Championship in 1987. Three B & H Gold Awards. Voted Young Cricketer of the Year 1988 by the Cricket Writers Club
Opinions on cricket: 'I think that the four-day game has been a great success, and hopefully one day we will play 16 four-day matches. You should only be allowed to contract and play one overseas player.'

LAST SEASON: BATTING

	I.	N.O.	R.	H.S.	AV.
TEST	2	0	13	10	6.50
1ST-CLASS	40	6	1472	126	43.29
INT					
RAL	12	1	354	92*	32.18
NAT.W.	3	0	121	64	40.33
B & H	6	0	335	115	55.83

CAREER: BATTING

	I.	N.O.	R.	H.S.	AV.
TEST	2	0	13	10	6.50
1ST-CLASS	122	15	4298	160	40.16
INT					
RAL	42	2	893	92*	22.32
NAT.W.	7	0	153	64	21.85
B & H	11	2	436	115	48.44

LAST SEASON: BOWLING

	O.	M.	R.	W.	AV.
TEST					
1ST-CLASS	18	4	55	0	–
INT					
RAL					
NAT.W.					
B & H	2	0	6	0	–

CAREER: BOWLING

	O.	M.	R.	W.	AV.
TEST					
1ST-CLASS	49.1	8	161	4	40.25
INT					
RAL					
NAT.W.					
B & H	2	0	6	0	–

Best batting performance: 160 Glamorgan v Somerset, Weston-super-Mare 1987
Best bowling performance: 3-21 Glamorgan v Oxford University, Oxford 1987

MAYS, C. S.   Surrey

Full Name: Christopher Sean Mays
Role: Right-hand bat, off-break bowler
Born: 11 May 1966, Brighton
Height: 5′ 10″ **Weight:** 11st 12lbs
Nickname: Doc
County debut: 1986 (Sussex), 1987 (Surrey)
1st-Class catches 1988: 2 (career 5)
Parents: Douglas and Joan
Family links with cricket: Father played for Sussex club and ground side
Education: Lancing College; Middlesex Hospital Medical School
Qualifications: 11 O-levels, 2 AO-levels, 3 A-levels. Final medical exams in June 1989
Jobs outside cricket: Full-time medical student
Off-season 1988–89: 'Starting my first house-surgeon's job in my medical pre-registration year, 1989–90.'
Overseas tours: Lancing College to Holland, 1979, 1981; Sussex YC to

LAST SEASON: BATTING

	I.	N.O.	R.	H.S.	AV.
TEST					
1ST-CLASS	1	1	13	13*	—
INT					
RAL					
NAT.W.					
B & H					

CAREER: BATTING

	I.	N.O.	R.	H.S.	AV.
TEST					
1ST-CLASS	9	4	39	13*	7.80
INT					
RAL					
NAT.W.					
B & H					

LAST SEASON: BOWLING

	O.	M.	R.	W.	AV.
TEST					
1ST-CLASS	25	2	102	1	102.00
INT					
RAL					
NAT.W.					
B & H					

CAREER: BOWLING

	O.	M.	R.	W.	AV.
TEST					
1ST-CLASS	293.5	54	1009	16	63.06
INT					
RAL					
NAT.W.					
B & H					

Barbados, 1982, 1985; NCA YC to Holland, 1983; NCA YC to Bermuda, 1985; England YC to West Indies, 1988
Cricketers particularly learnt from: Chris Waller, Don Smith, Les Lenham
Cricketers particularly admired: John Emburey
Other sports played: Golf, squash, hockey
Other sports followed: American football
Relaxations: Music, reading, photography
Extras: Has represented England Schools and MCC Schools. Left Sussex at end of 1986 season and joined Surrey. Hopes to continue to combine career as doctor and cricketer
Best batting performance: 13* Surrey v Essex, Chelmsford 1988
Best bowling performance: 3-77 Sussex v New Zealanders, Hove 1986

McEWAN, S. M. Worcestershire

Full Name: Steven Michael McEwan
Role: Right-hand bat, right-arm fast-medium bowler, slip fielder
Born: 5 May 1962, Worcester
Height: 6′ 1″ **Weight:** 13st 7lbs
Nickname: Mac, Maciz, Freddy
County debut: 1985
Place in bowling averages: —
(1987 98th av. 39.87)
1st-Class catches 1988: 1 (career 9)
Parents: Michael James and Valerie Jeanette
Marital status: Single
Family links with cricket: Father and uncle played club cricket
Education: Worcester Royal Grammar School

Qualifications: 6 O-levels, 3 A-levels. Technician's certificate in building
Jobs outside cricket: Assistant buyer, building trade; cricket coach
Off-season 1988–89: Playing and coaching in South Africa
Overseas teams played for: Birkenhead City, Auckland, 1985–87; Springs, Johannesburg 1988–89
Cricketers particularly learnt from: Dipak Patel, Basil D'Oliveira, Kapil Dev
Cricketers particularly admired: Richard Hadlee, Malcolm Marshall
Other sports played: Soccer

Other sports followed: American football
Injuries 1988: Hamstring
Relaxations: TV, reading
Extras: Took 10 wickets for 13 runs in an innings in 1983 for Worcester Nomads against Moreton-in-Marsh. Also broke school bowling record, 60 wickets, at WRGS, 1982
Opinions on cricket: 'In favour of four-day county cricket.'
Best batting performance: 13* Worcestershire v Oxford University, Oxford 1985
Best bowling performance: 4-43 Worcestershire v Lancashire, Worcester 1988

LAST SEASON: BATTING

	I.	N.O.	R.	H.S.	AV.
TEST					
1ST-CLASS	2	1	6	6	6.00
INT					
RAL	2	1	0	0	0.00
NAT.W.					
B & H					

CAREER: BATTING

	I.	N.O.	R.	H.S.	AV.
TEST					
1ST-CLASS	14	8	45	13*	7.50
INT					
RAL	5	3	13	7*	6.50
NAT.W.					
B & H					

LAST SEASON: BOWLING

	O.	M.	R.	W.	AV.
TEST					
1ST-CLASS	86	7	310	8	38.75
INT					
RAL	21	0	116	6	19.33
NAT.W.					
B & H					

CAREER: BOWLING

	O.	M.	R.	W.	AV.
TEST					
1ST-CLASS	530.5	79	1881	49	38.38
INT					
RAL	110	2	586	21	27.90
NAT.W.					
B & H					

107. What was unusual about the cap worn by Len Hutton in the final stages of The Oval Test match v Australia, in which England won The Ashes in 1953?

108. Who was top of the 1988 first-class bowling averages for Nottinghamshire?

MEDLYCOTT, K. T. Surrey

Full Name: Keith Thomas Medlycott
Role: Right-hand bat, slow left-arm bowler, short-leg fielder
Born: 12 May 1965, Whitechapel
Height: 5′ 11″ **Weight:** 12st 6lbs
Nickname: Medders
County debut: 1984
County cap: 1988
1st-Class 50s scored: 10
1st-Class 100s scored: 2
1st-Class 5 w. in innings: 10
1st-Class 10 w. in match: 4
Place in batting averages: 157th av. 23.08 (1987 113th av. 29.36)
Place in bowling averages: 43rd av. 24.05 (1987 110th av. 39.04)
Strike rate 1988: 51.57 (career 61.06)
1st-Class catches 1988: 27 (career 49)
Parents: Thomas Alfred and June Elizabeth
Marital status: Single
Family links with cricket: 'Father played club cricket for Colposa. Brother, Paul, played one game and scored one more than me!'
Education: Parmiters Grammar School
Qualifications: 2 O-levels
Jobs outside cricket: Coaching in South Africa for Waterkloof House Prep. School
Off-season 1988–89: Playing and coaching in South Africa
Cricketing superstitions or habits: 'Bad habit of talking rubbish before batting, which definitely annoys the coach!'
Overseas tours: Barbados, 1981, with London Schools
Overseas teams played for: Oostelikes CC 1983–88; Harlequins CC 1984–85
Cricketers particularly learnt from: Geoff Arnold, T. Sheppard, Chris Waller, T. Medlycott
Cricketers particularly admired: Bishan Bedi
Other sports played: Football, rugby, table tennis
Other sports followed: Any bar horse-racing
Injuries 1988: Missed one game with split finger
Extras: Scored 100 on debut (117* v Cambridge University) in 1984. Took first hat-trick of career against Hampshire 2nd XI, 1988. Capped in last game of season, against Kent
Opinions on cricket: 'There should be 16 four-day matches on wickets that have been prepared by groundsmen who are paid by the TCCB or an

equivalent body. Thereafter if any wickets are continually poor then that body must hire and fire until we get wickets that are good for cricket. I also believe that we should get more involved on the commercial side. We must look at other countries and see how they go about making cricket more interesting for players and public alike, e.g. South Africa and Australia.'

Best batting performance: 153 Surrey v Kent, The Oval 1987
Best bowling performance: 8-52 Surrey v Sussex, Hove 1988

LAST SEASON: BATTING

	I.	N.O.	R.	H.S.	AV.
TEST					
1ST-CLASS	29	5	554	77*	23.08
INT					
RAL	4	1	82	34	27.33
NAT.W.					
B & H					

LAST SEASON: BOWLING

	O.	M.	R.	W.	AV.
TEST					
1ST-CLASS	593.1	159	1660	69	24.05
INT					
RAL	14	0	72	3	24.00
NAT.W.					
B & H					

CAREER: BATTING

	I.	N.O.	R.	H.S.	AV.
TEST					
1ST-CLASS	83	18	1624	153	24.98
INT					
RAL	8	1	93	34	13.28
NAT.W.					
B & H					

CAREER: BOWLING

	O.	M.	R.	W.	AV.
TEST					
1ST-CLASS	1618.1	439	4691	159	29.50
INT					
RAL	20	0	132	4	33.00
NAT.W.					
B & H					

MENDIS, G. D. Lancashire

Full Name: Gehan Dixon Mendis
Role: Right-hand opening bat
Born: 24 April 1955, Colombo, Ceylon
Height: 5′ 8″ **Weight:** 11st
Nickname: Mendo, Dix
County debut: 1974 (Sussex), 1986 (Lancashire)
County cap: 1980 (Sussex), 1986 (Lancashire)
1000 runs in a season: 9
1st-Class 50s scored: 80
1st-Class 100s scored: 27
1st-Class 200s scored: 3
One-Day 50s: 30
One-Day 100s: 6
Place in batting averages: 54th av. 35.89 (1987 49th av. 38.61)
1st-Class catches 1988: 10 (career 110 + 1 stumping)

Parents: Sam Dixon Charles and Sonia Marcelle (both deceased)
Children: Hayley, 11 December 1982
Education: St Thomas College, Mount Lavinia, Sri Lanka; Brighton, Hove & Sussex Grammar School; Bede College, Durham University
Qualifications: BEd Mathematics, Durham; NCA coaching certificate
Jobs outside cricket: Teacher at Rosemead School, Littlehampton, Sussex; Richard Ellis, Perth, Western Australia; City Sales & Marketing Ltd, London. Self-employed
Off-season 1988–89: Financial adviser in Cheshire
Overseas tours: Maharaja Organisation XI to India 1980; Rohan Kanhai's Invitation XI to Pakistan 1981; numerous international teams to West Indies
Overseas teams played for: Maharaja Organisation XI in Sri Lanka 1980–81; Colombo CC; Sebastianites CC, and Mount Lawley CC, Western Australia; Nedlands CC, Perth
Cricketers particularly admired: Barry Richards, Richard Hadlee
Other sports played: 'None any more!'
Other sports followed: Formula One motor racing
Injuries 1988: 'Travelling by coach and being generally flabby and unfit.'
Relaxations: Music, 'getting away from cricket'
Extras: Played for TCCB XI in 1981. Has twice turned down invitations to play for Sri Lanka in order to be free to be chosen for England. Left Sussex at end of 1985 to join Lancashire. Played table tennis for Sussex at junior level
Opinions on cricket: 'None, any more, as cricketers and/or captains have not much say in the running of the game. Sign of old age, I guess!'
Best batting performance: 209* Sussex v Somerset, Hove 1984
Best bowling performance: 1-65 Sussex v Yorkshire, Hove 1985

LAST SEASON: BATTING

	I.	N.O.	R.	H.S.	AV.
TEST					
1ST-CLASS	42	4	1364	151	35.89
INT					
RAL	15	0	345	86	23.00
NAT.W.	2	0	68	64	34.00
B & H	4	0	156	61	39.00

LAST SEASON: BOWLING

	O.	M.	R.	W.	AV.
TEST					
1ST-CLASS	12	1	44	0	—
INT					
RAL					
NAT.W.					
B & H					

CAREER: BATTING

	I.	N.O.	R.	H.S.	AV.
TEST					
1ST-CLASS	487	46	15835	209*	35.90
INT					
RAL	150	14	3820	125*	28.08
NAT.W.	30	2	951	141*	33.96
B & H	49	1	1309	109	27.27

CAREER: BOWLING

	O.	M.	R.	W.	AV.
TEST					
1ST-CLASS	27.3	2	153	1	153.00
INT					
RAL					
NAT.W.					
B & H					

---

109. Who was top of the 1988 first-class bowling averages for Somerset?

Full Name: Tyrone Anthony Merrick
Role: Right-hand bat, right-arm fast-medium bowler
Born: 10 June 1963, Antigua
Height: 6'
County debut: 1987
1st-Class 50s scored: 2
1st-Class 5 w. in innings: 13
1st-Class 10 w. in match: 2
One-Day 50s: 1
Place in batting averages: 234th av. 14.22 (1987 212th av. 15.71)
Place in bowling averages: 26th av. 22.10 (1987 33rd av. 25.24)
Strike rate 1988: 42.32 (career 43.56)
1st-Class catches 1988: 5 (career 25)
Children: Anthea, 6 January 1987
Education: All Saints Primary and Secondary Schools
Jobs outside cricket: Physical Education Teacher
Off-season 1988–89: Playing in West Indies
Overseas tours: West Indies Youth Team to England 1982; West Indies B to Zimbabwe 1986
Overseas teams played for: Leeward Islands
Cricketers particularly learnt from: Andy Roberts, Eldine Baptiste
Other sports followed: Soccer, lawn tennis
Relaxations: Listening to music
Extras: Played for Rawtenstall in Lancashire League 1985 and 1986

LAST SEASON: BATTING

	I.	N.O.	R.	H.S.	AV.
TEST					
1ST-CLASS	21	3	256	34	14.22
INT					
RAL	4	0	28	19	7.00
NAT.W.	2	0	15	13	7.50
B & H	3	0	14	8	4.66

CAREER: BATTING

	I.	N.O.	R.	H.S.	AV.
TEST					
1ST-CLASS	74	14	909	74*	15.15
INT					
RAL	8	1	104	59	14.85
NAT.W.	2	0	15	13	7.50
B & H	4	1	27	13*	9.00

LAST SEASON: BOWLING

	O.	M.	R.	W.	AV.
TEST					
1ST-CLASS	458.3	105	1437	65	22.10
INT					
RAL	66.5	9	232	11	21.09
NAT.W.	21	7	39	3	13.00
B & H	38	7	95	5	19.00

CAREER: BOWLING

	O.	M.	R.	W.	AV.
TEST					
1ST-CLASS	1597.3	193	5233	220	23.78
INT					
RAL	120.1	16	458	20	22.90
NAT.W.	21	7	39	3	13.00
B & H	49	8	127	5	25.40

Best batting performance: 74* Warwickshire v Gloucestershire, Edgbaston 1987

Best bowling performance: 7-45 Warwickshire v Lancashire, Edgbaston 1987

METCALFE, A. A. Yorkshire

Full Name: Ashley Anthony Metcalfe
Role: Right-hand bat, off-break bowler
Born: 25 December 1963, Horsforth, Leeds
Height: 5′ 9½″ **Weight:** 11st 7lbs
County debut: 1983
County cap: 1986
1000 runs in a season: 3
1st-Class 50s scored: 25
1st-Class 100s scored: 11
1st-Class 200s scored: 1
One-Day 50s: 19
One-Day 100s: 1
Place in batting averages: 44th av. 37.71 (1987 101st av. 31.00)
1st-Class catches 1988: 5 (career 30)
Parents: Tony and Ann
Wife and date of marriage: Diane, 20 April 1986
Family links with cricket: Father played in local league; father-in-law Ray Illingworth (Yorkshire and England)
Education: Ladderbanks Middle School; Bradford Grammar School; University College, London
Qualifications: 9 O-levels, 3 A-levels, NCA Coaching Certificate
Jobs outside cricket: Worked for Grattan Mail Order Co, Paul Madeley's DIY
Off-season 1988–89: Working in England
Overseas tours: NCA tour of Denmark 1981
Overseas teams played for: Ringwood CC, Melbourne 1985–87
Cricketers particularly learnt from: Doug Padgett, Ray Illingworth, Don Wilson
Cricketers particularly admired: Barry Richards
Other sports played: Golf
Other sports followed: Most
Relaxations: 'Relaxing at home with my wife.'

Extras: 'I made 122 on my debut for Yorkshire against Nottinghamshire at Park Avenue in 1983. I was the youngest ever Yorkshire player to do so and it was the highest ever score by a Yorkshireman on debut.'
Opinions on cricket: 'Politics should not interfere with sport – South Africa should be eligible for Test cricket.'
Best batting performance: 216* Yorkshire v Middlesex, Headingley 1988
Best bowling performance: 2-18 Yorkshire v Warwickshire, Scarborough 1987

LAST SEASON: BATTING

	I.	N.O.	R.	H.S.	AV.
TEST					
1ST-CLASS	40	5	1320	216*	37.71
INT					
RAL	14	0	378	79	27.00
NAT.W.	2	1	74	74*	74.00
B & H	4	1	104	70	34.66

CAREER: BATTING

	I.	N.O.	R.	H.S.	AV.
TEST					
1ST-CLASS	152	10	4914	216*	34.60
INT					
RAL	61	2	1634	115*	22.87
NAT.W.	10	1	319	85	35.44
B & H	13	3	591	94*	59.10

LAST SEASON: BOWLING

	O.	M.	R.	W.	AV.
TEST					
1ST-CLASS	2.5	0	7	0	–
INT					
RAL					
NAT.W.					
B & H					

CAREER: BOWLING

	O.	M.	R.	W.	AV.
TEST					
1ST-CLASS	38.2	5	154	3	51.33
INT					
RAL					
NAT.W.	7	0	44	2	22.00
B & H					

METSON, C. P. Glamorgan

Full Name: Colin Peter Metson
Role: Right-hand bat, wicket-keeper
Born: 2 July 1963, Cuffley, Hertfordshire
Height: 5′ 6″ **Weight:** 10st 6lbs
Nickname: Dempster, Reggie, Jazzer
County debut: 1981 (Middlesex), 1987 (Glamorgan)
County cap: 1987 (Glamorgan)
1st-Class 50s scored: 3
Place in batting averages: 223rd av. 15.95 (1987 205th av. 16.43)
Parents: Denis Alwyn and Jean Mary
Marital status: Single
Family links with cricket: Father played good club cricket and for MCC; brother plays club cricket

Education: Stanborough School, Welwyn Garden City; Enfield Grammar School; Durham University
Qualifications: 10 O-levels, 5 A-levels, BA Hons Economic History, NCA Senior Coaching Award
Jobs outside cricket: Accounts clerk
Off-season 1988–89: Three months in Adelaide, three months in London
Cricketing superstitions or habits: 'Always put right pad on before left; try to use the same equipment right through the season if possible, especially wicket-keeping gloves. Try not to watch the cricket as a wicket always falls when I do.'
Overseas team played for: Payeham CC, Adelaide 1985–86, 1987–88
Cricketers particularly learnt from: Jack Robertson, Bob Taylor, Father, Don Bennett, Paul Downton
Cricketers particularly admired: Bob Taylor, Mike Brearley
Other sports played: Football, golf, tennis, hockey
Other sports followed: American football, golf, football
Injuries 1988: 'No injuries serious enough to make me miss any game.'
Relaxations: Computers, sleeping, wine, Indian, Chinese and Mexican food
Extras: Young Wicket-keeper of the Year 1981. Three Young England Tests v India 1981. Captain Durham University 1984, losing finalists in UAU competition. Beat Cambridge University twice. Middlesex 2nd XI Player of the Year 1984. Left Middlesex in March 1987 to replace Terry Davies at Glamorgan
Opinions on cricket: 'Cricket must find ways to market itself better, and in finding the sponsors, must give them value for money. Four-day cricket in 1988 looked to be a success, so I would encourage 16 four-day games, as long as the pitches lasted at least three days. Playing sessions could then be two hours long, with perhaps 100 overs minimum in the day.'
Best batting performance: 96 Middlesex v Gloucestershire, Uxbridge 1984

LAST SEASON: BATTING

	I.	N.O.	R.	H.S.	AV.
TEST					
1ST-CLASS	30	8	351	48	15.95
INT					
RAL	7	5	36	10*	18.00
NAT.W.	1	0	0	0	0.00
B & H	2	0	20	11	10.00

CAREER: BATTING

	I.	N.O.	R.	H.S.	AV.
TEST					
1ST-CLASS	98	24	1270	96	17.16
INT					
RAL	25	15	185	23*	18.50
NAT.W.	3	1	4	4*	2.00
B & H	4	0	27	11	6.75

LAST SEASON: WICKET KEEPING

	C.	ST.			
TEST					
1ST-CLASS	52	8			
INT					
RAL	18	6			
NAT.W.	3	–			
B & H	4	1			

CAREER: WICKET KEEPING

	C.	ST.			
TEST					
1ST-CLASS	149	16			
INT					
RAL	44	15			
NAT.W.	5	–			
B & H	6	2			

MIDDLETON, T. C.　　　　Hampshire

Full Name: Tony Charles
Middleton
Role: Right-hand bat,
slow left-arm bowler
Born: 1 February 1964, Winchester
Height 5′ 11″ **Weight:** 11 st
Nickname: Roo, Midders, TC
County debut: 1984
1st-Class 50s scored: 1
1st-Class catches 1988: 0 (career 8)
Parents: Peter and Molly
Marital status: Single
Family links with cricket: Brother
plays local club cricket in
Hampshire
Education: Weeke Infants and
Junior Schools; Montgomery of
Alamein Comprehensive, Winchester;
Peter Symonds Sixth Form College,
Winchester
Qualifications: 1 A-level, 5 O-levels
Jobs outside cricket: Worked for two winters as an electrical engineer
Cricketing superstitions or habits: Always wear spikes to bat in
Overseas teams played for: Club cricket for Durban Police, South Africa,
1984–85 and 1985–86
Cricketers particularly learnt from: 'Too many to name.'
Cricketers particularly admired: Barry Richards, Gordon Greenidge
Other sports played: Squash, football, badminton
Other sports followed: Football, rugby union
Relaxations: Watching and playing other sports
Extras: Played for England Schools 1982
Opinions on cricket: 'Sunday League should be increased to 50 overs with
normal run ups and only one knock-out cup plus play-offs for top Sunday
League sides. Hopefully the introduction of a full four-day Championship in
the near future will put an end to contrived results and "result" wickets.'

LAST SEASON: BATTING

	I.	N.O.	R.	H.S.	AV.
TEST					
1ST-CLASS	2	0	28	23	14.00
INT					
RAL					
NAT.W.					
B & H					

CAREER: BATTING

	I.	N.O.	R.	H.S.	AV.
TEST					
1ST-CLASS	19	3	366	68*	22.87
INT					
RAL					
NAT.W.					
B & H					

Best batting performance: 68* Hampshire v Somerset, Taunton 1986
Best bowling performance: 1-13 Hampshire v Middlesex, Lord's 1986

MILLER, G. Essex

Full Name: Geoffrey Miller
Role: Right-hand bat, off-break
bowler
Born: 8 September 1952,
Chesterfield
Height: 6′ 2″ **Weight:** 11st 6lbs
Nickname: Dusty
County debut: 1973 (Derbyshire),
1987 (Essex)
County cap: 1976 (Derbyshire),
1988 (Essex)
Benefit: 1985
Test debut: 1976
No. of Tests: 34
No. of One-Day Internationals: 25
1st-Class 50s scored: 69
1st-Class 100s scored: 2
1st-Class 5 w. in innings: 38
1st-Class 10 w. in match: 7
One-Day 50s: 17
Place in batting averages: 168th av. 22.17 (1987 221st av. 14.84)
Place in bowling averages: 78th av. 29.56 (1987 76th av. 31.09)
Strike rate 1988: 66.61 (career 64.99)
1st-Class catches 1988: 22 (career 294)
Parents: Keith and Gwen
Wife: Carol
Children: Helen Jane; Anna Louise; James Daniel
Family links with cricket: Father played local cricket in Chesterfield. Brother
plays for Chesterfield CC
Education: Chesterfield Grammar School
Qualifications: 5 O-levels
Jobs outside cricket: Owner of two sports shops
Off-season 1988–89: 'Running my sports shops.'
Overseas tours: With England Young Cricketers to India 1970–71 and West
Indies 1972; toured with England to India, Sri Lanka, Australia 1976–77;
Pakistan and New Zealand 1977–78; Australia 1978–79 and 1979–80 but had
to return December 1979 through injury; West Indies 1981; Australia and
New Zealand 1982–83

Cricketers particularly learnt from: Eddie Barlow, Ray Illingworth, Fred Titmus
Cricketers particularly admired: The late Ken Barrington
Other sports played: Golf, table tennis, football
Relaxations: 'Crosswords, reading, television, family life. Watching Chesterfield FC particularly, and all sports in general. Driving. Running my business. Indian food. Doing VAT.'
Extras: Became captain of Derbyshire half-way through 1979 season, but relinquished it half-way through 1981 season in favour of Barry Wood. Declined to sign for Derbyshire for 1982 season, and was released. Negotiated with several other counties, but signed again. Eventually left at end of 1986 season and joined Essex for 1987. Played table tennis for Derbyshire
Best batting performance: 130 Derbyshire v Lancashire, Old Trafford 1984
Best bowling performance: 8-70 Derbyshire v Leicestershire, Coalville 1982

LAST SEASON: BATTING

	I.	N.O.	R.	H.S.	AV.
TEST					
1ST-CLASS	21	4	377	77	22.17
INT					
RAL	6	2	106	31	26.50
NAT.W.	1	0	9	9	9.00
B & H	2	2	1	1*	—

LAST SEASON: BOWLING

	O.	M.	R.	W.	AV.
TEST					
1ST-CLASS	433	106	1153	39	29.56
INT					
RAL	82	8	316	13	24.30
NAT.W.	20.3	4	44	4	11.00
B & H	37	6	124	2	62.00

CAREER: BATTING

	I.	N.O.	R.	H.S.	AV.
TEST	51	4	1213	98*	25.80
1ST-CLASS	469	79	10235	130	26.24
INT	18	2	136	46	8.50
RAL	151	31	2474	84	20.61
NAT.W.	19	4	342	59*	22.80
B & H	52	12	1007	88*	25.17

CAREER: BOWLING

	O.	M.	R.	W.	AV.
TEST	280.1 484.4	79 140	1859	60	30.98
1ST-CLASS	256.2 8017.2	48 2254	21199	783	27.07
INT	13 194	1 19	813	25	32.52
RAL	936.3	66	3904	138	28.28
NAT.W.	226.3	52	597	22	27.13
B & H	525	102	1505	60	25.08

110. Who was top of the 1988 first-class bowling averages for Surrey?

111. Who was top of the 1988 first-class bowling averages for Sussex?

112. Who was top of the 1988 first-class bowling averages for Warwickshire?

MILLNS, D. J.   Nottinghamshire

Full Name: David James Millns
Role: Left-hand bat, right-arm
fast medium bowler, 1st slip fielder
Born: 27 February 1965, Mansfield
Height: 6′ 3″ **Weight:** 14st
Nickname: Ming, Rocket Man, Bulb
Head
County debut: 1988
1st-Class catches 1988: 4 (career 4)
Parents: Bernard and Brenda
Marital status: Single
Family links with cricket: Father
and elder brother Paul both play
for Clipstone WCC in Bassettlaw
League
Education: Garibaldi Comprehensive
Qualifications: 9 CSEs; Qualified
junior coach
Jobs outside cricket: Worked for
British Coal for three years as a linesman on the surveying staff at Clipstone
Colliery
Off-season 1988–89: Playing cricket for Uitenhage CC near Port Elizabeth
and coaching at Muir College for Boys also at Uitenhage
Cricketing superstitions or habits: 'Always try and walk out onto field behind
the captain.'
Overseas teams played for: Uitenhage CC, South Africa 1988–89
Cricketers particularly learnt from: John Birch, Clive Rice, Mike Hendrick,
Mike Bore

LAST SEASON: BATTING

	I.	N.O.	R.	H.S.	AV.
TEST					
1ST-CLASS	12	5	20	7*	2.85
INT					
RAL	1	1	0	0*	–
NAT.W.					
B & H					

CAREER: BATTING

	I.	N.O.	R.	H.S.	AV.
TEST					
1ST-CLASS	12	5	20	7*	2.85
INT					
RAL	1	1	0	0*	–
NAT.W.					
B & H					

LAST SEASON: BOWLING

	O.	M.	R.	W.	AV.
TEST					
1ST-CLASS	179	22	683	19	35.94
INT					
RAL	23	0	145	3	48.33
NAT.W.					
B & H					

CAREER: BOWLING

	O.	M.	R.	W.	AV.
TEST					
1ST-CLASS	179	22	683	19	35.94
INT					
RAL	23	0	145	3	48.33
NAT.W.					
B & H					

Cricketers particularly admired: Clive Rice, Franklyn Stephenson, Derek Randall

Other sports played: Football, snooker, golf ('to a poor standard')

Other sports followed: American football, skiing, Formula One motor racing

Injuries 1988: Shin sores

Relaxations: Television, watching films, walking, sleeping

Extras: Had two operations on each leg to cure shin sores in November 1987

Opinions on cricket: 'There should be a 14-day break in the middle of the season to allow all players a rest. South Africa should be allowed back into Test cricket. There should be 16 four-day games starting Tuesday, finish Friday, with another one-day competition on Saturdays. Perhaps a day–night series.'

Best batting performance: 7* Nottinghamshire v Hampshire, Basingstoke 1988

Best bowling performance: 3-37 Nottinghamshire v Glamorgan, Trent Bridge 1988

MOLES, A. J. Warwickshire

Full Name: Andrew James Moles

Role: Right-hand opening bat, right-arm medium bowler

Born: 12 February 1961, Solihull

Height: 5′ 10″ **Weight:** 13½st

Nickname: Molar

County debut: 1986

County cap: 1987

1000 runs in a season: 1

1st-Class 50s scored: 16

1st-Class 100s scored: 12

1st-Class 200s scored: 1

One-Day 50s: 6

One-Day 100s: 1

Place in batting averages: 70th av. 33.37 (1987 85th av. 33.27)

Place in bowling averages: —
(1987 124th av. 42.75)

1st-Class catches 1988: 12 (career 51)

Parents: Stuart Francis and Gillian Margaret

Wife and date of marriage: Jacquie, 17 December 1988

Family links with cricket: Brother plays for Solihull in the Midland Championship

Education: Finham Park Comprehensive, Coventry; Henley College of Further Education; Butts College of Further Education
Qualifications: 3 O-levels, 4 CSEs, Toolmaker/Standard Room Inspector City & Guilds 205 Pts I, II, III
Jobs outside cricket: Standard Room Inspector
Off-season 1988–89: 'Resting and getting married.'
Cricketing superstitions or habits: Put left pad on first. Never look back at stumps after being bowled
Overseas team: Griqualand West Cricket Union, South Africa 1985–86, 1987–88
Cricketers particularly learnt from: Dennis Amiss, Fred Gardner
Cricketers particularly admired: Dennis Amiss, Martin Crowe
Other sports played: Football
Injuries 1988: Broken thumb
Relaxations: Listening to music or a meal with friends and talking about cricket
Best batting performance: 200* Griqualand West v Northern Transvaal 1987–88
Best bowling performance: 3-21 Warwickshire v Oxford University, Oxford 1987

LAST SEASON: BATTING

	I.	N.O.	R.	H.S.	AV.
TEST					
1ST-CLASS	31	2	968	115	33.37
INT					
RAL	7	0	167	79	23.85
NAT.W.	2	0	25	25	12.50
B & H	5	0	148	68	29.60

LAST SEASON: BOWLING

	O.	M.	R.	W.	AV.
TEST					
1ST-CLASS					
INT					
RAL	4	0	32	0	–
NAT.W.					
B & H	6	0	31	1	31.00

CAREER: BATTING

	I.	N.O.	R.	H.S.	AV.
TEST					
1ST-CLASS	119	11	4499	200*	41.65
INT					
RAL	27	2	577	85	23.08
NAT.W.	6	0	179	127	29.83
B & H	8	0	228	72	28.50

CAREER: BOWLING

	O.	M.	R.	W.	AV.
TEST					
1ST-CLASS	397	88	1190	27	44.07
INT					
RAL	63	0	358	7	51.14
NAT.W.	15	0	81	0	–
B & H	24	0	115	2	57.50

113. Who was top of the 1988 first-class bowling averages for Worcestershire?

114. Who was top of the 1988 first-class bowling averages for Yorkshire?

MONKHOUSE, S.   Glamorgan

Full Name: Steven Monkhouse
Role: Right-hand bat, left-arm
fast-medium bowler, outfielder
Born: 24 November 1962, Bury
Height: 6′ 3″ **Weight:** 13st 7lbs
Nickname: Bob, Millstone, Monky
County debut: 1985 (Warwickshire),
1987 (Glamorgan)
1st-Class catches 1988: 0 (career 2)
Parents: Harold and May
Marital status: Single
Family links with cricket: Father
played in the Lancashire League
for Ramsbottom CC
Education: Derby Technical
Grammar School; Peel College
Qualifications: 7 O-levels,
BEC National Business Studies
Cert, NCA Coaching Certificate

Overseas tours: La Manga with Glamorgan CCC 1988
Overseas teams played for: Newtown District, Tasmania 1985–86, 1986–87
Cricketing superstitions or habits: 'I try to avoid them if I can!'
Cricketers particularly learnt from: Murray Bennett, Anton Ferreira
Cricketers particularly admired: Michael Holding, Ian Botham
Other sports played: 'Golf, snooker, darts, and a few others, but not
seriously.'
Injuries 1988: 'I was disillusioned for a while.'
Relaxations: 'Music, TV, and a few drinks with the lads.'
Extras: Signed for Glamorgan at end of 1986 season. Released at end of 1988

LAST SEASON: BATTING

	I.	N.O.	R.	H.S.	AV.
TEST					
1ST-CLASS	1	1	0	0*	–
INT					
RAL					
NAT.W.					
B & H					

LAST SEASON: BOWLING

	O.	M.	R.	W.	AV.
TEST					
1ST-CLASS	67	17	155	5	31.00
INT					
RAL					
NAT.W.					
B & H					

CAREER: BATTING

	I.	N.O.	R.	H.S.	AV.
TEST					
1ST-CLASS	12	5	30	15	4.28
INT					
RAL	3	1	0	0	0.00
NAT.W.					
B & H					

CAREER: BOWLING

	O.	M.	R.	W.	AV.
TEST					
1ST-CLASS	176	30	576	18	32.00
INT					
RAL	16	5	61	3	20.33
NAT.W.	12	3	32	5	6.40
B & H					

Opinions on cricket: 'Too many former players become team managers, coaches, etc., but do not have the ability to communicate, and get the best out of younger players. Second XI pitches are not up to the standard required for the cricket played on them. Also, second XI umpiring standards are not adequate.'

Best batting performance: 15 Glamorgan v Northamptonshire, Swansea 1987

Best bowling performance: 3-37 Glamorgan v Cambridge University, Cambridge 1988

MOORES, P. Sussex

Full Name: Peter Moores
Role: Right-hand bat, wicket-keeper
Born: 18 December 1962, Macclesfield, Cheshire
Height: 6' **Weight:** 12st 11lbs
Nickname: Stos, Stumper, Moorsey
County debut: 1983 (Worcestershire), 1985 (Sussex)
1st-Class 50s scored: 3
Place in batting averages: 204th av. 17.95 (1987 195th av. 17.50)
Parents: Bernard and Winifred
Marital status: Single
Family links with cricket: Three brothers, Anthony, Stephen and Robert all play local cricket
Education: King Edward VI School, Macclesfield

LAST SEASON: BATTING

	I.	N.O.	R.	H.S.	AV.
TEST					
1ST-CLASS	24	2	395	97*	17.95
INT					
RAL	8	3	88	34	17.60
NAT.W.	1	0	20	20	20.00
B & H					

CAREER: BATTING

	I.	N.O.	R.	H.S.	AV.
TEST					
1ST-CLASS	63	7	995	97*	17.76
INT					
RAL	17	9	126	34	15.75
NAT.W.	2	1	23	20	23.00
B & H					

LAST SEASON: WICKET KEEPING

	C.	ST.		
TEST				
1ST-CLASS	30	3		
INT				
RAL	5	2		
NAT.W.	2	–		
B & H				

CAREER: WICKET KEEPING

	C.	ST.		
TEST				
1ST-CLASS	68	9		
INT				
RAL	23	5		
NAT.W.	4	–		
B & H	1	–		

Qualifications: 7 O-levels, 3 A-levels. Senior NCA Coaching Award
Off-season 1988–89: Coaching in Orange Free State in South Africa
Overseas teams played for: Harare Sports Club, Zimbabwe 1984–85
Cricketers particularly learnt from: Don Wilson, Basil D'Oliveira
Cricketers particularly admired: Bob Taylor, Clive Lloyd, Alan Knott
Other sports played: Squash, football, swimming and most ball games
Other sports followed: Football, hockey
Relaxations: Old films, music, photography
Extras: On the MCC groundstaff in 1982 before joining Worcestershire in latter half of 1982 season. Joined Sussex in 1985
Opinions on cricket: 'I feel four-day cricket will be a good thing in that it will allow more genuine results and should also give more opportunities to younger players in the side.'
Best batting performance: 97* Sussex v Lancashire, Hove 1988

MORRIS, H. Glamorgan

Full Name: Hugh Morris
Role: Left-hand bat, right-arm medium bowler
Born: 5 October 1963, Cardiff
Height: 5′ 8″ **Weight:** 12st
Nickname: H, Banacek
County debut: 1981
County cap: 1986
1000 runs in a season: 2
1st-Class 50s scored: 32
1st-Class 100s scored: 6
One-Day 50s: 12
One-Day 100s: 2
Place in batting averages: 113th
av. 27.73 (1987 121st av. 28.34)
1st-Class catches 1988: 14 (career 52)
Parents: Roger and Anne
Marital status: Single
Family links with cricket: Brother
played for Wales U-19 and Glamorgan U-19. Father played league cricket. Cousin plays for Welsh Schools U-15
Education: Blundell's School; South Glamorgan Institute
Qualifications: 9 O-levels, 3 A-levels, 1 AO-level, BA(Hons), NCA Coaching Award
Cricketing superstitions or habits: Getting off 111. Put right pad on first
Overseas tours: With English Public Schoolboy tour to West Indies, 1980–81; to Sri Lanka 1982–83; to USA (Los Angeles) with Haverfordwest CC, 1984

Cricketers particularly learnt from: Alan Jones, Tom Cartwright, Kevin Lyons

Cricketers admired: Ian Botham, Javed Miandad, Viv Richards, Graeme Hick

Other sports played: Rugby, squash, golf

Other sports followed: Soccer

Injuries 1988: Dislocated finger; torn cartilege in right knee

Relaxations: Music, watching movies, having a few quiet pints, travelling

Extras: Highest schoolboy cricket average in 1979 (89.71), 1981 (184.6) and 1982 (149.2). Captain of England U-19 Schoolboys in 1981 and 1982. Played for Young England v Young West Indies 1982, and captained Young England v Australia. Won Gray-Nicholls 'Most Promising Schoolboy' Award 1981, and Young Cricketer of 1982. Played first-class rugby for Aberavon 1984–85 and South Glamorgan Institute scoring over 150 points. Appointed Glamorgan captain 1986 – the youngest ever for county. Scored most runs in Sunday League by a Glamorgan player – 586

Best batting performance: 143 Glamorgan v Oxford University, Oxford 1987

Best bowling performance: 1-6 Glamorgan v Oxford University, Oxford 1987

LAST SEASON: BATTING

	I.	N.O.	R.	H.S.	AV.
TEST					
1ST-CLASS	33	3	832	87	27.73
INT					
RAL	13	2	306	72*	27.81
NAT.W.	2	0	56	39	28.00
B & H	5	0	43	15	8.60

CAREER: BATTING

	I.	N.O.	R.	H.S.	AV.
TEST					
1ST-CLASS	185	21	5037	143	30.71
INT					
RAL	55	6	1489	100	30.38
NAT.W.	9	1	277	75	34.62
B & H	14	1	285	115	21.92

LAST SEASON: BOWLING

	O.	M.	R.	W.	AV.
TEST					
1ST-CLASS	4.3	0	58	0	–
INT					
RAL					
NAT.W.					
B & H	2	0	14	1	14.00

CAREER: BOWLING

	O.	M.	R.	W.	AV.
TEST					
1ST-CLASS	38.2	6	228	2	114.00
INT					
RAL					
NAT.W.					
B & H	2	0	14	1	14.00

115. Which Test cricketer had a biography published about him in 1988, entitled *Cricket Conjuror*?

116. Who was the 'Peter Pan' referred to in David Rayvern Allen's recent book *Peter Pan and Cricket*?

MORMS, J. E.   Derbyshire

Full Name: John Edward Morris
Role: Right-hand bat,
right-arm medium bowler
Born: 1 April 1964, Crewe
Height: 5′ 10½″ **Weight:** 13st 6lbs
Nickname: Animal
County debut: 1982
County cap: 1986
1000 runs in a season: 3
1st-Class 50s scored: 29
1st-Class 100s scored: 13
One-Day 50s: 11
One-Day 100s: 1
Place in batting averages: 45th
av. 37.62 (1987 76th av. 34.43)
1st-Class catches 1988: 6 (career 40)
Parents: George (Eddie) and Jean
Marital status: Single
Family links with cricket: Father
played for Crewe CC for many years as an opening bowler
Education: Shavington Comprehensive School; Dane Bank College of
Further Education
Qualifications: O-levels
Jobs outside cricket: Worked as a carpet fitter. PR officer for indoor cricket
centre
Overseas teams played for: Subiaco Floreat CC, Perth, Western Australia,
1986–87
Cricketers particularly learnt from: Tony Borrington, Phil Russell, Father
Other sports played: Football, basketball, snooker

LAST SEASON: BATTING

	I.	N.O.	R.	H.S.	AV.
TEST					
1ST-CLASS	37	5	1204	175	37.62
INT					
RAL	15	1	391	65	27.92
NAT.W.	3	1	100	43*	50.00
B & H	5	2	137	48*	45.66

LAST SEASON: BOWLING

	O.	M.	R.	W.	AV.
TEST					
1ST-CLASS	5.1	0	19	0	–
INT					
RAL					
NAT.W.					
B & H					

CAREER: BATTING

	I.	N.O.	R.	H.S.	AV.
TEST					
1ST-CLASS	194	12	6335	191	34.80
INT					
RAL	75	5	1761	104	25.15
NAT.W.	11	2	178	43*	19.77
B & H	21	3	440	65	24.44

CAREER: BOWLING

	O.	M.	R.	W.	AV.
TEST					
1ST-CLASS	73.3	7	453	3	151.00
INT					
RAL					
NAT.W.					
B & H					

Other sports followed: Athletics, motor racing
Relaxations: Movies, music, good food, fly-fishing
Best batting performance: 191 Derbyshire v Kent, Derby 1986
Best bowling performance: 1-13 Derbyshire v Yorkshire, Harrogate 1987

MORTENSEN, O. H.   Derbyshire

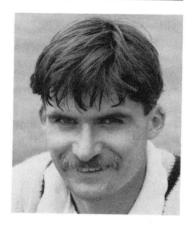

Full Name: Ole Henrik Mortensen
Role: Right-hand bat, right-arm fast-medium bowler
Born: 29 January 1958, Vejle, Denmark
Height: 6′ 4″ **Weight:** 14st 2lbs
Nickname: Stan (coined by Bob Taylor after England footballer Stan Mortenson), Blood-Axe
County debut: 1983
County cap: 1986
1st-Class 50s scored: 1
1st-Class 5 w. in innings: 11
1st-Class 10 w. in match: 1
Place in batting averages: 252nd av. 11.50 (1987 238th av. 12.00)
Place in bowling averages: 2nd av. 13.64 (1987 7th av. 19.70)
Strike rate 1988: 41.21 (career 51.28)
1st-Class catches 1988: 6 (career 26)
Parents: Will Ernst and Inge Wicka
Wife: Jette Jepmond
Children: Julie Jepmond, 30 August 1982
Family links with cricket: 'My small brother, Michael, used to play cricket. He is now a professional tennis player, and has played in Davis Cup for Denmark.'
Education: Brondbyoster School; Avedore School
Jobs outside cricket: Worked as a tax assistant in Denmark
Overseas tours: East Africa in 1976 with the Danish national side, and Scotland, Wales, Ireland and Holland
Overseas teams played for: Ellerslie, Auckland, New Zealand, 1983–84; Brighton CC, Melbourne 1985–86; Svanholm CC, Denmark
Cricketers particularly learnt from: Torben Jensen, Jorgen Janson, Peter Hargreaves and many others
Cricketers particularly admired: Dennis Lillee, Bob Taylor
Other sports played: Tennis, golf, football

Relaxations: Music, books, movies
Extras: *Derbyshire's Dane* by Peter Hargreaves, published 1984. Has played for Denmark. Only Dane currently playing first-class cricket
Opinions on cricket: 'Too much cricket; seam bowlers turn into robots by August.'
Best batting performance: 74* Derbyshire v Yorkshire, Chesterfield 1987
Best bowling performance: 6-27 Derbyshire v Yorkshire, Sheffield 1983

LAST SEASON: BATTING

	I.	N.O.	R.	H.S.	AV.
TEST					
1ST-CLASS	12	8	46	15	11.50
INT					
RAL	6	2	8	5	2.00
NAT.W.	2	2	0	0*	—
B & H	1	1	0	0*	—

CAREER: BATTING

	I.	N.O.	R.	H.S.	AV.
TEST					
1ST-CLASS	99	53	461	74*	10.02
INT					
RAL	30	21	40	5*	4.44
NAT.W.	7	5	19	11	9.50
B & H	4	2	5	3*	2.50

LAST SEASON: BOWLING

	O.	M.	R.	W.	AV.
TEST					
1ST-CLASS	233.3	73	464	34	13.64
INT					
RAL	86	9	277	9	30.77
NAT.W.	22.2	9	50	8	6.25
B & H	49	3	167	4	41.75

CAREER: BOWLING

	O.	M.	R.	W.	AV.
TEST					
1ST-CLASS	2153.4	533	5831	252	23.13
INT					
RAL	530.3	50	2033	71	28.63
NAT.W.	99	26	279	16	17.43
B & H	184.2	23	558	29	19.24

MOXON, M. D. Yorkshire

Full Name: Martyn Douglas Moxon
Role: Right-hand bat, right-arm medium bowler, slip fielder
Born: 4 May 1960, Barnsley
Height: 6' 1" **Weight:** 13st 7lbs
Nickname: Frog
County debut: 1981
County cap: 1984
Test debut: 1986
No. of Tests: 9
No. of One-Day Internationals: 8
1000 runs in a season: 4
1st-Class 50s scored: 46
1st-Class 100s scored: 20
One-Day 50s: 22
One-Day 100s: 1
Place in batting averages: 32nd
av. 41.25 (1987 43rd av. 40.03)
1st-Class catches 1988: 23 (career 124)
Parents: Audrey and Derek (deceased)

Wife and date of marriage: Sue, October 1985
Family links with cricket: Father and grandfather played local league cricket. Father was coach to Wombwell Cricket Lovers' Society
Education: Holgate Grammar School, Barnsley
Qualifications: 8 O-levels, 3 A-levels, HNC in Business Studies, NCA Coaching Award
Off-season 1988–89: 'Trying to get my golf handicap lowered.'
Jobs outside cricket: Bank clerk with Barclays Bank for two years before turning professional full-time
Cricketing superstitions or habits: Always put left pad on first
Overseas tours: Captain of North of England U-19 tour of Canada, 1979; with England to India and Australia 1984–85, England B tour to Sri Lanka 1986; England to Pakistan and New Zealand 1987–88
Overseas teams played for: Griqualand West, South Africa 1982–83 and 1983–84
Cricketers particularly learnt from: Doug Padgett, Phil Carrick, Steve Oldham
Cricketers particularly admired: Viv Richards
Other sports played: Football in the local league in the winter and golf
Other sports followed: 'Am a keen supporter of Barnsley FC.'
Relaxations: Listening to most types of music, having a drink with friends
Extras: Captained Yorkshire Schools U-15s and North of England U-15s. Played for Yorkshire Cricket Federation U-19s. Captained Yorkshire Senior Schools. Like Yorkshire colleagues, G. Stevenson and A. Sidebottom, he played for Wombwell Cricket Lovers' Society U-18 side which competes in the Joe Lumb U-18 Competition. At the time, made the highest score by a player on his Yorkshire debut – 116 v Essex (since overtaken by Ashley Metcalfe). First Yorkshire player to make centuries on his first two Championship games in Yorkshire: 116 v Essex at Headingley and 111 v Derbyshire at Sheffield. Changed from spectacles to contact lenses in 1981. Scored 153 in first 'Roses' innings. Picked for Lord's Test of 1984 v West Indies, but had to withdraw through injury and had to wait until 1986 to make Test debut

LAST SEASON: BATTING

	I.	N.O.	R.	H.S.	AV.
TEST	4	0	55	26	13.75
1ST-CLASS	35	3	1430	191	44.68
INT					
RAL	9	0	287	79	31.88
NAT.W.	2	1	42	33*	42.00
B & H	4	2	175	82*	87.50

CAREER: BATTING

	I.	N.O.	R.	H.S.	AV.
TEST	15	1	437	99	31.21
1ST-CLASS	247	17	8936	191	38.85
INT	8	0	174	70	21.75
RAL	53	5	1390	86	28.95
NAT.W.	13	4	500	82*	55.55
B & H	26	4	1057	106*	48.04

LAST SEASON: BOWLING

	O.	M.	R.	W.	AV.
TEST					
1ST-CLASS	6	2	15	0	–
INT					
RAL	27	0	153	1	153.00
NAT.W.					
B & H	10	1	23	2	11.50

CAREER: BOWLING

	O.	M.	R.	W.	AV.
TEST	8	2	30	0	–
1ST-CLASS	304.4	51	1070	18	59.44
INT					
RAL	67	2	383	4	95.75
NAT.W.	8	0	32	1	32.00
B & H	42	1	168	3	56.00

Best batting performance: 191 Yorkshire v Northamptonshire, Scarborough 1988
Best bowling performance: 3-26 D. B. Close's XI v Sri Lankans, Scarborough 1985

MUNTON, T. A. Warwickshire

Full Name: Timothy Alan Munton
Role: Right-hand bat, right-arm fast-medium bowler
Born: 30 July 1965, Melton Mowbray
Height: 6′ 6″ **Weight:** 14st
County debut: 1985
Nickname: Tiny, Herman
1st-Class 5 w. in innings: 4
Place in batting averages: —
(1987 247th av. 10.54)
Place in bowling averages: 31st
av. 22.76 (1987 33rd av. 25.43)
Strike rate 1988: 56.76 (career 55.53)
1st-Class catches 1988: 2 (career 6)
Parents names: Alan and Brenda
Wife and date of marriage: Helen, 20 September 1986
Education: Sarson High School, King Edward VII Upper School
Qualifications: 8 O-levels, 1 A-level; cricket coach

LAST SEASON: BATTING

	I.	N.O.	R.	H.S.	AV.
TEST					
1ST-CLASS	22	7	131	24*	8.73
INT					
RAL	2	2	6	6*	—
NAT.W.	1	1	0	0*	—
B & H	1	1	3	3*	—

CAREER: BATTING

	I.	N.O.	R.	H.S.	AV.
TEST					
1ST-CLASS	53	18	305	38	8.71
INT					
RAL	8	6	23	7*	11.50
NAT.W.	1	1	0	0*	—
B & H	4	4	9	6*	—

LAST SEASON: BOWLING

	O.	M.	R.	W.	AV.
TEST					
1ST-CLASS	435.1	126	1047	46	22.76
INT					
RAL	83	14	220	10	22.00
NAT.W.	21.4	3	83	0	—
B & H	22	0	79	1	79.00

CAREER: BOWLING

	O.	M.	R.	W.	AV.
TEST					
1ST-CLASS	1083	266	2979	117	25.46
INT					
RAL	218	19	909	31	29.32
NAT.W.	27.4	3	105	2	52.50
B & H	75	5	254	7	36.28

Overseas teams played for: Victoria University, Wellington, New Zealand 1985–86; Witswatersrand University, Johannesburg, 1986–87
Cricketers particularly learnt from: Ken Hughes
Cricketers particularly admired: Bob Willis, Clive Rice, Richard Hadlee
Other sports played: Basketball, soccer
Relaxations: Listening to music
Extras: Appeared for Leicestershire 2nd XI 1982–84
Best batting performance: 38 Warwickshire v Yorkshire, Scarborough 1987
Best bowling performance: 6-21 Warwickshire v Worcestershire, Edgbaston 1988

MURPHY, A. J. Lancashire

Full Name: Anthony John Murphy
Role: Right-hand bat,
right-arm medium bowler
Born: 6 August 1962, Manchester
Height: 6′ 0″ **Weight:** 13½st
Nickname: Audi, Headless,
Tramp, Compo
County debut: 1985
1st-Class catches 1988: 2 (career 6)
Parents: John Desmond and
Elizabeth Catherine
Marital status: Single
Family links with cricket: Brother
plays club cricket for Cheadle
Education: Xaverian College,
Manchester; Swansea University
Qualifications: 9 O-levels, 4 A-levels
Jobs outside cricket: Computer
operator for Barclays Bank.
Part-time store detective. Wool tester
Off-season 1988–89: Coaching in Tasmania for Ulveston CC
Overseas tours: Minor Counties U-25s to Kenya 1986
Overseas teams played for: Central Districts & Taradale CC, New Zealand,
1985–88
Cricketers particularly learnt from: Søren Henriksen, Mark Chadwick,
David Varey, Ian Davidson, Chris Maynard, Steve O'Shaughnessy
Cricketers particularly admired: Clive Lloyd, Michael Holding ('both great
ambassadors for cricket as well as great exponents of the game')
Other sports played: 'Many – but have become a master at none.'
Other sports followed: American football, dog and horse racing, Manchester
City FC

Relaxations: 'Flapping when raining during a game. Helping Chris Maynard back to fitness. Poetry and chamber music.'

Opinions on cricket: 'I feel four-day cricket can only succeed if the standard of wickets improves dramatically. At the moment, too many games do not last to their expected duration due to bad or under-prepared wickets. This is not helping English cricket, especially in the batting department. I also think that the ICC should make a decision, one way or the other, as to whether or not cricketers with links in South Africa can compete in international cricket or not, and this ruling should be adhered to by all members of the ICC, thus avoiding another farce like the on-off winter tour of India.'

Best batting performance: 6 Minor Counties v New Zealanders, Lakenham 1986

Best bowling performance: 4-115 Lancashire v Somerset, Taunton 1987

LAST SEASON: BATTING

	I.	N.O.	R.	H.S.	AV.
TEST					
1ST-CLASS	3	0	3	3	1.00
INT					
RAL					
NAT.W.					
B & H					

LAST SEASON: BOWLING

	O.	M.	R.	W.	AV.
TEST					
1ST-CLASS	100.5	18	318	6	53.00
INT					
RAL					
NAT.W.					
B & H					

CAREER: BATTING

	I.	N.O.	R.	H.S.	AV.
TEST					
1ST-CLASS	19	7	25	6	2.08
INT					
RAL	1	1	2	2*	–
NAT.W.					
B & H					

CAREER: BOWLING

	O.	M.	R.	W.	AV.
TEST					
1ST-CLASS	353.1	75	1268	33	38.42
INT					
RAL	6	0	33	1	33.00
NAT.W.					
B & H					

117. When Graeme Hick hit 1000 runs before the end of May in 1988, how many times had it been done before, and by whom?

118. Who said last season of whom: 'I keep telling him he is much better than his father'?

MYLES, S. D. Warwickshire

Full Name: Simon David Myles
Role: Right-hand bat,
right-arm medium bowler
Born: 2 June 1966, Mansfield
Height: 5′ 10″ **Weight:** 13st
Nickname: Slopey, Phoey
County debut: 1987 (Sussex),
1988 (Warwickshire)
1st-Class catches 1988: 0 (career 1)
Parents: David Wilson and
Carolyn Margaret
Marital status: Single
Family links with cricket: Both
younger brothers are keen
players and followers of
the game
Education: King George V School,
Hong Kong
Qualifications: 9 O-levels, 1 A-level,
NCA Coaching Certificate

Jobs outside cricket: Selling and surveying tennis courts in Hong Kong. Bicycle courier in Perth, Western Australia. Brickpaver's labourer
Off-season 1988–89: Playing for Nedlands CC in Perth, Western Australia
Cricketing superstitions or habits: 'Regularly – if I'm in for long enough – marking and remarking my guard. Getting through more than one season at the same county!'
Overseas tours: Hong Kong to Singapore and Malaysia 1983; to Bangladesh for South East Asian Cup 1984; to England for ICC Trophy 1986
Overseas team played for: Hong Kong domestic sides; Mount Lawley, Perth 1986–87, 1987–88
Cricketers particularly learnt from: David Clinton (schoolmaster), Geoff Boycott, Paul Parker
Cricketers particularly admired: Geoff Boycott, Richard Hadlee, Bob Taylor
Other sports played: All ball sports but particularly football
Other sports followed: Football (Derby County FC), most other sports
Injuries 1988: Severe abdominal blow forced him to lose 10 days cricket

LAST SEASON: BATTING

	I.	N.O.	R.	H.S.	AV.
TEST					
1ST-CLASS	7	0	111	39	15.85
INT					
RAL	1	0	32	32	32.00
NAT.W.					
B & H					

CAREER: BATTING

	I.	N.O.	R.	H.S.	AV.
TEST					
1ST-CLASS	10	1	130	39	14.44
INT					
RAL	6	1	57	32	11.40
NAT.W.					
B & H					

322

Relaxations: 'Golf, listening to music, watching a good film or just sleeping.'
Extras: Hong Kong Sportsboy of the Year 1984. Record ICC Trophy score of 172 in 1986. Released by Sussex at end of 1987 season. Joined Warwickshire in 1988 and released at end of season
Opinions on cricket: 'Despite the fact that some wickets have been sub-standard I think the four-day cricket played has given the opportunity for genuine matches to unfold. Surely that's got to be better than some of the farcical situations in which we attempt to achieve results in three-day cricket.'
Best batting performance: 39 Warwickshire v Leicestershire, Edgbaston 1988

NEALE, P. A.   Worcestershire

Full Name: Phillip Anthony Neale
Role: Right-hand bat, cover fielder
Born: 5 June 1954, Scunthorpe
Height: 5' 11" **Weight:** 11st 10lbs
Nickname: Phil
County debut: 1975
County cap: 1978
Benefit: 1988
1000 runs in a season: 8
1st-Class 50s scored: 76
1st-Class 100s scored: 26
One-Day 50s: 30
One-Day 100s: 2
Place in batting averages: 35th
av. 39.84 (1987 62nd av. 36.81)
1st-Class catches 1988: 8
(career 110)
Parents: Geoff and Margaret
Wife and date of marriage: Christine, 26 September 1976
Children: Kelly Joanne, 9 November 1979; Craig Andrew, 11 February 1982
Education: Frederick Gough Grammar School, Scunthorpe; John Leggot Sixth Form College, Scunthorpe; Leeds University
Qualifications: 10 O-levels, 2 A-levels, BA Hons Russian. Preliminary football and cricket coaching awards
Jobs outside cricket: Teacher, former professional footballer
Off-season 1988–89: Teaching cricket and soccer at Royal Grammar School, Worcester
Cricketing superstitions or habits: Left pad on first
Cricketers particularly learnt from: 'Most county players – you learn by watching'.
Cricketers particularly admired: Basil D'Oliveira, Norman Gifford, Alan Ormrod

Other sports played: Squash, golf ('badly')
Other sports followed: Most sports – mainly via TV
Injuries 1988: Broken finger; damaged shoulder ligaments
Relaxations: 'Reading, spending time with my family, trying to learn to play golf.'
Extras: Played for Lincolnshire 1973–74. Scored 100 runs before lunch v Warwickshire at Worcester, 1979. Captain 1983–. Testimonial season with Lincoln City 1984–85. Retired from full-time football 1985. Celebrated his benefit season by captaining Worcestershire to a County Championship and Sunday League double
Best batting performance: 167 Worcestershire v Sussex, Kidderminster, 1988
Best bowling performance: 1-15 Worcestershire v Derbyshire, Worcester 1976

LAST SEASON: BATTING

	I.	N.O.	R.	H.S.	AV.
TEST					
1ST-CLASS	31	5	1036	167	39.84
INT					
RAL	12	5	337	91	48.14
NAT.W.	5	0	228	98	45.60
B & H	4	0	132	91	33.00

LAST SEASON: BOWLING

	O.	M.	R.	W.	AV.
TEST					
1ST-CLASS	14	1	62	0	–
INT					
RAL					
NAT.W.					
B & H					

CAREER: BATTING

	I.	N.O.	R.	H.S.	AV.
TEST					
1ST-CLASS	482	70	14942	167	36.26
INT					
RAL	172	38	3910	102	29.17
NAT.W.	26	1	827	98	33.08
B & H	51	6	1384	128	30.75

CAREER: BOWLING

	O.	M.	R.	W.	AV.
TEST					
1ST-CLASS	59.5	4	275	1	275.00
INT					
RAL	8.2	0	50	2	25.00
NAT.W.					
B & H					

119. How old was Graeme Hick when he scored his first century?

120. Which wicket-keeper has made the most Test dismissals ever, and how many?

NEEDHAM, A.   Middlesex

Full Name: Andrew Needham
Role: Right-hand bat, off-break bowler
Born: 23 March 1957, Calow, Derbyshire
Height: 5' 10" **Weight:** 10st 7lbs
Nickname: Needers
County debut: 1977 (Surrey), 1987 (Middlesex)
County cap: 1985 (Surrey)
1000 runs in a season: 1
1st-Class 50s scored: 12
1st-Class 100s scored: 4
1st-Class 5 w. in innings: 6
One-Day 50s: 3
Place in batting averages: 75th av. 32.25 (1987 190th av. 18.22)
Place in bowling averages: — (1987 129th av. 45.41)
1st-Class catches 1988: 5 (career 50)
Parents: Thomas Robin and Peggy
Wife and date of marriage: Jane Marion, 1 November 1984
Education: Ecclesbourne Grammar School, Derbyshire; Paisley Grammar School, Scotland; Watford Grammar School
Qualifications: 6 O-levels
Off-season 1988–89: Working for family firm Needham and Needham Ltd
Cricketing superstitions or habits: Always put left pad on first
Overseas tours: Antigua with Surrey Young Cricketers 1977–78; Hong Kong, Singapore and Bangkok with Surrey 1979–80; Bangladesh with MCC

LAST SEASON: BATTING

	I.	N.O.	R.	H.S.	AV.
TEST					
1ST-CLASS	12	3	293	66*	32.55
INT					
RAL	5	0	100	39	20.00
NAT.W.	4	0	87	30	21.75
B & H					

CAREER: BATTING

	I.	N.O.	R.	H.S.	AV.
TEST					
1ST-CLASS	156	23	3077	138	23.13
INT					
RAL	50	8	778	55	18.52
NAT.W.	8	0	141	30	17.62
B & H	7	1	111	30	18.50

LAST SEASON: BOWLING

	O.	M.	R.	W.	AV.
TEST					
1ST-CLASS	113.4	19	399	8	49.87
INT					
RAL	36	1	151	6	25.16
NAT.W.	36	3	84	3	28.00
B & H					

CAREER: BOWLING

	O.	M.	R.	W.	AV.
TEST					
1ST-CLASS	1790.1	427	5373	124	43.33
INT					
RAL	215.1	10	1047	35	29.91
NAT.W.	84	8	257	12	21.41
B & H	30	3	99	0	—

1980–81; UAE with Barbican Touring Side 1983; South Africa with Alfred McAlpine 1983–84
Overseas teams played for: Glenwood Old Boys, Durban 1979–80 and 1984
Cricketers particularly learnt from: Fred Titmus
Cricketers particularly admired: Barry Richards
Other sports played: Squash and snooker
Other sports followed: Watches Chesterfield (football), horse racing and American football
Relaxations: Horses, cards, music, learning about wines
Extras: Left Surrey after 1986 season to join Middlesex. Retired at end of 1988 season to concentrate on his family sports marketing business
Best batting performance: 138 Surrey v Warwickshire, The Oval 1985
Best bowling performance: 6-30 Surrey v Oxford University, The Oval 1983

NEWELL, M. Nottinghamshire

Full Name: Michael Newell
Role: Right-hand opening bat, leg-break bowler, occasional wicket-keeper
Born: 25 February 1965, Blackburn
Height: 5′ 8″ **Weight:** 11st
Nickname: Sam, Tricky, Mott, Merrick
County debut: 1984
County cap: 1987
1000 runs in a season: 1
1st-Class 50s scored: 15
1st-Class 100s scored: 4
1st-Class 200s scored: 1
One-Day 50s: 2
Place in batting averages: 170th av. 21.76 (1987 46th av. 39.03)
1st-Class catches 1988: 28 (career 68 + 1 stumping)
Parents: Barry and Janet
Marital status: Single
Family links with cricket: Father chairman of Notts Unity CC. Brother Paul plays for Loughborough University.
Education: West Bridgford Comprehensive
Qualifications: 8 O-levels, 3 A-levels. NCA advanced coach
Jobs outside cricket: Part-time barman; has worked in children's home; packer at Gunn and Moore. Selling kit at Trent Bridge

Off-season 1988–89: Playing and coaching in Rotorua, New Zealand
Cricketing superstitions or habits: 'Always put right pad on first; always bat in short sweater and long-sleeved shirt. Wear the same whites if I am in form.'
Overseas tours: NCA U-19 tour to Holland 1983
Overseas teams played for: Nedland CC, Perth 1985–86
Cricketers particularly learnt from: Tim Robinson, Eddie Hemmings
Cricketers particularly admired: Franklyn Stephenson, John Birch
Other sports played: Football ('of a low standard'), indoor cricket
Other sports followed: Watches rugby union and football, horse racing
Relaxations: Good films, music and drinking at the Trent Bridge Inn
Extras: Carried his bat through the Nottinghamshire innings v Warwickshire, scoring 10 out of Nottinghamshire's 44 – the sixth-lowest individual score by a batsman playing all through an innings
Opinions on cricket: 'I feel that individuals should not be prevented from playing in South Africa, though rebel team tours are undoubtedly a danger to the future of Test cricket.'
Best batting performance: 203* Nottinghamshire v Derbyshire, Derby 1987
Best bowling performance: 2-38 Nottinghamshire v Sri Lankans, Trent Bridge 1988

LAST SEASON: BATTING

	I.	N.O.	R.	H.S.	AV.
TEST					
1ST-CLASS	37	3	740	105	21.76
INT					
RAL	7	0	175	58	25.00
NAT.W.	1	0	35	35	35.00
B & H	1	1	31	31*	–

LAST SEASON: BOWLING

	O.	M.	R.	W.	AV.
TEST					
1ST-CLASS	17.4	4	63	3	21.00
INT					
RAL					
NAT.W.	1	0	10	0	–
B & H					

CAREER: BATTING

	I.	N.O.	R.	H.S.	AV.
TEST					
1ST-CLASS	121	20	3074	203*	30.43
INT					
RAL	9	1	215	58	26.87
NAT.W.	3	0	97	60	32.33
B & H	3	1	83	31*	41.50

CAREER: BOWLING

	O.	M.	R.	W.	AV.
TEST					
1ST-CLASS	44.1	6	203	6	33.83
INT					
RAL					
NAT.W.	1	0	10	0	–
B & H					

121. Which wicket-keeper made the most Test stumpings ever, and how many?

122. Who was top of the 1988 first-class bowling averages for Kent?

NEWMAN, P. G.　　　　Derbyshire

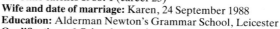

Full Name: Paul Geoffrey Newman
Role: Right-hand bat, right-arm
fast-medium bowler
Born: 10 January 1959,
Leicester
Height: 6' 2" **Weight:** 14st
Nickname: Judge
County debut: 1980
County cap: 1986
1st-Class 50s scored: 3
1st-Class 100s scored: 1
1st-Class 5 w. in innings: 5
One-Day 50s: 2
Place in batting averages: 232nd
av. 14.38 (1987 191st av. 17.94)
Place in bowling averages: 63rd
av. 27.14 (1987 26th av. 24.28)
Strike rate 1988: 58.26 (career 55.93)
1st-Class catches 1988: 1 (career 25)
Wife and date of marriage: Karen, 24 September 1988
Education: Alderman Newton's Grammar School, Leicester
Qualifications: 6 O-levels
Jobs outside cricket: Various temporary jobs
Cricketing superstitions or habits: Always wears wrist bands to bowl. Puts left
pad on first
Overseas tours: English Counties XI to Zimbabwe 1985
Overseas teams played for: Queensland Cricket Association Colts XI,
1981–82; Old Collegians and Pietermaritzburg, South Africa, 1983–84 and
1985–86

LAST SEASON: BATTING

	I.	N.O.	R.	H.S.	AV.
TEST					
1ST-CLASS	19	6	187	39	14.38
INT					
RAL	10	5	74	27*	14.80
NAT.W.	2	0	18	15	9.00
B & H	2	1	25	15*	25.00

CAREER: BATTING

	I.	N.O.	R.	H.S.	AV.
TEST					
1ST-CLASS	145	29	1843	115	15.88
INT					
RAL	51	16	499	52*	14.25
NAT.W.	8	2	108	35	18.00
B & H	18	8	208	56*	20.80

LAST SEASON: BOWLING

	O.	M.	R.	W.	AV.
TEST					
1ST-CLASS	339.5	81	950	35	27.14
INT					
RAL	91	4	418	13	32.15
NAT.W.	29.5	8	68	4	17.00
B & H	64	6	199	5	39.80

CAREER: BOWLING

	O.	M.	R.	W.	AV.
TEST					
1ST-CLASS	2656.5	507	8722	285	30.60
INT					
RAL	576.2	27	2593	86	30.15
NAT.W.	130.3	20	384	18	21.33
B & H	287.1	33	1059	34	31.14

Cricketers admired: John Snow, Richard Hadlee, Dennis Lillee
Other sports played: Golf, football
Other sports followed: Leicester City FC
Injuries 1988: Infected toe
Relaxations: Crosswords, music, watching Leicester FC, keeping up scrap-books, eating, socialising
Extras: Played for Leicestershire 2nd XI in 1978 and 1979, but was released. As a schoolboy, was a wicket-keeper. Took 50 wickets in his first season with Derbyshire. Won Commercial Union U-23 Bowling Award for 1981. Won Whitbread Scholarship to Brisbane, Australia 1981–82
Opinions on cricket: 'Having to listen to our wicket-keepers' opinions all season, most of us never have time to form any of our own.'
Best batting performance: 115 Derbyshire v Leicestershire, Chesterfield 1985
Best bowling performance: 8-29 Derbyshire v Yorkshire, Leeds 1988

NEWPORT, P. J. Worcestershire

Full Name: Philip John Newport
Role: Right-hand bat, right-arm fast-medium bowler, outfielder
Born: 11 October 1962, High Wycombe
Height: 6′ 2″ **Weight:** 13st 7lbs
Nickname: Newps, Spike, Schnozz
County debut: 1982
County cap: 1986
Test debut: 1988
No. of Tests: 1
1st-Class 50s scored: 6
1st-Class 5 w. in innings: 16
1st-Class 10 w. in match: 2
Place in batting averages: 124th av. 26.29 (1987 35th av. 41.07)
Place in bowling averages: 12th av. 19.82 (1987 126th av. 43.78)
Strike rate 1988: 38.74 (career 48.20)
1st-Class catches 1988: 8 (career 35)
Parents: John and Sheila Diana
Wife and date of marriage: Christine, 26 October 1985
Family links with cricket: 'Father is a good club cricketer, my younger brother Stewart played for High Wycombe CC.'
Education: Royal Grammar School, High Wycombe; Portsmouth Polytechnic

Qualifications: 8 O-levels, 3 A-levels, BA (Hons) Geography, basic coaching qualification

Jobs outside cricket: Schoolmaster at Worcester Royal Grammar School 1985–86

Off-season 1988–89: Chosen to tour with England on cancelled tour of India

Cricketing superstitions or habits: 'Always put a 10p piece in left pocket when batting.'

Overseas tours: With NCA to Denmark 1981

Overseas teams played for: Avis Vogelconn, New Plymouth, New Zealand 1986–87; Boland and Kraalfontein, Cape Town, South Africa 1987–88

Cricketers particularly admired: Batting of Graeme Hick; bowling of Malcolm Marshall; fielding of Gordon Lord

Other sports played: Soccer, rugby union, badminton, tennis, golf

Other sports followed: American football, sport in general

Injuries 1988: Lower back strain; missed one game

Relaxations: Listening to music, reading; in New Zealand surfing, water-skiing, horse riding

Extras: Had trial as schoolboy for Southampton FC. Played cricket for NAYC England Schoolboys 1981. Also for Buckinghamshire in Minor Counties in 1981. Took part in Minor Counties final 1982. Wears contact lens in left eye only

Opinions on cricket: 'Championship should be solely four-day cricket. Points be deducted for poor pitches, determined by umpires' report. One overseas player per county only to be replaced if injury rules him out for rest of season. Overseas tour for an England 'B'/U-25 side each winter. Better construction of cricketers' helmets and grilles. Names or numbers on players' shirts to help identification on Sunday only.'

Best batting performance: 86 Boland v Transvaal 'B', Stellenbosch, 1987–88

Best bowling performance: 8-52 Worcestershire v Middlesex, Lord's 1988

LAST SEASON: BATTING

	I.	N.O.	R.	H.S.	AV.
TEST	1	0	26	26	26.00
1ST-CLASS	24	8	421	77*	26.31
INT					
RAL	7	2	28	10*	5.60
NAT.W.	3	1	15	10*	7.50
B & H	4	1	30	11*	10.00

CAREER: BATTING

	I.	N.O.	R.	H.S.	AV.
TEST	1	0	26	26	26.00
1ST-CLASS	123	41	2147	86	26.18
INT					
RAL	27	11	194	26*	12.12
NAT.W.	7	2	60	25	12.00
B & H	9	3	56	15	9.33

LAST SEASON: BOWLING

	O.	M.	R.	W.	AV.
TEST	47.3	11	164	7	23.42
1ST-CLASS	553	118	1680	86	19.53
INT					
RAL	73	0	313	13	24.07
NAT.W.	46	4	146	4	36.50
B & H	39	3	129	4	32.25

CAREER: BOWLING

	O.	M.	R.	W.	AV.
TEST	47.3	11	164	7	23.42
1ST-CLASS	2515.2	409	8372	312	26.83
INT					
RAL	310	3	1457	48	30.35
NAT.W.	126.2	14	400	12	33.33
B & H	115	8	376	19	19.78

NICHOLAS, M. C. J.   Hampshire

Full Name: Mark Charles Jefford
Nicholas
Role: Right-hand bat, right-arm
medium bowler, slip fielder
Born: 29 September 1957, London
Height: 5′ 11½″ **Weight:** 12st 7lbs
Nickname: Skip, Cappy, Leader,
MCJ, Douglas
County debut: 1978
County cap: 1982
1000 runs in a season: 6
1st-Class 50s scored: 45
1st-Class 100s scored: 21
1st-Class 200s scored: 1
1st-Class 5 w. in innings: 1
One-Day 50s: 22
One-Day 100s: 1
Place in batting averages: 94th
av. 29.56 (1987 37th av. 40.79)
1st-Class catches 1988: 18 (career 145)
Parents: Anne
Marital status: Single
Family links with cricket: Grandfather (F.W.H.) played for Essex as batsman
and wicket-keeper and toured with MCC. Father played for Navy
Education: Fernden Prep School; Bradfield College
Qualifications: 9 O-levels, 3 A-levels
Jobs outside cricket: Worked in Classified Advertising for *The Observer*.
Selling for agencies. Writing for papers and magazines. PR agency
Off-season 1988–89: Working for PR agency. Tour to Barbados. Lots of golf
Cricketing superstitions or habits: 'Kit must fit. Not many superstitions left:
too few runs – though I do have favourite batting trousers and put my left pad
on first and . . .'
Overseas tours: Toured South Africa with Dragons (Public Schools team)
1976–77 as captain; with MCC to Bangladesh, February 1981; and to East and
Central Africa, October 1981; Dubai with *Cricketer* International XI,
November 1981; Dubai and Bahrain with 'England XI', March 1981; Sri
Lanka with England B 1986 as captain
Overseas teams played for: Captain of Southern Lakes in Australia 1978–79
and Grosvenor/Fynnland, Durban, 1982–83, 1983–84
Cricketers particularly learnt from: Barry Richards, Jimmy Gray
Cricketers particularly admired: John Snow
Other sports played: Regular football with Old Bradfieldians (Arthurian
League), golf, fives, squash

Injuries 1988: Torn thigh muscle on right leg; immobile for first two months of the season
Relaxations: Theatre, contemporary music, restaurants and wine
Extras: Appointed Hampshire captain 1985
Opinions on cricket: 'Too much cricket played too moderately. One of the one-day competitions should be abolished. Better pitches needed. Balls should have a smaller seam'
Best batting performance: 206* Hampshire v Oxford University, Oxford 1982
Best bowling performance: 5-45 Hampshire v Worcestershire, Southampton 1983

LAST SEASON: BATTING

	I.	N.O.	R.	H.S.	AV.
TEST					
1ST-CLASS	47	3	1301	132*	29.56
INT					
RAL	14	2	222	63*	18.50
NAT.W.	3	0	83	32	27.66
B & H	6	2	179	72	44.75

CAREER: BATTING

	I.	N.O.	R.	H.S.	AV.
TEST					
1ST-CLASS	378	45	10781	206*	32.37
INT					
RAL	113	18	2527	108	26.60
NAT.W.	24	1	584	63	25.39
B & H	38	4	852	74	25.05

LAST SEASON: BOWLING

	O.	M.	R.	W.	AV.
TEST					
1ST-CLASS	34	3	115	1	115.00
INT					
RAL	8	0	66	1	66.00
NAT.W.	1	0	3	0	–
B & H					

CAREER: BOWLING

	O.	M.	R.	W.	AV.
TEST					
1ST-CLASS	681.3	143	2159	49	44.06
INT					
RAL	265	2	1486	51	29.13
NAT.W.	76.2	8	315	9	35.00
B & H	144	9	641	19	33.75

NICHOLSON, N. G. Yorkshire

Full Name: Neil George Nicholson
Role: Left-hand bat
Born: 17 October 1963, Danby, Whitby, North Yorkshire
Height: 5' 8" **Weight:** 12st 7lbs
Nickname: Lorry
County debut: 1988
1st-Class catches 1988: 3 (career 3)
Parents: George and Jean
Wife and date of marriage: Alison, 27 October 1984
Children: Michael Neil, 5 February 1985; Ian John, 28 May 1986
Family links with cricket: Father played local league cricket around Danby
Education: Danby School; Eskdale School; Whitby School

Qualifications: 5 O-levels,
Process Operation Part I
Jobs outside cricket: Used to work for ICI as a storeman
Off-season 1988–89: Working for a carpet firm
Cricketers particularly learnt from: Martin McGuire, Maurice Hill, Doug Padgett
Cricketers particularly admired: Clive Lloyd
Other sports played: Golf, football
Other sports followed: Any but showjumping
Relaxations: Watching TV and gardening
Opinions on cricket: 'Cricketers should be allowed to play wherever they choose, i.e. in South Africa, and be sure of having no problems in the future, from any type of playing ban.'
Best batting performance: 16 Yorkshire v Cambridge University, Cambridge 1988

LAST SEASON: BATTING

	I.	N.O.	R.	H.S.	AV.
TEST					
1ST-CLASS	4	1	47	16	15.66
INT					
RAL					
NAT.W.					
B & H					

CAREER: BATTING

	I.	N.O.	R.	H.S.	AV.
TEST					
1ST-CLASS	4	1	47	16	15.66
INT					
RAL					
NAT.W.					
B & H					

NORTH, P. D. Glamorgan

Full Name: Philip David North
Role: Right-hand bat, slow left-arm bowler
Born: 16 May 1965, Newport, Gwent
Height: 5' 5" **Weight:** 9st 7lbs
Nickname: Philthy, Knobler, Big Fella
County debut: 1986
1st-Class catches 1988: 2 (career 4)
Parents: Arthur and Audrey
Marital status: Single
Family links with cricket: Father and uncles played club cricket
Education: St Julian's Comprehensive; Nash College of Further Education
Qualifications: 5 O-levels, TEC Mechanical Engineering, qualified toolmaker

Jobs outside cricket: Toolmaker with brake manufacturer (Lucas Girling in Cwmbran). Gardener and window cleaner in Australia. Indoor cricket umpire. Landscape gardener

Off-season 1988–89: Working as a financial consultant for Guardian Royal Exchange

Cricketing superstitions or habits: 'If I do well personally, or the team does, I try to wear the same kit the next day.'

Overseas teams played for: Southport CC, Brisbane 1985–86; Penrith CC, Sydney, 1986–87, 1987–88

Cricketers particularly learnt from: Don Shepherd, John Steele, Bill Pippen (Australia)

Cricketers particularly admired: Richard Hadlee, Graeme Hick

Other sports played: Golf

Other sports followed: Soccer, golf, most sports except horse-racing

Relaxations: Films, socialising, eating out, driving, quiet drinking

Extras: 'Nothing to do with cricket but when I was an apprentice with Lucas Girling, I machined three or four disc brakes that were on Richard Noble's "Thrust II" world land speed record-breaking car.'

Opinions on cricket: 'I think four-day cricket was a good success, but there is still too much travelling involved. Looking at next year's fixtures, it is getting worse rather than easier. Wickets *must* get better if we are to get the full benefit of four-day cricket.'

Best batting performance: 41* Glamorgan v Northamptonshire, Wellingborough 1988

Best bowling performance: 4-43 Glamorgan v Worcestershire, Neath 1987

LAST SEASON: BATTING

	I.	N.O.	R.	H.S.	AV.
TEST					
1ST-CLASS	7	3	107	41*	26.75
INT					
RAL	–	–	–	–	–
NAT.W.					
B & H					

LAST SEASON: BOWLING

	O.	M.	R.	W.	AV.
TEST					
1ST-CLASS	112.5	32	329	7	47.00
INT					
RAL	7	2	20	3	6.66
NAT.W.					
B & H					

CAREER: BATTING

	I.	N.O.	R.	H.S.	AV.
TEST					
1ST-CLASS	20	7	168	41*	12.92
INT					
RAL	1	0	0	0	0.00
NAT.W.					
B & H					

CAREER: BOWLING

	O.	M.	R.	W.	AV.
TEST					
1ST-CLASS	303	79	780	19	41.05
INT					
RAL	23	3	101	5	20.20
NAT.W.					
B & H					

123. Who was top of the 1988 first-class bowling averages for Lancashire?

Full Name: Timothy Joseph Gerard O'Gorman
Role: Right-hand bat
Born: 15 May 1967, Woking
Height: 6′ 2″ **Weight:** 11st 7lbs
County debut: 1987
1st-Class 50s scored: 1
Place in batting averages: 211th av. 16.88
1st-Class catches 1988: 5 (career 7)
Parents: Brian and Kathleen
Marital status: Single
Family links with cricket: Grandfather played for Surrey; father played for Nigeria
Education: St George's College, Weybridge, Surrey; Durham University
Qualifications: 12 O-levels, 3 A-levels
Jobs outside cricket: Working in solicitors' office during holidays
Overseas tours: St George's College to Zimbabwe 1984; Troubadours to Argentina 1987
Cricketers particularly learnt from: Father, Mike Edwards (Surrey)
Cricketers particularly admired: David Gower, Greg Chappell, Richard Hadlee
Other sports played: Hockey (England Schools U-16s and U-18s trialist), rugby (England Schools U-18 final trialist)
Other sports followed: Tennis, football, golf
Relaxations: Arts, theatre, music, movies
Extras: Surrey Young Cricketer of the Year 1984. Captained Surrey Young Cricketers for three years (1986 winners of Hilda Overy Trophy)
Best batting performance: 78 Derbyshire v Kent, Chesterfield 1988

LAST SEASON: BATTING

	I.	N.O.	R.	H.S.	AV.
TEST					
1ST-CLASS	9	0	152	78	16.88
INT					
RAL	1	0	14	14	14.00
NAT.W.					
B & H	4	0	108	43	27.00

CAREER: BATTING

	I.	N.O.	R.	H.S.	AV.
TEST					
1ST-CLASS	13	1	171	78	14.25
INT					
RAL	1	0	14	14	14.00
NAT.W.					
B & H	4	0	108	43	27.00

Full Name: Martin William Charles Olley
Role: Right-hand bat, wicket-keeper
Born: 27 November 1963, Romford
Height: 5′ 10½″ **Weight:** 10st 7lbs
County debut: 1983 (Northamptonshire), 1988 (Middlesex)
Parents: Robin and Shirley
Marital status: Single
Education: Goodrington School, Romford; Felsted School
Education: 6 O-levels, 2 A-levels
Jobs outside cricket: Working in family business
Overseas teams played for: Northern Districts, Sydney 1982–83
Cricketers particularly learnt from: Ray East, Bob Richards (Essex), Gordon Barker (Felsted School)
Cricketers particularly admired: Alan Knott, Bob Taylor, David Gower
Other sports played: Hockey

Extras: Played just one game for Northamptonshire in 1983. Made Minor Counties debut for Hertfordshire in 1984. Moved to Middlesex in 1988

LAST SEASON: BATTING

	I.	N.O.	R.	H.S.	AV.
TEST					
1ST-CLASS	5	1	69	27*	17.25
INT					
RAL					
NAT.W.					
B & H					

CAREER: BATTING

	I.	N.O.	R.	H.S.	AV.
TEST					
1ST-CLASS	6	1	77	27*	15.40
INT					
RAL					
NAT.W.					
B & H					

LAST SEASON: WICKET KEEPING

	C.	ST.			
TEST					
1ST-CLASS	9	–			
INT					
RAL					
NAT.W.					
B & H					

CAREER: WICKET KEEPING

	C.	ST.			
TEST					
1ST-CLASS	12	–			
INT					
RAL					
NAT.W.					
B & H					

ONTONG, R. C. Glamorgan

Full Name: Rodney Craig Ontong
Role: Right-hand bat,
off-break bowler
Born: 9 September 1955,
Johannesburg
County debut: 1975
County cap: 1979
Benefit: 1989
1000 runs in a season: 5
1st-Class 50s scored: 75
1st-Class 100s scored: 19
1st-Class 200s scored: 1
1st-Class 5 w. in innings: 32
1st-Class 10 w. in match: 4
One-Day 50s: 17
One-Day 100s: 1
Place in batting averages: 26th
av. 43.17 (1987 97th av. 34.39)
Place in bowling averages: 127th
av. 43.38 (1987 93rd av. 34.39)
Strike rate 1988: 98.19 (career 63.07)
1st-Class catches 1988: 7 (career 175)
Education: Selbourne College, East London, South Africa
Overseas teams played for: Made debut in 1972–73 for Border in Currie Cup
Competition. Transferred to Transvaal for 1976–77 season, before returning
to Border
Injuries 1988: Injured knee ligaments in a car crash in August
Extras: Took over Glamorgan captaincy during 1984, but resigned during
1986

LAST SEASON: BATTING

	I.	N.O.	R.	H.S.	AV.
TEST					
1ST-CLASS	25	8	734	120*	43.17
INT					
RAL	8	0	94	35	11.75
NAT.W.	2	0	48	40	24.00
B & H	4	1	69	26	23.00

CAREER: BATTING

	I.	N.O.	R.	H.S.	AV.
TEST					
1ST-CLASS	582	85	14842	204*	29.86
INT					
RAL	137	19	2771	100	23.48
NAT.W.	17	3	528	64	37.71
B & H	39	6	898	81	27.21

LAST SEASON: BOWLING

	O.	M.	R.	W.	AV.
TEST					
1ST-CLASS	395.1	94	1128	26	43.38
INT					
RAL	73	7	303	7	43.28
NAT.W.	32	0	100	3	33.33
B & H	55	7	174	3	58.00

CAREER: BOWLING

	O.	M.	R.	W.	AV.
TEST					
1ST-CLASS	8588.3	1992	24973	817	30.56
INT					
RAL	932	52	4210	130	32.38
NAT.W.	173	24	648	15	43.20
B & H	383.4	62	1237	48	25.77

Best batting performance: 204* Glamorgan v Middlesex, Swansea 1984
Best bowling performance: 8-67 Glamorgan v Nottinghamshire, Trent Bridge 1985

O'SHAUGHNESSY, S. J. Worcestershire

Full Name: Steven Joseph O'Shaughnessy
Role: Right-hand bat, right-arm medium bowler
Born: 9 September 1961, Bury
Height: 5′ 10½″
Nickname: Shauny
County debut: 1980 (Lancashire), 1988 (Worcestershire)
County cap: 1985 (Lancashire)
1000 runs in a season: 1
1st-Class 50s scored: 16
1st-Class 100s scored: 5
One-Day 50s: 13
One-Day 100s: 1
Place in batting averages: —
(1987 155th av. 22.91)
1st-Class catches 1988: 5 (career 57)
Education: Harper Green Secondary School, Farnworth, Lancashire
Overseas tours: Canada 1979 with NCA U-19 XI; West Indies 1980 with England Young Cricketers
Relaxations: Snooker

LAST SEASON: BATTING

	I.	N.O.	R.	H.S.	AV.
TEST					
1ST-CLASS	18	1	142	44	8.35
INT					
RAL	13	2	288	50	26.18
NAT.W.	4	0	122	62	30.50
B & H	2	0	20	12	10.00

CAREER: BATTING

	I.	N.O.	R.	H.S.	AV.
TEST					
1ST-CLASS	179	28	3709	159*	24.56
INT					
RAL	84	16	1622	101*	23.85
NAT.W.	18	4	386	62	27.57
B & H	26	1	596	90	23.84

LAST SEASON: BOWLING

	O.	M.	R.	W.	AV.
TEST					
1ST-CLASS	36	3	161	4	40.25
INT					
RAL	27	0	151	6	25.16
NAT.W.	3	0	15	0	—
B & H	1	0	4	0	—

CAREER: BOWLING

	O.	M.	R.	W.	AV.
TEST					
1ST-CLASS	1196.3	220	4108	114	36.03
INT					
RAL	478.1	14	2412	63	38.28
NAT.W.	138	13	578	13	44.46
B & H	184	32	671	25	26.84

Extras: Scored 100 in 35 minutes v Leicestershire, 11 September 1983 to equal fastest first-class century scored by Percy Fender in 1920. Released at end of 1987 season. Joined Worcestershire in 1988
Best batting performance: 159* Lancashire v Somerset, Bath 1984
Best bowling performance: 4-66 Lancashire v Nottinghamshire, Trent Bridge 1982

PALMER, G. V. Somerset

Full Name: Gary Vincent Palmer
Role: Right-hand bat, right-arm fast-medium bowler
Born: 1 November 1965, Taunton
Height: 6′ 1″ **Weight:** 11st 7lbs
Nickname: Pedlar
County debut: 1982
1st-Class 50s scored: 3
1st-Class 5 w. in innings: 1
One-Day 50s: 1
Place in batting averages: —
(1987 182nd av. 19.50)
Place in bowling averages: —
(1987 116th av. 40.06)
1st-Class catches 1988: 0 (career 30)
Parents: Kenneth Ernest and Joy Valerie
Marital status: Single
Family links with cricket: Father, K. E. Palmer, played for Somerset and England. Toured Pakistan with Commonwealth team, 1963. Test Umpire. Coach at Somerset CCC in winter. Grandfather did the double for 13 consecutive seasons in club cricket, and scored 25 centuries for Devizes CC
Education: North Town Junior School; Queen's College, Junior and Senior
Qualifications: SRA Part 1 Squash Coaching Certificate, NCA Cricket Coaching Award, GCEs
Jobs outside cricket: Squash coaching
Overseas tours: English Schools U-19 to Zimbabwe 1982–83; England Young Cricketers to West Indies 1984–85
Cricketers particularly learnt from: 'Learnt from my father from an early age.'
Cricketers particularly admired: Viv Richards, Joel Garner, Ian Botham
Other sports played: Squash
Relaxations: 'Listening to music – the up-to-date variety.'

Extras: Somerset U-19 Squash champion. Youngest professional ever; had summer contract with Somerset at 14. Captain of England U-15. English Schools U-16 Cricketer of the Year. Possibly youngest cricketer to play for England U-19. Made debut for Somerset 1st XI at 16. Opened his first-class career v Leicestershire by bowling two maidens

Best batting performance: 78 Somerset v Gloucestershire, Bristol 1983
Best bowling performance: 5-38 Somerset v Warwickshire, Taunton 1983

LAST SEASON: BATTING

	I.	N.O.	R.	H.S.	AV.
TEST					
1ST-CLASS	2	0	23	23	11.50
INT					
RAL	8	4	52	25*	13.00
NAT.W.	2	1	27	17	27.00
B & H	3	2	20	14	20.00

LAST SEASON: BOWLING

	O.	M.	R.	W.	AV.
TEST					
1ST-CLASS	18.2	2	54	1	54.00
INT					
RAL	46	1	280	11	25.45
NAT.W.	13	3	32	3	10.66
B & H	28.2	3	113	3	37.66

CAREER: BATTING

	I.	N.O.	R.	H.S.	AV.
TEST					
1ST-CLASS	70	11	903	78	15.30
INT					
RAL	32	15	272	33	16.00
NAT.W.	2	1	27	17	27.00
B & H	9	3	101	53	16.83

CAREER: BOWLING

	O.	M.	R.	W.	AV.
TEST					
1ST-CLASS	1128.2	182	4107	92	44.64
INT					
RAL	290	2	1561	57	27.38
NAT.W.	33	3	134	4	33.50
B & H	95.2	7	431	11	39.18

PARKER, P. W. G.   Sussex

Full Name: Paul William Giles Parker
Role: Right-hand bat, leg-break bowler, cover fielder
Born: 15 January 1956, Bulawayo, Rhodesia
Height: 5′ 10½″ **Weight:** 12st
Nickname: Porky, Polly
County debut: 1976
County cap: 1979
Benefit: 1988
Test debut: 1981
No. of Tests: 1
1000 runs in a season: 8
1st-Class 50s scored: 64
1st-Class 100s scored: 35
1st-Class 200s scored: 1
One-Day 50s: 40
One-Day 100s: 5
Place in batting averages: 39th av. 38.82 (1987 174th av. 20.17)

1st-Class catches 1988: 17 (career 199)
Parents: Anthony John and Margaret Edna
Wife and date of marriage: Teresa, 25 January 1980
Children: James William Ralph, 6 November 1980; Jocelyn Elizabeth, 10 September 1984
Family links with cricket: Father played for Essex 2nd XI. Uncle, David Green, played for Northamptonshire and Worcestershire. Two brothers, Guy and Rupert, 'very keen and active cricketers'. Father wrote *The Village Cricket Match* and was sports editor of ITN
Education: Collyer's Grammar School; St Catharine's College, Cambridge
Qualifications: MA (Cantab.)
Jobs outside cricket: Winter employment with Messrs Laing & Cruickshank (Stockbrokers), London
Overseas tours: Combined Oxford & Cambridge XI tour of Australia 1979–80
Overseas teams played for: Sturt CC, Adelaide, Australia, 1979–80; Natal, South Africa, 1980–81
Cricketers particularly learnt from: J. Denman, Sussex CCC
Other sports played: Most ball games
Relaxations: Reading, crosswords, bridge, music
Extras: Was selected for Cambridge for Varsity rugby match in 1977 but had to withdraw through injury. Was first reserve for England on Australia tour 1979–80. Appointed captain of Sussex 1988
Best batting performance: 215 Cambridge University v Essex, Cambridge 1976
Best bowling performance: 2-21 Sussex v Surrey, Guildford 1984

LAST SEASON: BATTING

	I.	N.O.	R.	H.S.	AV.
TEST					
1ST-CLASS	40	5	1359	124	38.82
INT					
RAL	14	1	526	90	40.46
NAT.W.	1	0	0	0	0.00
B & H	4	0	77	64	19.25

LAST SEASON: BOWLING

	O.	M.	R.	W.	AV.
TEST					
1ST-CLASS	1	0	1	1	1.00
INT					
RAL	0.1	0	4	0	–
NAT.W.					
B & H	0.2	0	3	0	–

CAREER: BATTING

	I.	N.O.	R.	H.S.	AV.
TEST	2	0	13	13	6.50
1ST-CLASS	484	68	14575	215	35.03
INT					
RAL	152	23	4053	121*	31.41
NAT.W.	31	4	900	109	33.33
B & H	53	4	1192	77	24.32

CAREER: BOWLING

	O.	M.	R.	W.	AV.
TEST					
1ST-CLASS	143.5	24	582	11	52.90
INT					
RAL	5.3	0	28	2	14.00
NAT.W.	2	0	17	1	17.00
B & H	1.2	0	6	2	3.00

124. Who was top of the 1988 first-class bowling averages for Leicestershire?

PARKS, R. J.   Hampshire

Full Name: Robert James Parks
Role: Right-hand bat, wicket-keeper
Born: 15 June 1959, Cuckfield, Sussex
Height: 5′ 7½″ **Weight:** 10st 7lbs
Nickname: Bobby
County debut: 1980
County cap: 1982
1st-Class 50s scored: 13
Place in batting averages: 226th av. 15.55 (1987 80th av. 33.63)
Parents: James and Irene
Wife and date of marriage: Amanda, 30 January 1982
Family links with cricket: Father, Jim Parks, played for Sussex and England, as did his grandfather, J. H. Parks. Uncle, H. W. Parks, also played for Sussex

Education: Eastbourne Grammar School; Southampton Institute of Technology
Qualifications: 9 O-levels, 1 A-level, OND and HND in Business Studies
Jobs outside cricket: Training in accountancy, working for Jardine Air Cargo; LEP International
Off-season 1988–89: Working for computer software company, Capsco International
Cricketing superstitions or habits: Left pad on first
Overseas tours: English Counties XI to Zimbabwe 1985
Cricketers particularly learnt from: Alan Knott, John Rice

LAST SEASON: BATTING

	I.	N.O.	R.	H.S.	AV.
TEST					
1ST-CLASS	35	8	420	38*	15.55
INT					
RAL	6	3	67	35*	22.33
NAT.W.	1	1	18	18*	–
B & H	3	1	33	23*	16.50

CAREER: BATTING

	I.	N.O.	R.	H.S.	AV.
TEST					
1ST-CLASS	224	57	3132	89	18.75
INT					
RAL	44	25	469	38*	24.68
NAT.W.	10	4	88	25	22.00
B & H	24	8	160	23*	10.00

LAST SEASON: WICKET KEEPING

	C.	ST.			
TEST					
1ST-CLASS	63	10			
INT					
RAL	17	3			
NAT.W.	6	1			
B & H	9				

CAREER: WICKET KEEPING

	C.	ST.			
TEST					
1ST-CLASS	501	62			
INT					
RAL	129	27			
NAT.W.	28	6			
B & H	47	5			

Cricketers particularly admired: Bob Taylor, Nick Pocock
Other sports played: Squash, football, golf
Other sports followed: 'Keen follower of Spurs, especially when they beat Arsenal.'
Relaxations: Stamp collecting, crosswords
Extras: Broke the Hampshire record for the number of dismissals in a match, v Derbyshire, 1982 (10 catches). Took over from Bob Taylor as stand-in wicket-keeper for England v New Zealand at Lord's after injury to Bruce French
Opinions on cricket: 'There is a serious danger that cricketers representing their countries are playing far too much international cricket which is proving detrimental to their fitness and performance at county level.'
Best batting performance: 89 Hampshire v Cambridge University, Cambridge 1984

PARSONS, G. J. Leicestershire

Full Name: Gordon James Parsons
Role: Left-hand bat, right-arm medium bowler, outfielder
Born: 17 October 1959, Slough
Height: 6' 1" **Weight:** 13st 7lbs
Nickname: Bullhead, Triangle, Vicar
County debut: 1978 (Leicestershire), 1986 (Warwickshire)
County cap: 1984 (Leicestershire), 1987 (Warwickshire)
50 wickets in a season: 2
1st-Class 50s scored: 19
1st-Class 5 w. in innings: 11
1st-Class 10 w. in match: 1
Place in batting averages: 197th av. 19.33 (1987 147th av. 24.82)
Place in bowling averages: 9th av. 19.06 (1987 100th av. 36.14)
Strike rate 1988: 47.17 (career 58.30)
1st-Class catches 1988: 1 (career 56)
Parents: Dave and Evelyn
Marital status: 'Still deciding.'
Family links with cricket: Father played club cricket
Education: Woodside County Secondary School, Slough
Qualifications: 5 O-levels

Jobs outside cricket: Worked as clerk at T. L. Bennett, Ratby, Leicester

Overseas tours: Australasia with Derrick Robins' U-23 XI 1979–80; ESCA tour to India 1977–78; Zimbabwe with Leicestershire 1981

Overseas teams played for: Maharaja in Sri Lanka, 1979, 1981–82, 1982–83; Boland, South Africa, 1983–84

Cricketers particularly learnt from: 'Alf Gover, Ken Higgs, Roger Tolchard and Andy Roberts have given me plenty of good advice plus too many to mention – particularly in the team.'

Cricketers particularly admired: Jonathan Agnew, Mike Garnham, David Allett

Other sports played: Golf, squash

Extras: Played for Leicester 2nd XI since 1976 and also for Buckinghamshire in 1977. Left Leicestershire after 1985 season and joined Warwickshire. Capped by Warwickshire while in plaster and on crutches. Released by Warwickshire at end of 1988 season and returned to his old county Leicestershire

Best batting performance: 76 Boland v Western Province B, Cape Town 1984–85

Best bowling performance: 9-72 Boland v Transvaal B, Johannesburg 1984–85

LAST SEASON: BATTING

	I.	N.O.	R.	H.S.	AV.
TEST					
1ST-CLASS	13	4	174	52	19.33
INT					
RAL	3	2	25	16*	25.00
NAT.W.	1	1	15	15*	—
B & H	1	0	3	3	3.00

LAST SEASON: BOWLING

	O.	M.	R.	W.	AV.
TEST					
1ST-CLASS	228	69	553	29	19.06
INT					
RAL	16	1	73	0	—
NAT.W.	12	0	35	0	—
B & H	18	1	67	2	33.50

CAREER: BATTING

	I.	N.O.	R.	H.S.	AV.
TEST					
1ST-CLASS	242	52	3647	76	19.19
INT					
RAL	57	18	429	26*	11.00
NAT.W.	11	2	105	23	11.66
B & H	19	8	189	29*	17.18

CAREER: BOWLING

	O.	M.	R.	W.	AV.
TEST					
1ST-CLASS	4314.4	916	13468	444	30.33
INT					
RAL	679.2	33	2986	99	30.16
NAT.W.	175.1	24	637	16	39.81
B & H	327.3	38	1160	41	28.29

125. Who was top of the 1988 first-class bowling averages for Middlesex?

126. Who was top of the 1988 first-class bowling averages for Northamptonshire?

PATTERSON, B. P.   Lancashire

Full Name: Balfour Patrick
Patterson
Role: Right-hand bat, right-arm
fast bowler, outfielder
Born: 15 September 1961, Portland,
Jamaica
Height: 6′ 2½″ **Weight:** 14st
Nickname: Balf, Pato
County debut: 1984
County cap: 1987
Test debut: 1985–86
No. of Tests: 13
No. of One-Day Internationals: 26
1st-Class 5 w. in innings: 15
1st-Class 10 w. in match: 2
Place in bowling averages: 50th
av. 25.28 (1987 44th av. 26.13)
Strike rate 1988: 47.04 (career 49.11)
1st-Class catches 1988: 1 (career 19)
Parents: Maurice and Emelda
Marital status: Single
Family links with cricket: Father and grandfather played for parish in Jamaica
Education: Happy Grove High School; Wolmers High School for Boys
Qualifications: Jamaica School Certificates, O-levels
Jobs outside cricket: Accounts clerk
Off-season 1988–89: Playing for West Indies in Australia
Overseas teams played for: Tasmania 1984–85
Cricketers particularly learnt from: Anderson Roberts
Cricketers particularly admired: Present West Indian team, Dennis Lillee

LAST SEASON: BATTING

	I.	N.O.	R.	H.S.	AV.
TEST	2	0	2	2	1.00
1ST-CLASS	5	2	58	23*	19.33
INT					
RAL					
NAT.W.					
B & H					

LAST SEASON: BOWLING

	O.	M.	R.	W.	AV.
TEST	74.5	13	270	4	67.50
1ST-CLASS	121.1	17	362	21	17.23
INT					
RAL					
NAT.W.					
B & H					

CAREER: BATTING

	I.	N.O.	R.	H.S.	AV.
TEST	15	8	56	21*	8.00
1ST-CLASS	80	29	307	29	6.01
INT	5	5	20	13*	–
RAL	2	2	5	3*	–
NAT.W.	2	1	4	4	4.00
B & H	2	2	18	15*	–

CAREER: BOWLING

	O.	M.	R.	W.	AV.
TEST	342.1	51	1354	47	28.80
1ST-CLASS	2031.4	324	6623	243	27.25
INT	226.3	17	992	51	19.45
RAL	22.2	0	98	5	19.60
NAT.W.	24	1	120	1	120.00
B & H	31	4	108	4	27.00

Other sports played: Basketball, football, squash and table tennis for fitness and pleasure
Other sports followed: Watches football
Relaxations: Swimming, listening to music, watching television
Best batting performance: 29 Lancashire v Northamptonshire, Northampton 1987
Best bowling performance: 7-24 Jamaica v Guyana, Kingston 1985–86

PENN, C. Kent

Full Name: Christopher Penn
Role: Left-hand bat, right-arm medium bowler
Born: 19 June 1963, Dover
Height: 6′ **Weight:** 14st 3lbs
Nickname: Penny, Cliff
County debut: 1982
County cap: 1987
1st-Class 50s scored: 4
1st-Class 100s scored: 1
1st-Class 5 w. in innings: 9
Place in batting averages: 159th av. 22.94 (1987 222nd av. 14.81)
Place in bowling averages: 45th av. 24.55 (1987 71st av. 30.60)
Strike rate 1988: 47.86 (career 55.62)
1st-Class catches 1988: 7 (career 31)
Parents: Reg and Brenda
Wife and date of marriage: Caroline, 22 March 1986
Family links with cricket: Father played club cricket for Dover CC for 26 years
Education: Dover Grammar School
Qualifications: 8 O-levels, 2 A-levels
Jobs outside cricket: Farm worker, car cleaner for hire company, financial consultant ('retired very quickly'), lumberjack
Off-season 1988–89: Coaching in Kent; working for the County on ground
Cricketing superstitions or habits: 'Luckily none!'
Overseas tours: NCA tour of Denmark 1981; Whitbread Scholarship to Australia 1982–83
Overseas teams played for: Koohinore Crescents, Johannesburg, 1981–82 and 1983–84; West Perth 1982–83; Johannesburg Municipals 1983–84; Wits University 1984–85

Cricketers particularly learnt from: 'My father, Colin Page, Brian Luckhurst, Barney Lock and many others.'
Cricketers particularly admired: Alan Knott, Dennis Lillee, Cliff Jamieson
Other sports played: Rugby, football, golf
Other sports followed: All sports
Injuries 1988: Shoulder
Relaxations: Music, art and art history, Indian food
Extras: Played for Young England and England Schools. Took hat-trick in first 2nd XI match v Middlesex when 16 years old
Opinions on cricket: 'Possibly too much car travel which could lead to a serious accident.'
Best batting performance: 115 Kent v Lancashire, Old Trafford 1984
Best bowling performance: 7-70 Kent v Middlesex, Lord's 1988

LAST SEASON: BATTING

	I.	N.O.	R.	H.S.	AV.
TEST					
1ST-CLASS	31	12	436	40	22.94
INT					
RAL	3	1	13	8	6.50
NAT.W.	1	0	0	0	0.00
B & H	2	1	8	5*	8.00

LAST SEASON: BOWLING

	O.	M.	R.	W.	AV.
TEST					
1ST-CLASS	646.1	143	1989	81	24.55
INT					
RAL	57.1	0	257	10	25.70
NAT.W.	32	6	77	5	15.40
B & H	26	1	112	3	37.33

CAREER: BATTING

	I.	N.O.	R.	H.S.	AV.
TEST					
1ST-CLASS	87	24	1265	115	20.07
INT					
RAL	27	6	164	40	7.80
NAT.W.	2	0	5	5	2.50
B & H	10	4	46	17	7.66

CAREER: BOWLING

	O.	M.	R.	W.	AV.
TEST					
1ST-CLASS	1613.1	312	5265	174	30.25
INT					
RAL	298.1	9	1465	51	28.72
NAT.W.	44	7	111	6	18.50
B & H	130.4	7	543	18	30.16

127. Who was the only batsman to score 1000 runs for Northamptonshire in 1988?

128. Who scored the first Test century for England, and when?

PETERS, N. H.   Surrey

Full Name: Nicholas Howard Peters
Role: Right-hand bat, right-arm
fast-medium bowler
Born: 21 February 1968, Guildford
Height: 6′ 3″ **Weight:** 13st 7lbs
Nickname: Bond-Machine, OO
County debut: 1988
1st-Class 5 w. in innings: 1
1st-Class 10 w. in match: 1
Place in batting averages: 249th
av. 12.14
Place in bowling averages: 67th
av. 28.05
Strike rate 1988: 49.11 (career 49.11)
1st-Class catches 1988: 5 (career 5)
Parents: Howard and Rosalind
Marital status: Single
Education: Humpty Dumpty Junior
School; Cranmore Preparatory
School, East Horsley; Sherborne School, Dorset
Qualifications: 8 O-levels, 2 A-levels; at present doing a degree in sports
science/history
Jobs outside cricket: Factory cleaner
Off-season 1988–89: Studying
Overseas tours: Surrey U-19s to Australia 1985
Cricketers particularly learnt from: Geoff Arnold
Cricketers particularly admired: Bill Wyman, Ian Botham
Other sports played: Basketball, cross-country, table tennis, tennis
Injuries 1988: Knee injury (patella tendinitis)

LAST SEASON: BATTING

	I.	N.O.	R.	H.S.	AV.
TEST					
1ST-CLASS	15	8	85	25*	12.14
INT					
RAL	4	2	5	4*	2.50
NAT.W.	–	–	–	–	–
B & H	1	1	1	1*	–

CAREER: BATTING

	I.	N.O.	R.	H.S.	AV.
TEST					
1ST-CLASS	15	8	85	25*	12.14
INT					
RAL	4	2	5	4*	2.50
NAT.W.	–	–	–	–	–
B & H	1	1	1	1*	–

LAST SEASON: BOWLING

	O.	M.	R.	W.	AV.
TEST					
1ST-CLASS	278.2	50	954	34	28.05
INT					
RAL	30.5	1	130	6	21.66
NAT.W.	21	3	78	3	26.00
B & H	30	3	101	3	33.66

CAREER: BOWLING

	O.	M.	R.	W.	AV.
TEST					
1ST-CLASS	278.2	50	954	34	28.05
INT					
RAL	30.5	1	130	6	21.66
NAT.W.	21	3	78	3	26.00
B & H	30	3	101	3	33.66

Relaxations: 'General relaxing, talking to Mark Frost and Graeme Brown who both have an unbelievable insight into present day cricket.'
Extras: Played for England Schools and NAYC
Opinions on cricket: '"No pain no gain." It is essential to always set yourself both short-term and long-term goals with maximum commitment and specificity.'
Best batting performance: 25* Surrey v Leicestershire, The Oval 1988
Best bowling performance: 6-31 Surrey v Warwickshire, The Oval 1988

PICK, R. A. Nottinghamshire

Full Name: Robert Andrew Pick
Role: Left-hand bat, right-arm fast-medium bowler
Born: 19 November 1963, Nottingham
Height: 5′ 10″ **Weight:** 13st
Nickname: Dad, Picky
County debut: 1983
County cap: 1987
1st-Class 50s scored: 2
1st-Class 5 w. in innings: 3
1st-Class 10 w. in match: 1
Place in batting averages: —
(1987 118th av. 15.40)
Place in bowling averages: —
(1987 74th av. 30.92)
1st-Class catches 1988: 1 (career 14)
Parents: Bob and Lillian
Family links with cricket: Father, uncles and cousins all play local cricket for Thrumpton CC
Education: Alderman Derbyshire Comprehensive; High Pavement College
Qualifications: 7 O-levels, 1 A-level, coaching qualification
Jobs outside cricket: Labourer; van driver; warehouse work
Off-season 1988–89: Working for O. Davis Ltd. and recovering from spinal injury
Overseas tours: Barbados with Keith Pont Benefit 1986
Overseas teams played for: Upper Hutt CC, New Zealand 1984–85; Taita CC, New Zealand 1986–87, 1987–88
Cricketers particularly admired: Bob White, Mike Hendrick, Mike Harris, Franklyn Stephenson
Other sports played: Football, fishing
Other sports followed: Ice-hockey, American football

Relaxations: 'As much fishing as possible and listening to a wide range of music; eating and drinking; going to the pictures.'
Extras: Played three Tests for Young England v Young Australia 1983. Played soccer for Nottingham Schoolboys
Injuries 1988: Operations for broken wrist and stress fracture in back
Opinions on cricket: 'Coloured clothing should be introduced for all one-day cricket.'
Best batting performance: 63 Nottinghamshire v Warwickshire, Nuneaton 1983
Best bowling performance: 6-68 Nottinghamshire v Yorkshire, Worksop 1986

LAST SEASON: BATTING

	I.	N.O.	R.	H.S.	AV.
TEST					
1ST-CLASS	4	1	31	19	10.33
INT					
RAL	1	1	1	1*	–
NAT.W.					
B & H	1	1	1	1*	–

CAREER: BATTING

	I.	N.O.	R.	H.S.	AV.
TEST					
1ST-CLASS	69	19	821	63	16.42
INT					
RAL	18	8	111	24	11.10
NAT.W.	8	6	63	34*	31.50
B & H	7	4	14	4	4.66

LAST SEASON: BOWLING

	O.	M.	R.	W.	AV.
TEST					
1ST-CLASS	74	14	334	9	37.11
INT					
RAL	22	0	134	2	67.00
NAT.W.					
B & H	23	3	95	2	47.50

CAREER: BOWLING

	O.	M.	R.	W.	AV.
TEST					
1ST-CLASS	1573.2	296	5479	156	35.12
INT					
RAL	350.2	12	1852	59	31.38
NAT.W.	156.1	17	572	22	26.00
B & H	136.5	12	558	18	31.00

PICKLES, C. S.   Yorkshire

Full Name: Christopher Stephen Pickles
Role: Right-hand bat, right-arm medium bowler
Born: 30 January 1966, Cleckheaton
Height: 6′ 1½″ **Weight:** 13st 7lbs
Nickname: Pick, Piccolo
County debut: 1985
1st-Class catches 1988: 1 (career 4)
Parents: Ronald Albert and Christine Mary
Wife and date of marriage: Janet Elizabeth, 22 October 1988
Family links with cricket: Father and brother both play local league cricket
Education: Whitcliffe Mount Comprehensive

Qualifications: Qualified cricket coach
Jobs outside cricket: Work in textiles
Off-season 1988–89: Working for Heckmondwike FB industrial carpet manufacturers
Overseas tours: NCA U-19 to Bermuda 1985
Overseas teams played for: City Cricket Club, Whangerai, New Zealand, 1986–87
Cricketers particularly learnt from: Ian Steen, Doug Padgett, Steve Oldham
Cricketers particularly admired: Geoff Boycott, Michael Holding
Other sports played: Rugby union
Other sports followed: Cleckheaton RFC
Injuries 1988: Fractured bone in ankle; had operation, but unsuccessful. Only played last two months of the season
Relaxations: 'Going out for a pint and then having some fish and chips.'
Opinions on cricket: 'Nobody should qualify as English unless they were born in this country.'
Best batting performance: 31* Yorkshire v Leicestershire, Bradford 1985
Best bowling performance: 2-31 Yorkshire v Kent, Scarborough 1985

LAST SEASON: BATTING

	I.	N.O.	R.	H.S.	AV.
TEST					
1ST-CLASS	2	1	3	3*	3.00
INT					
RAL	1	1	7	7*	–
NAT.W.					
B & H					

CAREER: BATTING

	I.	N.O.	R.	H.S.	AV.
TEST					
1ST-CLASS	5	2	55	31*	18.33
INT					
RAL	8	5	55	16*	18.33
NAT.W.					
B & H	1	1	13	13*	–

LAST SEASON: BOWLING

	O.	M.	R.	W.	AV.
TEST					
1ST-CLASS	16.2	5	58	0	–
INT					
RAL	8	2	19	2	9.50
NAT.W.					
B & H					

CAREER: BOWLING

	O.	M.	R.	W.	AV.
TEST					
1ST-CLASS	142.5	18	443	6	7.38
INT					
RAL	80	6	358	10	35.80
NAT.W.					
B & H	11	3	28	0	–

129. Who completed the 1000 runs and 100 wickets double in 1988?

130. Who won the Britannic County Championship in 1988?

PIENAAR, R. F.   Kent

Full Name: Roy Francois Pienaar
Role: Right-hand opening bat, right-arm fast-medium bowler
Born: 17 July 1961, Johannesburg
Height: 6′ 2″ **Weight:** 13st 6lbs
Nickname: Vitas
County debut: 1987
1st-Class 50s scored: 30
1st-Class 100s scored: 7
1st-Class 5 w. in innings: 3
One-Day 50s: 2
Place in batting averages: 47th av. 37.21 (1987 36th av. 40.87)
Place in bowling averages: 97th av. 32.27
Strike rate 1988: 67.38 (career 64.84)
1st-Class catches 1988: 5 (career 43)
Parents: Ron and Heather
Marital status: Single
Education: St Stithian's College, Johannesburg
Qualifications: Matriculation (Higher Grade); Bachelor of Commerce, University of Cape Town
Off-season 1988–89: Playing in South Africa
Cricketing superstitions or habits: Puts left pad on first
Overseas tours: Wanderers' Club to England 1977
Overseas teams played for: Transvaal, Western Province, Northern Transvaal, South Africa and Pakistan rebels in one-day internationals
Cricketers particularly learnt from: Peter Stringer

LAST SEASON: BATTING

	I.	N.O.	R.	H.S.	AV.
TEST					
1ST-CLASS	35	2	1228	144	37.21
INT					
RAL	10	1	244	84	27.11
NAT.W.	2	1	92	58*	92.00
B & H					

CAREER: BATTING

	I.	N.O.	R.	H.S.	AV.
TEST					
1ST-CLASS	173	10	5007	153	30.71
INT					
RAL	12	1	272	84	24.72
NAT.W.	2	1	92	58*	92.00
B & H					

LAST SEASON: BOWLING

	O.	M.	R.	W.	AV.
TEST					
1ST-CLASS	404.2	101	1162	36	32.27
INT					
RAL	61	1	293	11	26.63
NAT.W.	35	5	90	6	15.00
B & H					

CAREER: BOWLING

	O.	M.	R.	W.	AV.
TEST					
1ST-CLASS	1513	317	4431	140	31.65
INT					
RAL	79	1	383	14	27.35
NAT.W.	41	7	104	7	14.85
B & H					

Cricketers particularly admired: Barry Richards, Graeme Pollock
Other sports followed: Tennis, golf, rugby
Relaxations: Keeping fit, music, movies, wildlife
Extras: South African Cricketer of the Year 1983. Shared in record One-Day opening stand for South Africa v Australia of 154 with Jimmy Cook. Played for Worcestershire 2nd XI and Kidderminster in Birmingham League. Joined Kent mid-season in 1987 as their overseas player in place of the injured Eldine Baptiste
Best batting performance: 153 Kent v Derbyshire, Derby 1987
Best bowling performance: 5-24 Western Province v Natal, Durban 1981–82

PIERSON, A. R. K.   Warwickshire

Full Name: Adrian Roger Kirshaw Pierson
Role: Right-hand bat, off-break bowler
Born: 21 July 1963, Enfield, Middlesex
Height: 6′ 4½″ **Weight:** 12st
Nickname: Skirlog, Stick
County debut: 1985
1st-Class catches 1988: 1 (career 7)
Parents: Patrick Blake Kirshaw and Patricia Margaret
Marital status: Single
Education: Lochinver House Primary; Kent College, Canterbury; Hatfield Polytechnic
Qualifications: 8 O-levels, 2 A-levels, Advanced Coaching Certificate
Jobs outside cricket: Worked on light aircraft at Elstree Aerodrome, 1982
Cricketing superstitions or habits: Always puts left pad on first
Overseas tours: Barbados 1985 with Dennis Amiss Testimonial XI
Cricketers particularly learnt from: Don Wilson, Neal Abberley, Harry Birrell
Cricketers particularly admired: John Emburey, Phil Edmonds, Tony Greig
Other sports played: Hockey, golf, tennis
Other sports followed: All sports
Injuries 1988: Shoulder
Relaxations: Music, driving, reading
Extras: On Lord's groundstaff 1984–85

Opinions on cricket: 'One-day cricket could be played in coloured clothing with a white ball, making cricket more commercial. Try to draw more youngsters to the game by putting money into school and colts club cricket.'
Best batting performance: 42* Warwickshire v Northamptonshire, Northampton 1986
Best bowling performance: 3-23 Warwickshire v Worcestershire, Edgbaston 1988

LAST SEASON: BATTING

	I.	N.O.	R.	H.S.	AV.
TEST					
1ST-CLASS	12	7	57	18*	11.40
INT					
RAL	4	3	18	6	18.00
NAT.W.					
B & H	2	2	7	4*	–

LAST SEASON: BOWLING

	O.	M.	R.	W.	AV.
TEST					
1ST-CLASS	148.5	35	431	9	47.88
INT					
RAL	49.2	2	197	3	65.66
NAT.W.					
B & H	16	1	64	3	21.33

CAREER: BATTING

	I.	N.O.	R.	H.S.	AV.
TEST					
1ST-CLASS	29	16	189	42*	14.53
INT					
RAL	12	6	61	21*	10.16
NAT.W.	1	1	1	1*	–
B & H	2	2	7	4*	–

CAREER: BOWLING

	O.	M.	R.	W.	AV.
TEST					
1ST-CLASS	389.5	81	1312	24	54.66
INT					
RAL	134.2	6	604	10	60.40
NAT.W.	24	5	56	0	–
B & H	16	1	64	3	21.33

PIGOTT, A. C. S. Sussex

Full Name: Anthony Charles Shackleton Pigott
Role: Right-hand bat, right-arm fast bowler, slip fielder
Born: 4 June 1958, London
Height: 6' 1" **Weight:** 12st 6lbs
Nickname: Lester
County debut: 1978
County cap: 1982
Test debut: 1983–84
No. of Tests: 1
1st-Class 50s scored: 11
1st-Class 100s scored: 1
1st-Class 5 w. in innings: 18
1st-Class 10 w. in match: 1
One-Day 50s: 1
Place in batting averages: 131st av. 25.69 (1987 177th av. 19.82)
Place in bowling averages: 68th av. 28.08 (1987 84th av. 32.06)

Strike rate 1988: 50.83 (career 51.12)
1st-Class catches 1988: 16 (career 74)
Parents: Tom and Juliet
Marital status: Divorced
Children: Elliott, 15 March 1983
Family links with cricket: Father captained club side
Education: Harrow School
Qualifications: 5 O-levels, 2 A-levels; Junior Coaching Certificate
Jobs outside cricket: Sportsmaster at Claremont Prep School, Hastings. Owner of squash club at county ground
Off-season 1988–89: Looking after the squash courts
Overseas tours: With Derrick Robins' XI to Australasia 1980; part of England tour to New Zealand 1983–84
Overseas teams played for: Waverley CC, Sydney, Australia, 1976–77, 1977–78, 1979–80; Wellington, New Zealand, 1982–83 and 1983–84; Claremont, Cape Town, 1980–81, 1981–82
Cricketers particularly learnt from: Geoff Arnold
Cricketers particularly admired: Ian Botham, Imran Khan, John Snow
Other sports played: Squash, raquets, football, tennis, rugger
Injuries 1988: Three weeks off
Relaxations: 'My son.'
Extras: Public Schools Raquets champion 1975. Had operation on back, April 1981, missing most of season, and was told by a specialist he would never play cricket again. First three wickets in first-class cricket were a hat-trick. Postponed wedding to make Test debut when called into England party on tour of New Zealand. Originally going to Somerset for 1984 season, but then remained with Sussex. Was diagnosed as a diabetic after he lost 11lbs in two weeks in 1987, but recovered to take 74 wickets in 1988 season
Opinions on cricket: 'I think four-day cricket was successful. It would be even better if the wickets could be prepared to last four days.'
Best batting performance: 104* Sussex v Warwickshire, Edgbaston 1986
Best bowling performance: 7-74 Sussex v Northamptonshire, Eastbourne 1982

LAST SEASON: BATTING

	I.	N.O.	R.	H.S.	AV.
TEST					
1ST-CLASS	34	8	668	56	25.69
INT					
RAL	11	6	177	40	35.40
NAT.W.	1	0	53	53	53.00
B & H	1	0	1	1	1.00

LAST SEASON: BOWLING

	O.	M.	R.	W.	AV.
TEST					
1ST-CLASS	627	108	2078	74	28.08
INT					
RAL	82	1	427	18	23.72
NAT.W.	7	1	34	1	34.00
B & H	1	0	14	0	—

CAREER: BATTING

	I.	N.O.	R.	H.S.	AV.
TEST	2	1	12	8*	12.00
1ST-CLASS	183	40	2922	104*	20.43
INT					
RAL	46	20	436	49	16.76
NAT.W.	6	0	134	53	22.33
B & H	15	5	61	21	6.10

CAREER: BOWLING

	O.	M.	R.	W.	AV.
TEST	17	7	75	2	37.50
1ST-CLASS	3536.1	625	15341	415	36.96
INT					
RAL	602.1	19	2947	136	21.66
NAT.W.	108.4	16	364	17	21.41
B & H	193	22	841	31	27.12

POLLARD, P.   Nottinghamshire

Full Name: Paul Pollard
Role: Left-hand bat, right-arm
medium bowler
Born: 24 September 1968,
Carlton, Nottinghamshire
Height: 5′ 10′ **Weight:** 12st
Nickname: Polly
County debut: 1987
1st-Class 50s scored: 2
1st-Class 100s scored: 1
Place in batting averages: 121st
av. 26.75
1st-Class catches 1988: 6 (career 10)
Parents: Eric and Mary
Education: Gedling Comprehensive
Jobs outside cricket: Trainee
pub manager
Off-season 1988–89: Working
as a trainee manager
Overseas tours: Chesterfield CC to Barbados 1986
Overseas teams played for: Southern Districts, Brisbane, Australia 1987–88
Cricketers particularly learnt from: Clive Rice, Mike Bore, Gordon String-
fellow (the Nottinghamshire 2nd XI scorer and local cricketer)
Cricketers particularly admired: Clive Rice, Graeme Pollock, Richard Had-
lee, David Gower
Other sports played: Golf, snooker
Other sports followed: Ice-hockey, golf, football
Relaxations: Watching videos, playing golf
Extras: Made debut for Nottinghamshire 2nd XI in 1985
Best batting performance: 142 Nottinghamshire v Kent, Dartford 1988

LAST SEASON: BATTING

	I.	N.O.	R.	H.S.	AV.
TEST					
1ST-CLASS	17	1	428	142	26.75
INT					
RAL	4	0	85	25	21.25
NAT.W.					
B & H					

CAREER: BATTING

	I.	N.O.	R.	H.S.	AV.
TEST					
1ST-CLASS	24	1	560	142	24.34
INT					
RAL	4	0	85	25	21.25
NAT.W.					
B & H					

PONT, I. L. Essex

Full Name: Ian Leslie Pont
Role: Right-hand bat, right-arm fast-medium bowler, outfielder
Born: 28 August 1961, Brentwood
Height: 6′ 3″ **Weight:** 14st
Nickname: Pud, Puck, Pike, Ponty
County debut: 1982 (Nottinghamshire), 1985 (Essex)
1st-Class 50s scored: 1
1st-Class 5 w. in innings: 2
Place in batting averages: 138th av. 24.83
Place in bowling averages: 101st av. 33.12 (1987 97th av. 35.31)
Strike rate 1988: 55.00 (career 56.82)
1st-Class catches 1988: 2 (career 5)
Parents: Duncan and Eileen
Marital status: Single
Family links with cricket: Brother Keith retired from Essex CCC in 1986 after 16 years. Brother Kelvin on Lord's ground-staff
Education: Brentwood School, Essex
Qualifications: 7 O-levels, 3 A-levels, NCA Cricket Coach, qualified art historian
Jobs outside cricket: Sales executive for American Lettering Systems Co
Overseas tours: Public Schools to India 1978–79 and Australia 1979–80; NCA Young Cricketers to Canada 1980
Overseas teams played for: Bellville, Cape Town, 1981–82; Durban 1985–87; Natal A, 1985–86
Cricketers particularly learnt from: Richard Hadlee, Bob White, John Lever, Mike Bore
Cricketers particularly admired: Richard Hadlee, Wayne Daniel
Other sports played: Hockey, darts, javelin, baseball
Other sports followed: Watches golf, athletics, Manchester United FC
Relaxations: Impressionist paintings, particularly Monet, Manet, and Seurat
Extras: Spent time on Nottinghamshire staff before joining Essex. Also appeared for Buckinghamshire. Took hat-trick in 2nd XI match v Gloucestershire, 1985. Has come close to breaking world record for throwing the cricket ball. Took up the javelin with coaching from Fatima Whitbread's mother. Has also had trials as a pitcher with New York Yankees baseball team
Opinions on cricket: 'Four-day cricket will eventually prove to be a waste of time. Not enough county wickets will be able to last four days – most wickets are "result" wickets. The fourth day may prove to be a loss for the sponsors.

Sunday League or a new Saturday competition would or should be played in coloured clothing. Covered wickets ought to return.'

Best batting performance: 68 Essex v Cambridge University, Cambridge 1988
Best bowling performance: 5-103 Essex v Somerset, Taunton 1985
5-103 Essex v Surrey, The Oval 1988

LAST SEASON: BATTING

	I.	N.O.	R.	H.S.	AV.
TEST					
1ST-CLASS	8	2	149	68	24.83
INT					
RAL	5	1	98	36	24.50
NAT.W.					
B & H	–	–	–	–	–

CAREER: BATTING

	I.	N.O.	R.	H.S.	AV.
TEST					
1ST-CLASS	35	10	404	68	16.16
INT					
RAL	7	3	111	36	27.75
NAT.W.	1	1	7	7*	–
B & H	2	1	18	13*	18.00

LAST SEASON: BOWLING

	O.	M.	R.	W.	AV.
TEST					
1ST-CLASS	220	30	795	24	33.12
INT					
RAL	40.2	0	196	6	32.66
NAT.W.					
B & H	7	0	44	0	–

CAREER: BOWLING

	O.	M.	R.	W.	AV.
TEST					
1ST-CLASS	663	86	2505	70	35.78
INT					
RAL	110.2	1	471	16	29.43
NAT.W.	21	2	79	1	79.00
B & H	33.5	6	145	1	145.00

POOK, R. N. Essex

Full Name: Robert Neil Pook
Role: Right-hand bat, right-arm 'declaration' bowler, short-leg fielder
Born: 9 February 1967, Rainham, Essex
Height: 5' 10" **Weight:** 12st 4lbs
Nickname: Pooky, Spongehead
County debut: 1988
Parents: Sid and Hazel
Marital status: Single
Family links with cricket: Father keen club cricketer and enthusiastic youth coach
Education: Spring Farm Junior; The Chafford Senior
Qualifications: 5 O-levels, 3 CSE's; Coaching Certificate
Jobs outside cricket: Coach at the Ilford Cricket School. Also have worked in New Share Issues for bank

Off-season 1988–89: Playing in Brisbane, Australia
Cricketing superstitions or habits: 'I can't sit down waiting to bat for over five minutes. Bad habit.'

Overseas teams played for: Bathurst City Colts, Bathurst District 1986–87
Cricketers particularly learnt from: All at Essex
Other sports played: Club football, rugby
Other sports followed: Football (West Ham) and all other sports
Relaxations: Read when possible whilst listening to music and maybe enjoying a drink
Extras: Spent three years with MCC YC's
Best batting performance: 6 Essex v Cambridge University, Cambridge 1988

LAST SEASON: BATTING

	I.	N.O.	R.	H.S.	AV.
TEST					
1ST-CLASS	1	0	6	6	6.00
INT					
RAL					
NAT.W.					
B & H					

CAREER: BATTING

	I.	N.O.	R.	H.S.	AV.
TEST					
1ST-CLASS	1	0	6	6	6.00
INT					
RAL					
NAT.W.					
B & H					

POOLEY, M. W.   Gloucestershire

Full Name: Malcolm William Pooley
Role: Right-hand bat, right-arm medium bowler, out-fielder
Born: 27 July 1969, Truro
Height: 6′ **Weight:** 12st 1lb
Nickname: 'The Boy'
County debut: 1988
Place in batting averages: 201st av. 18.62
Place in bowling averages: 77th av. 29.53
Strike rate 1988: 59.38 (career 59.38)
Parents: Douglas John and Christine Wendy
Marital status: Single
Education: Pool Secondary School; Cornwall College
Qualifications: 4 O-levels, 6 CSE and City and Guilds in Sport and Recreation; NCA Coaching Certificate
Jobs outside cricket: Assistant PE teacher (YTS)
Off-season 1988–89: Part-time work in Cornwall
Overseas tours: Young England Cricketers, Youth World Cup, Australia 1988; England South, International Youth Tournament, Ireland 1987
Cricketers particularly learnt from: Graham Shephard, Graham Wiltshire (coaches at Gloucestershire CCC)

Cricketers particularly admired: Viv Richards, Ian Botham
Other sports played: Cornwall Schools U-16 football and rugby
Other sports followed: All sports
Relaxations: Music, films
Extras: Man of the tournament at the IYT in Ireland
Opinions on cricket: 'Lunch and tea break should be extended to an hour and half an hour respectively.'
Best batting performance: 38 Gloucestershire v Middlesex, Lord's 1988
Best bowling performance: 4-80 Gloucestershire v Kent, Bristol 1988

LAST SEASON: BATTING

	I.	N.O.	R.	H.S.	AV.
TEST					
1ST-CLASS	13	5	149	38	18.62
INT					
RAL	1	1	1	1*	–
NAT.W.					
B & H					

CAREER: BATTING

	I.	N.O.	R.	H.S.	AV.
TEST					
1ST-CLASS	13	5	149	38	18.62
INT					
RAL	1	1	1	1*	–
NAT.W.					
B & H					

LAST SEASON: BOWLING

	O.	M.	R.	W.	AV.
TEST					
1ST-CLASS	128.4	30	384	13	29.53
INT					
RAL	16	0	79	3	26.33
NAT.W.					
B & H					

CAREER: BOWLING

	O.	M.	R.	W.	AV.
TEST					
1ST-CLASS	128.4	30	384	13	29.53
INT					
RAL	16	0	79	3	26.33
NAT.W.					
B & H					

POTTER, L.   Leicestershire

Full Name: Laurie Potter
Role: Right-hand bat, slow left-arm bowler, slip fielder
Born: 7 November 1962, Bexleyheath, Kent
Height: 6′ 1″ **Weight:** 14st
Nickname: Potts, Liz, Lounge
County debut: 1981 (Kent), 1986 (Leicestershire)
1st-Class 50s scored: 25
1st-Class 100s scored: 5
One-Day 50s: 11
One-Day 100s: 2
Place in batting averages: 74th av. 32.77 (1987 144th av. 25.06)
1st-Class catches 1988: 13 (career 98)
Parents: Ronald Henry Ernest and Audrey Megan

Wife and date of marriage: Diana Frances, 28 September 1985
Family links with cricket: Father-in-law Kent 2nd XI scorer
Education: Kelmscott Senior High School, Perth, Western Australia
Qualifications: Australian leaving exams
Overseas tours: With Australian U-19 team to Pakistan 1981
Overseas teams played for: Australia U-19 team, West Perth CC, 1977–82; Griqualand West, 1984–85 and 1985–86 as captain; Harmony CC, South Africa 1987–88
Cricketers particularly learnt from: Norman O'Neill, Alan Beukas (Griqualand West), Brian Luckhurst, Peter Willey
Cricketers particularly admired: Norman O'Neill
Other sports played: Australian rules football, soccer, squash
Other sports followed: Football
Injuries 1988: Broken finger
Relaxations: Music, watching movies (cinema), reading, following sports
Extras: Captained Australia U-19 team to Pakistan 1981. Played for Young England v Young India 1981. Parents emigrated to Australia when he was 4. His mother wrote to Kent in 1978 asking for trial for him. Captained Young Australia as well as Young England. Decided to leave Kent after 1985 season and joined Leicestershire
Best batting performance: 165* Griqualand West v Border, East London 1984–85
Best bowling performance: 4-52 Griqualand West v Boland, Stellenbosch 1985–86

LAST SEASON: BATTING

	I.	N.O.	R.	H.S.	AV.
TEST					
1ST-CLASS	34	7	885	107	32.77
INT					
RAL	14	2	366	66*	30.50
NAT.W.	2	0	44	22	22.00
B & H	3	1	66	37*	33.00

LAST SEASON: BOWLING

	O.	M.	R.	W.	AV.
TEST					
1ST-CLASS	98.4	26	293	8	36.62
INT					
RAL	8	0	54	1	54.00
NAT.W.	12	4	31	1	31.00
B & H	11	1	28	0	–

CAREER: BATTING

	I.	N.O.	R.	H.S.	AV.
TEST					
1ST-CLASS	187	22	4589	165*	27.81
INT					
RAL	67	6	1706	105	27.96
NAT.W.	7	0	166	45	23.71
B & H	14	1	341	112	26.23

CAREER: BOWLING

	O.	M.	R.	W.	AV.
TEST					
1ST-CLASS	927.1	229	2625	76	34.53
INT					
RAL	101.5	4	478	20	23.90
NAT.W.	26	7	66	2	33.00
B & H	43	3	207	3	69.00

131. Who won the Refuge Assurance League in 1988?

132. Who scored the fastest first-class century in 1988?

133. Who won the NatWest Trophy in 1988?

PRICHARD, P. J.   Essex

Full Name: Paul John Prichard
Role: Right-hand bat,
cover/mid-wicket fielder
Born: 7 January 1965, Brentwood
Height: 5′ 10″ **Weight:** 11st 7lbs
Nickname: Prich, Dilch,
Ditch, Pablo, Pilch
County debut: 1984
County cap: 1986
1000 runs in a season: 2
1st-Class 50s scored: 33
1st-Class 100s scored: 2
One-Day 50s: 6
One-Day 100s: 1
Place in batting averages: 40th
av. 38.77 (1987 84th av. 33.38)
1st-Class catches 1988: 12 (career 58)
Parents: John and Margaret

Wife: Alicia
Family links with cricket: Father played club cricket in Essex
Education: Brentwood County High School
Qualifications: NCA Senior Coaching Award
Jobs outside cricket: Worked for shipping company
Off-season 1988–89: Playing and coaching in Sydney
Overseas tours: Kingfishers tour of South Africa 1981
Overseas teams played for: VOB Cavaliers, Cape Town, 1981–82; Sutherland
CC, Sydney 1985–86, 1987–88
Cricketers particularly learnt from: All at Essex
Cricketers particularly admired: 'Too many to mention.'
Other sports played: Golf
Other sports followed: American football
Relaxations: 'Sailing my boat, listening to music.'
Best batting performance: 147* Essex v Nottinghamshire, Chelmsford 1986

LAST SEASON: BATTING

	I.	N.O.	R.	H.S.	AV.
TEST					
1ST-CLASS	39	8	1202	97	38.77
INT					
RAL					
NAT.W.	2	0	77	77	38.50
B & H	6	2	127	68*	31.75

CAREER: BATTING

	I.	N.O.	R.	H.S.	AV.
TEST					
1ST-CLASS	162	20	4645	147*	32.71
INT					
RAL					
NAT.W.	8	0	250	94	31.25
B & H	15	3	330	68*	27.50

Full Name: Alan Paul Pridgeon
Role: Right-hand bat, right-arm medium bowler
Born: 22 February 1954, Wall Heath, Staffordshire
Height: 6′ 3″ **Weight:** 13st 2lbs
Nickname: Pridge
County debut: 1972
County cap: 1980
Benefit: 1989
1st-Class 50s scored: 1
1st-Class 5 w. in innings: 10
1st-Class 10 w. in match: 1
Place in bowling averages: 93rd av. 31.52 (1987 86th av. 32.85)
Strike rate 1988: 76.14 (career 67.88)
1st-Class catches 1988: 3 (career 82)
Parents: Albert Ernest and Sybil Ruby
Wife and date of marriage: Jane, 7 October 1978
Children: Laura, 8 August 1983; Benjamin Mark, 8 August 1985
Education: Summerhill Secondary Modern, Kingswinford, West Midlands
Qualifications: 6 CSEs, Qualified FA Coach, Qualified NCA Coach
Jobs outside cricket: Semi-professional footballer, salesman; has worked for Manpower Commission
Cricketing superstitions or habits: 'Hate batting while Sylvester Clarke is bowling.'
Overseas tours: Worcestershire CC to Barbados 1980
Overseas teams played for: Howick and Pakuranga, New Zealand, 1983–84

LAST SEASON: BATTING

	I.	N.O.	R.	H.S.	AV.
TEST					
1ST-CLASS	11	3	31	11	3.87
INT					
RAL	1	1	2	2*	–
NAT.W.	–	–	–	–	–
B & H	2	1	6	5*	6.00

LAST SEASON: BOWLING

	O.	M.	R.	W.	AV.
TEST					
1ST-CLASS	266.3	58	662	21	31.52
INT					
RAL	84.4	4	327	26	12.57
NAT.W.	10	1	35	1	35.00
B & H	33	6	91	2	45.50

CAREER: BATTING

	I.	N.O.	R.	H.S.	AV.
TEST					
1ST-CLASS	216	83	1164	67	8.75
INT					
RAL	50	28	144	17	6.54
NAT.W.	10	7	38	13*	12.66
B & H	20	11	81	13*	9.00

CAREER: BOWLING

	O.	M.	R.	W.	AV.
TEST					
1ST-CLASS	5951.4	1234	17218	526	32.73
INT					
RAL	1053	51	4687	160	29.29
NAT.W.	175.2	31	517	15	34.46
B & H	416.2	48	1595	34	46.91

Cricketers particularly learnt from: Viv Richards, Dennis Lillee, Norman Gifford

Cricketers particularly admired: Steve Perryman

Other sports played: Semi-professional footballer for Dudley Town FC, West Midlands League; golf, snooker, tennis

Other sports followed: Horse racing

Relaxations: Horse racing, taking dog (Muffin) for walks

Extras: He is the county's longest-serving player. Finished top of Refuge Assurance League bowling averages in 1988

Best batting performance: 67 Worcestershire v Warwickshire, Worcester 1984

Best bowling performance: 7-35 Worcestershire v Oxford University, Oxford 1976

PRINGLE, D. R. Essex

Full Name: Derek Raymond Pringle
Role: Right-hand bat, right-arm fast-medium bowler, 1st slip fielder
Born: 18 September 1958, Nairobi
Height: 6′ 5″ **Weight:** 15¾st
Nickname: Ignell, Suggs
County debut: 1978
County cap: 1982
Test debut: 1982
No. of Tests: 19
No. of One-Day Internationals: 20
1st-Class 50s scored: 32
1st-Class 100s scored: 8
1st-Class 5 w. in innings: 16
1st-Class 10 w. in match: 1
One-Day 50s: 21
Place in batting averages: 198th av. 19.11 (1987 112th av. 29.37)
Place in bowling averages: 58th av. 26.17 (1987 46th av. 26.45)
Strike rate 1988: 71.90 (career 60.10)
1st-Class catches 1988: 5 (career 111)
Parents: Donald James (deceased) and Doris May
Marital status: Single
Family links with cricket: Father represented Kenya and East Africa (played in World Cup 1975)
Education: St Mary's School, Nairobi; Felsted School, Essex; Cambridge University (Fitzwilliam College)
Qualifications: 8 O-levels, 3 A-levels, MA Cantab.

Jobs outside cricket: T-shirt designer

Cricketing superstitions or habits: 'None now; too many ducks have seen to that.'

Overseas tours: With England Schools to India 1978–79; Oxbridge tour of Australia 1979–80; England to Australia and New Zealand 1982–83; England B tour to Sri Lanka 1986

Cricketers particularly learnt from: My father, Gordon Barker, 'Tonker' Taylor, Keith Fletcher

Cricketers particularly admired: 'Neil Foster for his flexible philosophy about bowling and life.'

Other sports played: Squash, golf

Other sports followed: Watches rugby union

Relaxations: 'Modern music, especially The Smiths, New Order, Billy Bragg and The The, photography, conchology, pub discussions over a pint of Adnams. Good novels: Kunderg, Naipaul, Garcia Marquez etc.'

Extras: 'Took all ten wickets for Nairobi Schools U-13½ v Up Country Schools U-13½. Captain of Cambridge 1982 season. Extra in *Chariots of Fire*. Once went shark hunting with Chris Smith of Hampshire (a recklessly brave fellow) in the Maldive Islands.'

Opinions on cricket: 'If four-day cricket will allow more days off in order to mentally prepare oneself for each match, then I'm all for it. Uncovered wickets don't suit our batsmen so scrap that idea. Our spinners have also bowled far less than normal, so wet wickets don't always equal more spin. Inception of up-to-date technologies in order to reduce umpiring errors, as there is too much at stake (particularly at international level) to merely grin and accept bad decisions, i.e. off-the-field panel of three watching replays, electrode implants in ball, pads, bat etc, anything to aid the umpires who are now in a very high-pressure situation.'

Best batting performance: 128 Essex v Kent, Chelmsford 1988

Best bowling performance: 7-32 Essex v Middlesex, Chelmsford 1983

LAST SEASON: BATTING

	I.	N.O.	R.	H.S.	AV.
TEST	8	0	66	39	8.25
1ST-CLASS	19	0	450	128	23.68
INT	3	2	81	39	81.00
RAL	8	1	77	40	11.00
NAT.W.	2	1	86	80*	86.00
B & H	4	0	100	51	25.00

LAST SEASON: BOWLING

	O.	M.	R.	W.	AV.
TEST	136.5	36	373	14	26.64
1ST-CLASS	378.3	75	1119	43	26.02
INT	44	9	129	6	21.50
RAL	57	1	235	14	16.78
NAT.W.	14.5	2	35	1	35.00
B & H	65.4	5	260	9	28.88

CAREER: BATTING

	I.	N.O.	R.	H.S.	AV.
TEST	33	3	479	63	15.96
1ST-CLASS	266	52	6077	128	28.39
INT	16	6	284	49*	28.40
RAL	71	17	1416	81*	26.22
NAT.W.	20	5	425	80*	28.33
B & H	43	7	1077	68	29.91

CAREER: BOWLING

	O.	M.	R.	W.	AV.
TEST	538.4	121	1501	43	34.90
1ST-CLASS	4400.1	1065	11937	450	26.52
INT	187.2	20	852	20	42.60
RAL	599.2	26	2821	99	28.49
NAT.W.	205.2	39	614	25	24.56
B & H	462	50	1665	65	25.61

PRINGLE, M. W. Sussex

Full Name: Meyrick Wayne Pringle
Role: Right-hand bat, right-arm fast bowler, all rounder
Born: 22 June 1966, Adelaide, South Africa
Height: 6′ 4″ **Weight:** 13st 4lbs
Nickname: Perky, Magnum
County debut: 1987
1st-Class 50s scored: 1
1st-Class 5 w. in innings: 1
1st-Class catches 1988: 1 (career 4)
Parents: Errol and Sheila
Marital status: Single
Education: Dale College; Kingswood College, South Africa
Qualifications: Matriculation
Jobs outside cricket: Professional cricket coach
Cricketing superstitions or habits: Left pad on first, Nelsons 111, 222 etc
Overseas tours: Kingswood College to England, Holland and Channel Islands 1984
Overseas teams played for: Orange Free State 1986–87
Cricketers particularly learnt from: Percy Davis
Cricketers particularly admired: Imran Khan, Richard Hadlee, Malcolm Marshall
Other sports played: Rugby, squash
Other sports followed: Rugby, tennis, golf
Relaxations: Fishing, stamp collecting, watching videos, music

LAST SEASON: BATTING

	I.	N.O.	R.	H.S.	AV.
TEST					
1ST-CLASS	7	0	104	35	14.85
INT					
RAL	1	0	11	11	11.00
NAT.W.					
B & H	1	1	19	19*	–

CAREER: BATTING

	I.	N.O.	R.	H.S.	AV.
TEST					
1ST-CLASS	22	4	289	50*	16.05
INT					
RAL	1	0	11	11	11.00
NAT.W.					
B & H	1	1	19	19*	–

LAST SEASON: BOWLING

	O.	M.	R.	W.	AV.
TEST					
1ST-CLASS	131	23	458	8	57.25
INT					
RAL	9.4	0	46	3	15.33
NAT.W.					
B & H	9	2	33	1	33.00

CAREER: BOWLING

	O.	M.	R.	W.	AV.
TEST					
1ST-CLASS	344.4	59	1153	32	36.03
INT					
RAL	9.4	0	46	3	15.33
NAT.W.					
B & H	9	2	33	1	33.00

Extras: Opened bowling for South African Schools 1983 and 1984; opened bowling for Orange Free State in Currie Cup Competition 1986–87. Released by Sussex at end of 1988 season
Opinions on cricket: 'Sportsmanship.'
Best batting performance: 50* Eastern Province 'B' v Border, Port Elizabeth 1987–88
Best bowling performance: 6-33 Eastern Province 'B' v Western Province 'B', Cape Town 1987–88

PRINGLE, N. J.   Somerset

Full Name: Nicholas John Pringle
Role: Right-hand bat, right-arm medium bowler, cover fielder
Born: 20 September 1966, Weymouth, Dorset
Height: 5' 11" **Weight:** 12st
Nickname: Pring
County debut: 1986
1st-Class 50s scored: 3
Place in batting averages: 166th av. 22.18 (1987 172nd av. 20.41)
1st-Class catches 1988: 8 (career 9)
Parents: Marion and Guy Pease
Marital status: Single
Education: Priorswood Comprehensive, Taunton; Taunton School
Qualifications: 8 O-levels, 1 A-level. NCA Coaching Award
Overseas tours: Taunton School to Sri Lanka 1983
Overseas teams played for: Mossman CC, Sydney, 1986–87
Cricketers particularly learnt from: Martin Crowe, Don Wilson, John Jameson
Cricketers particularly admired: Martin Crowe, Richard Hadlee, Viv Richards, Greg Chappell
Other sports played: Football
Other sports followed: Rugby, American football, anything except horse racing
Relaxations: Gardeners Arms, Taunton, reading, watching videos and sport
Extras: On Lord's ground staff 1986. Called up from there by Somerset for his debut
Opinions on cricket: 'I think that there should be cricket apprenticeships,

similar to that of the Lord's groundstaff around the counties. This way young cricketers learn about other aspects of the game and perform duties that in years to come they can look back at, and not take things for granted, which these days, with all the money and sponsorship involved in cricket, is very easy to do. I would like to see four-day cricket, 16 games a year, on uncovered wickets without the bowlers run-ups being covered.'

Best batting performance: 79 Somerset v Warwickshire, Edgbaston 1987
Best bowling performance: 2-35 Somerset v Glamorgan, Weston-super-Mare 1987

LAST SEASON: BATTING

	I.	N.O.	R.	H.S.	AV.
TEST					
1ST-CLASS	15	4	244	54	22.18
INT					
RAL	3	0	34	10	11.33
NAT.W.	1	0	17	17	17.00
B & H					

LAST SEASON: BOWLING

	O.	M.	R.	W.	AV.
TEST					
1ST-CLASS	13	1	40	1	40.00
INT					
RAL	2	0	10	0	–
NAT.W.					
B & H					

CAREER: BATTING

	I.	N.O.	R.	H.S.	AV.
TEST					
1ST-CLASS	35	5	612	79	20.40
INT					
RAL	6	1	71	22	14.20
NAT.W.	1	0	17	17	17.00
B & H					

CAREER: BOWLING

	O.	M.	R.	W.	AV.
TEST					
1ST-CLASS	116	15	429	5	85.80
INT					
RAL	5	0	28	0	–
NAT.W.					
B & H					

RADFORD, N. V.　　Worcestershire

Full Name: Neal Victor Radford
Role: Right-hand bat, right-arm fast-medium bowler, gully fielder
Born: 7 June 1957, Luanshya, Zambia
Height: 5′ 11″ **Weight:** 12st 4lbs
Nickname: Radiz, Vic
County debut: 1980 (Lancashire), 1985 (Worcestershire)
County cap: 1985 (Worcestershire)
Test debut: 1986
No. of Tests: 3
No. of One-Day Internationals: 6
1st-Class 50s scored: 4
1st-Class 5 w. in innings: 34
1st-Class 10 w. in match: 6
Place in batting averages: 165th av. 22.22 (1987 243rd av. 11.58)

Place in bowling averages: 48th av. 24.92 (1987 10th av. 20.81)
Strike rate 1988: 48.23 (career 48.49)
1st-Class catches 1988: 13 (career 93)
Parents: Victor Reginald and Edith Joyce
Wife: Lynne
Children: Luke Anthony, 20th November 1988
Family links with cricket: Brother Wayne pro for Gowerton (SWCA) and Glamorgan 2nd XI. Also played for Orange Free State in Currie Cup
Education: Athlone Boys High School, Johannesburg
Qualifications: Matriculation and university entrance. NCA Advanced Coach
Jobs outside cricket: Auditor
Off-season 1988–89: 'Relaxing in the sun.'
Cricketing superstitions or habits: 'Nelson and left pad on first.'
Overseas teams played for: Transvaal 1979–87; South African Schools XI; South African Army
Overseas tours: With England to New Zealand and Australia 1988
Cricketers particularly admired: Vincent van der Bijl
Other sports played: Golf, squash
Other sports followed: All sports
Injuries 1988: 'A touch of old age creeping in . . . but no serious injuries!'
Relaxations: Music, TV, films
Extras: Only bowler to take 100 first-class wickets in 1985. First player to 100 wickets in 1987. Took most first-class wickets in 1987 with 109. One of *Wisden*'s Five Cricketers of the Year, 1985
Opinions on cricket: 'We play too much cricket! A cut down will result in better standard all round. Have a day off for travelling as the majority of injuries and stiffness are caused by travelling hundreds of miles immediately after matches. I do feel as a professional working person, one should be entitled to accept work where one so desires.'
Best batting performance: 76* Lancashire v Derbyshire, Blackpool 1981
Best bowling performance: 9-70 Worcestershire v Somerset, Worcester 1986

LAST SEASON: BATTING

	I.	N.O.	R.	H.S.	AV.
TEST					
1ST-CLASS	15	6	200	65	22.22
INT	–	–	–	–	–
RAL	6	4	44	21*	22.00
NAT.W.	2	0	8	5	4.00
B & H	4	3	52	37*	–

LAST SEASON: BOWLING

	O.	M.	R.	W.	AV.
TEST					
1ST-CLASS	570.5	101	1770	71	24.92
INT	11	2	29	0	–
RAL	87	2	398	18	22.11
NAT.W.	41.3	3	161	3	53.66
B & H	43	6	138	10	13.80

CAREER: BATTING

	I.	N.O.	R.	H.S.	AV.
TEST	4	1	21	12*	7.00
1ST-CLASS	179	45	2248	76*	16.77
INT	3	2	0	0*	0.00
RAL	47	24	453	48*	19.69
NAT.W.	9	2	90	37	12.85
B & H	15	7	147	37*	18.37

CAREER: BOWLING

	O.	M.	R.	W.	AV.
TEST	113	15	351	4	87.75
1ST-CLASS	5277.5	1024	16570	663	24.99
INT	58	5	230	2	115.00
RAL	531	24	2403	107	22.45
NAT.W.	178	23	587	26	22.57
B & H	216	28	751	29	25.89

RAMPRAKASH, M. R.   Middlesex

Full Name: Mark Ravin Ramprakash
Role: Right-hand bat
Born: 5 September 1969,
Bushey, Herts
Height: 5' 9" **Weight:** 11½st
Nickname: Ramps
County debut: 1987
1st-Class 50s scored: 5
One-Day 50s: 3
1st-Class catches 1988: 2 (career 8)
Parents: Jennifer and Deo
Marital status: Single
Family links with cricket: Father
played club cricket in Guyana
Education: Gayton High School;
Harrow Weald College
Qualifications: 5 O-levels
Cricketing superstitions or habits:
Left pad on first
Overseas tours: England U-19s to Sri Lanka 1987
Cricketers particularly learnt from: Jack Robertson, Don Bennett
Cricketers particularly admired: All the great all-rounders
Other sports played: Football
Other sports followed: Snooker, tennis
Relaxations: Watching good comedy films and westerns
Extras: Won Best U-15 Schoolboy of 1985 by Cricket Society. Won Gray
Nicholls Award for Best Young Cricketer 1986. Did not begin to play cricket
until he was nine years old. Made debut for Middlesex age 17 in April 1987 v
Yorkshire, making 17 and 63*. Played for Middlesex Under-11s and Under-
13s. Played for Bessborough CC at age 13. Played for ESCA Under-15s v
Public Schools, 1984. Played in NCA Guernsey Festival Tournament and
scored 204*. Played for Young England in the last two Tests against Sri Lanka
in 1986. Played for Middlesex 2nd XI at age 16. In one weekend in June 1986,
he scored 148* on the Saturday and 140 on the Sunday for Bessborough CC.
In 1987, played for Stanmore CC and made 186* on his debut. Opportunities
to play for Middlesex were severely restricted during 1987 and 1988 by the fact

LAST SEASON: BATTING	I.	N.O.	R.	H.S.	AV.
TEST					
1ST-CLASS	13	4	421		46.77
INT					
RAL	1	0	51	51	51.00
NAT.W.	1	0	56	56	56.00
B & H					

CAREER: BATTING	I.	N.O.	R.	H.S.	AV.
TEST					
1ST-CLASS	27	7	742	71	37.10
INT					
RAL	8	1	190	82*	27.14
NAT.W.	1	0	56	56	56.00
B & H					

that he was still at school studying for A-levels. Man of the Match in Middlesex's NatWest Trophy Final win 1988, on his debut in the competition. Cricket Society's Most Promising Player of the Year 1988
Opinions on cricket: 'Wickets should be covered at all times.'
Best batting performance: 71 Middlesex v Essex, Chelmsford 1987

RANDALL, D. W.   Nottinghamshire

Full Name: Derek William Randall
Role: Right-hand bat, cover fielder
Born: 24 February 1951, Retford, Nottinghamshire
Height: 5' 8½" **Weight:** 11st
Nickname: Arkle, Rags
County debut: 1972
County cap: 1973
Benefit: 1983 (£42,000)
Test debut: 1976–77
No. of Tests: 47
No. of One-Day Internationals: 49
1000 runs in a season: 11
1st-Class 50s scored: 136
1st-Class 100s scored: 38
1st-Class 200s scored: 3
One-Day 50s: 54
One-Day 100s: 6
Place in batting averages: 38th
av. 38.97 (1987 71st av. 35.00)
1st-Class catches 1988: 9 (career 301)
Parents: Frederick and Mavis
Wife and date of marriage: Elizabeth, September 1973
Children: Simon, June 1977
Family links with cricket: Father played local cricket – 'tried to bowl fast off a long run and off the wrong foot too!'
Education: Sir Frederick Milner Secondary Modern School, Retford
Qualifications: ONC mechanical engineering, mechanical draughtsman
Jobs outside cricket: Coaching
Overseas tours: India, Sri Lanka and Australia 1976–77; Pakistan and New Zealand 1977–78; Australia 1978–79, Australia and India 1979–80; Australia and New Zealand 1982–83; New Zealand and Pakistan 1983–84
Overseas teams played for: North Perth, Australia
Cricketers particularly learnt from: Sir Gary Sobers, Tom Graveney (boyhood idol), Reg Simpson

Other sports played: Football, squash, golf
Relaxations: Listening to varied selection of tapes. Family man
Extras: Played in one John Player League match in 1971 for Nottinghamshire. Before joining Nottinghamshire staff, played for Retford CC in the Bassetlaw League, and helped in Championship wins of 1968 and 1969. One of the finest fielders in cricket. Scored 174 in Centenary Test v Australia 1977. Renowned for his untidiness in the dressing room. One of *Wisden*'s Five Cricketers of the Year, 1979
Best batting performance: 237 Nottinghamshire v Derbyshire, Trent Bridge 1988
Best bowling performance: 3-15 Nottinghamshire v MCC, Lord's 1982

LAST SEASON: BATTING

	I.	N.O.	R.	H.S.	AV.
TEST					
1ST-CLASS	37	4	1286	237	38.97
INT					
RAL	14	1	460	68	35.38
NAT.W.	2	2	153	149*	–
B & H	3	0	97	69	32.33

LAST SEASON: BOWLING

	O.	M.	R.	W.	AV.
TEST					
1ST-CLASS					
INT					
RAL					
NAT.W.	1	0	20	0	–
B & H					

CAREER: BATTING

	I.	N.O.	R.	H.S.	AV.
TEST	79	5	2470	174	33.37
1ST-CLASS	604	57	20785	237	37.99
INT	45	5	1067	88	26.68
RAL	193	26	5343	123	31.99
NAT.W.	34	5	858	149*	29.58
B & H	73	11	2144	103*	34.58

CAREER: BOWLING

	O.	M.	R.	W.	AV.
TEST	2	0	3	0	–
1ST-CLASS	69.5	5	380	12	31.66
INT	0.2	0	2	1	2.00
RAL					
NAT.W.	2	0	23	0	–
B & H	2.5	0	5	0	–

RATCLIFFE, J. D.   Warwickshire

Full Name: Jason David Ratcliffe
Role: Opening bat, right-arm medium-pace bowler, slip fielder
Born: 19 June 1969, Solihull
Height: 6′ 4″ **Weight:** 12st 7lbs
Nickname: Ratters, Roland
County debut: 1988
1st-Class catches 1988: 2 (career 2)
Parents: David and Sheila
Marital status: Single
Family links with cricket: Father (D. P. Ratcliffe) played for Warwickshire 1956–62
Education: Meadow Green Primary School; Sharmons Cross Secondary School; Solihull Sixth Form College
Qualifications: 6 O-levels,

Off-season 1988–89: 'Searching for winter employment.'
Cricketers particularly learnt from: Father, Warwickshire coaches
Cricketers particularly admired: Geoff Boycott, Dennis Amiss
Other sports played: Football, squash, snooker
Other sports followed: Most sports
Relaxations: 'Listening to music, reading, walking my dogs (three Golden Retrievers).'
Best batting performance: 16 Warwickshire v Sussex, Hove 1988

LAST SEASON: BATTING

	I.	N.O.	R.	H.S.	AV.
TEST					
1ST-CLASS	4	0	31	16	7.75
INT					
RAL					
NAT.W.					
B & H					

CAREER: BATTING

	I.	N.O.	R.	H.S.	AV.
TEST					
1ST-CLASS	4	0	31	16	7.75
INT					
RAL					
NAT.W.					
B & H					

REEVE, D. A. Warwickshire

Full Name: Dermot Alexander Reeve
Role: Right-hand bat, right-arm fast-medium bowler, fields anywhere
Born: 2 April 1963, Hong Kong
Height: 6' 0" **Weight:** 12st
Nickname: Ears
County debut: 1983 (Sussex), 1988 (Warwickshire)
County cap: 1986 (Sussex)
1st-Class 50s scored: 11
1st-Class 100s scored: 2
1st-Class 5 w. in innings: 5
One-Day 50s: 1
Place in batting averages: 174th av. 21.55 (1987 39th av. 40.40)
Place in bowling averages: 90th av. 31.25 (1987 67th av. 29.52)
Strike rate 1988: 73.00 (career 63.62)
1st-Class catches 1988: 11 (career 62)
Parents: Alexander James and Monica
Wife and date of marriage: Julie, 20 December 1986
Children: Emily Kaye, 14 September 1988
Family links with cricket: Father captain of school XI, brother Mark an improving club cricketer

Education: King George V School, Kowloon, Hong Kong
Qualifications: 7 O-levels
Jobs outside cricket: Cricket coach
Off-season 1988–89: In Perth, Western Australia, recovering from shoulder operation
Cricketing superstitions or habits: 'Hot bath every morning.'
Overseas tours: Hong Kong to Malaysia and Singapore 1980; Hong Kong British Forces to Malaysia 1982; MCC to Holland and Denmark 1983
Overseas teams played for: Claremont-Cottesloe CC, Western Australia, 1982–85; Mount Lawley CC, Perth, 1985–88
Cricketers particularly learnt from: Don Wilson, David Clinton, John Barclay
Cricketers particularly admired: John Barclay, Chris Cowdrey, Malcolm Marshall
Other sports played: Golf
Other sports followed: Most sports
Injuries 1988: Broken thumb, shoulder injury
Relaxations: Music, videos, beach, swimming
Extras: Formerly on Lord's groundstaff. Represented Hong Kong in the ICC Trophy competition June 1982. Hong Kong Cricketer of the Year 1980–81. Hong Kong's Cricket Sports Personality of the Year 1981. Man of the Match in 1986 NatWest Final. Silk Cut Challenge Finalist. Moved from Sussex to Warwickshire in 1988
Opinions on cricket: 'Four-day cricket on covered wickets, 100 overs a day, 16 matches. More one-day internationals in England. Over rate fines too strict'
Best batting performance: 119 Sussex v Surrey, Guildford 1984
Best bowling performance: 7-37 Sussex v Lancashire, Lytham 1987

LAST SEASON: BATTING

	I.	N.O.	R.	H.S.	AV.
TEST					
1ST-CLASS	23	3	431	103	21.55
INT					
RAL	10	3	225	69	32.14
NAT.W.	1	0	13	13	13.00
B & H	5	3	49	20*	24.50

CAREER: BATTING

	I.	N.O.	R.	H.S.	AV.
TEST					
1ST-CLASS	124	34	2192	119	24.35
INT					
RAL	38	13	405	69	16.20
NAT.W.	8	5	76	26*	25.33
B & H	15	7	152	30*	19.00

LAST SEASON: BOWLING

	O.	M.	R.	W.	AV.
TEST					
1ST-CLASS	292	71	750	24	31.25
INT					
RAL	82.3	4	359	18	19.94
NAT.W.	3	2	2	0	–
B & H	26	2	98	2	49.00

CAREER: BOWLING

	O.	M.	R.	W.	AV.
TEST					
1ST-CLASS	2788.3	719	7478	263	28.43
INT					
RAL	475.3	15	2214	87	25.44
NAT.W.	126.5	29	623	16	38.93
B & H	153.4	16	667	18	37.05

RHODES, S. J.   Worcestershire

Full Name: Steven John Rhodes
Role: Right-hand bat, wicket-keeper
Born: 17 June 1964, Bradford
Height: 5′ 8″ **Weight:** 11st 10lbs
Nickname: Wilf, Bumpy
County debut: 1981 (Yorkshire),
1985 (Worcestershire)
County cap: 1988 (Worcestershire)
1st-Class 50s scored: 10
1st-Class 100s scored: 1
One-Day 50s: 1
Place in batting averages: 129th
av. 25.95 (1987 158th av. 22.66)
Parents: Bill and Norma
Marital status: Single
Family links with cricket: Father
played for Nottinghamshire 1961–64
Education: Bradford Moor Junior
School; Lapage St Middle; Carlton-
Bolling Comprehensive, Bradford
Qualifications: 4 O-levels, cricket coaching certificate
Jobs outside cricket: Trainee manager in sports retailer in winters of 1980–81
and 1981–82. Cucumber picker in Queensland
Off-season 1988–89: 'Moving house!' Picked for cancelled England tour to
India
Cricketing superstitions or habits: 'I like to make sure I am not last out of the
changing room when fielding.'
Overseas tours: England 'B' to Sri Lanka 1986
Overseas teams played for: Past Brothers Cricket Club, Bundaberg, Queens-
land, Australia, 1982–83 and 1983–84, and Bundaberg Cricket Association
Cricketers particularly learnt from: Phil Carrick, Doug Padgett, Tim Curtis,
Father
Cricketers particularly admired: Alan Knott ('seemed to have lots of time
with his keeping'), Bob Taylor, Graeme Hick
Other sports played: Golf
Other sports followed: Rugby league (Bradford Northern)
Extras: Played for Young England v Young Australia in 1983. Youngest
wicket-keeper to play for Yorkshire. Holds record for most victims in an
innings for Young England. Played for England Schools U-15s. Released by
Yorkshire to join Worcestershire at end of 1984 season. Record 29 Sunday
League dismissals in 1988
Opinions on cricket: 'The four-day game feels to be more like a game of
cricket, with sides bowling teams out twice to win a game, even if it means

spending a long time in the field. (Sixteen four-day games must be the answer providing that the wickets are satisfactory.) All one-day games should be 50 overs. That way all starts can be 11 a.m.'

Best batting performance: 108 Worcestershire v Derbyshire, Derby 1988

LAST SEASON: BATTING

	I.	N.O.	R.	H.S.	AV.
TEST					
1ST-CLASS	33	10	597	108	25.95
INT					
RAL	8	1	108	36	15.42
NAT.W.	5	2	20	9	6.66
B & H	4	1	90	43*	30.00

CAREER: BATTING

	I.	N.O.	R.	H.S.	AV.
TEST					
1ST-CLASS	137	45	2521	108	27.40
INT					
RAL	45	10	782	46	22.34
NAT.W.	12	6	88	32*	14.66
B & H	16	4	255	51*	21.25

LAST SEASON: WICKET KEEPING

	C.	ST.			
TEST					
1ST-CLASS	70	8			
INT					
RAL	26	3			
NAT.W.	8	1			
B & H	6	–			

CAREER: WICKET KEEPING

	C.	ST.			
TEST					
1ST-CLASS	245	28			
INT					
RAL	71	15			
NAT.W.	21	3			
B & H	28	4			

RICHARDS, C. J. Surrey

Full Name: Clifton James Richards
Role: Right-hand bat, wicket-keeper
Born: 10 August 1958, Penzance
Height: 5′ 11″ **Weight:** 11st 8lbs
Nickname: Jack
County debut: 1976
County cap: 1978
Benefit: 1988
Test debut: 1986–87
No. of Tests: 8
No. of One-Day Internationals: 22
1000 runs in a season: 1
1st-Class 50s scored: 37
1st-Class 100s scored: 8
One-Day 50s: 7
One-Day 100s: 3
Place in batting averages: 30th
av. 41.61 (1987 61st av. 36.90)
Parents: Clifton and Elizabeth June
Wife: Birgitta, 27 September 1980
Family links with cricket: Father a member of Penzance CC and Surrey CCC
Education: Humphry Davy Grammar School, Penzance
Qualifications: 7 O-levels

Jobs outside cricket: Trainee electrical engineer, apprentice draughtsman
Cricketing superstitions or habits: Always last out of the dressing room when fielding
Overseas tours: Australia with Derrick Robins' U-23 XI in 1979–80; Far East with Surrey CCC in 1978–79; England to India 1981–82; New Zealand and Australia 1988
Overseas teams played for: Klaas Vervelde XI, 1981
Other sports played: Tennis, golf, rugby, skiing, ice-skating, sailing
Other sports followed: Most sports, especially American and other foreign sports
Relaxations: Reading, television, driving
Extras: Left Surrey at end of 1988 season
Best batting performance: 172* Surrey v Kent, The Oval 1987
Best bowling performance: 2-42 Surrey v Somerset, The Oval 1985

LAST SEASON: BATTING

	I.	N.O.	R.	H.S.	AV.
TEST	4	0	13	8	3.25
1ST-CLASS	21	4	861	102*	50.64
INT					
RAL	14	2	423	105*	35.25
NAT.W.	4	1	94	50	31.33
B & H	3	1	23	19	11.50

LAST SEASON: BOWLING

	O.	M.	R.	W.	AV.
TEST					
1ST-CLASS	4	1	26	0	—
INT					
RAL					
NAT.W.					
B & H					

CAREER: BATTING

	I.	N.O.	R.	H.S.	AV.
TEST	13	0	285	133	21.92
1ST-CLASS	358	87	7727	172*	28.51
INT	16	3	154	50	11.84
RAL	116	26	1914	113	21.26
NAT.W.	21	6	429	105*	28.60
B & H	36	10	372	45	14.30

CAREER: BOWLING

	O.	M.	R.	W.	AV.
TEST					
1ST-CLASS	47	4	224	5	44.80
INT					
RAL					
NAT.W.					
B & H					

LAST SEASON: WICKET KEEPING

	C.	ST.
TEST	3	
1ST-CLASS	60	1
INT		
RAL	8	2
NAT.W.	8	—
B & H	3	1

CAREER: WICKET KEEPING

	C.	ST.
TEST	20	1
1ST-CLASS	583	71
INT	16	1
RAL	94	36
NAT.W.	38	5
B & H	48	6

134. Who won the Refuge Assurance Cup in 1988?

135. Which current Test cricketer had an exhibition of his drawings in the summer of 1988?

RIPLEY, D.   Northamptonshire

Full Name: David Ripley
Role: Right-hand bat, wicket-keeper
Born: 13 September 1966, Leeds
Height: 5′ 11″ **Weight:** 11st 7lbs
Nickname: Rippers, Rips, Spud
County debut: 1984
County cap: 1987
1st-Class 50s scored: 2
1st-Class 100s scored: 2
Place in batting averages: 212th
av. 16.70 (1987 145th av. 24.94)
Parents: Arthur and Brenda
Marital status: Engaged to Jackie
Education: Woodlesford Primary;
Royds High, Leeds
Qualifications: 5 O-levels, NCA
Coaching Certificate
Family links with cricket: 'My Mum
once made the teas at Farsley CC.'

Jobs outside cricket: Manager of Gard Sports, Northampton
Off-season 1988–89: Working in Gard Sports Shop, Northampton
Cricketing superstitions or habits: 'If having a good run will not have my hair cut; left pad on first. Like to be last out of changing room. The number 111.'
Overseas tours: To West Indies with England Young Cricketers 1984–85
Overseas teams played for: Poverty Bay Cricket Association, New Zealand, 1985–86
Cricketers particularly learnt from: Brian Reynolds, Jim Yardley, Ian Stein, Billy Rhodes, Roy Wills

LAST SEASON: BATTING

	I.	N.O.	R.	H.S.	AV.
TEST					
1ST-CLASS	33	6	451	49	16.70
INT					
RAL	8	4	91	24*	22.75
NAT.W.	1	0	1	1	1.00
B & H			2	38	30	38.00

CAREER: BATTING

	I.	N.O.	R.	H.S.	AV.
TEST					
1ST-CLASS	107	23	1590	134*	18.92
INT					
RAL	28	14	282	36*	20.14
NAT.W.	6	2	44	27*	11.00
B & H	10	3	151	33	21.57

LAST SEASON: WICKET KEEPING

	C.	ST.
TEST		
1ST-CLASS	80	7
INT		
RAL	6	2
NAT.W.	1	–
B & H	2	1

CAREER: WICKET KEEPING

	C.	ST.
TEST		
1ST-CLASS	179	36
INT		
RAL	22	8
NAT.W.	12	2
B & H	13	3

Cricketers particularly admired: Alan Knott, Bob Taylor, Ian Botham, Dennis Lillee
Other sports played: Soccer, golf, pool
Other sports followed: Soccer (Leeds United) and rugby league (Castleford)
Relaxations: Music, eating out
Extras: Finished top of wicket-keepers' dismissals list for 1988 with 87 victims
Best batting performance: 134* Northamptonshire v Yorkshire, Scarborough 1986
Best bowling performance: 2-89 Northamptonshire v Essex, Ilford 1987

ROBERTS, B.   Derbyshire

Full Name: Bruce Roberts
Role: Right-hand bat, right-arm medium bowler, slip fielder, occasional wicket-keeper
Born: 30 May 1962, Lusaka, Zambia
Height: 6′ 1½″ **Weight:** 14st
County debut: 1984
County cap: 1986
1000 runs in a season: 2
1st-Class 50s scored: 34
1st-Class 100s scored: 10
1st-Class 5 w. in innings: 1
One-Day 50s: 14
One-Day 100s: 2
Place in batting averages: 125th av. 26.25 (1987 26th av. 43.23)
1st-Class catches 1988: 15 (career 118 + 1 stumping)
Parents: Arthur William and Sara Ann
Marital status: Single
Family links with cricket: Father played for Orange Free State
Education: Ruzawi, Peterhouse; Prince Edward, Zimbabwe
Qualifications: O-levels, Coaching qualifications
Overseas teams played for: Transvaal B 1982–88
Cricketers particularly learnt from: 'My father and Ali Bacher.'
Cricketers particularly admired: Imran Khan, Michael Holding
Other sports played: Swimming, squash, jogging
Other sports followed: Rugby, athletics, golf
Relaxations: Family, music, TV
Best batting performance: 184 Derbyshire v Sussex, Chesterfield 1987

Best bowling performance: 5-68 Transvaal B v Northern Transvaal B, Johannesburg 1986–87

LAST SEASON: BATTING

	I.	N.O.	R.	H.S.	AV.
TEST					
1ST-CLASS	39	4	919	71	26.25
INT					
RAL	16	3	367	59	28.23
NAT.W.	3	0	87	57	29.00
B & H	6	2	84	44	21.00

LAST SEASON: BOWLING

	O.	M.	R.	W.	AV.
TEST					
1ST-CLASS	103	22	307	9	34.11
INT					
RAL	33	1	251	13	19.30
NAT.W.	3	0	5	0	—
B & H	5	1	12	0	—

CAREER: BATTING

	I.	N.O.	R.	H.S.	AV.
TEST					
1ST-CLASS	252	23	7184	184	31.37
INT					
RAL	66	12	1713	101*	31.72
NAT.W.	10	1	220	60	24.44
B & H	22	5	585	100	34.41

CAREER: BOWLING

	O.	M.	R.	W.	AV.
TEST					
1ST-CLASS	849.1	158	2863	86	33.29
INT					
RAL	134.4	2	886	40	22.15
NAT.W.	23	2	104	2	52.00
B & H	35	3	163	4	40.75

LAST SEASON: WICKET KEEPING

	C.	ST.
TEST		
1ST-CLASS		
INT		
RAL		
NAT.W.		
B & H		

CAREER: WICKET KEEPING

	C.	ST.
TEST		
1ST-CLASS		
INT		
RAL		
NAT.W.	2	—
B & H	8	1

ROBINSON, J. D. Surrey

Full Name: Jonathan David Robinson
Role: Left-hand bat, right-arm medium bowler, cover fielder,
Born: 3 August 1966, Epsom Surrey
Height: 5′ 10½″ **Weight:** 12st 4lbs
Nickname: Robbo, JR
County debut: 1988
1st-Class catches 1988: 1 (career 1)
Parents: Peter and Wendy
Marital status: Single
Family links with cricket: Father played for Cambridge University
Education: Danes Hill Preparatory School; Lancing College; West Sussex Institute of Higher Education
Qualifications: 6 O-levels,

3 A-levels, BA degree in Sports Studies, Cricket coaching award

Jobs outside cricket: Marketing/sales in film company
Off-season 1988–89: Travel, work
Cricketing superstitions or habits: Left pad on first, lucky shirt
Overseas tours: School tour to Holland 1981; Melbourne, Sydney and Adelaide 1983; Esher CC to Barbados, 1988
Cricketers particularly learnt from: Father, David Smith, Geoff Arnold, Don Smith
Cricketers particularly admired: Ian Botham, Richard Hadlee, Trevor Jesty
Other sports played: Soccer, squash, tennis, golf, swimming, running
Other sports followed: All the above plus horse racing (brother is a trainer)
Relaxations: Theatre, restaurants, TV, music, pubs, all sports, cinema, clubs, friends, travel
Extras: Did a major study about the commercialisation of cricket at college
Opinions on cricket: 'Too much cricket, therefore smaller crowds at championship matches. One-day game keeps many clubs above water financially. Second XI wickets often poor and under-prepared – bad because young players coming up are learning trade on poor surfaces.'
Best batting performance: 20 Surrey v Nottinghamshire, Trent Bridge 1988
Best bowling performance: 2-41 Surrey v Worcestershire, The Oval 1988

LAST SEASON: BATTING

	I.	N.O.	R.	H.S.	AV.
TEST					
1ST-CLASS	5	2	55	20	18.33
INT					
RAL	1	0	14	14	14.00
NAT.W.					
B & H					

LAST SEASON: BOWLING

	O.	M.	R.	W.	AV.
TEST					
1ST-CLASS	22	4	105	3	35.00
INT					
RAL	9.2	0	70	0	–
NAT.W.					
B & H					

CAREER: BATTING

	I.	N.O.	R.	H.S.	AV.
TEST					
1ST-CLASS	5	2	55	20	18.33
INT					
RAL	1	0	14	14	14.00
NAT.W.					
B & H					

CAREER: BOWLING

	O.	M.	R.	W.	AV.
TEST					
1ST-CLASS	22	4	105	3	35.00
INT					
RAL	9.2	0	70	0	–
NAT.W.					
B & H					

136. On what occasion did the Australian bowler, Ernest Jones, say 'Sorry, Doc, she slipped'?

137. Which former county cricketer once said: 'Ah reckon, Mr Cardus, tha's invented me'?

ROBINSON, M. A.   Northamptonshire

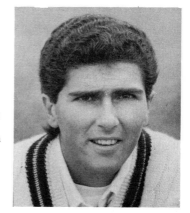

Full Name: Mark Andrew Robinson
Role: Right-hand bat, right-arm
fast-medium bowler
Born: 23 November 1966, Hull
Height: 6′ 3″ **Weight:** 12st 12lbs
Nickname: Smokey, Coddy, Robbo
County debut: 1987
Place in bowling averages: 34th
av. 22.93
Strike rate 1988: 52.52 (career 56.20)
1st-Class catches 1988: 3 (career 4)
Parents: Joan Margaret and Malcolm
Marital status: Single
Family links with cricket: Maternal
grandfather an established local
cricketer
Education: Fifth Avenue Primary;
Endike Junior High; Hull Grammar
School
Qualifications: 6 O-levels, 2 A-levels, 1st NCA Cricket Coaching Award
Jobs outside cricket: Jeweller, sports shop assistant, employee at Hull indoor
cricket stadium
Off-season 1988–89: Playing for East Christchurch-Shirley CC and Canter-
bury, New Zealand, as part of scholarship
Cricketing superstitions or habits: Refuses to walk on the pitch sixth in line
Overseas tours: North of England U-19s to Bermuda 1985
Overseas teams played for: East Christchurch-Shirley CC, 1987–88
Cricketers particularly learnt from: Fred Cowell, Ken Lake, Doug Ferguson,
Dave Rees, Bob Carter, Duncan Wild, Dennis Lillee
Cricketers particularly admired: Dennis Lillee, Richard Hadlee, Duncan
Wild
Other sport played: Football (Hull Schools and Humberside U-19), indoor
cricket (National League), tennis
Other sports followed: Hull City FC, and all sports
Injuries 1988: 'General wear and tear.'
Relaxations: Movies, soap operas, reading, music, hot baths
Extras: Took part in Leeds to London relay run around all county headquar-
ters, in aid of Leukaemia Research. Took hat-trick with first three balls of
innings in Yorkshire League, playing for Hull v Doncaster. First time this has
been done for 71 years. First player to win Yorkshire U-19s Bowler of the
Season Award in two successive years. Won player of the month award
August/September 1988
Opinions on cricket: 'Politics and sport should not mix. Cricketers should

have freedom of movement to be able to earn their living where they wish. Counties should make more effort to help players find winter employment.'

Best batting performance: 19* Northamptonshire v Essex, Chelmsford 1988
Best bowling performance: 4-19 Northamptonshire v Glamorgan, Wellingborough 1988

LAST SEASON: BATTING

	I.	N.O.	R.	H.S.	AV.
TEST					
1ST-CLASS	17	7	37	19*	3.70
INT					
RAL	2	0	0	0	0.00
NAT.W.					
B & H					

LAST SEASON: BOWLING

	O.	M.	R.	W.	AV.
TEST					
1ST-CLASS	402.4	85	1055	46	22.93
INT					
RAL	21.4	0	113	2	56.50
NAT.W.					
B & H					

CAREER: BATTING

	I.	N.O.	R.	H.S.	AV.
TEST					
1ST-CLASS	23	9	41	19*	2.92
INT					
RAL	4	1	1	1*	—
NAT.W.					
B & H					

CAREER: BOWLING

	O.	M.	R.	W.	AV.
TEST					
1ST-CLASS	552.4	110	1556	59	26.37
INT					
RAL	55.1	1	280	3	93.33
NAT.W.					
B & H					

ROBINSON, P. E. — Yorkshire

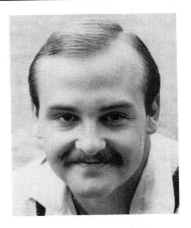

Full Name: Phillip Edward Robinson
Role: Right-hand bat, slip or cover fielder
Born: 3 August 1963, Keighley
Height: 5' 11" **Weight:** 12½st
Nickname: Red Robbo, Billy
County debut: 1984
County cap: 1988
1000 runs in a season: 1
1st-Class 50s scored: 23
1st-Class 100s scored: 2
One-Day 50s: 7
Place in batting averages: 79th av. 31.70 (1987 51st av. 38.27)
1st-Class catches 1988: 21 (career 45)
Parents: Keith and Lesley
Wife: Jane
Family links with cricket: Father played and brothers play in Bradford League
Education: Long Lee Primary; Hartington Middle; Greenhead Grammar
Qualifications: 2 O-levels

Cricketing superstitions or habits: 'Always put my left pad on first.'
Overseas teams played for: Southland, New Zealand 1987–88
Cricketers particularly learnt from: 'I learn from all cricketers.'
Cricketers particularly admired: Gary Sobers, Geoff Boycott
Other sports played: Football, golf, squash, tennis
Other sports followed: 'I follow most sports.'
Relaxations: Crosswords, reading, playing sports
Extras: Scored the highest score by a Yorkshire 2nd XI player of 233 in 1983 v Kent at Canterbury
Best batting performance: 129* Yorkshire v Nottinghamshire, Sheffield 1988

LAST SEASON: BATTING

	I.	N.O.	R.	H.S.	AV.
TEST					
1ST-CLASS	40	3	1173	129*	31.70
INT					
RAL	15	3	387	51	32.25
NAT.W.	–	–	–	–	–
B & H	2	0	40	34	20.00

CAREER: BATTING

	I.	N.O.	R.	H.S.	AV.
TEST					
1ST-CLASS	106	13	3192	129*	34.32
INT					
RAL	56	6	1369	78*	27.38
NAT.W.	3	0	66	66	22.00
B & H	5	0	99	42	19.80

ROBINSON, R. T.   Nottinghamshire

Full Name: Robert Timothy Robinson
Role: Right-hand opening bat, cover fielder
Born: 21 November 1958, Sutton-in-Ashfield, Nottinghamshire
Height: 5′ 11″ **Weight:** 12st 4lbs
Nickname: Robbo, Chop
County debut: 1978
County cap: 1983
Test debut: 1984–85
No. of Tests: 28
No. of One-Day Internationals: 26
1000 runs in a season: 6
1st-Class 50s scored: 70
1st-Class 100s scored: 30
1st-Class 200s scored: 1
One-Day 50s: 32
One-Day 100s: 3
Place in batting averages: 42nd av. 38.51 (1987 45th av. 39.06)
1st-Class catches 1988: 17 (career 122)
Parents: Eddy and Christine
Wife and date of marriage: Trisha, 2 November 1985

Children: Philip, 14 December 1986
Family links with cricket: Father, uncle, cousin and brother all played local cricket. Brother played for Nottinghamshire Schoolboys
Education: Dunstable Grammar School; High Pavement College, Nottingham; Sheffield University
Qualifications: Degree in Accounting and Financial Management
Jobs outside cricket: Trainee accountant. Working in Commercial Department, Nottinghamshire CCC
Cricketing superstitions or habits: Always puts left pad on first. Keeps himself to himself when batting
Overseas tours: NCA U-19 tour 1976; England to India and Australia 1984–85 and West Indies 1986; World Cup, India, Pakistan and New Zealand 1987–88
Overseas teams played for: Durban Collegians, South Africa, 1980–81
Cricketers particularly learnt from: Clive Rice
Cricketers particularly admired: Most successful players
Other sports played: Soccer, golf, squash, tennis
Other sports followed: Soccer, rugby
Injuries 1988: Broken hand
Relaxations: Television, reading, playing with son
Extras: Played for Northants 2nd XI in 1974–75 and for Nottinghamshire 2nd XI in 1977. Had soccer trials with Portsmouth, Chelsea and QPR. Plays in contact lenses. One of *Wisden*'s Five Crickets of the Year, 1985
Opinions on cricket: 'Fewer overseas players, four-day county championship, and better batting wickets.'
Best batting performance: 207 Nottinghamshire v Warwickshire, Trent Bridge 1983
Best bowling performance: 1-22 Nottinghamshire v Northamptonshire, Northampton 1982

LAST SEASON: BATTING

	I.	N.O.	R.	H.S.	AV.
TEST	2	1	53	34*	53.00
1ST-CLASS	33	3	1141	134*	38.03
INT	1	0	13	13	13.00
RAL	11	0	366	100	33.27
NAT.W.	1	0	30	30	30.00
B & H	4	0	133	60	33.25

CAREER: BATTING

	I.	N.O.	R.	H.S.	AV.
TEST	47	5	1589	175	37.83
1ST-CLASS	332	41	11959	207	41.09
INT	26	0	597	83	22.96
RAL	103	9	2816	100	29.95
NAT.W.	22	2	882	139	44.10
B & H	39	3	1167	120	32.41

LAST SEASON: BOWLING

	O.	M.	R.	W.	AV.
TEST					
1ST-CLASS	4	0	38	0	–
INT					
RAL					
NAT.W.					
B & H					

CAREER: BOWLING

	O.	M.	R.	W.	AV.
TEST	1	1	0	0	–
1ST-CLASS	22	0	165	2	82.50
INT					
RAL					
NAT.W.					
B & H					

Full Name: Paul Gerard Peter Roebuck
Role: Right-hand bat, right-arm
medium bowler
Born: 13 October 1963, Bath
Height: 6′ 0″ **Weight:** 13st 7lbs
County debut: 1984 (Gloucestershire),
1988 (Glamorgan)
1st-Class 50s scored: 3
1st-Class catches 1988: 1 (career 5)
Parents: James and Elizabeth
Marital status: Single
Family links with cricket: Brother
plays for Somerset. Mother and
sister both played for Oxford
University Ladies
Education: Millfield School;
Emmanuel College, Cambridge
Qualifications: MA(Cantab.)
Cricketing superstitions or habits:
If does well on one day, tries to do the same next day
Cricketers particularly admired: Mike Procter, Ian Botham
Other sports played: Tennis, golf, squash
Other sports followed: Tottenham Hotspur FC
Injuries 1988: Back injury
Relaxations: 'Reading good literature; a wide range of music.'
Opinions on cricket: 'There are many who would have liked to play profes-
sional cricket. Those who are fortunate enough to be able to do so, should try
to set an example while on the field of play, since it is their actions that will
be watched and copied.'

LAST SEASON: BATTING

	I.	N.O.	R.	H.S.	AV.
TEST					
1ST-CLASS	4	0	60	46	15.00
INT					
RAL					
NAT.W.					
B & H					

LAST SEASON: BOWLING

	O.	M.	R.	W.	AV.
TEST					
1ST-CLASS					
INT					
RAL					
NAT.W.					
B & H					

CAREER: BATTING

	I.	N.O.	R.	H.S.	AV.
TEST					
1ST-CLASS	38	8	771	82	25.70
INT					
RAL					
NAT.W.					
B & H	7	1	132	33	22.00

CAREER: BOWLING

	O.	M.	R.	W.	AV.
TEST					
1ST-CLASS	75.5	17	269	6	44.83
INT					
RAL					
NAT.W.					
B & H	25	1	86	1	86.00

Best batting performance: 82 Cambridge University v Somerset, Taunton 1985
Best bowling performance: 2-44 Cambridge University v Kent, Cambridge 1983

ROEBUCK, P. M.   Somerset

Full Name: Peter Michael Roebuck
Role: Right-hand bat, right-arm
leg-break bowler, slip fielder
Born: 6 March 1956, Oxford
Height: 6′ 0″ **Weight:** 13st 5lbs
Nickname: Professor
County debut: 1974
County cap: 1978
1000 runs in a season: 7
1st-Class 50s scored: 76
1st-Class 100s scored: 24
1st-Class 200s scored: 1
1st-Class 5 w. in innings: 1
One-Day 50s: 27
One-Day 100s: 3
Place in batting averages: 109th
av. 28.37 (1987 10th av. 49.95)
1st-Class catches 1988: 6 (career 143)

Parents: James and Elizabeth
Marital status: Single
Family links with cricket: Mother and sister both played for Oxford University Ladies. Younger brother, Paul, played for ESCA U-15 and now plays for Glamorgan
Education: Park School, Bath; Millfield School; Emmanuel College, Cambridge University
Qualifications: 1st Class Hons degree in law
Jobs outside cricket: Teacher, author and freelance journalist
Off-season 1988–89: 'Writing a book, working as a reporter in Australia (*Sydney Morning Herald*), hopefully visiting Sudan in March.'
Cricketing superstitions or habits: 'I try to play straight with varying degrees of success.'
Overseas tours: Toured in Australia with Combined Oxford & Cambridge XI 1979–80.
Overseas teams played for: Played in Perth, Australia, 1979–80; also in Corfu, Sydney and Fiji
Cricketers particularly learnt from: Viv Richards, Martin Crowe

Cricketers particularly admired: R. J. O. Meyer, Keith Fletcher

Other sports played: 'Tennis, kayaking, soccer with Somerset CCC soccer team (apart from heading, trapping, tackling and shooting, I play OK).'

Other sports followed: 'Not synchronised swimming – I follow Bath Rugby (since 12 years of age) and Somerset cricket.'

Injuries 1988: 'Too numerous to mention.' (He cited his susceptibility to injury as the reason for voluntarily relinquishing the county captaincy in August)

Relaxations: 'Reginald Perrin books, Clint Eastwood films, music of all kinds from Fauré Requiem to the works of Mr Springsteen.'

Extras: Cambridge blue 1975–76–77. Plays in spectacles. Youngest Minor County cricketer, playing for Somerset 2nd XI at age of 13. Shared in 4th wicket partnership record for county of 251 with I. V. A. Richards v Surrey at Weston-super-Mare in 1977. Books: *Slice of Cricket, It Never Rains* and *It Sort of Clicks*. Articles in *Sunday Times, Independent, Guardian*, 'and anyone else who asks'. Founder member of campaign for fair play. Appointed captain in 1986. One of *Wisden*'s Five Cricketers of the Year, 1988. Resigned captaincy during 1988 season

Opinions on cricket: 'It is a very good game when you are doing well.'

Best batting performance: 221* Somerset v Nottinghamshire, Trent Bridge 1986

Best bowling performance: 6-50 Cambridge University v Kent, Canterbury 1977

LAST SEASON: BATTING

	I.	N.O.	R.	H.S.	AV.
TEST					
1ST-CLASS	19	3	454	112*	28.37
INT					
RAL	11	0	248	64	22.54
NAT.W.	2	0	69	47	34.50
B & H	2	0	46	42	23.00

LAST SEASON: BOWLING

	O.	M.	R.	W.	AV.
TEST					
1ST-CLASS	28.4	2	106	1	106.00
INT					
RAL					
NAT.W.					
B & H					

CAREER: BATTING

	I.	N.O.	R.	H.S.	AV.
TEST					
1ST-CLASS	458	70	14186	221*	36.56
INT					
RAL	138	22	3572	105	30.79
NAT.W.	31	2	805	98	27.75
B & H	50	6	1202	120	27.31

CAREER: BOWLING

	O.	M.	R.	W.	AV.
TEST					
1ST-CLASS	814.1	203	2349	44	53.38
INT					
RAL	12.3	0	65	2	32.50
NAT.W.					
B & H	8.2	1	23	2	11.50

138. Who made the highest first-class score in England and what was it?

139. What was the second highest first-class score made in England, and who made it?

ROMAINES, P. W.   Gloucestershire

Full Name: Paul William Romaines
Role: Right-hand opening bat,
off-break bowler
Born: 25 December 1955, Bishop
Auckland, Co Durham
Height: 6′ 0″ **Weight:** 12st 8lbs
Nickname: Canny, Human
County debut: 1975 (Northampton-
shire), 1982 (Gloucestershire)
County cap: 1983 (Gloucestershire)
1000 runs in a season: 3
1st-Class 50s scored: 36
1st-Class 100s scored: 13
One-Day 50s: 19
One-Day 100s: 2
Place in batting averages: 122nd
av. 26.52 (1987 119th av. 28.60)
1st-Class catches 1988: 12 (career 62)
Parents: George and Freda
Wife and date of marriage: Julie Anne, 1979
Children: Claire Louise
Family links with cricket: Father played local cricket and is still an avid
watcher. Grandfather, W. R. Romaines, represented Durham in Minor
Counties cricket, and played v Australia in 1926
Education: Leeholme School, Bishop Auckland
Qualifications: 8 O-levels, NCA Qualified Coach
Jobs outside cricket: Sales representative
Overseas teams played for: Griqualand West 1984–85; De Beers CC 1984–85;
Gordon CC, Sydney 1981–2, 1982–3

LAST SEASON: BATTING

	I.	N.O.	R.	H.S.	AV.
TEST					
1ST-CLASS	39	3	955	101*	26.52
INT					
RAL	13	2	341	78*	31.00
NAT.W.	3	1	56	20	28.00
B & H					

LAST SEASON: BOWLING

	O.	M.	R.	W.	AV.
TEST					
1ST-CLASS	0.1	0	6	0	–
INT					
RAL					
NAT.W.					
B & H					

CAREER: BATTING

	I.	N.O.	R.	H.S.	AV.
TEST					
1ST-CLASS	282	21	7570	186	29.00
INT					
RAL	80	7	2173	105	29.76
NAT.W.	15	2	380	82	29.23
B & H	16	1	554	125	36.93

CAREER: BOWLING

	O.	M.	R.	W.	AV.
TEST					
1ST-CLASS	36.5	2	217	3	72.33
INT					
RAL					
NAT.W.					
B & H					

Cricketers particularly learnt from: Peter Willey, Barry Dudleston, David Graveney

Cricketers particularly admired: Zaheer Abbas, Graham Gooch, Clive Radley, Gordon Greenidge

Other sports played: Squash, golf, soccer

Other sports followed: Athletics

Relaxations: 'Listening to music, having a good pint, antiques, people, writing letters, good conversation.'

Extras: Debut for Northamptonshire 1975. Played Minor County cricket with Durham 1977–1981. Joined Gloucestershire in 1982

Opinions on cricket: 'Four-day cricket in 1988 has been a success, and it should be continued. Over rate fines too strict; they should be reviewed.'

Best batting performance: 186 Gloucestershire v Warwickshire, Nuneaton 1982

Best bowling performance: 3-42 Gloucestershire v Surrey, The Oval, 1985

ROSE, G. D.   Somerset

Full Name: Graham David Rose

Role: Right-hand bat, right-arm fast-medium bowler, 1st slip

Born: 12 April 1964, Tottenham

Height: 6′ 4″ **Weight:** 14st 7lbs

Nickname: Rosie

County debut: 1985 (Middlesex), 1987 (Somerset)

County cap: 1988

1st-Class 50s scored: 3

1st-Class 5 w. in innings: 3

One-Day 50s: 2

Place in batting averages: 189th av. 20.26 (1987 146th av. 24.73)

Place in bowling averages: 61st av. 26.77 (1987 36th av. 25.68)

Strike rate 1988: 53.14 (career 50.19)

1st-Class catches 1988: 11 (career 21)

Parents: William and Edna

Wife and date of marriage: Teresa Julie, 19 September 1987

Family links with cricket: Father and brother played club cricket in North London

Education: Northumberland Park School, Tottenham

Qualifications: 6 O-levels, 4 A-levels. NCA Coaching Certificate

Jobs outside cricket: 'Many and various – for example, bricklayer's mate, tele-researcher, wool sampler.'
Off-season 1988–89: Playing and coaching for Paarl CC, South Africa
Overseas tours: ESCA U-19 to Zimbabwe; Haringey Cricket College to West Indies 1986; NCA South to Holland 1983
Overseas teams played for: Carey Park, Western Australia, 1984–85; Fremantle, Perth, 1986–87; Paarl CC, South Africa 1988–89
Cricketers particularly learnt from: Jack Robertson, Ted Jackson, Father, Ron Booth
Cricketers particularly admired: Steve Waugh, Wayne Daniel, Richard Hadlee
Other sports: Golf, squash
Other sports followed: 'Follow Spurs for my sins.'
Relaxations: Music – Dire Straits, Beatles, Pink Floyd, U2
Extras: Played for Young England v Young Australia 1983. Took 6 wickets for 41 on Middlesex debut. Joined Somerset for 1987 season and scored 95 on debut
Opinions on cricket: 'Four-day cricket was definitely a success, but something has to be done about the state of the pitches to see that games can last four days. Over-rate fines should not be levied if quotas are reached by 6.30 pm. Counties should do more to find winter employment for their players, especially the younger ones.'
Best batting performance: 95 Somerset v Lancashire, Taunton 1987
Best bowling performance: 6-41 Middlesex v Worcestershire, Worcester 1985

LAST SEASON: BATTING

	I.	N.O.	R.	H.S.	AV.
TEST					
1ST-CLASS	25	6	385	69*	20.26
INT					
RAL	14	3	304	93*	27.63
NAT.W.	2	0	11	8	5.50
B & H	3	1	46	22*	23.00

CAREER: BATTING

	I.	N.O.	R.	H.S.	AV.
TEST					
1ST-CLASS	56	11	948	95	21.06
INT					
RAL	29	5	542	93*	22.58
NAT.W.	3	0	37	26	12.33
B & H	8	1	106	42	15.14

LAST SEASON: BOWLING

	O.	M.	R.	W.	AV.
TEST					
1ST-CLASS	504.5	116	1526	57	26.77
INT					
RAL	97	1	454	16	28.37
NAT.W.	21	3	73	2	36.50
B & H	41	3	158	5	31.60

CAREER: BOWLING

	O.	M.	R.	W.	AV.
TEST					
1ST-CLASS	928.4	190	2921	111	26.31
INT					
RAL	261.3	11	1125	32	35.15
NAT.W.	32.5	7	103	4	25.75
B & H	95	7	383	14	27.35

140. Who made the third highest first-class score in England, and what was it?

ROSEBERRY, M. A.　　　Middlesex

Full Name: Michael Anthony
Roseberry
Role: Right-hand bat, right-arm
occasional off-break and swing
bowler, close-to-wicket fielder
Born: 28 November 1966,
Houghton-le-Spring, Sunderland
Height: 6' 0" **Weight:** 14st
Nickname: Zorro
County debut: 1985
1st-Class 50s scored: 4
Place in batting averages: 176th
av. 21.44 (1987 148th av. 24.54)
1st-Class catches 1988: 5 (career 13)
Parents: Matthew and Jean
Marital status: Single
Family links with cricket: Uncle,
Peter Wyness, played for Royal
Navy; brother Andrew has just
joined Leicester
Education: Tonstall Preparatory School; Durham School
Qualifications: 5 O-levels, 1 A-level
Jobs outside cricket: 'Last winter I coached rugby at my old school as well as
basketball.'
Off-season 1988–89: Playing cricket for Melville in Perth, Western Australia
Cricketing superstitions or habits: 'Tend to put my front batting pad on first.'
Overseas tours: Durham School 1st XI to Barbados, 1983; Young England to
West Indies, 1985; Kenya with Minor Counties U-25, 1986
Overseas teams played for: Fremantle, Perth, Western Australia, 1986

LAST SEASON: BATTING

	I.	N.O.	R.	H.S.	AV.
TEST					
1ST-CLASS	21	3	386	67	21.44
INT					
RAL	2	0	23	13	11.50
NAT.W.					
B & H					

CAREER: BATTING

	I.	N.O.	R.	H.S.	AV.
TEST					
1ST-CLASS	43	7	830	70*	23.05
INT					
RAL	9	0	177	27	19.66
NAT.W.					
B & H	2	0	8	6	4.00

LAST SEASON: BOWLING

	O.	M.	R.	W.	AV.
TEST					
1ST-CLASS	11.4	1	61	2	30.50
INT					
RAL					
NAT.W.					
B & H					

CAREER: BOWLING

	O.	M.	R.	W.	AV.
TEST					
1ST-CLASS	16.4	1	86	2	43.00
INT					
RAL					
NAT.W.					
B & H					

Cricketers particularly learnt from: Alec Coxon (ex-England and Yorkshire bowler), Don Wilson and Gordon Jenkins (MCC Indoor School), Mike Gatting

Cricketers particularly admired: Ian Botham, Geoff Boycott

Other sports played: 'Rugby, squash, snooker and whatever takes my fancy.'

Other sports followed: Football, golf

Relaxations: Snooker, music

Extras: Won Lord's Taverners/MCC Cricketer of the Year 1983. Won Sunday Sun/Dixon Sport Cricketer of the Year 1983. Won Cricket Societies' Wetherall Award 1983, 1984. Won Cricket Societies' Award for Best Young Cricketer of the Year 1984 and Frank Morris Memorial Award 1984. Won Cricket Society award for best all-rounder in schools cricket twice

Opinions on cricket: 'The position on overseas players should be tightened up as it has got well out of hand. Hopefully four-day cricket will come in on a permanent basis.'

Best batting performance: 70* Middlesex v Northamptonshire, Northampton 1986

Best bowling performance: 1-1 Middlesex v Sussex, Hove 1988

RUSSELL, R. C.　　　　Gloucestershire

Full Name: Robert Charles Russell
Role: Left-hand bat, wicket-keeper
Born: 15 August 1963, Stroud
Height: 5′ 8½″ **Weight:** 9st 8lbs
Nickname: Jack, Bob (after great England wicket-keeper, Bob Taylor), Whispering Gloves
County debut: 1981
County cap: 1985
Test debut: 1988
No. of Tests: 1
No. of One-Day Internationals: 2
1st-Class 50s scored: 15
One-Day 50s: 3
One-Day 100s: 1
Place in batting averages: 82nd av. 30.96 (1987 127th av. 27.51)
Parents: John and Jennifer
Wife and date of marriage: Aileen Ann, 6 March 1985
Children: Stepson, Marcus Anthony; Elizabeth Ann, March 1988

Education: Uplands County Primary School; Archway Comprehensive School
Qualifications: 7 O-levels, 2 A-levels
Jobs outside cricket: Carpet fitter, runs own carpet business; professional artist
Off-season 1988–89: 'Working for Goodyer Associates as an artist, running carpet business, working on second book *A Match Drawn*, published by Goodyer Associates of Nuneaton.'
Cricketing superstitions or habits: 'The numbers 37 and 87. In general try to make clothing and equipment last as long as possible.'
Overseas tours: Denmark with NCA Young Cricketers 1981; with Gloucestershire to Barbados 1985; Mendip Acorns Pacific tour 1984; England to Pakistan 1987; Gloucestershire to Sri Lanka 1987
Overseas teams played for: Takapuna CC, New Zealand, 1983–85
Cricketers particularly learnt from: Alan Knott, Bob Taylor
Cricketers particularly admired: Alan Knott, Bob Taylor
Other sports played: 'Occasional football; snooker, when time!'
Other sports followed: Football, snooker
Injuries 1988: Missed game v Sussex in April because of tooth trouble
Relaxations: Drawing, sketching, painting (oil and watercolour). Watching comedy, Rory Bremner and Phil Cool especially
Extras: Record for most dismissals in a match for first-class debut: 8 (7 caught, 1 stumped) for Gloucestershire v Sri Lankans at Bristol, 1981. Youngest wicket-keeper for Gloucestershire (17 years 307 days). Represented Young England v Young West Indies in the Agatha Christie 'Test Match' series, 1982. Played for Duchess of Norfolk's XI v West Indies at Arundel in 1984. Joint holder of world record for hat-trick of catches (v Surrey at The Oval 1986). Youngest wicket-keeper to score Sunday League hundred (v Worcestershire at Hereford 1986). Had a three-week exhibition of his drawings in Bristol in 1988. Published a book of his work entitled *A Cricketer's Art* (1988)
Best batting performance: 94 England v Sri Lanka, Lord's 1988

LAST SEASON: BATTING

	I.	N.O.	R.	H.S.	AV.
TEST	1	0	94	94	94.00
1ST-CLASS	35	8	773	72	28.62
INT	–	–	–	–	–
RAL	7	1	88	28	14.66
NAT.W.	1	0	4	4	4.00
B & H		0	11	11	11.00

CAREER: BATTING

	I.	N.O.	R.	H.S.	AV.
TEST	1	0	94	94	94.00
1ST-CLASS	196	48	3566	72	24.09
INT	1	1	2	2*	–
RAL	49	16	813	108	24.63
NAT.W.	11	3	146	39	18.25
B & H	14	3	126	36*	11.45

LAST SEASON: WICKET KEEPING

	C.	ST.
TEST	3	–
1ST-CLASS	54	12
INT		
RAL	15	1
NAT.W.	3	–
B & H	3	–

CAREER: WICKET KEEPING

	C.	ST.
TEST	3	–
1ST-CLASS	307	62
INT	3	
RAL	58	15
NAT.W.	16	5
B & H	24	7

SABINE, D. J. Kent

Full Name: David John Sabine
Role: Right-hand bat, medium-fast bowler, cover, outfielder
Born: 2 June 1966, Papakora, Auckland, New Zealand
Height: 5′ 11½″ **Weight:** 12st 7lbs
Nickname: Sabs, Abbo
County debut: 1988
Parents: Barry and Rita
Marital status: Single
Education: St Thomas's RC Primary School, Canterbury; St Anselm's RC Comprehensive, Canterbury; Canterbury College of Technology
Qualifications: 2 O-levels; 5 CSEs; Diploma in Building Engineering; Senior Cricket Coaching Award
Jobs outside cricket: Working for architectural surveyors (C. Tomlin Associates, Canterbury)
Off-season 1988–89: Setting up building and labouring partnership
Cricketing superstitions or habits: Puts left pad on first
Overseas tours: Kent U-17s to Canada 1983; NCA Tournament in Bermuda 1985
Overseas teams played for: Parnell Cricket Club, Auckland 1986–87
Cricketers particularly learnt from: Colin Page, Geoff Rabone, Wilf Slack
Cricketers particularly admired: Richard Hadlee, Geoff Rabone
Other sports played: Football, squash, golf
Other sports followed: Any kind of sport
Injuries 1988: Back trouble
Relaxations: Gentle running
Opinions on cricket: 'Sponsorship found to aid 2nd XIs playing same championship as 1st XIs.'
Best batting performance: 7 Kent v West Indians, Canterbury 1988

LAST SEASON: BATTING

	I.	N.O.	R.	H.S.	AV.
TEST					
1ST-CLASS	2	0	8	7	4.00
INT					
RAL	–	–	–	–	–
NAT.W.					
B & H					

CAREER: BATTING

	I.	N.O.	R.	H.S.	AV.
TEST					
1ST-CLASS	2	0	8	7	4.00
INT					
RAL	–	–	–	–	–
NAT.W.					
B & H					

SADIQ, Z. A. — Surrey

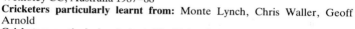

Full Name: Zahid Asa Sadiq
Role: Right-hand bat
Born: 6 May 1965, Nairobi
Height: 5′ 11″ **Weight:** 11st 2lbs
Nickname: Zeidi, Munch, Shag
County debut: 1987
1st-Class 50s scored: 1
One-Day 50s: 1
1st-Class catches 1988: 2 (career 2)
Parents: Mohammed Sadiq
Marital status: Single
Education: Rutlish School
Qualifications: 2 O-levels
Off-season 1988–89: Playing cricket in Australia
Cricketing superstitions or habits: Left pad on first
Overseas teams played for: Claremont CC, Australia, 1986–87; Wembley CC, Australia 1987–88
Cricketers particularly learnt from: Monte Lynch, Chris Waller, Geoff Arnold
Cricketers particularly admired: Viv Richards, Monte Lynch, Imran Khan
Other sports played: Squash, rugby
Other sports followed: Rugby
Relaxations: Listening to music, parties
Best batting performance: 64 Surrey v Cambridge University, Cambridge 1988

LAST SEASON: BATTING

	I.	N.O.	R.	H.S.	AV.
TEST					
1ST-CLASS	6	0	135	64	22.50
INT					
RAL	9	0	154	53	17.11
NAT.W.					
B & H					

CAREER: BATTING

	I.	N.O.	R.	H.S.	AV.
TEST					
1ST-CLASS	6	0	135	64	22.50
INT					
RAL	10	0	154	53	15.40
NAT.W.					
B & H					

141. True or false: all three highest individual first-class scores in England were made against Somerset?

SAXELBY, K.   Nottinghamshire

Full Name: Kevin Saxelby
Role: Right-hand bat, right-arm
fast medium bowler
Born: 23 February 1959, Worksop
Height: 6′ 2″ **Weight:** 14st
Nickname: Sax, Sacko, Nasty
County debut: 1978
County cap: 1984
1st-Class 50s scored: 1
1st-Class 5 w. in innings: 6
1st-Class 10 w. in match: 1
Place in bowling averages: 131st
av. 49.23 (1987 49th av. 27.19)
Strike rate 1988: 86.58 (career 60.61)
1st-Class catches 1988: 4 (career 24)
Parents: George Kenneth and
Hilda Margaret
Wife: Peta Jean Wendy
Children: Craig Robert, 6 June 1985
Family links with cricket: Father played in local league cricket. Brother
played for NAYC and Nottinghamshire 2nd XI, and is to be taken on to
Nottinghamshire staff for 1989 season
Education: Magnus Grammar School, Newark
Qualifications: 10 O-levels, 4 A-levels
Jobs outside cricket: Farmer
Off-season 1988–89: Working on family farm
Overseas teams played for: North Perth, Australia 1979–80; Durban Collegians, South Africa 1980–81; Alma-Marist, Cape Town 1982–83
Cricketers particularly admired: Dennis Lillee, John Snow

LAST SEASON: BATTING

	I.	N.O.	R.	H.S.	AV.
TEST					
1ST-CLASS	13	2	47	17	4.27
INT					
RAL	2	2	4	2*	–
NAT.W.	–	–	–	–	–
B & H	1	0	1	1	1.00

CAREER: BATTING

	I.	N.O.	R.	H.S.	AV.
TEST					
1ST-CLASS	120	36	989	59*	11.77
INT					
RAL	31	21	138	23*	13.80
NAT.W.	4	3	25	12	25.00
B & H	12	7	53	13*	10.60

LAST SEASON: BOWLING

	O.	M.	R.	W.	AV.
TEST					
1ST-CLASS	245.2	42	837	17	49.22
INT					
RAL	52.4	1	288	6	48.00
NAT.W.	24	0	116	2	58.00
B & H	31	5	125	6	20.83

CAREER: BOWLING

	O.	M.	R.	W.	AV.
TEST					
1ST-CLASS	2778.2	650	8628	275	31.37
INT					
RAL	588	24	2895	108	26.80
NAT.W.	183.1	22	683	27	25.29
B & H	278.4	32	1063	42	25.30

Other sports played: Rugby union
Other sports followed: 'Most sports except soccer and anything to do with horses.'
Injuries 1988: Knee injury
Relaxations: Gardening, DIY
Opinions on cricket: 'I believe there should be no limit on over rates in four-day cricket, in order to encourage quick bowling as opposed to seam bowling.'
Best batting performance: 59* Nottinghamshire v Derbyshire, Chesterfield 1982
Best bowling performance: 6-49 Nottinghamshire v Sussex, Trent Bridge 1987

SCOTT, C. W.   Nottinghamshire

Full Name: Christopher Wilmot Scott
Role: Right-hand bat, wicket-keeper
Born: 23 January 1964, Lincoln
Height: 5′ 8″ **Weight:** 10st 11lbs
Nickname: George, Ginge
County debut: 1981
County cap: 1988
1st-Class 50s scored: 3
Place in batting averages: 210th av. 16.95 (1987 193rd av. 17.85)
Parents: Kenneth and Kathleen
Wife and date of marriage: Jacqueline, 18 March 1989
Family links with cricket: Father and brothers play for Collingham CC
Education: Robert Pattinson Comprehensive School, North Hykeham, Lincoln
Qualifications: 4 O-levels, 2 CSEs, coaching certificate
Jobs outside cricket: Farming
Off-season 1988–89: Coaching locally and working at Trent Bridge
Cricketing superstitions or habits: 'I never say anything to the outgoing batsman as I walk in to bat.'
Overseas teams played for: Poverty Bay CC, New Zealand 1983–84; Queensland University, Australia 1985–86, 1987–88
Cricketers particularly learnt from: Bruce French, Pasty Harris, Bob White
Cricketers particularly admired: Ian Botham above all, but many others
Other sports played: Rugby union

Other sports followed: Soccer
Injuries 1988: 'Managed to get away with just one broken finger, despite playing many games at Trent Bridge.'
Relaxations: Watching films, listening to records
Extras: One of the youngest players to play for Nottinghamshire in County Championship team – made debut at 17 years 157 days. Ten catches against Derbyshire, May 1988, broke Nottinghamshire record for catches in a match
Opinions on cricket: 'I find four-day cricket very long and boring especially having to bowl 110 overs a day. I would like the three-day game to stay.'
Best batting performance: 78 Nottinghamshire v Cambridge University, Cambridge 1983

LAST SEASON: BATTING

	I.	N.O.	R.	H.S.	AV.
TEST					
1ST-CLASS	27	6	356	63*	16.95
INT					
RAL	3	2	23	13*	23.00
NAT.W.	–	–	–	–	–
B & H		1	28	18	14.00

CAREER: BATTING

	I.	N.O.	R.	H.S.	AV.
TEST					
1ST-CLASS	59	13	1016	78	22.08
INT					
RAL	8	3	83	26	16.60
NAT.W.	–	–	–	–	–
B & H	3	1	28	18	14.00

LAST SEASON: WICKET KEEPING

	C.	ST.			
TEST					
1ST-CLASS	49	2			
INT					
RAL	8	–			
NAT.W.	3	–			
B & H	1	–			

CAREER: WICKET KEEPING

	C.	ST.			
TEST					
1ST-CLASS	116	7			
INT					
RAL	18	1			
NAT.W.	4	–			
B & H	1	–			

SCOTT, R. J.   Hampshire

Full Name: Richard James Scott
Role: Left-hand bat, right-arm medium pace bowler, 'short-leg fielder, allowing C. Smith to retire to third man'
Born: 2 November 1963, Bournemouth
Height: 5′ 11″ **Weight:** 14st
Nickname: Gazza, Scotty
County debut: 1985
1st-Class 50s scored: 2
1st-Class 100s scored: 1
Place in batting averages: 136th av. 24.93
1st-Class catches 1988: 9 (career 9)
Parents: Andrew and Ann
Marital status: Single

Family links with cricket: 'Dad played for Colehill. Two brothers also play for same side in Dorset league.'

Education: Queen Elizabeth School, Wimborne

Qualifications: 2 O-levels, CSEs, coaching award

Jobs outside cricket: Worked for father's building firm before turning professional

Off-season 1988–89: Playing for Pirates CC, Durban, South Africa; coaching Indians, coloureds and blacks – Pirates is the main multi-racial club in South Africa

Cricketing superstitions or habits: 'Always put right pad on first.'

Overseas teams played for: Glenwood Old Boys, Durban, 1984–85, 1985–86; Pirates CC, Durban, 1987–88

Cricketers particularly learnt from: Chris and Robin Smith

Cricketers particularly admired: Chris Smith, Ian Botham, Malcolm Marshall

Other sports played: Golf (with a hefty slice), football, snooker

Other sports followed: Golf, football

Relaxations: 'Like to relax down any nice pub. Also like taking dog for walks deep in Dorset countryside.'

Extras: Played Minor Counties cricket for Dorset since 1981. Represented Minor Counties Cricket Association in 1985

Opinions on cricket: 'Four-day game a revelation. Best side will always win Championship.'

Best batting performance: 107* Hampshire v Sri Lankans, Southampton 1988

LAST SEASON: BATTING

	I.	N.O.	R.	H.S.	AV.
TEST					
1ST-CLASS	16	1	374	107*	24.93
INT					
RAL	2	0	10	6	5.00
NAT.W.					
B & H	1	0	41	41	41.00

CAREER: BATTING

	I.	N.O.	R.	H.S.	AV.
TEST					
1ST-CLASS	16	1	374	107*	24.93
INT					
RAL	6	1	89	48	17.80
NAT.W.	1	0	0	0	0.00
B & H	1	0	41	41	41.00

142. Who came top of the Derbyshire first-class batting averages in 1988?

143. Who came top of the Essex first-class batting averages in 1988?

SCRIVEN, T. J. A. Somerset

Full Name: Timothy John
Adam Scriven
Role: Right-hand bat, slow
left-arm bowler
Born: 15 December 1965,
High Wycombe
Height: 6′ 3″ **Weight:** 14st
Nickname: Sammy, Spiv
County debut: 1988
Parents: John Richard and
Hilary Margaret
Marital status: Single
Family links with cricket: Father
played 2nd XI cricket for Hampshire
as well as Minor County cricket
for Buckinghamshire. Brother Jeremy
plays club cricket
Education: RGS, High Wycombe
Qualifications: 6 O-levels;
qualified cricket coach
Jobs outside cricket: Insurance clerk, groundsman at a sports centre
Off-season 1988–89: Playing in New Zealand
Cricketing superstitions or habits: Left pad on first
Overseas teams played for: Marist CC, New Plymouth, New Zealand 1986–
87; Marist CC and Taranaki 1987–88
Cricketers particularly learnt from: Father, Richard Williams, Peter Robin-
son
Cricketers particularly admired: Wayne Larkins, Steve Waugh, Barry
Richards, Phil Edmonds, Steven Boock

LAST SEASON: BATTING

	I.	N.O.	R.	H.S.	AV.
TEST					
1ST-CLASS	2	0	11	7	5.50
INT					
RAL					
NAT.W.					
B & H					

LAST SEASON: BOWLING

	O.	M.	R.	W.	AV.
TEST					
1ST-CLASS	96	25	237	3	79.00
INT					
RAL					
NAT.W.					
B & H					

CAREER: BATTING

	I.	N.O.	R.	H.S.	AV.
TEST					
1ST-CLASS	2	0	11	7	5.50
INT					
RAL					
NAT.W.					
B & H					

CAREER: BOWLING

	O.	M.	R.	W.	AV.
TEST					
1ST-CLASS	96	25	237	3	79.00
INT					
RAL					
NAT.W.					
B & H					

Other sports played: Golf, football, hockey
Other sports followed: Likes to watch and follow most sports
Injuries 1988: Slight back strain
Relaxations: Watching films, music, going for a drink
Extras: On the Northamptonshire staff 1985–87. Released by Somerset at end of 1988 season
Opinions on cricket: '16 four-day games should be played in the County Championship. Spinners should be given every encouragement by the counties, with slow bowling clinics being organised, etc.'
Best batting performance: 7 Somerset v Derbyshire, Weston-super-Mare 1988
Best bowling performance: 1-40 Somerset v Derbyshire, Weston-super-Mare 1988

SHARMA, R. Derbyshire

Full Name: Rajesh Sharma
Role: Right-hand bat, off-break bowler, slip or short-leg fielder
Born: 27 June 1962, Kenya
Height: 6′ 3″ **Weight:** 13st
Nickname: Reg
County debut: 1985
1st-Class 50s scored: 6
1st-Class 100s scored: 1
1st-Class 5 w. in innings: 1
Place in batting averages: 107th av. 28.63 (1987 137th av. 25.91)
Place in bowling averages: —
(1987 123rd av. 42.66)
1st-Class catches 1988: 5 (career 44)
Parents: M. R. and R. D.
Marital status: Single
Family links with cricket: Younger brother has played 2nd XI cricket for Kent
Education: Parkland School for Boys
Qualifications: CSEs and O-levels
Jobs outside cricket: Family business (retail trade)
Overseas teams played for: Mudgreeba, Queensland 1982–83; Helensvale, Queensland 1983–84
Cricketers particularly learnt from: Ron Harland (played for Bexley CC)
Cricketers particularly admired: Viv Richards
Other sports played: Snooker and golf
Other sports followed: Football and snooker

Relaxations: 'Spending lots of time with my dogs, Simba, Sable and Bruno.'
Opinions on cricket: 'I believe that overseas players have improved the standard of county cricket and their experience has helped younger players. However, I fail to understand the fairness of one county being allowed to have more overseas players than others. When each county is allowed an equal number of overseas players the standards will improve even more.'
Best batting performance: 111 Derbyshire v Yorkshire, Chesterfield 1987
Best bowling performance: 6-80 Derbyshire v Gloucestershire, Bristol 1987

LAST SEASON: BATTING

	I.	N.O.	R.	H.S.	AV.
TEST					
1ST-CLASS	14	3	315	80	28.63
INT					
RAL	8	1	121	33	17.28
NAT.W.	1	0	4	4	4.00
B & H	–	–	–	–	–

LAST SEASON: BOWLING

	O.	M.	R.	W.	AV.
TEST					
1ST-CLASS	218.2	49	593	7	84.71
INT					
RAL	27	3	135	5	27.00
NAT.W.	13	2	33	1	33.00
B & H					

CAREER: BATTING

	I.	N.O.	R.	H.S.	AV.
TEST					
1ST-CLASS	70	15	1441	111	26.20
INT					
RAL	23	6	303	37	17.82
NAT.W.	5	0	50	21	10.00
B & H	1	0	2	2	2.00

CAREER: BOWLING

	O.	M.	R.	W.	AV.
TEST					
1ST-CLASS	565.1	128	1640	33	49.69
INT					
RAL	80	8	410	9	45.55
NAT.W.	46	7	146	5	29.20
B & H					

SHARP, K. Yorkshire

Full Name: Kevin Sharp
Role: Left-hand bat, off-break bowler
Born: 6 April 1959, Leeds
Height: 5′ 10″ **Weight:** 12st 9lbs
Nickname: Lambsy, Poodle
County debut: 1976
County cap: 1982
1000 runs in a season: 1
1st-Class 50s scored: 41
1st-Class 100s scored: 14
One-Day 50s: 23
One-Day 100s: 3
Place in batting averages: 162nd
av. 22.52 (1987 132nd av. 26.75)
1st-Class catches 1988: 9 (career 97)
Parents: Gordon and Joyce
Wife and date of marriage: Karen,
1 October 1983

Children: Amy Lauren, 28 December 1985
Family links with cricket: Father played with Woodhouse in Leeds League for many years. Young brother, David, now playing local cricket
Education: Abbey Grange C of E High School, Leeds
Qualifications: CSE Grade I Religious Education. Coaching award
Jobs outside cricket: Plasterer's labourer, warehouseman, driver for film company
Overseas tours: Derrick Robins' XI to Australasia 1980
Overseas teams played for: Subiaco Floreat CC, Perth, Australia; De Beers CC, Griqualand West, 1981–82
Cricketers particularly learnt from: Doug Padgett, Geoff Boycott, Phil Carrick
Cricketers particularly admired: Richard Hadlee, Malcolm Marshall
Other sports played: Golf, squash
Other sports followed: Snooker, soccer
Injuries 1988: Troubled disc in back
Relaxations: Decorating and maintaining the house
Extras: 260* v Young West Indies 1977. Rested during latter part of 1980 season on medical advice. Captain of England U-19 v West Indies U-19 1978 at Worcester. Winston Churchill Travelling Fellowship to Australia for two months, 1978. 'I took the first wicket of my career in 1984 – a feat I never thought possible.'
Opinions on cricket: 'Would like to see more Englishmen playing for England. Would like to see Graham Gooch and company left alone because of their contact with South Africa. Why should English players be made scapegoats when South Africans are left well alone?'
Best batting performance: 181 Yorkshire v Gloucestershire, Harrogate 1986
Best bowling performance: 2-13 Yorkshire v Glamorgan, Bradford 1984

LAST SEASON: BATTING

	I.	N.O.	R.	H.S.	AV.
TEST					
1ST-CLASS	19	0	428	128	22.52
INT					
RAL	10	0	309	56	30.90
NAT.W.	1	0	21	21	21.00
B & H	1	0	75	75	75.00

CAREER: BATTING

	I.	N.O.	R.	H.S.	AV.
TEST					
1ST-CLASS	329	29	9132	181	30.44
INT					
RAL	118	11	2852	114	26.65
NAT.W.	12	2	213	50	21.30
B & H	6	1	200	75	40.00

LAST SEASON: BOWLING

	O.	M.	R.	W.	AV.
TEST					
1ST-CLASS	1	0	11	0	–
INT					
RAL					
NAT.W.					
B & H					

CAREER: BOWLING

	O.	M.	R.	W.	AV.
TEST					
1ST-CLASS	196.2	43	802	12	66.83
INT					
RAL	0.1	0	1	0	–
NAT.W.	10	0	47	4	11.75
B & H					

SHASTRI, R. — Glamorgan

Full Name: Ravishankar Shastri
Role: Right-hand bat, slow
left-arm bowler, close fielder
Born: 27 May 1962, Bombay
Height: 6′ 3½″ **Weight:** 13st 1lb
Nickname: Shas
County debut: 1987
Test debut: 1980–81
No. of Tests: 58
No. of One-Day Internationals: 101
1st-Class 50s scored: 37
1st-Class 100s scored: 14
1st-Class 200s scored: 1
1st-Class 5 w. in innings: 14
1st-Class 10 w. in match: 3
One-Day 50s: 22
One-Day 100s: 2
Place in batting averages: 66th
av. 33.82 (1987 37th av. 40.26)
Place in bowling averages: 113th
av. 33.45 (1987 83rd av. 31.91)
Strike rate 1988: 91.30 (career 84.38)
1st-Class catches 1988: 5 (career 82)
Parents: Jayadritha and Lakshmi
Marital status: Single
Qualifications: Bachelor of Commerce, Bombay University
Jobs outside cricket: Public relations executive
Off-season 1988–89: Playing for India
Cricketing superstitions or habits: Left pad and left boot on first

LAST SEASON: BATTING

	I.	N.O.	R.	H.S.	AV.
TEST					
1ST-CLASS	19	2	575	157	33.82
INT					
RAL	14	6	513	84*	64.12
NAT.W.	3	2	103	59*	103.00
B & H	6	2	117	55	29.25

CAREER: BATTING

	I.	N.O.	R.	H.S.	AV.
TEST	86	12	2568	142	34.70
1ST-CLASS	125	21	4536	200*	45.36
INT	81	16	2067	102	31.80
RAL	26	7	762	84*	40.10
NAT.W.	5	2	140	59*	46.66
B & H	9	2	167	55	23.85

LAST SEASON: BOWLING

	O.	M.	R.	W.	AV.
TEST					
1ST-CLASS	304.2	91	709	20	35.45
INT					
RAL	67	1	339	11	30.81
NAT.W.	31	2	103	8	12.87
B & H	61	6	215	3	71.66

CAREER: BOWLING

	O.	M.	R.	W.	AV.
TEST	2175.1	581	4911	127	38.66
1ST-CLASS	3042.2	812	6933	244	28.41
INT	799.2	47	3283	101	32.50
RAL	151	5	660	17	38.82
NAT.W.	34.1	3	108	9	12.00
B & H	94	8	332	4	83.00

Overseas tours: Young India to Sri Lanka 1980 and England 1981; India to England 1982, 1983, 1986; to West Indies 1983; to New Zealand 1981; to Australia 1985, 1986; to Pakistan 1982, 1983, 1984; to Sri Lanka 1985; to Zimbabwe 1984

Overseas teams played for: Bombay 1979–88

Cricketers particularly learnt from: Chandu Borde, Sunil Gavaskar, Gary Sobers

Cricketers particularly admired: Imran Khan, Viv Richards, Richard Hadlee, Gundappa Vishwanath, Gary Sobers, Gordon Greenidge

Other sports played: Swimming, tennis, chess

Other sports followed: Tennis, athletics

Relaxations: Watching sports, films, listening to music

Extras: Has batted at every number for India except No. 11. Hit six sixes in an over off Tank Raj for Bombay v Baroda at Bombay 1984–85 on the way to highest first-class score of 200*. Played in MCC Bicentenary Test

Opinions on cricket: 'We must have neutral umpires.'

Best batting performance: 200* Bombay v Baroda, Bombay 1984–85

Best bowling performance: 9-101 Bombay v Rest of India, Indore 1981–82

SHAW, C. Yorkshire

Full Name: Christopher Shaw

Role: Right-hand bat, right-arm fast-medium bowler

Born: 17 February 1964, Hemsworth

Height: 6′ 1″ **Weight:** 12st 7lbs

Nickname: Sandy

County debut: 1984

1st-Class 5 w. in innings: 3

Place in batting averages: 240th av. 13.07

Place in bowling averages: 100th av. 33.08

Strike rate 1988: 66.23 (career 67.02)

1st-Class catches 1988: 2 (career 9)

Parents: Brian and Betty

Wife and date of marriage: Karen, 3 October 1987

Family links with cricket: Father good local league cricketer

Education: Sharlston Junior School; Crofton High School

Qualifications: 5 CSEs, Qualified Cricket Coach

Jobs outside cricket: Electrician

Off-season 1988–89: Working and coaching in Headingley Cricket School
Overseas tours: Holland with NCA U-19s (North of England) 1983; Barbados with Yorkshire Cricket Association 1984
Overseas teams played for: Epuni-Cambridge CC, New Zealand 1985–86
Cricketers particularly learnt from: Father, Doug Padgett, Steve Oldham
Cricketers particularly admired: Dennis Lillee
Other sports played: Golf
Other sports followed: Likes watching all sports; keen supporter of Featherstone Rovers RLFC
Relaxations: Playing golf, listening to music
Extras: On debut at Lord's took 4-68 v Middlesex. Took 5-41 in second JPL match v Hampshire at Bournemouth. His county captain, Phil Carrick, says of Shaw: 'He is a joy to captain. He will always give you everything he's got.'
Best batting performance: 31 Yorkshire v Nottinghamshire, Sheffield 1988
Best bowling performance: 6-64 Yorkshire v Lancashire, Leeds 1987

LAST SEASON: BATTING

	I.	N.O.	R.	H.S.	AV.
TEST					
1ST-CLASS	25	12	170	31	13.07
INT					
RAL	4	4	32	13*	–
NAT.W.	1	0	1	1	1.00
B & H	1	1	4	4*	–

CAREER: BATTING

	I.	N.O.	R.	H.S.	AV.
TEST					
1ST-CLASS	58	27	340	31	10.96
INT					
RAL	15	8	117	26	16.71
NAT.W.	4	1	9	6*	3.00
B & H	1	1	4	4*	–

LAST SEASON: BOWLING

	O.	M.	R.	W.	AV.
TEST					
1ST-CLASS	507.5	110	1522	46	33.08
INT					
RAL	105.1	7	410	9	21.57
NAT.W.	24	9	49	5	9.80
B & H	22	6	60	2	30.00

CAREER: BOWLING

	O.	M.	R.	W.	AV.
TEST					
1ST-CLASS	1374	295	4101	123	33.34
INT					
RAL	252.4	12	1142	45	25.37
NAT.W.	66.1	17	194	11	17.63
B & H	22	6	60	2	30.00

144. Who came top of the Glamorgan first-class batting averages in 1988?

145. Who came top of the Gloucestershire first-class batting averages in 1988?

SIDEBOTTOM, A. Yorkshire

Full Name: Arnold Sidebottom
Role: Right-hand bat, right-arm
fast-medium bowler, outfielder
Born: 1 April 1954, Barnsley
Height: 6′ 2″ **Weight:** 13st 10lbs
Nickname: Woofer, Red Setter, Arnie
County debut: 1973
County cap: 1980
Benefit: 1988
Test debut: 1985
No. of Tests: 1
1st-Class 50s scored: 13
1st-Class 100s scored: 1
1st-Class 5 w. in innings: 18
1st-Class 10 w. in match: 2
One-Day 50s: 1
Place in batting averages: 116th
av. 27.21 (1987 207th av. 16.31)
Place in bowling averages: 16th
av. 20.68 (1987 65th av. 29.32)
Strike rate 1988: 48.69 (career 51.10)
1st-Class catches 1988: 5 (career 51)
Parents: Jack and Florence
Wife and date of marriage: Gillian, 17 June 1977
Children: Ryan Jay, 1978; Dale, 1980
Family links with cricket: Father good cricketer
Education: Barnsley Broadway Grammar School
Jobs outside cricket: Professional footballer with Manchester United for five
years, Huddersfield Town for two years and Halifax Town

LAST SEASON: BATTING

	I.	N.O.	R.	H.S.	AV.
TEST					
1ST-CLASS	24	5	517	55	27.21
INT					
RAL	6	2	32	10	8.00
NAT.W.	1	0	10	10	10.00
B & H	1	0	2	2	2.00

CAREER: BATTING

	I.	N.O.	R.	H.S.	AV.
TEST	1	0	2	2	2.00
1ST-CLASS	233	56	4040	124	22.82
INT					
RAL	71	24	750	52*	15.95
NAT.W.	13	5	183	45	22.87
B & H	25	8	235	32	13.82

LAST SEASON: BOWLING

	O.	M.	R.	W.	AV.
TEST					
1ST-CLASS	511.2	137	1303	63	20.68
INT					
RAL	95.2	4	413	9	45.88
NAT.W.	24	4	51	3	17.00
B & H	22	5	55	0	–

CAREER: BOWLING

	O.	M.	R.	W.	AV.
TEST	18.4	3	65	1	65.00
1ST-CLASS	4436.2	981	12687	522	24.30
INT					
RAL	901.1	40	3899	130	29.99
NAT.W.	198.2	27	558	34	16.41
B & H	425.4	68	1372	65	21.10

Overseas tours: Rebel England team to South Africa 1982
Cricketers particularly learnt from: Father, Doug Padgett, Geoff Boycott
Cricketers particularly admired: Steve Oldham, David Bairstow, Graham Stevenson
Other sports played: Professional football, tennis, table tennis, badminton
Other sports followed: Most sports
Relaxations: Watching television, horse racing, playing with sons
Extras: Banned from Test cricket for three years for joining rebel team to South Africa in 1982. Injured toe during Test debut in 1985 and not picked for England again
Best batting performance: 124 Yorkshire v Glamorgan, Cardiff 1977
Best bowling performance: 8-72 Yorkshire v Leicestershire, Middlesbrough 1986

SIMMONS, J.   Lancashire

Full Name: Jack Simmons
Role: Right-hand bat, off-break bowler, slip fielder
Born: 28 March 1941, Clayton-le-Moors, nr Accrington
Height: 6′ 1″ **Weight:** 15st 7lbs
Nickname: Simmo, Flat Jack
County debut: 1968
County cap: 1971
Benefit: 1980 (£128,000)
1st-Class 50s scored: 39
1st-Class 100s scored: 6
1st-Class 5 w. in innings: 41
1st-Class 10 w. in match: 6
One-Day 50s: 6
Place in batting averages: 191st av. 20.11 (1987 233rd av. 13.26)
Place in bowling averages: 46th av. 24.57 (1987 13th av. 21.26)
Strike rate 1988: 59.90 (career 64.18)
1st-Class catches 1988: 11 (career 337)
Parents: Robert and Ada
Wife and date of marriage: Jacqueline, 23 March 1963
Children: Kelly Louise, 28 January 1979
Family links with cricket: Father, Robert, played for Enfield in Lancashire League. Grandfather, Robert, also played for Enfield from 1887, giving 92 years' association with the same club

Education: Accrington Technical School; Blackburn Technical College
Qualifications: 5 O-levels, ONC, City & Guilds in Quantities
Jobs outside cricket: Draughtsman with Accrington Brick & Tile Co Ltd, and Lancashire County Surveyors' Department. Sports Agency (Jack Simmons Ltd). Travel company with Murray Birnie. Director of Bowlers Leisure Centre and Conference Centre, with six indoor cricket courts, eight bowling lanes, two 5-a-side pitches, 16 snooker tables, new hi-tech gym and four bars, in Trafford Park, Manchester
Off-season 1988–89: Working at 'Bowlers'. Holiday in Tenerife. Taking Blackpool CC Under 17s Centenary Tour to Australia for 17 days, playing in Sydney, Melbourne and Tasmania.
Cricketing superstitions or habits: 'I always like to be last on the field. To do the same things again if successful once, i.e. clothes or eating habits.'
Overseas tours: Zimbabwe and South Africa with Whitbread Wanderers 1975; Mike Brearley Invitation XI to Calcutta 1981; New York 1985 with C. Lloyd Lancashire XI; MCC to Bermuda 1987
Overseas teams played for: Tasmania 1972–79 (where he is 'a bit of a folk hero'). Captained Tasmania to Gillette Cup for first time in 1979, and when they first entered Sheffield Shield (1978)
Cricketers particularly learnt from: 'Coached by Clyde Walcott when I was a youngster. Learnt from Clive Lloyd with Lancashire. Jack Bond, Ray Illingworth, plus many more off-spinners.'
Cricketers particularly admired: 'Clive Lloyd (great team man), Viv Richards, Chappell brothers and great bowlers, Dennis Lillee and Michael Holding.'
Other sports played: Golf, indoor cricket
Other sports followed: Football, horse racing
Injuries 1988: Bad back
Relaxations: Soccer, golf, horse racing, eating, playing cards, watching television and going on holiday
Extras: 'I didn't play for a couple of years because I broke my leg three times

LAST SEASON: BATTING

	I.	N.O.	R.	H.S.	AV.
TEST					
1ST-CLASS	27	9	362	57*	20.11
INT					
RAL	7	6	33	20*	33.00
NAT.W.	2	0	6	6	3.00
B & H	2	2	39	31*	—

CAREER: BATTING

	I.	N.O.	R.	H.S.	AV.
TEST					
1ST-CLASS	553	141	9360	112	22.71
INT					
RAL	178	56	1924	65	15.77
NAT.W.	36	14	460	54*	20.90
B & H	52	21	665	64	21.45

LAST SEASON: BOWLING

	O.	M.	R.	W.	AV.
TEST					
1ST-CLASS	629	159	1548	63	24.57
INT					
RAL	104	4	515	15	34.33
NAT.W.	21	3	62	3	20.66
B & H	39	4	172	3	57.33

CAREER: BOWLING

	O.	M.	R.	W.	AV.
TEST					
1ST-CLASS	446.2 / 10422.4	94 / 2455	27735	1030	26.92
INT					
RAL	1833.2	136	7704	290	26.56
NAT.W.	588.5	106	1727	76	22.72
B & H	678.2	134	1983	75	26.44

in ten months and the previous year broke my arm quite badly, all playing soccer – except one broken leg, which was broken going down to the football ground just after I had it out of plaster for the first time.' Made debut for 2nd XI in 1959. Hat-trick v Nottinghamshire, Liverpool 1977. Director of Burnley FC. Published autobiography *Flat Jack* in 1986. One of *Wisden*'s Five Cricketers of the Year, 1984. Reached 1000 first-class wickets in career in 1988

Opinions on cricket: 'Cricket fines can become a farce, with players thinking of fines when they should be concentrating on cricket. If four-day cricket comes in throughout the season, on average, too many result pitches, especially for quick bowlers. Like to see lbw changed to encourage leg-spinners.'

Best batting performance: 112 Lancashire v Sussex, Hove 1970
Best bowling performance: 7-59 Tasmania v Queensland, Brisbane 1978–79

SLACK, W. N. Middlesex

Full Name: Wilfred Norris Slack
Role: Left-hand opening bat, right-arm medium bowler, short-leg fielder
Born: 12 December 1954, Troumaca, St Vincent, West Indies
Height: 6′ **Weight:** 13st
Nickname: Slacky, Bishop, Tutu
County debut: 1977
County cap: 1981
Test debut: 1985–86
No. of Tests: 3
No. of One-Day Internationals: 2
1000 runs in a season: 7
1st-Class 50s scored: 75
1st-Class 100s scored: 22
1st-Class 200s scored: 3
One-Day 50s: 28
One-Day 100s: 2
Place in batting averages: 23rd av. 45.48 (1987 47th av. 38.95)
1st-Class catches 1988: 10 (career 173)
Parents: Grafton and Doreen
Education: Wellesbourne Secondary, High Wycombe
Qualifications: City & Guilds in Radio and TV mechanics, NCA Advanced Coach
Jobs outside cricket: Digital electronics test engineer
Overseas tours: To Pakistan with Rohan Kanhai's World XI 1981; England B

to Sri Lanka 1986 and then joined England tour of West Indies 1986; England to Australia 1986–87

Overseas teams played for: Played in Auckland, New Zealand, 1979–80; World XI in Pakistan 1981; Windward Islands in Shell Shield 1981–83

Cricketers particularly learnt from: Don Bennett, Clive Radley

Other sports played: Basketball for Bucks and Wycombe Pirates; tennis, squash, badminton, football, athletics

Relaxations: Building electronic projects. Relaxing in a sauna. Travelling

Extras: Played for Buckinghamshire in 1976. At 16 played for Wycombe Colts. Played for Freith in Haigh Village Cricket Competition. Then joined High Wycombe; then Buckinghamshire in 1976; then Middlesex in 1977. Qualified to play for both West Indies and England. Died tragically from a heart attack in January 1989 after collapsing at the crease whilst batting for the touring Cavaliers XI in an exhibition match in The Gambia

Best batting performance: 248* Middlesex v Worcestershire, Lord's 1981

Best bowling performance: 3-17 Middlesex v Leicestershire, Uxbridge 1982

LAST SEASON: BATTING

	I.	N.O.	R.	H.S.	AV.
TEST					
1ST-CLASS	32	5	1228	163*	45.48
INT					
RAL	11	3	320	77*	40.00
NAT.W.	5	0	76	56	15.20
B & H	4	0	94	47	23.50

LAST SEASON: BOWLING

	O.	M.	R.	W.	AV.
TEST					
1ST-CLASS	2	1	14	0	–
INT					
RAL	3	0	25	0	–
NAT.W.					
B & H					

CAREER: BATTING

	I.	N.O.	R.	H.S.	AV.
TEST	6	0	81	52	13.50
1ST-CLASS	392	40	13869	248*	39.40
INT	2	0	43	34	21.50
RAL	95	13	2353	101*	28.69
NAT.W.	26	1	827	98	33.08
B & H	36	4	895	110	27.96

CAREER: BOWLING

	O.	M.	R.	W.	AV.
TEST					
1ST-CLASS	234.5	44	688	21	32.76
INT					
RAL	176.4	1	878	34	25.82
NAT.W.	84	6	317	8	39.62
B & H	7	0	34	0	–

146. Who came top of the Hampshire first-class batting averages in 1988?

147. Who came top of the Kent first-class batting averages in 1988?

Full Name: Gladstone Cleophas Small

Role: Right-hand bat, right-arm fast-medium bowler

Born: 18 October 1961, St George, Barbados

Height: 5′ 11″ **Weight:** 12st

Nickname: Gladys

County debut: 1980

County cap: 1982

Test debut: 1986

No. of Tests: 5

No. of One-Day Internationals: 25

1st-Class 50s scored: 4

1st-Class 5 w. in innings: 24

1st-Class 10 w. in match: 2

Place in batting averages: 134th av. 25.18 (1987 209th av. 16.06)

Place in bowling averages: 13th av. 20.06 (1987 79th av. 31.38)

Strike rate 1988: 47.11 (career 54.13)

1st-Class catches 1988: 7 (career 53)

Parents: Chelston and Gladys

Marital status: Married

Family links with cricket: Cousin, Milton Small, toured England with West Indies in 1984

Education: Mosely School; Hall Green Technical College, Birmingham

Qualifications: 2 O-levels

Overseas tours: With Young England to New Zealand 1979–80; Derrick Robins' XI tour of Australia, Tasmania and New Zealand 1980; Rohan Kanhai International XI tour of Pakistan 1981; England to Australia, 1986–87; World Cup 1987; England to Pakistan, Australia and New Zealand 1987–88

Overseas teams played for: Balwyn CC, Melbourne 1982–83, 1984–85; South Australia and West Torrens, Adelaide 1985–86

Cricketers particularly learnt from: David Brown (manager at Warwickshire)

Cricketers particularly admired: Dennis Lillee, Malcolm Marshall, Richard Hadlee, Bob Willis

Other sports played: Golf, tennis

Other sports followed: Athletics, golf, tennis, soccer

Relaxations: 'Playing a round of golf really relaxes me; listening to music and relaxing with my wife.'

Extras: In 1980, became youngest bowler to take five JPL wickets in one innings. Was called up for England Test squad v Pakistan at Edgbaston, July 1982, but did not play. Bowled 18-ball over v Middlesex in August 1982, with 11 no balls

Opinions on cricket: 'The introduction of four-day Championship cricket will improve the first-class game in that teams would have to bowl out the opposition twice instead of relying on contrived results. For four-day cricket to be successful, clubs must be made to produce good, hard cricketing wickets that would be beneficial to both batsmen and bowlers.'

Best batting performance: 70 Warwickshire v Lancashire, Old Trafford 1988
Best bowling performance: 7-15 Warwickshire v Nottinghamshire, Edgbaston 1988

LAST SEASON: BATTING

	I.	N.O.	R.	H.S.	AV.
TEST	2	1	12	7	12.00
1ST-CLASS	27	6	542	70	25.80
INT	1	1	7	7*	–
RAL	9	2	41	13	5.85
NAT.W.	1	0	12	12	12.00
B & H	2	0	3	2	1.50

CAREER: BATTING

	I.	N.O.	R.	H.S.	AV.
TEST	7	3	61	21*	15.25
1ST-CLASS	233	54	2670	70	14.91
INT	10	5	33	8	6.60
RAL	50	17	258	40*	7.81
NAT.W.	12	5	116	33	16.57
B & H	19	5	79	19*	5.64

LAST SEASON: BOWLING

	O.	M.	R.	W.	AV.
TEST	37.5	6	140	4	35.00
1ST-CLASS	590.2	164	1465	76	19.27
INT	30	3	76	6	12.66
RAL	86.3	4	346	16	21.62
NAT.W.	10	1	32	0	–
B & H	26	3	79	0	–

CAREER: BOWLING

	O.	M.	R.	W.	AV.
TEST	180.3	49	454	20	22.70
1ST-CLASS	4746	979	14685	526	27.91
INT	237	15	941	27	34.85
RAL	687	47	3107	141	22.03
NAT.W.	188.1	35	637	23	27.69
B & H	284.2	47	1053	34	30.97

148. Which West Indian has the record amount from a benefit year?

149. Which Australian was one of only two players ever to score a century in both his first-class and his Test debuts?

SMITH, C. L. Hampshire

Full Name: Christopher Lyall Smith
Role: Right-hand bat, off-spin bowler
Born: 15 October 1958, Durban, South Africa
Height: 5′ 11″ **Weight:** 13st 10lbs
Nickname: Kippy
County debut: 1979 (Glamorgan), 1980 (Hampshire)
County cap: 1981 (Hampshire)
Test debut: 1983
No. of Tests: 9
No. of One-Day Internationals: 4
1000 runs in a season: 7
1st-Class 50s scored: 63
1st-Class 100s scored: 34
1st-Class 200s scored: 1
1st-Class 5 w. in innings: 1
One-Day 50s: 32
One-Day 100s: 3
Place in batting averages: 53rd av. 35.90 (1987 17th av. 46.03)
1st-Class catches 1988: 14 (career 138)
Parents: John Arnold and Elaine Jessie
Marital status: Single
Family links with cricket: Grandfather, Vernon Lyall Shearer, played for Natal; brother, Robin, also plays for Hampshire
Education: Northlands High School, Durban, South Africa
Qualifications: Matriculation (2 A-level equivalents)
Jobs outside cricket: 'Running Chris Smith Sports Entertainment which specialises in corporate entertaining. Also run a travel business and am involved with Car Phone Group's activities around Hampshire.'
Overseas tours: Toured UK with Kingsmead Mynahs (Natal U-25s under another name) 1976; with England to New Zealand and Pakistan 1983–84; England B to Sri Lanka 1986
Overseas teams played for: Kingsmead Mynahs; Natal Schools 1975; South African Schools 1976; Natal B (debut 1978)
Cricketers particularly admired: Barry Richards, Grayson Heath (coach in South Africa)
Other sports played: League squash, golf (15 handicap)
Other sports followed: Watches football (Southampton FC)
Relaxations: Walking in the countryside with my dog or lying on the beach, swimming, listening to music
Extras: Made debut for Glamorgan in 1979. Played for Gorseinon in South

Wales League in 1979. Made Hampshire debut 1980. Captained Hampshire 2nd XI in 1981. Became eligible to play for England in 1983. One of *Wisden*'s Five Cricketers of the Year, 1983

Opinions on cricket: 'Still feel the game is undersold and that too few clubs employ successful, proven, get-up-and-go marketing managers. Welcome four-day cricket as it should help to produce more potential Test players.'

Best batting performance: 217 Hampshire v Warwickshire, Edgbaston 1987
Best bowling performance: 5-69 Hampshire v Sussex, Southampton 1988

LAST SEASON: BATTING

	I.	N.O.	R.	H.S.	AV.
TEST					
1ST-CLASS	43	3	1436	124*	35.90
INT					
RAL	14	4	265	70	26.50
NAT.W.	4	1	268	117	89.33
B & H	7	2	201	70*	40.20

LAST SEASON: BOWLING

	O.	M.	R.	W.	AV.
TEST					
1ST-CLASS	49	1	171	5	34.20
INT					
RAL					
NAT.W.	3	0	27	2	13.50
B & H					

CAREER: BATTING

	I.	N.O.	R.	H.S.	AV.
TEST	14	1	392	91	30.15
1ST-CLASS	354	45	12967	217	41.96
INT	4	0	109	70	27.25
RAL	88	17	2779	95	39.12
NAT.W.	20	4	756	140*	47.25
B & H	25	4	647	82*	30.80

CAREER: BOWLING

	O.	M.	R.	W.	AV.
TEST	17	4	39	3	13.00
1ST-CLASS	641.5	115	2414	40	60.35
INT	6	0	28	2	14.00
RAL	3.3	1	10	2	5.00
NAT.W.	15	3	59	5	11.80
B & H					

SMITH, D. M. Sussex

SMITH, D. M. — Sussex

Full Name: David Mark Smith
Role: Left-hand bat, right-arm fast-medium bowler
Born: 9 January 1956, Balham
Height: 6' 4" **Weight:** 15st
Nickname: Smudger, Tom
County debut: 1973 (Surrey), 1984 (Worcestershire)
County cap: 1980 (Surrey), 1984 (Worcestershire)
Test debut: 1985–86
No. of Tests: 2
No. of One-Day Internationals: 1
1000 runs in a season: 4
1st-Class 50s scored: 48
1st-Class 100s scored: 19
One-Day 50s: 26
One-Day 100s: 4
Place in batting averages: 18th av. 48.86 (1987 53rd av. 37.95)

416

1st-Class catches 1988: 3 (career 142)
Parents: Dennis Henry and Tina
Wife and date of marriage: Jacqui, 7 January 1977
Children: Sarah Jane Louise, 4 April 1982
Family links with cricket: Father plays cricket for the BBC
Education: Battersea Grammar School
Qualifications: 3 O-levels
Jobs outside cricket: Two years with insurance company, one year with Harrods, one year spent in Zimbabwe, two years with building firm. Contracts manager, painting and decorating firm
Cricketing superstitions or habits: 'No room for them all.'
Overseas tours: West Indies with England 1986
Overseas teams played for: Sydney University, Australia, 1980–81, 1982–83
Cricketers particularly learnt from: Mickey Stewart, Graham Roope
Cricketers particularly admired: Graham Gooch, Malcolm Marshall, Ian Botham
Other sports played: Football, motor racing
Relaxations: 'I own my own racing car.'
Extras: Played for Surrey 2nd XI in 1972. Was not retained after 1977 but was re-instated in 1978. Top of Surrey first-class batting averages in 1982. Sacked by Surrey during 1983 season. Joined Worcestershire in 1984. Rejoined Surrey in 1987. Released by Surrey at end of 1988 season. Joined Sussex for 1989
Best batting performance: 189* Worcestershire v Kent, Worcester, 1984
Best bowling performance: 3-40 Surrey v Sussex, The Oval 1976

LAST SEASON: BATTING

	I.	N.O.	R.	H.S.	AV.
TEST					
1ST-CLASS	18	5	630	157*	48.46
INT					
RAL	9	0	282	75	31.33
NAT.W.	2	0	49	44	24.50
B & H	2	0	187	85	46.75

LAST SEASON: BOWLING

	O.	M.	R.	W.	AV.
TEST					
1ST-CLASS					
INT					
RAL					
NAT.W.					
B & H					

CAREER: BATTING

	I.	N.O.	R.	H.S.	AV.
TEST	4	0	80	47	20.00
1ST-CLASS	353	71	10085	189*	35.76
INT	1	1	10	10*	–
RAL	124	26	2708	87*	27.63
NAT.W.	27	5	1027	109	46.68
B & H	50	9	1550	126	37.80

CAREER: BOWLING

	O.	M.	R.	W.	AV.
TEST					
1ST-CLASS	456	96	1520	30	50.66
INT					
RAL	124.5	6	606	12	50.50
NAT.W.	31	6	118	4	29.50
B & H	56	4	266	8	33.25

---

150. Which Indian was one of only two players ever to score a century in both his first-class and Test debuts?

SMITH, N. M. K.　　　　　Warwickshire

Full Name: Neil Michael Knight Smith
Role: Right-hand bat, off-spin bowler, slip fielder
Born: 27 July 1967, Solihull
Height: 6′ **Weight:** 12½st
Nickname: Smudge, Kit, Alpha
County debut: 1987
1st-Class catches 1988: 0 (career 1)
Parents: Mike (M.J.K.) and Diana
Marital status: Single
Family links with cricket: Father captained Warwickshire and England
Education: Warwick School
Qualifications: 3 O-levels (Maths, English, French); cricket coach Grade 1
Off-season 1988–89: 'In Perth for six months, coaching and playing.'
Cricketing superstitions or habits: 'I always say see you in a minute when leaving the pavilion to go out to bat.'
Overseas tours: South America 1987; Barbados 1987–88
Cricketers particularly learnt from: Father
Cricketers particularly admired: David Gower, John Emburey
Other sports played: Rugby, squash, golf, tennis
Other sports followed: Any sport
Relaxations: Music, television, watching sport
Best batting performance: 23 Warwickshire v Lancashire, Southport 1987
　　　　　　　　　　　　　23 Warwickshire v Nottinghamshire, Worksop 1987
Best bowling performance: 2-73 Warwickshire v Lancashire, Southport 1987

LAST SEASON: BATTING

	I.	N.O.	R.	H.S.	AV.
TEST					
1ST-CLASS	1	0	3	3	3.00
INT					
RAL	3	0	5	3	1.66
NAT.W.					
B & H					

CAREER: BATTING

	I.	N.O.	R.	H.S.	AV.
TEST					
1ST-CLASS	5	1	59	23	14.75
INT					
RAL	4	0	27	22	6.75
NAT.W.					
B & H					

LAST SEASON: BOWLING

	O.	M.	R.	W.	AV.
TEST					
1ST-CLASS					
INT					
RAL	4	0	19	0	–
NAT.W.					
B & H					

CAREER: BOWLING

	O.	M.	R.	W.	AV.
TEST					
1ST-CLASS	42	6	152	4	38.00
INT					
RAL	11	0	64	1	64.00
NAT.W.					
B & H					

SMITH, P. A. Warwickshire

Full Name: Paul Andrew Smith
Role: Right-hand bat, right-arm
fast-medium bowler, cover fielder
Born: 15 April 1964, Newcastle-
on-Tyne
Height: 6′ 2″ **Weight:** 12st
Nickname: Smithy, Jim
County debut: 1982
County cap: 1986
1000 runs in a season: 2
1st-Class 50s scored: 36
1st-Class 100s scored: 2
One-Day 50s: 4
Place in batting averages: 152nd
av. 23.56 (1987 183rd av. 19.46)
Place in bowling averages: 39th
av. 23.47 (1987 133rd av. 46.05)
Strike rate 1988: 42.91 (career 59.41)
1st-Class catches 1988: 3 (career 38)
Parents: Kenneth and Joy
Wife and date of marriage: Caroline, 31 July 1987
Children: Oliver James, 5 February 1988
Family links with cricket: Father played for Leicestershire and Northumber-
land. Both brothers played for Warwickshire
Education: Heaton Grammar School, Newcastle
Qualifications: 5 O-levels
Jobs outside cricket: Warehouseman 1985–86. Works for *Birmingham Post
and Mail* in winters
Off-season 1988–89: Working for *Birmingham Post and Mail*
Cricketing superstitions or habits: 'Sometimes use lucky kit again. It
varies.'
Overseas teams played for: Florida, Johannesburg, 1982–83; Belgrano CC,
Argentina 1983–84; Carlton, Melbourne, 1984–85
Cricketers particularly learnt from: Father, Dennis Amiss, David Brown,
Bob Willis
Cricketers particularly admired: Ian Botham, David (Vic) Thorne, Wayne
Larkins, Dennis Amiss
Other sports played: Occasional squash
Other sports followed: Anything but horse racing
Injuries 1988: Thigh strain, two broken fingers
Relaxations: Listening to music (Rolling Stones, The Doors, David Lee
Roth), reading music books, American cars
Extras: Along with Andy Moles set a new world record for most consecutive

50+ partnerships in first 12 innings together. 'In the past two years I have had more new helmets than bats.'

Opinions on cricket: 'I think four-day cricket is a really good idea, *but* wickets for those games must be good and not green fliers. Would like to see batting gloves improved as there seem to be more and more broken fingers.'

Best batting performance: 119 Warwickshire v Worcestershire, Edgbaston 1986

Best bowling performance: 4-25 Warwickshire v Lancashire, Edgbaston 1985

LAST SEASON: BATTING

	I.	N.O.	R.	H.S.	AV.
TEST					
1ST-CLASS	27	4	542	84*	23.56
INT					
RAL	10	1	165	48	18.33
NAT.W.	2	0	11	6	5.50
B & H	5	0	76	43	15.20

CAREER: BATTING

	I.	N.O.	R.	H.S.	AV.
TEST					
1ST-CLASS	213	24	5252	119	27.78
INT					
RAL	68	18	1079	56	21.58
NAT.W.	14	2	270	79	22.50
B & H	21	3	299	43	16.61

LAST SEASON: BOWLING

	O.	M.	R.	W.	AV.
TEST					
1ST-CLASS	164.3	20	540	23	23.47
INT					
RAL	46.1	4	219	8	27.37
NAT.W.	21	3	73	3	24.33
B & H	15.2	0	83	0	—

CAREER: BOWLING

	O.	M.	R.	W.	AV.
TEST					
1ST-CLASS	1287.2	159	5428	130	41.75
INT					
RAL	302.2	9	1638	50	32.76
NAT.W.	82.4	6	317	12	26.41
B & H	72.3	4	342	10	34.20

SMITH, R. A. — Hampshire

Full Name: Robin Arnold Smith
Role: Right-hand bat, wrist spinner, gully fielder
Born: 13 September 1963, Durban, South Africa
Height: 5′ 11¾″ **Weight:** 15st 3lbs
Nickname: The Judge
County debut: 1982
County cap: 1985
Test debut: 1988
No. of Tests: 3
No of One-Day Internationals: 3
1000 runs in a season: 3
1st-Class 50s scored: 35
1st-Class 100s scored: 14
1st-Class 200s scored: 1
One-Day 50s: 15
One-Day 100s: 3
Place in batting averages: av. 39.88 (1987 13th av. 48.27)

1st-Class catches 1988: 15 (career 87)
Parents: John Arnold and Elaine Jessie
Wife and date of marriage: Katherine, 21 September 1988
Family links with cricket: Grandfather played for Natal in Currie Cup. Brother Chris plays for Hampshire, Natal and England
Education: Northlands Boys High, Durban
Qualifications: 'Highly qualified.' Qualified saddler
Jobs outside cricket: Financial adviser
Off-season 1988–89: Skiing in Switzerland
Cricketing superstitions or habits: 'A few beers the night before a game.'
Overseas teams played for: Natal in South African Currie Cup season 1980–84; Perth, Western Australia
Cricketers particularly learnt from: Brother Chris, Barry Richards, Mike Procter
Cricketers particularly admired: Malcolm Marshall, Allan Border, Graeme Hick
Other sports played: Squash, golf, snow and water skiing
Other sports followed: Soccer, athletics, most sports
Injuries 1988: Tore calf muscle in Fourth Test v West Indies
Relaxations: 'Reading Jeffrey Archer novels, trout fishing, siestas, keeping fit and spending as much time as possible with my lovely wife!'
Extras: Played rugby for Natal Schools, 1980. South Africa Schools Cricket, 1979–80. Still holds nineteen school athletics records and two South African schools records in shot putt and 100 metre hurdles
Opinions on cricket: 'I think four-day cricket so far has been a great success. I think the standard of umpiring in England is of a very high quality in comparison to umpiring in other parts of the world.'
Best batting performance: 209* Hampshire v Essex, Southampton 1987
Best bowling performance: 2-11 Hampshire v Surrey, Southampton 1985

LAST SEASON: BATTING

	I.	N.O.	R.	H.S.	AV.
TEST	6	1	145	57	29.00
1ST-CLASS	36	7	1211	141*	41.75
INT	1	0	9	9	9.00
RAL	12	0	317	57	26.41
NAT.W.	4	0	115	40	28.75
B & H	6	2	163	87*	40.75

LAST SEASON: BOWLING

	O.	M.	R.	W.	AV.
TEST					
1ST-CLASS	6.1	1	35	0	–
INT					
RAL					
NAT.W.					
B & H					

CAREER: BATTING

	I.	N.O.	R.	H.S.	AV.
TEST	6	1	145	57	29.00
1ST-CLASS	222	41	7188	209*	39.71
INT	1	0	9	9	9.00
RAL	54	9	1732	104	38.48
NAT.W.	11	1	416	110	41.60
B & H	17	3	487	81	34.78

CAREER: BOWLING

	O.	M.	R.	W.	AV.
TEST					
1ST-CLASS	100.3	15	443	9	49.22
INT					
RAL					
NAT.W.	2.5	0	13	2	6.50
B & H	1	0	2	0	–

Full Name: Nicholas Jason Speak
Role: Right-hand opening bat, off-break bowler, slip fielder
Born: 21 October 1966, Manchester
Height: 6′ 0″ **Weight:** 11st
Nickname: Speaky
County debut: 1987
1st-Class catches 1988: 2 (career 2)
Parents: John and Irene
Marital status: Single
Family links with cricket: Father was league professional in Lancashire and Yorkshire
Education: Parrswood High School and Sixth Form College
Qualifications: 5 O-levels; NCA Coaching Certificate
Jobs outside cricket: YTS with Lancashire CCC (1986)
Cricketing superstitions or habits: 'Still practising with my local club during the week.'
Overseas tours: NAYC North (for International Youth Competition) to Bermuda 1985; Lancashire CCC pre-season tour to Jamaica 1987
Overseas teams played for: Taradale CC, Napier, New Zealand 1985; Napier Old Boys CC (contracted player), New Zealand 1986 and 1987
Cricketers particularly learned from: Harry Pilling, Alan Ormrod, David Hughes
Cricketers particularly admired: Clive Lloyd, Geoff Boycott, Richard Hadlee, Martin Crowe, Ian Botham
Other sports played: Football, lacrosse, golf
Other sports followed: Golf, tennis, American football
Relaxations: General interest in all sports, music, reading
Opinions on cricket: 'One overseas player per county, with a minimum of a five-year contract. The return of spin bowlers to county and Test cricket. To

LAST SEASON: BATTING

	I.	N.O.	R.	H.S.	AV.
TEST					
1ST-CLASS	2	0	45	35	22.50
INT					
RAL					
NAT.W.					
B & H					

CAREER: BATTING

	I.	N.O.	R.	H.S.	AV.
TEST					
1ST-CLASS	4	0	49	35	12.25
INT					
RAL	1	0	13	13	13.00
NAT.W.					
B & H					

have more U-25 matches at county level. To see return of South Africa to Test cricket. To see Holland reach Test level, along with Zimbabwe.'
Best batting performance: 35 Lancashire v Gloucestershire, Old Trafford 1988

SPEIGHT, M. P. Sussex

Full Name: Martin Peter Speight
Role: Right-hand bat, wicket-keeper/close fielder
Born: 24 October 1967, Walsall
Height: 5′ 10¼″ **Weight:** 10st 10lbs
Nickname: Sprog, Hoover
County debut: 1986
1st-Class 50s scored: 2
One-Day 50s: 1
Place in batting averages: 195th av. 19.84
1st-Class catches 1988: 5 (career 11)
Parents: Peter John and Valerie
Marital status: Single
Education: Hassocks' Infants School; The Windmill's School, Hassocks; Hurstpierpoint College Junior and Senior Schools; Durham University
Qualifications: 13 O-levels, 3 A-levels; halfway through Degree in Archaeology/Ancient History
Jobs outside cricket: Student
Off-season 1988–89: Student at Durham University (last year)
Cricketing superstitions or habits: Left pad on first
Overseas tours: NCA to Bermuda 1985; Hurstpierpoint College to India 1985–86; England YCs Tour to Sri Lanka 1987; Durham University to Barbados 1988 (hockey)
Cricketers particularly learnt from: Derek Semmence (coach at Hurstpierpoint College), Paul Parker
Cricketers particularly admired: Viv Richards, David Gower, Dennis Lillee
Other sports played: Hockey, squash, rowing, golf, tennis
Other sports followed: Golf, tennis, football
Relaxations: Music, TV, drawing, oil paintings (landscapes)
Extras: 148* v Sutton Valence Old Boys, Brewer's Cup Final (1988); Member of Durham University UAU Winners (1987), Runners Up (1988); Member of Combined Universities' XI in B & H Cup (1987, 1988)
Opinions on cricket: 'Over rates put undue pressure on bowlers and team as a

whole (especially towards end of season if below required rate). One overseas player per county *only* under contract/able to play. Individuals should be allowed to coach in South Africa (a valuable source of income and experience for many players during the winter months).'

Best batting performance: 58 Sussex v Hampshire, Southampton 1988
Best bowling performance: 1-2 Sussex v Middlesex, Hove 1988

LAST SEASON: BATTING

	I.	N.O.	R.	H.S.	AV.
TEST					
1ST-CLASS	13	0	258	58	19.84
INT					
RAL	4	0	87	37	21.75
NAT.W.					
B & H		0	128	83	32.00

CAREER: BATTING

	I.	N.O.	R.	H.S.	AV.
TEST					
1ST-CLASS	15	0	279	58	18.60
INT					
RAL	4	0	87	37	21.75
NAT.W.					
B & H	6	0	151	83	25.16

LAST SEASON: WICKET KEEPING

	C.	ST.		
TEST				
1ST-CLASS				
INT				
RAL				
NAT.W.				
B & H	3	–		

CAREER: WICKET KEEPING

	C.	ST.		
TEST				
1ST-CLASS				
INT				
RAL	1	–		
NAT.W.				
B & H	6	–		

STANDING, D. K. Sussex

Full Name: David Kevin Standing
Role: Right-hand bat, off-break bowler
Born: 21 October 1963, Brighton
Height: 5′ 7″ **Weight:** 11st
Nickname: Uppers, Theo, Gummy
County debut: 1983
1st-Class 50s scored: 5
Place in batting averages: —
(1987 201st av. 17.03)
1st-Class catches 1988: 0 (career 17)
Parents: David Eric and Valerie Mavis
Marital status: Single
Family links with cricket: Father was good local cricketer
Education: Tideway School, Newhaven; Brighton and Hove VI Form
Qualifications: 9 O-levels, 1 A-level, coaching certificate
Jobs outside cricket: Crown Financial Management

Overseas tours: Sussex Young Cricketers to West Indies (as captain) 1983
Cricketers particularly learnt from: Paul Parker
Cricketers particularly admired: Greg Chappell
Other sports played: Golf (as much as possible)
Relaxations: Reading, music, drinking – anything other than cricket
Extras: Captained England Schools U-15. Played for England Schools U-19. Released by Sussex at end of 1988 season
Opinions on cricket: 'Too much cricket played. Welcome four-day county cricket. Uncovered pitches have caused more hours spent in the pavilion and have done nothing to encourage young spinners as fast bowlers can still stand up.'
Best batting performance: 65 Sussex v Warwickshire, Edgbaston 1986
Best bowling performance: 2-28 Sussex v New Zealand, Hove 1986

LAST SEASON: BATTING

	I.	N.O.	R.	H.S.	AV.
TEST					
1ST-CLASS	3	0	13	9	4.33
INT					
RAL	1	1	2	2*	–
NAT.W.	1	0	4	4	4.00
B & H	3	2	43	42*	43.00

CAREER: BATTING

	I.	N.O.	R.	H.S.	AV.
TEST					
1ST-CLASS	70	10	1130	65	18.83
INT					
RAL	3	2	14	8*	14.00
NAT.W.	3	2	5	4	5.00
B & H	3	2	43	42*	43.00

LAST SEASON: BOWLING

	O.	M.	R.	W.	AV.
TEST					
1ST-CLASS					
INT					
RAL	17	0	107	3	35.66
NAT.W.					
B & H	17.5	1	73	3	24.33

CAREER: BOWLING

	O.	M.	R.	W.	AV.
TEST					
1ST-CLASS	230.5	42	725	6	120.83
INT					
RAL	54.1	1	283	10	28.30
NAT.W.	17	3	54	2	27.00
B & H	18.5	1	80	3	26.66

151. Who is Chief Executive of the Test and County Cricket Board?

152. Who has hit the most first-class sixes in an English season and how many?

STANLEY, N. A.   Northamptonshire

Full Name: Neil Alan Stanley
Role: Right-hand bat, right-arm medium bowler
Born: 16 May 1968, Bedford
Height: 6′ 3″ **Weight:** 14st 4lbs
Nickname: Giz, Stanners
County debut: 1988
1st-Class 50s scored: 3
1st-Class catches 1988: 4 (career 4)
Parents: Jack and Julie Margaret
Marital status: Single
Education: Bedford Modern School
Qualifications: 7 O-levels, NCA senior coaching award
Jobs outside cricket: Postman, chicken farmer
Off-season 1988–89: Working in Bedford
Cricketing superstitions or habits:
'Change bats if not scoring runs; left pad first, chew gum when batting.'
Overseas tours: Bedford Modern School to Barbados 1983; Young England to Youth World Cup, Australia 1988
Cricketers particularly learnt from: Bob Carter, Brian Reynolds, all at Northampton
Cricketers particularly admired: Ian Botham, Wayne Larkins
Other sports played: Table tennis (for Bedfordshire), football, golf
Other sports followed: Snooker
Injuries 1988: Broken right thumb
Relaxations: Listening to music, watching Clint Eastwood films
Opinions on cricket: 'Too much cricket played. Clubs should make more effort to find employment in UK for players during the winter. Politics should be kept out of cricket. A higher percentage of 2nd XI games should be played on first-class grounds.'
Best batting performance: 66 Northamptonshire v Oxford University, Oxford 1988

LAST SEASON: BATTING

	I.	N.O.	R.	H.S.	AV.
TEST					
1ST-CLASS	12	2	263	66	26.30
INT					
RAL	7	3	65	18	16.25
NAT.W.					
B & H	2	0	13	8	6.50

CAREER: BATTING

	I.	N.O.	R.	H.S.	AV.
TEST					
1ST-CLASS	12	2	263	66	26.30
INT					
RAL	7	3	65	18	16.25
NAT.W.					
B & H	2	0	13	8	6.50

STEPHENSON, F. D.   Nottinghamshire

Full Name: Franklyn Dacosta Stephenson
Role: Right-arm fast bowler, right-hand bat
Born: 8 April 1959, Barbados
Height: 6′ 4″ **Weight:** 13st 7lbs
Nickname: Cookie, Stevo
County debut: 1982 (Gloucestershire), 1988 (Nottinghamshire)
County cap: 1988 (Nottinghamshire)
1st-Class 50s scored: 12
1st-Class 100s scored: 3
1st-Class 5 w. in innings: 16
1st-Class 10 w. in match: 4
Place in batting averages: 102nd av. 29.08
Place in bowling averages: 8th av. 18.31
Strike rate 1988: 39.32 (career 42.09)
1st-Class catches 1988: 10 (career 29)

Parents: Leonard Young and Violet
Wife: Julia
Children: Amanda
Education: St John Baptist Mixed School; Samuel Jackson Prescod Polytechnic
Jobs outside cricket: Hotel porter. Golf pro in Barbados
Off-season 1988–89: Playing cricket at home in Barbados
Overseas tours: With West Indies Under-19s to England, 1978
Overseas teams played for: Tasmania 1981–82; Barbados
Cricketers particularly admired: Charles Griffith, Collis King
Other sports played: Lawn tennis, golf (off scratch)
Other sports followed: Athletics
Injuries 1988: Broken nose by Kevin Curran of Gloucestershire in May caused him to miss two matches
Relaxations: Movies, card games, pool and snooker.
Extras: After being introduced to English League Cricket in 1979 with Littleborough in the Central Lancashire League, had three consecutive success-filled championships. In 1980 with Royton, took 100 wickets and scored 621 runs (first time in 66 years); with Rawtenstall in 1981 and 1982, took 105 wickets and 559 runs, and over 100 wickets and over 500 runs respectively; and also participated in Barbados 10th Shell Shield championship victory in 16 years in 1982. Top of Gloucestershire first-class bowling averages in 1982. Banned for life by West Indies for taking part in two rebel tours of South Africa. In 1988, did the double when he scored 1018 first-class

runs and took 125 first-class wickets. Britannic Assurance Player of the Year, 1988

Opinions on cricket: 'I fail to see how the further limitation of overseas players can be the answer to the lack of outstanding English players; or, for that matter the low gate receipts being experienced by the county clubs. I think that a lot more can be done to promote and sell the game in England; and along those lines I think that the English officials can take a hint from Australian cricket authorities especially with Test tours etc. I don't think it will do much for the players–officials relationship when the umpires are asked to run to Lord's shouting "dissent" every time a player sneezes too hard on the field of play.'

Best batting performance: 165 Barbados v Leeward Islands, Basseterre 1981–82

Best bowling performance: 7–56 Nottinghamshire v Northamptonshire, Trent Bridge 1988

LAST SEASON: BATTING

	I.	N.O.	R.	H.S.	AV.
TEST					
1ST-CLASS	35	0	1018	117	29.08
INT					
RAL	12	3	147	43	16.33
NAT.W.	–	–	–	–	–
B & H	3	0	21	10	7.00

CAREER: BATTING

	I.	N.O.	R.	H.S.	AV.
TEST					
1ST-CLASS	82	5	1991	165	25.85
INT					
RAL	19	5	239	43	17.07
NAT.W.	1	0	7	7	7.00
B & H	3	0	21	10	7.00

LAST SEASON: BOWLING

	O.	M.	R.	W.	AV.
TEST					
1ST-CLASS	819.1	196	2289	125	18.31
INT					
RAL	96	11	419	22	19.04
NAT.W.	22	7	74	3	24.66
B & H	43.2	6	113	6	18.83

CAREER: BOWLING

	O.	M.	R.	W.	AV.
TEST					
1ST-CLASS	1648.4	368	4850	235	20.63
INT					
RAL	160	16	707	36	19.63
NAT.W.	44	11	136	7	19.42
B & H	43.2	6	113	6	18.33

153. Whose record did Ian Botham break for the fastest Test double of 1000 runs and 100 wickets?

154. Who was chosen as Wombwell Cricket Lovers 'Cricketer of the Year' 1988?

STEPHENSON, J. P. Essex

Full Name: John Patrick Stephenson
Role: Right-hand opening bat, right-arm medium bowler
Born: 14 March 1965, Stebbing
Height: 6' 1" **Weight:** 12½st
Nickname: Stanley, Svensson
County debut: 1985
1st-Class 50s scored: 12
One-Day 50s: 2
Place in batting averages: 100th av. 29.29 (1987 130th av. 27.10)
1st-Class catches 1988: 13 (career 30)
Parents: Patrick and Eve
Marital status: Single
Family links with cricket: 'Father member of Rugby Meteors Cricketer Cup winning side in 1973. Three brothers in Felstead 1st XI; Guy played for Essex 2nd XI; Mark and Paul play for Rickling Green and Felstead Robins, as does Father; Mum does my whites!'
Education: Felstead Prep School; Felstead Senior School; Durham University
Qualifications: 7 O-levels, 3 A-levels; NCA Coaching Award; General Arts BA
Jobs outside cricket: Refrigeration engineering with Cullen and Sons 1987; resident tutor Melbourne CEGS 1987–88; groundsman, Fitzroy CC, 1984
Off-season 1988–89: Playing for Boland in South Africa
Cricketing superstitions or habits: 'They change with my form.'
Overseas tours: Zimbabwe 1982–83 with ESCA U-19s; Barbados with Keith Pont Benefit 1986
Overseas teams played for: Fitzroy CC, Melbourne 1983–84; Fitzroy-Doncaster 1987–88; Crusaders CC 1983–84, 1987–88; Boland 1988–89
Cricketers particularly learnt from: Gordon Barker, Ray East, Keith Fletcher, Graham Gooch
Cricketers particularly admired: Graham Gooch, Brian Hardie and many others
Other sports played: Squash, hockey, snooker, golf
Other sports followed: Most except horse racing and synchronised swimming
Relaxations: Music – The Smiths, and many other bands, including New Order, Talk Talk, Prefab, Bible, Minds; keeping fit; Stan Barstow; P. G. Wodehouse
Extras: Scored 1100 runs in 2nd XI and 791 in 1st XI in 1988. Awarded 2nd XI

cap in 1984 when leading run-scorer with Essex 2nd XI. Young Player of the Year 1985 for Essex CCC. Captained Durham University to victory in UAU Competition 1986. Captain of Combined Universities team 1987 in the first year that it was drawn from all universities

Opinions on cricket: 'Four-day cricket to stay and hopefully take over as long as wickets improve across the country. Less 40-over cricket. Abolish 5-over rule for substitute fielders. One registered overseas player per county. No restraint of trade.'

Best batting performance: 99 Essex v Leicestershire, Chelmsford 1988
Best bowling performance: 2-66 Essex v Surrey, The Oval 1988

LAST SEASON: BATTING

	I.	N.O.	R.	H.S.	AV.
TEST					
1ST-CLASS	31	4	791	99	29.29
INT					
RAL	6	2	44	22*	11.00
NAT.W.	1	1	31	31*	—
B & H					

CAREER: BATTING

	I.	N.O.	R.	H.S.	AV.
TEST					
1ST-CLASS	80	8	1967	99	27.31
INT					
RAL	17	4	260	45	20.00
NAT.W.	4	1	92	55	30.66
B & H	3	0	119	75	39.66

LAST SEASON: BOWLING

	O.	M.	R.	W.	AV.
TEST					
1ST-CLASS	71.2	16	212	5	42.40
INT					
RAL	18.2	1	92	1	92.00
NAT.W.					
B & H					

CAREER: BOWLING

	O.	M.	R.	W.	AV.
TEST					
1ST-CLASS	98.3	19	311	6	51.83
INT					
RAL	18.2	1	92	1	92.00
NAT.W.					
B & H	16	0	75	2	37.50

STEWART, A. J. Surrey

Full Name: Alec James Stewart
Role: Right-hand bat, right-arm medium bowler, occasional wicket-keeper
Born: 8 April 1963, Merton
Nickname: Stewie
Height: 5′ 11″ **Weight:** 12st
County debut: 1981
County cap: 1985
1000 runs in a season: 4
1st-Class 50s scored: 39
1st-Class 100s scored: 10
One-Day 50s: 11
One-Day 100s: 1
Place in batting averages: 62nd av. 34.68 (1987 52nd av. 38.09)
1st-Class catches 1988: 25 (career 125 + 3 stumpings)

Parents: Michael James and Sheila Marie Macdonald
Marital status: Single
Family links with cricket: Father played for England (1962–64) and Surrey (1954–72). Brother Neil plays club cricket and Surrey 2nd XI; sister, Judy, plays for Malden Wanderers Ladies XI
Education: Tiffin Grammar School
Qualifications: 4 O-levels
Jobs outside cricket: Sales rep for Slater-Gartrell Sports, Western Australia
Off-season 1988–89: Playing for Midland-Guildford CC in Australia
Cricketing superstitions or habits: 'Always put left foot on to cricket field first, when going out to bat.'
Overseas tours: 1980–81 tour of Australia with Surrey U-19
Overseas teams played for: Midland-Guildford CC, Western Australia 1981–88
Cricketers particularly learnt from: Geoff Arnold, Kevin Gartrell
Cricketers particularly admired: Geoff Boycott, Alan Knott
Other sports played: All sports
Other sports followed: All sports, watches Chelsea FC
Injuries 1988: Broken thumb
Relaxations: Music, Perth beaches
Opinions on cricket: 'Four-day cricket is a must. Standard of pitches should be the highest standard possible.'
Best batting performance: 166 Surrey v Kent, The Oval 1986

LAST SEASON: BATTING

	I.	N.O.	R.	H.S.	AV.
TEST					
1ST-CLASS	32	3	1006	133	34.68
INT					
RAL	12	0	339	60	28.25
NAT.W.	4	1	214	107*	71.33
B & H	4	1	150	57*	50.00

CAREER: BATTING

	I.	N.O.	R.	H.S.	AV.
TEST					
1ST-CLASS	183	19	6029	166	36.76
INT					
RAL	64	7	1264	86	22.17
NAT.W.	11	2	420	107*	46.66
B & H	16	2	318	63*	22.71

155. Who took all 10 wickets in an innings for Western Province v Orange Free State in the 1987–88 Currie Cup?

156. Which player hit most first-class sixes in the English 1988 season, and how many?

Full Name: Alastair Caleb Storie
Role: Right-hand bat, right-arm medium bowler, short-leg fielder
Born: 25 July 1965, Glasgow
Height: 5′ 8″ **Weight:** 10st
Nickname: Ally, Wolf, Ratsky
County debut: 1985 (Northamptonshire), 1987 (Warwickshire)
1st-Class 50s scored: 6
1st-Class 100s scored: 1
One-Day 50s: 3
Place in batting averages: 207th av. 17.00 (1987 156th av. 22.77)
1st-Class catches 1988: 6 (career 28)
Parents: Hank and Jenny
Marital status: Single
Family links with cricket: Father played club cricket in Glasgow and Johannesburg
Education: St Stithians College, Johannesburg; UNISA Correspondence University
Qualifications: JMB Matriculation; BA English I and English II; NCA coaching certificate
Off-season 1988–89: Studying in England
Cricketing superstitions or habits: Always puts left pad on first
Overseas teams played for: Transvaal Schools 1978–83; Transvaal B 1984; Orange Free State 1987–88
Cricketers particularly learnt from: Willie Watson, Peter Stringer, Richard Lumb
Cricketers particularly admired: Clive Rice, Dennis Amiss, Wayne Larkins
Other sports played: Represented South Africa U-19 hockey team 1982–83
Other sports followed: Football, rugby union, hockey
Injuries 1988: Dislocated finger
Relaxations: Music, reading, stock market
Extras: First Northamptonshire batsman to score a 100 on first-class debut. Left to join Warwickshire for 1987 season. Scored 50s on both B & H and Sunday League debuts. Took five catches in an innings v Leicestershire at Edgbaston 1988. Released after 1988 season
Opinions on cricket: 'Part of the reason England have a strong one-day side but a comparatively weak Test side is because we are channelled towards one-day cricket through a financial need. Four-day cricket is a good idea as it

will assist in the development of Test cricketers, provided we play on a higher standard of pitches'

Best batting performance: 106 Northamptonshire v Hampshire, Northampton 1985

LAST SEASON: BATTING

	I.	N.O.	R.	H.S.	AV.
TEST					
1ST-CLASS	17	2	255	68	17.00
INT					
RAL					
NAT.W.	2	0	4	3	2.00
B & H					

CAREER: BATTING

	I.	N.O.	R.	H.S.	AV.
TEST					
1ST-CLASS	75	12	1350	106	21.42
INT					
RAL	4	0	86	55	21.50
NAT.W.	4	2	44	24*	22.00
B & H	3	0	142	66	47.33

STOVOLD, A. W.   Gloucestershire

Full Name: Andrew Willis-Stovold
Role: Right-hand bat, wicket-keeper
Born: 19 March 1953, Bristol
Height: 5' 7" **Weight:** 12st 4lbs
Nickname: Stumper, Squeak, Stov, Stovers, Stubble
County debut: 1973
County cap: 1976
Benefit: 1987 (£75,000)
1000 runs in a season: 8
1st-Class 50s scored: 96
1st-Class 100s scored: 19
1st-Class 200s scored: 1
One-Day 50s: 34
One-Day 100s: 4
Place in batting averages: 60th av. 35.02 (1987 152nd av. 24.09)
1st-Class catches 1988: 14 (career 284)
Parents: Lancelot Walter and Dorothy Patricia
Wife and date of marriage: Kay Elizabeth, 30 September 1978
Children: Nicholas, 18 June 1981; Neil, 24 February 1983
Family links with cricket: Father played local club cricket for Old Down CC. Brother, Martin, also played county cricket for Gloucestershire
Education: Filton High School; Loughborough College of Education
Qualifications: Certificate of Education
Jobs outside cricket: Teacher at Tockington Manor Prep School
Cricketing superstitions or habits: 'Keeping the same routine until I have a bad run, then trying something else. Always prepare for batting in the same order.'

Overseas tours: England Schools to India 1970–71; England Young Cricketers to West Indies 1972

Overseas teams played for: Orange Free State 1974–76

Cricketers particularly admired: Mike Procter, Barry Richards, Richard Hadlee

Other sports played: Football, golf

Other sports followed: Rugby, hunting, horse racing

Relaxations: Gardening, walking

Extras: Writes a weekly article for *Gloucestershire Echo*. His 1987 benefit produced a record £75,000 for a Gloucestershire player

Opinions on cricket: 'Worried about the sudden increase in player "transfers". We must not let it get too much like football.'

Best batting performance: 212* Gloucestershire v Northamptonshire, Northampton 1982

Best bowling performance: 1-0 Gloucestershire v Derbyshire, Bristol 1976

LAST SEASON: BATTING

	I.	N.O.	R.	H.S.	AV.
TEST					
1ST-CLASS	39	2	1296	136	35.02
INT					
RAL	12	1	230	43*	20.90
NAT.W.	3	1	163	104*	81.50
B & H	4	0	133	78	33.25

LAST SEASON: BOWLING

	O.	M.	R.	W.	AV.
TEST					
1ST-CLASS					
INT					
RAL					
NAT.W.					
B & H					

CAREER: BATTING

	I.	N.O.	R.	H.S.	AV.
TEST					
1ST-CLASS	613	35	17417	212*	30.13
INT					
RAL	176	21	3703	98*	23.89
NAT.W.	32	3	1089	104*	37.55
B & H	60	8	1937	123	37.25

CAREER: BOWLING

	O.	M.	R.	W.	AV.
TEST					
1ST-CLASS	52.3	8	218	4	54.50
INT					
RAL					
NAT.W.					
B & H					

LAST SEASON: WICKET KEEPING

	C.	ST.
TEST		
1ST-CLASS		
INT		
RAL		
NAT.W.		
B & H		

CAREER: WICKET KEEPING

	C.	ST.
TEST		
1ST-CLASS	284	45
INT		
RAL	85	13
NAT.W.	17	5
B & H	37	4

157. Which player hit the second most first-class sixes in the English 1988 season, and how many?

158. Which player failed by only one run to hit 1000 first-class runs in the 1988 English season?

SUCH, P. M.   Leicestershire

Full Name: Peter Mark Such
Role: Right-hand bat, off-spin bowler
Born: 12 June 1964, Helensburgh,
Scotland
Height: 6′ **Weight:** 11st 7lbs
Nickname: Suchy
County debut: 1982
(Nottinghamshire), 1987
(Leicestershire)
1st-Class 5 w. in innings: 6
Place in bowling averages: 106th
av. 34.00 (1987 72nd av. 30.63)
Strike rate 1988: 74.30 (career 63.20)
1st-Class catches 1988: 0 (career 37)
Parents: John and Margaret
Marital status: Single
Family links with cricket: Father
and brother village cricketers
Education: Lantern Lane Primary
School; Harry Carlton Comprehensive
Qualifications: 9 O-levels, 3 A-levels. Qualified Cricket Coach (Senior)
Jobs outside cricket: Van driver, handyman, administration assistant
Off-season 1988–89: Working for rental company
Overseas teams played for: Kempton Park CC, South Africa 1982–83;
Bathurst CC, New South Wales 1985–86
Cricketers particularly learnt from: Bob White, Eddie Hemmings
Cricketers particularly admired: Richard Hadlee
Other sports played: Hockey, golf
Other sports followed: American football and most other sports

LAST SEASON: BATTING

	I.	N.O.	R.	H.S.	AV.
TEST					
1ST-CLASS	6	2	9	6	2.25
INT					
RAL	–	–	–	–	–
NAT.W.					
B & H					

LAST SEASON: BOWLING

	O.	M.	R.	W.	AV.
TEST					
1ST-CLASS	123.5	22	340	10	34.00
INT					
RAL	7	0	53	2	26.50
NAT.W.					
B & H					

CAREER: BATTING

	I.	N.O.	R.	H.S.	AV.
TEST					
1ST-CLASS	73	28	109	16	2.42
INT					
RAL	1	1	0	0*	–
NAT.W.					
B & H					

CAREER: BOWLING

	O.	M.	R.	W.	AV.
TEST					
1ST-CLASS	2022.4	549	5755	192	29.97
INT					
RAL	42	1	274	5	54.80
NAT.W.					
B & H	33	1	151	4	37.75

Relaxations: Music, TV, films, playing golf, gardening, reading
Extras: Played for Young England v Young Australia in three 'Tests' in 1983. Represented TCCB v New Zealand 1986. Left Nottinghamshire at end of 1986 season. Joined Leicestershire for 1987
Best batting performance: 16 Nottinghamshire v Middlesex, Lord's 1984
Best bowling performance: 6-123 Nottinghamshire v Kent, Trent Bridge 1983

SWALLOW, I. G. — Yorkshire

Full Name: Ian Geoffrey Swallow
Role: Right-hand bat, off-break bowler, cover or slip fielder
Born: 18 December 1962, Barnsley
Height: 5′ 7″ **Weight:** 10st
Nickname: Chicken, Swal
County debut: 1983
1st-Class 50s scored: 1
1st-Class 100s scored: 1
1st-Class 5 w. in innings: 1
Place in batting averages: 183rd av. 20.70 (1987 67th av. 35.57)
1st-Class catches 1988: 5 (career 23)
Parents: Geoffrey and Joyce
Marital status: Single
Family links with cricket: Father and brother both played for Elsecar Village CC
Education: Hayland Kirk, Balk, Comprehensive School; Barnsley Technical College

LAST SEASON: BATTING

	I.	N.O.	R.	H.S.	AV.
TEST					
1ST-CLASS	19	2	352	48*	20.70
INT					
RAL					
NAT.W.	–	–	–	–	–
B & H					

CAREER: BATTING

	I.	N.O.	R.	H.S.	AV.
TEST					
1ST-CLASS	62	16	1009	114	21.93
INT					
RAL	1	0	2	2	2.00
NAT.W.	–	–	–	–	–
B & H	3	2	18	10*	18.00

LAST SEASON: BOWLING

	O.	M.	R.	W.	AV.
TEST					
1ST-CLASS	88	15	311	2	155.50
INT					
RAL					
NAT.W.					
B & H					

CAREER: BOWLING

	O.	M.	R.	W.	AV.
TEST					
1ST-CLASS	855.5	193	2542	48	52.95
INT					
RAL	4	0	31	0	–
NAT.W.					
B & H	36	4	151	2	75.50

Qualifications: 3 O-levels
Jobs outside cricket: Storeman
Cricketing superstitions or habits: Always puts left pad on first
Overseas teams played for: Sunshine CC, Melbourne 1985–86, 1986–87
Cricketers particularly learnt from: Doug Padgett, Phil Carrick, Steve Oldham
Cricketers particularly admired: Viv Richards, John Emburey
Other sports played: Football and most sports for fun
Other sports followed: Barnsley FC, all sports
Relaxations: Sport in general
Extras: Took hat-trick v Warwickshire 2nd XI 1984. Figures: 4-3-2-4
Best batting performance: 114 Yorkshire v MCC, Scarborough 1987
Best bowling performance: 7-95 Yorkshire v Nottinghamshire, Trent Bridge 1987

SYKES, J. F.   Middlesex

Full Name: James Frederick Sykes
Role: Right-hand bat, off-break bowler, slip or gully fielder
Born: 30 December 1965, Shoreditch
Height: 6′ 2″ **Weight:** 13st 7lbs
Nickname: Eric, Sykesy
County debut: 1983
1st-Class 50s scored: 3
1st-Class 100s scored: 1
One-Day 50s: 1
Place in batting averages: 146th av. 24.33
1st-Class catches 1988: 3 (career 15)
Parents: James and Kathleen
Education: Bow Comprehensive
Qualifications: 1 O-level
Jobs outside cricket: Coaching in South Africa for 2 weeks
Cricketing superstitions or habits: 49, 99
Overseas tours: England U-19 to West Indies 1984–85
Cricketers particularly learnt from: John Emburey, Don Bennett, Graham Barlow, Wayne Daniel
Cricketers particularly admired: Clive Radley, Neil Williams
Other sports played: Squash, football

Best batting performance: 126 Middlesex v Cambridge University, Cambridge 1985
Best bowling performance: 4-49 Middlesex v Glamorgan, Cardiff 1987

LAST SEASON: BATTING

	I.	N.O.	R.	H.S.	AV.
TEST					
1ST-CLASS	13	1	292	88	24.33
INT					
RAL	8	3	131	57	26.20
NAT.W.					
B & H	1	0	24	24	24.00

CAREER: BATTING

	I.	N.O.	R.	H.S.	AV.
TEST					
1ST-CLASS	34	6	655	126	23.39
INT					
RAL	16	4	196	57	16.33
NAT.W.					
B & H	1	0	24	24	24.00

LAST SEASON: BOWLING

	O.	M.	R.	W.	AV.
TEST					
1ST-CLASS	60	9	205	1	205.00
INT					
RAL	44.1	2	224	8	28.00
NAT.W.					
B & H					

CAREER: BOWLING

	O.	M.	R.	W.	AV.
TEST					
1ST-CLASS	366.2	78	1110	26	42.69
INT					
RAL	130.1	3	566	20	28.30
NAT.W.					
B & H					

TAVARÉ, C. J. Kent

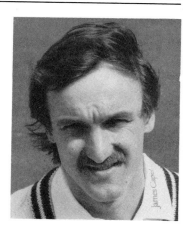

Full Name: Christopher James Tavaré
Role: Right-hand bat, off-break bowler, slip fielder
Born: 27 October 1954, Orpington
Height: 6′ 1½″ **Weight:** 12st 12lbs
Nickname: Tav, Rowdy
County debut: 1974
County cap: 1978
Benefit: 1988
Test debut: 1980
No. of Tests: 30
No. of One-Day Internationals: 29
1000 runs in a season: 12
1st-Class 50s scored: 103
1st-Class 100s scored: 35
One-Day 50s: 44
One-Day 100s: 8
Place in batting averages: 28th av. 42.02 (1987 87th av. 33.05)
1st-Class catches 1988: 29 (career 328)
Parents: Andrew and June
Wife and date of marriage: Vanessa, 22 March 1980

Family links with cricket: Father, uncle Jack Tavaré, and uncle, Derrick Attwood, all played school and club cricket, father and Uncle Jack at Chatham House, father and Uncle Derrick at Bickley Park CC. Elder brother, Stephen, and younger brother, Jeremy, both play cricket
Education: Sevenoaks School; Oxford University
Qualifications: Zoology degree
Jobs outside cricket: Consultant, N. M. Schroder Financial Management Ltd
Off-season 1988–89: Working for Schroders and completing benefit year
Overseas tours: England to India and Sri Lanka 1981–82; England to Australia and New Zealand 1982–83; England to New Zealand and Pakistan 1983–84
Overseas teams played for: University of Western Australia, Perth, 1977–78; West Perth CC for half a season 1978–79
Other sports followed: 'Take an interest in most sports, especially American football in winter.'
Relaxations: Music, zoology, films, gardening, woodwork, golf
Extras: Played for England Schools v All-India Schools at Birmingham in 1973, scoring 124*. Oxford University cricket blue 1975–76–77. Whitbread Scholarship to Perth, Australia, 1978–79. Suffers from asthma and hay-fever. Was top-scorer with 82* and Man of the Match, on debut for England in 55-over match v West Indies at Headingley, May 1980. Captain of Kent 1983–84. Rejected Kent's offer of a new contract for 1989
Best batting performance: 168* Kent v Essex, Chelmsford 1982
Best bowling performance: 1-3 Kent v Hampshire, Canterbury 1986

LAST SEASON: BATTING

	I.	N.O.	R.	H.S.	AV.
TEST					
1ST-CLASS	36	2	1429	138*	42.02
INT					
RAL	13	4	290	82*	32.22
NAT.W.	2	1	55	49	55.00
B & H	4	0	88	31	22.00

LAST SEASON: BOWLING

	O.	M.	R.	W.	AV.
TEST					
1ST-CLASS					
INT					
RAL					
NAT.W.					
B & H					

CAREER: BATTING

	I.	N.O.	R.	H.S.	AV.
TEST	55	2	1753	149	33.07
1ST-CLASS	497	57	16785	168*	38.14
INT	28	2	720	83*	27.69
RAL	156	23	4291	136*	32.26
NAT.W.	28	4	926	118*	38.58
B & H	70	4	1878	143	28.45

CAREER: BOWLING

	O.	M.	R.	W.	AV.
TEST	5	3	11	0	—
1ST-CLASS	102.5	15	514	5	102.80
INT	2	0	3	0	—
RAL					
NAT.W.					
B & H					

159. Who scored the first Test century ever?

TAYLOR, L. B.   Leicestershire

Full Name: Leslie Brian Taylor
Role: Right-hand bat, right-arm
fast-medium bowler
Born: 25 October 1953, Earl Shilton,
Leicestershire
Height: 6′ 3½″ **Weight:** 14st 7lbs
Nickname: Les
County debut: 1977
County cap: 1981
Benefit: 1989
Test debut: 1985
No. of Tests: 2
No. of One-Day Internationals: 2
1st-Class 50s scored: 1
1st-Class 5 w. in innings: 18
1st-Class 10 w. in match: 1
Place in bowling averages: 66th

av. 27.62 (1987 42nd av. 25.95)
Strike rate 1988: 55.62 (career 52.43)
1st-Class catches 1988: 4 (career 48)
Parents: Peggy and Cyril
Wife and date of marriage: Susan, 12 July 1973
Children: Jamie, 24 June 1976; Donna, 10 November 1978; Suzy, 3 June 1981
Family links with cricket: Relation of the late Sam Coe, holder of highest
individual score for Leicestershire, 252* v Northamptonshire at Leicester in
1914
Education: Heathfield High School, Earl Shilton
Qualifications: Qualified carpenter and joiner

LAST SEASON: BATTING

	I.	N.O.	R.	H.S.	AV.
TEST					
1ST-CLASS	16	6	111	60	11.10
INT					
RAL	5	2	10	5*	3.33
NAT.W.					
B & H	–	–	–	–	–

CAREER: BATTING

	I.	N.O.	R.	H.S.	AV.
TEST	1	1	1	1*	–
1ST-CLASS	180	77	1000	60	9.70
INT	1	1	1	1*	–
RAL	34	24	109	15*	10.90
NAT.W.	6	5	18	6*	18.00
B & H	10	5	18	5	3.60

LAST SEASON: BOWLING

	O.	M.	R.	W.	AV.
TEST					
1ST-CLASS	324.3	72	967	35	27.62
INT					
RAL	74.5	0	379	15	25.26
NAT.W.					
B & H	5	0	23	1	23.00

CAREER: BOWLING

	O.	M.	R.	W.	AV.
TEST	63.3	11	178	4	44.50
1ST-CLASS	4804.1	1174	13565	553	24.52
INT	14	3	47	0	
RAL	805.5	58	3543	165	21.47
NAT.W.	146.1	23	496	30	16.53
B & H	302	57	984	51	19.29

Overseas tours: South America with Derrick Robins' XI in 1978–79; West Indies with England 1986
Overseas teams played for: Natal 1982–84
Other sports: Swimming and football
Relaxations: Game-shooting and fox-hunting with the Atherstone Hunt
Extras: Was banned from Test cricket for three years for joining rebel England tour of South Africa in 1982
Opinions on cricket: 'Should not be subjected to over-rate fines in one-day cricket.'
Best batting performance: 60 Leicestershire v Essex, Chelmsford 1988
Best bowling performance: 7-28 Leicestershire v Derbyshire, Leicester 1981

TAYLOR, N. R. Kent

Full Name: Neil Royston Taylor
Role: Right-hand bat, off-break bowler, outfielder
Born: 21 July 1959, Farnborough, Kent
Height: 6' 1" **Weight:** 13st 10lbs
Nickname: Map
County debut: 1979
County cap: 1982
1000 runs in a season: 5
1st-Class 50s scored: 39
1st-Class 100s scored: 20
One-Day 50s: 14
One-Day 100s: 4
Place in batting averages: 117th av. 27.20 (1987 60th av. 37.14)
1st-Class catches 1988: 17 (career 101)
Parents: Leonard and Audrey
Wife and date of marriage: Jane Claire, 25 September 1982
Children: Amy Louise, 7 November 1985; Lauren, 21 July 1988
Family links with cricket: Brother Colin played for Kent U-19s. Father played club cricket
Education: Cray Valley Technical High School
Qualifications: 8 O-levels, 2 A-levels, NCA Coaching Certificate
Jobs outside cricket: Insurance broker, and working in Civil Service
Off-season 1988–89: Coaching
Cricketing superstitions or habits: Always puts batting gear on in same order. Wears same gear when scoring runs

Overseas tours: With England Schools Team to India 1977–78; Kent to Vancouver 1979
Overseas teams played for: Randburg, Johannesburg, 1980–86; coach at St Stithian's College 1981–86
Cricketers particularly learnt from: Bob Woolmer, Mark Benson, Chris Tavaré
Cricketers particularly admired: Alan Knott, Gary Sobers, Barry Richards
Other sports played: Rugby (played for Kent U-21 XV), golf
Other sports followed: 'Anything – but not horses!'
Injuries 1988: Chipped bone in little finger of left hand caused him to miss last part of the season
Relaxations: Listening to records, lying in bed reading the Sunday newspapers. Reading autobiographies, Robert Ludlum, Frederick Forsyth, Wilbur Smith. Listening to music: Level 42, Phil Collins, U2; watching TV
Extras: Made 110 on debut for Kent CCC v Sri Lanka, 1979. Won four Man of the Match awards in first five matches. Scored highest score by Kent player in Benson and Hedges cricket: 121 v Sussex and Somerset. Scored three successive centuries in B & H. Played for England B v Pakistan, 1982. Fielded twice as 12th man for England v India in 1982 and West Indies in 1988, both matches at The Oval
Opinions on cricket: 'The type of pitches we play on must be improved. Perhaps the groundsmen could be employed by the TCCB, so that they do not feel pressured by their county club. They can then produce their best pitch, instead of inferior ones!'
Best batting performance: 155* Kent v Glamorgan, Cardiff 1983
Best bowling performance: 2-20 Kent v Somerset, Canterbury 1985

LAST SEASON: BATTING

	I.	N.O.	R.	H.S.	AV.
TEST					
1ST-CLASS	37	3	925	114	27.20
INT					
RAL	13	0	372	85	28.61
NAT.W.	3	0	53	41	17.66
B & H	4	0	293	137	73.25

CAREER: BATTING

	I.	N.O.	R.	H.S.	AV.
TEST					
1ST-CLASS	301	39	8834	155*	33.71
INT					
RAL	69	6	1654	85	26.25
NAT.W.	14	0	371	85	26.50
B & H	25	1	1094	137	45.58

LAST SEASON: BOWLING

	O.	M.	R.	W.	AV.
TEST					
1ST-CLASS	8	4	7	1	7.00
INT					
RAL					
NAT.W.					
B & H					

CAREER: BOWLING

	O.	M.	R.	W.	AV.
TEST					
1ST-CLASS	236.3	41	795	15	53.00
INT					
RAL					
NAT.W.	9	3	19	0	–
B & H	2	1	5	0	–

160. Which current first-class umpire is also an art teacher and a former professional soccer player?

Full Name: Geoffrey Alan Tedstone
Role: Right-hand bat, wicket-keeper
Born: 19 January 1961, Southport
Height: 5' 6½" **Weight:** 10½st
Nickname: Ted
County debut: 1982
1st-Class 50s scored: 3
One-Day 50s: 1
Place in batting averages: 200th av. 18.87
Parents: Ken and Win
Wife and date of marriage: Jane, 17 September 1988
Family links with cricket: Sister, Janet Aspinall, plays for England Ladies. Father played club cricket for Leamington. Brother Roger plays for Leamington
Education: Warwick School; St Pauls College, Cheltenham
Qualifications: 6 O-levels, 4 A-levels, BEd degree, qualified teacher, FA coach
Jobs outside cricket: PE teacher
Off-season 1988–89: Teaching at Emscote Lawn School, Warwick
Overseas tours: Young England to West Indies 1980; British Colleges to West Indies 1981; Dennis Amiss XI to Barbados 1985; Geoff Humpage Benefit tour to Barbados 1987
Overseas teams played for: Union High School, South Africa 1982–83
Cricketers particularly learnt from: 'My Dad'

LAST SEASON: BATTING

	I.	N.O.	R.	H.S.	AV.
TEST					
1ST-CLASS	8	0	151	50	18.87
INT					
RAL	–	–	–	–	–
NAT.W.					
B & H	–	–	–	–	–

LAST SEASON: WICKET KEEPING

	C.	ST.
TEST		
1ST-CLASS	7	1
INT		
RAL	2	2
NAT.W.		
B & H	–	–

CAREER: BATTING

	I.	N.O.	R.	H.S.	AV.
TEST					
1ST-CLASS	45	7	641	67*	16.86
INT					
RAL	5	2	74	31*	24.66
NAT.W.	1	1	55	55*	–
B & H	–	–	–	–	–

CAREER: WICKET KEEPING

	C.	ST.
TEST		
1ST-CLASS	49	10
INT		
RAL	10	2
NAT.W.	–	–
B & H	–	–

Cricketers particularly admired: Dennis Amiss, Bob Taylor
Other sports played: Hockey for Coventry and Warwickshire
Other sports followed: Soccer (Wolverhampton Wanderers FC)
Injuries 1988: Dislocated and broken finger; torn cartilege
Relaxations: Playing or watching most sports, listening to music, watching films, being sociable
Extras: 'I changed last season from being a tireless medium pace net bowler into a tiresome non-turning off-spin net bowler!' Released by Warwickshire at end of 1988 season
Opinions on cricket: 'Released at the end of 1988, I spent eight thoroughly enjoyable years with Warwickshire, where I have been fortunate to play with and against some great players, and to make many good friends.'
Best batting performance: 67* Warwickshire v Cambridge University, Cambridge 1983

TENNANT, L.   Leicestershire

Full Name: Lloyd Tennant
Role: Right-hand bat, right-arm
medium bowler, outfielder
Born: 9 April 1968, Walsall
Height: 5′ 11″ **Weight:** 12st 7lbs
Nickname: Charmaine (after
the Tennent Lager advert)
County debut: 1986
1st-Class catches 1988: 0 (career 1)
Parents: Dennis and Jean
Marital status: Single
Family links with cricket:
Father played local club cricket
as opening bowler
Education: Shellfield
Comprehensive School
Qualifications: 8 CSEs
Jobs outside cricket:
Fencing and bricklaying

Off-season 1988–89: Working for GBG Fencing Ltd
Cricketing superstitions or habits: Wearing favourite gear. Always puts left boot on first
Overseas tours: England U-19 to Sri Lanka 1986–87
Cricketers particularly learnt from: Ken Higgs, Alan Townsend
Cricketers particularly admired: Ian Botham, Malcolm Marshall
Other sports played: Football

Relaxations: Listening to music, watching TV
Opinions on cricket: 'Politics should be kept out of the game.'
Best batting performance: 12* Leicestershire v Sussex, Leicester 1986
Best bowling performance: 1-0 Leicestershire v Warwickshire, Edgbaston 1988

LAST SEASON: BATTING

	I.	N.O.	R.	H.S.	AV.
TEST					
1ST-CLASS	2	1	3	3	3.00
INT					
RAL	4	3	28	17*	28.00
NAT.W.					
B & H					

LAST SEASON: BOWLING

	O.	M.	R.	W.	AV.
TEST					
1ST-CLASS	7	2	19	1	19.00
INT					
RAL	42	3	170	5	34.00
NAT.W.					
B & H					

CAREER: BATTING

	I.	N.O.	R.	H.S.	AV.
TEST					
1ST-CLASS	4	2	16	12*	8.00
INT					
RAL	5	4	30	17*	30.00
NAT.W.					
B & H					

CAREER: BOWLING

	O.	M.	R.	W.	AV.
TEST					
1ST-CLASS	34	6	110	3	36.66
INT					
RAL	75	5	315	11	28.63
NAT.W.					
B & H					

TERRY, V. P. Hampshire

Full Name: Vivian Paul Terry
Role: Right-hand bat, right-arm medium bowler, slip or cover fielder
Born: 14 January 1959, Osnabruck, West Germany
Height: 6′ 0″ **Weight:** 13st 6lbs
County debut: 1978
County cap: 1983
Test debut: 1984
No. of Tests: 2
1000 runs in a season: 5
1st-Class 50s scored: 45
1st-Class 100s scored: 16
One-Day 50s: 22
One-Day 100s: 6
Place in batting averages: 95th av. 29.55 (1987 27th av. 43.18)
1st-Class catches 1988: 33 (career 156)
Parents: Michael and Patricia
Wife and date of marriage: Bernadette, 4 June 1986

Children: Siobhan Catherine, 13 September 1987
Education: Durlston Court, Barton-on-Sea, Hampshire; Millfield School, Somerset
Qualifications: 8 O-levels, 1 A-level, cricket coach
Jobs outside cricket: Worked in a fish factory, apple picker, estate agent, coach
Off-season 1988–89: Working for Braziers, a building company
Overseas tours: ESCA tour to India 1977–78; Gordon Greenidge benefit tour to Paris and Isle of Wight; English Counties tour to Zimbabwe 1985
Overseas teams played for: Sydney 1978–79; in New Zealand 1980–81; Durban Collegians 1982–83
Cricketers particularly learnt from: Chris Smith
Cricketers particularly admired: Gordon Greenidge, Chris Smith, Viv and Barry Richards, Malcolm Marshall, Gary Sobers
Other sports played: Golf, squash, soccer
Other sports followed: Most sports
Injuries 1988: Hit in the eye by a squash ball and out for two weeks
Relaxations: Music, sport
Opinions on cricket: 'Why don't the authorities do what most people feel should be done – 16 four-day games? It's obvious we play too much cricket, and because of this one tends to "drift" at times. In such circumstances, every game does not seem crucial.'
Best batting performance: 190 Hampshire v Sri Lankans, Southampton 1988

LAST SEASON: BATTING

	I.	N.O.	R.	H.S.	AV.
TEST					
1ST-CLASS	43	3	1182	190	29.55
INT					
RAL	14	0	328	77	23.42
NAT.W.	4	0	239	83	59.75
B & H	6	2	311	109	77.75

CAREER: BATTING

	I.	N.O.	R.	H.S.	AV.
TEST	3	0	16	3	5.33
1ST-CLASS	248	28	7678	190	34.90
INT					
RAL	100	14	2643	142	30.73
NAT.W.	17	1	679	165*	42.43
B & H	31	3	1001	109	35.75

161. Which current umpire used to be a detective?

162. Which counties did Dickie Bird play for?

163. Which current umpire scored a century in his first Test?

Full Name: David James Thomas
Role: Left-hand bat, left-arm
fast-medium bowler
Born: 30 June 1959, Solihull,
Warwickshire
Height: 6′ 0″ **Weight:** 13st 6lbs
Nickname: Teddy
County debut: 1977 (Surrey),
1988 (Gloucestershire)
County cap: 1982 (Surrey)
50 wickets in a season: 2
1st-Class 50s scored: 8
1st-Class 100s scored: 2
1st-Class 5 w. in innings: 7
1st-Class 10 w. in match: 1
One-Day 50s: 6
Place in batting averages: —
(1987 184th av. 18.69)
Place in bowling averages: —
(1987 105th av. 37.27)

1st-Class catches 1988: 1 (career 50)
Parents: Howard James and Heather
Wife and date of marriage: Miranda, 20 February 1982
Children: Christopher James Owen, 4 May 1986
Family links with cricket: Father played for RAF. Brother, Howard, played
for Bucks U-19 and now club cricket
Education: Licensed Victuallers' School, Slough
Jobs outside cricket: Salesman for Securicor Communications and PR for
Europa Communications
Off-season 1988–89: Working for own sports promotion company, Thomas
Promotions
Overseas tours: Surrey CCC tour of the Far East and Antigua; *Cricketer*
International to Dubai; Whitbread Scholarship in Australia 1982–83
Overseas teams played for: Northern Transvaal 1980–81; Natal 1983–84
Cricketers particularly admired: Mike Procter, Robin Jackman, Imran Khan,
Graham Monkhouse
Other sports played: Golf, squash
Injuries 1988: Back problem and groin injury, leading to retirement half-way
through season
Relaxations: Theatre, pubs, watching Chelsea FC
Extras: Played for England U-19 v West Indies U-19, and for Derrick Robins'
XI v New Zealand U-25 XI. Released by Surrey at end of 1987 season and

joined Gloucestershire on a two-year contract in 1988. Retired in 1988 because of injury

Best batting performance: 119 Surrey v Nottinghamshire, The Oval 1983
Best bowling performance: 6-36 Surrey v Somerset, The Oval 1984

LAST SEASON: BATTING

	I.	N.O.	R.	H.S.	AV.
TEST					
1ST-CLASS	4	1	77	57*	25.66
INT					
RAL	3	1	34	29	17.00
NAT.W.					
B & H	1	1	12	12*	

CAREER: BATTING

	I.	N.O.	R.	H.S.	AV.
TEST					
1ST-CLASS	193	41	3044	119	20.02
INT					
RAL	73	16	1090	72	19.12
NAT.W.	16	5	279	65	25.36
B & H	15	3	120	22	10.00

LAST SEASON: BOWLING

	O.	M.	R.	W.	AV.
TEST					
1ST-CLASS	53.4	9	174	7	24.85
INT					
RAL	12	0	56	0	–
NAT.W.					
B & H	8	0	45	0	–

CAREER: BOWLING

	O.	M.	R.	W.	AV.
TEST					
1ST-CLASS	3567.3	750	11415	336	33.97
INT					
RAL	640.5	37	3008	90	33.42
NAT.W.	201.5	24	737	23	32.04
B & H	204.3	29	780	16	48.75

THOMAS, J. G.   Northamptonshire

Full Name: John Gregory Thomas
Role: Right-hand bat, right-arm fast bowler
Born: 12 August 1960, Trebanos, Swansea
Height: 6′ 3″ **Weight:** 14st
Nickname: Blodwen
County debut: 1979 (Glamorgan)
County cap: 1986 (Glamorgan)
Test debut: 1985–86
No. of Tests: 5
No. of One-Day Internationals: 3
1st-Class 50s scored: 5
1st-Class 100s scored: 2
1st-Class 5 w. in innings: 10
1st-Class 10 w. in match: 1
Place in batting averages: 142nd av. 24.52 (1987 119th av. 15.38)
Place in bowling averages: 94th av. 31.89 (1987 63rd av. 29.16)
Strike rate 1988: 52.79 (career 53.81)
1st-Class catches 1988: 5 (career 53)
Parents: Illtyd and Margaret

Marital status: Single
Family links with cricket: Father played village cricket
Education: Cwmtawe Comprehensive School; South Glamorgan Institute of Higher Education
Qualifications: Qualified teacher, advanced cricket coach
Cricketing superstitions or habits: The number 111
Overseas tours: West Indies with British Colleges 1982; West Indies with England 1986
Overseas teams played for: Border Cricket Union, South Africa; Eastern Province, 1987–88
Other sports followed: Watches rugby
Relaxations: Any sport, music
Extras: Bowling award for four wickets or more most times in 1983. Having never hit a first-class century before, hit two in August 1988. Signed for Northamptonshire in 1989
Best batting performance: 110 Glamorgan v Warwickshire, Edgbaston 1988
Best bowling performance: 6-68 Glamorgan v Nottinghamshire, Trent Bridge 1988

LAST SEASON: BATTING

	I.	N.O.	R.	H.S.	AV.
TEST					
1ST-CLASS	26	5	515	110	24.52
INT					
RAL	11	3	69	25	8.62
NAT.W.	3	2	22	12*	22.00
B & H	3	1	48	18	24.00

CAREER: BATTING

	I.	N.O.	R.	H.S.	AV.
TEST	10	4	83	31*	13.83
1ST-CLASS	177	31	2467	110	16.89
INT	3	2	1	1*	1.00
RAL	63	14	590	37	12.04
NAT.W.	10	3	150	34	21.42
B & H	17	2	155	32	10.33

LAST SEASON: BOWLING

	O.	M.	R.	W.	AV.
TEST					
1ST-CLASS	422.2	62	1531	48	31.89
INT					
RAL	86.3	8	372	15	24.80
NAT.W.	28.5	2	97	3	32.33
B & H	55.4	8	181	7	25.85

CAREER: BOWLING

	O.	M.	R.	W.	AV.
TEST	129	18	504	10	50.40
1ST-CLASS	3180.3	557	11297	359	31.46
INT	26	2	144	3	48.00
RAL	470.1	31	2266	87	26.04
NAT.W.	79.5	7	292	9	32.44
B & H	195	25	761	25	30.44

164. Which current umpire played for England and has a son playing for Somerset?

165. Which famous former West Indian Test player is President of the West Indies Cricket Board of Control?

THORNE, D. A. Warwickshire

Full Name: David Anthony Thorne
Role: Right-hand bat, left-arm medium bowler, slip fielder
Born: 12 December 1964, Coventry
Height: 5′ 11″ **Weight:** 12st
Nickname: Strop, Thorney
County debut: 1983
1st-Class 50s scored: 16
1st-Class 100s scored: 2
1st-Class 5 w. in innings: 1
One-Day 50s: 1
Place in batting averages: 151st av. 23.58
1st-Class catches 1988: 17 (career 49)
Parents: Dennis and Barbara
Marital status: Single
Family links with cricket:
Father is a qualified coach in Warwickshire area, and was a very good club player. Brothers, Robert and Philip, both played for Warwickshire Schools. Mother played for Hinckley Ladies
Education: Bablake School, Coventry; Keble College, Oxford
Qualifications: 10 O-levels, 3 A-levels, BA (2.1) in Modern History; MCC coaching certificate
Jobs outside cricket: Components packager for Quinton Hazell car components. Worked as a labourer on building site pre-season 1983. Teaching
Off-season 1988–89: Working for McCann Erickson, the advertising agency
Cricketing superstitions or habits: 'Always left pad on first. If I get runs I try to wear the same shirt and trousers no matter how dirty until I fail again.'

LAST SEASON: BATTING

	I.	N.O.	R.	H.S.	AV.
TEST					
1ST-CLASS	25	1	566	76	23.58
INT					
RAL	8	4	191	59*	47.75
NAT.W.	1	0	20	20	20.00
B & H					

CAREER: BATTING

	I.	N.O.	R.	H.S.	AV.
TEST					
1ST-CLASS	103	15	2389	124	27.14
INT					
RAL	29	10	409	59*	21.52
NAT.W.	4	0	70	21	17.50
B & H	15	3	204	36*	17.00

LAST SEASON: BOWLING

	O.	M.	R.	W.	AV.
TEST					
1ST-CLASS	3	0	11	0	–
INT					
RAL					
NAT.W.					
B & H					

CAREER: BOWLING

	O.	M.	R.	W.	AV.
TEST					
1ST-CLASS	699.5	154	2065	41	50.36
INT					
RAL	95.5	1	580	13	44.61
NAT.W.	1	0	4	0	–
B & H	60.3	4	251	1	251.00

Overseas tours: Oxbridge to Hong Kong and Australia 1985–86. Barbados tours with Dennis Amiss 1985, and Geoff Humpage 1987

Cricketers particularly learnt from: 'Dennis Amiss, Dermot Reeve, Dean Hoffmann and above all my Father.'

Cricketers particularly admired: Rob Weir, Dennis Amiss, Paul Smith, Norman Gifford

Other sports played: Rugby, golf, football

Other sports followed: 'Football, any sports except horse racing.'

Relaxations: Listening to music, reading biographies and non-fiction. Watching good films

Extras: 'Hit for 26 in 3rd over in first John Player League game by Trevor Jesty. Was out first ball on first-class debut v Oxford University. Once took 7 for 7 in a school's first XI match including a hat-trick and all seven bowled. Secretary OUCC 1985, captain 1986. Scored unbeaten 100 in 1986 Varsity Match only to lose off last ball to a leg-bye. Suspended for one match in mid-July

Opinions on cricket: 'There is too much cricket played in this country. Four-day cricket is an excellent idea, but the pitches must be improved. That is what is wrong, above all, with English cricket at the moment. There should only be one overseas player per county.'

Best batting performance: 124 Oxford University v Zimbabwe, Oxford 1985

Best bowling performance: 5-39 Oxford University v Cambridge University, Lord's 1984

THORPE, G. P. Surrey

Full Name: Graham Paul Thorpe
Role: Left-hand bat, right-arm medium bowler
Born: 1 August 1969, Farnham
Height: 5′ 10″ **Weight:** 12st
Nickname: Chalky, Chelsea
County debut: 1988
1st-Class 100s scored: 1
1st-Class catches 1988: 3 (career 3)
Parents: Geoff and Toni
Marital status: Single
Family links with cricket: 'Both brothers play cricket, so does Dad.'
Education: Weydon Comprehensive; Farnham College
Qualifications: 6 O-levels, PE Diploma

Jobs outside cricket: Working for wine merchant
Off-season 1988–89: Playing football, training and working
Cricketers particularly learnt from: Graham Clinton, David Smith
Cricketers particularly admired: Ian Botham, Viv Richards, Mark Rampra-kash
Other sports played: Football, squash
Other sports followed: Football
Relaxations: 'Watching most sports, playing a bit of golf and squash, seeing my girlfriend Maria, and talking life to James Boiling. Enjoy watching comedy programmes.'
Extras: Played England Schools cricket U-15 and U-19 and England Schools football U-18
Opinions: 'To work hard and aim high.'
Best batting performance: 100* Surrey v Cambridge University, Cambridge 1988
Best bowling performance: 2-33 Surrey v Leicestershire, The Oval 1988

LAST SEASON: BATTING

	I.	N.O.	R.	H.S.	AV.
TEST					
1ST-CLASS	6	2	158	100*	39.50
INT					
RAL	1	0	15	15	15.00
NAT.W.					
B & H					

LAST SEASON: BOWLING

	O.	M.	R.	W.	AV.
TEST					
1ST-CLASS	30	3	77	4	19.25
INT					
RAL	4	1	25	0	–
NAT.W.					
B & H					

CAREER: BATTING

	I.	N.O.	R.	H.S.	AV.
TEST					
1ST-CLASS	6	2	158	100*	39.50
INT					
RAL	1	0	15	15	15.00
NAT.W.					
B & H					

CAREER: BOWLING

	O.	M.	R.	W.	AV.
TEST					
1ST-CLASS	30	3	77	4	19.25
INT					
RAL	4	1	25	0	–
NAT.W.					
B & H					

166. Which club, founded in 1872, plays at Walker Park?

167. Which famous actor, who died in 1988, asked in his will that his ashes be scattered over the ground at Lord's?

TODD, P. A.   Glamorgan

Full Name: Paul Adrian Todd
Role: Right-hand bat
Born: 12 March 1953, Morton, Nottinghamshire
Height: 6′ 1″ **Weight:** 13st 9lbs
Nickname: Toddy
County debut:
1972 (Nottinghamshire),
1987 (Glamorgan)
County cap: 1977 (Nottinghamshire)
1000 runs in a season: 3
1st-Class 50s scored: 41
1st-Class 100s scored: 9
One-Day 50s: 4
One-Day 100s: 1
Place in batting averages: —
(1987 190th av. 19.58)
1st-Class catches 1988: 0 (career 119)
Parents: Tom and Joan
Marital status: Single
Family links with cricket: Brother played for Nottinghamshire Colts and Nottinghamshire 2nd XI
Education: Edward Cludd, Southwell
Jobs outside cricket: Process worker for British Sugar
Off-season 1988–89: Working for British Sugar
Overseas teams played for: Woodridge College, Port Elizabeth, South Africa 1964–65; Nedlands CC, Perth, Western Australia 1978–79; Avendale CC, Cape Town, South Africa 1981–82
Cricketers particularly admired: Richard Hadlee
Other sports played: Football, golf
Other sports followed: All sports
Relaxations: Stamp collecting
Extras: Left Nottinghamshire in 1982. Played for Lincolnshire 1985–87. Joined Glamorgan during 1987 season. Released by Glamorgan at end of 1988 season

LAST SEASON: BATTING

	I.	N.O.	R.	H.S.	AV.
TEST					
1ST-CLASS					
INT					
RAL	3	0	47	38	15.66
NAT.W.	1	0	2	2	2.00
B & H					

CAREER: BATTING

	I.	N.O.	R.	H.S.	AV.
TEST					
1ST-CLASS	302	16	7663	178	26.79
INT					
RAL	97	1	1635	79	17.03
NAT.W.	11	0	347	105	31.54
B & H	36	1	709	59	20.25

Best batting performance: 178 Nottinghamshire v Gloucestershire, Trent Bridge 1975

TOPLEY, T. D. Essex

Full Name: Thomas Donald Topley
Role: Right-hand bat, right-arm fast-medium bowler
Born: 25 February 1964, Canterbury
Height: 6′ 3″ **Weight:** 13st 8lbs
Nickname: Toppers
County debut: 1985 (Surrey), 1985 (Essex)
County cap: 1988 (Essex)
1st-class 50s scored: 2
1st-Class 5 w. in innings: 9
1st-Class 10 w. in match: 2
Place in batting averages: 230th av. 14.68 (1987 167th av. 21.00)
Place in bowling averages: 53rd av. 25.60 (1987 51st av. 28.00)
Strike rate 1988: 49.72 (career 51.02)
1st-Class catches 1988: 8 (career 20)
Parents: Tom and Rhoda
Marital status: Single
Family links with cricket: Brother, Peter, played for Kent (1972–75). Father played for Royal Navy
Education: Royal Hospital School, Holbrook, Suffolk
Qualifications: 6 O-levels, NCA Coach at Intermediate level
Jobs outside cricket: Exporting to the Gulf States. Worked for CK & P, shipping forwarders
Off-season 1988–89: 'Staying in England and hibernating!'
Overseas tours: Keith Pont Benefit tour to Barbados 1986
Overseas teams played for: Natal Midlands & Noodsburg, South Africa 1985–86; Griqualand West, South Africa 1987–88
Cricketers particularly learnt from: Don Wilson, Geoff Arnold, and all at Essex
Cricketers particularly admired: John Lever, Richard Hadlee, Graham Gooch, Stuart Turner
Other sports played: Rugby, football, badminton and all ball sports
Injuries 1988: Shin soreness and sprained right ankle
Relaxations: Photography, food, travelling
Extras: Spent three years prior to joining Essex on the MCC Young Pro-

fessionals at Lord's. As 12th man held famous Test match 'catch' for England v West Indies at Lord's: unfortunately, did not count as his foot was over the boundary. Also appeared for Surrey during 1985

Opinions on cricket: 'Certainly in favour of four-day games, but we must prepare better pitches, without uneven bounce. I would like to see the introduction of an England 'B' side and even 'U-25' side.'

Best batting performance: 66 Essex v Yorkshire, Leeds 1987
Best bowling performance: 7-75 Essex v Derbyshire, Chesterfield 1988

LAST SEASON: BATTING

	I.	N.O.	R.	H.S.	AV.
TEST					
1ST-CLASS	22	6	235	56*	14.68
INT					
RAL	8	1	43	23	6.14
NAT.W.	–	–	–	–	–
B & H	1	1	6	6*	–

CAREER: BATTING

	I.	N.O.	R.	H.S.	AV.
TEST					
1ST-CLASS	62	16	761	66	16.54
INT					
RAL	15	5	77	23*	7.70
NAT.W.	3	1	25	15*	12.50
B & H	2	2	9	6*	–

LAST SEASON: BOWLING

	O.	M.	R.	W.	AV.
TEST					
1ST-CLASS	538.4	87	1664	65	25.60
INT					
RAL	89	3	406	20	20.30
NAT.W.	9	1	17	1	17.00
B & H	55	2	222	10	22.20

CAREER: BOWLING

	O.	M.	R.	W.	AV.
TEST					
1ST-CLASS	1471.1	291	4364	173	25.22
INT					
RAL	227	14	947	41	23.09
NAT.W.	61.2	9	188	12	15.66
B & H	98	12	344	16	21.50

TREMLETT, T. M.   Hampshire

Full Name: Timothy Maurice Tremlett
Role: Right-hand bat, right-arm medium bowler
Born: 26 July 1956, Wellington, Somerset
Height: 6' 2" **Weight:** 13st 7lbs
Nickname: Hurricane, Trooper, R2
County debut: 1976
County cap: 1983
50 wickets in a season: 4
1st-Class 50s scored: 17
1st-Class 100s scored: 1
1st-Class 5 w. in innings: 11
Place in batting averages: 336th av. 13.87 (1987 231st av. 13.41)
Place in bowling averages: 36th av. 23.28 (1987 6th av. 19.54)
Strike rate 1988: 53.78 (career 58.60)

1st-Class catches 1988: 3 (career 72)
Parents: Maurice Fletcher and Melina May
Wife and date of marriage: Carolyn Patricia, 28 September 1979
Children: Christopher Timothy, 2 September 1981; Alastair Jonathan, 1 February 1983; Benjamin Paul, 2 May 1984
Family links with cricket: Father played for Somerset and for England against West Indies in the West Indies 1947–48. Captained Somerset 1958–60. Younger brother plays local club cricket for Deanery CC
Education: Bellemoor Secondary Modern; Richard Taunton Sixth-Form College
Qualifications: 5 O-levels, 1 A-level. Advanced Coaching Certificate
Jobs outside cricket: One winter spent labouring on building site for muscle-building ('did not seem to work'). Furrier in father-in-law's business
Cricketing superstitions or habits: 'I always like to be the last to leave the dressing room when taking the field plus always walk round the large table on the right-hand side in our dressing room before taking the field. This has replaced leaving the dressing room last as most of our players rarely get out on time!'
Overseas tours: English Counties tour to Zimbabwe 1985; England B to Sri Lanka 1986
Overseas teams played for: Oudtshoorn Teachers' Training College, Western Cape, South Africa 1978–79
Cricketers particularly learnt from: 'My father, and in general watching and listening to other cricketers, first-class or club players.'
Cricketers particularly admired: Vincent van der Bijl, Mike Hendrick, Malcolm Marshall, Richard Hadlee
Other sports played: Golf (7 handicap), table tennis, squash, swimming, badminton
Injuries 1988: Cracked bone in right wrist and stress fracture in lower back
Relaxations: Collecting cricket books and records, gardening, cinema
Extras: Member of local cricket club, Deanery. Batted in almost every position for Hants in batting order from 1 to 11 in 1979. Captained both his school and sixth-form college at cricket

LAST SEASON: BATTING

	I.	N.O.	R.	H.S.	AV.
TEST					
1ST-CLASS	10	2	111	38	13.87
INT					
RAL	1	0	8	8	8.00
NAT.W.					
B & H					

LAST SEASON: BOWLING

	O.	M.	R.	W.	AV.
TEST					
1ST-CLASS	125.3	35	326	14	23.28
INT					
RAL	27	0	143	6	23.83
NAT.W.					
B & H					

CAREER: BATTING

	I.	N.O.	R.	H.S.	AV.
TEST					
1ST-CLASS	236	59	3609	102*	20.38
INT					
RAL	54	24	314	35	10.46
NAT.W.	13	4	142	43*	15.77
B & H	25	10	213	36*	14.20

CAREER: BOWLING

	O.	M.	R.	W.	AV.
TEST					
1ST-CLASS	4131.3	1190	10010	423	23.66
INT					
RAL	876.4	36	4083	161	25.36
NAT.W.	213.2	37	697	28	24.89
B & H	325.5	50	1063	46	23.10

Opinions on cricket: 'With ever increasing numbers of top-class cricketers withdrawing from international fixtures, the cricketing authorities will hopefully begin to reduce the amount of cricket played in this country, especially one-day cricket. With the emphasis still geared towards one-day matches, specialists are still outnumbered heavily by bits-and-pieces performers, with young spin-bowlers particularly at a disadvantage. To ensure that the highest standards are maintained, the structure of English fiirst-class cricket is in further need of streamlining.'

Best batting performance: 102* Hampshire v Somerset, Taunton 1985
Best bowling performance: 6-53 Hampshire v Somerset, Weston-super-Mare 1987

TRUMP, H. R. J. Somerset

Full Name: Harvey Russell John Trump
Role: Right-hand bat, off-spin bowler
Born: 11 October 1968, Taunton
Height: 6' 1" **Weight:** 13st
Nickname: Trumptonian, Snagger
County debut: 1988
Place in bowling averages: 72nd av. 29.00
Strike rate 1988: 67.50 (career 67.50)
1st-Class catches 1988: 7 (career 7)
Marital status: Single
Education: Edgarley Hall (Millfield Jnr School); Millfield School; Chester College of Higher Education
Qualifications: 7 O-levels, 2 A-levels
Off-season 1988–89: Studying for degree at Chester College in PE and History
Overseas tours: England Young Cricketers to Sri Lanka; England Young Cricketers to Australia for Junior World Cup; NCA (South) to Northern Ireland for U-19 ICC Tournament
Cricketers particularly learnt from: Vic Marks, Steve Waugh
Cricketers particularly admired: John Emburey, Vic Marks, Viv Richards
Other sports played: Hockey especially, and most other ball games
Other sports followed: Hockey
Relaxations: Reading, walking
Extras: Played county hockey for Somerset U-19s

Opinions on cricket: 'I believe it would be good to introduce four-day cricket throughout the whole season. Also bring in two/three-day games at junior levels, e.g. U-15/19s, especially county.'
Best batting performance: 48 Somerset v Hampshire, Taunton 1988
Best bowling performance: 4-17 Somerset v Kent, Canterbury 1988

LAST SEASON: BATTING

	I.	N.O.	R.	H.S.	AV.
TEST					
1ST-CLASS	11	1	62	48	6.20
INT					
RAL	1	0	4	4	4.00
NAT.W.					
B & H					

LAST SEASON: BOWLING

	O.	M.	R.	W.	AV.
TEST					
1ST-CLASS	270	74	696	24	29.00
INT					
RAL					
NAT.W.					
B & H					

CAREER: BATTING

	I.	N.O.	R.	H.S.	AV.
TEST					
1ST-CLASS	11	1	62	48	6.20
INT					
RAL	1	0	4	4	4.00
NAT.W.					
B & H					

CAREER: BOWLING

	O.	M.	R.	W.	AV.
TEST					
1ST-CLASS	270	74	696	24	29.00
INT					
RAL					
NAT.W.					
B & H					

TUFNELL, P. C. R.   Middlesex

Full Name: Philip Clive Roderick Tufnell
Role: Right-hand bat, slow left-arm spinner
Born: 29 April 1966, Hadley Wood, Hertfordshire
Height: 6' 0" **Weight:** 11st 8lbs
Nickname: Tuffers, Brucie
County debut: 1986
1st-Class 5 w. in innings: 1
Place in bowling averages: 126th av. 42.32 (1987 68th av. 29.81)
Strike rate 1988: 104.00 (career 87.30)
1st-Class catches 1988: 5 (career 11)
Parents: Sylvia and Alan
Wife and date of marriage: Alison Jane, 5 October 1986
Education: Highgate School; Southgate School
Qualifications: O-level in Art; City & Guilds Silversmithing
Jobs outside cricket: Silversmith, mini-cabbing
Overseas tours: Young England tour to the West Indies 1985

Cricketers particularly learnt from: Jack Robertson, Gordon Jenkins, Don Wilson

Cricketers particularly admired: Clive Radley, Derek Underwood

Other sports played: Snooker, hack around at golf

Other sports followed: American football

Relaxations: 'Taking Alison and her friend Elaine shopping. Finding excuses to get out of buying a round.'

Extras: MCC Young Cricketer of the Year 1984. Middlesex uncapped Bowler of the Year 1987

Opinions on cricket: 'Tea should be longer. Keep uncovered wickets.'

Best batting performance: 20 Middlesex v Kent, Lord's 1988

Best bowling performance: 6-60 Middlesex v Kent, Canterbury 1987

LAST SEASON: BATTING

	I.	N.O.	R.	H.S.	AV.
TEST					
1ST-CLASS	12	4	44	20	5.50
INT					
RAL	–	–	–	–	–
NAT.W.	–	–	–	–	–
B & H					

CAREER: BATTING

	I.	N.O.	R.	H.S.	AV.
TEST					
1ST-CLASS	27	9	97	20	5.38
INT					
RAL	–	–	–	–	–
NAT.W.	–	–	–	–	–
B & H					

LAST SEASON: BOWLING

	O.	M.	R.	W.	AV.
TEST					
1ST-CLASS	433.2	119	1058	25	42.32
INT					
RAL	14	1	62	1	62.00
NAT.W.	12	4	29	3	9.66
B & H					

CAREER: BOWLING

	O.	M.	R.	W.	AV.
TEST					
1ST-CLASS	916.4	226	2521	63	40.01
INT					
RAL	14	1	62	1	62.00
NAT.W.	12	4	29	3	9.66
B & H					

168. What is the title of Dickie Bird's latest book?

169. Who was top of the first-class batting averages in England in 1988 and what was his average?

TURNER, D. R. Hampshire

Full Name: David Roy Turner
Role: Left-hand bat, right-arm medium bowler, out-fielder
Born: 5 February 1949, Corsham, nr Chippenham, Wiltshire
Height: 5′ 6″ **Weight:** 11st 8lbs
Nickname: Birdy, Fossil
County debut: 1966
County cap: 1970
Benefit: 1981 (£23,011)
1000 runs in a season: 9
1st-Class 50s scored: 87
1st-Class 100s scored: 28
One-Day 50s: 59
One-Day 100s: 5
Place in batting averages: 58th av. 35.41 (1987 12th av. 49.18)
1st-Class catches 1988: 5 (career 189)
Parents: Robert Edward and Evelyn Peggy
Wife and date of marriage: Henriette, 18 February 1977
Children: Nicola Marianna, 15 March 1984
Education: Chippenham Boys' High School
Qualifications: 5 O-levels
Off-season 1988–89: Becoming involved in the shoe business
Overseas tours: With Derrick Robins' XI to South Africa 1972–73
Overseas teams played for: Western Province in the winning 1977–78 Currie Cup Competition side; player-coach for Paarl Cricket Club, South Africa 1972–80, 1982–85
Cricketers particularly learnt from: Roy Marshall
Cricketers particularly admired: Mike Procter
Other sports played: Golf, football, athletics
Injuries 1988: None
Relaxations: Chess, gardening, reading, television, watching war films
Extras: Played for Wiltshire in 1965. Took a hat-trick in a Lambert & Butler 7-a-side floodlit tournament at Ashton Gate, Bristol on 17 September 1981 v Glamorgan. Captained school at soccer, rugger and cricket. Also ran for school in cross-country and athletics. Shared in an unbeaten partnership of 283 with C. G. Greenidge, a record in any one-day competition, in Benson & Hedges Cup, Hampshire v Minor Counties South at Amersham in 1973. Scored a career best 184* v Gloucestershire in 1987, 18 years since previous best Championship score
Opinions on cricket: 'I would like the cricket authorities to try for one season,

16 four-day Championship matches, coupled with a Saturday 60-overs limited cricket league, along with the usual Sunday League. There should be tighter controls on overseas players. They should scrap the no-substitute rule. Perhaps substitutes should only be allowed at the discretion of the umpires. In four-day cricket, they should increase the follow-on figure from 150 to 175. Also, captains should be given the chance to choose any roller they wish.'

Best batting performance: 184* Hampshire v Gloucestershire, Gloucester 1987

Best bowling performance: 2-7 Hampshire v Glamorgan, Bournemouth 1981

LAST SEASON: BATTING

	I.	N.O.	R.	H.S.	AV.
TEST					
1ST-CLASS	40	6	1204	150*	35.41
INT					
RAL	15	3	573	103*	47.75
NAT.W.	4	0	42	35	10.50
B & H	6	1	95	31	19.00

LAST SEASON: BOWLING

	O.	M.	R.	W.	AV.
TEST					
1ST-CLASS	0.2	0	8	0	–
INT					
RAL					
NAT.W.					
B & H					

CAREER: BATTING

	I.	N.O.	R.	H.S.	AV.
TEST					
1ST-CLASS	679	70	18641	184*	30.60
INT					
RAL	239	23	6429	114	29.76
NAT.W.	37	4	963	100*	29.18
B & H	72	11	2083	123*	34.14

CAREER: BOWLING

	O.	M.	R.	W.	AV.
TEST					
1ST-CLASS	100	27	346	9	38.44
INT					
RAL	1.3	0	11	0	–
NAT.W.	1	0	4	0	–
B & H	0.2	0	4	0	–

VAN ZYL, C. J. P. G.   Glamorgan

Full Name: Cornelius Johannes Petrus Gerhardus Van Zyl
Role: Right-hand bat, right-arm fast-medium bowler
Born: 1 October 1961, Bloemfontein, South Africa
Nickname: Cornie
County debut: 1987
1st-Class 5 w. in innings: 9
1st-Class 10 w. in match: 2
1st-Class catches 1988: 1 (career 13)
Education: University of Orange Free State
Overseas teams played for: Orange Free State 1981–89
Extras: Released by Glamorgan at end of 1988 season

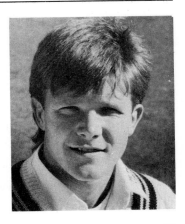

Best batting performance: 49 Orange Free State v Natal B, Bloemfontein 1984–85
Best bowling performance: 8-84 Orange Free State v Northern Transvaal B, Bloemfontein 1984–85

LAST SEASON: BATTING

	I.	N.O.	R.	H.S.	AV.
TEST					
1ST-CLASS	5	1	30	11	7.50
INT					
RAL					
NAT.W.					
B & H					

CAREER: BATTING

	I.	N.O.	R.	H.S.	AV.
TEST					
1ST-CLASS	75	15	744	49	15.18
INT					
RAL					
NAT.W.					
B & H	1	0	5	5	5.00

LAST SEASON: BOWLING

	O.	M.	R.	W.	AV.
TEST					
1ST-CLASS	114.1	30	339	3	113.00
INT					
RAL					
NAT.W.					
B & H					

CAREER: BOWLING

	O.	M.	R.	W.	AV.
TEST					
1ST-CLASS	1453.2	355	4390	204	21.51
INT					
RAL					
NAT.W.					
B & H	11	2	45	1	45.00

WALKER, A.　　Northamptonshire

Full Name: Alan Walker
Role: Left-hand bat, right-arm fast-medium bowler, outfielder
Born: 7 July 1962, Emley, nr Huddersfield
Height: 5′ 11″ **Weight:** 12st 7lbs
Nickname: Walks, Wacky
County debut: 1983
County cap: 1987
1st-Class 5 w. in innings: 2
Place in batting averages: 179th av. 21.30 (1987 214th av. 15.60)
Place in bowling averages: 52nd av. 25.55 (1987 11th av. 21.06)
Strike rate 1988: 51.75 (career 58.09)
1st-Class catches 1988: 7 (career 32)
Parents: Malcolm and Enid
Wife and date of marriage: Janice, 17 September 1983
Education: Emley Junior School; Kirkburton Middle School; Shelley High School
Qualifications: 2 O-levels, 4 CSEs, qualified coal-face worker

Jobs outside cricket: Miner; worked in iron foundry
Off-season 1988–89: Labouring
Cricketing superstitions or habits: Puts left boot on first, right pad on first, wears the same thing next day if successful the day before
Overseas tours: Denmark with NCA U-19s (North of England) 1980
Overseas teams played for: Uitenhage, South Africa 1984–85, 1986–87
Cricketers particularly learnt from: David Steele, Nick Cook, Winston Davis, Dennis Lillee
Cricketers particularly admired: Dennis Lillee, Richard Hadlee
Other sports played: Football
Other sports followed: Rugby league (Wakefield Trinity), football (Huddersfield Town)
Relaxations: 'Watching TV, listening to music, DIY, having a pint.'
Extras: Took part in a sponsored drive to every first-class headquarters, including Oxford, Cambridge and Arundel, in one day, with four other members of the club, raising money for Cat-scan appeal and the cricket club
Best batting performance: 41* Northamptonshire v Warwickshire, Edgbaston 1987
Best bowling performance: 6-50 Northamptonshire v Lancashire, Northampton 1986

LAST SEASON: BATTING

	I.	N.O.	R.	H.S.	AV.
TEST					
1ST-CLASS	20	10	213	40*	21.30
INT					
RAL	4	2	10	4*	5.00
NAT.W.	1	0	7	7	7.00
B & H	1	1	0	0*	–

LAST SEASON: BOWLING

	O.	M.	R.	W.	AV.
TEST					
1ST-CLASS	465.5	98	1380	54	25.55
INT					
RAL	76	3	383	14	27.35
NAT.W.	11.5	2	37	1	37.00
B & H	36.2	4	143	6	23.83

CAREER: BATTING

	I.	N.O.	R.	H.S.	AV.
TEST					
1ST-CLASS	78	40	543	41*	14.28
INT					
RAL	11	5	51	13	8.50
NAT.W.	3	1	11	7	5.50
B & H	6	5	30	15*	30.00

CAREER: BOWLING

	O.	M.	R.	W.	AV.
TEST					
1ST-CLASS	2004.2	411	6187	207	29.88
INT					
RAL	418.4	22	1935	77	25.12
NAT.W.	100.4	15	353	14	25.21
B & H	184.1	13	819	23	35.60

170. Which Englishman was highest in the first-class batting averages in 1988?

171. How many first-class wickets did Franklyn Stephenson take in 1988?

WALSH, C. A.   Gloucestershire

Full Name: Courtney Andrew Walsh
Role: Right-hand bat, right-arm
fast bowler
Born: 30 October 1962, Kingston,
Jamaica
Height: 6′ 5½″ **Weight:** 13st 7lbs
Nickname: Mark, Walshy, Shorty
County debut: 1984
County cap: 1985
Test debut: 1984–85
No. of Tests: 25
No. of One-Day Internationals: 54
1st-Class 50s scored: 2
1st-Class 5 w. in innings: 34
1st-Class 10 w. in match: 6
Place in bowling averages: 111th
av. 34.55 (1987 34th av. 25.53)
Strike rate 1988: 77.44 (career 45.49)
1st-Class catches 1988: 3 (career 43)
Parents: Erick and Joan Wollaston
Marital status: Single
Education: Excelsior High School
Qualifications: GCE and CXL
Off-season 1988–89: Touring with West Indies in Australia
Overseas tours: West Indies Young Cricketers to Zimbabwe 1983; West
Indies to England 1984; to Australia 1984–85; to Pakistan 1986; World Cup
1987; to England 1988
Overseas teams played for: Jamaica

LAST SEASON: BATTING

	I.	N.O.	R.	H.S.	AV.
TEST	5	3	26	9*	13.00
1ST-CLASS	2	0	5	4	2.50
INT	2	1	20	18	20.00
RAL					
NAT.W.					
B & H					

CAREER: BATTING

	I.	N.O.	R.	H.S.	AV.
TEST	30	11	189	18*	9.94
1ST-CLASS	133	31	1092	52	10.70
INT	16	7	70	18	7.77
RAL	21	4	148	35	8.70
NAT.W.					
B & H	6	3	30	8	10.00

LAST SEASON: BOWLING

	O.	M.	R.	W.	AV.
TEST	157.2	40	412	12	34.33
1ST-CLASS	75	15	210	6	35.00
INT	33	6	100	1	100.00
RAL					
NAT.W.					
B & H					

CAREER: BOWLING

	O.	M.	R.	W.	AV.
TEST	802.4	174	2190	87	25.17
1ST-CLASS	3435.5	577	10573	472	22.40
INT	476.3	47	1828	64	28.56
RAL	272.5	20	1121	53	21.15
NAT.W.	93	11	318	14	22.71
B & H	114.3	13	407	14	29.07

Cricketers particularly learnt from: Michael Holding, Andy Roberts, Malcolm Marshall, George Headley
Cricketers particularly admired: Michael Holding, Viv Richards, Lawrence Rowe
Other sports played: Football
Other sports followed: Basketball, track and field events
Relaxations: Music, reading, watching TV
Extras: Took record 10-43 in Jamaican school cricket in 1979. Played in MCC Bicentenary Test 1987. On tour, he has the reputation as an insatiable collector of souvenirs. David Graveney, when captaining Gloucestershire, reckoned Walsh was the 'best old-ball bowler in the world'. One of *Wisden*'s Five Cricketers of the Year, 1986
Best batting performance: 52 Gloucestershire v Yorkshire, Bristol 1986
Best bowling performance: 9-72 Gloucestershire v Somerset, Bristol 1986

WARD, D. M. Surrey

Full Name: David Mark Ward
Role: Right-hand bat,
off-break bowler, gully fielder
Born: 10 February 1961, Croydon
Height: 6′ **Weight:** 13st 2lbs
Nickname: Cocker, Wardy, Jaws,
Gnasher, Chad, Pianoman
County debut: 1985
1st-Class 50s scored: 8
1st-Class 100s scored: 2
One-Day 50s: 3
Place in batting averages: 79th
av. 31.40 (1987 194th av. 17.80)
1st-Class catches 1988: 22 (career 32)
Parents: Thomas and Dora Kathleen
Marital status: Single
Family links with cricket:
'Grandad played for the
"Duke of York XI", Croydon.'

Education: Haling Manor High School; Croydon Technical College
Qualifications: 2 O-levels, Advanced City and Guilds in Carpentry and Joinery
Jobs outside cricket: Carpenter. Working in Chinese take-away
Off-season 1988–89: Working as carpenter. Tour to Jersey. Playing golf
Cricketing superstitions or habits: Marks across corner of non-striking crease with bat

Overseas tours: Barbados 1985 with Surrey; Dubai 1988 with Surrey
Overseas teams played for: Caulfield CC, Australia 1984–85, 1985–86 and 1986–87; Sunshine CC, Australia 1987–88
Cricketers particularly learnt from: Geoff Arnold, Graham Clinton, Geoff Howarth, Monte Lynch, Chris Waller, M. Frost
Cricketers particularly admired: Graham Gooch, Ian Botham, Viv Richards, John Goodey (Banstead CC), Geoff Howarth, Keith Ebdon (Chipstead and Coulsdon CC)
Other sports played: Football, snooker, table tennis
Other sports followed: Charlton FC – 'seem to spend most of the time with my hands over my eyes!'
Relaxations: Eating out, watching TV, movies, jazz, golf, greyhound racing
Opinions on cricket: 'Avoid the politics and get on with the game!'
Best batting performance: 143 Surrey v Derbyshire, Derby 1985

LAST SEASON: BATTING

	I.	N.O.	R.	H.S.	AV.
TEST					
1ST-CLASS	36	6	942	126	31.40
INT					
RAL	13	3	216	48*	21.60
NAT.W.	4	0	33	27	8.25
B & H	3	0	12	7	4.00

CAREER: BATTING

	I.	N.O.	R.	H.S.	AV.
TEST					
1ST-CLASS	62	10	1499	143	28.82
INT					
RAL	37	8	665	73*	22.93
NAT.W.	4	0	33	27	8.25
B & H	3	0	12	7	4.00

WARD, T. R.   Kent

Full Name: Trevor Robert Ward
Role: Right-hand opening bat
Born: 18 January 1968, Farningham, Kent
Height: 5′ 11″ **Weight:** 12st 11lbs
Nickname: Wardy, Cher
County debut: 1986
1st-Class 50s scored: 3
Place in batting averages: 80th av. 21.29
1st-Class catches 1988: 9 (career 9)
Parents: Robert Henry and Hazel Ann
Marital status: Single
Family links with cricket: Father played a little village cricket with Farningham
Education: Anthony Roper County Primary; Hextable Comprehensive

Qualifications: 7 O-levels
Jobs outside cricket: Worked in building trade; sports shop assistant
Off-season 1988–89: Labouring
Cricketing superstitions or habits: Puts left pad on first
Overseas tours: NCA to Bermuda 1985; Young England to Sri Lanka 1987; Young England to Australia 1988 for Youth World Cup
Overseas teams played for: Scarborough CC, Perth, Western Australia 1986–87
Cricketers particularly learnt from: Alan Ealham, Derek Aslett, Colin Page, Graham Saville
Cricketers particularly admired: Viv Richards, Richard Hadlee, Derek Underwood, Graham Gooch
Other sports played: Football, golf, squash, rugby, badminton, fishing
Other sports followed: American football, fishing, golf
Injuries 1988: 'Knee injury kept me out for two weeks.'
Relaxations: Watching films, playing golf, fishing
Opinions on cricket: 'Less cricket, with more four-day games. And with four-day cricket, there must be better batting wickets, to ensure the matches go the full distance.'
Best batting performance: 72 Kent v Surrey, Guildford 1988

LAST SEASON: BATTING

	I.	N.O.	R.	H.S.	AV.
TEST					
1ST-CLASS	17	0	362	72	21.29
INT					
RAL	5	0	56	25	11.20
NAT.W.	2	0	35	34	17.50
B & H					

CAREER: BATTING

	I.	N.O.	R.	H.S.	AV.
TEST					
1ST-CLASS	21	1	422	72	21.10
INT					
RAL	5	0	56	25	11.20
NAT.W.	2	0	35	34	17.50
B & H					

172: How many first-class wickets did Graeme Hick take in 1988: 9, 21, or 37?

173. How many runs did Len Hutton make at The Oval Test v Australia in 1938?

WARNER, A. E.   Derbyshire

Full Name: Allan Esmond Warner
Role: Right-hand bat, right-arm
fast bowler, outfielder
Born: 12 May 1959, Birmingham
Height: 5′ 8″ **Weight:** 10st
Nickname: Esis
County debut: 1982 (Worcestershire),
1985 (Derbyshire)
County cap: 1987
1st-Class 50s scored: 10
1st-Class 5 w. in innings: 2
One-Day 50s: 1
Place in batting averages: 224th
av. 15.78 (1987 187th av. 18.50)
Place in bowling averages: 57th
av. 26.15 (1987 64th av. 29.31)
Strike rate 1988: 60.68 (career 62.13)
1st-Class catches 1988: 4 (career 26)
Parents: Edgar and Sarah
Children: Alvin, 6 September 1980
Education: Tabernacle School, St Kitts, West Indies
Qualifications: CSE Maths
Jobs outside cricket: Bricklaying
Cricketers particularly learnt from: John Browny, Henry Benjamin
Cricketers particularly admired: Malcolm Marshall, Michael Holding
Other sports played: Football, table tennis
Other sports followed: Football, boxing and athletics
Relaxations: Watching movies, music (soul, reggae and calypso)
Extras: Released by Worcestershire at end of 1984 and joined Derbyshire

LAST SEASON: BATTING

	I.	N.O.	R.	H.S.	AV.
TEST					
1ST-CLASS	25	6	300	45	15.78
INT					
RAL	13	1	103	18	8.58
NAT.W.	1	0	9	9	9.00
B & H	2	0	17	13	8.50

LAST SEASON: BOWLING

	O.	M.	R.	W.	AV.
TEST					
1ST-CLASS	445	104	1151	44	26.15
INT					
RAL	98.4	2	578	15	38.53
NAT.W.	20	5	65	1	65.00
B & H	65.5	6	266	9	29.55

CAREER: BATTING

	I.	N.O.	R.	H.S.	AV.
TEST					
1ST-CLASS	140	27	2131	91	18.85
INT					
RAL	53	12	500	68	12.19
NAT.W.	5	0	66	32	13.20
B & H	15	5	102	24*	10.20

CAREER: BOWLING

	O.	M.	R.	W.	AV.
TEST					
1ST-CLASS	1988.1	384	6337	192	33.00
INT					
RAL	441.3	10	2352	80	29.40
NAT.W.	73.1	9	294	7	42.00
B & H	278.2	18	984	33	29.81

Best batting performance: 91 Derbyshire v Leicestershire, Chesterfield 1986
Best bowling performance: 5-27 Worcestershire v Glamorgan, Worcester 1984

WASIM AKRAM   Lancashire

Full Name: Wasim Akram
Role: Left-hand bat, left-arm fast-medium bowler
Born: 3 June 1966, Lahore, Pakistan
Height: 6′ 3″ **Weight:** 12st 7lbs
County debut: 1988
Test debut: 1984–85
No. of Tests: 25
No. of One-Day Internationals: 57
1st-Class 50s scored: 7
1st-Class 100s scored: 1
Place in batting averages: 81st av. 31.00
Place in bowling averages: 20th av. 21.48
Strike rate 1988: 56.45 (career 62.56)
1st-Class catches 1988: 2 (career 21)
Education: Islamia College
Off-season 1988–89: Touring with Pakistan
Overseas teams: Lahore Zone
Overseas tours: With Pakistan to New Zealand, 1984–85; Sri Lanka, 1984–85; India, 1986–87; England, 1987

LAST SEASON: BATTING

	I.	N.O.	R.	H.S.	AV.
TEST					
1ST-CLASS	18	2	496	116*	31.00
INT					
RAL	7	2	126	29	25.20
NAT.W.	2	0	23	14	11.50
B & H	3	0	42	23	14.00

LAST SEASON: BOWLING

	O.	M.	R.	W.	AV.
TEST					
1ST-CLASS	291.4	76	666	31	21.48
INT					
RAL	65.3	3	264	14	18.85
NAT.W.	20	2	65	4	16.25
B & H	30.4	1	109	3	36.33

CAREER: BATTING

	I.	N.O.	R.	H.S.	AV.
TEST	31	6	410	66	16.40
1ST-CLASS	36	8	778	116*	27.78
INT	34	6	297	48*	10.60
RAL	7	2	126	29	25.20
NAT.W.	2	0	23	14	11.50
B & H	3	0	42	23	14.00

CAREER: BOWLING

	O.	M.	R.	W.	AV.
TEST	829	206	2098	76	27.60
1ST-CLASS	776.5	169	2045	78	26.21
INT	465.2	46	1788	68	26.29
RAL	65.3	3	264	14	18.85
NAT.W.	20	2	65	4	16.25
B & H	30.4	1	109	3	36.33

Extras: His second first-class match was playing for Pakistan on tour in New Zealand. Imran Khan wrote of him: 'I have great faith in Wasim Akram. I think he will become a great all-rounder, as long as he realises how much hard work is required. His batting needs attention, but he has the advantage of thinking like a lower order batsman: he doesn't have the problems of being a frustrated opening bat. As a bowler he is extremely gifted, and has it in him to be the best left-armer since Alan Davidson.'

Best batting performance: 116* Lancashire v Somerset, Old Trafford 1988
Best bowling performance: 7-50 Pakistan v New Zealand, Rawalpindi 1984

WATKIN, S. L. Glamorgan

Full Name: Steven Llewellyn Watkin
Role: Right-hand bat, right-arm fast-medium bowler
Born: 13 September 1964, Duffryn, Rhondda, nr Port Talbot
Height: 6′ 3″ **Weight:** 12st 8lbs
Nickname: Watty, Banger
County debut: 1986
1st-Class 5 w. in innings: 2
Place in bowling averages: 87th av. 30.93
Strike rate 1988: 68.80 (career 67.93)
1st-Class catches 1988: 1 (career 1)
Parents: John and Sandra
Marital status: Single
Family links with cricket: Father and brother played
Education: Cymer Afan Comprehensive; Swansea College of Further Education; South Glamorgan Institute of Higher Education
Qualifications: 8 O-levels, 2 A-levels, BA degree in Human Movement Studies
Overseas tours: British Colleges to West Indies 1987
Overseas teams played for: Potchefstroom University, South Africa, 1987–88
Cricketers you have particularly learnt from: Tom Cartwright, Alan Jones, Barry Lloyd
Cricketers you have particularly admired: Richard Hadlee, Dennis Lillee
Other sports played: Football, tennis, basketball
Other sports followed: All sports except horse racing
Relaxations: Watching TV, listening to music, a few beers

Opinions on cricket: 'Four-day cricket is here to stay. It produces better cricket, and less results coming from captain's agreements.'
Best batting performance: 23 Glamorgan v Worcestershire, Abergavenny 1988
Best bowling performance: 8–59 Glamorgan v Warwickshire, Edgbaston 1988

LAST SEASON: BATTING

	I.	N.O.	R.	H.S.	AV.
TEST					
1ST-CLASS	19	7	115	23	9.58
INT					
RAL	1	1	1	1*	–
NAT.W.					
B & H	1	1	4	4*	–

CAREER: BATTING

	I.	N.O.	R.	H.S.	AV.
TEST					
1ST-CLASS	19	7	115	23	9.58
INT					
RAL	2	1	8	7	8.00
NAT.W.					
B & H	1	1	4	4*	–

LAST SEASON: BOWLING

	O.	M.	R.	W.	AV.
TEST					
1ST-CLASS	527.3	127	1423	46	30.93
INT					
RAL	29	2	121	7	17.28
NAT.W.					
B & H	3	0	25	0	–

CAREER: BOWLING

	O.	M.	R.	W.	AV.
TEST					
1ST-CLASS	543.3	128	1505	48	31.35
INT					
RAL	41	2	180	8	22.50
NAT.W.					
B & H	3	0	25	0	–

WATKINSON, M. Lancashire

Full Name: Michael Watkinson
Role: Right-hand bat, right-arm medium or off-break bowler
Born: 1 August 1961, Westhoughton
Height: 6′ 1½″ **Weight:** 13st
Nickname: Winker
County debut: 1982
County cap: 1987
1st-Class 50s scored: 21
1st-Class 100s scored: 1
1st-Class 5 w. in innings: 11
One-Day 50s: 4
Place in batting averages: 173rd av. 21.68 (1987 79th av. 33.73)
Place in bowling averages: 109th av. 34.21 (1987 18th av. 23.47)
Strike rate 1988: 74.71 (career 65.42)
1st-Class catches 1988: 15 (career 61)
Parents: Albert and Marian
Wife and date of marriage: Susan, 12 April 1986
Education: Rivington and Blackrod High School, Horwich
Qualifications: 8 O-levels, HTC Civil Engineering

Jobs outside cricket: Draughtsman
Overseas teams played for: Woder Valley CC, Canberra, 1984–85
Cricketers particularly learnt from: Paul Allott, Steve O'Shaughnessy
Cricketers particularly admired: Clive Lloyd, Imran Khan
Other sports played: Football
Extras: Played for Cheshire CCC in Minor Counties, and NatWest Trophy (v Middlesex) 1982. Man of the Match in the first ever Refuge Assurance Cup Final 1988
Best batting performance: 106 Lancashire v Surrey, Southport 1985
Best bowling performance: 7-25 Lancashire v Sussex, Lytham 1987

LAST SEASON: BATTING

	I.	N.O.	R.	H.S.	AV.
TEST					
1ST-CLASS	39	4	759	85*	21.68
INT					
RAL	15	2	347	58	26.69
NAT.W.	2	0	11	9	5.50
B & H	4	1	102	70*	34.00

CAREER: BATTING

	I.	N.O.	R.	H.S.	AV.
TEST					
1ST-CLASS	170	23	3465	106	23.57
INT					
RAL	60	21	840	58	21.53
NAT.W.	12	3	163	56	18.11
B & H	15	3	190	70*	15.83

LAST SEASON: BOWLING

	O.	M.	R.	W.	AV.
TEST					
1ST-CLASS	647.3	153	1779	52	34.21
INT					
RAL	106.5	6	537	17	31.58
NAT.W.	24	2	98	2	49.00
B & H	38	2	166	1	166.00

CAREER: BOWLING

	O.	M.	R.	W.	AV.
TEST					
1ST-CLASS	2606.1	551	8017	239	33.54
INT					
RAL	529.5	29	2525	81	31.17
NAT.W.	167.5	16	660	14	47.14
B & H	211.1	18	881	27	32.62

WAUGH, M. E.   Essex

Full Name: Mark Edward Waugh
Role: Right-hand bat, right-arm medium pace bowler
Born: 2 June 1965, Canterbury, New South Wales
Height: 5′ 9¾″ **Weight:** 13st 7lbs
Nickname: Junior
County debut: 1988
1st-Class 50s scored: 9
1st-Class 100s scored: 4
1st-Class catches 1988: 2 (career 30)
Parents: Rodger and Beverley
Marital status: Single
Family links with cricket: Uncle a very good District player. Twin-brother Stephen plays for Australia and played for Somerset in 1988.

Younger brother Dean playing in Bolton League with Astley Bridge in 1989

Education: East Hills Boys High School

Qualifications: Higher School Certificate, cricket coach

Jobs outside cricket: Sales assistant, ML Sporting Goods 1983; Sales and Promotions, Kingsgrove Sports Store 1984–88

Off-season 1988–89: Playing cricket for New South Wales

Overseas tours: With New South Wales to Zimbabwe 1986, 1987; with New South Wales to New Zealand 1986

Overseas teams played for: New South Wales 1985, 1986, 1987

Cricketers particularly learnt from: 'Allan Border for his determination and attitude towards the game. Bob Simpson, especially for his fielding techniques.'

Cricketers particularly admired: Doug Walters, Allan Border

Other sports played: Golf, tennis, soccer

Other sports followed: Any sport

Injuries 1988: 'None this season, but I have had stress fractures in my back.'

Relaxations: 'Sleeping, horse racing, going for a quiet week or weekend away from cricket with my girlfriend.'

Extras: Only twins to score hundreds in the same innings of a first-class match (Stephen and Mark). Chosen as New South Wales Cricketer of the Year, 1988

Opinions on cricket: 'I believe there is too much cricket for the professional in England. The strain on fast bowlers particularly in playing five or six days a week will shorten their careers greatly and affect their performances while playing. I also believe compared to other professional sports (e.g. soccer, golf, tennis) cricketers are poorly paid considering the life-span of their careers.'

Best batting performance: 116 New South Wales v Tasmania, Sydney 1987–88

Best bowling performance: 4-130 New South Wales v Queensland 1985–86

LAST SEASON: BATTING

	I.	N.O.	R.	H.S.	AV.
TEST					
1ST-CLASS	4	0	178	86	44.50
INT					
RAL	3	0	120	103	40.00
NAT.W.					
B & H					

CAREER: BATTING

	I.	N.O.	R.	H.S.	AV.
TEST					
1ST-CLASS	40	6	1503	116	44.20
INT					
RAL	3	0	120	103	40.00
NAT.W.					
B & H					

LAST SEASON: BOWLING

	O.	M.	R.	W.	AV.
TEST					
1ST-CLASS	12	0	75	0	–
INT					
RAL	13	1	68	2	34.00
NAT.W.					
B & H					

CAREER: BOWLING

	O.	M.	R.	W.	AV.
TEST					
1ST-CLASS	237.4	52	730	20	36.50
INT					
RAL	13	1	68	2	34.00
NAT.W.					
B & H					

WAUGH, S. R. Somerset

Full Name: Stephen Rodger Waugh
Role: Right-hand bat, right-arm medium bowler
Born: 2 June 1965, Canterbury, New South Wales
Nickname: Melon
County debut: 1987
Test debut: 1985–86
No. of Tests: 18
No. of One-Day Internationals: 58
1000 runs in a season: 1
1st-Class 50s scored: 19
1st-Class 100s scored: 11
1st-Class 5 w. in innings: 2
One-Day 50s: 10
One-Day 100s: 2
Place in batting averages: 3rd av. 73.00

1st-Class catches 1988: 20 (career 80)
Parents: Rodger and Beverley
Family links with cricket: Twin-brother Mark plays for Essex. Uncle a very good District player. Younger brother Dean playing in Bolton League in 1989
Education: East Hills Boys High School
Off-season 1988–89: Playing for New South Wales and Australia
Overseas tours: Young Australia to Zimbabwe; Australia to New Zealand; India 1986–87; India and Pakistan for World Cup 1987
Overseas team played for: New South Wales
Extras: Played for Nelson in Lancashire League 1987. Signed by Somerset

LAST SEASON: BATTING

	I.	N.O.	R.	H.S.	AV.
TEST					
1ST-CLASS	24	6	1314	161	73.00
INT					
RAL	10	2	534	140*	66.75
NAT.W.	2	0	21	21	10.50
B & H	3	1	161	79	80.50

CAREER: BATTING

	I.	N.O.	R.	H.S.	AV.
TEST	27	4	676	79*	29.39
1ST-CLASS	74	13	3218	170	52.75
INT	52	15	1321	83*	35.70
RAL	10	2	534	140*	66.75
NAT.W.	2	0	21	21	10.50
B & H	3	1	161	79	80.50

LAST SEASON: BOWLING

	O.	M.	R.	W.	AV.
TEST					
1ST-CLASS	23	5	60	3	20.00
INT					
RAL	20	0	114	2	57.00
NAT.W.	22	3	96	4	24.00
B & H	14	1	63	2	31.50

CAREER: BOWLING

	O.	M.	R.	W.	AV.
TEST	323.2	87	885	28	31.60
1ST-CLASS	599.3	119	1743	60	29.05
INT	437.1	18	1926	70	27.51
RAL	20	0	114	2	57.00
NAT.W.	22	3	96	4	24.00
B & H	14	1	63	2	31.50

during season as overseas player to cover for the injured Martin Crowe. Only twins, with brother Mark, both to score a century in same first-class match. First played for New South Wales at age 19, and for Australia at age 20. Played for Essex 2nd XI on Esso scholarship in 1985. Had to leave Somerset in August 1988 to prepare for Australia's tour of Pakistan.
Best batting performance: 170 New South Wales v Victoria, Sydney 1987–88
Best bowling performance: 5-50 New South Wales v Tasmania, Sydney 1987–88

WELLS, A. P. Sussex

Full Name: Alan Peter Wells
Role: Right-hand bat, right-arm medium bowler, cover fielder
Born: 2 October 1961, Newhaven
Height: 6′ 0″ **Weight:** 12st 4lbs
Nickname: Morph, Bomber
County debut: 1981
County cap: 1986
1000 runs in a season: 3
1st-Class 50s scored: 30
1st-Class 100s scored: 8
One-Day 50s: 14
Place in batting averages: 61st av. 34.75 (1987 93rd av. 32.06)
1st-Class catches 1988: 18 (career 76)
Parents: Ernest William Charles and Eunice Mae
Marital status: Single
Family links with cricket: Father played for many years for local club. Eldest brother, Ray, plays club cricket. Brother of C. M. Wells of Sussex
Education: Tideway Comprehensive, Newhaven
Qualifications: 5 O-levels, NCA Coaching Certificate
Jobs outside cricket: Laboratory assistant. Coached in South Africa
Cricketing superstitions or habits: 'Have to put bat at junction of return and popping crease at the end of each over. Never stand inside the return crease when backing up. When repairing wicket count how many times I tap ground. Double whirl of arms with bat when going in to bat. Plus many more.'
Overseas tours: NCA U-19 tour of Canada, 1979
Cricketers particularly learnt from: Father, Chris Waller, Roger Marshall, Les Lenham
Other sports played: Table tennis, squash, darts, snooker, tennis

Relaxations: Listening to music, eating out, drinking in country pubs
Extras: Played for England Young Cricketers v India 1981
Best batting performance: 161* Sussex v Kent, Hove 1987
Best bowling performance: 3-67 Sussex v Worcestershire, Worcester 1987

LAST SEASON: BATTING

	I.	N.O.	R.	H.S.	AV.
TEST					
1ST-CLASS	42	5	1286	120	34.75
INT					
RAL	14	0	294	51	21.00
NAT.W.	1	0	0	0	0.00
B & H	4	0	125	53	31.25

LAST SEASON: BOWLING

	O.	M.	R.	W.	AV.
TEST					
1ST-CLASS	14	1	54	1	54.00
INT					
RAL					
NAT.W.					
B & H	1.5	0	15	0	–

CAREER: BATTING

	I.	N.O.	R.	H.S.	AV.
TEST					
1ST-CLASS	225	37	5856	161*	31.14
INT					
RAL	85	12	1772	71*	24.27
NAT.W.	13	3	147	55	14.70
B & H	22	2	583	72	29.15

CAREER: BOWLING

	O.	M.	R.	W.	AV.
TEST					
1ST-CLASS	70	5	322	5	64.40
INT					
RAL	10.2	0	69	4	17.25
NAT.W.	1	0	1	0	–
B & H	10	1	72	3	24.00

WELLS, C. M.   Sussex

Full Name: Colin Mark Wells
Role: Right-hand bat, right-arm medium bowler
Born: 3 March 1960, Newhaven
Height: 6′ 0″ **Weight:** 13st
Nickname: Bomber, Dougie
County debut: 1979
County cap: 1982
No. of One-Day Internationals: 2
1000 runs in a season: 6
1st-Class 50s scored: 43
1st-Class 100s scored: 17
1st-Class 200s scored: 1
1st-Class 5 w. in innings: 4
One-Day 50s: 19
One-Day 100s: 2
Place in batting averages: 141st av. 24.54 (1987 19th av. 45.50)
Place in bowling averages: 108th av. 34.16 (1987 66th av. 29.44)
Strike rate 1988: 74.58 (career 69.67)
1st-Class catches 1988: 8 (career 67)
Parents: Ernest William Charles and Eunice Mae

Wife and date of marriage: Celia, 25 September 1982

Family links with cricket: Father, Billy, had trials for Sussex and played for Sussex Cricket Association. Eldest brother, Ray, plays club cricket and youngest brother, Alan, plays for Sussex

Education: Tideway Comprehensive School, Newhaven

Qualifications: 9 O-levels, 2 CSEs, 1 A-level, MCC Intermediate Coaching Certificate

Jobs outside cricket: Working as a cellular telephone salesman for F. Smith & Co. of Horsham

Cricketing superstitions or habits: Left boot and left pad on first

Overseas tours: With England to Sharjah 1985

Overseas teams played for: Border, 1980–81; Western Province 1984–85

Other sports played: Football, rugby, hockey, basketball, tennis, table tennis

Relaxations: Sea-angling, philately, listening to music

Extras: Played in three John Player League matches in 1978. Was recommended to Sussex by former Sussex player, Ian Thomson. Highest 4th wicket partnership of 256 for Sussex v Glamorgan with Imran Khan. Vice captain since 1988

Opinions on cricket: 'Strongly believe that we cram in too much cricket, which must have a detrimental effect on all, especially the fast bowlers, particularly long term.'

Best batting performance: 203 Sussex v Hampshire, Hove 1984

Best bowling performance: 6-34 Sussex v Lancashire, Lytham 1987

LAST SEASON: BATTING

	I.	N.O.	R.	H.S.	AV.
TEST					
1ST-CLASS	41	4	908	109*	24.54
INT					
RAL	14	3	377	85	34.27
NAT.W.	1	0	0	0	0.00
B & H	4	0	45	26	11.25

LAST SEASON: BOWLING

	O.	M.	R.	W.	AV.
TEST					
1ST-CLASS	534.3	119	1469	43	34.16
INT					
RAL	87	10	308	7	44.00
NAT.W.	6	0	19	1	19.00
B & H	16	0	86	3	28.66

CAREER: BATTING

	I.	N.O.	R.	H.S.	AV.
TEST					
1ST-CLASS	339	53	9580	203	33.49
INT					
RAL	120	19	2887	104*	28.58
NAT.W.	20	3	405	76	23.82
B & H	37	4	836	101*	25.33

CAREER: BOWLING

	O.	M.	R.	W.	AV.
TEST					
1ST-CLASS	3460.2	805	9855	298	33.07
INT					
RAL	687.2	52	2544	96	26.50
NAT.W.	155.4	23	443	12	36.91
B & H	188	26	677	24	28.20

174. Which county cricket club was founded earlier, Yorkshire or Lancashire?

175. Who is the only Dutch-born player in county cricket?

WELLS, V. J.   Kent

Full Name: Vincent John Wells
Role: Right-hand bat, right-arm
medium pace bowler, wicket-keeper
Born: 6 August 1965, Dartford
Height: 6′ 1″ **Weight:** 12st 11lbs
Nickname: Wellsy
County debut: 1987
1st-Class catches 1988: 1 (career 1)
Parents: Pat and Jack
Marital status: Single
Family links with cricket: Brother
plays club cricket in Kent League
Education: Downs School, Dartford;
Sir William Nottidge School
Qualifications: 1 O-level, 8 CSEs
Jobs outside cricket: Ex-partner of
sportshop
Off-season 1988–89: Coaching
for Avendale CC, South Africa

Overseas teams played for: Parnell CC, Auckland, New Zealand 1986;
Avendale CC 1986–87, 1988–89
Cricketers particularly learnt from: Colin Page, Bob Woolmer, Malcolm Bell
Cricketers particularly admired: David Gower, Ian Botham
Other sports played: Football
Other sports followed: Most sports
Relaxations: 'Eating out with my girlfriend Debbie; reading.'
Extras: Was a schoolboy footballer with Leyton Orient
Best batting performance: 6 Kent v West Indians, Canterbury 1988
Best bowling performance: 1-51 Kent v West Indians, Canterbury 1988

LAST SEASON: BATTING

	I.	N.O.	R.	H.S.	AV.
TEST					
1ST-CLASS	2	0	6	6	3.00
INT					
RAL	1	1	10	10*	–
NAT.W.					
B & H	1	1	15	15*	–

CAREER: BATTING

	I.	N.O.	R.	H.S.	AV.
TEST					
1ST-CLASS	2	0	6	6	3.00
INT					
RAL	2	1	12	10*	12.00
NAT.W.					
B & H	1	1	15	15*	–

LAST SEASON: BOWLING

	O.	M.	R.	W.	AV.
TEST					
1ST-CLASS	14	4	51	1	51.00
INT					
RAL	22	1	68	7	9.71
NAT.W.					
B & H	7	1	33	0	–

CAREER: BOWLING

	O.	M.	R.	W.	AV.
TEST					
1ST-CLASS	14	4	51	1	51.00
INT					
RAL	22	1	68	7	9.71
NAT.W.					
B & H	7	1	33	0	–

WESTON, M. J. Worcestershire

Full Name: Martin John Weston
Role: Right-hand bat, right-arm medium bowler
Born: 8 April 1959, Worcester
Height: 6' 1" **Weight:** 14st 7lbs
Nickname: Wesso, Shag
County debut: 1979
County cap: 1986
1000 runs in season: 1
1st-Class 50s scored: 24
1st-Class 100s scored: 3
One-Day 50s: 8
One-Day 100s: 1
Place in batting averages: 118th
av. 27.05 (1987 160th av. 22.42)
Place in bowling averages: 60th
av. 26.33
Strike rate 1988: 62.00 (career 81.20)
1st-Class catches 1988: 15 (career 62)
Parents: John Franklyn and Sheila Margaret
Marital status: Single
Education: St George's C of E Junior; Samuel Southall Secondary Modern
Qualifications: City & Guilds and Advance Crafts in Bricklaying
Overseas tours: 1980 tour to Barbados with Worcestershire CCC
Cricketers particularly learnt from: Basil D'Oliveira
Other sports played: Football, squash
Relaxations: Horse racing
Best batting performance: 145* Worcestershire v Northamptonshire, Worcester 1984

LAST SEASON: BATTING

	I.	N.O.	R.	H.S.	AV.
TEST					
1ST-CLASS	24	5	514	95*	27.05
INT					
RAL	9	4	188	72	37.60
NAT.W.	5	2	129	45*	43.00
B & H	1	0	50	50	50.00

CAREER: BATTING

	I.	N.O.	R.	H.S.	AV.
TEST					
1ST-CLASS	207	16	4716	145*	24.69
INT					
RAL	80	12	1354	109	19.91
NAT.W.	13	4	277	45*	30.77
B & H	26	0	501	56	19.26

LAST SEASON: BOWLING

	O.	M.	R.	W.	AV.
TEST					
1ST-CLASS	124	31	320	12	26.66
INT					
RAL	74	5	234	11	21.27
NAT.W.	26.3	4	110	4	27.50
B & H	8.1	0	27	1	27.00

CAREER: BOWLING

	O.	M.	R.	W.	AV.
TEST					
1ST-CLASS	879.4	207	2559	65	39.36
INT					
RAL	308.3	11	1381	44	31.38
NAT.W.	74.2	11	286	9	31.77
B & H	78.1	7	286	10	28.60

Best bowling performance: 4-24 Worcestershire v Warwickshire, Edgbaston 1988

WHITAKER, J. J.   Leicestershire

Full Name: John James Whitaker
Role: Right-hand bat,
off-break bowler
Born: 5 May 1962, Skipton,
Yorkshire
Height: 6′ 0″ **Weight:** 13st
County debut: 1983
County cap: 1986
Test debut: 1986–87
No. of Tests: 1
No. of One-Day Internationals: 2
1000 runs in a season: 5
1st-Class 50s scored: 35
1st-Class 100s scored: 15
1st-Class 200s scored: 1
One-Day 50s: 9
One-Day 100s: 3
Place in batting averages: 52nd

av. 35.97 (1987 64th av. 36.61)
1st-Class catches 1988: 16 (career 83)
Parents: John and Anne
Family links with cricket: Father plays club cricket for Skipton
Education: Uppingham School
Qualifications: 7 O-levels
Jobs outside cricket: Employee of Whitakers Chocolates Ltd; groundsman, Adelaide 1982–83; cricket coach and farmer, Tasmania 1983
Overseas tours: Australia 1981–82 with Uppingham School; England to Australia 1986–87
Overseas teams played for: Glenelg CC, Adelaide 1982–83; Old Scotch CC, Tasmania 1983–84; Somerset West, South Africa 1984–85
Cricketers particularly learnt from: Maurice Hallam (coach at Uppingham), Brian Davison
Cricketers particularly admired: Geoff Boycott, Dennis Amiss
Other sports played: Rugby, hockey, tennis, golf, squash
Other sports followed: Football, Leicester Tigers rugby
Injuries 1988: Back, shoulder and knee strains
Relaxations: Discos, music, reading, eating out
Extras: One of *Wisden*'s Five Cricketers of the Year, 1986

Opinions on cricket: 'Too many wickets are sub-standard. There is too much first-class cricket.'
Best batting performance: 200* Leicestershire v Nottinghamshire, Leicester 1986
Best bowling performance: 1-41 Leicestershire v Essex, Leicester 1986

LAST SEASON: BATTING

	I.	N.O.	R.	H.S.	AV.
TEST					
1ST-CLASS	39	5	1223	145	35.97
INT					
RAL	13	2	238	51	21.63
NAT.W.	2	0	14	14	7.00
B & H	2	0	23	16	11.50

CAREER: BATTING

	I.	N.O.	R.	H.S.	AV.
TEST	1	0	11	11	11.00
1ST-CLASS	198	28	6702	200*	39.42
INT	2	1	48	44*	48.00
RAL	58	8	1618	132	32.36
NAT.W.	11	0	437	155	39.72
B & H	19	2	364	73*	21.41

WHITTICASE, P.   Leicestershire

Full Name: Philip Whitticase
Role: Right-hand bat, wicket-keeper
Born: 15 March 1965, Birmingham
Height: 5′ 8″ **Weight:** 10st 7lbs
Nickname: Jasper, Tracy, Roland Rat
County debut: 1984
County cap: 1987
1st-Class 50s scored: 9
Place in batting averages: 128th av. 21.31 (1987 226th av. 14.04)
Parents: Larry Gordon and Ann
Marital status: Single
Family links with cricket: Grandfather and Father club cricketers (both wicket-keepers)
Education: Buckpool Secondary; Crestwood Comprehensive
Qualifications: 5 O-levels, 4 CSEs, coaching certificate
Jobs outside cricket: Inland Revenue, Linkbronze Ltd
Overseas teams played for: South Bunbury, Western Australia 1984–86
Cricketers particularly learnt from: D. Collins (Stourbridge CC), members of Leicestershire staff
Cricketers particularly admired: Bob Taylor, Alan Knott, Philip DeFreitas, Dennis Amiss
Other sports played: Football, table tennis, golf. Used to be on schoolboy forms with Birmingham City FC
Relaxations: Football, golf, listening to music. 'I'm interested in most sports.

Playing cards is amusing especially when Les Taylor and John Agnew are involved. A good night out.'

Extras: Played for MCC v Scotland 1985. Took two catches in Paddy Clift's hat-trick v Derby at Chesterfield 1985. Was Derek Underwood's last first-class victim

Opinions on cricket: 'I would like to see 16 four-day games, so that you play every county just once, during the week. Have the weekends purely for one-day cricket, Refuge League on a Sunday, and have a new competition on a Saturday, possibly involving coloured clothing.'

Best batting performance: 71 Leicestershire v Somerset, Leicester 1988

LAST SEASON: BATTING

	I.	N.O.	R.	H.S.	AV.
TEST					
1ST-CLASS	32	10	469	71	21.31
INT					
RAL	7	1	51	21	8.50
NAT.W.	2	1	28	23	28.00
B & H	2	0	6	4	3.00

CAREER: BATTING

	I.	N.O.	R.	H.S.	AV.
TEST					
1ST-CLASS	98	23	1558	71	20.77
INT					
RAL	18	5	132	29*	10.15
NAT.W.	5	1	67	32	16.75
B & H	7	2	87	36	17.40

LAST SEASON: WICKET KEEPING

	C.	ST.
TEST		
1ST-CLASS	70	4
INT		
RAL	17	1
NAT.W.	3	–
B & H	2	–

CAREER: WICKET KEEPING

	C.	ST.
TEST		
1ST-CLASS	187	7
INT		
RAL	35	4
NAT.W.	10	–
B & H	16	–

WILD, D. J.   Northamptonshire

Full Name: Duncan James Wild
Role: Left-hand bat, right-arm medium bowler, cover fielder
Born: 28 November 1962, Northampton
Height: 6' 0" **Weight:** 12st 7lbs
Nickname: Oscar, Wildy
County debut: 1980
County cap: 1986
1st-Class 50s scored: 13
1st-Class 100s scored: 4
One-Day 50s: 5
Place in batting averages: 218th av. 16.26 (1987 110th av. 29.47)
Place in bowling averages: 91st av. 31.27 (1987 136th av. 48.27)
Strike rate 1988: 62.61 (career 81.07)

1st-Class catches 1988: 3 (career 33)
Parents: John and Glenys
Marital status: Single
Family links with cricket: Father played for Northamptonshire
Education: Cherry Orchard Middle; Northampton School for Boys
Qualifications: 7 O-levels. Diploma in international trade
Jobs outside cricket: Law costs draughtsman, manufacturer's agent
Overseas tours: England Young Cricketers to West Indies 1980
Cricketers particularly learnt from: Wayne Larkins, Bob Carter
Cricketers particularly admired: David Gower, Richard Hadlee, Geoff Cook
Other sports played: Squash, golf, snooker
Other sports followed: Rugby, rallying
Extras: Played for England Young Cricketers v Young India in 3-Test series 1981. Also for Young England v Young West Indies, 1982
Best batting performance: 144 Northamptonshire v Lancashire, Southport 1984
Best bowling performance: 4-4 Northamptonshire v Cambridge University, Cambridge 1986

LAST SEASON: BATTING

	I.	N.O.	R.	H.S.	AV.
TEST					
1ST-CLASS	27	1	423	75	16.26
INT					
RAL	10	3	266	91	38.00
NAT.W.	1	0	11	11	11.00
B & H	2	0	1	1	0.50

CAREER: BATTING

	I.	N.O.	R.	H.S.	AV.
TEST					
1ST-CLASS	148	21	3315	144	26.10
INT					
RAL	57	19	798	91	21.00
NAT.W.	9	0	48	11	5.33
B & H	19	7	229	48	19.08

LAST SEASON: BOWLING

	O.	M.	R.	W.	AV.
TEST					
1ST-CLASS	187.5	37	563	18	31.27
INT					
RAL	70	4	364	10	36.40
NAT.W.	9	3	12	1	12.00
B & H	16	0	66	5	13.20

CAREER: BOWLING

	O.	M.	R.	W.	AV.
TEST					
1ST-CLASS	878.2	179	2836	65	43.63
INT					
RAL	429.1	13	2065	73	28.28
NAT.W.	122.3	16	424	14	30.28
B & H	101.5	5	398	14	28.42

176. Who is the only West German-born player in county cricket?

177. What is the highest individual score ever officially recorded?

WILLEY, P.   Leicestershire

Full Name: Peter Willey
Role: Right-hand bat,
off-break bowler, all-rounder
Born: 6 December 1949, Sedgefield,
Co Durham
Height: 6′ 1″ **Weight:** 13st
Nickname: Chin, Will
County debut: 1966
(Northamptonshire), 1984
(Leicestershire)
County cap: 1971
(Northamptonshire), 1984
(Leicestershire)
Benefit: 1981 (£31,400)
Test debut: 1976
No. of Tests: 25
No. of One-Day Internationals: 26
1000 runs in a season: 8
1st-Class 50s scored: 89
1st-Class 100s scored: 41
1st-Class 200s scored: 1
1st-Class 5 w. in innings: 25
1st-Class 10 w. in match: 3
One-Day 50s: 59
One-Day 100s: 9
Place in batting averages: 135th av. 25.07 (1987 77th av. 33.94)
Place in bowling averages: 125th av. 42.26 (1987 90th av. 34.11)
Strike rate 1988: 107.68 (career 74.45)
1st-Class catches 1988: 12 (career 208)
Parents: Oswald and Maisie
Wife and date of marriage: Charmaine, 23 September 1971
Children: Heather Jane, 11 September 1985
Family links with cricket: Father played local club cricket in County Durham
Education: Secondary School, Seaham, County Durham
Jobs outside cricket: Has worked as a groundsman, labourer and in a shoe factory
Off-season 1988–89: Working in a local warehouse of electrical products
Overseas tours: Toured Australia with England 1979–80; West Indies, 1981 and 1986
Overseas teams played for: Eastern Province, South Africa, 1982–85
Cricketers particularly learnt from: Bishan Bedi, Geoffrey Boycott
Other sports played: Golf, shooting
Other sports followed: Football, golf, rugby

Relaxations: Reading, taking Irish Setter for long walks and shooting, gardening

Extras: With Wayne Larkins, received 2016 pints of beer (seven barrels) from a brewery in Northampton as a reward for their efforts in Australia with England in 1978–79. Hit a six off his first ball v Middlesex in JPL, 26 July 1981. Shared in 4th wicket partnership record for county, 370 with R. T. Virgin v Somerset at Northampton in 1976. Youngest player ever to play for Northamptonshire CCC at 16 years 180 days v Cambridge in 1966. Banned from Test cricket for three years for joining England rebel tour of South Africa in 1982. Left Northamptonshire at end of 1983 and moved to Leicestershire as vice-captain. Appointed Leicestershire captain for 1987. Resigned captaincy at end of season

Opinions on cricket: 'Wickets must improve at every ground. It is the only way to get good cricketers. Four-day cricket won't make people better cricketers. Young players have things made too easy for them.'

Best batting performance: 227 Northamptonshire v Somerset, Northampton 1976

Best bowling performance: 7-37 Northamptonshire v Oxford University, Oxford 1975

LAST SEASON: BATTING

	I.	N.O.	R.	H.S.	AV.
TEST					
1ST-CLASS	40	1	978	130	25.07
INT					
RAL	11	0	168	43	15.27
NAT.W.	2	0	22	15	11.00
B & H	3	0	98	59	32.66

LAST SEASON: BOWLING

	O.	M.	R.	W.	AV.
TEST					
1ST-CLASS	341	106	803	19	42.26
INT					
RAL	78	4	316	7	45.14
NAT.W.	24	1	92	0	–
B & H	31.5	3	101	4	25.25

CAREER: BATTING

	I.	N.O.	R.	H.S.	AV.
TEST	50	6	1184	102*	26.90
1ST-CLASS	773	102	20797	227	30.99
INT	24	1	538	64	23.39
RAL	235	18	5975	107	27.53
NAT.W.	44	6	1275	154*	33.55
B & H	60	11	1576	88*	32.16

CAREER: BOWLING

	O.	M.	R.	W.	AV.
TEST	181.5	49	456	7	65.14
1ST-CLASS	32.6 8532.3	13 2362	20427	684	29.86
INT	171.5	9	659	13	50.69
RAL	1373.2	118	5565	206	27.01
NAT.W.	431.3	57	1331	31	42.93
B & H	551.3	88	1521	42	36.21

178. Which county captain has a degree in Russian and was a professional footballer?

179. What current England Test cricketer always keeps a 10p piece in his left pocket when batting?

WILLIAMS, N. F. Middlesex

Full Name: Neil Fitzgerald
Williams
Role: Right-hand bat, right-arm
fast-medium bowler
Born: 2 July 1962, Hopewell,
St Vincent, West Indies
Height: 5′ 11″ **Weight:** 11st 7lbs
Nickname: Joe
County debut: 1982
County cap: 1984
Benefit: 1989
50 wickets in a season: 2
1st-Class 50s scored: 6
1st-Class 5 w. in innings: 6
1st-Class 10 w. in match: 1
Place in batting averages: 184th
av. 20.66 (1987 235th av. 12.80)
Place in bowling averages: 5th
av. 17.05 (1987 129th av. 44.23)
Strike rate 1988: 35.70 (career 53.90)
1st-Class catches 1988: 1 (career 26)
Parents: Alexander and Aldreta
Marital status: Single

Family links with cricket: 'Uncle Joe was 12th man for St Vincent and plays 1st
Division cricket.'
Education: Cane End Primary School, St Vincent; Acland Burghley School,
Tufnell Park
Qualifications: School Leavers Certificate, 6 O-levels, 1 A-level
Overseas tours: English Counties to Zimbabwe 1985

LAST SEASON: BATTING

	I.	N.O.	R.	H.S.	AV.
TEST					
1ST-CLASS	11	2	186	63*	20.66
INT					
RAL	4	3	96	43	96.00
NAT.W.	1	1	8	8*	–
B & H	3	0	18	12	6.00

CAREER: BATTING

	I.	N.O.	R.	H.S.	AV.
TEST					
1ST-CLASS	122	30	1823	67	19.81
INT					
RAL	30	11	309	43	16.26
NAT.W.	7	3	36	10	9.00
B & H	15	3	148	20	12.33

LAST SEASON: BOWLING

	O.	M.	R.	W.	AV.
TEST					
1ST-CLASS	178.3	33	511	30	17.03
INT					
RAL	55	2	242	16	15.12
NAT.W.	12.1	4	24	2	12.00
B & H	48	3	186	3	62.00

CAREER: BOWLING

	O.	M.	R.	W.	AV.
TEST					
1ST-CLASS	2677.2	488	8674	298	29.10
INT					
RAL	388.3	11	1747	68	25.69
NAT.W.	89.1	15	301	13	23.15
B & H	251.4	26	964	26	37.07

Overseas teams played for: Windward Islands 1983; Tasmania 1983–84
Cricketers particularly learnt from: Wilf Slack, Roland Butcher, Wayne Daniel
Cricketers particularly admired: Viv Richards, Andy Roberts, Michael Holding, Dennis Lillee, Malcolm Marshall, Lawrence Rowe
Other sports followed: Most
Relaxations: Reggae, soca, soul, cinema
Extras: Was on stand-by for England in New Zealand and Pakistan 1983–84
Best batting performance: 67 Middlesex v Cambridge University, Cambridge 1985
Best bowling performance: 7-55 English Counties XI v Zimbabwean XI, Harare 1984–85

WILLIAMS, R. G. Northamptonshire

Full Name: Richard Grenville Williams
Role: Right-hand bat, off-break bowler, all-rounder
Born: 10 August 1957, Bangor, Caernarvonshire
Height: 5' 6" **Weight:** 12st
Nickname: Chippy
County debut: 1974
County cap: 1979
Benefit: 1989
1000 runs in a season: 6
1st-Class 50s scored: 50
1st-Class 100s scored: 17
1st-Class 5 w. in innings: 9
One-Day 50s: 21
Place in batting averages: 67th av. 33.80 (1987 20th av. 44.90)
Place in bowling averages: 80th av. 29.69 (1987 35th av. 25.65)
Strike rate 1988: 60.18 (career 70.28)
1st-Class catches 1988: 8 (career 89)
Parents: Gordon and Rhianwen
Wife and date of marriage: Helen Laura, 24 April 1982
Family links with cricket: Father played for Caernarvonshire and North Wales
Education: Ellesmere Port Grammar School
Jobs outside cricket: Qualified carpenter (self-employed)

Off-season 1988–89: Preparing for benefit year

Overseas tours: Australasia in 1980 with Derrick Robins' U-23 XI; West Indies with England Young Cricketers 1976; Zimbabwe with English Counties 1985

Overseas teams played for: Stockton CC and Belmont CC in Sydney, Australia on Whitbread Scholarship. Also played in New Zealand

Other sports played: Golf

Injuries 1988: Torn cartilage

Relaxations: Fly fishing, shooting, trout fishing

Extras: Debut for 2nd XI in 1972 aged 14 years 11 months. Made maiden century in 1979 and then scored four centuries in five innings. Hat-trick v Gloucestershire, at Northampton 1980. Was first player to score a century against the 1980 West Indies touring team. Was stand-by for England in India 1981

Best batting performance: 175* Northamptonshire v Leicestershire, Leicester 1980

Best bowling performance: 7-73 Northamptonshire v Cambridge University, Cambridge 1980

LAST SEASON: BATTING

	I.	N.O.	R.	H.S.	AV.
TEST					
1ST-CLASS	34	9	845	119	33.80
INT					
RAL	9	1	139	55	17.37
NAT.W.	1	0	3	3	3.00
B & H	3	1	94	75	47.00

LAST SEASON: BOWLING

	O.	M.	R.	W.	AV.
TEST					
1ST-CLASS	331	72	980	33	29.69
INT					
RAL	35	0	192	8	24.00
NAT.W.	5	2	10	1	10.00
B & H	25	2	75	3	25.00

CAREER: BATTING

	I.	N.O.	R.	H.S.	AV.
TEST					
1ST-CLASS	399	56	10835	175*	31.58
INT					
RAL	124	21	2371	82	23.01
NAT.W.	26	5	491	94	23.38
B & H	34	8	859	83	33.03

CAREER: BOWLING

	O.	M.	R.	W.	AV.
TEST					
1ST-CLASS	3924.2	998	11132	335	33.22
INT					
RAL	419.2	25	2010	73	27.53
NAT.W.	165	24	501	26	19.26
B & H	201	27	679	23	29.52

180. Which current county cricketer has worked as a lumberjack?

181. What have Voce, Statham, Lindwall, Trueman, Lillee and Holding got in common, apart from being Test fast bowlers?

Full Name: Anthony John Wright
Role: Right-hand bat, off-break
bowler, short-leg or slip fielder
Born: 27 July 1962, Stevenage
Height: 6′ 1″ **Weight:** 13st 7lbs
Nickname: Billy, Horace
County debut: 1980
County cap: 1987
1000 runs in a season: 2
1st-Class 50s scored: 25
1st-Class 100s scored: 4
One-Day 50s: 10
Place in batting averages: 83rd
av. 30.92 (1987 120th av. 28.38)
1st-Class catches 1988: 14 (career 67)
Parents: Michael and Patricia
Wife and date of marriage: Rachel,
21 December 1986
Children: Hannah, 3 April 1988
Education: Alleyn's School, Stevenage
Qualifications: 6 O-levels
Jobs outside cricket: Sales rep for Allied Breweries
Overseas tours: Barbados 1980, 1985, 1986 and 1988 with Gloucestershire
Overseas teams played for: Port Melbourne 1981–85
Cricketers particularly learnt from: Barry Dudleston
Cricketers particularly admired: Viv Richards, Ian Botham, Javed Miandad,
Malcolm Marshall
Other sports played: Rugby, golf, soccer
Off-season 1988–89: 'Making as much money as possible! Playing rugby in
Bristol.'
Injuries 1988: Back trouble
Other sports followed: 'Most sports except snooker and darts.'
Relaxations: Eating out, drinking socially, listening to music, reading news-
papers, playing golf
Opinions on cricket: 'Four-day cricket was very enjoyable and in my opinion

LAST SEASON: BATTING

	I.	N.O.	R.	H.S.	AV.
TEST					
1ST-CLASS	42	1	1268	137	30.92
INT					
RAL	9	1	273	81	34.12
NAT.W.	3	0	66	55	22.00
B & H	4	0	87	66	21.75

CAREER: BATTING

	I.	N.O.	R.	H.S.	AV.
TEST					
1ST-CLASS	199	13	4899	161	26.33
INT					
RAL	47	5	712	81	16.95
NAT.W.	10	0	397	88	39.70
B & H	11	0	210	66	19.09

quite successful. Advertising restrictions on players should be relaxed to try to get more money into the game for the average pro. I struggle to see our sponsor's name from 22 yards, let alone from the boundary!'

Best batting performance: 161 Gloucestershire v Glamorgan, Bristol 1987

WRIGHT, J. G.   Derbyshire

Full Name: John Geoffrey Wright
Role: Left-hand opening bat, right-arm medium bowler
Born: 5 July 1954, Darfield, New Zealand
Height: 6′ 1″ **Weight:** 12st 7lbs
Nickname: Shake
County debut: 1977
County cap: 1977
Benefit: 1987 (£52,168)
Test debut: 1977–78
No. of Tests: 58
No. of One-Day Internationals: 110
1000 runs in a season: 6
1st-Class 50s scored: 105
1st-Class 100s scored: 47
One-Day 50s: 34
One-Day 100s: 5
Place in batting averages: 27th av. 42.89 (1987 59th av. 37.20)
1st-Class catches 1988: 1 (career 172)
Parents: Geoff and Helen
Wife and date of marriage: Susan, 1984
Family links with cricket: Father played first-class cricket for Canterbury, New Zealand
Education: Christ's College, Christchurch, New Zealand; University of Otago, Dunedin, New Zealand
Qualifications: BSc in Biochemistry
Off-season 1988–89: Playing for New Zealand, as captain, and Canterbury
Cricketing superstitions or habits: 'Ironed shirts are bad luck.'
Overseas tours: With New Zealand to England 1978, 1986; Australia 1980–81; Sri Lanka and Pakistan 1984–85; West Indies 1985; World Cup 1987; India 1988
Overseas teams played for: Northern Districts, Canterbury, New Zealand
Cricketers particularly learnt from: Eddie Barlow, David Steele

Cricketers particularly admired: 'Cutter' Curtayne, Allan Border, Malcolm Marshall
Other sports played: Rugby, golf
Other sports followed: Horse racing, tennis, rugby – 'most sports'
Relaxations: Music
Extras: Holds record of seven centuries for Derbyshire in a season – beating record of six held by Peter Kirsten in previous season, after record of five had stood for 49 years. Vice-captain of New Zealand 1984. Captain of New Zealand 1987. Awarded MBE in Queen's Birthday Honours 1988. Retired from county cricket at end of 1988 season
Opinions on cricket: 'From a cricket point of view, I feel that the implementation of some four-day games this summer was a tremendous success. Finally, I would like to say that I thoroughly enjoyed my 12 years of county cricket. I was privileged and fortunate to get that opportunity; may I wish both players and umpires all the very best for the future.'
Best batting performance: 192 Canterbury v Central Districts, New Plymouth 1986–87

LAST SEASON: BATTING

	I.	N.O.	R.	H.S.	AV.
TEST					
1ST-CLASS	20	1	815	154*	42.89
INT					
RAL	2	0	19	15	9.50
NAT.W.					
B & H					

CAREER: BATTING

	I.	N.O.	R.	H.S.	AV.
TEST	103	4	3343	141	33.76
1ST-CLASS	546	37	20849	192	40.96
INT	109	1	2926	101	27.09
RAL	93	6	2729	108	31.36
NAT.W.	12	2	555	87*	55.50
B & H	30	2	1005	102	35.89

WYATT, J. G. Somerset

Full Name: Julian George Wyatt
Role: Right-hand bat, off-break bowler
Born: 19 June 1963, Paulton, Somerset
Height: 5′ 10″ **Weight:** 12st
Nickname: Jules, Earp, Harold
County debut: 1983
1st-Class 50s scored: 12
1st-Class 100s scored: 3
One-day 50s: 5
Place in batting averages: 156th av. 23.12 (1987 157th av. 22.72)
1st-Class catches 1988: 9 (career 27)
Parents: Christopher Hedley and Dinah Ruby

Marital status: Single
Family links with cricket: 'None,
really, though my Dad played a six-a-side match two years ago!'
Education: Farrington Gurney Primary; Wells Cathedral School, Somerset
Qualifications: 5 O-levels, NCA Senior Coaching Certificate
Jobs outside cricket: Brandon Tool Hire 1980–83; van driver; shelf-stacker, etc.
Off-season 1988–89: Playing in Australia for Kew CC in Melbourne
Cricketing superstitions or habits: Right pad on first
Overseas tours: Barbados with Somerset 1985
Overseas teams played for: Kew CC, Melbourne 1984–85; Manley CC, Sydney 1987–88; Kew, 1988–89
Cricketers particularly admired: Brian Rose, Peter Denning, Colin Dredge, Trevor Gard, David Gower
Other sports played: Squash, football
Other sports followed: Rugby, soccer, horse racing
Relaxations: 'Socialising at local pubs. Sport.'
Opinions on cricket: 'Over-rate fines should be abolished. It is unfair that a side can be fined even though it has bowled its allotted overs in a day.'
Best batting performance: 145 Somerset v Oxford University, Oxford 1985
Best bowling performance: 1-0 Somerset v Sussex, Hove 1984

LAST SEASON: BATTING

	I.	N.O.	R.	H.S.	AV.
TEST					
1ST-CLASS	26	1	578	69	23.12
INT					
RAL	9	0	261	89	29.00
NAT.W.	1	0	8	8	8.00
B & H	2	0	99	55	49.50

CAREER: BATTING

	I.	N.O.	R.	H.S.	AV.
TEST					
1ST-CLASS	111	5	2743	145	25.87
INT					
RAL	24	2	472	89	21.45
NAT.W.	3	0	11	8	3.66
B & H	6	0	138	55	23.00

182. When Graeme Hick made 410 runs in April 1988, whose record was he breaking?

183. Who is the current President of MCC?

UMPIRES

BALDERSTONE, J. C.

Full Name: John Christopher Balderstone
Role: Right-hand bat, slow left-arm bowler, slip fielder
Born: 16 November 1940, Huddersfield, Yorkshire
Height: 6′ 2″ **Weight:** 12st 7lbs
Nickname: Baldy, Chris, Dad
Parents: Frank and Jenny
Counties: Yorkshire, Leicestershire
County debut: 1961 (Yorkshire), 1971 (Leicestershire)
County cap: 1973 (Leicestershire)
Testimonial: 1984 (£64,470 jointly with Ken Higgs)
Test debut: 1976
No. of Tests: 2
1000 runs in a season: 11
1st-Class 50s scored: 102
1st-Class 100s scored: 32
1st-Class 5 w. in innings: 5
One-day 50s: 32
One-day 100s: 5
1st-Class catches: 210
Best batting performance: 181* Leicestershire v Gloucestershire, Leicester 1984
Best bowling performance: 6-25 Leicestershire v Hampshire, Southampton 1978
Appointed to 1st-Class list: 1988
Wife and date of marriage: Madeline, April 1962
Children: Sally Victoria, 15 September 1970; Michael James, 3 January 1973

CAREER: BATTING

	I.	N.O.	R.	H.S.	AV.
TEST	4	0	39	35	9.75
1ST-CLASS	615	61	18995	181*	34.28
INT					
RAL	125	23	2673	96	26.20
NAT.W.	32	2	891	119*	29.70
B & H	57	12	2059	113*	45.76

CAREER: BOWLING

	O.	M.	R.	W.	AV.
TEST	16	0	80	1	80.00
1ST-CLASS	3187	957	8080	309	26.14
INT					
RAL	58.3	2	296	12	24.66
NAT.W.	48	12	176	11	16.00
B & H	30	4	103	5	20.60

Education: Paddock County School, Huddersfield
Qualifications: Advanced cricket coach, soccer coach
Jobs outside cricket: Professional footballer with Huddersfield Town, Carlisle United, Doncaster Rovers, Queen of the South, Enderby Town. Representative for a sports shop
Overseas tours: With Leicester to Zimbabwe 1981 and to Oman 1984
Cricketers particularly learnt from: 'Everyone.'
Other sports: Golf, professional football
Relaxations: Do-it-yourself, golf, reading and all sports
Extras: Played for Yorkshire 1961–70. Once played first-class cricket match and a league football match on the same day, 15 September 1975 (Leicestershire v Derbyshire at Chesterfield 11.30 am to 6.30 pm and Doncaster Rovers v Brentford at Doncaster 7.30 pm to 9.10 pm). Former Chairman of Cricketers' Association

BIRD, H. D.

Full Name: Harold Dennis Bird
Role: Right-hand opening bat
Born: 19 April 1933, Barnsley
Height: 5' 10½" **Weight:** 11st 6lbs
Nickname: Dickie
Parents: James Harold and Ethel
Counties: Yorkshire, Leicestershire
County debut: 1956 (Yorkshire), 1960 (Leicestershire)
County cap: 1960 (Leicestershire)
1000 runs in a season: 1
1st-Class 50s scored: 14
1st-Class 100s scored: 2
1st-Class catches: 20
Best batting performance: 181* Yorkshire v Glamorgan, Bradford 1959
Appointed to 1st-Class list: 1969
Appointed to Test panel: 1972
No. of Tests umpired: 37
No. of One-Day Internationals umpired: 62
Marital status: Bachelor
Education: Raley School, Barnsley
Jobs outside cricket: 'Cricket is my life.'

Off-season 1988–89: Umpiring in Sharjah, international matches between West Indies, Pakistan, and India. After-dinner speaking

Cricketing superstitions or habits: Twitch of the shoulders. Wearing a distinctive white cap
Other sports followed: Football
Cricketers particularly learnt from: Johnny Wardle, Sir Gubby Allen
Cricketers particularly admired: Sir Garfield Sobers, Dennis Lillee, Viv Richards
Relaxations: 'Listening to Barbra Streisand and Diana Ross records.'
Opinions on cricket: 'The greatest game in the world. A game to be enjoyed by young and old. I have consistently advocated playing through all light unless the umpire is convinced there is a genuine physical danger to the batsman.'
Extras: Awarded MBE, June 1986. Only man to umpire in three World Cup Finals, 1975, 1979 and 1983. Voted Yorkshire Personality of the Year, 1977. Umpired Centenary Test Match, England v Australia, 1980. Umpired Queen's Silver Jubilee Test Match, England v Australia, Lord's 1977. Author of *Not Out* (1978), *That's Out* (1985), *From the Pavilion End* (1988). Member of the TCCB Cricket Committee

CAREER: BATTING

	I.	N.O.	R.	H.S.	AV.
TEST					
1ST-CLASS	170	10	3314	181*	20.71
INT					
RAL					
NAT.W.	2	0	9	7	4.50
B & H					

CAREER: BOWLING

	O.	M.	R.	W.	AV.
TEST					
1ST-CLASS	8	2	22	0	–
INT					
RAL					
NAT.W.					
B & H					

184. What is relevant to cricket about the dedication of Robert Carter's novel *Armada*?

185. What current Australian Test cricketer played for Nostell in the Leeds League in 1988?

BOND, J. D.

Full Name: John David Bond
Role: Right-hand bat
Born: 6 May 1932, Kersley,
Lancashire
Nickname: Jackie
Counties: Lancashire,
Nottinghamshire
County debut: 1955 (Lancashire),
1974 (Nottinghamshire)
County cap: 1961 (Lancashire)
Benefit: 1970 (£7,230)
1000 runs in a season: 2
1st-Class 50s scored: 54
1st-Class 100s scored: 14
1st-Class catches: 223
Best batting performance: 157
Lancashire v Hampshire, Old
Trafford 1962
Appointed to 1st-Class list: 1988
Education: Bolton School
Extras: Lancashire, under his captaincy, won Gillette Cup 1970, 1971, 1972.
Won John Player League, 1969, 1970. Scored 2125 first-class runs in 1962.
Missed part of 1963 with a broken wrist. Was captain of Lancashire 1968–72.
Cricket Manager of Lancashire from 1980–86

CAREER: BATTING

	I.	N.O.	R.	H.S.	AV.
TEST					
1ST-CLASS	548	80	12125	157	25.90
INT					
RAL	42	12	416	43	13.87
NAT.W.	17	4	181	35*	13.92
B & H	3	0	16	14	5.33

CAREER: BOWLING

	O.	M.	R.	W.	AV.
TEST					
1ST-CLASS	12.1	1	69	0	–
INT					
RAL					
NAT.W.					
B & H					

186. Who came top of the Lancashire first-class batting averages in
1988?

187. Who came top of the Leicestershire first-class batting averages
in 1988?

CONSTANT, D. J.

Full Name: David John Constant
Role: Left-hand bat, slow
left-arm bowler
Born: 9 November 1941,
Bradford-on-Avon, Wiltshire
Nickname: Connie
Counties: Kent 1961–63,
Leicestershire 1965–68
County debut: 1961 (Kent),
1965 (Leicestershire)
1st-Class 50s scored: 6
1st-Class catches: 33
Best batting performance: 80
Leicestershire v Gloucestershire,
Bristol 1966
Appointed to 1st-Class list: 1969
Appointed to Test panel: 1971
No. of Tests umpired: 34
**No. of One-day Internationals
umpired:** 27

CAREER: BATTING

	I.	N.O.	R.	H.S.	AV.
TEST					
1ST-CLASS	93	14	1517	80	19.20
INT					
RAL					
NAT.W.	1	0	5	5	–
B & H					

CAREER: BOWLING

	O.	M.	R.	W.	AV.
TEST					
1ST-CLASS	12.3	3	36	1	–
INT					
RAL					
NAT.W.					
B & H					

188. Who came top of the Middlesex first-class batting averages in 1988?

189. Who came top of the Northamptonshire first-class batting averages in 1988?

DUDLESTON, B.

Full Name: Barry Dudleston
Role: Right-hand bat, slow
left-arm bowler
Born: 16 July 1945, Bebington,
Cheshire
Height: 5′ 9″ **Weight:** 11st 8lbs
Nickname: Danny
Parents: Percy and Dorothy Vera
Counties: Leicestershire,
Gloucestershire
County debut: 1966 (Leicestershire),
1981 (Gloucestershire)
County cap: 1969 (Leicestershire)
Benefit: 1980 (£25,000)
1000 runs in a season: 8
1st-Class 100s scored: 31
1st-Class 200s scored: 1
1st-Class catches: 234
One-Day 50s: 21
One-Day 100s: 4

Best batting performance: 202 Leicestershire v Derbyshire, Leicester 1979
Best bowling performance: 4-6 Leicestershire v Surrey, Leicester 1972
Appointed to 1st-Class list: 1984
Parents: Percy and Dorothy Vera
Wife and date of marriage: Lindsey Vivien Stratford, 5 April 1980
Children: Sharon Louise, 29 October 1968
Education: Stockport School
Qualifications: O-levels. Junior Coaching Certificate. Shell marketing exams
Jobs outside cricket: Retail and commercial representative for Shell
Overseas tours: With Derrick Robins' XI to Rhodesia
Overseas teams played for: Rhodesia 1966–67 to 1979–80 in Currie Cup
competition
Cricketers particularly learnt from: Vinoo Mankad
Cricket records: Leicestershire CCC 1st wicket record of 390, 7th wicket
record of 206, with Jack Birkenshaw v Kent at Canterbury in 1969. Fastest to
1000 runs in Currie Cup ever for Rhodesia, 2nd fastest of all time in Currie
Cup. Highest score by overseas player on debut in South Africa, 142 v
Western Province
Relaxations: Bridge and philately, watching all sports, red wine
Extras: England Under-25. Has suffered badly from broken fingers. Broke
fingers on same hand three times in 1978. Made debut for Leicestershire in
1966, gaining county cap in 1969. Released by Leicestershire at end of 1980
season and made debut for Gloucestershire 1981

Opinions on cricket: 'Now we are playing on covered wickets I should like to see a Championship programme of 16 four-day games, two one-day matches and a day off per week, which would then be a balanced programme.'

CAREER: BATTING

	I.	N.O.	R.	H.S.	AV.
TEST					
1ST-CLASS	501	47	14747	202	32.48
INT					
RAL	123	8	2490	152	24.41
NAT.W.	18	1	586	125	34.47
B & H	42	5	1171	90	31.65

CAREER: BOWLING

	O.	M.	R.	W.	AV.
TEST					
1ST-CLASS	406	87	1365	47	29.04
INT					
RAL	1	0	4	0	—
NAT.W.	3	0	14	0	—
B & H					

EELE, P. J.

Full Name: Peter James Eele
Role: Left-hand bat,
wicket-keeper
Born: 27 January 1935, Taunton
Height: 5' 6" **Weight:** 11st
County: Somerset
County debut: 1958
Benefit: 1969
1st-Class 100s scored: 1
1st-Class catches: 87 +
19 stumpings
Best batting performance:
103* Somerset v Pakistan Eaglets,
Taunton 1969
Appointed to 1st-Class list: 1981
Marital status: Single
Education: Taunton School

190. Who came top of the Nottinghamshire first-class batting averages in 1988?

191. Who came top of the Somerset first-class batting averages in 1988?

EVANS, D. G. L.

Full Name: David Gwillim Lloyd Evans
Role: Right-hand bat, wicket-keeper
Born: 27 July 1933, Lambeth
County: Glamorgan
County debut: 1956
County cap: 1959
Benefit: 1969 (£3,500)
Best batting performance: 46* Glamorgan v Oxford University, Oxford 1961
Appointed to 1st-Class list: 1971
Appointed to Test panel: 1981

CAREER: BATTING

	I.	N.O.	R.	H.S.	AV.
TEST					
1ST-CLASS	364	91	2875	46*	10.53
INT					
RAL					
NAT.W.	2	0	9	8	4.50
B & H					

CAREER: WICKET KEEPING

	C.	ST.			
TEST					
1ST-CLASS	503	55			
INT					
RAL					
NAT.W.	4	–			
B & H					

192. Who came top of the Surrey first-class batting averages in 1988?

193. Who came top of the Sussex first-class batting averages in 1988?

194. Who came top of the Warwickshire first-class batting averages in 1988?

HAMPSHIRE, J. H.

Full Name: John Harry Hampshire
Role: Right-hand bat, leg-break bowler
Born: 10 February 1941, Thurnscoe
Height: 6′ **Weight:** 13st
Nickname: Hamp
Parents: Jack and Vera
Counties: Yorkshire, Derbyshire
County debut: 1961 (Yorkshire), 1982 (Derbyshire)
County cap: 1963 (Yorkshire), 1982 (Derbyshire)
Test debut: 1969
No. of Tests: 8
1000 runs in a season: 15
1st-Class 50s scored: 142
1st-Class 100s scored: 43
1st-Class catches: 445
1st-Class 5 w. in innings: 1
One-Day 50s: 39
One-Day 100s: 7
Appointed to 1st-Class list: 1985
Education: Oakwood Technical High School, Rotherham
Wife and date of marriage: Judith Ann, 4 September 1964
Children: Ian Christopher, 6 January 1969; Paul Wesley, 12 February 1972
Family links with cricket: Father and brother, Alan, both played for Yorkshire
Jobs outside cricket: Coaching
Off-season 1988–89: Cricket coach at McEwan's Cricket Centre, Houghton-le-Spring, Durham
Other sports played: Golf
Relaxations: Gardening, reading
Extras: Scored 107 in his first Test Match v West Indies at Lord's
Best batting performance: 183* Yorkshire v Sussex 1971
Best bowling performance: 7-52 Yorkshire v Glamorgan 1963

CAREER: BATTING

	I.	N.O.	R.	H.S.	AV.
TEST	16	1	403	107	26.67
1ST-CLASS	908	111	27063	183*	33.96
INT	3	1	48	25*	24.00
RAL	172	20	4994	119	32.85
NAT.W.	33	5	930	110	33.21
B & H	45	6	1091	85*	27.97

CAREER: BOWLING

	O.	M.	R.	W.	AV.
TEST					
1ST-CLASS	16.6 402.5	1 85	1637	30	54.57
INT					
RAL	4	1	22	1	—
NAT.W.	2	0	4	0	—
B & H					

HARRIS, J. H.

Full Name: John Humphrey
Harris
Role: Left-hand bat, right-arm
fast-medium bowler
Born: 13 February 1936, Taunton
County: Somerset
County debut: 1952 (at
16 years 99 days)
1st-Class catches: 6
Best batting performance: 41
Somerset v Worcestershire,
Taunton 1957
Best bowling performance: 3-29
Somerset v Worcestershire,
Bristol 1959
Appointed to 1st-Class list: 1983
Extras: Played for Suffolk
1960–62 and Devon 1975

CAREER: BATTING

	I.	N.O.	R.	H.S.	AV.
TEST					
1ST-CLASS	18	4	154	41	11.00
INT					
RAL					
NAT.W.					
B & H					

CAREER: BOWLING

	O.	M.	R.	W.	AV.
TEST					
1ST-CLASS	217.2	42	619	19	32.57
INT					
RAL					
NAT.W.					
B & H					

195. Who came top of the Worcestershire first-class batting averages in 1988?

196. Who came top of the Yorkshire first-class batting averages in 1988?

HARRIS, M. J.

Full Name: Michael John Harris
Role: Right-hand bat, wicket-keeper, leg-break bowler
Born: 25 May 1944, St Just-in-Roseland, Cornwall
Height: 6′ 1″ **Weight:** 15st
Nickname: Pasty
Parents: Winnie and Dick
Counties: Middlesex, Nottinghamshire
County debut: 1964 (Middlesex), 1969 (Nottinghamshire)
County cap: 1970 (Nottinghamshire)
Benefit: 1977
1000 runs in a season: 11
1st-Class 50s scored: 98
1st-Class 100s scored: 40
1st-Class 200s scored: 1
Wife and date of marriage:
Danielle Ruth, 10 September 1969
Children: Jodene, Elizabeth, Richard
Family links with cricket: Father and uncles on both sides played top village cricket
Education: Gerrans C/P
Qualifications: MCC Advanced Coach. SRA Squash Coach
Jobs outside cricket: Squash club manager
Cricketing superstitions or habits: Left boot and pad go on first
Overseas tours: With Derrick Robins' XI to West Indies 1974; with International Wanderers to South Africa and Rhodesia in 1974
Overseas teams played for: Eastern Province in 1971–72 Currie Cup Competition; Wellington in New Zealand Shell Shield Competition 1975–76
Appointed to 1st-Class list: On reserve list
Cricket records: Scored nine centuries in 1971 to equal county record. Shared in first wicket partnership record for Middlesex, 312 with W. E. Russell v Pakistan, Lord's 1967
Cricketers particularly learnt from: Eric Russell of Middlesex

CAREER: BATTING

	I.	N.O.	R.	H.S.	AV.
TEST					
1ST-CLASS	581	58	19196	201*	36.70
INT					
RAL	139	31	3303	104*	30.58
NAT.W.	25	1	579	101	24.13
B & H	34	7	925	101	34.26

CAREER: BOWLING

	O.	M.	R.	W.	AV.
TEST					
1ST-CLASS	1047.5	229	3459	79	43.78
INT					
RAL	6.4	1	41	3	13.67
NAT.W.					
B & H	9	0	46	1	—

Other sports played: Squash, golf, football
Extras: Made debut for Middlesex in 1964. Left staff after 1968 to join Nottinghamshire in 1969. Scored 2,238 at an average of 50.86 in 1971. Scored two centuries in a match twice in 1971, 118 and 123 v Leicestershire at Leicester, and 107 and 131* v Essex at Chelmsford

HASSAN, S. B.

Full Name: Sheikh Basharat Hassan
Role: Right-hand bat, right-arm medium bowler, occasional wicket-keeper
Born: 24 March 1944, Nairobi, Kenya
Height: 5′ 11″ **Weight:** 11st
Nickname: Basher, Scooby Doo
Parents: Haji Sarwar Hussain (deceased) and Sairan Sheikh
County: Nottinghamshire
County debut: 1966
County cap: 1970
Benefit: 1978
1000 runs in a season: 5
1st-Class 50s scored: 80
1st-Class 100s scored: 15
One-Day 50s scored: 36
One-Day 100s scored: 4
1st-Class catches: 308 + 1 stumping

Best batting performance: 182* Nottinghamshire v Gloucestershire, Trent Bridge 1977
Best bowling performance: 3-33 Nottinghamshire v Lancashire, Old Trafford 1976
Wife: Dorothy Ann
Children: Jamil Hassan, 22 October 1980; Sarah Jane Hassan, 30 June 1982
Family links with cricket: Father and brothers played
Education: City High School, Nairobi; Kenya Polytechnic
Qualifications: City and Guilds in Printing; Advanced Coaching Certificate
Jobs outside cricket: Sales representative for a printing firm
Off-season 1988–89: Working for Nottinghamshire CCC in their marketing department
Cricketing superstitions or habits: 'Never take off my "necklace" which was given to me by my father.'
Overseas tours: Kenya 1967; West Indies 1974; Dubai 1982; Bermuda 1987

Overseas teams played for: Kenya 1960–66; East Africa 1961–66
Appointed to 1st-Class list: On reserve list
Cricketers particularly learnt from: M. J. K. Smith, M. Ali (Kenya), Sir Garfield Sobers, Tom Graveney
Cricketers particularly admired: Richard Hadlee, Viv Richards, Garfield Sobers
Other sports played: Hockey, golf, football
Other sports followed: Athletics, golf, football, hockey
Relaxations: 'TV, gardening, going for long walks with my pet dog (Sheik) and listening to music.'
Extras: Played first Test for Kenya at age of 15½, the youngest in the country. Made debut for East Africa Invitation XI v MCC 1963–64. Played for Kenya against touring sides. Scored a century with the aid of a runner v Kent at Canterbury in 1977. Best sprinter at Nottinghamshire. Short-listed for Kenyan Olympic team in 1960. Announced retirement in 1985 while fielding substitute for England in Trent Bridge Test v Australia

CAREER: BATTING

	I.	N.O.	R.	H.S.	AV.
TEST					
1ST-CLASS	549	54	14394	182*	29.07
INT					
RAL	196	21	5168	120*	29.53
NAT.W.	27	1	568	79	–
B & H	48	7	1070	99*	26.09

CAREER: BOWLING

	O.	M.	R.	W.	AV.
TEST					
1ST-CLASS	141.2	35	407	6	67.83
INT					
RAL	16.3	0	131	2	65.60
NAT.W.	7.1	2	20	3	6.66
B & H					

HOLDER, J. W.

Full Name: John Wakefield Holder
Role: Right-arm fast bowler
Born: 19 March 1945, Barbados
Height: 6′ **Weight:** 13½st
Nickname: Benson, Hod
Parents: Charles and Carnetta
County: Hampshire
County debut: 1968
50 wickets in a season: 1
1st-Class 5 w. in innings: 5
1st-Class 10 w. in match: 1
1st-Class catches: 12
Best batting performance: 33 Hampshire v Sussex, Hove 1971
Best bowling performance: 6-49 and 7-79 (in same match) Hampshire v Gloucestershire, Gloucester 1972
Appointed to 1st-Class list: 1983

Wife: Glenda
Children: Christopher, 1968; Nigel, 1970
Family links with cricket: 'Both my sons played for Royston in the Central Lancashire League. They want to play county cricket. Father taught me to play.'
Education: St Giles Boys School; Combermere High School, Barbados
Qualifications: 3 O-levels. MCC Advanced Coach
Jobs outside cricket: Part-time cricket coach. Training as driving instructor
Off-season 1988–89: Becoming a fully qualified driving instructor
Overseas tours: Coached in Eastern Goldfields for Western Australian Cricket Association 1987–88
Cricketers particularly learnt from: Wes Hall, Everton Weekes
Cricketers particularly admired: Sir Garfield Sobers, Dennis Lillee, Richard Hadlee
Other sports followed: Manchester United FC, boxing
Relaxations: Watching documentaries about wildlife. Would like to become an accomplished after-dinner speaker
Extras: Holds best bowling performance ever for Rothmans International Cavaliers cricket matches. Playing for Hampshire Cavaliers, took 6-7 at Tichbourne Park, 1968. Between 1974 and 1982, played professional league cricket in Lancashire and Yorkshire. One first-class hat-trick, Hampshire v Kent 1972, 'but finished with 3 for 100!'
Opinions on cricket: 'There has been much argument about the need for a neutral international panel of umpires for Test cricket. The emphasis should be on competence rather than neutrality. The captains of the Test-playing countries know who the best umpires are. If there is going to be a panel, the captains should get together officially and put forward to the ICC the names of who they regard as the best umpires internationally.'

CAREER: BATTING

	I.	N.O.	R.	H.S.	AV.
TEST					
1ST-CLASS	49	14	374	33	10.68
INT					
RAL	21	7	87	25	6.21
NAT.W.	2	0	4	3	2.00
B & H	3	1	23	14	11.50

CAREER: BOWLING

	O.	M.	R.	W.	AV.
TEST					
1ST-CLASS	1183	229	3415	139	24.56
INT					
RAL	237	14	984	38	25.89
NAT.W.	47	10	144	5	28.80
B & H	26	4	85	3	28.33

197. Why were 22 players all on the field at the same time in the match between Worcestershire and Northamptonshire, at Worcester on 1 August 1988?

198. What was unusual about Phil Romaines' innings for Gloucestershire v Warwickshire at Cheltenham in August 1988?

HOLDER, V. A.

Full Name: Vanburn Alonza Holder
Role: Right-hand bat, right arm fast medium bowler
Born: 8 October 1945, St Michael, Barbados
Nickname: Van
County: Worcestershire
County debut: 1968
County cap: 1970
Test debut: 1969
Number of Tests: 40
Benefit: 1979. £25,000
1st-Class 50s scored: 4
1st-Class 100s scored: 1
1st-Class 5 w. in innings: 38
1st-Class 10 w in match: 3
1st-Class catches: 98
Best batting performance: 122
Barbados v Trinidad, Bridgetown 1973–74
Best bowling performance: 7-40 Worcestershire v Glamorgan, Cardiff 1974
Appointed to 1st-Class list: 1988
Overseas tours: With West Indies to England 1969, 1973, and 1976; India, Sri Lanka and Pakistan 1974–75; Australia 1975–76; India and Sri Lanka 1978–79 as vice-captain
Overseas teams played for: Barbados in Shell Shield Competition
Extras: Made debut for Barbados 1966–67 in Shell Shield Competition

CAREER: BATTING

	I.	N.O.	R.	H.S.	AV.
TEST	59	11	682	42	14.21
1ST-CLASS	295	70	2877	122	12.79
INT	6	1	64	30	12.80
RAL	61	15	323	35*	7.02
GILLETTE	14	5	79	25*	8.78
B & H	17	8	67	17*	7.44

CAREER: BOWLING

	O.	M.	R.	W.	AV.
TEST	166.6 1293	21 346	3629	109	33.27
1ST-CLASS	160.3 7499	27 1736	19556	838	23.34
INT	7.5 103.2	1 8	454	19	23.89
RAL	864.5	99	2970	176	16.88
GILLETTE	197.3	34	604	22	27.45
B & H	238.4	44	691	37	18.68

> 199. Who did Peter May, as chairman of England selectors in 1988, give as an example of cricketing talent damaged by too many overseas players in the English county game?

JONES, A. A.

Full Name: Allan Arthur Jones
Role: Left-arm fast bowler
Born: 9 December 1947, Horley,
Surrey
Height: 6′ 3½″ **Weight:** 14st
Nickname: Jonah, Buckets
Parents: Leslie and Hazel
Counties: Sussex, Somerset,
Middlesex, Glamorgan
County debut: 1966 (Sussex),
1970 (Somerset), 1976 (Middlesex),
1980 (Glamorgan)
County cap: 1972 (Somerset),
1976 (Middlesex)
50 wickets in a season: 4
1st-Class 5 w. in innings: 23
1st-Class 10 w. in match: 3
1st-Class catches: 50
Best batting performance: 33

Middlesex v Kent, Canterbury 1978
Best bowling performance: 9-51 Somerset v Sussex, Hove 1976
Appointed to 1st-Class list: 1985
Wife and date of marriage: Marilyn, 1979
Children: Clare Michelle, 4 July 1979
Education: St John's College, Horsham
Qualifications: 5 O-levels. MCC 'A' coach, NCA staff coach
Jobs outside cricket: 'None at present.'
Off-season 1988–89: 'Playing lots of golf.'
Cricketers particularly learnt from: Brian Close, Mike Brearley, Tom Cartwright
Cricketers particularly admired: Brian Close, Barry Richards, John Snow
Other sports followed: 'All sports.'
Relaxations: Horse racing, cinema, reading
Opinions on cricket: 'I think there is too much one-day cricket played at present. Although it has its place and has brought money into the game, one-day cricket has undoubtedly lowered the standard of cricket as a whole.

CAREER: BATTING

	I.	N.O.	R.	H.S.	AV.
TEST					
1ST-CLASS	216	68	799	33	5.40
INT					
RAL	56	27	90	18*	3.10
NAT.W.	9	6	13	5*	4.33
B & H	18	8	51	14	5.10

CAREER: BOWLING

	O.	M.	R.	W.	AV.
TEST					
1ST-CLASS	4994.1	997	15414	549	28.08
INT					
RAL	952.1	99	3995	187	21.36
NAT.W.	167	14	658	29	22.68
B & H	352.2	60	1115	65	17.15

Also I am of the opinion that overseas players should be banned completely, or only allowed to play one-day cricket. That way we might be able to find more than just a dozen decent players in this country. As for cricket correspondents, most of them should take a look at their own knowledge of the game, and be seen to be watching, rather than just copying the scorecards. Also it might be good if they stuck to writing about cricket, and not cricketers.'

JULIAN, R.

Full Name: Raymond Julian
Role: Right-hand bat, wicket-keeper
Born: 23 August 1936, Cosby, Leicestershire
Height: 5′ 11″ **Weight:** 11st 4lbs
Nickname: Julie
Parents: George Ernest and Doris
County: Leicestershire
County debut: 1953
County cap: 1961
1st-Class 50s scored: 2
1st-Class catches: 382
Best batting performance: 51 Leicestershire v Worcestershire, Worcester 1962
Wife and date of marriage: Ruth Ann, 30 April 1958
Children: Peter, 1 February 1958; John, 13 October 1960; David, 15 October 1963; Paul, 22 September 1967
Family links with cricket: Father and two brothers all played local club cricket; two sons also play
Education: Wigston Secondary Modern School
Jobs outside cricket: Painter and decorator, cricket kit salesman
Off-season 1988–89: Cricket coaching
Overseas tours: MCC to West Africa, 1975, as wicket-keeper and umpire
Cricketers particularly learnt from: Keith Andrew
Cricketers particularly admired: Gary Sobers, Keith Andrew, Willie Watson, Ray Illingworth
Other sports played: Ex-1st-Class football referee (local), linesman on Southern League for four seasons, refereed one FA Cup match. Football goalkeeper
Relaxations: Gardening, listening to Johnny Mathis records
Extras: Youngest player to make debut (age 15) for Leicestershire v Glouces-

tershire, Bristol 1953. Gave 8 lbw decisions on the trot, Glamorgan v Sussex, Cardiff 1986. Played for Army 1955–57. Three Benson & Hedges semi-finals, one Gillette Cup semi-final

Opinions on cricket: 'In favour of four-day cricket, and a Saturday league of 55 overs.'

CAREER: BATTING

	I.	N.O.	R.	H.S.	AV.
TEST					
1ST-CLASS	288	23	2581	51	9.73
INT					
RAL					
NAT.W.	3	0	6	4	2.00
B & H					

CAREER: WICKET KEEPING

	C.	ST.
TEST		
1ST-CLASS	381	40
INT		
RAL		
NAT.W.	–	–
B & H		

KITCHEN, M. J.

Full Name: Mervyn John Kitchen
Role: Left-hand bat, right-arm medium bowler
Born: 1 August 1940, Nailsea, Somerset
County: Somerset
County debut: 1960
County cap: 1966
Benefit: 1973 (£6000)
1000 runs in a season: 7
1st-Class 50s scored: 68
1st-Class 100s scored: 17
One-Day 50s: 22
One-Day 100s: 1
1st-Class catches: 157
Best batting performance: 189 Somerset v Pakistan, Taunton 1967
Appointed to 1st-Class list: 1982
Education: Backwell Secondary Modern, Nailsea

CAREER: BATTING

	I.	N.O.	R.	H.S.	AV.
TEST					
1ST-CLASS	612	32	15230	189	26.25
INT					
RAL	111	10	2069	82	20.48
NAT.W.	27	1	815	116	31.34
B & H	25	1	504	70	21.00

CAREER: BOWLING

	O.	M.	R.	W.	AV.
TEST					
1ST-CLASS	30.1	7	109	2	54.50
INT					
RAL	17.5	0	89	4	22.25
NAT.W.	3	2	8	1	–
B & H					

LEADBEATER, B.

Full Name: Barrie Leadbeater
Role: Right-hand opening bat,
right-arm medium bowler,
slip fielder
Born: 14 August 1943, Leeds
Height: 6′ **Weight:** 13st
Nickname: Leady
Parents: Ronnie (deceased) and Nellie
County: Yorkshire
County debut: 1966
County cap: 1969
Benefit: 1980 (£33,846 shared
with G. A. Cope)
1st-Class 50s scored: 27
1st-Class 100s scored: 1
One-Day 50s: 11
1st-Class catches: 82
Best batting performance: 140*
Yorkshire v Hampshire, Portsmouth
1976
Appointed to 1st-Class list: 1981
Wife and date of marriage: Jacqueline, 18 September 1971
Children: Richard Barrie, 23 November 1972; Michael Spencer, 21 March
1976; Daniel Mark Ronnie, 19 June 1981
Family links with cricket: Father played works cricket
Education: Brownhill County Primary; Harehills Secondary Modern, Leeds
Qualifications: 2 O-levels (English and Maths)
Jobs outside cricket: Coach, driver
Off-season 1988–89: Driver for Supercook Group
Cricketing superstitions or habits: 'As a player always touched down behind
my crease at the end of an over.'
Overseas tours: Duke of Norfolk's XI to West Indies 1970
Overseas teams played for: Johannesburg Municipals 1978–79
Cricketers particularly learnt from: Brian Close, Willie Watson, Arthur
Mitchell, Maurice Leyland
Cricketers particularly admired: Colin Cowdrey, Clive Rice, Richard
Hadlee, Gary Sobers, Michael Holding
Other sports played: Golf, table tennis, snooker
Other sports followed: Rugby union, most other sports
Injuries 1988: 'Sore ears from all the appealing!'
Relaxations: Family, car maintenance, music, DIY
Opinions on cricket: 'Disappointed in players who lack self-control and
professional pride and set bad examples to young players and public alike.

Public should be regularly and properly informed during stoppages in play. Stoppages for bad light cause more frustration for public, players and not least, umpires and a change in regulations may be needed soon if the game is to retain its support and credibility.'

CAREER: BATTING

	I.	N.O.	R.	H.S.	AV.
TEST					
1ST-CLASS	241	29	5373	140*	25.34
INT					
RAL	68	14	1423	86*	26.35
NAT.W.	9	0	155	76	17.22
B & H	21	5	601	90	37.56

CAREER: BOWLING

	O.	M.	R.	W.	AV.
TEST					
1ST-CLASS	5	1	5	1	5.00
INT					
RAL	8.5	0	38	2	19.00
NAT.W.					
B & H					

MEYER, B. J.

Full Name: Barrie John Meyer
Role: Right-hand bat, wicket-keeper
Born: 21 August 1932, Bournemouth
Height: 5' 10½" **Weight:** 12st 7lbs
Nickname: BJ
County: Gloucestershire
County debut: 1957
County cap: 1958
1st-Class 50s scored: 11
Best batting performance: 63 Gloucestershire v Indians, 1959; Gloucestershire v Oxford University, 1962; Gloucestershire v Sussex, 1964
Appointed to 1st-Class list: 1973
Appointed to Test panel: 1978
No. of Tests umpired: 20
No. of One-Day Internationals umpired: 17
Wife and date of marriage: Gillian, 4 September 1965
Children: Stephen Barrie, Christopher John, Adrian Michael
Education: Boscombe Secondary, Bournemouth
Jobs outside cricket: Ex-salesman
Off-season 1988–89: Coaching umpires in South Africa
Overseas tours: Gloucestershire to Bermuda 1960
Cricketers particularly learnt from: Andy Wilson of Gloucestershire
Cricketers particularly admired: Keith Andrew, Bob Taylor
Other sports played: Ex-professional footballer, golf (7 handicap)
Relaxations: Music, reading

CAREER: BATTING

	I.	N.O.	R.	H.S.	AV.
TEST					
1ST-CLASS	569	190	5367	63	14.16
INT					
RAL	16	3	65	15	5.00
NAT.W.	9	2	69	21	9.86
B & H					

CAREER: BOWLING

	O.	M.	R.	W.	AV.
TEST					
1ST-CLASS	5	1	28	0	–
INT					
RAL					
NAT.W.					
B & H					

CAREER: WICKET-KEEPING

	C.	ST.
TEST		
1ST-CLASS	708	117
INT		
RAL	31	2
NAT.W.	16	3
B & H		

OSLEAR, D. O.

Full Name: Donald Osmund Oslear
Born: 3 March 1929, Cleethorpes
Height: 6′ **Weight:** 13st 6lbs
Parents: John Osmund and
Violet Maude
Appointed to 1st-Class list: 1975
Appointed to Test panel: 1980
No. of Tests umpired: 5
**No. of One-Day Internationals
umpired:** 9
Marital status: Divorced
Children: Sara Elizabeth,
25 February 1960
Family links with cricket: 'Father,
younger brother and myself
all played for Cleethorpes CC.
Brother still plays and captains
2nd XI, aged 53.'
Education: Elliston Street
Secondary School, Cleethorpes

Qualifications: Member of General Council ACU. Training Officer of ACU.
Member of TCCB Electronic Aids Committee
Jobs outside cricket: Fishing Industry in Grimsby. Lecturing to umpires
overseas
Off-season 1988–89: Lecturing and umpiring in Israel and Zimbabwe
Cricketers particularly admired: Garth Le Roux, Ray Illingworth, Mike
Brearley

Other sports followed: Anything which England are engaged in
Relaxations: The study of cricket law and the changes in the laws over the years. Reading cricket books
Extras: The only English umpire to have 'stood' in Test Matches, who has not played county cricket. Played soccer for Grimsby and ice-hockey for Grimsby and an England Select side. Life member of the Association of Cricket Umpires. Training Officer of the ACU. Member of General Council of ACU. 'In 1988, I figured in two instances where the striker has been stumped off a wide ball. In all my career, I have never seen it happen before.'

PALMER, K. E.

Full Name: Kenneth Ernest Palmer
Role: Right-hand bat, right-arm fast-medium bowler, all-rounder
Born: 22 April 1937, Winchester
Height: 5′ 10″ **Weight:** 13st
Nickname: Pedlar
Parents: Harry and Cecilia
County: Somerset
County debut: 1955
County cap: 1958
Test debut: 1965
No. of Tests: 1
1000 runs in a season: 1
50 wickets in a season: 6
1st-Class 50s scored: 27
1st-Class 100s scored: 2
1st-Class 5 w. in innings: 46
1st-Class 10 w. in match: 5
1st-Class catches: 156
Best batting performance: 125* Somerset v Northamptonshire, Northampton 1961
Best bowling performance: 9-57 Somerset v Nottinghamshire, Trent Bridge 1963
Appointed to 1st-Class list: 1972
Appointed to Test panel: 1978
No. of Tests umpired: 16
No. of One-Day Internationals umpired: 8
Wife and date of marriage: Joy Valerie, 6 September 1962
Children: Gary, 1 November 1965
Family links with cricket: Son Gary professional cricketer with Somerset. Brother umpire on first-class list and also played for Somerset
Jobs outside cricket: Coached cricket for Somerset for some time

Other sports played: Squash
Relaxations: 'I enjoy watching my son play cricket on the rare occasions that I get the opportunity.'
Extras: Toured with Commonwealth side to Pakistan, 1962. Toured West Indies with Denis Compton's team January 1963. 'I had the opportunity to see him score 100 in great style with a straw hat on!' Umpired in two Benson & Hedges Finals and two NatWest Finals. Also twice on World Cup panel in England. Won Carling Single Wicket Competition in 1961. Did the 'double' in 1961: 114 wickets and 1036 runs. Batting with former Australia and Somerset cricketer (and former Test umpire) Bill Alley, holds 6th wicket partnership record for Somerset. Wife, Joy, is a PE teacher

CAREER: BATTING

	I.	N.O.	R.	H.S.	AV.
TEST	1	0	10	10	–
1ST-CLASS	480	105	7751	125*	20.66
INT					
RAL	6	1	28	14	5.60
NAT.W.	13	4	109	35	12.11
B & H					

CAREER: BOWLING

	O.	M.	R.	W.	AV.
TEST	63	7	189	1	–
1ST-CLASS	7260.4	1767	18304	865	21.16
INT					
RAL	59	6	282	11	25.64
NAT.W.	163.3	35	451	23	19.60
B & H					

PALMER, R.

Full Name: Roy Palmer
Role: Right-hand bat, right-arm fast-medium bowler
Born: 12 July 1942, Devizes, Wiltshire
County: Somerset
County debut: 1965
50 wickets in a season: 1
1st-Class 50s scored: 1
1st-Class 5 w. in innings: 4
1st-Class catches: 25
Best batting performance: 84 Somerset v Leicestershire, Taunton 1967
Best bowling performance: 6-45 Somerset v Middlesex, Lord's 1967
Appointed to 1st-Class list: 1980

CAREER: BATTING

	I.	N.O.	R.	H.S.	AV.
TEST					
1ST-CLASS	110	32	1037	84	13.29
INT					
RAL	19	2	168	25	9.88
NAT.W.	9	2	30	11	4.28

CAREER: BOWLING

	O.	M.	R.	W.	AV.
TEST					
1ST-CLASS	1697.1	336	5439	172	31.62
INT					
RAL	220	14	963	37	26.03
NAT.W.	148.1	19	532	30	17.73

Family links with cricket: Brother Ken played for Somerset and is also a first-class umpire. Nephew, Gary, plays for Somerset
Education: Southbroom Secondary Modern

PLEWS, N. T.

Full Name: Nigel Trevor Plews
Born: 5 September 1934, Nottingham
Height: 6′ 6½″ **Weight:** 16st 12lbs
Appointed to 1st-Class list: 1982
Appointed to Test panel: 1986
(one-day panel)
No. of One-Day Internationals umpired: 1
Wife and date of marriage: Margaret, 1956
Children: Elaine, 1961; Douglas, 1964
Education: Mundella Grammar School, Nottingham
Qualifications: School Certificate, Royal Society of Arts, Advanced Book-keeping
Jobs outside cricket: Nottingham City Police for 25 years as a Det. Sgt in Fraud Squad
Off-season 1987–88: Employed off season by international chartered accountants Spicer and Oppenheim in insolvency work
Other sports played: Table tennis, swimming
Other sports followed: Rugby
Relaxations: Hill walking, reading, travel
Extras: Did not play first-class cricket

200. What was unusual about the England team for the Fifth Test v West Indies at The Oval in 1988?

RHODES, H. J.

Full Name: Harold James Rhodes
Role: Right-hand bat, right-arm fast bowler
Born: 22 July 1936, Hadfield, Derbyshire
Height: 6′ 2″ **Weight:** 14st 7lbs
Nickname: Dusty
Parents: Bert and Vera
County: Derbyshire
County debut: 1953
County cap: 1958
Test debut: 1959
No. of Tests: 2
50 wickets in a season: 11
1st-Class 5 w. in innings: 42
1st-Class 10 w. in match: 4
1st-Class catches: 86
Best batting performance: 48 Derbyshire v Middlesex, Chesterfield 1958

Best bowling performance: 7-38 Derbyshire v Warwickshire, Edgbaston 1965
Appointed to 1st-Class list: On reserve list 1985 and 1986
Wife and date of marriage: Barbara 17 September 1960
Children: Marcus, 31 May 1961; Julie, 26 September 1962; Simon, 9 March 1968; Jonathan, 24 August 1969
Family links with cricket: Father was first-class and Test umpire
Education: Vernon High School, Derby
Jobs outside cricket: Mortgage manager, Abbey Life Assurance Co.
Off-season 1988–89: Mortgage manager full-time
Overseas tours: South Africa 1959 with Denis Compton's Commonwealth team; Round the World 1960, with R. Benaud's Commonwealth team; to West Indies with E. W. Swanton's Commonwealth team; Round the World 1967 with Mickey Stewart's Commonwealth team; MCC to Far East 1983
Cricketers particularly learnt from: Les Jackson, Cliff Gladwin
Cricketers particularly admired: Brian Statham, Richard Hadlee, F. S. Trueman
Other sports followed: Rugby, soccer
Relaxations: Reading, gardening
Extras: Top of first-class bowling averages 1965 – 119 wickets, av. 11.09. Test career ruined by throwing controversy, cleared 1968 after eight years of deliberations. Autobiography published March 1987. Senior cricket coach at Lord's Indoor School
Opinions on cricket: 'Too much cricket played. Would like to see semi-

professional system: this would give better security for players, and would give an opportunity for *all* to participate. Uncovered wickets to bring back skills and provide more interesting games for spectators. Except for a few, cricket is a badly paid sport.'

CAREER: BATTING

	I.	N.O.	R.	H.S.	AV.
TEST	1	1	0	0*	–
1ST-CLASS	398	142	2427	48	9.48
INT					
RAL	11	5	23	6*	3.83
NAT.W.	10	6	84	26*	21.00
B & H	5	2	17	8*	5.66

CAREER: BOWLING

	O.	M.	R.	W.	AV.
TEST	74.5	10	244	9	27.11
1ST-CLASS	9128.4	2425	20901	1064	19.64
INT					
RAL	242.4	32	933	38	24.55
NAT.W.	173.4	41	435	22	19.77
B & H	98	18	302	11	27.45

SHEPHERD, D. R.

Full Name: David Robert Shepherd
Role: Right-hand bat, right-arm medium bowler
Born: 27 December 1940, Bideford, Devon
County: Gloucestershire
County debut: 1965
County cap: 1969
Benefit: 1978 (shared with J. Davey)
1000 runs in a season: 2
1st-Class 50s scored: 55
1st-Class 100s scored: 12
One-Day 50s: 18
One-Day 100s: 2
1st-Class catches: 95
Best batting performance: 153 Gloucestershire v Middlesex, Bristol 1968
Appointed to 1st-Class list: 1981
Appointed to Test panel: 1985
Education: Barnstaple GS; St Luke College, Exeter

CAREER: BATTING

	I.	N.O.	R.	H.S.	AV.
TEST					
1ST-CLASS	476	40	10672	153	24.47
INT					
RAL	118	9	2274	100	20.86
NAT.W.	24	3	457	72*	21.76
B & H	30	5	580	81	23.20

CAREER: BOWLING

	O.	M.	R.	W.	AV.
TEST					
1ST-CLASS	32.4	4	106	2	53.00
INT					
RAL	1	0	6	0	–
NAT.W.	0.2	0	4	0	–
B & H					

Extras: Superstitious enough to stand on one leg when the score is on a 'Nelson'. Only Gloucestershire player to score a hundred on first-class debut

TAYLOR, K.

Full Name: Kenneth Taylor
Role: Right-hand opening bat, cover point fielder
Born: 21 August 1935
Height: 5′ 9½″ **Weight:** 13st
Nickname: K.Ty (Katy)
Parents: Harold and Amy
County: Yorkshire
County debut: 1953
County cap: 1957
Benefit: 1968 (£6301)
1000 runs in a season: 6
1st-Class 50s scored: 68
1st-Class 100s scored: 15
1st-Class 200s scored: 1
1st-Class 5 w. in innings: 1
Best batting performance: 203*
Yorkshire v Warwickshire, Edgbaston 1961
Best bowling performance: 6-75 Yorkshire v Lancashire, Old Trafford 1961
Family links with cricket: Son, Nicholas, was on playing staff with Surrey and Somerset, 1986
Wife and date of marriage: Avril, 26 March 1960
Children: Nicholas Simon, 2 June 1963; James Cameron 5 June 1966
Education: Huddersfield School of Art; Slade College of Art; London University
Qualifications: NDD Art, Slade certificate
Jobs outside cricket: Professional footballer with Huddersfield Town AFC 1953–68, art teacher, cricket coach
Off-season 1988–89: Teaching art, painting and drawing at Beeston Hall School
Overseas tours: Jim Swanton's Commonwealth side to India 1963–64; MCC to Bangladesh 1978–79
Overseas teams played for: Auckland, New Zealand 1963–64
Cricketers particularly learnt from: Sir Len Hutton
Cricketers particularly admired: Sir Len Hutton, Sir Gary Sobers
Other sports played: Golf, tennis
Other sports followed: Absolutely everything
Relaxations: Photography

Extras: Youngest player to play first-class cricket and First Division soccer: at age 17 played for Yorkshire v Northamptonshire at Headingley, 24 June 1953; at age 18 played for Huddersfield v Liverpool, 6 June 1954. His 160 runs is the highest score by a Yorkshire player in a county match against the Australian tourists this century, in 1964. Scored four goals in one game for Huddersfield v West Ham

CAREER: BATTING

	I.	N.O.	R.	H.S.	AV.
TEST	5	0	57	24	11.40
1ST-CLASS	519	36	12996	203*	26.90
INT					
RAL					
NAT.W.	10	0	134	30	13.40
B & H					

CAREER: BOWLING

	O.	M.	R.	W.	AV.
TEST	2	0	6	0	–
1ST-CLASS	1769.5	607	3757	131	28.67
INT					
RAL					
NAT.W.	61	12	168	11	15.27
B & H					

THOMPSETT, D. S.

Full Name: Donald Stanley Thompsett
Born: 8 April 1935, Piltdown, Sussex
Height: 6′ 1″ **Weight:** 13st
Appointed to 1st-Class list: On reserve list since 1985
Parents: John and Dorothy
Wife and date of marriage: Valerie, 10 October 1957
Children: Glen, Clifford, Steven, Debbie and Linzie
Family links with cricket: Sons Cliff and Steve play club cricket for Chippenham in Western League
Education: Secondary
Jobs outside cricket: Poultry farmer
Off-season 1988–89: Working on farm
Other sports played: Bowls, football
Relaxations: Walking, gardening and reading
Extras: No first-class playing experience. Played local club cricket from the age of 11 years. Umpired at club level since 1974. Appointed to Minor Counties umpires list in 1978. Appointed to 1st-Class reserve list 1985. Umpired 2nd XI 1st-Class Championship matches since 1979. Debut in 1st-Class Championship Essex v Derbyshire, Colchester 1985. 'My fifth year

on the reserve list. This must be a record of some kind! In that time, I've been asked to stand in 41 first-class matches.'

Opinions on cricket: 'Like many people I do feel that we have opened the floodgates for too many overseas players, therefore depriving us of some 25 or 30 places for youngsters coming into the game throughout the country.'

WHITE, R. A.

Full Name: Robert Arthur White
Role: Left-hand bat, off-break bowler, all-rounder
Born: 6 October 1936, Fulham
Height: 5′ 9½″ **Weight:** 12st 4lbs
Nickname: Knocker
Counties: Middlesex, Nottinghamshire
County debut: 1958 (Middlesex), 1966 (Nottinghamshire)
County cap: 1963 (Middlesex), 1966 (Nottinghamshire)
1000 runs in a season: 1
50 wickets in a season: 2
1st-Class 50s scored: 50
1st-Class 100s scored: 5
1st-Class 5 w. in innings: 28
1st-Class 10 w. in match: 4
1st-Class catches: 190
Best batting performance: 116*
Nottinghamshire v Surrey, The Oval 1967
Best bowling performance: 7-41 Nottinghamshire v Derbyshire, Ilkeston 1971
Appointed to 1st-Class list: 1982
Wife: Janice
Children: Robin, Vanessa
Education: Chiswick Grammar School
Qualifications: Matriculation
Jobs outside cricket: Self-employed salesman
Cricketers particularly learnt from: 'I tried to learn from everyone I encountered.'
Cricketers particularly admired: 'Garfield Sobers more than anyone.'
Other sports played: Golf – very indifferently
Other sports followed: All sports, soccer, ice-hockey and racing in particular
Relaxations: Theatre-going
Extras: Independent coaching trips to South Africa, 1959, 1960, 1966, 1967,

1968. Together with M. J. Smedley, had the Nottinghamshire 6th wicket partnership of 204, v Surrey, at The Oval, 1966

Opinions on cricket: 'Too controversial to go into print.'

CAREER: BATTING

	I.	N.O.	R.	H.S.	AV.
TEST					
1ST-CLASS	642	105	12452	116*	23.19
INT					
RAL	78	28	844	86*	16.88
NAT.W.	20	1	284	39	14.95
B & H	21	9	251	52*	20.92

CAREER: BOWLING

	O.	M.	R.	W.	AV.
TEST					
1ST-CLASS	7946	2219	21138	693	30.50
INT					
RAL	607	54	2448	103	23.76
NAT.W.	147	15	488	14	34.86
B & H	234.5	32	800	19	42.11

WHITEHEAD, A. G. T.

Full Name: Alan Geoffrey
Thomas Whitehead
Role: Left-hand bat, slow
left-arm bowler
Born: 28 October 1940, Butleigh,
Somerset
County: Somerset
County debut: 1957
1st-Class 5 w. in innings: 3
1st-Class catches: 20
Best batting performance: 15
Somerset v Hampshire,
Southampton 1959
Best bowling performance: 6-74
Somerset v Sussex, Eastbourne 1959
Appointed to 1st-Class list: 1970
Appointed to Test panel: 1982
No. of Tests umpired: 4

CAREER: BATTING

	I.	N.O.	R.	H.S.	AV.
TEST					
1ST-CLASS	49	25	137	15	5.71
INT					
RAL					
NAT.W.					
B & H					

CAREER: BOWLING

	O.	M.	R.	W.	AV.
TEST					
1ST-CLASS	846.4	250	2306	67	34.42
INT					
RAL					
NAT.W.					
B & H					

WIGHT, P. B.

Full Name: Peter Bernard Wight
Role: Right-hand bat, off-break bowler
Born: 25 June 1930, Georgetown, British Guyana
County: Somerset
County debut: 1953
County cap: 1954
Benefit: 1963 (£5000)
1000 runs in a season: 10
1st-Class 50s scored: 207
1st-Class 100s scored: 26
1st-Class 200s scored: 2
1st-Class 5 w. in innings: 1
1st-Class catches: 204
Best batting performance: 222*
Somerset v Kent, Taunton 1959
Best bowling performance: 6-29
Somerset v Derbyshire, Chesterfield 1957
Appointed to 1st-Class list: 1966
Family links with cricket: Brother G. L. played for West Indies. Brothers H. A. and N. played for British Guyana

CAREER: BATTING

	I.	N.O.	R.	H.S.	AV.
TEST					
1ST-CLASS	590	53	17773	222*	33.10
INT					
RAL					
NAT.W.	6	0	56	38	9.33
B & H					

CAREER: BOWLING

	O.	M.	R.	W.	AV.
TEST					
1ST-CLASS	789.1	224	2262	68	33.26
INT					
RAL					
NAT.W.					
B & H					

NOW YOU KNOW WHO'S WHO, WHY NOT FIND OUT WHAT'S WHAT?

Talk to Refuge about Life Assurance, Investments, Car Insurance, Mortgages, Pensions or House and Home Insurance.

Refuge ASSURANCE PLC

REFUGE HOUSE, ALDERLEY ROAD,
WILMSLOW, CHESHIRE SK9 1PF.

THE CRICKETERS' WHO'S WHO QUIZ

Competition Form

To celebrate the 10th anniversary of *The Cricketers' Who's Who*, Collins Willow are offering three marvellous cricket prizes to those readers who supply the most number of correct answers to the quiz questions throughout the book. All three winners will receive two tickets to a Sunday League game of their choice, courtesy of Refuge Assurance, together with a copy of the prestigious *Treasures of Lord's*, the first title in the new MCC Cricket Library.

Please send the entry form below, together with your answers to the quiz questions on a separate sheet of paper, to the following address:

Victoria Singer
Collins Willow
8 Grafton Street
London W1X 3LA

The closing date for entries is 30 June 1989. The winners will be notified of their prizes by 14 July. No correspondence will be entered into and the decision of the judges will be final. In the event of a tie in the number of correct answers supplied, the winning entries will be drawn out of a hat.

Name: ....

Address: ....

....

....

Where you bought the book: ....

Preferred Sunday League venue: ....

Please remember to enclose your list of answers written out clearly on a separate sheet of paper.